Also by William and Stephanie Laska

Extra Easy Keto: 7 Days to Ketogenic Weight Loss on a Low Carb Diet by Stephanie Laska (St. Martin's Essentials, 2023)

The DIRTY, LAZY, KETO® 5-Ingredient Cookbook: 100 Easy-Peasy Recipes Low in Carbs, Big on Flavor by Stephanie Laska, MEd, and William Laska (Simon & Schuster, 2021)

The DIRTY, LAZY, KETO® No Time to Cook Cookbook: 100 Easy Recipes Ready in Under 30 Minutes by Stephanie Laska, MEd, and William Laska (Simon & Schuster, 2021)

The DIRTY, LAZY, KETO® Dirt Cheap Cookbook: 100 Easy Recipes to Save Money & Time! by Stephanie Laska, MEd, and William Laska (Simon & Schuster, 2020)

The DIRTY, LAZY, KETO® Cookbook: 100 Affordable Recipes, All Less Than 10g Net Carbs! by Stephanie Laska, MEd, and William Laska (Simon & Schuster, 2020)

DIRTY, LAZY, KETO® (Revised and Expanded) Get Started Losing Weight While Breaking the Rules by Stephanie Laska (St. Martin's Essentials, 2020)

DIRTY, LAZY, KETO® Fast Food Guide: 10 Carbs or Less by William Laska and Stephanie Laska, MEd (2018)

Keto Diet Restaurant Guide:

Eat Healthy and Stay in Ketosis, Dining Out on a Low Carb Diet

William Laska & Stephanie Laska, MEd

For additional resources, visit the author's website:

https://dirtylazyketo.com

First Edition. 2022

ISBN-13: 9798435860153

Dedication

William (Bill)

To all those out there who have spent time in the healthy eating "trenches." Those unfortunate souls who endure the daily struggle to stay on their diet plan. It's hard enough to plan and execute low-carb eating in the safety of your own home, but what about out there "in the wild"? This book was conceived and written with those moments in mind. Now you are covered both in *and out* of your kitchen!

Of course, none of this would be possible without the "Grand Ketoess" Stephanie Laska, who has fought this lengthy weight loss war for decades. We are all eternally grateful for her unwavering persistence through the initial regret and humiliation of failure to that low-carb spark that started her keto journey to success and happiness (and a 140 pound weight loss!).

Stephanie

To all of you who are tired of trying to be perfect, I dedicate this book to you. Have you been meal planning up the wazoo? Striving for a homecooked dinner every night? Strict dieting without ever a break? Not anymore. Let's stop holding ourselves to saint-like standards that are impossible to meet.

We put too much pressure on ourselves. Who says we have to cook for ourselves from scratch (or even cook at all)? Not me. There's another way to eat low-carb and live a healthy lifestyle (which may or may not include a cocktail – shhh!). Come out to eat with me. I'm going to show you how.

Keto Diet Restaurant Guide Superstar Award

Only an elite group of restaurants were awarded the coveted *Keto Diet Restaurant Guide* Superstar Award. These establishments make choosing low-carb food easy. They go above and beyond, providing clear and accurate nutrition facts about their menu. Their websites offer bonus tools, like customizable online food calculators, and some even go so far as to call out their low-carb options specifically. Thank you!

Keto Diet Restaurant Guide Superstar restaurants make it easy for us to stay on track with a ketogenic lifestyle.

Table of Contents

Preface

Choosing low-carb foods at home is easy. Rephrase! It's *easierrrrrrr* to eat healthier at home compared to eating out at a restaurant. Don't believe me? Just open your pantry. All of the food you see includes a nutrition facts label. The information is right in front of you. There's no mystery about what's inside. Picking and choosing the "right" snacks is much simpler when you don't have to guess what you're eating.

Nutrition facts and ingredient lists are our best way to determine what to eat. Does a food contain sugar or white flour? No thanks. Too many net carbs for your liking? Pass! Accurate information leads to informed decision-making. But we aren't always at home. What then?

Once you leave the sanctuary of your kitchen, all bets are off. It's hard to stay on track when eating on the run. Trying to order low-carb foods gets complicated. *Fast.* When someone else is preparing your food and nutrition labels are nowhere to be found, you are bound to feel lost.

How do YOU handle dining out while "doing keto"?

Option One: Pester the wait staff with a million and one questions. "Is this keto?" "IS THIS KETO?" (Expect plenty of blank stares and "Huhs?").

Option Two: Frantically scour the internet for advice about what to order (while everyone else in your party is "yackin' it up" and enjoying cocktails). You may or may not find out anything useful –just frustration.

Option Three: Order something plain, predictable, and boring (because at least you know it's healthy). Inside, you might feel resentful and miserable. So not fair!

Option Four: Give up.

Even with the best of intentions, we often find ourselves in a pickle when dining out. But when it comes to our health, there's no such thing as a free lunch (pardon the pun). Excuses, even legitimate ones, won't sway your metabolism. Did spotty internet prevent you from checking a restaurant's online menu? Your waistline doesn't care. P.S. There are no exceptions made for birthdays or vacations either. Sad, I know!

What we choose to eat - at home AND on the road – has consequences. (Don't get mad at me; I didn't make the rules.) Whether you choose french fries or a side salad, that's up to you: your body, your choice. However, if you're looking for guidance about choosing low-carb food on the run and could use some helpful advice, know you've come to the right place.

My motivation here isn't to shame or "tsk tsk" anyone about food. I only want to share what I have learned. With all the facts, we can do better. Empower yourself. Know what you are eating. Make the "right" decisions about what to eat - *for you.*

Introduction

I spent decades of my life weighing almost 300 pounds. Since absolutely NONE of the diets I tried over the years yielded positive results, I gave up. I lacked faith that my weight would ever change.

It's not that I hadn't tried.

I listened carefully to my family doctor when he counseled me how to lose weight. He told me to eat a low-calorie, low-fat diet and get plenty of exercise. I obeyed (for a while, anyway). The process was miserable. I drove myself crazy by weighing and measuring every morsel of food on my plate. Despite my best efforts, *I totally bombed*.

Following his advice caused me to *gain*, not lose, weight. Oatmeal, fat-free cottage cheese, or a bowl of grapefruit for breakfast? YUCK. I never felt full or satisfied. I would tolerate these foods temporarily while listening to my stomach rumble. I wanted a donut! I blamed myself for not having enough self-control and would eventually quit (ending up worse off than when I started). This left me hangry and hopeless.

My life changed for the better once I stumbled upon the benefits of a low-carb ketogenic lifestyle. I toyed around with the principles of ketosis and implemented them in a no-nonsense way. I learned how to make the keto diet my own. A year and a half later, I found myself 140 pounds lighter. My body weight was literally cut in half. Ridiculous, I know!

Dramatic weight loss was only part of my keto transformation. I gained more energy, slept better, and stopped having migraines. My emotional health improved, too. Inside, I felt stronger. For the first time (as in ever), I was happy in my own skin. My self-esteem and confidence levels soared.

As you might suspect, people around me started asking questions.

"How did you lose so much weight, Stephanie?"

DIRTY, LAZY, KETO® – DLK for short – describes my methodology in a nutshell. I created a relaxed, flexible "keto-ish" diet (still high-fat, moderate protein, low-carb) but without strict or unnecessary rules. I played dirty fighting my obesity *and* won.

I knew in my heart that I couldn't be the only one struggling. I had to tell others! I'm so passionate about this lifestyle – you'll find DIRTY, LAZY, KETO is all I ever talk about. Whether through one of my cookbooks, YouTube videos, or "how-to" guides[1], I will do whatever it takes to help someone else become successful (even touching on embarrassing or shameful topics). And I'm just getting started.

First, I realized there was one topic I hadn't spent enough time on. Eating out. *Not everyone likes to cook!* Dining out (or having meals delivered) has become routine, not an exception, in today's culture. For many, it's the new normal.

Dining Out Doom?

Just because you eat out a lot (or occasionally) doesn't mean you can't follow a ketogenic diet. It's not that black or white. You don't have to be a professional chef or hire a meal delivery service to achieve your health goals. Perfection on keto is overrated, people. Let go of false assumptions and rigid standards. It's okay to feel some anxiety about changing the way you eat while still making progress.

"I want to lose weight and feel better, but I don't know where to start."

"Eating healthy at restaurants is darn-near impossible."

"There are no keto-friendly restaurants in my area."

"I hate to cook. I should give up."

"Finding nutrition info for a restaurant is time-consuming and confusing."

"I don't want to order weird diet food (at work, on a date, social event)."

"I'm too busy to figure this out."

"I have no clue what to order!"

Ignorance, Not Bliss

No more pretending. You and I both know that we are always responsible for what we eat, no matter who prepares the meal. When dining out, "I didn't know what was in it" is not a valid excuse.

We can't ignore the health ramifications of eating restaurant food so often. Convenience is king (don't you LOVE food delivery?), but admit it. Such service comes with unexpected costs. I'm not just talking about your wallet here. Temptation abounds, and we often overeat. *So much deliciousness, so little time.* Serving sizes are *ginormous*. And the food is so tasty! It's no wonder many of us get caught up in the moment.

To complicate matters, many of us look at restaurant meals as a dieting loophole. I admit falling victim to a self-sabotaging mentality like this in my past. When I was a size 24/26, I considered the restaurant experience a free-for-all. Dining out was a treat. Sometimes, a reward. Since I was paying good money, I felt I "deserved" to eat whatever I wanted. *This never ended well!*

---

[1] For beginners, I recommend *DIRTY, LAZY, KETO® (revised and expanded) Get Started Losing Weight While Breaking the Rules* by Stephanie Laska (St. Martin's Essentials, 2020) and *Extra Easy Keto: 7 Days to Ketogenic Weight Loss on a Low Carb Diet* by Stephanie Laska (St. Martin's Essentials, 2023).

I had to change my thinking during my weight loss journey. It didn't matter if I was at home or on a cruise ship (the buffets!); I realized that eating healthy wasn't a punishment. It was a gift! Once I learned how to order DIRTY, LAZY, KETO-type foods, I no longer felt deprived.

You can learn to do this too.

WHERE Can You Find a Keto-Friendly Restaurant?

When I asked this question to my DIRTY, LAZY, KETO Facebook support group, I had an "a-ha" moment. My goal was to start a discussion about dining out while on keto; however, the response was *crickets*. One brave soul (nervously) shared that a mom-and-pop restaurant in her town made "the most amazing cheese shell tacos." Other than that, no one else chimed in.

Hmmm. The lack of response made me wonder. *Do people NOT know where to find a keto-friendly restaurant? Do people go out to eat and throw up their hands about what to order?*

I didn't mean for the question to be so perplexing. I assumed everyone knew how to eat low-carb on the go. Keto is much more than sugar-free bakery items and cheese shell tacos (although they sound delicious). I realized I had some work to do.

Restaurant Round-Up

We've got one mission here. Restaurants! Our plan is to spotlight low-carb foods at a variety of establishments. *What to eat and where to eat it!* While we include a few fast food options, that's not our focus here (there's already a DIRTY, LAZY, KETO book for that[2].) Here we include primarily sit-down, franchise restaurants.

Plus, you'll find plenty of support. If your lifestyle includes takeout, delivery, or dining out, rest assured, you can maintain a ketogenic lifestyle. The trick is figuring out *what* and *how* to order. With the help of the *Keto Diet Restaurant Guide*, choosing low-carb foods has never been easier!

Prepare to be shocked – you won't find turn-your-nose-up "diet" food here. It's quite the opposite. Identified foods are savory and scrumptious. Breakfast, lunch, dinner, and drinks? Check! All meals are covered. (There are even a few desserts. *Ooooh, la la!*)

You won't have to worry if a restaurant is keto-friendly or not. All of the groundwork is done for you. We will share personal suggestions and explain how to cut carbs from the existing menu. You'll walk away with strategies applicable to any restaurant, anywhere. **The *Keto Diet Restaurant Guide* will support your efforts to stay in ketosis, lose weight, and be healthy – however you define your goal.**

Want to peek inside? Here's what you can expect:

- Comprehensive research - 60+ popular chain restaurants included!
- A complete directory of keto-friendly food and drinks, all "10 grams of net carbs or less."
- Full nutrient profile for each entrée (calories, fat, protein, net carbs).
- "Special Order Tips" and secret tricks for cutting carbs off the existing menu.
- Fun and support. Learn which restaurants make it easier to "do keto" – the *Keto Diet Restaurant Guide* Superstar Award gives it away!

Discover a variety of delicious low-carb foods to support your keto lifestyle. The *Keto Diet Restaurant Guide*

---

[2] *DIRTY, LAZY, KETO Fast Food Guide: 10 Carbs or Less* by William Laska and Stephanie Laska (2018)

contains everything you need to know in one handy-dandy place. Staying on track with the keto lifestyle becomes simplified. *No more scrolling, stressing, or guessing!* Stop second-guessing yourself about what to eat or worrying about where to go. Get the food you want *the way you want it.*

Take a Restaurant Road Trip

Alongside my ah-mazing husband, William (Bill) Laska (co-author of *The DIRTY, LAZY, KETO Cookbook* series and *DIRTY, LAZY, KETO Fast Food Guide*), we set out to find some answers. We targeted more than 60 popular sit-down chain restaurants across America[3] (all tastes and budgets considered). Our goal was to identify as many low-carb foods as possible. Was this information easy to find? *No ma'am. No sir!* But there was no giving up. We rolled up our sleeves, tucked napkins in our shirts, and remained optimistic.

Our research concluded that keto-friendly foods exist in every town and every restaurant across this great nation of ours. It didn't matter what kind of chain we investigated (steak houses, Italian, Mexican, diners, burger joints, etc.). We found foods and flavors that would appeal to anyone. Exciting, right? This revelation, my friends, deserves a hip hip, hurray!

Since we're celebrating, let me pause and give a shout-out to Bill (who made all of this happen). He analyzed restaurant menus, studied countless websites, and scrutinized entrée ingredients. At the same time, he cross-compared nutrition facts for accuracy[4]. All in the name of discovering low-carb opportunities. My hero! And he didn't stop there.

To ensure that this information will be useful for you, Bill grouped the findings by meal type (breakfast, lunch, etc.) followed by category (appetizers, sandwiches, drinks, and so on). Logical and organized, with macronutrients and calories to boot. (Whew.) If that wasn't enough, he wrote a brief summary for each restaurant, highlighting tips for ordering and advice for how to best navigate their menu. Don't skip over those intros -some of the comments are a hoot!

While Bill was busy doing 99.9% of the work, I participated in an entirely different role —as the designated taste-tester (this required less math). Together, we went on quite a tasty adventure. Here is what we found.

Eat-O, Keto Everywhere!

Finding a keto-friendly restaurant is not as hard as you might think. Spoiler alert —they are on every street corner. All restaurants (yep, every single one) have low-carb options on their menu (though you may have to squint or get creative to find them). Entrees are probably not labeled "keto," but they do exist. *HOW do you find them? WHERE do you look on the menu?* Herein lies the challenge.

When picking out keto-friendly foods on a menu, some restaurants make it more difficult than others. I recently dined at a Nuevo-Mexican restaurant that appeared to be serving only casseroles. Beans, corn, and rice? Everything I saw coming out of the kitchen looked mixed on the plate. Not surprisingly, I panicked. *What could I eat?*

I politely approached the waiter, "This isn't on the menu, but... Would it be possible to order (any kind of) grilled fish with vegetables?"

---

[3] Sidebar: Don't fret if some of these chains aren't in your community. Entrée suggestions and low-carb tips apply to similar restaurants. You may not have an IHOP per se, but what about a regular 'ole diner?

[4] If you spot a discrepancy, be sure to let us (and the restaurant) know so they can fix their website.

He shook his head no.

"Sorry, ma'am. We have to stick to the menu. Plus, we don't serve vegetables."

Wait, WHAT?!? First of all, who is he calling *ma'am*? (Do I look that old?) And secondly, what kind of restaurant doesn't serve VEGETABLES!?!

This disappointing situation was probably a one-off (let's hope so – y'all). Nonetheless, I learned some valuable lessons. Apparently, not everyone knows their food groups (a salad IS a vegetable, *hellooooo!*). And second, if you want to get anywhere, speaking a restaurant's language is essential. Instead of trying to invent a meal, I should have modified an existing entrée from this restaurant's menu. I might have had more luck that way.

Order Off the Menu

Always be prepared to order off the menu (in some shape or form). Here is where the *Keto Diet Restaurant Guide* is beneficial. All the necessary lingo describing what and how to order? It's right here, spelled out for you. Pick out what sounds good and read it out loud, word for word, to whoever is taking down your order. *Done!*

Start by flipping through this interactive book. Look for inspiration about where to eat or go directly to the restaurant you've picked out. Choose an entrée that tickles your fancy. Can't decide? Check out the "Author Favorite" for a subtle nudge. Either way, you'll be able to make a fast decision since the pertinent nutrition information is at your fingertips (calories, fat, protein, net carbs). Since every item is "10 grams net carbs or less," there's no temptation to go off plan.

Special Orders & Modifications

Standalone "10 grams of net carbs or less" menu items are few and far between. A chicken Caesar salad or a Denver omelet? Even traditional lower-carb menu items like this need to be ordered "with a twist" to cut back on carbs.

"Hold the croutons! No toast!" Most restaurants are happy to accommodate reasonable requests. Ask nicely, and substitutions, swaps, and omissions are usually not a problem. We will walk you through how to do this. Pay attention to the "Special Order Tips" provided throughout the *Keto Diet Restaurant Guide*. Use the provided verbiage when placing your order. That's it! Sit back and relax with confidence. These instructions match the calorie and macronutrient information provided. Problem solved. Feel free to customize your order and make alterations (but understand this will affect the stated nutritional outcome).

You'll even find specific carb-cutting tips for tweaking a restaurant's noteworthy dishes here – no need to feel deprived or left out when the rest of your party is ordering what's popular. Select what to eat from the list of "10 grams of net carbs or less" menu items, order with the provided tips, and you are good to go. Easy-peasy. With so many low-carb options available, you can't go wrong. Prep for success by familiarizing yourself with the terms and phrases used throughout the guide (explained here in the Glossary).

Glossary

No Bread, Bunless, Breadless, Lettuce-Wrapped – consider these terms interchangeable (and words to live by when enjoying burgers or sandwiches).

Remove Breading – This instruction is a "last resort." Some entrees are premade (or prepared off-site) with breading. In these rare instances, you cannot order the food in any other way. Do your best to remove the coating.

Easy – Not to be confused with "light" (which often describes low-fat food). I use the term "easy" to refer to quantity. The instruction "easy" here means to use a small amount.

Super Easy – This implies you use an extremely small amount. Sometimes a menu item automatically comes with sauce, and you'll have to scrape it off (I warned you we would be getting creative). If the sauce is served on the side, use the bare minimum to add flavor to your meal.

Half-Serving – To include more crowd-pleasing favorites (soups, chilis, etc.) in the list of "10 grams of net carbs or less," I occasionally recommend ordering (or consuming) half a serving. Sometimes the option is provided on a restaurant's menu. Know that I included this option sparingly. As a hearty-eater myself, a half-serving doesn't fill me up!

Full-Rack or Half-Rack – used exclusively to describe ordering a full-rack or half-rack of ribs.

Without or No – Skip this food altogether. Ask the kitchen NOT to put it on your plate. (Should the server forget and serve your meal with Fries, for example, be assertive about sending the plate back to the kitchen for prompt removal.)

Substitute – In lieu of high-carb, high-starch side dishes (bread, pasta, roll, rice, french fries, potatoes, grits, toast, tortilla, etc.), ask for a healthier vegetable swap (like a side salad or steamed low-carb veggie). If there is an upcharge, pay it. Your health is worth the extra dollar or two!

*That's Not Keto! – You'll find all sorts of surprising foods listed here. Some might fall into the dirty keto category (alcohol, diet soda, sugar-free syrup). But that's not all. Don't be shocked when you see higher-carb foods included (you may have assumed they were off-limits). I'm not telling you whether you should eat these foods or not. What fits your macros or daily carb spend is up to you. Sure, there are consequences to eating higher-carb foods, but it's my philosophy not to criticize the choices of another, and I ask that you do the same. Respect the judgment-free zone. No keto police allowed.

Author Favorite – This category is just for fun. If this meal sounds appealing to you and the macros are a fit, consider trying one of Bill or Stephanie's favorite meals listed for each chain restaurant.

Keto Diet Restaurant Guide Superstar Award 🔘 – Wow! This restaurant makes it easy to "do keto." We want to thank these establishments for providing transparency about nutrition facts on their websites. Customizable food calculators (for ingredient additions and deletions) make eating healthier here a dream. Be sure to thank them with your patronage.

Research Methodology

Restaurants are not always forthcoming with nutrition information. Case in point, only an elite list earned the esteemed *Keto Diet Restaurant Guide* Superstar Award. The vast majority trail light years behind. This discrepancy made our job a bit of a challenge. Because of this unique situation, most of our research is unauthorized and unofficial.

We did not test food or drinks in laboratories. Much of our analysis was conducted by comparing and contrasting the public information shared by each restaurant, though named restaurants did not endorse this publication. Net carb calculations and menu recommendations are provided at the authors' discretion. Should you stumble upon a discrepancy, keep in mind there are both regional and seasonal menu offerings, not to mention website updates (we hope!).

Menus, as you know, are fluid. Offerings are subject to change, as are proprietary recipes, ingredients, and geographical restaurant suppliers. Expect some variability among different locations. Even among chain restaurants, serving sizes and menus may differ. Because of these many variables, calculating restaurant nutrition information will never be a perfect science.

Bottom line? Our hearts are in the right place. Every effort was made to provide the most accurate information possible based on exhaustive online and in-person research at the time of publication.

The Keto Mindset

"Not knowing" every detail about food can be stressful for many people. So much uncertainty. *What if I make a mistake?* Take a deep breath. Changing your lifestyle is hard, I know! Instead of trying to be perfect, do your best. Don't sweat over minutia beyond your control. Use this material to help you make the best decision possible, given the circumstances and information in front of you.

In the spirit of keeping things as uncomplicated as possible, you'll notice there are no partial decimal amounts here. Fractions round appropriately up or down. There is no talk of weighing or measuring food either (bringing a food scale to a restaurant? How weird!). Go ahead and eyeball your serving sizes. Relax a little and trust yourself.

Over time, you'll develop more confidence. Keywords or phrases on menus will start to jump out at you. Sugar is sneaky, remember? It hides behind many names. Study the provided "Carby Word Bank" located at the end of this chapter. Stop and investigate when you see these terms describe an entrée or restaurant special. These terms *might* indicate it's higher in carbs (but not always). It's possible you may need to avoid an offending ingredient or make a special request. Read carefully. Ask questions. Once you learn to decode a menu, deciding what to eat becomes more manageable. With practice, it gets easier, even automatic.

You don't have to have all the answers – jump right in. Don't let perfect be the enemy of good. Will you make mistakes? Probably. Expect them to happen. Forgive yourself, learn from the experience, then keep plugging along. No biggie. Every step you make toward eating healthier is worthwhile. No matter your health goals, making informed decisions about your eating is the first step to getting there.

Carby Watch-Outs

Read Menus Carefully

Spot Higher Carb Clues

Investigate

Ask Questions

Exercise Caution

Avoid Sugar & Flour

Be Assertive When Ordering

Carby Word Bank

Exercise caution, or at least investigate when descriptors like these are used on a menu.
As you discover more, add to the list.

A la mode
Agave
Angel hair
Apple
Apple juice
Applesauce
Au gratin
Baby corn
Bagel
Baguette
Baked potato
Banana
Barbecue
Battered
BBQ
Beans
Beer
Beignet
Biscuit
Black bean
Blintz
Bran
Bread
Bread bowl
Breadcrumbs
Breaded
Breading
Breadstick
Brown rice
Brown sauce
Brown sugar
Brownie
Bruschetta
Buckwheat
Bun
Burrito
Buttermilk
Butterscotch
Cake
Calzone
Candied
Candied nuts
Candy
Cantaloupe
Caramel
Carrot
Catsup
Cereal
Cheesecake
Cherry
Chicken noodle
Chile relleno

Chili
Chimichanga
Chips
Chocolate
Chow Mein
Chowder
Citrus
Cobbler
Cocktail sauce
Coconut
Cone
Cookie
Corn
Cornbread
Corn chips
Corn dog
Corn flakes
Corn on the cob
Corn salsa
Corn starch
Corn tortilla
Cotton candy
Country fried
Crackers
Craisin
Cranberry
Cranberry juice
Creamed corn
Crisp
Crispy
Croissant
Crouton
Crumb
Crumble
Crunch
Crunchy
Crust
Crusted
Cupcake
Daiquiri
Dal
Danish
Dates
Deep dish
Deep fried
Dessert
Dip
Dipped
Donut
Doughnut
Dressing
Dumpling

Egg roll
Enchilada
Etouffee
Fat-free
Fettuccini
Fig
Flambée
Flatbread
Flautas
Flour
Flour tortilla
French dressing
French fry
French toast
Fried
Fried rice
Fries
Frosted
Frosting
Frozen yogurt
Fruit
Fruit cocktail
Fry
Fudge
Gelato
Glaze
Gnocchi
Graham cracker
Grain
Granola
Grape
Grapefruit
Green peas
Grits
Guava
Gumbo
Hard-shell
Hash browns
Hawaiian
Hoagie
Home fries
Homestyle
Homestyle pot
Hominy
Honey
Honey mustard
Hush puppies
Ice cream
Icing
Jam
Jambalaya
Jell-O

Keto Diet Restaurant Guide

Jelly	Pastry	Sesame sticks
Juice	Peach	Shell
Kahlua	Pear	Sherbet
Katsu	Peas	Slider
Ketchup	Piccata	Smoothie
Kidney bean	Pie	Soda
Kiwi	Pilaf	Soft drinks
Korean	Pineapple	Soft taco
Lasagna	Pinto bean	Sourdough
Lassi	Pita	Spaghetti
Latte	Pizza	Steak fries
Lentils	Plantains	Steel cut oats
Linguini	Plum	Strudel
Lo Mein	Polynesian	Stuffed
Low-fat	Popcorn	Stuffing
Mac and cheese	Pot pie	Sugar
Macaroni	Potato	Sundae
Malt	Potato chips	Sweet
Mandarin	Potato salad	Sweet and sour
Mango	Potato soup	Sweet pickle
Manicotti	Potsticker	Sweet potato
Maple	Praline	Sweet tea
Margarita	Preserves	Sweetened
Marshmallow	Pretzel	Syrup
Mashed potato	Pudding	Taco
Melon	Quesadilla	Taquito
Milk	Quiche	Tator tots
Milkshake	Quinoa	Tempura
Millet	Raisin	Teriyaki
Mocha	Ramen	Toast
Molasses	Rangoon	Torte
Muffin	Ravioli	Tortellini
Multi-grain	Refried beans	Tortilla
Muscat	Relish	Tortilla chips
Naan	Rice	Tots
Nachos	Rice noodles	Tropical
Navy bean	Rice sticks	Udon
Noodles	Riesling	Tortilla strips
Oat	Rigatoni	Waffle
Oatmeal	Risotto	Waldorf
Onion rings	Roll	Watermelon
Orange	Rolled oats	Wheat
Orange juice	Roux	Whole-grain
Oriental	Russian dressing	Won ton
Paella	Saltines	Wrap
Pancake	Samosa	Yam
Panini	Sandwich	Yogurt (sweetened)
Panko	Sangria	Ziti
Papaya	Sauce	
Parfait	Scampi	
Pasta	Scone	

1. Breakfast & Diners

Chapter 1

IHOP
Waffle House
Dunkin'
Tim Hortons
Bob Evans

Denny's
Panera Bread
Black Bear Diner
Big Boy

IHOP

IHOP gets a much-deserved *Keto Diet Restaurant Guide* Superstar Award for its website's customizable Nutrition Calculator and Interactive Nutrition Menu. Give these valuable online tools a try! Manipulate a menu item by adding or subtracting ingredients (to reduce carbs and make the food more keto-friendly).

Special Order Tips

Most locations have sugar-free syrup available and will bring it out upon request. Be sure to read the nutrition information on the bottle to ensure it fits within your daily carb budget. For some reason, they do not list this item on the menu, so I chose not to include it in my analysis below.

According to the Interactive Nutrition Menu, the regular omelet mixture (not egg white mixture) has wheat flour AND sugar in it (8 grams of carbs per serving), so I am recommending egg white omelets since they have <1 gram of carb per serving. I wonder if this is an error on their part (why would the regular omelet have flour and sugar but not the egg white omelet?).

Order all burgers and sandwiches with "no bread." Be wary of the available "Add-Ons" since they are often an unnecessary source of net carbs.

Feel free to customize your order. Restaurants are usually happy to accommodate reasonable customer requests. The exception is when the item has been premade or was prepared off-site. Note that any alterations on your end will change the provided nutrition information. Adjust accordingly.

Avoid pancakes, toast, fries, potatoes, rice, pasta, bread, hash browns, grits, beans, tortillas, etc. Ask the server to substitute a side salad or a side of steamed/grilled vegetables.

You'll notice some menu items indicate a half-serving size. Don't worry; there will only be a few! A smaller portion size allowed us to include more (higher-carb) crowd-pleasing favorites like soups or chilis.

Author Favorite

Breakfast: Huevos Rancheros, no beans and tortillas, easy salsa. 16 oz. chilled Sobe Yumberry Pomegranate Life Water to drink. 660 calories, 35g fat, 6g net carbs, 23g protein

Lunch: Bunless Jalapeño Kick Steakburgers, substitute House Salad with easy ranch dressing for the fries. 16 oz. Diet Pepsi to drink. 1100 calories, 84g fat, 7g net carbs, 41g protein

Dinner: Sirloin Steak Tips, no potatoes, no corn, no glaze/sauce with Broccoli Florets and House Salad with ranch dressing on the side. 20 oz. unsweetened iced tea to drink. 1215 calories, 77g fat, 16g net carbs, 53g protein

BREAKFAST (No Bread, No Potatoes)

Combos (No Pancakes, No Hash Browns, No Bread)

2g net carbs: Quick 2-Egg Breakfast 210 calories, 14g fat, 2g protein
3g net carbs: Grilled Steak & Eggs, no gravy, remove breading, 720 calories, 50g fat, 41g protein
3g net carbs: T-Bone Steak & Eggs (10 oz.) 740 calories, 28g fat, 62g protein
4g net carbs: Breakfast Sampler 890 calories, 57g fat, 32g protein
4g net carbs: Grilled Chicken & Eggs, no gravy, no breading/remove breading, 750 calories, 43g fat,
    32g protein
4g net carbs: Loco Moco, no rice, easy gravy 870 calories, 32g fat, 37g protein
4g net carbs: Split Decision Breakfast 910 calories, 60g fat, 27g protein
4g net carbs: T-Bone Steak & Eggs (12 oz.) 830 calories, 37g fat, 67g protein
5g net carbs: 2 x 2 x 2 250 calories, 15g fat, 9g protein
5g net carbs: Sirloin Tips & Eggs, no glaze or seasonings 970 calories, 51g fat, 49g protein
6g net carbs: Eggs Benedict, easy Hollandaise 870 calories, 51g fat, 40g protein
6g net carbs: Huevos Rancheros, no tortillas, no beans, easy salsa 660 calories, 35g fat, 23g protein
6g net carbs: Machaca, no tortillas, no tortilla strips, no salsa 1,100 calories, 81g fat, 49g protein
7g net carbs: Monster Mummy Burrito, no tortilla, no cheese sauce 1,110 calories, 76g fat, 56g protein
8g net carbs: Migas, no tortillas, no tortilla strips, no salsa 1,030 calories, 77g fat, 39g protein
8g net carbs: Smokehouse Combo 1,020 calories, 73g fat, 27g protein

Egg White Omelets

5g net carbs: Big Steak Egg White Omelet, no salsa 1,030 calories, 69g fat, 66g protein
6g net carbs: Bacon Temptation Egg White Omelet, no Queso Sauce 1,190 calories, 90g fat, 72g protein
6g net carbs: Colorado Egg White Omelet, no salsa 1,250 calories, 98g fat, 74g protein
6g net carbs: Spinach & Mushroom Egg White Omelet, no Hollandaise 910 calories, 71g fat, 47g protein
7g net carbs: Chicken Fajita Egg White Omelet, no Roasted Poblano, Red Peppers & Onion 900 calories, 57g fat, 74g protein
7g net carbs: Spicy Poblano Egg White Omelet, no Poblano Hollandaise 1,010 calories, 75g fat, 56g protein

Build Your Own Omelets[5]

0g net carbs: Diced Bacon 80 calories, 6g fat, 6g protein
1g net carbs: Egg Whites (3) 100 calories, 3g fat, 18g protein
1g net carbs: Avocado 80 calories, 7g fat, 1g protein
1g net carbs: Diced Ham 35 calories, 1g fat, 5g protein
1g net carbs: Pepper Jack Cheese 160 calories, 13g fat, 10g protein
1g net carbs: Pork Sausage Link 200 calories, 20g fat, 5g protein
1g net carbs: Sauteed Mushrooms 70 calories, 7g fat, 2g protein
1g net carbs: Sauteed Spinach 80 calories, 7g fat, 2g protein
1g net carbs: Sharp White Cheddar Cheese 170 calories, 14g fat, 10g protein
1g net carbs: Sour Cream 60 calories, 6g fat, 1g protein
1g net carbs: Tomato 10 calories, 0g fat, 1g protein
2g net carbs: American Cheese 100 calories, 8g fat, 5g protein
2g net carbs: Sauteed Green Peppers & Onions 70 calories, 7g fat, 0g protein
2g net carbs: Shredded Cheddar Cheese 230 calories, 18g fat, 13g protein
2g net carbs: Shredded Cheese Blend 220 calories, 17g fat, 13g protein
2g net carbs: Swiss Cheese 110 calories, 9g fat, 8g protein
3g net carbs: Fire Roasted Poblano Salsa 20 calories, 0g fat, 1g protein
8g net carbs: Regular Eggs Mixture (2 eggs) 400 calories, 28g fat, 28g protein

Bowls (No Hash Browns, Egg Whites Only)

3g net carbs: The Classic Egg White Bowl with Bacon 870 calories, 65g fat, 42g protein
5g net carbs: Spicy Shredded Beef Egg White Bowl, no Roasted Poblano, Red Peppers & Onion, no cheese sauce, 900 calories, 42g fat, 45g protein
6g net carbs: The Classic Egg White Bowl with Sausage 910 calories, 73g fat, 35g protein
7g net carbs: Big Country Egg White Bowl, no gravy, no Roasted Poblano, Red Peppers & Onion 1,020 calories, 76g fat, 45g protein
7g net carbs: New Mexico Egg White Chicken Bowl, no Rice & Barley, no queso sauce, no salsa 940 calories, 46g fat, 47g protein
7g net carbs: Spicy Poblano Egg White Fajita Bowl, no Roasted Poblano, Red Peppers & Onion, no queso sauce 1,050 calories, 75g fat, 55g protein
8g net carbs: Southwest Chicken Egg White Bowl, no queso sauce, no salsa 1,100 calories, 79g fat, 57g protein

---

[5] Regular omelets are higher in carbs due to the flour and sugar IHOP adds to the egg mixture.

Breakfast Add-Ons

Choice of Eggs (1 Egg)

0g net carbs: Poached Egg 60 calories, 4g fat, 6g protein
0g net carbs: Scrambled Egg White 30 calories, 1g fat, 6g protein
1g net carbs: Hardboiled Egg 80 calories, 5g fat, 6g protein
1g net carbs: Scrambled Egg 110 calories, 9g fat, 7g protein
2g net carbs: Fried Egg 60 calories, 3g fat, 6g protein

Choice of Eggs (2 Eggs)

1g net carbs: Hardboiled Egg 160 calories, 11g fat, 13g protein
1g net carbs: Poached Egg 130 calories, 8g fat, 11g protein
1g net carbs: Scrambled Egg 220 calories, 17g fat, 14g protein
1g net carbs: Scrambled Egg White 60 calories, 2g fat, 11g protein
3g net carbs: Fried Egg 120 calories, 6g fat, 12g protein

Choice of Eggs (3 Eggs)

1g net carbs: Poached Egg 190 calories, 13g fat, 17g protein
1g net carbs: Scrambled Egg White 100 calories, 2g fat, 17g protein
2g net carbs: Hardboiled Egg 230 calories, 16g fat, 19g protein
2g net carbs: Scrambled Egg 320 calories, 26g fat, 21g protein
5g net carbs: Fried Egg 180 calories, 9g fat, 18g protein

Choice of Meat (2 Pieces)

0g net carbs: Bacon 90 calories, 8g fat, 6g protein
0g net carbs: Turkey Sausage Link 90 calories, 7g fat, 8g protein
1g net carbs: Pork Sausage Link 200 calories, 20g fat, 5g protein
1g net carbs: Turkey Bacon 60 calories, 4g fat, 5g protein
2g net carbs: Ham 60 calories, 1g fat, 10g protein

Choice of Meat (4 Pieces)

1g net carbs: Bacon 190 calories, 15g fat, 12g protein
1g net carbs: Pork Sausage Link 410 calories, 40g fat, 10g protein
1g net carbs: Turkey Sausage Link 190 calories, 13g fat, 17g protein
2g net carbs: Turkey Bacon 120 calories, 8g fat, 10g protein
4g net carbs: Ham 120 calories, 2g fat, 20g protein

Sides

1g net carbs: Avocado 80 calories, 7g fat, 1g protein
2g net carbs: Spam (2 slices) 170 calories, 14g fat, 8g protein
3g net carbs: Spam (4 slices) 340 calories, 29g fat, 16g protein
4g net carbs: Ham (1 slice) 120 calories, 2g fat, 20g protein

7g net carbs: Fresh Fruit[6], Half-Serving, 50 calories, 0g fat, 1g protein

LUNCH

Ultimate Steakburgers (No Bread with House Salad, No Dressing)

3g net carbs: Mega Monster Cheeseburger, no IHOP sauce 1,060 calories, 72g fat, 60g protein
3g net carbs: The Classic with Bacon and Grilled Chicken, easy IHOP sauce 620 calories, 29g fat, 47g protein
3g net carbs: The Classic with Grilled Chicken 520 calories, 21g fat, 41g protein
3g net carbs: The Classic, easy IHOP sauce 670 calories, 42g fat, 33g protein
4g net carbs: Big Brunch with Grilled Chicken, no Potato Cake 840 calories, 43g fat, 54g protein
4g net carbs: Big Brunch, no Potato Cake 990 calories, 64g fat, 46g protein
4g net carbs: Cowboy BBQ, no BBQ sauce, no onion rings 950 calories, 54g fat, 41g protein
5g net carbs: The Classic with Bacon, easy IHOP sauce 770 calories, 49g fat, 38g protein
6g net carbs: Cowboy BBQ with Grilled Chicken, no BBQ sauce, no onion rings 790 calories, 33g fat, 50g protein
6g net carbs: Jalapeño Kick 1,000 calories, 74g fat, 41g protein
7g net carbs: Jalapeño Kick with Grilled Chicken 850 calories, 53g fat, 50g protein

Sandwiches (No Bread, with House Salad, No Dressing)

4g net carbs: Spicy Buffalo Grilled Chicken Sandwich 630 calories, 31g fat, 29g protein
4g net carbs: Turkey Cheddar Club 1,190 calories, 76g fat, 59g protein
5g net carbs: BLTA 1,170 calories, 84g fat, 32g protein
6g net carbs: Ham & Egg Melt 960 calories, 51g fat, 57g protein
7g net carbs: Philly Cheese Steak Stacker 820 calories, 46g fat, 46g protein

Salads

3g net carbs: House Salad (without dressing), 30 calories, 0g fat, 2g protein
9g net carbs: Grilled Chicken & Veggie Salad with ranch dressing 600 calories, 35g fat, 38g protein

Salad Dressing

2g net carbs: Ranch, 2 oz. 290 calories, 31g fat, 1g protein
6g net carbs: Balsamic Vinaigrette, 1 oz. 200 calories, 16g fat, 0g protein
6g net carbs: Honey Mustard, 1 oz. 230 calories, 20g fat, 1g protein

DINNER

Entrees (with House Side Salad as Side, No Dressing)

2g net carbs: T-Bone Steak (10 oz.), no potatoes 560 calories, 24g fat, 56g protein
3g net carbs: T-Bone Steak (12 oz.), no potatoes 650 calories, 32g fat, 61g protein
4g net carbs: Grilled Tilapia, no Rice & Barley Medley 11 calories, 2g fat, 44g protein
4g net carbs: Pot Roast, no corn, no potatoes, no gravy 790 calories, 44g fat, 40g protein

---

[6] *That's Not Keto!* – You'll find all sorts of surprising foods listed here. I'm not telling you whether you should eat these foods or not. What fits your macros or daily carb spend is up to you. No keto police allowed.

5g net carbs: Boneless Grilled Buffalo Chicken Strips 460 calories, 21g fat, 42g protein
6g net carbs: Cheesy Chicken Bacon Ranch with Grilled Chicken, no Queso Sauce, no Rice & Barley Medley 680 calories, 60g fat, 95g protein
6g net carbs: Roasted Turkey Breast, no potatoes, no Lingonberries, easy gravy 710 calories, 26g fat, 51g protein
7g net carbs: Sirloin Steak Tips, no potatoes, no corn, no glaze/sauce 860 calories, 46g fat, 47g protein

Sides

2g net carbs: Broccoli Florets 25 calories, 0g fat, 3g protein

Choice of Dipping Sauce (2 oz.)

2g net carbs: Buttermilk Ranch 290 calories, 31g fat, 1g protein
8g net carbs: IHOP Sauce 220 calories, 21g fat, 1g protein

DRINKS

0g net carbs: Coke Zero, 16 oz. 0 calories, 0g fat, 0g protein
0g net carbs: Diet Coke, 16 oz. 0 calories, 0g fat, 0g protein
0g net carbs: Diet Pepsi, 16 oz. 0 calories, 0g fat, 0g protein
0g net carbs: Hot Tea, Golden Chamomile, unsweetened, 8 oz. 0 calories, 0g fat, 0g protein
0g net carbs: Hot Tea, Organic Green, unsweetened, 8 oz. 0 calories, 0g fat, 1g protein
0g net carbs: International House Roast Coffee, unsweetened, 8 oz. 0 calories, 0g fat, 0g protein
0g net carbs: International House Roast Decaf Coffee, unsweetened, 8 oz. 0 calories, 0g fat, 0g protein
0g net carbs: Sobe Yumberry Pomegranate Life Water, 16 oz. bottle 0 calories, 0g fat, 0g protein
1g net carbs: Hot Tea, Decaf, unsweetened, 8 oz. 0 calories, 0g fat, 0g protein
1g net carbs: Hot Tea, English Breakfast, unsweetened, 8 oz. 0 calories, 0g fat, 0g protein
2g net carbs: Iced Tea, unsweetened, 16 oz. 5 calories, 0g fat, 0g protein
2g net carbs: Iced Tea, unsweetened, 20 oz. 10 calories, 0g fat, 0g protein
7g net carbs: Tomato Juice[7], 8 oz. 50 calories, 0g fat, 2g protein

---

[7] *That's Not Keto!* – You'll find all sorts of surprising foods listed here. I'm not telling you whether you should eat these foods or not. What fits your macros or daily carb spend is up to you. No keto police allowed.

Waffle House

With a name like Waffle House, you would guess that the low-carb options are limited, but I was surprised. There are several dishes with grilled chicken as the protein. Even better, I COULD NOT find any breaded chicken options. Bravo, Waffle House!

Waffle House has a half-baked customizable nutrition calculator on its website. However, for our purposes, it's not very useful. For example, the calculator cannot remove bread/buns from any meal or burger/sandwich option. On the other hand, they provide a detailed PDF of Full Nutritional's. Bottom line? You've got to crunch the numbers yourself.

Feel free to customize orders to your liking. Usually, restaurants are happy to accommodate reasonable customer requests (they are used to patrons asking for deletions/substitutions by now). The exception is when the item was premade or was prepared off-site, which is often the case with chain restaurants (think frozen breaded shrimp or wings pre-seasoned with BBQ sauce).

Special Order Tips

All burgers and sandwiches should be ordered "bunless" (without the bread) or "lettuce wrapped" to match the nutrition information provided. Be wary of the available "Add-Ons" since they are often an unnecessary source of net carbs. These items are analyzed in their "regular" form as described on the menu. Any alterations will change their calorie and macronutrient amount.

Avoid all fries, potatoes, rice, pasta, bread, etc. Ask the server to substitute a side salad or a side of steamed/grilled vegetables.

I couldn't find any information on the website regarding the salad dressings, so I omitted them from my calculations. The only reference I could find was a photo of a salad with dressing packets. So not helpful!

Author Favorite

Breakfast: All-Star Special™ with no bread or hash browns. 8 oz. Dark Roast Coffee, unsweetened to drink. 385 calories, 26g fat, 4g net carbs, 22g protein

Lunch: Bunless Angus 1/4 lb. Cheeseburger Deluxe with Garden Side Salad, no dressing. 16 oz. Diet Coke to drink. 655 calories, 45g fat, 7g net carbs, 24g protein

Dinner: Sirloin Dinner topped with Bert's Chili. Garden Side Salad with no dressing and sliced tomatoes on the side. 16 oz. Alice's Iced Tea™, unsweetened on ice to drink. 760 calories, 33g fat, 18g net carbs, 39g protein

BREAKFAST (No Bread, No Potatoes, No Grits)

2g net carbs: 2 Egg Breakfast 370 calories, 24g fat, 24g protein
2g net carbs: Cheese 'N Eggs 290 calories, 10g fat, 18g protein
3g net carbs: Grilled Chicken & Eggs 560 calories, 42g fat, 47g protein
3g net carbs: Ham Egg & Cheese Bowl 375 calories, 25g fat, 24g protein
3g net carbs: T-Bone & Eggs 820 calories, 64g fat, 129g protein
4g net carbs: All-Star Special™ 380 calories, 26g fat, 22g protein
4g net carbs: Country Ham & Eggs 830 calories, 42g fat, 93g protein
4g net carbs: Meat Lover's Pork Chops & Eggs 610 calories, 45g fat, 51g protein
4g net carbs: Pork Chops & Eggs 570 calories, 43g fat, 47g protein
5g net carbs: Bacon Egg & Cheese Bowl 330 calories, 22g fat, 23g protein
5g net carbs: Meat Lover's Grilled Chicken & Eggs 580 calories, 44g fat, 49g protein
5g net carbs: Sausage Egg & Cheese Bowl 360 calories, 24g fat, 22g protein
6g net carbs: Steak & Eggs 760 calories, 56g fat, 64g protein

Toddle House© Omelet Breakfasts (No Bread, No Potatoes)

2g net carbs: Cheese Omelet Breakfast 470 calories, 33g fat, 27g protein
3g net carbs: Ham & Cheese Omelet Breakfast 570 calories, 37g fat, 37g protein
4g net carbs: Cheesesteak Omelet Breakfast 580 calories, 41g fat, 43g protein
4g net carbs: Fiesta Omelet Breakfast 565 calories, 38g fat, 40g protein

Build Your Own Omelet Breakfast (No Bread, No Potatoes)

0g net carbs: Bacon 90 calories, 8g fat, 5g protein
0g net carbs: Cheesesteak 130 calories, 7g fat, 16g protein
0g net carbs: Sausage 130 calories, 12g fat, 5g protein
1g net carbs: Grilled Chicken 140 calories, 2g fat, 29g protein
1g net carbs: Melted American Cheese 100 calories, 8g fat, 5g protein
1g net carbs: Sliced Tomatoes 10 calories, 0g fat, 1g protein
2g net carbs: 2 Eggs Scrambled 400 calories, 38g fat, 12g protein
2g net carbs: Grilled Mushrooms 20 calories, 0g fat, 2g protein
2g net carbs: Grilled Tomatoes 5 calories, 0g fat, 0g protein
2g net carbs: Hickory Smoked Ham 60 calories, 1g fat, 9g protein
2g net carbs: Jalapeño Peppers 10 calories, 0g fat, 0g protein

2g net carbs: Sautéed Onions 15 calories, 0g fat, 0g protein

Egg Sandwiches (No Bread)

1g net carbs: Bacon Sandwich 240 calories, 4g fat, 19g protein
3g net carbs: Sausage Sandwich 270 calories, 13g fat, 12g protein
4g net carbs: Egg & Cheese Sandwich 270 calories, 12g fat, 13g protein
4g net carbs: Egg Sandwich 220 calories, 8g fat, 10g protein
4g net carbs: Grilled Ham Sandwich 530 calories, 36g fat, 23g protein
4g net carbs: Ham & Egg Sandwich 450 calories, 33g fat, 28g protein
4g net carbs: Ham, Egg & Cheese Sandwich 330 calories, 11g fat, 25g protein
4g net carbs: Sausage & Egg Sandwich 360 calories, 20g fat, 18g protein
4g net carbs: Sausage, Egg & Cheese Sandwich 410 calories, 24g fat, 21g protein
4g net carbs: Texas Bacon, Egg & Cheese Melt 480 calories, 32g fat, 20g protein
4g net carbs: Texas Ham, Egg & Cheese Melt 380 calories, 15g fat, 28g protein
5g net carbs: Bacon & Egg Sandwich 590 calories, 39g fat, 18g protein
5g net carbs: Bacon, Egg & Cheese Sandwich 390 calories, 25g fat, 14g protein
5g net carbs: Texas Egg & Cheese Melt 700 calories, 41g fat, 33g protein
5g net carbs: Texas Sausage, Egg & Cheese Melt 730 calories, 51g fat, 26g protein

Breakfast Toppings

0g net carbs: Melted American Cheese 50 calories, 4g fat, 3g protein
2g net carbs: Grilled Mushrooms 20 calories, 0g fat, 2g protein
2g net carbs: Grilled Tomatoes 5 calories, 0g fat, 0g protein
2g net carbs: Hickory Smoked Ham 60 calories, 1g fat, 9g protein
2g net carbs: Jalapeño Peppers 10 calories, 0g fat, 0g protein
2g net carbs: Sautéed Onions 15 calories, 0g fat, 0g protein
6g net carbs: Bert's Chili™ 80 calories, 3g fat, 5g protein
8g net carbs: Sausage Gravy 90 calories, 5g fat, 1g protein

Breakfast Sides

0g net carbs: Bacon (3 strips) 140 calories, 12g fat, 8g protein
0g net carbs: Country Ham (1 slice) 210 calories, 9g fat, 32g protein
1g net carbs: Large Bacon (5 strips) 230 calories, 19g fat, 13g protein
1g net carbs: Large Sausage (3 patties) 390 calories, 36g fat, 15g protein
1g net carbs: Sausage (2 patties) 260 calories, 24g fat, 10g protein
1g net carbs: Tomatoes, sliced 10 calories, 0g fat, 1g protein
7g net carbs: City Ham (1 slice) 110 calories, 2g fat, 15g protein

LUNCH (No Hashbrowns)

4g net carbs: Cheesesteak Melt Bowl 520 calories, 45g fat, 39g protein
4g net carbs: Grilled Chicken Melt Bowl 530 calories, 41g fat, 34g protein

100% Angus Beef Hamburgers (No Bread)

3g net carbs: Angus 1/4 lb. Hamburger Deluxe 560 calories, 41g fat, 19g protein

4g net carbs: Angus 1/4 lb. Cheeseburger Deluxe 620 calories, 45g fat, 22g protein
5g net carbs: Double Angus 1/4 lb. Cheeseburger Deluxe 890 calories, 66g fat, 40g protein
5g net carbs: "Original" Angus Hamburger 465 calories, 33g fat, 11g protein
5g net carbs: "Original" Angus Cheeseburger 515 calories, 37g fat, 14g protein
5g net carbs: Double "Original" Angus Hamburger 575 calories, 42g fat, 18g protein
6g net carbs: Double "Original" Angus Cheeseburger 625 calories, 46g fat, 21g protein

Sandwiches (No Bread)

3g net carbs: Grilled Cheese Sandwich 330 calories, 21g fat, 10g protein
3g net carbs: Grilled Chicken Bacon Cheese Sandwich Deluxe 630 calories, 38g fat, 41g protein
3g net carbs: Grilled Chicken Sandwich Deluxe 490 calories, 26g fat, 33g protein
3g net carbs: Ham & Cheese Sandwich (Lettuce & Tomato) 295 calories, 8g fat, 22g protein
4g net carbs: BLT Sandwich 275 calories, 13g fat, 12g protein
4g net carbs: Waffle Sandwich (Ham and Cheese) 380 calories, 18g fat, 26g protein
5g net carbs: Texas Bacon Lover's BLT Sandwich 635 calories, 44g fat, 19g protein

Texas Melts (No Bread)

6g net carbs: Texas Grilled Chicken Melt 660 calories, 35g fat, 41g protein
6g net carbs: Texas Cheesesteak™ Melt 650 calories, 40g fat, 28g protein
6g net carbs: Texas Angus Patty Melt 730 calories, 50g fat, 26g protein

DINNER (No Bread, No Hashbrowns, Garden Salad, No Dressing)

Classic Dinners

5g net carbs: Grilled Chicken Dinner 565 calories, 21g fat, 37g protein
5g net carbs: Pork Chop Dinner 1005 calories, 49g fat, 84g protein
6g net carbs: Country Ham Dinner 635 calories, 28g fat, 40g protein
6g net carbs: Meat Lovers Grilled Chicken Dinner 705 calories, 24g fat, 66g protein
6g net carbs: Meat Lovers Pork Chop Dinner 1295 calories, 64g fat, 122g protein

USDA Choice Steak Dinners

5g net carbs: T-Bone Dinner 725 calories, 37g fat, 42g protein
6g net carbs: Sirloin Dinner 615 calories, 30g fat, 29g protein

Add-Ons

0g net carbs: Bacon (2 strips) 90 calories, 8g fat, 5g protein
6g net carbs: Bert's Chili™ as a Topping 80 calories, 3g fat, 5g protein

Salads (No Dressing)

3g net carbs: Garden Side Salad 35 calories, 0g fat, 2g protein
5g net carbs: Grilled Chicken Salad 175 calories, 2g fat, 31g protein

Dinner Sides

0g net carbs: Bacon (3 strips) 140 calories, 12g fat, 8g protein
0g net carbs: Country Ham (1 slice) 210 calories, 9g fat, 32g protein
1g net carbs: Large Bacon (5 strips) 230 calories, 19g fat, 13g protein
1g net carbs: Large Sausage (3 patties) 390 calories, 36g fat, 15g protein
1g net carbs: Sausage (2 patties) 260 calories, 24g fat, 10g protein
1g net carbs: Tomatoes, sliced 10 calories, 0g fat, 1g protein
7g net carbs: City Ham (1 slice) 110 calories, 2g fat, 15g protein
8g net carbs: Sausage Gravy 90 calories, 5g fat, 1g protein

DRINKS

0g net carbs: Diet Coke, 16 oz. 0 calories, 0g fat, 0g protein
0g net carbs: Alice's Iced Tea™, unsweetened, 16 oz. 0 calories, 0g fat, 0g protein
0g net carbs: Hot Tea, unsweetened, 8 oz. 5 calories, 0g fat, 0g protein
0g net carbs: Classic Blend Coffee, unsweetened, 8 oz. 5 calories, 0g fat, 0g protein
0g net carbs: Dark Roast Coffee, unsweetened, 8 oz. 5 calories, 0g fat, 0g protein
0g net carbs: Decaf Coffee, unsweetened, 8 oz. 5 calories, 0g fat, 0g protein

Dunkin'

In my book, Dunkin' should be reserved for the *staunchest* keto-er. It takes some iron-clad conviction to forgo the donuts, bagels, and sugar-laden coffee drinks. Temptation is everywhere you look! You can even smell the deliciousness from the drive-thru window.

Dunkin' has a limited customizable nutrition calculator on its website, and it is not very useful. Bread (as an ingredient) cannot be removed from sandwiches or wraps. It's not possible to separate sauces from an entrée either. They have a detailed Nutrition Guide PDF that will help you be in control of your carb intake.

Those thinking a drink order will be a clear choice will have to guess again. There's some suspicion here too! The Dunkin' website is a bit unclear about beverage serving size. Would you believe there is no mention ANYWHERE about the number of ounces inside small, medium, large, or extra-large drinks? A general search online doesn't help either; sizes are all over the place. Weird.

Special Order Tips

Order all burgers and sandwiches "bunless" (without the bread) or "lettuce wrapped" to match the estimated nutrition information provided. Be wary of the available "Add-Ons" since they are often an unnecessary source of net carbs. These items are analyzed in their "regular" form as described on the menu. Any alterations will change their calorie and macronutrient amount.

Avoid all bagels, croissants, bread, muffins, potatoes, wraps, rice, pasta, bread, etc. Ask the server to substitute a side salad or a side of steamed/grilled vegetables.

Listen up everybody, we have some dessert items comin' up. They are the Munchkins and they are listed in the Breakfast section. They are sugary donut hole singles that range from 6-10 net carbs each. Come On, we deserve an exorbitant treat every now and then don't we?

Author Favorite

All Day Breakfast: Breadless Kosher Sweet Black Pepper Bacon Breakfast Sandwich. Unsweetened Medium Cold Brew Coffee over ice to drink. 680 calories, 43g fat, 6g net carbs, 21g protein

ALL DAY BREAKFAST

Breadless Croissant Stuffers

4g net carbs: Chicken, Bacon & Cheese Croissant Stuffer 330 calories, 18g fat, 14g protein

Munchkins[8]

6g net carbs: Cinnamon Munchkins*, 1 Donut Hole 60 calories, 3g fat, 2g protein
6g net carbs: Old Fashioned Munchkins*, 1 Donut Hole 50 calories, 3g fat, 1g protein
7g net carbs: Glazed Munchkins*, 1 Donut Hole 60 calories, 3g fat, 1g protein
7g net carbs: Powdered Munchkins*, 1 Donut Hole 60 calories, 3g fat, 1g protein
8g net carbs: Glazed Chocolate Munchkins*, 1 Donut Hole 60 calories, 3g fat, 1g protein
8g net carbs: Glazed Old Fashioned Munchkins*, 1 Donut Hole 70 calories, 3g fat, 1g protein
8g net carbs: Jelly Munchkins*, 1 Donut Hole 60 calories, 3g fat, 1g protein
9g net carbs: Glazed Blueberry Munchkins*, 1 Donut Hole 60 calories, 3g fat, 1g protein
10g net carbs: Cornbread Munchkins*, 1 Donut Hole 70 calories, 2g fat, 1g protein

Omelet Bites

7g net carbs: Bacon & Cheddar Omelet Bites (2) 280 calories, 19g fat, 17g protein
7g net carbs: Egg White & Veggie Omelet Bites (2) 180 calories, 11g fat, 0g protein

Snacking Bacon

10g net carbs: Sweet Black Pepper Snacking Bacon (8 Pieces) 190 calories, 12g fat, 10g protein

Breadless Stuffed Bagel Minis

5g net carbs: Stuffed Bagel Minis*, No Bread, Plain (2) 240 calories, 10g fat, 7g protein
5g net carbs: Stuffed Bagel Minis*, No Bread, Chive & Onion (2) 240 calories, 9g fat, 8g protein
6g net carbs: Stuffed Bagel Minis*, No Bread, Everything (2) 260 calories, 12g fat, 8g protein

Hash Browns

6g net carbs: Hash Browns* (3 Pieces) 55 calories, 3g fat, 1g protein

---

[8] *That's Not Keto!* – You'll find all sorts of surprising foods listed here. I'm not telling you whether you should eat these foods or not. What fits your macros or daily carb spend is up to you. No keto police allowed.

Breakfast Sandwiches (No Bread, No Tortillas)

3g net carbs: Chicken Croissant Sandwich 650 calories, 36g fat, 28g protein
3g net carbs: Egg and Cheese Wake-Up Wrap 180 calories, 10g fat, 7g protein
3g net carbs: Kosher Egg and Cheese 340 calories, 14g fat, 14g protein
3g net carbs: Kosher Tuna Salad 510 calories, 17g fat, 24g protein
3g net carbs: Kosher Veggie Bacon Wake-Up Wrap 200 calories, 12g fat, 8g protein
3g net carbs: Sausage, Egg, and Cheese Wake-Up Wrap 290 calories, 21g fat, 10g protein
3g net carbs: Sourdough Breakfast Sandwich 650 calories, 32g fat, 31g protein
4g net carbs: Bacon, Egg, and Cheese Wake-Up Wrap 220 calories, 13g fat, 10g protein
4g net carbs: Chicken Biscuit 460 calories, 22g fat, 21g protein
4g net carbs: Double Sausage Breakfast Sandwich 900 calories, 54g fat, 33g protein
4g net carbs: Kosher Egg and Cheese Wake Up Wrap 170 calories, 10g fat, 7g protein
4g net carbs: Kosher Grilled Cheese with Veggie Bacon 480 calories, 27g fat, 5g protein
4g net carbs: Kosher Sourdough Breakfast Sandwich 660 calories, 34g fat, 29g protein
4g net carbs: Sausage Biscuit 490 calories, 34g fat, 13g protein
4g net carbs: Sausage, Egg, and Cheese 720 calories, 52g fat, 21g protein
4g net carbs: Kosher Sweet Black Pepper Bacon Breakfast Sandwich 650 calories, 41g fat, 23g protein
5g net carbs: Kosher Sweet Black Pepper Bacon Wake-Up Wrap 280 calories, 17g fat, 12g protein
5g net carbs: Kosher Veggie Bacon Egg and Cheese 510 calories, 17 g fat, 21g protein
5g net carbs: Kosher Veggie Sausage Wake-Up Wrap 210 calories, 11g fat, 11g protein
5g net carbs: Spam Breakfast Sandwich 630 calories, 42g fat, 20g protein
6g net carbs: Bacon, Egg, and Cheese 560 calories, 36g fat, 18g protein
6g net carbs: Egg and Cheese 500 calories, 31g fat, 15g protein
6g net carbs: Kosher Dunkin' Double Veggie Sausage Sandwich 600 calories, 18g fat, 37g protein
6g net carbs: Kosher Sweet Black Pepper Bacon Breakfast Sandwich 670 calories, 43g fat, 21g protein
6g net carbs: Kosher Tuna Melt 630 calories, 42g fat, 24g protein
6g net carbs: Kosher Veggie Sausage Egg and Cheese 570 calories, 33g fat, 23g protein
6g net carbs: Sweet Black Pepper Bacon Wake-Up Wrap 280 calories, 18g fat, 13g protein
6g net carbs: Turkey Sausage Sandwich 460 calories, 22g fat, 26g protein
6g net carbs: Turkey Sausage Wake Up Wrap 240 calories, 15g fat, 11g protein
7g net carbs: Biscuit, Bacon, Egg, and Cheese 490 calories, 31g fat, 17g protein
7g net carbs: Tomato Pesto Grilled Cheese 520 calories, 22g fat, 20g protein

Condiments

0g net carbs: Butter (1 pat) 35 calories, 4g fat, 0g protein
0g net carbs: Butter Spread with Canola Oil (1 Portion) 100 calories, 11g fat, 0g protein

Cream Cheese Spread

2g net carbs: Garden Veggie Cream Cheese Spread (1 packet) 100 calories, 10g fat, 2g protein
3g net carbs: Classic Plain Cream Cheese Spread (1 packet) 120 calories, 12g fat, 2g protein
9g net carbs: Strawberry Cream Cheese Spread (1 packet) 130 calories, 10g fat, 2g protein

DRINKS

Hot Coffee (Unsweetened Unless Otherwise Indicated)

0g net carbs: Box 'O Joe® 1 Small Cup 5 calories, 0g fat, 0g protein
0g net carbs: Hot Coffee, Small 5 calories, 0g fat, 0g protein
0g net carbs: Hot Coffee, Medium 5 calories, 0g fat, 1g protein
0g net carbs: Hot Coffee, Large 5 calories, 0g fat, 1g protein
0g net carbs: Hot Coffee, Extra Large 5 calories, 0g fat, 1g protein
0g net carbs: Hot Coffee with Coconut Milk, Small 10 calories, 1g fat, 0g protein
0g net carbs: Hot Coffee with Coconut Milk, Medium 15 calories, 1g fat, 1g protein
1g net carbs: Hot Coffee with Coconut Milk, Extra Large 25 calories, 2g fat, 1g protein
1g net carbs: Hot Coffee with Coconut Milk, Large 20 calories, 1g fat, 1g protein
1g net carbs: Hot Coffee with Cream, Small 60 calories, 6g fat, 1g protein
1g net carbs: Hot Coffee with Cream, Medium 90 calories, 9g fat, 2g protein
1g net carbs: Hot Coffee with Whole Milk, Small 20 calories, 1g fat, 1g protein
2g net carbs: Hot Coffee with Almond Milk, Small 15 calories, 0g fat, 0g protein
2g net carbs: Hot Coffee with Cream, Extra Large 150 calories, 15g fat, 3g protein
2g net carbs: Hot Coffee with Cream, Large 120 calories, 12g fat, 2g protein
2g net carbs: Hot Coffee with Skim Milk, Medium 20 calories, 0g fat, 2g protein
2g net carbs: Hot Coffee with Skim Milk, Small 15 calories, 0g fat, 1g protein
2g net carbs: Hot Coffee with Whole Milk, Medium 30 calories, 1g fat, 2g protein
3g net carbs: Hot Coffee with Oat Milk, Small 15 calories, 0g fat, 1g protein
3g net carbs: Hot Coffee with Skim Milk, Large 25 calories, 0g fat, 3g protein
3g net carbs: Hot Coffee with Whole Milk, Extra Large 50 calories, 2g fat, 3g protein
3g net carbs: Hot Coffee with Whole Milk, Large 40 calories, 2g fat, 2g protein
4g net carbs: Hot Coffee with Almond Milk, Medium 25 calories, 1g fat, 1g protein
4g net carbs: Hot Coffee with Oat Milk, Medium 30 calories, 1g fat, 1g protein
4g net carbs: Hot Coffee with Skim Milk, Extra Large 30 calories, 0g fat, 3g protein
5g net carbs: Hot Coffee with Almond Milk, Large 35 calories, 1g fat, 1g protein
6g net carbs: Café Au Lait with Skim Milk, Small 45 calories, 0g fat, 4g protein
6g net carbs: Café Au Lait with Whole Milk, Small 80 calories, 4g fat, 4g protein
7g net carbs: Hot Coffee with Almond Milk, Extra Large 45 calories, 1g fat, 1g protein
7g net carbs: Hot Coffee with Oat Milk, Large 45 calories, 1g fat, 1g protein
9g net carbs: Café Au Lait with Skim Milk, Medium 70 calories, 0g fat, 7g protein
9g net carbs: Café Au Lait with Whole Milk, Medium 110 calories, 6g fat, 6g protein
9g net carbs: Hot Coffee with Oat Milk, Extra Large 60 calories, 1g fat, 1g protein

Cold Brew Coffee (Unsweetened Unless Otherwise Indicated)

0g net carbs: Cold Brew Coffee, Small 5 calories, 0g fat, 0g protein
0g net carbs: Cold Brew Coffee, Medium 5 calories, 0g fat, 0g protein
0g net carbs: Cold Brew Coffee, Large 5 calories, 0g fat, 1g protein
1g net carbs: Cold Brew Coffee with Cream, Small 60 calories, 6g fat, 1g protein
1g net carbs: Vanilla Cream Cold Brew, Small 60 calories, 6g fat, 1g protein
1g net carbs: Cold Brew Coffee with Cream, Medium 90 calories, 9g fat, 2g protein
2g net carbs: Coconut Almond Milk Cold Brew, Small 15 calories, 0g fat, 0g protein
2g net carbs: Cold Brew Coffee with Cream, Large 120 calories, 12g fat, 2g protein
2g net carbs: Vanilla Cream Cold Brew, Medium 100 calories, 9g fat, 2g protein
2g net carbs: Vanilla Cream Cold Brew, Large 130 calories, 12g fat, 2g protein

3g net carbs: Cold Brew Coffee with Oat Milk, Small 15 calories, 0g fat, 1g protein
4g net carbs: Coconut Almond Milk Cold Brew, Medium 30 calories, 1g fat, 1g protein
4g net carbs: Cold Brew Coffee with Oat Milk, Medium 30 calories, 1g fat, 1g protein
6g net carbs: Coconut Almond Milk Cold Brew, Large 45 calories, 1g fat, 1g protein
7g net carbs: Cold Brew Coffee with Oat Milk, Large 50 calories, 1g fat, 1g protein

Hot Americano (Unsweetened Unless Otherwise Indicated)

1g net carbs: Americano, Small 5 calories, 0g fat, 0g protein
2g net carbs: Americano, Large 10 calories, 0g fat, 0g protein
2g net carbs: Americano, Medium 10 calories, 0g fat, 0g protein

Hot Cappuccino (Unsweetened Unless Otherwise Indicated)

7g net carbs: Cappuccino with Skim Milk, Small 45 calories, 0g fat, 4g protein
7g net carbs: Cappuccino with Whole Milk, Small 80 calories, 4g fat, 4g protein
10g net carbs: Cappuccino with Skim Milk, Medium 70 calories, 0g fat, 6g protein

Hot Espresso (Unsweetened Unless Otherwise Indicated)

0g net carbs: Hot Espresso Single Shot 5 calories, 0g fat, 0g protein

Hot Latte (Unsweetened Unless Otherwise Indicated)

2g net carbs: Hot Latte with Coconut Milk, Small 35 calories, 3g fat, 0g protein
3g net carbs: Hot Latte with Coconut Milk, Medium 50 calories, 4g fat, 1g protein
4g net carbs: Hot Latte with Coconut Milk, Large 70 calories, 6g fat, 1g protein
9g net carbs: Hot Latte with Whole Milk, Small 120 calories, 6g fat, 6g protein
10g net carbs: Hot Latte with Skim Milk, Small 70 calories, 0g fat, 6g protein
10g net carbs: Hot Latte with Almond Milk, Small 70 calories, 2g fat, 1g protein

Hot Macchiato (Unsweetened Unless Otherwise Indicated)

2g net carbs: Hot Macchiato with Coconut Milk, Small 30 calories, 2g fat, 0g protein
3g net carbs: Hot Macchiato with Coconut Milk, Medium 40 calories, 3g fat, 0g protein
3g net carbs: Hot Macchiato with Coconut Milk, Large 50 calories, 4g fat, 1g protein
7g net carbs: Hot Macchiato with Whole Milk, Small 80 calories, 4g fat, 4g protein
7g net carbs: Hot Macchiato with Skim Milk, Small 50 calories, 0g fat, 4g protein
10g net carbs: Hot Macchiato with Whole Milk, Medium 120 calories, 6g fat, 6g protein

Iced Americano (Unsweetened Unless Otherwise Indicated)

1g net carbs: Iced Americano, Small 5 calories, 0g fat, 0g protein
2g net carbs: Iced Americano, Medium 10 calories, 0g fat, 0g protein
2g net carbs: Iced Americano, Large 10 calories, 0g fat, 0g protein

Iced Cappuccino (Unsweetened Unless Otherwise Indicated)

7g net carbs: Iced Cappuccino with Skim Milk, Small 45 calories, 0g fat, 4g protein
7g net carbs: Iced Cappuccino with Whole Milk, Small 80 calories, 4g fat, 4g protein
10g net carbs: Iced Cappuccino with Skim Milk, Medium 70 calories, 0g fat, 6g protein
10g net carbs: Iced Cappuccino with Whole Milk, Medium 120 calories, 6g fat, 6g protein

Iced Café Au Lait (Unsweetened Unless Otherwise Indicated)

6g net carbs: Iced Café Au Lait with Skim Milk, Small 45 calories, 0g fat, 4g protein
6g net carbs: Iced Café Au Lait with Whole Milk, Small 80 calories, 4g fat, 4g protein
9g net carbs: Iced Café Au Lait with Skim Milk, Medium 60 calories, 0g fat, 6g protein
9g net carbs: Iced Café Au Lait with Whole Milk, Medium 110 calories, 6g fat, 6g protein

Iced Coffee (Unsweetened Unless Otherwise Indicated)

0g net carbs: Iced Coffee with Coconut Milk, Small 10 calories, 1g fat, 0g protein
0g net carbs: Iced Coffee with Coconut Milk, Medium 15 calories, 1g fat, 1g protein
0g net carbs: Iced Coffee, Small 5 calories, 0g fat, 0g protein
0g net carbs: Iced Coffee, Medium 5 calories, 0g fat, 0g protein
0g net carbs: Iced Coffee, Large 5 calories, 0g fat, 1g protein
1g net carbs: Iced Coffee with Cream, Small 60 calories, 6g fat, 0g protein
1g net carbs: Iced Coffee with Cream, Medium 90 calories, 9g fat, 0g protein
1g net carbs: Iced Coffee with Coconut Milk, Large 20 calories, 1g fat, 1g protein
1g net carbs: Iced Coffee with Whole Milk, Small 20 calories, 1g fat, 1g protein
2g net carbs: Iced Coffee with Almond Milk, Small 15 calories, 0g fat, 0g protein
2g net carbs: Iced Coffee with Cream, Large 120 calories, 12g fat, 0g protein
2g net carbs: Iced Coffee with Skim Milk, Medium 20 calories, 0g fat, 0g protein
2g net carbs: Iced Coffee with Skim Milk, Small 15 calories, 0g fat, 0g protein
2g net carbs: Iced Coffee with Whole Milk, Medium 30 calories, 1g fat, 2g protein
3g net carbs: Iced Coffee with Oat Milk, Small 15 calories, 0g fat, 0g protein
3g net carbs: Iced Coffee with Skim Milk, Large 25 calories, 0g fat, 0g protein
3g net carbs: Iced Coffee with Whole Milk, Large 40 calories, 2g fat, 3g protein
4g net carbs: Iced Coffee with Almond Milk, Medium 25 calories, 1g fat, 1g protein
4g net carbs: Iced Coffee with Oat Milk, Medium 30 calories, 1g fat, 0g protein
5g net carbs: Iced Coffee with Almond Milk, Large 35 calories, 1g fat, 1g protein
7g net carbs: Iced Coffee with Oat Milk, Large 45 calories, 1g fat, 0g protein

Iced Latte (Unsweetened Unless Otherwise Indicated)

2g net carbs: Iced Latte with Coconut Milk, Small 35 calories, 3g fat, 0g protein
3g net carbs: Iced Latte with Coconut Milk, Medium 50 calories, 4g fat, 1g protein
4g net carbs: Iced Latte with Coconut Milk, Large 70 calories, 6g fat, 1g protein
9g net carbs: Iced Latte with Whole Milk, Small 120 calories, 6g fat, 6g protein
10g net carbs: Iced Latte with Skim Milk, Small 70 calories, 0g fat, 2g protein

Iced Macchiato (Unsweetened Unless Otherwise Indicated)

2g net carbs: Iced Macchiato with Coconut Milk, Small 30 calories, 2g fat, 2g protein

3g net carbs: Iced Macchiato with Coconut Milk, Large 50 calories, 4g fat, 1g protein
3g net carbs: Iced Macchiato with Coconut Milk, Medium 40 calories, 3g fat, 0g protein
7g net carbs: Iced Macchiato with Skim Milk, Small 50 calories, 0g fat, 7g protein
7g net carbs: Iced Macchiato with Whole Milk, Small 80 calories, 4g fat, 4g protein
10g net carbs: Iced Macchiato with Whole Milk, Medium 120 calories, 6g fat, 10g protein

Hot Tea (Unsweetened Unless Otherwise Indicated)

0g net carbs: Bold Breakfast Black Tea, Large 0 calories, 0g fat, 0g protein
0g net carbs: Bold Breakfast Black Tea, Medium 0 calories, 0g fat, 0g protein
0g net carbs: Bold Breakfast Black Tea, Small 0 calories, 0g fat, 0g protein
0g net carbs: Chamomile Fields Herbal Infusion, Large 0 calories, 0g fat, 0g protein
0g net carbs: Chamomile Fields Herbal Infusion, Medium 0 calories, 0g fat, 0g protein
0g net carbs: Chamomile Fields Herbal Infusion, Small 0 calories, 0g fat, 0g protein
0g net carbs: Cool Mint Herbal Infusion, Large 0 calories, 0g fat, 0g protein
0g net carbs: Cool Mint Herbal Infusion, Medium 0 calories, 0g fat, 0g protein
0g net carbs: Cool Mint Herbal Infusion, Small 0 calories, 0g fat, 0g protein
0g net carbs: Decaf Breakfast Black Tea, Large 0 calories, 0g fat, 0g protein
0g net carbs: Decaf Breakfast Black Tea, Medium 0 calories, 0g fat, 0g protein
0g net carbs: Decaf Breakfast Black Tea, Small 0 calories, 0g fat, 0g protein
0g net carbs: Harmony Leaf Green Tea, Large 0 calories, 0g fat, 0g protein
0g net carbs: Harmony Leaf Green Tea, Medium 0 calories, 0g fat, 0g protein
0g net carbs: Harmony Leaf Green Tea, Small 0 calories, 0g fat, 0g protein
0g net carbs: Hibiscus Kiss Herbal Infusion, Large 0 calories, 0g fat, 0g protein
0g net carbs: Hibiscus Kiss Herbal Infusion, Medium 0 calories, 0g fat, 0g protein
0g net carbs: Hibiscus Kiss Herbal Infusion, Small 0 calories, 0g fat, 0g protein

Iced Green Tea (Unsweetened)

0g net carbs: Iced Green Tea Unsweetened, Small 5 calories, 0g fat, 0g protein
0g net carbs: Iced Green Tea Unsweetened, Medium 5 calories, 0g fat, 1g protein
0g net carbs: Iced Green Tea Unsweetened, Large 5 calories, 0g fat, 1g protein
1g net carbs: Iced Tea Unsweetened, Small 5 calories, 0g fat, 0g protein
1g net carbs: Iced Tea Unsweetened, Medium 5 calories, 0g fat, 0g protein
2g net carbs: Iced Tea Unsweetened, Large 5 calories, 0g fat, 0g protein
2g net carbs: Iced Tea Unsweetened Blueberry Flavored Tea, Small 10 calories, 0g fat, 0g protein
3g net carbs: Iced Tea Unsweetened Blueberry Flavored Tea, Medium 15 calories, 0g fat, 0g protein
5g net carbs: Iced Tea Unsweetened Blueberry Flavored Tea, Large 20 calories, 0g fat, 0g protein
3g net carbs: Iced Tea Unsweetened Raspberry Flavored, Small 10 calories, 0g fat, 0g protein
4g net carbs: Iced Tea Unsweetened Raspberry Flavored, Medium 15 calories, 0g fat, 0g protein
5g net carbs: Iced Tea Unsweetened Raspberry Flavored, Large 20 calories, 0g fat, 0g protein

Tim Hortons

Tim Hortons earns themselves a *Keto Diet Restaurant Guide* Superstar Award for having a beneficial customizable nutrition calculator on their website. It is not on their main page, timhortons.com, so Google "Tim Hortons nutrition information" for their "Nutrition & Wellness Information" page. There is a "Find a Menu Item" search bar toward the top where you can search for a specific item like "latte" or a whole category like "breakfast." For example, in the breakfast sandwich section, you can remove the bread and see how it affects its macronutrients or total calories. Fun, right?

Keep in mind that Tim Hortons is a "coffee and donut" focused restaurant, so as you can guess, the low-carb options are limited.

Special Order Tips

When ordering coffees or teas with dairy (think lattes or cappuccinos), always ask for full cream (avoid skim or low-fat milk); heavy whipping cream (HWC) is lowest in carbs.

Order all burgers and sandwiches with "no bread." Menu items served "bunless" or "lettuce wrapped" will match the estimated nutrition information provided. Be wary of the available "Add-Ons" since they are often an unnecessary source of net carbs. These items are analyzed in their "regular" form as described on the menu. Any alterations will change their calorie and macronutrient amounts.

Feel free to customize orders to your liking. Usually, restaurants are happy to accommodate reasonable customer requests (they are used to patrons asking for deletions/substitutions by now). The exception is when the item has been premade or was prepared off-site, which is often the case with chain restaurants (think frozen breaded shrimp or wings pre-seasoned with BBQ sauce).

You'll notice some menu items indicate a half-serving size. Don't worry; there will only be a few! A smaller portion size allowed us to include more (higher-carb) crowd-pleasing favorites from Tim Hortons like soups or chilis.

Author Favorite

Breakfast: Breadless Steak and Four-Cheese Bagel Breakfast Sandwich with 16 oz. Iced Coffee with cream, unsweetened. 580 calories, 17g fat, 5g net carbs, 28g protein

Lunch & Dinner: Breadless Turkey Bacon Club with 16 oz. Brewed Iced Tea unsweetened over ice. 625 calories, 31g fat, 5g net carbs, 30g protein

BREAKFAST (No Bread, No Wrap)

2g net carbs: Aged Cheddar Biscuit 540 calories, 37g fat, 20g protein
2g net carbs: Angus Steak and Egg 400 calories, 20g fat, 21g protein
2g net carbs: Croissant Breakfast Sandwich 600 calories, 42g fat, 19g protein
2g net carbs: Simply Bacon 365 calories, 16g fat, 22g protein
2g net carbs: Simply Sausage 320 calories, 14g fat, 18g protein
3g net carbs: Turkey Sausage Breakfast Sandwich 350 calories, 16g fat, 20g protein
4g net carbs: Bacon Breakfast Sandwich 420 calories, 23g fat, 19g protein
4g net carbs: Farmer's Breakfast Grilled Wrap 680 calories, 42g fat, 21g protein
4g net carbs: Sausage Breakfast Sandwich 317 calories, 26g fat, 13g protein
4g net carbs: Steak and Four-Cheese Bagel Breakfast Sandwich 510 calories, 17g fat, 27g protein
5g net carbs: Bagel BELT 560 calories, 24g fat, 24g protein
5g net carbs: Steak & Cheddar Grilled Breakfast Wrap 440 calories, 21g fat, 22g protein

LUNCH & DINNER (No Bread, No Wrap)

3g net carbs: Chicken Fajita Grilled Wrap 430 calories, 19g fat, 28g protein
3g net carbs: Chipotle Chicken Wrap 520 calories, 16g fat, 15g protein
3g net carbs: Steak Fajita Grilled Wrap 430 calories, 20g fat, 26g protein
4g net carbs: Chipotle Chicken Bacon Wrap 548 calories, 17g fat, 16g protein
4g net carbs: Ham & Swiss Sandwich 498 calories, 14g fat, 19g protein
4g net carbs: Tuna Salad Sandwich 455 calories, 17g fat, 25g protein
5g net carbs: Chicken Salad Sandwich 417 calories, 15g fat, 24g protein
5g net carbs: Turkey Bacon Club 625 calories, 31g fat, 30g protein

Soups

6g net carbs: Hearty Vegetable Soup, small, Half-Serving 40 calories, 0g fat, 4g protein
7g net carbs: Chili[9], small, Half-Serving 160 calories, 9g fat, 23g protein
7g net carbs: Roasted Red Pepper & Gouda Soup, small, Half-Serving 110 calories, 7g fat, 6g protein

DRINKS

0g net carbs: Diet Coke 16 oz. 0 calories, 0g fat, 0g protein
0g net carbs: Diet Coke 22 oz. 0 calories, 0g fat, 0g protein
0g net carbs: Diet Coke 32 oz. 0 calories, 0g fat, 0g protein

Coffee & Tea (Unsweetened Unless Otherwise Indicated)

0g net carbs: Dark Roast Coffee 15 oz. 5 calories, 0g fat, 0g protein
0g net carbs: Dark Roast Coffee 20 oz. 5 calories, 0g fat, 1g protein
0g net carbs: Dark Roast Coffee 24 oz. 5 calories, 0g fat, 1g protein
0g net carbs: Original Blend Coffee 10 oz. 5 calories, 0g fat, 0g protein
0g net carbs: Original Blend Coffee 15 oz. 5 calories, 0g fat, 0g protein
0g net carbs: Original Blend Coffee 20 oz. 5 calories, 0g fat, 0g protein
0g net carbs: Original Blend Coffee 24 oz. 5 calories, 0g fat, 1g protein
0g net carbs: Decaffeinated Coffee 10 oz. 5 calories, 0g fat, 0g protein
0g net carbs: Decaffeinated Coffee 15 oz. 5 calories, 0g fat, 0g protein
0g net carbs: Decaffeinated Coffee 20 oz. 5 calories, 0g fat, 1g protein
0g net carbs: Decaffeinated Coffee 24 oz. 5 calories, 0g fat, 1g protein
2g net carbs: Latte with cream 10 oz. 60 calories, 0g fat, 8g protein
3g net carbs: Latte with cream 15 oz. 90 calories, 0g fat, 10g protein
4g net carbs: Latte with cream 20 oz. 120 calories, 0g fat, 13g protein
3g net carbs: Cappuccino with cream 10 oz. 60 calories, 0g fat, 73g protein
5g net carbs: Cappuccino with cream 15 oz. 90 calories, 0g fat, 73g protein
6g net carbs: Cappuccino with cream 20 oz. 120 calories, 0g fat, 73g protein
1g net carbs: Espresso Shot 0 calories, 0g fat, 0g protein
1g net carbs: Iced Coffee with cream 16 oz. 42 calories, 4g fat, 1g protein
1g net carbs: Iced Coffee with cream 20 oz. 69 calories, 7g fat, 1g protein
2g net carbs: Iced Coffee with cream 32 oz. 85 calories, 8g fat, 1g protein
2g net carbs: New French Vanilla Cold Brew- 16 oz. 90 calories, 0g fat, 1g protein
0g net carbs: Steeped Hot Tea made with Whole Leaf 10 oz. 0 calories, 0g fat, 0g protein
0g net carbs: Steeped Hot Tea made with Whole Leaf 15 oz. 0 calories, 0g fat, 0g protein
0g net carbs: Steeped Hot Tea made with Whole Leaf 20 oz. 0 calories, 0g fat, 0g protein
0g net carbs: Steeped Hot Tea made with Whole Leaf 24 oz. 0 calories, 0g fat, 0g protein
0g net carbs: Brewed Iced Tea 16 oz. 0 calories, 0g fat, 0g protein
0g net carbs: Brewed Iced Tea 24 oz. 0 calories, 0g fat, 0g protein
0g net carbs: Brewed Iced Tea 32 oz. 0 calories, 0g fat, 0g protein

---

[9] *That's Not Keto!* – You'll find all sorts of surprising foods listed here. I'm not telling you whether you should eat these foods or not. What fits your macros or daily carb spend is up to you. No keto police allowed.

Bob Evans

Bob Evans is another restaurant that only covers calorie count on their website when a menu item is clicked. Again, to determine how many net carbs are in each menu item (and its components), we will have to dig into the online "Nutrition Guide" PDF.

Feel free to customize orders to your liking. Usually, restaurants are happy to accommodate reasonable customer requests (they are used to patrons asking for deletions/substitutions by now). The exception is when the item has been premade or was prepared off-site, which is often the case with chain restaurants (think frozen breaded shrimp or wings pre-seasoned with BBQ sauce).

Special Order Tips

Order all burgers and sandwiches with "no bread." Menu items served "bunless" or "lettuce wrapped" will match the estimated nutrition information provided. Be wary of the available "Add-Ons" since they are often an unnecessary source of net carbs. These items are analyzed in their "regular" form as described on the menu. Any alterations will change their stated calorie and macronutrient amounts.

Avoid all fries, potatoes, rice, pasta, bread, etc. Ask the server to substitute a side salad or a side of steamed/grilled vegetables.

You'll notice a few half-serving recommendations here. This exception allowed us to expand the offerings to include a few more Bob Evans customer favorites.

Author Favorite

Breakfast: Whole Hog, Freshly Cracked Eggs with Sausage Links with 5 oz. Hot Tea-Unsweetened. 560 calories, 45g fat, 7g net carbs, 30g protein

Lunch: Breadless Double Cheese Pot Roast Dip, no gravy with Green Beans with Ham on the side. 16 oz. Diet Pepsi to drink. 840 calories, 51g fat, 6g net carbs, 46g protein

Dinner: Lemon Pepper Sole Fillets with Broccoli and Green Beans with Ham on the side. 16 oz. Unsweetened Freshly Brewed Iced Tea to drink. 465 calories, 33g fat, 14g net carbs, 26g protein

BREAKFAST (Substitute a Breakfast Meat for the Potatoes & Breads)

1g net carbs: Sunrise with Freshly Cracked Eggs and Bacon 390 calories, 30g fat, 26g protein
1g net carbs: The Big Egg Breakfast 420 calories, 34g fat, 22g protein
1g net carbs: The Everything Breakfast 490 calories, 40g fat, 24g protein
1g net carbs: Whole Hog, Freshly Cracked Eggs with Sausage Links 520 calories, 44g fat, 28g protein
2g net carbs: The Farmer's Choice- Original, Egg Whites with Hickory Smoked Ham 160 calories, 3g fat, 29g protein
3g net carbs: Mini Sampler with Scrambled Eggs and Hardwood-Smoked Bacon 350 calories, 25g fat, 27g protein
3g net carbs: Rise & Shine, Egg Whites with Bacon 250 calories, 14g fat, 25g protein
3g net carbs: The Farmer's Choice- Double Meat, Scrambled Eggs with Bacon and Sausage Patties 690 calories, 43g fat, 31g protein
4g net carbs: Classic Breakfast with Egg Whites and sausage patties 140 calories, 12g fat, 35g protein
4g net carbs: Homestead Farmer, Scrambled Eggs with Turkey Links, no gravy 300 calories, 18g fat, 32g protein
4g net carbs: Sirloin Steak & Farm- Freshly Cracked Eggs 590 calories, 36g fat, 58g protein

Omelets

3g net carbs: Three Meat Omelet, no tomatoes 1210 calories, 94g fat, 70g protein
5g net carbs: Western Omelet, easy bell peppers 650 calories, 50g fat, 40g protein
5g net carbs: Build Your Own Omelet, 2 eggs, bacon, Monterey Jack, Mushrooms, Onions, and Spinach 810 calories, 31g fat, 29g protein

Skillets

5g net carbs: Everything Breakfast 1130 calories, 73g fat, 57g protein
5g net carbs: Pot Roast Hash with Scrambled Eggs, no Home Fries 740 calories, 50g fat, 42g protein
6g net carbs: Sunshine Skillet, no gravy, no Home Fries 760 calories, 49g fat, 35g protein
6g net carbs: Ham Benedict with Freshly Cracked Eggs, easy fruit[10] 620 calories, 40g fat, 36g protein

Farmhouse Breakfast Sides

1g net carbs: Egg Whites (2) 60 calories, 0g fat, 12g protein

---

[10] *That's Not Keto!* – You'll find all sorts of surprising foods listed here. I'm not telling you whether you should eat these foods or not. What fits your macros or daily carb spend is up to you. No keto police allowed.

1g net carbs: Freshly Cracked Eggs (2) 200 calories, 16g fat, 13g protein
1g net carbs: Scrambled (2) 160 calories, 11g fat, 14g protein
1g net carbs: Bacon (2 slices) 90 calories, 7g fat, 6g protein
1g net carbs: Cheddar Cheese 110 calories, 10g fat, 7g protein
1g net carbs: Green Onions 0 calories, 0g fat, 1g protein
1g net carbs: Sour Cream 30 calories, 3g fat, 1g protein

Breakfast Meat

0g net carbs: Bob Evans Sausage (3 links) 190 calories, 16g fat, 9g protein
1g net carbs: Hardwood-Smoked Bacon (4 slices) 190 calories, 14g fat, 13g protein
2g net carbs: Bob Evans Sausage (2 patties) 320 calories, 26g fat, 19g protein
2g net carbs: Hickory-Smoked Ham (2 slices) 100 calories, 2g fat, 17g protein
2g net carbs: Turkey Sausage Links (2 links) 140 calories, 7g fat, 18g protein

LUNCH

Sandwiches (No Bread)

3g net carbs: Farmhouse Grilled Chicken, no honey mustard 630 calories, 27g fat, 41g protein
3g net carbs: Slow-Roasted Turkey Bacon Melt 670 calories, 33g fat, 45g protein
3g net carbs: All American BLT 570 calories, 33g fat, 35g protein
4g net carbs: Double Cheese Pot Roast Dip, no gravy 810 calories, 49g fat, 44g protein

Big Farm Burgers (No Bread)

3g net carbs: Bacon Cheeseburger 810 calories, 48g fat, 46g protein
5g net carbs: Rise & Shine Burger, no hash browns, no maple honey 1300 calories, 77g fat, 51g protein
5g net carbs: Steakhouse Burger, easy A1 sauce 1040 calories, 60g fat, 66g protein

Pick Two Combos (No Bread)

6g net carbs: Slow Roasted Turkey Bacon Melt (Lettuce Wrap), Half-Serving, with Farmhouse Garden
     Side Salad, no croutons, no dressing 360 calories, 29g fat, 26g protein
7g net carbs: All American BLT (Lettuce Wrap), Half-Serving, with Farmhouse Garden Side Salad, no
     croutons, no dressing 460 calories, 35g fat, 37g protein

Farmhouse Sides

1g net carbs: Bacon 90 calories, 7g fat, 6g protein
1g net carbs: Cheddar Cheese 110 calories, 10g fat, 7g protein
1g net carbs: Green Onions 0 calories, 1g fat, 1g protein
1g net carbs: Sour Cream 30 calories, 3g fat, 1g protein
2g net carbs: Green Beans with Ham 30 calories, 2g fat, 2g protein
3g net carbs: Farmhouse Garden Side Salad, no croutons 160 calories, 11g fat, 17g protein
3g net carbs: Hickory-Smoked Ham 100 calories, 9g fat, 18g protein
5g net carbs: Broccoli 110 calories, 10g fat, 3g protein

Salads (No Crackers)

3g net carbs: Grilled Chicken Cobb Salad 360 calories, 21g fat, 27g protein
4g net carbs: Cranberry Pecan Grilled Chicken Salad, easy cranberries[11] 260 calories, 15g fat, 19g protein
5g net carbs: Chicken Salad Plate, no fruit 470 calories, 27g fat, 10g protein
5g net carbs: Farmhouse Garden Salad, no croutons 290 calories, 23g fat, 17g protein
6g net carbs: Bob Evans Wildfire® Grilled Chicken Salad, no corn, no tortilla strips 350 calories, 19g fat, 27g protein
6g net carbs: Cobb Salad with Small Blue Cheese Dressing 390 calories, 28g fat, 26g protein
7g net carbs: Strawberry Salad, easy strawberries 260 calories, 14g fat, 20g protein
8g net carbs: Farmhouse Garden Side Salad, no dressing 110 calories, 4g fat, 6g protein

Salad Dressing

1g net carbs: Small Buttermilk Ranch 100 calories, 10g fat, 0g protein
2g net carbs: Large Buttermilk Ranch 210 calories, 21g fat, 0g protein
2g net carbs: Light Berry Dressing 90 calories, 2g fat, 1g protein
2g net carbs: Small Blue Cheese Dressing 140 calories, 15g fat, 1g protein
2g net carbs: Small Italian 70 calories, 7g fat, 0g protein
4g net carbs: Large Blue Cheese Dressing 280 calories, 30g fat, 2g protein
4g net carbs: Large Italian 150 calories, 14g fat, 1g protein
6g net carbs: Small French 140 calories, 13g fat, 0g protein
6g net carbs: Small Wildfire Ranch 80 calories, 6g fat, 0g protein
8g net carbs: Small Colonial 150 calories, 14g fat, 0g protein

DINNER (No Rolls)

5g net carbs: Lemon Pepper Sole Fillets 320 calories, 21g fat, 21g protein
6g net carbs: Herb Rubbed Turkey, no bread & celery dressing, no cranberry relish 520 calories, 40g fat, 37g protein
6g net carbs: Sirloin and Grilled Shrimp, easy Cocktail Sauce 620 calories, 38g fat, 43g protein
6g net carbs: Mushroom and Onion Chopped Steak, no mashed potatoes, easy gravy 530 calories, 43g fat, 31g protein
7g net carbs: USDA Choice Sirloin 660 calories, 45g fat, 47g protein
8g net carbs: Fork-Tender Pot Roast, no mashed potatoes, no carrots, easy gravy 950 calories, 62g fat, 38g protein
9g net carbs: Grilled to Perfection Chicken with Broccoli and Green Beans with Ham 410 calories, 16g fat, 60g protein
9g net carbs: Homestyle Boneless Fried Chicken, no breading/remove breading with Broccoli and Green Beans with Ham 720 calories, 39g fat, 71g protein

Dinner Bell Plates $8 (Substitute Green Beans with Ham for Mashed Potatoes)

2g net carbs: Lemon Pepper Sole Filet 360 calories, 28g fat, 20g protein
4g net carbs: Smaller Portion Turkey & Dressing, no dressing, no cranberry relish 420 calories, 32g fat, 31g protein

---

[11] *That's Not Keto!* – You'll find all sorts of surprising foods listed here. I'm not telling you whether you should eat these foods or not. What fits your macros or daily carb spend is up to you. No keto police allowed.

5g net carbs: Grilled Chicken Breast Meal 280 calories, 18g fat, 45g protein
6g net carbs: Mushroom & Onion Chopped Steak, easy gravy 630 calories, 46g fat, 47g protein
7g net carbs: Hickory-Smoked Ham Steaks 540 calories, 36g fat, 30g protein

Add-Ons

1g net carbs: Grilled Chicken 140 calories, 2g fat, 27g protein

DRINKS

0g net carbs: Coffee-Unsweetened, 5 oz. 5 calories, 0g fat, 1g protein
0g net carbs: Decaf Coffee-Unsweetened, 5 oz. 0 calories, 0g fat, 1g protein
0g net carbs: Diet Pepsi, 16 oz. 0 calories, 0g fat, 0g protein
0g net carbs: Tropicana Light Lemonade, 16 oz. 5 calories, 0g fat, 0g protein
1g net carbs: Hot Tea-Unsweetened, 5 oz. 0 calories, 0g fat, 0g protein
2g net carbs: Freshly Brewed Iced Tea- Unsweetened, 16 oz. 5 calories, 0g fat, 0g protein
7g net carbs: Tomato Juice[12] Small, 8 oz. 40 calories, 1g fat, 2g protein

---

[12] *That's Not Keto!* – You'll find all sorts of surprising foods listed here. I'm not telling you whether you should eat these foods or not. What fits your macros or daily carb spend is up to you. No keto police allowed.

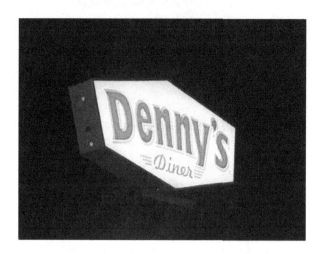

Denny's

Denny's is all about carby comfort food. The keto choices here are limited, folks. They lose points for not having ANY grilled chicken sandwiches or even grilled chicken lunch or dinner entrees. They only have breaded and fried chicken breasts and tenders.

Denny's does not have a customizable nutrition calculator on their website, but they have a detailed Nutritional Guide PDF that will help you control your carb intake. Feel free to customize orders to your liking. Usually, restaurants are happy to accommodate customer requests (they are used to patrons asking for deletions or substitutions by now). The exception is when the item has been premade, or was prepared off-site, which is often the case with chain restaurants (think frozen breaded shrimp or wings pre-seasoned with BBQ sauce).

Special Order Tips

Order all burgers and sandwiches with "no bread." Menu items served "bunless" or "lettuce wrapped" will match the estimated nutrition information provided. Be wary of the available "Add-Ons" since they are often an unnecessary source of net carbs. These items are analyzed in their "regular" form as described on the menu. Any alterations on your part will change the stated calorie and macronutrient amounts.

Avoid all fries, potatoes, rice, pasta, bread, etc. Ask the server to substitute a side salad or a side of steamed/grilled vegetables.

Author Favorite

Breakfast: Mile High Denver Omelet, no bell peppers & no onions; substitute bread and potatoes with sausage link (1) and bacon strips (2). 8 oz. coffee unsweetened to drink. 950 calories, 73g fat, 7g net carbs, 57g protein

Lunch: Bunless Flamin' 5-Pepper Burger with easy 5-Pepper sauce and Garden Side Salad with 1.5 oz. ranch dressing, no croutons. 12 oz. Diet Coke to drink. 1440 calories, 102g fat, 10g net carbs, 56g protein

Dinner: Crazy Spicy Sizzlin' Skillet, no Pepper Jack queso with Broccoli and Garden Side Salad with ranch dressing, no croutons on the side. 16 oz. chilled bottle of Dasani®. 1585 calories, 117g fat, 14g net carbs, 70g protein

BREAKFAST (No Bread, No Potatoes)

Slams

3g net carbs: Original Grand Slam® 11 oz. 700 calories, 34g fat, 22g protein
4g net carbs: All-American Slam® 15 oz. 930 calories, 69g fat, 44g protein
5g net carbs: Fit Slam® 15 oz. 450 calories, 12g fat, 27g protein
6g net carbs: Lumberjack Slam® 19 oz. 990 calories, 45g fat, 37g protein
7g net carbs: Grand Slam Slugger® 19 oz. 710 calories, 34g fat, 22g protein

Build Your Own Grand Slam (4 Items)

1g net carbs: Bacon (2 strips) 100 calories, 8g fat, 7g protein
1g net carbs: Eggs, Boiled (2) 4 oz. 130 calories, 8g fat, 0g protein
1g net carbs: Eggs, Fried (2) 4 oz. 190 calories, 16g fat, 11g protein
1g net carbs: Eggs, Scrambled (2) 4 oz. 220 calories, 17g fat, 14g protein
1g net carbs: Egg Whites (2) 4 oz. 80 calories, 1g fat, 13g protein
1g net carbs: Sausage Links (2) 150 calories, 15g fat, 5g protein
1g net carbs: Turkey Bacon (2 strips) 70 calories, 4g fat, 7g protein
3g net carbs: Grilled Ham (1 slice) 3 oz. 110 calories, 4g fat, 14g protein

Omelets

6g net carbs: Mile High Denver Omelet, no bell peppers & no onions 13 oz. 670 calories, 48g fat, 44g protein
7g net carbs: Loaded Veggie Omelet 12 oz. 500 calories, 38g fat, 29g protein
8g net carbs: Philly Cheesesteak Omelet 13 oz. 710 calories, 53g fat, 47g protein
8g net carbs: Ultimate Omelet® 12 oz. 720 calories, 59g fat, 37g protein

Build Your Own Omelet

1g net carbs: Omelet, Egg White, plain 7 oz. 110 calories, 1g fat, 20g protein
2g net carbs: Omelet, plain 7 oz. 340 calories, 26g fat, 21g protein
0g net carbs: Cheddar Cheese 1 oz. 80 calories, 6g fat, 5g protein
0g net carbs: Fresh Spinach 0.5 oz. 5 calories, 0g fat, 0g protein
0g net carbs: Sausage link (1) 1.5 oz. 180 calories, 17g fat, 6g protein
0g net carbs: Swiss Cheese (1 slice) 80 calories, 6g fat, 6g protein
1g net carbs: American Cheese (1 slice) 80 calories, 7g fat, 4g protein
1g net carbs: Bacon (2 strips) 100 calories, 8g fat, 7g protein
1g net carbs: Caramelized Onions 1 oz. 70 calories, 7g fat, 0g protein
1g net carbs: Fresh Avocado 1 serv 90 calories, 8g fat, 1g protein
1g net carbs: Jalapeños 1 oz. 5 calories, 0g fat, 0g protein

1g net carbs: Sautéed Mushrooms 1 oz. 50 calories, 6g fat, 1g protein
1g net carbs: Tomatoes 2 oz. 10 calories, 0g fat, 0g protein
1g net carbs: Turkey Bacon (2 strips) 70 calories, 4g fat, 7g protein
2g net carbs: Pico de Gallo 2 oz. 15 calories, 0g fat, 1g protein
3g net carbs: Fire-Roasted Bell Peppers & Onions 2 oz. 70 calories, 6g fat, 0g protein
3g net carbs: Ham 3 oz. 110 calories, 4g fat, 14g protein
4g net carbs: Chorizo Sausage 3 oz. 330 calories, 27g fat, 17g protein
5g net carbs: Pepper Jack Queso 2 oz. 100 calories, 7g fat, 3g protein

Signature Breakfasts (No Bread)

3g net carbs: Supreme Sizzlin' Skillet 10 oz. 580 calories, 45g fat, 15g protein
4g net carbs: Classic Benny Breakfast, easy Hollandaise sauce 15 oz. 830 calories, 52g fat, 31g protein
4g net carbs: Moons Over My Hammy® 960 calories, 56g fat, 44g protein
4g net carbs: Prime Rib Benny Breakfast, easy Hollandaise sauce 1020 calories, 65g fat, 50g protein
4g net carbs: T-Bone Steak & Eggs 18 oz. 670 calories, 38g fat, 53g protein
5g net carbs: Southwestern Benny Breakfast, easy Hollandaise sauce, easy 5-pepper sauce 17 oz. 950 calories, 60g fat, 36g protein
5g net carbs: The Grand Slamwich®, no maple spice spread 20 oz. 1320 calories, 81g fat, 52g protein
6g net carbs: Santa Fe Sizzlin' Skillet 10 oz. 720 calories, 55g fat, 26g protein

Breakfast Sides

0g net carbs: Egg White (1) 2 oz. 40 calories, 0g fat, 7g protein
0g net carbs: Egg, Boiled (1) 2 oz. 60 calories, 4g fat, 6g protein
0g net carbs: Egg, Fried (1) 2 oz. 90 calories, 8g fat, 6g protein
1g net carbs: Egg, Scrambled (1) 2 oz. 110 calories, 9g fat, 7g protein
1g net carbs: Sausage Links (4) 310 calories, 29g fat, 10g protein
2g net carbs: Bacon Strips (4) 210 calories, 16g fat, 14g protein
2g net carbs: Turkey Bacon Strips (4) 140 calories, 8g fat, 15g protein
3g net carbs: Grilled Ham (1 slice) 3 oz. 110 calories, 4g fat, 14g protein

$2 $4 $6 $8 Value Menu® (No Bread)

3g net carbs: Classic Bunless Burger 690 calories, 50g fat, 39g protein
5g net carbs: Triple Play Breakfast 13 oz. 650 calories, 14g fat, 15g protein
7g net carbs: Cowboy Chopped Steak 7 oz. 510 calories, 36g fat, 32g protein
7g net carbs: Everyday Value Slam® 450 calories, 11g fat, 10g protein

Condiments

0g net carbs: Whipped Margarine 0.5 oz. 40 calories, 4g fat, 0g protein
1g net carbs: Buffalo Sauce 1.5 oz. 110 calories, 12g fat, 0g protein
1g net carbs: Sour Cream 1 oz. 45 calories, 4g fat, 1g protein
2g net carbs: Brown Gravy 1 oz. 10 calories, 0g fat, 0g protein
2g net carbs: Country Gravy 1 oz. 20 calories, 1g fat, 0g protein
2g net carbs: Pico de Gallo 2 oz. 15 calories, 0g fat, 1g protein
3g net carbs: Tomato Sauce 1.5 oz. 25 calories, 1g fat, 1g protein

5g net carbs: Creamer[13] - Hazelnut or French Vanilla 13 ml 30 calories, 1g fat, 0g protein
6g net carbs: Maple-Flavored Syrup, sugar-free 2 oz. 15 calories, 0g fat, 0g protein
8g net carbs: Nashville Hot Sauce 1.5 oz. 70 calories, 4g fat, 0g protein
9g net carbs: Diner Q Sauce 1.5 oz. 220 calories, 21g fat, 0g protein

LUNCH

Burgers (No Bread, No Fries)

2g net carbs: Double Cheeseburger 15 oz. 920 calories, 52g fat, 61g protein
3g net carbs: Bourbon Bacon Burger, super easy bourbon sauce 15 oz. 880 calories, 50g fat, 53g protein
3g net carbs: Flamin' 5-Pepper Burger, easy 5-pepper sauce 15 oz. 1000 calories, 66g fat, 47g protein
4g net carbs: America's Diner Single, easy Diner Q sauce 10 oz. 820 calories, 50g fat, 38g protein
4g net carbs: Bacon Avocado Cheeseburger 15 oz. 1020 calories, 69g fat, 48g protein
5g net carbs: America's Diner Double, easy Diner Q sauce 15 oz. 1220 calories, 80g fat, 69g protein
5g net carbs: Slamburger™ with cheese, no sauce, no hash browns 11 oz. 840 calories, 47g fat, 45g protein

Build Your Own Bunless Burger

0g net carbs: 100% Beef Patty 320 calories, 24g fat, 26g protein
6g net carbs: Beyond Burger Patty 270 calories, 19g fat, 20g protein
0g net carbs: Aged White Cheddar Cheese (1 slice) 80 calories, 7g fat, 5g protein
0g net carbs: Mayo 0.5 oz. 100 calories, 11g fat, 0g protein
0g net carbs: Pickles (4 slices) 0 calories, 0g fat, 0g protein
0g net carbs: Swiss Cheese (1 slice) 80 calories, 6g fat, 6g protein
1g net carbs: American Cheese (1 slice) 80 calories, 7g fat, 4g protein
1g net carbs: Bacon Strips (2) 100 calories, 8g fat, 7g protein
1g net carbs: Caramelized Onions 1 oz. 70 calories, 7g fat, 0g protein
1g net carbs: Fresh Avocado 1 serv 90 calories, 8g fat, 1g protein
1g net carbs: Jalapeños 1 oz. 5 calories, 0g fat, 0g protein
1g net carbs: Lettuce 1 oz. 5 calories, 0g fat, 0g protein
1g net carbs: Sautéed Mushrooms 1 oz. 50 calories, 6g fat, 1g protein
2g net carbs: Red Onions, raw (3 rings) 5 calories, 0g fat, 0g protein
2g net carbs: Tomato (2 slices) 5 calories, 0g fat, 0g protein
6g net carbs: Diner Q Sauce 1 oz. 150 calories, 14g fat, 0g protein

Melts & Handhelds (No Bread, No Fries)

4g net carbs: The Super Bird® 11 oz. 680 calories, 35g fat, 46g protein
5g net carbs: Cali Club Sandwich 15 oz. 890 calories, 55g fat, 44g protein
6g net carbs: The Big Dipper Melt 17 oz. 1140 calories, 69g fat, 65g protein
7g net carbs: Diner Classic Patty Melt, no Diner Q sauce 13 oz. 1100 calories, 70g fat, 46g protein

---

[13] *That's Not Keto!* – You'll find all sorts of surprising foods listed here. I'm not telling you whether you should eat these foods or not. What fits your macros or daily carb spend is up to you. No keto police allowed.

Salads

4g net carbs: Garden Side Salad, no croutons, no dressing 7 oz. 170 calories, 9g fat, 8g protein
3g net carbs: House Salad, no croutons, no dressing 10 oz. 190 calories, 9g fat, 9g protein
4g net carbs: Cobb Salad, no potato sticks, no dressing 14 oz. 480 calories, 34g fat, 22g protein

Salad Add-Ons

1g net carbs: Fresh Avocado 1 serv 90 calories, 8g fat, 1g protein
2g net carbs: Prime Rib 2.5 oz. 140 calories, 8g fat, 14g protein
2g net carbs: Wild Alaska Salmon 7 oz. 350 calories, 23g fat, 32g protein

Salad Dressing

1g net carbs: Blue Cheese Dressing 1 oz. 100 calories, 10g fat, 1g protein
2g net carbs: Ranch Dressing 3 oz. 390 calories, 42g fat, 0g protein
3g net carbs: Italian Dressing 1 oz. 13 calories, 0g fat, 6g protein
5g net carbs: Thousand Island Dressing 1 oz. 115 calories, 11g fat, 1g protein
8g net carbs: Balsamic Vinaigrette 1 oz. 38 calories, 4g fat, 7g protein
8g net carbs: French Dressing 1 oz. 87 calories, 6g fat, 5g protein
8g net carbs: Honey Mustard Dressing 1 oz. 120 calories, 10g fat, 7g protein

DINNER (No Bread, No Potatoes)

2g net carbs: Sirloin Steak 10 oz. 530 calories, 25g fat, 49g protein
3g net carbs: T-Bone Steak 13 oz. 680 calories, 38g fat, 57g protein
4g net carbs: Wild Alaska Salmon 9 oz. 540 calories, 31g fat, 37g protein
5g net carbs: Crazy Spicy Sizzlin' Skillet, no Pepper Jack queso 19 oz. 990 calories, 66g fat, 59g protein
5g net carbs: Mama D's Pot Roast Bowl, no carrots 22 oz. 760 calories, 32g fat, 54g protein
6g net carbs: Grilled Steak with gravy 14 oz. 960 calories, 56g fat, 35g protein
6g net carbs: Sliced Turkey 15 oz. 760 calories, 30g fat, 54g protein
7g net carbs: Brooklyn Spaghetti & Meatballs, no pasta, easy tomato sauce 24 oz. 1080 calories, 51g fat, 40g protein

Dinner Sides

2g net carbs: Fresh Sautéed Zucchini & Squash 3 oz. 70 calories, 6g fat, 1g protein
3g net carbs: Broccoli 4 oz. 35 calories, 0g fat, 3g protein

DRINKS

0g net carbs: Diet Coke 12 oz. 0 calories, 0g fat, 0g protein
0g net carbs: Coffee, unsweetened 8 oz. 0 calories, 0g fat, 0g protein
0g net carbs: Hot Tea / Herbal Tea, unsweetened 8 oz. 0 calories, 0g fat, 0g protein

Panera Bread

Panera's online ordering system includes a *pretty* decent "customizable" menu, but it has some limitations. Yes, you can add or subtract bread from sandwiches, but the provided nutrition information is limited to *calories* only. So 1980s! What about fat, protein, fiber, and carbohydrates? Panera doesn't think these details are worth sharing front and center. This information is buried. You'll need a calculator, reading glasses, and an afternoon off work to study their nutrition information PDF. Oh wait – *I did all of that for you!*

Extreme caution is needed when dining at a restaurant with the word "bread" in its name. Go breadless on the sandwiches, pass on the chips, and RUN (don't walk) past the bakery counter. Plug your nose if necessary. The smell of freshly made bagels can be intoxicating.

Special Order Tips

Order all sandwiches with "no bread." Avoid all bagels, croissants, chips, muffins, pastries, cookies, etc. Ask the server to substitute a side salad or a side of steamed/grilled vegetables. Not available? Try asking for a pickle.

Be wary of the available "Add-Ons" since they are often an unnecessary source of net carbs.

Feel free to customize your order. Restaurants are usually happy to accommodate reasonable customer requests. The exception is when the item has been premade or was prepared off-site. Note that any alterations on your end will change the provided nutrition information. Adjust accordingly.

Author Favorite

Breakfast: Breadless Bacon, Scrambled Egg, Tomato & Cheese with 20 oz. Iced Caffe Latte with Almond Milk to drink. 368 calories, 24g fat, 9g net carbs, 36g protein

Lunch & Dinner: Cup Ten Vegetable Soup to start. Asian Sesame with Chicken Salad, no sesame seeds, no wonton strips with 20 oz. Plum Ginger Hibiscus Tea over ice. 470 calories, 23g fat, 14g net carbs, 30g protein

BREAKFAST (No Bread)

1g net carbs: Bacon, Over Easy Egg & Cheese 330 calories, 19g fat, 23g protein
1g net carbs: Egg Whites & Cheese 280 calories, 5g fat, 18g protein
1g net carbs: Over Easy Egg & Cheese 310 calories, 15g fat, 18g protein
2g net carbs: Bacon, Scrambled Egg & Cheese 350 calories, 21g fat, 25g protein
2g net carbs: Scrambled Egg & Cheese 330 calories, 16g fat, 20g protein
3g net carbs: Bacon, Scrambled Egg, Tomato & Cheese 360 calories, 21g fat, 29g protein
3g net carbs: Sausage, Over Easy Egg & Cheese 320 calories, 26g fat, 27g protein
4g net carbs: Asiago Bacon, Egg & Cheese 260 calories, 24g fat, 21g protein
4g net carbs: Avocado, Egg White & Spinach 250 calories, 14g fat, 19g protein
4g net carbs: Chipotle Chicken, Scrambled Egg & Avocado 370 calories, 27g fat, 29g protein
4g net carbs: Sausage, Scrambled Egg & Cheese 340 calories, 28g fat, 29g protein

Breakfast Add-Ons

0g net carbs: Chipotle Aioli Sauce for Breakfast Sandwiches, 1 Serving 45 calories, 4g fat, 0g protein
0g net carbs: Over Easy Egg (1) 70 calories, 5g fat, 6g protein
1g net carbs: Egg Whites (1) 35 calories, 0g fat, 6g protein
1g net carbs: Mustard Horseradish Sauce for Breakfast Sandwiches, 1 Serving 20 calories, 2g fat, 0g protein
1g net carbs: Scrambled Egg (1) 100 calories, 7g fat, 8g protein

Spreads

2g net carbs: Chive & Onion Cream Cheese Spread, 1 oz. 130 calories, 10g fat, 6g protein
4g net carbs: Plain Cream Cheese Spread, 1.75 oz. 180 calories, 17g fat, 2g protein

LUNCH & DINNER

Sandwiches (No Bread)

4g net carbs: Turkey 510 calories, 19g fat, 31g protein
4g net carbs: Roasted Turkey & Avocado BLT 660 calories, 54g fat, 43g protein
6g net carbs: Tuna Salad 740 calories, 32g fat, 35g protein
6g net carbs: Steak & White Cheddar Panini, easy pickled red onions 620 calories, 45g fat, 47g protein
7g net carbs: Bacon Turkey Bravo 660 calories, 41g fat, 50g protein
6g net carbs: Chipotle Chicken Avocado Melt, no Peppadew peppers 740 calories, 49g fat, 46g protein
6g net carbs: Toasted Frontega Chicken 620 calories, 38g fat, 43g protein
6g net carbs: Mediterranean Veggie, no Peppadew peppers, no Hummus 540 calories, 12g fat, 21g protein
7g net carbs: Smokehouse BBQ Chicken 620 calories, 29g fat, 45g protein

8g net carbs: Napa Almond Chicken Salad, easy Chicken Salad 550 calories, 25g fat, 22g protein

Sandwich (Protein Only)

0g net carbs: Double Meat- Smoked Chicken 100 calories, 2g fat, 21g protein
1g net carbs: Double Meat- 4 Half Bacon Slices 100 calories, 7g fat, 6g protein
1g net carbs: Double Meat- 6 Half Bacon Slices 140 calories, 11g fat, 10g protein
1g net carbs: Double Meat- Steak 140 calories, 5g fat, 22g protein
2g net carbs: Double Meat- Roasted Turkey 110 calories, 3g fat, 19g protein
2g net carbs: Double Meat- Tuna Salad 340 calories, 27g fat, 21g protein
3g net carbs: Double Meat- Sliced Turkey 120 calories, 3g fat, 21g protein
8g net carbs: Double Meat- Teriyaki Chicken 270 calories, 13g fat, 27g protein
10g net carbs: Double Meat- Napa Chicken Salad 320 calories, 24g fat, 13g protein

Sides & Grab-n-Go

0g net carbs: Hard Boiled Egg (1) 70 calories, 5g fat, 6g protein
1g net carbs: Pickle Spear (1) 5 calories, 0g fat, 0g protein
8g net carbs: Tomato Basil Cucumber Salad, 1 Serving 90 calories, 6g fat, 1g protein

Salads (No Dressing Unless Otherwise Indicated)

4g net carbs: Caesar, no croutons 140 calories, 25g fat, 10g protein
4g net carbs: Caesar with Chicken, no croutons 440 calories, 27g fat, 29g protein
6g net carbs: Fuji Apple with Chicken, no apple chips, easy dressing 560 calories, 35g fat, 27g protein
6g net carbs: Southwest Chile Lime Ranch with Chicken, no black bean and no corn salsa, no masa crisps 670 calories, 34g fat, 35g protein
7g net carbs: Asian Sesame with Chicken, no sesame seeds, no wonton strips 410 calories, 22g fat, 27g protein
8g net carbs: Green Goddess Cobb with Chicken, easy dressing, no pickled red onions 500 calories, 30g fat, 37g protein
10g net carbs: Greek 390 calories, 34g fat, 8g protein

Salad Add-Ons

1g net carbs: Bacon Pieces- 1 Double Portion 80 calories, 6g fat, 5g protein
3g net carbs: Grilled Chicken- 1 Double Portion 110 calories, 2g fat, 19g protein

Salad Dressing (3 Tbsp)

1g net carbs: Greek Dressing 230 calories, 25g fat, 0g protein
2g net carbs: Caesar 170 calories, 18g fat, 1g protein
4g net carbs: Green Goddess 80 calories, 7g fat, 2g protein
4g net carbs: Asian Sesame Vinaigrette 90 calories, 8g fat, 0g protein
5g net carbs: BBQ Ranch 140 calories, 13g fat, 1g protein
3g net carbs: Chile Lime Rojo Ranch 90 calories, 8g fat, 2g protein
10g net carbs: White Balsamic Vinaigrette flavored with Apple 160 calories, 13g fat, 0g protein

Warm Bowls (Substitute Salad Greens for Cilantro Lime Brown Rice and Quinoa)

3g net carbs: Teriyaki Chicken & Broccoli Bowl, easy teriyaki glaze 300 calories, 16g fat, 22g protein
3g net carbs: Baja Bowl with Chicken, no black bean and no corn salsa 330 calories, 14g fat, 28g protein
3g net carbs: Mediterranean Bowl, no Hummus 220 calories, 12g fat, 19g protein
3g net carbs: Mediterranean Bowl with Chicken, no Hummus 280 calories, 16g fat, 24g protein
3g net carbs: Baja Bowl, no black bean and no corn salsa 220 calories, 9g fat, 22g protein

Soups

7g net carbs: Ten Vegetable Soup, Cup 60 calories, 1g fat, 3g protein
8g net carbs: Homestyle Chicken Noodle Soup[14], Cup 60 calories, 1g fat, 6g protein
9g net carbs: Thai Style Chicken Soup, Cup 160 calories, 9g fat, 7g protein

DRINKS

0g net carbs: Diet Coke 20 oz. 0 calories, 0g fat, 0g protein
0g net carbs: Diet Coke 30 oz. 0 calories, 0g fat, 0g protein
0g net carbs: Diet Coke 20 oz. bottle 0 calories, 0g fat, 0g protein
0g net carbs: Coke Zero 20 oz. 0 calories, 0g fat, 0g protein
0g net carbs: Coke Zero 20 oz. bottle 0 calories, 0g fat, 0g protein
0g net carbs: Coke Zero 30 oz. 0 calories, 0g fat, 0g protein
0g net carbs: Diet Pepsi 12 oz. can 0 calories, 0g fat, 0g protein
0g net carbs: Diet Pepsi 20 oz. 0 calories, 0g fat, 0g protein
0g net carbs: Diet Pepsi 20 oz. bottle 0 calories, 0g fat, 0g protein
0g net carbs: Caffeine-Free Diet Pepsi 20 oz. 0 calories, 0g fat, 0g protein
1g net carbs: Caffeine-Free Diet Pepsi 30 oz. 0 calories, 0g fat, 0g protein
1g net carbs: Diet Pepsi 30 oz. 0 calories, 0g fat, 0g protein
0g net carbs: Diet Mountain Dew 12 oz. can 0 calories, 0g fat, 0g protein
1g net carbs: Diet Mountain Dew 20 oz. 10 calories, 0g fat, 0g protein
1g net carbs: Diet Mountain Dew 30 oz. 15 calories, 0g fat, 0g protein
0g net carbs: Diet Dr. Pepper 20 oz. 0 calories, 0g fat, 0g protein
1g net carbs: Diet Dr. Pepper 30 oz. 0 calories, 0g fat, 0g protein

0g net carbs: Bubly Sparkling Water, Lemon 12 oz. 0 calories, 0g fat, 0g protein
0g net carbs: Bubly Sparkling Water, Lime 12 oz. 0 calories, 0g fat, 0g protein
0g net carbs: Dasani Lemon 16 oz. bottle 0 calories, 0g fat, 0g protein
0g net carbs: Dasani Lime 16 oz. bottle 0 calories, 0g fat, 0g protein
0g net carbs: Tropicana Light Lemonade 20 oz. 5 calories, 0g fat, 0g protein
0g net carbs: Tropicana Light Lemonade 30 oz. 10 calories, 0g fat, 0g protein
0g net carbs: SoBe Life Water Yumberry Pomegranate 20 oz. 0 calories, 0g fat, 0g protein
1g net carbs: SoBe Life Water Yumberry Pomegranate 30 oz. 5 calories, 0g fat, 0g protein

Teas & Coffees (Unsweetened Unless Otherwise Indicated)

0g net carbs: Black Tea 20 oz. 10 calories, 0g fat, 2g protein

---

[14] *That's Not Keto!* – You'll find all sorts of surprising foods listed here. I'm not telling you whether you should eat these foods or not. What fits your macros or daily carb spend is up to you. No keto police allowed.

0g net carbs: Black Tea 30 oz. 12 calories, 0g fat, 2g protein
0g net carbs: Earl Greyer Tea 8 oz. 0 calories, 0g fat, 0g protein
0g net carbs: Earl Greyer Decaf Tea 8 oz. 0 calories, 0g fat, 0g protein
0g net carbs: Blackberry Sage Tea 8 oz. 0 calories, 0g fat, 0g protein
0g net carbs: British Breakfast Decaf Tea 8 oz. 0 calories, 0g fat, 0g protein
0g net carbs: British Breakfast Tea 8 oz. 0 calories, 0g fat, 0g protein
0g net carbs: Cinnamon Plum Tea 8 oz. 0 calories, 0g fat, 0g protein
0g net carbs: Plum Ginger Hibiscus Tea 20 oz. 0 calories, 0g fat, 0g protein
0g net carbs: Plum Ginger Hibiscus Tea 30 oz. 0 calories, 0g fat, 0g protein
0g net carbs: Ginger Peach Tea 8 oz. 0 calories, 0g fat, 0g protein
0g net carbs: Honey Ginseng Green Tea 8 oz. 0 calories, 0g fat, 0g protein
0g net carbs: Orange Ginger Mint Tea 8 oz. 0 calories, 0g fat, 0g protein
0g net carbs: Gold Peak Iced Tea 18.5 oz. 10 calories, 0g fat, 2g protein

2g net carbs: Cafe Blend Light Roast Coffee 12 oz. 15 calories, 0g fat, 1g protein
3g net carbs: Cafe Blend Light Roast Coffee 16 oz. 20 calories, 0g fat 1g protein
4g net carbs: Cafe Blend Light Roast Coffee 20 oz. 25 calories, 0g fat, 1g protein
2g net carbs: 100% Colombian Dark Roast Coffee 12 oz. 10 calories, 0g fat, 1g protein
3g net carbs: 100% Colombian Dark Roast Coffee 16 oz. 12 calories, 0g fat, 1g protein
3g net carbs: 100% Colombian Dark Roast Coffee 20 oz. 15 calories, 0g fat, 1g protein
2g net carbs: Iced 100% Colombian Dark Roast Coffee 12 oz. 10 calories, 0g fat, 1g protein
2g net carbs: Iced 100% Colombian Dark Roast Coffee 16 oz. 12 calories, 0g fat, 1g protein
3g net carbs: Iced 100% Colombian Dark Roast Coffee 20 oz. 15 calories, 0g fat, 1g protein
3g net carbs: Iced 100% Colombian Dark Roast Coffee 30 oz. 20 calories, 0g fat, 1g protein
2g net carbs: Hazelnut Flavored Coffee 12 oz. 15 calories, 0g fat, 1g protein
3g net carbs: Hazelnut Flavored Coffee 16 oz. 20 calories, 0g fat, 1g protein
4g net carbs: Hazelnut Flavored Coffee 20 oz. 25 calories, 0g fat, 2g protein
3g net carbs: Decaf Coffee 12 oz. 15 calories, 0g fat, 0g protein
2g net carbs: Cold Brew Coffee 16 oz. 10 calories, 0g fat, 1g protein
3g net carbs: Cold Brew Coffee 20 oz. 15 calories, 0g fat, 1g protein
2g net carbs: Espresso 2 oz. 10 calories, 0g fat, 1g protein
2g net carbs: Americano 16 oz. 10 calories, 0g fat, 1g protein
6g net carbs: Caffe Latte with Almond Milk 20 oz. 80 calories, 3g fat, 7g protein
6g net carbs: Iced Caffe Latte with Almond Milk 20 oz. 80 calories, 3g fat, 7g protein

Coffee Shots/Pumps/Substitutions

1g net carbs: Additional Shot of Espresso 1 oz. 5 calories, 0g fat, 0g protein
1g net carbs: Additional Shot of Espresso Decaf 5 calories, 0g fat, 0g protein
2g net carbs: Substitute Almond Milk 8 oz. 40 calories, 30g fat, 1g protein
5g net carbs: Additional Shot of Madagascar Vanilla Syrup[15] 20 calories, 0g fat, 0g protein
5g net carbs: Cane Sugar Syrup* 1 pump 15 calories, 0g fat, 0g protein
6g net carbs: Additional Shot of Cinnamon Bark Flavored Syrup* 25 calories, 0g fat, 0g protein
6g net carbs: Substitute Skim Milk 4 oz. 80 calories, 0g fat, 4g protein

---

[15] *That's Not Keto!* – You'll find all sorts of surprising foods listed here. I'm not telling you whether you should eat these foods or not. What fits your macros or daily carb spend is up to you. No keto police allowed.

Black Bear Diner

Black Bear Diner does not have a customizable nutrition calculator on its website. However, they do have a detailed "Nutritional Menu" PDF available. While you have to crunch the numbers, this tool allows you to take control of your carb intake.

Feel free to customize orders to your liking. Usually, restaurants are happy to accommodate reasonable customer requests (they are used to patrons asking for deletions/substitutions by now). The exception is when the item has been premade or was prepared off-site, which is often the case with chain restaurants (think frozen breaded shrimp or wings pre-seasoned with BBQ sauce).

Special Order Tips

Order all burgers and sandwiches with "no bread." Menu items served "bunless" or "lettuce wrapped" will match the estimated nutrition information provided. Be wary of the available "Add-Ons" since they are often an unnecessary source of net carbs. These items are analyzed in their "regular" form as described on the menu. Any alterations will change their calorie and macronutrient amounts.

Avoid all fries, potatoes, rice, pasta, bread, etc. Ask the server to substitute a side salad or a side of steamed/grilled vegetables.

Don't get hoodwinked by Dr. Praeger's Veggie Patty, and get it into your mind that this disaster is healthy. It has a whopping 18 grams of net carbs (for the patty only).

Note the Chicken Strips are breaded, so unless you want to get your fingers dirty trying to remove the coating, stay away.

You'll notice some menu items indicate a half-serving size. Don't worry; there will only be a few! A smaller portion size allowed us to include more (higher-carb) crowd-pleasing traditional favorites like Black Bear Diner soups or sandwiches.

Author Favorite

Breakfast: Joe's Hobo Omelet with Corned Beef Hash and 2 Hot Patty Sausages on the side. 16 oz. Iced Cold Brew Coffee, unsweetened, to drink. 1640 calories, 126g fat, 17g net carbs, 104g protein

Lunch: Bunless Bob's Big Bear Burger with Dinner Salad (without dressing) on the side. 16 oz. Diet Pepsi to drink. 1320 calories, 78g fat, 8g net carbs, 66g protein

Dinner: Santa Maria Tri-Tip with Italian Green Beans and Steamed Mixed Vegetables on the side. 6 oz. glass House Wine, Red, Merlot to drink. 730 calories, 35g fat, 13g net carbs, 57g protein

BREAKFAST (No Bread, No Potatoes, No Grits, No Fruit)

3g net carbs: Bear's Choice (2 Eggs) 130 calories, 8g fat, 12g protein
4g net carbs: New York Steak 10 oz. & Eggs 750 calories, 56g fat, 38g protein
5g net carbs: The Grizz 1720 calories, 71g fat, 65g protein
6g net carbs: Bigfoot Chicken Fried Steak, nonbreaded & Eggs 1180 calories, 70g fat, 46g protein

2-Egg Omelets & Scrambles (No Bread, No Potatoes, No Grits, No Fruit)

3g net carbs: Shasta Scramble 360 calories, 26g fat, 21g protein
3g net carbs: The Original ScramBOWL, easy gravy 1160 calories, 67g fat, 62g protein
4g net carbs: Southern Scramble, easy gravy 1160 calories, 74g fat, 43g protein

3-Egg Omelets & Scrambles (No Biscuit)

2g net carbs: California Omelet 480 calories, 35g fat, 31g protein
2g net carbs: Joe's Hobo Omelet 620 calories, 42g fat, 46g protein
3g net carbs: Bruce's Meat Lover's Omelet 690 calories, 48g fat, 51g protein
3g net carbs: Denver Omelet 460 calories, 28g fat, 37g protein
3g net carbs: Vegetarian Omelet 400 calories, 25g fat, 30g protein

Classic 2-Egg Combos (No Bread, No Potatoes, No Grits, No Fruit)

3g net carbs: Scrambled Eggs (2) 140 calories, 8g fat, 12g protein
4g net carbs: Chicken Sausage and Eggs, Low Range 412 calories, 31g fat, 27g protein
4g net carbs: New York Steak and Eggs 212 calories, 16g fat, 12g protein
4g net carbs: Thick-Cut Smoked Bacon and Eggs 470 calories, 34g fat, 34g protein
5g net carbs: Chicken Fried Steak, remove breading, and Eggs 750 calories, 40g fat, 42g protein
5g net carbs: Chicken Sausage and Eggs, High Range 454 calories, 34g fat, 31g protein
5g net carbs: Link Sausage and Eggs 380 calories, 31g fat, 21g protein
6g net carbs: Hot Patty Sausage and Eggs 760 calories, 64g fat, 35g protein

6g net carbs: Mild Patty Sausage and Eggs 750 calories, 64g fat, 35g protein
7g net carbs: Chorizo Breakfast Burrito Bowl, no tortilla 1240 calories, 77g fat, 41g protein
7g net carbs: Hickory Smoked Ham & Eggs 600 calories, 17g fat, 34g protein
8g net carbs: Breakfast Sliders, breadless, easy gravy 1400 calories, 55g fat, 58g protein

Bear's Benedicts (No Bread, No Potatoes, No Grits, No Fruit)

5g net carbs: Classic Eggs Benedict, easy Hollandaise sauce 700 calories, 37g fat, 31g protein
7g net carbs: California Bacon Benedict, easy Hollandaise sauce 850 calories, 63g fat, 37g protein

Breakfast Burrito (No Bread, No Potatoes, No Grits, No Tortilla)

6g net carbs: Chorizo Breakfast Burrito 400 calories, 27g fat, 23g protein

Breakfast Extras

0g net carbs: Thick-Cut Bacon (4 strips) 320 calories, 26g fat, 22g protein
1g net carbs: Eggs (3) 190 calories, 13g fat, 17g protein
1g net carbs: Link Sausage (2) 160 calories, 15g fat, 6g protein
3g net carbs: Hot Patty Sausage (2) 620 calories, 56g fat, 24g protein
3g net carbs: Mild Patty Sausage (2) 610 calories, 55g fat, 23g protein
6g net carbs: Corned Beef Hash 400 calories, 28g fat, 34g protein
6g net carbs: Ham Steak (1 slice), no glaze, 6 oz. 220 calories, 8g fat, 22g protein

Little Less (No Bread, No Potatoes)

3g net carbs: Egg (1) and Bacon (2 strips) 170 calories, 11g fat, 12g protein
4g net carbs: Egg (1) and Sausage (2) 240 calories, 19g fat, 12g protein
6g net carbs: Ham & Cheese Omelet 270 calories, 16g fat, 23g protein
8g net carbs: Egg (1) and Ham (1 slice) 190 calories, 8g fat, 17g protein

LUNCH

Burgers (No Bread, No Side, No Housemade Thousand Island Dressing)

4g net carbs: Bacon Cheddar Burger 940 calories, 60g fat, 51g protein
4g net carbs: Shasta Cheeseburger 520 calories, 35g fat, 36g protein
5g net carbs: Bob's Big Bear Burger 1290 calories, 78g fat, 64g protein
5g net carbs: Western BBQ Burger, no BBQ sauce, no onion rings 1230 calories, 60g fat, 48g protein
6g net carbs: California Burger 1000 calories, 61g fat, 47g protein
6g net carbs: Chili Cheddar Cheeseburger, easy chili 475 calories, 41g fat, 44g protein
7g net carbs: Parmesan Sourdough Cheeseburger 960 calories, 63g fat, 54g protein
8g net carbs: Ciabatta Bear Burger 1145 calories, 62g fat, 64g protein

Add-Ons

0g net carbs: Bacon (2 strips) 90 calories, 7g fat, 6g protein
0g net carbs: Cheese, Monterey Jack, 4 oz. 210 calories, 17g fat, 14g protein

0g net carbs: Cheese, pepper jack (2 slices) 170 calories, 13g fat, 9g protein
1g net carbs: Cheese, Mozzarella, whole milk, 4 oz. 170 calories, 13g fat, 12g protein
1g net carbs: Cheese, Swiss (2 slices) 170 calories, 13g fat, 11g protein
2g net carbs: Cheese, cheddar, 4 oz. 230 calories, 19g fat, 13g protein
4g net carbs: Cheese, American (2 slices) 140 calories, 11g fat, 7g protein

Specialty/Signature Sandwiches (No Bread, No Side)

4g net carbs: Tri-Tip Dip 490 calories, 16g fat, 41g protein
4g net carbs: Turkey Club Sandwich 660 calories, 26g fat, 31g protein
5g net carbs: BBQ Brisket, no sauce 880 calories, 42g fat, 62g protein
5g net carbs: Grilled Chicken Bacon Ranch Wrap, no tortilla 760 calories, 52g fat, 49g protein
6g net carbs: The Reuben, easy sauerkraut, substitute bacon ranch dressing for thousand island 970 calories, 60g fat, 55g protein
6g net carbs: Tri-Tip Dip Deluxe 680 calories, 29g fat, 53g protein
7g net carbs: Chicken Avocado Club 900 calories, 40g fat, 57g protein
7g net carbs: New York Steak Sandwich, no sauce 740 calories, 27g fat, 50g protein

Little Less (No Bread, No Side)

3g net carbs: Club Sandwich 540 calories, 24g fat, 28g protein
4g net carbs: BLT 560 calories, 29g fat, 24g protein
4g net carbs: Chicken Sandwich, Half-Serving 470 calories, 26g fat, 21g protein
5g net carbs: Ham Sandwich, Half-Serving 300 calories, 11g fat, 15g protein
5g net carbs: Small Patty Melt 620 calories, 45g fat, 60g protein
5g net carbs: Tuna Melt 670 calories, 53g fat, 41g protein
6g net carbs: Turkey Sandwich, Half-Serving 290 calories, 10g fat, 24g protein
8g net carbs: Tuna Sandwich, Half-Serving 480 calories, 29g fat, 25g protein

Super Salads (No Dressing Unless Otherwise Indicated)

3g net carbs: Grilled Chicken Cobb Salad, no croutons 660 calories, 53g fat, 49g protein
5g net carbs: Tuna Chef Salad with Bacon Ranch Dressing, no carrots 520 calories, 31g fat, 32g protein
6g net carbs: Bacon Cheeseburger Salad with bacon ranch dressing 840 calories, 64g fat, 45g protein
6g net carbs: Beef Taco Salad, no tostada bowl, no beans 1340 calories, 75g fat, 72g protein
6g net carbs: Grilled Chicken Taco Salad, no tostada bowl, no beans 1120 calories, 53g fat, 70g protein

Salad Dressing (3 oz. Unless Otherwise Indicated)

2g net carbs: Bacon Ranch Dressing 500 calories, 53g fat, 2g protein
3g net carbs: Bleu Cheese Dressing, Housemade 370 calories, 38g fat, 3g protein
4g net carbs: Fat-Free Italian Dressing, 1 oz. 48 calories, 0g fat, 3g protein
7g net carbs: Fat-Free Honey Dijon Dressing, 1 oz. 43 calories, 0g fat, 0g protein
8g net carbs: Thousand Island Dressing, Housemade 300 calories, 29g fat, 0g protein
9g net carbs: Balsamic Vinaigrette Dressing 270 calories, 24g fat, 0g protein

Soups (1 Cup)

4g net carbs: Saltine Crackers[16] (1 Packet) 25 calories, 1g fat, 0g protein
8g net carbs: Classic Broccoli Cheese, Half-Serving 150 calories, 11g fat, 2g protein
9g net carbs: Classic Chicken Noodle*, Half-Serving 80 calories, 2g fat, 12g protein
9g net carbs: Classic Minestrone*, Half-Serving 60 calories, 2g fat, 4g protein
9g net carbs: Tomato Bisque with Basil, Half-Serving 130 calories, 9g fat, 3g protein

Salad Dressing (2 oz.)

1g net carbs: Bacon Ranch Dressing 330 calories, 35g fat, 1g protein
2g net carbs: Bleu Cheese Dressing, Housemade 250 calories, 26g fat, 2g protein
5g net carbs: Thousand Island Dressing, Housemade 200 calories, 19g fat, 0g protein
6g net carbs: Balsamic Vinaigrette Dressing 180 calories, 16g fat, 0g protein
8g net carbs: Fat-Free Italian Dressing 96 calories, 0g fat, 6g protein

DINNER

Breakfast for Dinner (No Bread, No Side, No Potatoes, No Grits)

5g net carbs: Grilled Chicken & Eggs, no fruit 700 calories, 60g fat, 51g protein
6g net carbs: N.Y. Steak & Eggs 1070 calories, 97g fat, 181g protein
6g net carbs: Smoked Beef Brisket & Eggs 1030 calories, 82g fat, 177g protein
6g net carbs: Smoked Beef Brisket Benedict, easy Hollandaise Sauce 1140 calories, 86g fat, 173g protein
8g net carbs: Chopped Steak & Eggs, easy gravy 1460 calories, 94g fat, 183g protein

Full-Course Dinner (No Bread, with House Salad, No Dressing, Green Beans as Side, No Soup, No Potatoes)

4g net carbs: Roasted Turkey, easy gravy, no cranberry sauce 470 calories, 19g fat, 62g protein
6g net carbs: Homestyle Grilled Chicken, easy gravy 810 calories, 52g fat, 56g protein
6g net carbs: Housemade Meatloaf, easy Ketchup, no beef gravy, no onion rings 1170 calories, 81g fat, 3g protein
6g net carbs: Slow-Cooked Pot Roast, no potatoes, no gravy 460 calories, 41g fat, 43g protein
7g net carbs: Bigfoot Chicken Fried Steak, remove breading, easy gravy 1180 calories, 67g fat, 46g protein

Steaks & Such (No Bread, with House Salad, No Dressing, Green Beans as Side, No Soup, No Potatoes)

3g net carbs: Rib Eye Steak 590 calories, 45g fat, 68g protein
3g net carbs: Santa Maria Tri-Tip 400 calories, 20g fat, 52g protein
5g net carbs: New York Steak, no onion rings 640 calories, 19g fat, 67g protein
6g net carbs: Smoked Beef Brisket 510 calories, 33g fat, 1g protein

---

[16] *That's Not Keto!* – You'll find all sorts of surprising foods listed here. I'm not telling you whether you should eat these foods or not. What fits your macros or daily carb spend is up to you. No keto police allowed.

Dinner Deals (No Bread, No Potatoes, No Sides)

6g net carbs: Open-Faced Hot Turkey Sandwich, breadless, no cranberry sauce 880 calories, 19g fat, 54g protein
7g net carbs: Blackened Salmon 740 calories, 17g fat, 57g protein
7g net carbs: Grilled Fish & Chips, remove breading, no coleslaw 740 calories, 103g fat, 33g protein

Weekly Specials (No Bread, No Potatoes, No Soup, No Sides)

7g net carbs: Prime Rib, Friday/Saturday after 4 pm, easy gravy 1460 calories, 110g fat, 72g protein

Little Less (No Side)

3g net carbs: Santa Maria Tri-Tip 240 calories, 12g fat, 31g protein
7g net carbs: Housemade Meatloaf Dinner, easy ketchup, no onion rings, easy gravy 790 calories, 73g fat, 28g protein
8g net carbs: Slow-Cooked Pot Roast Dinner, easy gravy 250 calories, 58g fat, 31g protein

Super Salads (No Dressing Unless Otherwise Indicated)

3g net carbs: Grilled Chicken Cobb Salad, no croutons 660 calories, 53g fat, 49g protein
5g net carbs: Tuna Chef Salad with Bacon Ranch Dressing, no carrots 520 calories, 31g fat, 32g protein
6g net carbs: Bacon Cheeseburger Salad with bacon ranch dressing 840 calories, 64g fat, 45g protein
6g net carbs: Beef Taco Salad, no tostada bowl, no beans 1340 calories, 75g fat, 72g protein
6g net carbs: Grilled Chicken Taco Salad, no tostada bowl, no beans 1120 calories, 53g fat, 70g protein

Salad Dressing (2 oz. Unless Otherwise Indicated)

1g net carbs: Bacon Ranch Dressing 330 calories, 35g fat, 1g protein
2g net carbs: Bleu Cheese Dressing, Housemade 250 calories, 26g fat, 2g protein
5g net carbs: 1000 Island Dressing, Housemade 200 calories, 19g fat, 0g protein
6g net carbs: Balsamic Vinaigrette Dressing 180 calories, 16g fat, 0g protein
8g net carbs: Fat-Free Italian Dressing 30 calories, 0g fat, 0g protein
10g net carbs: Fat-Free Honey Dijon Dressing, 1 oz. 45 calories, 0g fat, 0g protein

Extras

2g net carbs: Italian Green Beans 80 calories, 6g fat, 2g protein
3g net carbs: Dinner Salad (without dressing) 30 calories, 0g fat, 2g protein
4g net carbs: Mixed Vegetables 110 calories, 9g fat, 3g protein
5g net carbs: Seasonal Vegetables: Zucchini, Squash, Red Bell Pepper 120 calories, 10g fat, 2g protein

Add-Ons

1g net carbs: Cheddar & Bacon 200 calories, 16g fat, 12g protein
3g net carbs: Bleu Cheese and Mushrooms 210 calories, 16g fat, 13g protein

Soups (1 Cup)

8g net carbs: Classic Broccoli Cheese, Half-Serving 150 calories, 11g fat, 2g protein
9g net carbs: Classic Chicken Noodle[17], Half-Serving 80 calories, 2g fat, 12g protein
9g net carbs: Classic Minestrone*, Half-Serving 60 calories, 2g fat, 4g protein
9g net carbs: Tomato Bisque with Basil, Half-Serving 130 calories, 9g fat, 3g protein

Soup Add On

4g net carbs: Saltine Crackers* (1 Packet) 25 calories, 1g fat, 0g protein

DESSERT

8g net carbs: Strawberries and whipped cream 70 calories, 4g fat, 0g protein

DRINKS

0g net carbs: Diet Pepsi, 16 oz. 0 calories, 0g fat, 0g protein
0g net carbs: Iced Tea, unsweetened, 16 oz. 0 calories, 0g fat, 0g protein
0g net carbs: Hot Tea, unsweetened, 8 oz. 0 calories, 0g fat, 0g protein
0g net carbs: Hot Coffee, unsweetened, 8 oz. 0 calories, 0g fat, 0g protein
0g net carbs: Iced Cold Brew Coffee, unsweetened, 16 oz. 0 calories, 0g fat, 0g protein

Wine

3g net carbs: House Wine, Red, Pinot Noir, 6 oz. 146 calories, 0g fat, 0g protein
3g net carbs: House Wine, White, Sauvignon Blanc, 6 oz. 135 calories, 0g fat, 0g protein
4g net carbs: House Wine, Red, Cabernet Sauvignon, 6 oz. 155 calories, 0g fat, 0g protein
4g net carbs: House Wine, Red, Merlot, 6 oz. 140 calories, 0g fat, 0g protein
4g net carbs: House Wine, White, Chardonnay, 6 oz. 150 calories, 0g fat, 0g protein

---

[17] *That's Not Keto!* – You'll find all sorts of surprising foods listed here. I'm not telling you whether you should eat these foods or not. What fits your macros or daily carb spend is up to you. No keto police allowed.

Big Boy

Big Boy is "Big on Breakfast- Served All Day," so if that's your sort of thing, this is your place. Comfort food is king at Big Boy, with many breaded and fried options. *(Definitely not a "keto forward" operation, tho!)*

Ignore the "Nutrition Information" link at the bottom of all of the menu pages on the Big Boy website. It is supposedly "under construction," so there is no help there. They don't have a customizable nutrition calculator either, so you need to look up each menu item online and find the description with the list of ingredients. Now customize (add/delete ingredients) to your liking.

Special Order Tips

Order all burgers and sandwiches with "no bread." Menu items served "bunless" or "lettuce wrapped" will match the estimated nutrition information provided. Be wary of the available "Add-Ons" since they are often an unnecessary source of net carbs. These items are analyzed in their "regular" form as described on the menu. Any alterations on your end will change the stated calorie and macronutrient amounts.

Feel free to customize orders to your liking. Usually, restaurants are happy to accommodate reasonable customer requests (they are used to patrons asking for deletions/substitutions by now). The exception is when the item has been premade or was prepared off-site, which is often the case with chain restaurants (think frozen breaded shrimp or wings pre-seasoned with BBQ sauce).

In general, avoid all fries, potatoes, rice, pasta, bread, etc. Ask the server to substitute a side salad or a side of steamed/grilled vegetables.

Author Favorite

Breakfast: Farmers Omelet and an 8 oz. Hot Tea, unsweetened to drink. 500 calories, 69g fat, 8g net carbs, 35g protein

Lunch & Dinner: Bunless Best Cheeseburger on The Planet® (how could I pass this up?), no relish with green beans, a Side Greek Salad, and no croutons. 16 oz. Diet Mt. Dew to drink. 1310 calories, 60g fat, 17g net carbs, 59g protein

BREAKFAST (No Bread, No Hash Browns, No Fresh Fruit)

4g net carbs: Steak & Eggs, no steak sauce 530 calories, 39g fat, 25g protein
5g net carbs: Breakfast Quesadilla, no tortilla 420 calories, 29g fat, 31g protein
5g net carbs: Bacon Avocado Benedict Breakfast 560 calories, 29g fat, 35g protein

Omelets & Scrambles

3g net carbs: Mushroom Swiss Scramble 520 calories, 24g fat, 28g protein
4g net carbs: Mini Blockbuster 460 calories, 37g fat, 46g protein
4g net carbs: Santa Fe Scramble 620 calories, 32g fat, 30g protein
4g net carbs: Steak & Eggs Blockbuster 450 calories, 28g fat, 24g protein
5g net carbs: Classic Blockbuster 730 calories, 49g fat, 40g protein
6g net carbs: Ham & Cheese Omelet 930 calories, 52g fat, 35g protein
6g net carbs: Mediterranean 660 calories, 39g fat, 37g protein
6g net carbs: Southern, easy gravy 810 calories, 42g fat, 36g protein
6g net carbs: The Works Scramble 640 calories, 36g fat, 34g protein
7g net carbs: Meat Lovers 840 calories, 46g fat, 46g protein
7g net carbs: Spanish Omelet 1130 calories, 51g fat, 44g protein
7g net carbs: Western Omelet 1080 calories, 54g fat, 56g protein
8g net carbs: Farmers 500 calories, 69g fat, 35g protein

Breakfast Sandwiches (No Bread)

2g net carbs: Sausage Biscuit 380 calories, 30g fat, 12g protein
6g net carbs: Bacon and Egg Sandwich 490 calories, 5g fat, 15g protein
6g net carbs: Sausage, Egg 'n Cheese Biscuit 480 calories, 37g fat, 19g protein

Breakfast A La Carte & Sides

0g net carbs: Bacon (2 strips) 80 calories, 7g fat, 5g protein
0g net carbs: Egg (1) 70 calories, 5g fat, 6g protein
0g net carbs: Egg white (1) 90 calories, 5g fat, 6g protein
0g net carbs: Sausage Link (1) 90 calories, 8g fat, 3g protein
0g net carbs: Sausage Patty-Regular (1) 180 calories, 17g fat, 7g protein
1g net carbs: Breakfast Ham (1 slice) 70 calories, 2g fat, 12g protein
2g net carbs: Sausage Patty-Large (1) 200 calories, 19g fat, 7g protein
3g net carbs: Glier's® Goetta 180 calories, 12g fat, 8g protein
3g net carbs: Turkey Sausage (1) 140 calories, 8g fat, 6g protein
7g net carbs: Breakfast Burrito, no tortilla 720 calories, 45g fat, 30g protein

9g net carbs: Grape Jelly[18] 35 calories, 0g fat, 0g protein

LUNCH & DINNER

Big Boy Burgers (No Bread)

2g net carbs: Small Cheeseburger 530 calories, 35g fat, 21g protein
2g net carbs: Small Hamburger 480 calories, 31g fat, 19g protein
3g net carbs: 1/4 lb. Cheeseburger 690 calories, 47g fat, 35g protein
3g net carbs: 1/4 lb. Hamburger 600 calories, 40g fat, 31g protein
3g net carbs: Big Boy Burger 580 calories, 44g fat, 34g protein
3g net carbs: Primetime BLT Cheeseburger 1020 calories, 63g fat, 53g protein
4g net carbs: Bacon Cheeseburger 810 calories, 57g fat, 41g protein
4g net carbs: Brawny Lad 390 calories, 22g fat, 31g protein
4g net carbs: Primetime Cheeseburger 930 calories, 54g fat, 49g protein
5g net carbs: Primetime Mushroom & Swiss 710 calories, 32g fat, 48g protein
6g net carbs: Super Big Boy Burger 660 calories, 84g fat, 63g protein
6g net carbs: Swiss Miss 490 calories, 46g fat, 35g protein
6g net carbs: Turkey Burger 580 calories, 16g fat, 18g protein
7g net carbs: Bacon Triple 550 calories, 41g fat, 39g protein
7g net carbs: Best Cheeseburger on The Planet®, no relish 900 calories, 58g fat, 54g protein
7g net carbs: Green Chile Burger 780 calories, 48g fat, 42g protein
7g net carbs: Mushroom Swiss Burger 710 calories, 31g fat, 48g protein
7g net carbs: Patty Melt 1280 calories, 45g fat, 43g protein
8g net carbs: Frontier Burger 760 calories, 38g fat, 44g protein
8g net carbs: Steakhouse Burger, no haystack onions, easy A1 Sauce 760 calories, 38g fat, 46g protein

Sandwiches (No Bread)

4g net carbs: Ham Melt 340 calories, 13g fat, 25g protein
4g net carbs: Pork Tenderloin 420 calories, 25g fat, 18g protein
4g net carbs: Slim Jim®, no sauce 510 calories, 17g fat, 24g protein
4g net carbs: Tuna Salad Sandwich 510 calories, 41g fat, 13g protein
5g net carbs: Bacon, Lettuce & Tomato Sandwich 535 calories, 32g fat, 21g protein
5g net carbs: Cheese Steak 610 calories, 19g fat, 44g protein
5g net carbs: Grilled Chicken Club Wrap 800 calories, 48g fat, 42g protein
5g net carbs: Hot Turkey 670 calories, 22g fat, 35g protein
5g net carbs: Philly Chicken 570 calories, 17g fat, 39g protein
5g net carbs: Triple-Decker Turkey Club 750 calories, 19g fat, 44g protein
6g net carbs: Big Boy Sandwich 680 calories, 34g fat, 44g protein
6g net carbs: Ham Sandwich Hot or Cold 430 calories, 28g fat, 19g protein
6g net carbs: Honey Mustard Grilled Chicken Sandwich, easy honey mustard 810 calories, 27g fat, 29g protein
6g net carbs: The Dolly Grilled Chicken Sandwich® 540 calories, 27g fat, 49g protein
7g net carbs: Buddie Boy 510 calories, 30g fat, 24g protein
7g net carbs: Buffalo Ranch Grilled Chicken Sandwich 1270 calories, 32g fat, 33g protein
7g net carbs: Grilled Chicken Breast 530 calories, 34g fat, 27g protein

---

[18] *That's Not Keto!* – You'll find all sorts of surprising foods listed here. I'm not telling you whether you should eat these foods or not. What fits your macros or daily carb spend is up to you. No keto police allowed.

7g net carbs: Hot Roast Beef 720 calories, 25g fat, 38g protein
7g net carbs: Large Tuna Melt 810 calories, 50g fat, 26g protein
7g net carbs: The Spicy Dolly Grilled Chicken Sandwich® 620 calories, 27g fat, 42g protein
8g net carbs: Corned Beef Reuben, no dressing 1010 calories, 78g fat, 52g protein
8g net carbs: Turkey Club Wrap 810 calories, 48g fat, 45g protein

Add-Ons

0g net carbs: Hamburger Patty - 1/4 lb. 280 calories, 18g fat, 27g protein
0g net carbs: Hamburger Patty - Small 140 calories, 9g fat, 14g protein
1g net carbs: American Cheese 45 calories, 4g fat, 2g protein
1g net carbs: Swiss Cheese 50 calories, 4g fat, 3g protein
3g net carbs: Turkey Burger - 5.3 oz. Patty 300 calories, 27g fat, 24g protein
4g net carbs: Grilled Chicken Breast 220 calories, 10g fat, 29g protein

Condiments

0g net carbs: Butter (1 pat) 115 calories, 13g fat, 0g protein
0g net carbs: Butter, Whipped 50 calories, 6g fat, 0g protein
0g net carbs: Chipotle Mayonnaise 120 calories, 13g fat, 0g protein
0g net carbs: Frisch's Mayonnaise 120 calories, 13g fat, 0g protein
0g net carbs: Frisch's Tartar Sauce Packets 80 calories, 8g fat, 0g protein
0g net carbs: Heinz® Mustard, yellow, classic Packets 5 calories, 0g fat, 0g protein
0g net carbs: Parmesan Cheese 20 calories, 2g fat, 2g protein
1g net carbs: Heinz® Mustard, yellow, classic 5 calories, 0g fat, 0g protein
2g net carbs: Frisch's Tartar Sauce 190 calories, 20g fat, 0g protein
2g net carbs: Remoulade Sauce 80 calories, 8g fat, 0g protein
3g net carbs: Smuckers® Grape Jelly Packets, sugar-free 10 calories, 0g fat, 0g protein
3g net carbs: Smuckers® Strawberry Jelly Packets, sugar-free 10 calories, 0g fat, 0g protein
5g net carbs: Heinz® Ketchup[19] 20 calories, 0g fat, 0g protein
8g net carbs: Smuckers® Apple Butter* Packets 30 calories, 0g fat, 0g protein
9g net carbs: BBQ Sauce* 45 calories, 0g fat, 0g protein
9g net carbs: Smuckers® Grape Jelly* Packets 35 calories, 0g fat, 0g protein
9g net carbs: Smuckers® Strawberry Jelly* Packets 35 calories, 0g fat, 0g protein

Entrees (No Bread, No Rice, No Pasta)

3g net carbs: Hot Turkey Dinner 230 calories, 12g fat, 23g protein
5g net carbs: Sesame-Ginger Glazed Salmon, easy glaze 370 calories, 15g fat, 14g protein

Salad Bar (1 oz. Unless Otherwise Indicated)

0g net carbs: Lettuce Salad Bar Blend, 2 cups, 10 calories, 0g fat, 0g protein
0g net carbs: Bar Spinach Leaves, 2 cups, 15 calories, 0g fat, 2g protein
0g net carbs: Bacon Bits, .5 oz., 70 calories, 5g fat, 4g protein
0g net carbs: Hard-boiled Egg (1) 45 calories, 3g fat, 4g protein

---

[19] *That's Not Keto!* – You'll find all sorts of surprising foods listed here. I'm not telling you whether you should eat these foods or not. What fits your macros or daily carb spend is up to you. No keto police allowed.

0g net carbs: Jalapeños 10 calories, 0g fat, 0g protein
0g net carbs: Sugar-free Jell-O®, 1 cup, 10 calories, 0g fat, 14g protein
1g net carbs: Broccoli 10 calories, 0g fat, 1g protein
1g net carbs: Cauliflower 5 calories, 0g fat, 1g protein
1g net carbs: Cucumbers 5 calories, 0g fat, 0g protein
1g net carbs: Grape Tomatoes 5 calories, 0g fat, 0g protein
1g net carbs: Green Peppers 5 calories, 0g fat, 0g protein
1g net carbs: Mushrooms 5 calories, 0g fat, 1g protein
1g net carbs: Pepperoncini 10 calories, 0g fat, 0g protein
2g net carbs: Beets 10 calories, 0g fat, 0g protein
2g net carbs: Red Onions 10 calories, 0g fat, 0g protein
2g net carbs: Salsa, 2oz., 10 calories, 0g fat, 0g protein
3g net carbs: Sunflower Seeds 80 calories, 7g fat, 3g protein
5g net carbs: Croutons* 30 calories, 1g fat, 1g protein
8g net carbs: Cantaloupe*, 1/2 cup 40 calories, 0g fat, 1g protein

Salads

3g net carbs: Large Garden Salad with grilled chicken breast, no croutons 280 calories, 18g fat, 17g protein
4g net carbs: Grilled Chicken Caesar Salad, no croutons 850 calories, 8g fat, 9g protein
4g net carbs: Ham and Cheese Salad, no croutons 350 calories, 21g fat, 31g protein
4g net carbs: House Salad, no croutons, no dressing 200 calories, 6g fat, 8g protein
4g net carbs: Michigan Apple Salad, no apples, no dried cranberries 900 calories, 7g fat, 18g protein
5g net carbs: Greek Salad, no chickpeas 550 calories, 6g fat, 10g protein

Salad Add-Ons

0g net carbs: Chicken Breast Grilled for Salads 110 calories, 1g fat, 23g protein

Salad Dressing

0g net carbs: French Dressing, Fat-Free 35 calories, 0g fat, 0g protein
1g net carbs: Buttermilk Ranch Dressing 100 calories, 10g fat, 0g protein
2g net carbs: Balsamic Vinaigrette Dressing 70 calories, 7g fat, 0g protein
2g net carbs: Blue Cheese Dressing 100 calories, 10g fat, 1g protein
2g net carbs: Italian Dressing 25 calories, 1g fat, 0g protein
6g net carbs: Thousand Island Dressing 140 calories, 15g fat, 0g protein

Soups

5g net carbs: Chili[20], Cup 140 calories, 8g fat, 10g protein
5g net carbs: Spicy Chicken Tortilla Soup*, Cup 120 calories, 9g fat, 8g protein
6g net carbs: Bean Soup*, Cup 70 calories, 2g fat, 4g protein
8g net carbs: Cream of Broccoli Soup 160 calories, 4g fat, 1g protein
9g net carbs: Vegetable Soup, Cup 60 calories, 1g fat, 2g protein
10g net carbs: Spicy Chicken Tortilla Soup*, Bowl 336 calories, 13g fat, 17g protein

---

[20] *That's Not Keto!* – You'll find all sorts of surprising foods listed here. I'm not telling you whether you should eat these foods or not. What fits your macros or daily carb spend is up to you. No keto police allowed.

Sides

2g net carbs: Side Caesar Salad, no croutons 300 calories, 0g fat, 2g protein
3g net carbs: Cottage Cheese 80 calories, 1g fat, 14g protein
4g net carbs: Seasonal Vegetables 55 calories, 0g fat, 4g protein
4g net carbs: Side Greek Salad, no croutons 360 calories, 0g fat, 3g protein
4g net carbs: Side House Salad, no croutons 30 calories, 0g fat, 2g protein
5g net carbs: Brown Gravy 50 calories, 4g fat, 1g protein
6g net carbs: Green Beans 50 calories, 2g fat, 2g protein
8g net carbs: Coleslaw, 4 oz. 180 calories, 15g fat, 1g protein

DESSERT

6g net carbs: Ice Cream, half-serving (half-scoop), 55 calories, 3g fat, 1g protein

Dessert Add-Ons

0g net carbs: Rich's® Whipped Topping 20 calories, 2g fat, 0g protein
0g net carbs: Reddi Wip® Whipped Topping 15 calories, 1g fat, 0g protein

DRINKS

0g net carbs: Coffee, unsweetened, 8 oz. 0 calories, 0g fat, 0g protein
0g net carbs: Decaffeinated Coffee, unsweetened, 8 oz. 0 calories, 0g fat, 0g protein
0g net carbs: Diet Pepsi, 16 oz. 0 calories, 0g fat, 0g protein
0g net carbs: Hot Tea, unsweetened, 8 oz. 0 calories, 0g fat, 0g protein
0g net carbs: Iced Tea, unsweetened, 16 oz. 0 calories, 0g fat, 0g protein
1g net carbs: Diet Mt. Dew, 16 oz. 5 calories, 0g fat, 0g protein
9g net carbs: Tomato Juice* 8 oz. 45 calories, 0g fat, 1g protein

2. Burgers & Sandwiches

Shake Shack ◉

Shake Shack gets a *Keto Diet Restaurant Guide* Superstar Award for having a robust website that lets you add and subtract toppings (click on menu items on the main page and then click Customize). The online Nutritional Information PDF gives us the macronutrients for the "Martin's Potato Roll," which is the bun on all the burgers. Ditch that bun and automatically reduce the total net carbs for the burger by 24 grams (31 grams for the Gluten Free Bun). They even offer a Lettuce Wrap (Remove Bun) option for all burgers and sandwiches. Thank you, Shake Shack!

Speaking of sandwiches, Shake Shack may have the most impressive assortment of burgers in this entire book. Who else can boast truffle sauce, green chilies, crispy shallots, or brats on a BURGER? Be sure to avoid the bunless Veggie Shack, though, as the patty alone has about 27 grams of net carbs. Dang. I hope you are not a chicken lover because all the options at Shake Shack (sandwiches and bites) are prepared "crispy," AKA breaded. No chicken dishes are listed here.

Salad aficionado? Then Shake Shack is the wrong place for you. There are absolutely no salad options available. Plan accordingly.

As you might expect from the restaurant's name, you'll notice a plethora of shake options on the menu. Look away! Unfortunately, there are no sugar-free options for these cups of deliciousness. Disappointing, I know, but I don't think we were expecting any, were we? Those kinds of surprises are few and far between.

Special Order Tips

Order all burgers and sandwiches with "no bread." Menu items served "bunless" or "lettuce wrapped" will match the estimated nutrition information provided. Be wary of the available "Add-Ons" since they are often an unnecessary source of net carbs. These items are analyzed in their "regular" form as described on the menu. Any alterations will change the stated calorie and macronutrient amounts.

Feel free to customize orders to your liking. Usually, restaurants are happy to accommodate reasonable customer requests (they are used to patrons asking for deletions/substitutions by now). The exception is when the item has been premade or was prepared off-site, which is often the case with chain restaurants.

Author Favorite

Breakfast: Bunless Sausage and Egg Breakfast Sandwich with 12 oz. Fresh Brewed Iced Tea, unsweetened to drink. 345 calories, 19g fat, 3g net carbs, 17g protein

Lunch & Dinner: Bunless Golden State Single with 6 oz. Shack White Wine to drink. 525 calories, 37g fat, 6g net carbs, 25g protein

BREAKFAST (No Bread)

2g net carbs: Bacon and Egg Breakfast Sandwich 400 calories, 23g fat, 15g protein
2g net carbs: Egg and Cheese Breakfast Sandwich 230 calories, 22g fat, 14g protein
2g net carbs: Sausage and Egg Breakfast Sandwich 340 calories, 19g fat, 17g protein
3g net carbs: Bacon and Egg Breakfast Sandwich (Double Egg) 490 calories, 30g fat, 26g protein
3g net carbs: Egg and Cheese Breakfast Sandwich (Double Egg) 320 calories, 29g fat, 22g protein
3g net carbs: Sausage and Egg Breakfast Sandwich (Double Egg) 430 calories, 25g fat, 25g protein

LUNCH & DINNER

Burgers (No Bread)

0g net carbs: Double Hamburger 560 calories, 30g fat, 25g protein
0g net carbs: Single Hamburger 370 calories, 18g fat, 15g protein
1g net carbs: Bacon Cheeseburger, double 760 calories, 47g fat, 46g protein
1g net carbs: Bacon Cheeseburger, single 500 calories, 29g fat, 25g protein
1g net carbs: Double Cheeseburger 700 calories, 42g fat, 45g protein
1g net carbs: Grilled Cheese 320 calories, 18g fat, 15g protein

1g net carbs: Single Cheeseburger 340 calories, 24g fat, 24g protein
2g net carbs: Golden State Single 360 calories, 37g fat, 25g protein
2g net carbs: Mound City Double 780 calories, 48g fat, 26g protein
2g net carbs: Single ShackBurger 300 calories, 30g fat, 24g protein
3g net carbs: Avocado Bacon Burger, Single 570 calories, 32g fat, 27g protein
3g net carbs: Brat Burger, Single, no sauce 460 calories, 61g fat, 26g protein
3g net carbs: Double ShackBurger 760 calories, 48g fat, 44g protein
3g net carbs: Golden State Double 740 calories, 56g fat, 45g protein
3g net carbs: Link Burger 280 calories, 46g fat, 26g protein
3g net carbs: Lockhart Link Burger 380 calories, 56g fat, 25g protein
3g net carbs: Roadside Double Burger, easy onions 770 calories, 46g fat, 27g protein
4g net carbs: Avocado Bacon Burger, Double 810 calories, 52g fat, 47g protein
4g net carbs: Black Truffle Burger, single, no crispy shallots 510 calories, 48g fat, 36g protein
4g net carbs: Brat Burger, Double, no sauce 850 calories, 73g fat, 46g protein
4g net carbs: Double SmokeShack 830 calories, 53g fat, 47g protein
4g net carbs: Green Chile CheddarShack, Double 750 calories, 46g fat, 46g protein
4g net carbs: Green Chile CheddarShack, Single 470 calories, 26g fat, 26g protein
4g net carbs: Link Burger, Double 530 calories, 64g fat, 36g protein
4g net carbs: Link Burger, Triple 790 calories, 82g fat, 47g protein
4g net carbs: Lockhart Link Burger, Double 740 calories, 74g fat, 35g protein
4g net carbs: Single SmokeShack 370 calories, 35g fat, 28g protein
5g net carbs: Black Truffle Burger, double, no crispy shallots 780 calories, 67g fat, 56g protein
5g net carbs: Lockhart Link Burger, Triple 1300 calories, 92g fat, 46g protein
5g net carbs: Slap Shot Burger, Double, no sauce 680 calories, 40g fat, 46g protein
5g net carbs: Slap Shot Burger, Single, no sauce 490 calories, 27g fat, 26g protein

Burger Add-Ons

0g net carbs: Bacon (2 Slices) 70 calories, 4g fat, 11g protein
0g net carbs: Burger Patty 190 calories, 12g fat, 10g protein
0g net carbs: Herb Mayonnaise 90 calories, 10g fat, 13g protein
0g net carbs: Lettuce 1 calorie, 0g fat, 0g protein
0g net carbs: Lettuce Wrap 5 calories, 0g fat, 0g protein
0g net carbs: Onion 5 calories, 0g fat, 0g protein
0g net carbs: Pickle 1 calorie, 0g fat, 0g protein
0g net carbs: ShackSauce 60 calories, 6g fat, 9g protein
0g net carbs: Tomato 5 calories, 0g fat, 0g protein
1g net carbs: American Cheese 70 calories, 6g fat, 10g protein
1g net carbs: Black Truffle Sauce 140 calories, 14g fat, 10g protein
2g net carbs: Cherry Peppers 10 calories, 0g fat, 2g protein
4g net carbs: Honey Mustard 180 calories, 19g fat, 4g protein
7g net carbs: Crispy Shallots 110 calories, 8g fat, 0g protein

Flat-Top Dogs (No Bread)

1g net carbs: Hot Dog 350 calories, 22g fat, 26g protein
4g net carbs: Garden Dog 180 calories, 3g fat, 7g protein
6g net carbs: Shackmeister Cheddar Brat 690 calories, 51g fat, 26g protein
7g net carbs: Publican Pork Sausage 660 calories, 47g fat, 26g protein

Flat-Top Dog Add-Ons

1g net carbs: Cheese Sauce 80 calories, 7g fat, 7g protein
2g net carbs: Sausage Link (1) 240 calories, 20g fat, 10g protein

DRINKS

0g net carbs: Diet Coke 12 oz. 0 calories, 0g fat, 0g protein
0g net carbs: Diet Coke 20 oz. 0 calories, 0g fat, 0g protein
0g net carbs: Coke Zero 12 oz. 0 calories, 0g fat, 0g protein
0g net carbs: Coke Zero 20 oz. 0 calories, 0g fat, 0g protein
0g net carbs: Diet Dr. Pepper 12 oz. 0 calories, 0g fat, 0g protein
0g net carbs: Diet Dr. Pepper 20 oz. 0 calories, 0g fat, 0g protein
0g net carbs: Diet Pepsi 12 oz. 0 calories, 0g fat, 0g protein
0g net carbs: Diet Pepsi 20 oz. 0 calories, 0g fat, 0g protein
0g net carbs: Pepsi Zero Sugar 12 oz. 0 calories, 0g fat, 0g protein
0g net carbs: Pepsi Zero Sugar 20 oz. 0 calories, 0g fat, 0g protein
0g net carbs: Diet Mountain Dew 12 oz. 0 calories, 0g fat, 0g protein
1g net carbs: Diet Mountain Dew 20 oz. 10 calories, 0g fat, 0g protein
0g net carbs: Shack2O Water 16 oz. bottle 0 calories, 0g fat, 0g protein
0g net carbs: Sparkling Shack2O Water 16 oz. bottle 0 calories, 0g fat, 0g protein
1g net carbs: Organic Iced Tea, unsweetened 12 oz. 4 calories, 0g fat, 0g protein
1g net carbs: Fresh Brewed Iced Tea, unsweetened 12 oz. 4 calories, 0g fat, 0g protein
2g net carbs: Fresh Brewed Iced Tea, unsweetened 20 oz. 6 calories, 0g fat, 0g protein

Wine

4g net carbs: Shack White 6 oz. 165 calories, 0g fat, 0g protein
5g net carbs: Shack Red 6 oz. glass 150 calories, 0g fat, 0g protein
5g net carbs: Shack White Can 8.4 oz. 185 calories, 0g fat, 0g protein
6g net carbs: Shack Red Can 8.4 oz. 175 calories, 0g fat, 0g protein
6g net carbs: Shack Sparkling Can 8.4 oz. 170 calories, 0g fat, 0g protein
9g net carbs: Shack Rosé Can 8.4 oz. 180 calories, 0g fat, 0g protein

Smashburger

Smashburger is another rockstar in the interactive menu department, so it easily earns a *Keto Diet Restaurant Guide* Superstar Award. It allows you to adjust the maximum carbs to something more reasonable when searching menu items, PLUS they have a very robust interactive menu.

Click Nutrition in the Menu drop-down on the main page at smashburger.com. Select your local Smashburger location, and the "Set Your Preferences" window will open up. The third drop-down is the "Set Nutritional Goals" section, where you can adjust the maximum allowable for any macronutrient (including carbs). Next, click the "Show me only what I can eat" box at the bottom and click "Save & Go!" This is where you will find the interactive menu where you can play with toppings for all menu options and immediately see the effect on calories, protein, fat, and carbohydrates. They even have an option for "On Lettuce, No Bun" in the Bun Choice drop-down. (As you can tell, I get excited about these things.)

Adjusting the carbs to capture only foods that fit your daily carb budget is magical. Remember that the vast majority of food items I list in this book are regular, higher net carb items that I tweaked with special order requests to lower the carbs.

If you're looking for something lite to eat, note that only one salad dressing is available at Smashburger (ranch) and two available salads, the Cobb Salad and the Bacon Ranch Salad. The ranch dressing shows 6 grams of net carbs (that's pretty high for ranch) so order it "easy." Lastly, don't be fooled by "healthy" sounding menu items; for example, the Black Bean (Veggie) patty has a whopping 19 grams of net carbs!

If you are like me and LOVE spicy food, Smashburger is a jalapeño lovers delight. If you're not sure you can handle the heat, order peppers on the side and test them out before going "buck-wild."

Special Order Tips

Order all burgers and sandwiches with "no bread." Menu items served "bunless" or "lettuce wrapped" will match the estimated nutrition information provided. Be wary of the available "Add-Ons" since they are often an unnecessary source of net carbs. These items are analyzed in their "regular" form as described on the menu. Any alterations will change their stated calorie and macronutrient amounts.

All sides of fries, tots, etc. should be avoided and substituted with salad greens or steamed/grilled vegetables to match the provided nutrition information.

Feel free to customize orders to your liking. Usually, restaurants are happy to accommodate reasonable customer requests (they are used to patrons asking for deletions/substitutions by now). The exception is when the item has been premade or prepared off-site, which is often the case with chain restaurants.

Author Favorite

Lunch & Dinner: Lettuce wrapped Double Spicy Jalapeño Baja Turkey, no Jalapeños with Side Salad with easy ranch and 20 oz. Diet Coke to drink. 725 calories, 57g fat, 7g net carbs, 41g protein

LUNCH & DINNER

Craft Your Own Burger/Sandwich (No Bread, Lettuce Wrapped)

Protein

0g net carbs: Beef-double 500 calories, 38g fat, 42g protein
0g net carbs: Beef-single 250 calories, 19g fat, 21g protein
0g net carbs: Turkey-double 380 calories, 30g fat, 28g protein
0g net carbs: Turkey-single 190 calories, 15g fat, 14g protein
1g net carbs: Grilled Chicken 160 calories, 8g fat, 27g protein
3g net carbs: Veggie (lettuce, tomato, & red onion) 10 calories, 0g fat, 0g protein

Cheese

0g net carbs: Aged Cheddar-double 160 calories, 14g fat, 5g protein

0g net carbs: Aged Cheddar-single 80 calories, 7g fat, 5g protein
0g net carbs: Aged Swiss-double 160 calories, 12g fat, 12g protein
0g net carbs: Aged Swiss-single 80 calories, 6g fat, 6g protein
0g net carbs: Smoked Cheddar-double 180 calories, 14g fat, 10g protein
0g net carbs: Smoked Cheddar-single 90 calories, 7g fat, 5g protein
1g net carbs: American-single 90 calories, 6g fat, 3g protein
1g net carbs: Pepperjack-single 80 calories, 6g fat, 5g protein
2g net carbs: American-double 180 calories, 12g fat, 6g protein
2g net carbs: Blue Crumbles-single 100 calories, 10g fat, 6g protein
2g net carbs: Pepperjack-double 160 calories, 12g fat, 10g protein
4g net carbs: Blue Crumbles-double 200 calories, 20g fat, 12g protein

Sauce

0g net carbs: Chicken Mayo 100 calories, 11g fat, 0g protein
0g net carbs: Mayo 100 calories, 11g fat, 0g protein
0g net carbs: Truffle Mayo 100 calories, 11g fat, 0g protein
1g net carbs: Ranch 50 calories, 5g fat, 0g protein
1g net carbs: Spicy Chipotle 90 calories, 9g fat, 0g protein
2g net carbs: Smash Sauce 70 calories, 7g fat, 0g protein
3g net carbs: Yellow Mustard 0 calories, 0g fat, 0g protein
4g net carbs: Ketchup[21] 15 calories, 0g fat, 0g protein
9g net carbs: BBQ sauce* 35 calories, 0g fat, 0g protein

Toppings

0g net carbs: Applewood Smoked Bacon (2 slices) 45 calories, 4g fat, 3g protein
0g net carbs: Fresh Sliced Avocado 25 calories, 3g fat, 0g protein
0g net carbs: Fried Egg (1) 110 calories, 9g fat, 6g protein
0g net carbs: Grilled Onions 25 calories, 3g fat, 0g protein
0g net carbs: Lettuce 0 calories, 0g fat, 0g protein
0g net carbs: Pickles 0 calories, 0g fat, 0g protein
1g net carbs: Guacamole 40 calories, 4g fat, 0g protein
1g net carbs: Red Onions 5 calories, 0g fat, 0g protein
1g net carbs: Sautéed Crimini Mushrooms 45 calories, 4g fat, 0g protein
2g net carbs: Tomato 5 calories, 0g fat, 0g protein
3g net carbs: Fresh Jalapeños 10 calories, 0g fat, 0g protein
3g net carbs: Smoked Brisket 150 calories, 8g fat, 14g protein

Signature Burgers (No Bread, Lettuce Wrapped)

1g net carbs: Double Truffle Mushroom Swiss 790 calories, 63g fat, 54g protein
1g net carbs: Truffle Mushroom Swiss, 460 calories, 38g fat, 27g protein
3g net carbs: Avocado Bacon Club 480 calories, 42g fat, 24g protein
3g net carbs: Bacon Smash 490 calories, 40g fat, 27g protein
3g net carbs: Double Avocado Bacon Club 730 calories, 61g fat, 45g protein
3g net carbs: Double Smoked Bacon Brisket 970 calories, 71g fat, 74g protein

---

[21] *That's Not Keto!* – You'll find all sorts of surprising foods listed here. I'm not telling you whether you should eat these foods or not. What fits your macros or daily carb spend is up to you. No keto police allowed.

3g net carbs: Smoked Bacon Brisket 630 calories, 45g fat, 48g protein

4g net carbs: Classic Smash, no ketchup, easy Smash Sauce 420 calories, 32g fat, 24g protein

4g net carbs: Double Bacon Smash 880 calories, 69g fat, 54g protein

5g net carbs: BBQ Bacon Cheddar, no Haystack Onions, easy BBQ sauce 410 calories, 30g fat, 29g protein

5g net carbs: Double BBQ Bacon Cheddar, no Haystack Onions, easy BBQ sauce 740 calories, 56g fat, 55g protein

5g net carbs: Double Classic Smash, no ketchup, easy Smash Sauce 760 calories, 57g fat, 48g protein

6g net carbs: Colorado Smash, no Cheese Spread 480 calories, 39g fat, 27g protein

6g net carbs: Double Spicy Jalapeño Baja, easy jalapeños, no tomatoes 790 calories, 63g fat, 52g protein

6g net carbs: Spicy Jalapeño Baja, easy jalapeños, no tomatoes 470 calories, 38g fat, 26g protein

7g net carbs: Double Colorado Smash, no Cheese Spread 810 calories, 64g fat, 53g protein

Grilled Chicken Sandwiches (No Bread, Lettuce Wrapped)

2g net carbs: Truffle Mushroom Swiss Grilled Chicken 370 calories, 27g fat, 33g protein

4g net carbs: Avocado Bacon Club Grilled Chicken 390 calories, 31g fat, 30g protein

4g net carbs: Bacon Smash Grilled Chicken 400 calories, 29g fat, 33g protein

4g net carbs: Classic Smash Grilled Chicken, no ketchup, easy Smash Sauce 270 calories, 19g fat, 27g protein

5g net carbs: BBQ Bacon Cheddar Grilled Chicken, no Haystack Onions, easy BBQ sauce 290 calories, 19g fat, 39g protein

7g net carbs: Spicy Jalapeño Baja Grilled Chicken, easy jalapeños, no tomatoes 370 calories, 27g fat, 32g protein

Turkey Burgers (No Bread, Lettuce Wrapped)

1g net carbs: Double Truffle Mushroom Swiss Turkey 670 calories, 55g fat, 40g protein

1g net carbs: Truffle Mushroom Swiss Turkey 400 calories, 34g fat, 20g protein

3g net carbs: Avocado Bacon Club Turkey 420 calories, 38g fat, 17g protein

3g net carbs: Bacon Smash Turkey 430 calories, 36g fat, 20g protein

3g net carbs: Double Avocado Bacon Club Turkey 610 calories, 54g fat, 31g protein

4g net carbs: BBQ Bacon Cheddar Turkey, no Haystack Onions, easy BBQ sauce 320 calories, 26g fat, 22g protein

4g net carbs: Double Bacon Smash Turkey 760 calories, 61g fat, 40g protein

4g net carbs: Double BBQ Bacon Cheddar Turkey, no Haystack Onions, easy BBQ sauce 590 calories, 48g fat, 41g protein

5g net carbs: Classic Smash Turkey, no ketchup, easy Smash Sauce 290 calories, 21g fat, 17g protein

6g net carbs: Double Classic Smash Turkey, no ketchup, easy Smash Sauce 570 calories, 42g fat, 34g protein

6g net carbs: Spicy Jalapeño Baja Turkey, no jalapeños 410 calories, 34g fat, 19g protein

7g net carbs: Double Spicy Jalapeño Baja Turkey, no jalapeños 680 calories, 55g fat, 38g protein

Salads

4g net carbs: Classic Cobb, no dressing 310 calories, 24g fat, 21g protein

4g net carbs: Beef Classic Cobb, no dressing 560 calories, 43g fat, 42g protein

4g net carbs: Turkey Classic Cobb, no dressing 500 calories, 39g fat, 35g protein

5g net carbs: Grilled Chicken Classic Cobb, no dressing 470 calories, 32g fat, 48g protein

5g net carbs: Bacon Ranch Salad, no Haystack onions, easy ranch dressing 300 calories, 25g fat, 12g protein

5g net carbs: Beef Bacon Ranch Salad, no Haystack onions, easy ranch dressing 550 calories, 44g fat,

33g protein
6g net carbs: Grilled Chicken Bacon Ranch Salad, no Haystack onions, easy ranch dressing 460 calories, 33g fat, 39g protein

Salad Dressing

6g net carbs: Ranch 310 calories, 30g fat, 0g protein

Sides

2g net carbs: Side Salad, easy ranch dressing 45 calories, 2g fat, 3g protein
9g net carbs: Crispy Brussels Sprouts with easy Ranch 250 calories, 21g fat, 5g protein

DRINKS

0g net carbs: Coke Zero 16 oz. bottle 0 calories, 0g fat, 0g protein
0g net carbs: Coke Zero 20 oz. fountain 0 calories, 0g fat, 0g protein
0g net carbs: Coke Zero 30 oz. fountain 0 calories, 0g fat, 0g protein
0g net carbs: Dasani 16 oz. bottle 0 calories, 0g fat, 0g protein
0g net carbs: Diet Coke 16 oz. bottle 0 calories, 0g fat, 0g protein
0g net carbs: Diet Coke 20 oz. fountain 0 calories, 0g fat, 0g protein
0g net carbs: Diet Coke 30 oz. fountain 0 calories, 0g fat, 0g protein
0g net carbs: Honest Unsweetened Iced Tea 20 oz. fountain 0 calories, 0g fat, 0g protein
0g net carbs: Honest Unsweetened Iced Tea 30 oz. fountain 0 calories, 0g fat, 0g protein
0g net carbs: Smart Water 16 oz. 0 calories, 0g fat, 0g protein
1g net carbs: Cold Brew Coffee Unsweetened 12 oz. 5 calories, 0g fat, 0g protein

Beer & Seltzer

2g net carbs: White Claw Black Cherry 12 oz. 100 calories, 0g fat, 0g protein
2g net carbs: White Claw Mango 12 oz. 100 calories, 0g fat, 0g protein
3g net carbs: Miller Lite 12 oz. 96 calories, 0g fat, 1g protein
5g net carbs: Coors Light 12 oz. 102 calories, 0g fat, 1g protein

The Habit Burger Grill

The Habit Burger Grill gets a high-five for listing a Lettuce Wrap Charburger on their "Nutritional Information" document on their website and even lists "ICEBERG LETTUCE (for wrap)" as one of their "Bread Options" along with 5 other breads. This makes calculating net carbs (and other pertinent information) for all the burgers and sandwiches a snap. Find out which bread is called for (seeded bun, sourdough, ciabatta, etc.) and subtract those macronutrients and calories from what is listed. Should you add back lettuce, as in "lettuce wrapped," those nutrition details can be easily added to the running total (personally, I count lettuce as a freebie).

The Habit Burger Grill does not have a customizable nutrition calculator on its website. However, they have a detailed "Nutritional Information" page that will help you control your carb intake. Feel free to customize orders to your liking. Usually, restaurants are happy to accommodate reasonable customer requests (they are used to patrons asking for deletions/substitutions). The exception is when the item has been premade or prepared off-site, which is often the case with chain restaurants.

Special Order Tips

Order all burgers and sandwiches with "no bread." Menu items served "bunless" or "lettuce wrapped" will match the estimated nutrition information provided. Be wary of the available "Add-Ons" since they are often an unnecessary source of net carbs. These items are analyzed in their "regular" form as described on the menu. Any alterations will change their stated calorie and macronutrient totals.

If going the veggie patty route with your burger, remember that the Impossible patty has 6 grams of net carbs and the Veggie Burger patty has 13 grams of net carbs. Substitute salad for french fries no matter what burger or sandwich you order. Or, give the Roasted Garlic Cauliflower side a try. It's the bomb!

Don't be fooled by the alluring tempura green bean "fries" offered at Habit Grill. I've made that mistake (green beans and all). But at 27 grams of net carbs per 5 oz. serving? That's a hard pass, my friend. Sad!

You'll notice some menu items indicate a half-serving size. Don't worry; there will only be a few. A smaller portion size allowed us to include additional (higher-carb) crowd-pleasing favorites.

Author Favorite

Lunch & Dinner: Ahi Tuna Caesar Salad, no croutons, no teriyaki glaze on the tuna with 8 oz. Diet Coke to drink. 720 calories, 34g fat, 7g net carbs, 49g protein

LUNCH & DINNER

Charburgers (No Bread, Lettuce Wrapped)

2g net carbs: Iceberg Lettuce (wrap only) 12 calories, 0g fat, 1g protein[22] For Reference, (note footnote below)
1g net carbs: Charburger, no caramelized onions 352 calories, 19g fat, 18g protein
2g net carbs: Bacon Charburger, no caramelized onions 630 calories, 44g fat, 27g protein
2g net carbs: Charburger with Cheese, no caramelized onions 392 calories, 22g fat, 21g protein
3g net carbs: Double Charburger, no caramelized onions 640 calories, 55g fat, 39g protein
4g net carbs: Portabella Charburger, no caramelized onions 640 calories, 76g fat, 33g protein
7g net carbs: Santa Barbara Charburger, no caramelized onions 730 calories, 69g fat, 52g protein

Sandwiches (No Bread, Lettuce Wrapped)

2g net carbs: Iceberg Lettuce (wrap only) 12 calories, 0g fat, 1g protein For Reference, (note footnote below)
4g net carbs: Chargrilled Ahi Tuna Sandwich, no teriyaki glaze 390 calories, 10g fat, 28g protein
4g net carbs: Chicken Club 730 calories, 39g fat, 47g protein
4g net carbs: Grilled Chicken Sandwich, no BBQ or teriyaki sauce 590 calories, 23g fat, 29g protein
4g net carbs: Tenderloin Steak Sandwich, no BBQ or teriyaki sauce 800 calories, 36g fat, 57g protein
7g net carbs: Veggie Burger (Vegan), Half-Serving, no sweet mustard dressing 235 calories, 6g fat, 28g protein

Salads

2g net carbs: Side Salad, no dressing, no croutons 70 calories, 3g fat, 3g protein
4g net carbs: Garden Salad, no dressing, no carrots or croutons 140 calories, 5g fat, 6g protein
5g net carbs: Side Caesar Salad, no croutons 220 calories, 15g fat, 6g protein
5g net carbs: Grilled Chicken Salad, no dressing, no carrots & croutons 410 calories, 15g fat, 35g protein
5g net carbs: Caesar Salad, no croutons 470 calories, 29g fat, 4g protein
5g net carbs: Chicken Caesar Salad, no croutons 690 calories, 39g fat, 45g protein
5g net carbs: Tenderloin Caesar Salad, no croutons, no BBQ or teriyaki sauce 675 calories, 35g fat, 41g protein
6g net carbs: Garden Salad with Tenderloin, no dressing/sauce, no carrots or croutons 680 calories, 28g fat,

---

[22] I suspect this amount of net carbs is an error, but it's pulled directly from the restaurant's website.

41g protein

6g net carbs: Southwest BBQ Chicken Salad, no BBQ sauce, no corn, no pickled red onions 690 calories, 39g fat, 43g protein

7g net carbs: Ahi Tuna Caesar Salad, no croutons, no teriyaki glaze 720 calories, 34g fat, 49g protein

7g net carbs: Super Food Salad, no quinoa, no carrots, no Craisins®, easy dressing 780 calories, 41g fat, 40g protein

7g net carbs: Garden Salad with Ahi Tuna, no dressing, no carrots or croutons, no teriyaki glaze 740 calories, 32g fat, 45g protein

8g net carbs: Santa Barbara Cobb 690 calories, 50g fat, 47g protein

Sides

5g net carbs: Roasted Garlic Cauliflower 100 calories, 6g fat, 4g protein

Add-Ons

0g net carbs: Bacon (2 Strips) 100 calories, 9g fat, 4g protein

0g net carbs: Butter Blend Spread, 2 Tsp 50 calories, 5g fat, 1g protein

0g net carbs: Mayonnaise, 1 Tbsp 100 calories, 12g fat, 0g protein

0g net carbs: Seasoned Grilled Beef Patty 225 calories, 20g fat, 15g protein

0g net carbs: White American Cheese (1 Slice) 70 calories, 5g fat, 4g protein

1g net carbs: American Cheese (1 Slice) 70 calories, 6g fat, 4g protein

1g net carbs: Avocado (1 Scoop) 90 calories, 8g fat, 1g protein

1g net carbs: Crumbled Blue Cheese, 2 Tbsp 50 calories, 4g fat, 3g protein

1g net carbs: Crumbled Feta Cheese, 2 Tbsp 70 calories, 6g fat, 4g protein

1g net carbs: Pickled Red Onion 10 calories, 1g fat, 0g protein

1g net carbs: Sautéed Portabella Mushrooms 2 oz. 120 calories, 13g fat, 1g protein

1g net carbs: Whipped Cream, 2 Tbsp 15 calories, 2g fat, 0g protein

2g net carbs: Caramelized Onions 14 calories, 1g fat, 0g protein

2g net carbs: Seasoned Grilled Chicken Breast 220 calories, 11g fat, 30g protein

3g net carbs: Pineapple[23] (1 Slice) 10 calories, 0g fat, 0g protein

5g net carbs: Quinoa* 1oz. 30 calories, 1g fat, 1g protein

6g net carbs: Croutons* (About 6 Croutons) 12g 40 calories, 1g fat, 1g protein

6g net carbs: Fire Roasted Corn* 30 calories, 0g fat, 1g protein

6g net carbs: Impossible Patty 240 calories, 14g fat, 19g protein

6g net carbs: Seasoned Grilled Tenderloin Steak 320 calories, 12g fat, 46g protein

7g net carbs: Craisins®*, 2 Tbsp 40 calories, 0g fat, 0g protein

7g net carbs: Seasoned Chargrilled Ahi Tuna 80g 130 calories, 1g fat, 23g protein

7g net carbs: Veggie Burger Patty, Half-Serving 85 calories, 3g fat, 7g protein

10g net carbs: Ancho BBQ Sauce 50 calories, 2g fat, 0g protein

10g net carbs: Applesauce* Cup, Unsweetened 50 calories, 0g fat, 0g protein

Sauces & Salad Dressing (2 Tablespoons)

1g net carbs: Blue Cheese Dressing, 80 calories, 8g fat, 1g protein

1g net carbs: Caesar Salad Dressing, 180 calories, 20g fat, 1g protein

---

[23] *That's Not Keto!* – You'll find all sorts of surprising foods listed here. I'm not telling you whether you should eat these foods or not. What fits your macros or daily carb spend is up to you. No keto police allowed.

1g net carbs: Kale Pesto Vinaigrette, 130 calories, 14g fat, 0g protein
1g net carbs: Red Wine Vinaigrette, 150 calories, 17g fat, 0g protein
1g net carbs: Roasted Garlic Aioli, 180 calories, 21g fat, 1g protein
1g net carbs: Tartar Sauce, 160 calories, 17g fat, 0g protein
2g net carbs: Cilantro Lime Ranch, 120 calories, 10g fat, 1g protein
2g net carbs: Hidden Valley® Ranch Dressing, 120 calories, 12g fat, 1g protein
3g net carbs: Fat-Free Italian Dressing, 12 calories, 0g fat, 0g protein
3g net carbs: House Dressing (Balsamic & Olive Oil), 160 calories, 17g fat, 0g protein
3g net carbs: Spicy Red Pepper Sauce (Boom), 150 calories, 17g fat, 0g protein
3g net carbs: Thousand Island Dressing, 130 calories, 13g fat, 0g protein
6g net carbs: Sweet Mustard Dressing (Vegan), 140 calories, 14g fat, 0g protein
7g net carbs: Italian Dressing, 110 calories, 10g fat, 0g protein
8g net carbs: Teriyaki Sauce[24], 334 calories, 0g fat, 0g protein

DRINKS

0g net carbs: Diet Coke, 8 oz. 0 calories, 0g fat, 0g protein
0g net carbs: Tropical Tea, unsweetened, 8 oz. 0 calories, 0g fat, 2g protein
0g net carbs: Dasani Water, 16 oz. bottle 0 calories, 0g fat, 0g protein
1g net carbs: Minute Maid Light Lemonade, 8 oz. 5 calories, 0g fat, 0g protein
1g net carbs: Minute Maid Light Pomegranate Lemonade, 8 oz. 5 calories, 0g fat, 0g protein
1g net carbs: Black Tea, unsweetened, 8 oz. 2 calories, 0g fat, 0g protein
1g net carbs: Citrus Green Tea, unsweetened, 8 oz. 2 calories, 0g fat, 0g protein

---

[24] *That's Not Keto!* – You'll find all sorts of surprising foods listed here. I'm not telling you whether you should eat these foods or not. What fits your macros or daily carb spend is up to you. No keto police allowed.

Red Robin

Red Robin is, first and foremost, a burger place. They have a vast assortment of burgers that makes up half of their food menu offerings. Sandwiches and regular entrees are available but scarce. There is a veritable cornucopia of adult beverage options; many are keto-friendly. Cheers to that! They even have a cauliflower pizza crust that passes my inspection. A slice of from a 10" Cauliflower Crust Very Vegy™ boasts just 7 grams of net carbs (84 calories, 28g fat, 22g protein). Not too shabby for a slice of pizza, eh? 10" Pizzas = 14 slices per pie.

My favorite part of their website is their NUTRITIONAL GUIDE (click Nutrition at the bottom of the home page), where you can find the make-your-own-burger (the section cleverly named FUN WITH BUNS). They break out the macronutrients for all their bread options and the other burger ingredients. You can create your own bunless or lettuce-wrapped burger and know exactly what you are getting nutritionally.

Special Order Tips

Order all burgers and sandwiches with "no bread." Be wary of the available "Add-Ons" since they are often an unnecessary source of net carbs. Any alterations will change the provided nutrition information.

Feel free to customize your order. Usually, restaurants are happy to accommodate reasonable customer requests (they are used to customers' asking for deletions/substitutions). The exception is when the item has been premade or prepared off-site (think frozen breaded shrimp or chicken wings).

Avoid all fries, potatoes, rice, pasta, bread, etc. Ask the server to substitute a side salad or a side of steamed/grilled vegetables.

Author Favorite

Lunch & Dinner: Scorpion Wings, no BBQ sauce to start. Bunless Red's Tavern Double® Burger, no sauce with Steamed Broccoli on the side. 5 oz. 14 Hands Merlot to drink. 1403 calories, 86g fat, 15g net carbs, 73g protein

LUNCH & DINNER

Apps (Appetizers)

2g net carbs: Wings Red's Bold Bone-In with ranch 680 calories, 70g fat, 34g protein
4g net carbs: Scorpion Wings, no BBQ sauce 650 calories, 70g fat, 34g protein
7g net carbs: Bar Wings with Buzzard Sauce 860 calories, 88g fat, 73g protein

Red Robin's Finest Burgers (No Bread, Lettuce Wrapped)

5g net carbs: Smoke & Pepper™ 690 calories, 40g fat, 49g protein
6g net carbs: The Master Cheese, no sauce 790 calories, 45g fat, 47g protein
7g net carbs: The MadLove Burger, no jalapeño relish, no candied bacon 960 calories, 57g fat, 65g protein
8g net carbs: Black & Bleu, easy cheese sauce 750 calories, 53g fat, 39g protein

Gourmet Burgers (No Bread, Lettuce Wrapped)

3g net carbs: Keep It Simple Beef 540 calories, 24g fat, 35g protein
4g net carbs: Guacamole Bacon 820 calories, 57g fat, 52g protein
4g net carbs: Red Robin Gourmet Cheeseburger, no pickle relish 710 calories, 47g fat, 40g protein
5g net carbs: The Wedgie™ Burger 540 calories, 34g fat, 40g protein
6g net carbs: Burnin' Love, no Fried jalapeño 810 calories, 61g fat, 42g protein
6g net carbs: Royal Red Robin 1000 calories, 77g fat, 55g protein
7g net carbs: Bacon Cheeseburger 890 calories, 67g fat, 49g protein
7g net carbs: Burnin' Love Chicken, no Fried jalapeño 740 calories, 43g fat, 43g protein
7g net carbs: Sautéed 'Shroom 670 calories, 40g fat, 48g protein
8g net carbs: Monster Burger, no pickle relish 1020 calories, 77g fat, 73g protein
8g net carbs: Scorpion Gourmet Burger, no fried jalapeños 950 calories, 57g fat, 43g protein
9g net carbs: Impossible Burger 760 calories, 40g fat, 33g protein

Tavern Burgers (No Bread, Lettuce Wrapped)

4g net carbs: Red's Tavern Double®, no sauce 600 calories, 35g fat, 36g protein
5g net carbs: The Big Tavern, no sauce 630 calories, 43g fat, 40g protein
6g net carbs: Haystack Tavern Double™, no onion straws 690 calories, 42g fat, 37g protein
6g net carbs: The Big Haystack, no onion straws 820 calories, 58g fat, 40g protein

Sandwiches & Wraps (No Bread, Lettuce Wrapped, No Fries)

4g net carbs: BLTA Croissant 680 calories, 40g fat, 31g protein
4g net carbs: Caesar's Chicken (grilled) Wrap, no wrap, no croutons 720 calories, 50g fat, 33g protein
4g net carbs: Grilled Turkey Burger 550 calories, 25g fat, 31g protein
5g net carbs: Simply Grilled Chicken Sandwich 370 calories, 6g fat, 35g protein

6g net carbs: Grilled California Chicken Sandwich 650 calories, 36g fat, 51g protein

Entrees

6g net carbs: Ensenada Chicken™ Platter, One Chicken Breast 210 calories, 7g fat, 29g protein
8g net carbs: Ensenada Chicken™ Platter 390 calories, 14g fat, 57g protein

Pizza (10" Pizza = 14 slices per pie)

7g net carbs: Cauliflower Crust Very Vegy™ (slice) 84 calories, 28g fat, 22g protein

Salads (No Croutons)

1g net carbs: House Salad 100 calories, 5g fat, 5g protein
4g net carbs: Avo-Cobb-O Salad 510 calories, 18g fat, 50g protein
5g net carbs: Mighty Caesar 760 calories, 62g fat, 36g protein
6g net carbs: Caesar Salad 230 calories, 21g fat, 4g protein
6g net carbs: Simply Grilled Chicken Salad 280 calories, 8g fat, 35g protein

Dipping Sauces

2g net carbs: Buzzard 140 calories, 15g fat, 0g protein
3g net carbs: Fresh Salsa 15 calories, 0g fat, 0g protein
4g net carbs: Ranch 260 calories, 27g fat, 1g protein
5g net carbs: Chipotle Aioli 410 calories, 44g fat, 0g protein
6g net carbs: Bistro Sauce 140 calories, 13g fat, 0g protein
7g net carbs: Red's Secret Tavern Sauce™ 190 calories, 18g fat, 0g protein
8g net carbs: Roasted Garlic Aioli 410 calories, 42g fat, 1g protein

Substitutions & Sides

0g net carbs: Bacon (2 strips) 100 calories, 7g fat, 10g protein
0g net carbs: Cucumber Slices (3) 0 calories, 0g fat, 0g protein
0g net carbs: Fried Egg 90 calories, 7g fat, 6g protein
1g net carbs: Tomato Slices (2) 5 calories, 0g fat, 0g protein
2g net carbs: Green Chile side 10 calories, 0g fat, 0g protein
2g net carbs: Onion Rings (Raw) 280 calories, 1g fat, 6g protein
2g net carbs: Pickle Slices 5 calories, 0g fat, 0g protein
2g net carbs: Sautéed Onions 25 calories, 1g fat, 0g protein
3g net carbs: Bacon Bits 140 calories, 9g fat, 12g protein
3g net carbs: Mayonnaise 1oz. 250 calories, 26g fat, 0g protein
3g net carbs: Red Onion 10 calories, 0g fat, 0g protein
3g net carbs: Steamed Broccoli 30 calories, 1g fat, 3g protein
8g net carbs: Sautéed Mushrooms 140 calories, 7g fat, 7g protein

Protein

0g net carbs: Gourmet Burger Patty 290 calories, 20g fat, 27g protein

0g net carbs: Grilled Chicken Patty 120 calories, 1g fat, 27g protein
0g net carbs: Tavern Patty 130 calories, 9g fat, 12g protein
2g net carbs: Turkey Patty 230 calories, 15g fat, 21g protein
6g net carbs: Impossible Burger Patty 240 calories, 14g fat, 19g protein

DRINKS

0g net carbs: Diet Coke, 16 oz. 0 calories, 0g fat, 0g protein
0g net carbs: Coca-Cola Zero, 16 oz. 0 calories, 0g fat, 0g protein
0g net carbs: AHA Blueberry and Pomegranate Sparkling Water, 16 oz. 0 calories, 0g fat, 0g protein
0g net carbs: AHA Blueberry and Pomegranate Sparkling Water, 16 oz. 0 calories, 0g fat, 0g protein
0g net carbs: Fresh-Brewed Iced Tea, unsweetened 16 oz. 0 calories, 0g fat, 0g protein
0g net carbs: Dasani Water Bottle 0 calories, 0g fat, 0g protein
8g net carbs: Fresh-Brewed Tea, Sugar-free Peach, 16 oz. 0 calories, 0g fat, 0g protein
8g net carbs: Fresh-Brewed Tea, Sugar-free Raspberry, 16 oz. 0 calories, 0g fat, 0g protein

Beer & Seltzer

2g net carbs: Truly Wild Berry Hard Seltzer, 12 oz. Can 100 calories, 0g fat, 0g protein
3g net carbs: Michelob Ultra, 12 oz. 95 calories, 0g fat, 1g protein
3g net carbs: Miller Lite, 12 oz. 96 calories, 0g fat, 1g protein
4g net carbs: Michelob Ultra, 16 oz. 130 calories, 0g fat, 1g protein
4g net carbs: Miller Lite, 16 oz. 130 calories, 0g fat, 1g protein
5g net carbs: Coors Light, 12 oz. 102 calories, 0g fat, 1g protein
6g net carbs: Michelob Ultra, 22 oz. 170 calories, 0g fat, 2g protein
6g net carbs: Miller Lite, 22 oz. 180 calories, 0g fat, 2g protein
7g net carbs: Bud Light, 12 oz. 110 calories, 0g fat, 1g protein
7g net carbs: Coors Light, 16 oz. 140 calories, 0g fat, 1g protein
9g net carbs: Bud Light, 16 oz. 140 calories, 0g fat, 1g protein
9g net carbs: Coors Light, 22 oz. 190 calories, 0g fat, 2g protein

Wine

3g net carbs: Ecco Domani Pinot Grigio, 5 oz. 110 calories, 0g fat, 0g protein
3g net carbs: Ecco Domani Pinot Grigio, 6 oz. 130 calories, 0g fat, 0g protein
5g net carbs: Ecco Domani Pinot Grigio, 9 oz. 200 calories, 0g fat, 0g protein
3g net carbs: Cupcake Vineyards Chardonnay, 5 oz. 130 calories, 0g fat, 0g protein
4g net carbs: Cupcake Vineyards Chardonnay, 6 oz. 160 calories, 0g fat, 0g protein
5g net carbs: Cupcake Vineyards Chardonnay, 9 oz. 230 calories, 0g fat, 0g protein
4g net carbs: 14 Hands Merlot, 5 oz. 123 calories, 0g fat, 0g protein
5g net carbs: 14 Hands Merlot, 6 oz. 150 calories, 0g fat, 0g protein
8g net carbs: 14 Hands Merlot, 9 oz. 220 calories, 0g fat, 0g protein
4g net carbs: Dark Horse Cabernet Sauvignon, 5 oz. 140 calories, 0g fat, 0g protein
5g net carbs: Dark Horse Cabernet Sauvignon, 6 oz. 160 calories, 0g fat, 0g protein
8g net carbs: Dark Horse Cabernet Sauvignon, 9 oz. 240 calories, 0g fat, 0g protein

Dave & Buster's

Let's face it, Dave & Buster's was created with one thing in mind, to provide a place for grownups to sit down and relax while their children run off and play. The environment (and ridiculous alcohol menu) provides the adults with much-needed solace. The kids will inevitably run off and enjoy the games and rides while parents decompress after a busy day, usually with a drink in hand. Don't get me wrong; I'm a HUGE fan of happy hour, but it can be challenging to remain carb-smart while imbibing. Need a recommendation? Try a low-carb hard seltzer (like White Claw) or a sugar-free cocktail made with (unflavored) hard alcohol and diet soda.

If the drinks or games aren't enough of a draw, lettuce-wrapped burgers and zoodles (zucchini noodles) are part of the standard menu at Dave & Buster's. Really! Though I wish their website functionality shared the same enthusiasm for healthy eating. Their online menu lacks any nutrition information. What are they hiding? It's hard to say since they simply aren't telling us.

Special Order Tips

Order all burgers and sandwiches with "no bread." Menu items served "bunless" or "lettuce wrapped" will match the estimated nutrition information provided. Be wary of the available "Add-Ons" since they are often an unnecessary source of net carbs. These items are analyzed in their "regular" form as described on the menu. Any alterations will change the stated calories and macronutrients.

Avoid all fries, rice, pasta, bread, etc. Ask the server to substitute a side salad or side of steamed/grilled vegetables. How about the Roasted Cauliflower (Pregame Bites)? At the very least, check out the zoodle (zucchini noodle) options. C'mon!

Feel free to customize orders to your liking. Usually, restaurants are happy to accommodate reasonable customer requests (they are used to patrons asking for deletions/substitutions). The exception is when the item has been premade or prepared off-site, which is sometimes the case with chain restaurants.

Author Favorite

Lunch & Dinner: Korean Sticky Ribs with easy spicy Korean BBQ sauce to start. Fire-Grilled Steak with Bacon-Wrapped Shrimp & Lobster Sauce with Fresh Seasonal Vegetables on the side. Grey Goose Martini to drink. 1304 calories, 92g fat, 14g net carbs, 75g protein

LUNCH & DINNER

Shareables & Snackables

6g net carbs: Ancho Caesar Grilled Chicken Lettuce Wraps, no croutons 544 calories, 37g fat, 40g protein

Pregame Bites

2g net carbs: Buffalo Wings, regular with Ranch, remove breading 666 calories, 47g fat, 20g protein
2g net carbs: Roasted Cauliflower 120 calories, 2g fat, 5g protein
5g net carbs: Brussels & Bacon with Ranch 891 calories, 81g fat, 17g protein
5g net carbs: Korean Sticky Ribs, easy spicy Korean BBQ sauce 526 calories, 47g fat, 28g protein

Sliders (No Bread, No French Fries)

4g net carbs: Turkey Club Sliders 239 calories, 24g fat, 44g protein
5g net carbs: Smashed Bar Burgers 392 calories, 35g fat, 45g protein

Burgers & Sandwiches (No Bread, No French Fries)

6g net carbs: Mucho Loco Moco, no rice 746 calories, 82g fat, 77g protein
6g net carbs: Philly French Dip 520 calories, 24g fat, 27g protein
6g net carbs: The Super Stack 1149 calories, 82g fat, 92g protein
7g net carbs: Buster's Cheeseburger 864 calories, 58g fat, 53g protein
7g net carbs: Mushroom Stout Burger, no bacon jam 560 calories, 34g fat, 32g protein
7g net carbs: Triple Bacon Burger 764 calories, 66g fat, 41g protein
8g net carbs: All-American Cheeseburger 550 calories, 45g fat, 31g protein
8g net carbs: Beastmode Bacon Burger, no cheese sauce, no bacon jam 660 calories, 49g fat, 45g protein
8g net carbs: Chicken Avocado Club 510 calories, 31g fat, 19g protein

Burgers & Sandwich Add-Ons

0g net carbs: Applewood Smoked Bacon (2 slices) 90 calories, 7g fat, 5g protein
1g net carbs: Avocado 80 calories, 7g fat, 1g protein

Handhelds (No Bread, No French Fries)

4g net carbs: Green Chile Chicken Lettuce wraps 524 calories, 78g fat, 54g protein

4g net carbs: Grilled Chicken Avocado Ranch Sandwich 539 calories, 64g fat, 52g protein
6g net carbs: Grilled Chicken Sandwich 564 calories, 64g fat, 50g protein
7g net carbs: The Philly Cheesesteak 607 calories, 62g fat, 70g protein

Entrees (Substitute Steamed Vegetables for Pasta/Potatoes)

3g net carbs: Slow-Cooked Smokehouse BBQ Ribs, Full-Rack, no BBQ sauce 724 calories, 65g fat, 128g protein
4g net carbs: Slow-Cooked Smokehouse BBQ Ribs, Half-Rack, easy BBQ sauce 667 calories, 45g fat, 65g protein
5g net carbs: JR's Kalbi Beef 797 calories, 65g fat, 32g protein
7g net carbs: Bistro Steak & Shrimp 674 calories, 47g fat, 45g protein
7g net carbs: Grilled Chicken & Baby Kale Caesar 800 calories, 57g fat, 64g protein
7g net carbs: Tuscan Chicken Alfredo 420 calories, 48g fat, 42g protein
8g net carbs: Fire-Grilled Steak with Bacon-Wrapped Shrimp & Lobster Sauce 607 calories, 43g fat, 47g protein
8g net carbs: Fire-Grilled Steak 419 calories, 43g fat, 48g protein
8g net carbs: New York Strip 506 calories, 50g fat, 67g protein
8g net carbs: Sirloin Steak 417 calories, 39g fat, 43g protein

Entrée Add-Ons

1g net carbs: Grilled Shrimp (5) 67 calories, 1g fat, 14g protein
1g net carbs: Bacon-Wrapped Shrimp (3) 137 calories, 10g fat, 12g protein

Plates (Substitute Steamed Vegetables for Pasta/Potatoes/Rice)

3g net carbs: Chimichurri Bowl, no pickled red cabbage 340 calories, 17g fat, 12g protein
4g net carbs: Fire-Grilled Atlantic Salmon 320 calories, 16g fat, 17g protein
4g net carbs: Fresh Fish 414 calories, 27g fat, 63g protein
5g net carbs: Grilled Chicken Chimichurri Bowl, no pickled red cabbage 440 calories, 21g fat, 26g protein
5g net carbs: Sautéed Shrimp Chimichurri Bowl, no pickled red cabbage 420 calories, 19g fat, 21g protein
5g net carbs: Shrimp & Asparagus Primavera 530 calories, 35g fat, 2g protein
6g net carbs: Grilled Steak Chimichurri Bowl, no pickled red cabbage 460 calories, 27g fat, 28g protein
6g net carbs: Lemon Garlic Shrimp 480 calories, 41g fat, 2g protein
7g net carbs: Simply Grilled Chicken 613 calories, 38g fat, 59g protein
7g net carbs: Simply Grilled Salmon 433 calories, 36g fat, 60g protein
8g net carbs: Bang Bang Chicken, Zoodles, no sauce 734 calories, 95g fat, 51g protein

Noodles & Zoodles[25] (Substitute Steamed Vegetables for Pasta/Potatoes/Rice)

3g net carbs: Fresh Tomato & Basil Linguine Zoodles 472 calories, 38g fat, 9g protein
4g net carbs: The Ultimate Mac & Cheese Zoodles 554 calories, 64g fat, 7g protein
5g net carbs: Tuscan Chicken Alfredo Zoodles 766 calories, 43g fat, 77g protein
6g net carbs: Fresh Tomato & Basil Linguine Zoodles with Shrimp 510 calories, 39g fat, 18g protein
7g net carbs: Bistro Steak & Shrimp with Lobster Alfredo Linguine Zoodles 674 calories, 47g fat, 55g protein
7g net carbs: Linguine Zoodles & Meatballs 752 calories, 72g fat, 50g protein
8g net carbs: Fresh Tomato & Basil Linguine Zoodles with Chicken 684 calories, 56g fat, 54g protein

---

[25] Just making sure you saw that zucchini noodles are available here. Zoodles, people. ZOODLES!

Side Salads (No Croutons, No Dressing)

5g net carbs: Fresh Garden Salad 145 calories, 11g fat, 9g protein
7g net carbs: Parmesan Caesar Salad 224 calories, 20g fat, 8g protein

Salads (No Croutons, No Dressing)

5g net carbs: Southern Cobb Salad with grilled chicken, no corn 560 calories, 29g fat, 39g protein
6g net carbs: Kale Caesar Salad 287 calories, 23g fat, 39g protein
6g net carbs: Kale Caesar Salad with grilled chicken 487 calories, 33g fat, 49g protein
6g net carbs: Kale Caesar Salad with grilled steak 517 calories, 35g fat, 52g protein
6g net carbs: Kale Caesar Salad with sautéed Shrimp 387 calories, 28g fat, 47g protein
7g net carbs: Fire-Grilled Steak Salad, no pecans 435 calories, 48g fat, 43g protein

Salad Dressings (2 oz.)

0g net carbs: Roasted Garlic Caesar 280 calories, 30g fat, 2g protein
2g net carbs: Avocado Jalapeño Ranch 222 calories, 22g fat, 2g protein
2g net carbs: Bleu Cheese 280 calories, 30g fat, 2g protein
2g net carbs: Buttermilk Ranch 220 calories, 22g fat, 0g protein
3g net carbs: Ancho Chile Caesar 263 calories, 27g fat, 3g protein
6g net carbs: Balsamic herb Vinaigrette 220 calories, 22g fat, 0g protein

Soup

4g net carbs: Tomato Feta Soup, cup 4 oz. 66 calories, 4g fat, 2g protein
9g net carbs: Tomato Feta Soup, bowl 8 oz. 131 calories, 7g fat, 4g protein

Sidekicks

3g net carbs: Fresh-Made Guacamole 4 oz. 187 calories, 17g fat, 2g protein
3g net carbs: Sauteed Zucchini Noodles (Zoodles) 168 calories, 15g fat, 3g protein
4g net carbs: Fresh Seasonal Vegetables 66 calories, 7g fat, 1g protein
6g net carbs: Parmesan Bacon Brussels Sprouts 424 calories, 38g fat, 8g protein

DRINKS

0g net carbs: Diet Coke, 20 oz. 0 calories, 0g fat, 0g protein
0g net carbs: Coke Zero, 20 oz. 0 calories, 0g fat, 0g protein
0g net carbs: San Pellegrino, 16.9 oz. bottle 0 calories, 0g fat, 0g protein
0g net carbs: Nestlé Waters Regional Spring Water, 16.9 oz. bottle 0 calories, 0g fat, 0g protein
0g net carbs: Regular Coffee, unsweetened, 11 oz. 3 calories, 0g fat, 0g protein
0g net carbs: Decaf Coffee, unsweetened, 11 oz. 3 calories, 0g fat, 0g protein
0g net carbs: Hot Tea, unsweetened, 11 oz. 0 calories, 0g fat, 0g protein
0g net carbs: Iced Tea, unsweetened, 20 oz. 0 calories, 0g fat, 0g protein
2g net carbs: Red Bull, Sugar-free, 8.4 oz. can 10 calories, 0g fat, 0g protein

Beer & Seltzer

2g net carbs: White Claw Black Cherry, 12 oz. can 100 calories, 0g fat, 0g protein
2g net carbs: Truly Wild Berry, 12 oz. can 100 calories, 0g fat, 0g protein

4g net carbs: Michelob Ultra, 16 oz. 127 calories, 0g fat, 1g protein
5g net carbs: Michelob Ultra, 22 oz. 175 calories, 0g fat, 2g protein
4g net carbs: Miller Lite, 16 oz. 128 calories, 0g fat, 1g protein
6g net carbs: Miller Lite, 22 oz. 176 calories, 0g fat, 2g protein
7g net carbs: Corona, Light, 16 oz. 130 calories, 0g fat, 1g protein
9g net carbs: Corona, Light, 22 oz. 179 calories, 0g fat, 2g protein
7g net carbs: Coors Light, 16 oz. 136 calories, 0g fat, 1g protein
10g net carbs: Coors Light, 22 oz. 193 calories, 0g fat, 2g protein
9g net carbs: Bud Light, 16 oz. 147 calories, 0g fat, 2g protein
10g net carbs: Bud Light, 22 oz. 188 calories, 0g fat, 2g protein

Wine

3g net carbs: Lunetta Prosecco (split), 5 oz. 126 calories, 0g fat, 0g protein
5g net carbs: Barefoot Rosé (split), 93.5 mL 75 calories, 0g fat, 2g protein
5g net carbs: Robert Mondavi Private Selection Cabernet Sauvignon, 9.0 oz. 138 calories, 0g fat, 0g protein
6g net carbs: Ecco Domani Pinot Grigio, 5 oz. 225 calories, 0g fat, 0g protein
6g net carbs: Meiomi Pinot Noir, 9.0 oz. 218 calories, 0g fat, 0g protein
6g net carbs: Santa Margherita Pinot Grigio, 5 oz. 219 calories, 0g fat, 0g protein
8g net carbs: 14 Hands Hot to Trot Red Blend, 9.0 oz. 225 calories, 0g fat, 0g protein
8g net carbs: Franciscan Estate Cabernet Sauvignon, 9.0 oz. 219 calories, 0g fat, 0g protein
8g net carbs: La Marca Prosecco, 5 oz. 506 calories, 0g fat, 0g protein
9g net carbs: Alamos Malbec, 9.0 oz. 252 calories, 0g fat, 0g protein

Cocktails

0g net carbs: Crown & Diet Sprite 96 calories, 0g fat, 1g protein
0g net carbs: Jack & Diet Coke 97 calories, 0g fat, 0g protein
0g net carbs: Rum & Diet Coke 99 calories, 0g fat, 0g protein
0g net carbs: Vodka Soda 86 calories, 0g fat, 0g protein
1g net carbs: Grey Goose Martini 171 calories, 2g fat, 0g protein
1g net carbs: Tequila Soda 101 calories, 0g fat, 0g protein
10g net carbs: Hendrick's Gin & Tonic 133 calories, 0g fat, 0g protein
10g net carbs: Jameson & Ginger 122 calories, 0g fat, 0g protein

Vodka (1.5 oz.)

0g net carbs: Absolut 98 calories, 0g fat, 0g protein
0g net carbs: Absolut Citron 98 calories, 0g fat, 0g protein
0g net carbs: Grey Goose 99 calories, 0g fat, 0g protein
0g net carbs: Ketel One 97 calories, 0g fat, 0g protein
0g net carbs: Tito's Handmade Vodka 98 calories, 0g fat, 0g protein

Tequila, 100% Agave (1.5 oz.)

0g net carbs: Hornitos Reposado 101 calories, 0g fat, 0g protein
0g net carbs: Patron Reposado 110 calories, 0g fat, 0g protein
0g net carbs: Patron Silver 110 calories, 0g fat, 0g protein
0g net carbs: Sauza Blue Silver 101 calories, 0g fat, 0g protein
3g net carbs: Effen Blood Orange 102 calories, 0g fat, 0g protein

Gin (1.5 oz.)

0g net carbs: Bombay Sapphire 117 calories, 0g fat, 0g protein
0g net carbs: Hendrick's 107 calories, 0g fat, 0g protein
0g net carbs: Tanqueray 111 calories, 0g fat, 0g protein

Bourbon/Whiskey (1.5 oz.)

0g net carbs: Bulleit Rye Whiskey 109 calories, 0g fat, 0g protein
0g net carbs: Crown Royal Whisky 96 calories, 0g fat, 0g protein
0g net carbs: Jack Daniel's Tennessee Whiskey 97 calories, 0g fat, 0g protein
0g net carbs: Jameson Irish Whiskey 98 calories, 0g fat, 0g protein
0g net carbs: Jim Beam Bourbon 101 calories, 0g fat, 0g protein
0g net carbs: Maker's Mark Bourbon 114 calories, 0g fat, 0g protein
0g net carbs: Woodford Reserve Bourbon 110 calories, 0g fat, 0g protein
4g net carbs: Southern Comfort Whiskey 98 calories, 0g fat, 0g protein
5g net carbs: Crown Royal Regal Apple Whisky 103 calories, 0g fat, 0g protein
6g net carbs: Firefly Strawberry Moonshine 76 calories, 0g fat, 0g protein
10g net carbs: Fireball Cinnamon Whisky 124 calories, 0g fat, 0g protein

Scotch (1.5 oz.)

0g net carbs: The Glenlivet 98 calories, 0g fat, 0g protein
0g net carbs: Johnnie Walker Black 98 calories, 0g fat, 0g protein

Cognac/Brandy (1.5 oz.)

0g net carbs: Hennessy V.S 97 calories, 0g fat, 0g protein
0g net carbs: Rémy Martin V.S.O.P. 99 calories, 0g fat, 0g protein
7g net carbs: Tuaca Originale Italiano 116 calories, 0g fat, 0g protein

Rum (1.5 oz.)

0g net carbs: Bacardi Superior Rum 99 calories, 0g fat, 0g protein
0g net carbs: Myers Original Dark Rum 96 calories, 0g fat, 0g protein
1g net carbs: Captain Morgan Original Spiced Rum 87 calories, 0g fat, 0g protein
8g net carbs: Malibu Coconut 83 calories, 0g fat, 0g protein

Fuddruckers

Fuddruckers gets a much-deserved *Keto Diet Restaurant Guide* Superstar Award due to its keto-friendly PDF Nutrition Guide. It breaks out the burger bun options so customers can easily calculate the macronutrients with or *without* bread (most restaurant websites don't give you this option). Additionally, Fuddruckers' online ordering tool allows you to choose not one but TWO low-carb, bunless options; "Bed of Lettuce" or "No Bread." So exciting!

Feel free to customize orders to your liking. Usually, restaurants are happy to accommodate reasonable customer requests (they are used to customers asking for deletions/substitutions by now). The exception is when the item has been premade or prepared off-site, which is sometimes the case at chain restaurants.

Special Order Tips

Don't be fooled by Fuddrucker's Veggie Burger (not Beyond Burger). Sure, it might sound healthy (the word veggie and all), but a glance at the restaurant's Nutrition Guide shows it has 23 grams of net carbs. That's a lot! Consider the 100% beef patty or Grilled Chicken patty instead.

Order all burgers and sandwiches with "no bread." Menu items served "bunless" or "lettuce wrapped" matches the estimated nutrition information provided. Be wary of the available "Add-Ons" since they are often an unnecessary source of net carbs. Any alterations will change the provided nutrition information.

Author Favorite

Lunch & Dinner: Breadless Ribeye Steak Sandwich, no onion rings with Side Caesar Salad with Caesar Dressing, no croutons. 16 oz. Diet Coke to drink. 693 calories, 16g fat, 5g net carbs, 39g protein

LUNCH & DINNER

Appetizers

10g net carbs: Buffalo Wings (6) 713 calories, 25g fat, 24g protein

Build Your Own World Famous Burger (No Bread)

Burger Patty

2g net carbs: 1/4 lb. Regular Burger Patty 475 calories, 26g fat, 21g protein
2g net carbs: 1/3 lb. Original (small) Burger Patty 525 calories, 29g fat, 25g protein
2g net carbs: 1/2 lb. Classic (medium) Burger Patty 790 calories, 33g fat, 30g protein
2g net carbs: 2/3 lb. Fudd Buster (large) Burger 930 calories, 37g fat, 35g protein
2g net carbs: 1 lb. Legend Burger 1387 calories, 41g fat, 39g protein

Burger Toppings

0g net carbs: Bleu Cheese 80 calories, 6g fat, 5g protein
0g net carbs: Cheddar Cheese 80 calories, 7g fat, 5g protein
0g net carbs: Fried Egg 120 calories, 10g fat, 6g protein
0g net carbs: Lettuce 1 calorie, 0g fat, 0g protein
0g net carbs: Onion 5 calories, 0g fat, 0g protein
0g net carbs: Provolone Cheese 70 calories, 6g fat, 5g protein
0g net carbs: Smoke House Bacon (2 strips) 90 calories, 8g fat, 5g protein
0g net carbs: Swiss Cheese 80 calories, 6g fat, 6g protein
1g net carbs: Grilled Jalapeños 50 calories, 5g fat, 0g protein
1g net carbs: Pepper Jack Cheese 90 calories, 8g fat, 5g protein
1g net carbs: Tomato 5 calories, 0g fat, 0g protein
2g net carbs: American Cheese 140 calories, 12g fat, 7g protein
2g net carbs: Grilled Onions 60 calories, 3g fat, 1g protein
3g net carbs: Fresh Guacamole 40 calories, 3g fat, 1g protein
3g net carbs: Grilled Mushrooms 160 calories, 14g fat, 4g protein

3g net carbs: Sliced Avocado 160 calories, 15g fat, 2g protein

Specialty Burgers (No Bread)

2g net carbs: 1/3 lb. American Melt Burger 342 calories, 17g fat, 22g protein
5g net carbs: 1/2 lb. BBQ Pork Burger, easy BBQ sauce 886 calories, 21g fat, 30g protein

4g net carbs: 1/4 lb. Bacon Cheddar Burger 744 calories, 14g fat, 40g protein
4g net carbs: 1/3 lb. Bacon Cheddar Burger 771 calories, 17g fat, 50g protein
5g net carbs: 1/2 lb. Bacon Cheddar Burger 1007 calories, 23g fat, 52g protein
5g net carbs: 2/3 lb. Bacon Cheddar Burger 913 calories, 27g fat, 55g protein

2g net carbs: 1/4 lb. Bacon Bleu Burger 754 calories, 14g fat, 30g protein
2g net carbs: 1/3 lb. Bacon Bleu Burger 771 calories, 17g fat, 37g protein
3g net carbs: 1/2 lb. Bacon Bleu Burger 807 calories, 23g fat, 42g protein
4g net carbs: 2/3 lb. Bacon Bleu Burger 853 calories, 26g fat, 50g protein

6g net carbs: 1/3 lb. BBQ Burger, easy BBQ sauce 750 calories, 40g fat, 53g protein
6g net carbs: 1/2 lb. BBQ Burger, easy BBQ sauce 998 calories, 53g fat, 67g protein

2g net carbs: 1/4 lb. Tex Mex Burger 605 calories, 14g fat, 31g protein
3g net carbs: 1/3 lb. Tex Mex Burger 692 calories, 16g fat, 36g protein
3g net carbs: 1/2 lb. Tex Mex Burger 746 calories, 19g fat, 41g protein
4g net carbs: 2/3 lb. Tex Mex Burger 852 calories, 24g fat, 52g protein

5g net carbs: 1/3 lb. Hangover Burger 774 calories, 45g fat, 42g protein
6g net carbs: 1/2 lb. Hangover Burger 1001 calories, 57g fat, 55g protein

3g net carbs: 1/4 lb. Inferno Burger 716 calories, 12g fat, 39g protein
3g net carbs: 1/3 lb. Inferno Burger 755 calories, 15g fat, 42g protein
4g net carbs: 1/2 lb. Inferno Burger 803 calories, 20g fat, 52g protein
5g net carbs: 2/3 lb. Inferno Burger 896 calories, 24g fat, 60g protein

5g net carbs: 1/4 lb. Bourbon Burger, easy sauce 692 calories, 15g fat, 41g protein
5g net carbs: 1/3 lb. Bourbon Burger, easy sauce 743 calories, 17g fat, 51g protein
7g net carbs: 1/2 lb. Bourbon Burger, easy sauce 867 calories, 23g fat, 57g protein
7g net carbs: 2/3 lb. Bourbon Burger, easy sauce 921 calories, 28g fat, 61g protein

5g net carbs: 1/4 lb. Mushroom Swiss Melt Burger 705 calories, 14g fat, 38g protein
5g net carbs: 1/3 lb. Mushroom Swiss Melt Burger 749 calories, 17g fat, 48g protein
6g net carbs: 1/2 lb. Mushroom Swiss Melt Burger 1062 calories, 22g fat, 51g protein
6g net carbs: 2/3 lb. Mushroom Swiss Melt Burger 845 calories, 28g fat, 59g protein

2g net carbs: 1/4 lb. Three Cheese Burger 689 calories, 21g fat, 40g protein
2g net carbs: 1/3 lb. Three Cheese Burger 756 calories, 26g fat, 51g protein
3g net carbs: 1/2 lb. Three Cheese Burger 829 calories, 30g fat, 54g protein
3g net carbs: 2/3 lb. Three Cheese Burger 855 calories, 35g fat, 62g protein

4g net carbs: 1/4 lb. The Works Burger 806 calories, 17g fat, 47g protein
4g net carbs: 1/3 lb. The Works Burger 857 calories, 20g fat, 57g protein

5g net carbs: 1/2 lb. The Works Burger 933 calories, 25g fat, 60g protein
6g net carbs: 2/3 lb. The Works Burger 998 calories, 30g fat, 68g protein

6g net carbs: Beyond Burger 725 calories, 23g fat, 31g protein

Exotic Burgers (No Bread)

3g net carbs: Ribeye Steak Sandwich, no onion rings 456 calories, 11g fat, 31g protein
3g net carbs: 1/2 lb. Buffalo Burger 692 calories, 12g fat, 35g protein
4g net carbs: 1/2 lb. Elk Burger 515 calories, 7g fat, 32g protein
4g net carbs: 1/2 lb. American Kobe Burger 908 calories, 21g fat, 32g protein

Chicken & More (No Bread)

2g net carbs: Bacon and Swiss Grilled Chicken Sandwich 1041 calories, 16g fat, 29g protein
3g net carbs: Green Chili Grilled Chicken Sandwich 740 calories, 10g fat, 42g protein
3g net carbs: Mushroom Turkey Burger 960 calories, 20g fat, 35g protein
3g net carbs: Original Grilled Chicken Sandwich 501 calories, 6g fat, 23g protein
4g net carbs: Buffalo Grilled Chicken Sandwich 620 calories, 5g fat, 31g protein
4g net carbs: Turkey Burger 870 calories, 18g fat, 31g protein
5g net carbs: Turkey Swiss Burger 981 calories, 23g fat, 32g protein
6g net carbs: California Turkey Burger 1172 calories, 29g fat, 38g protein
6g net carbs: Mushroom Swiss Turkey Burger 1071 calories, 25g fat, 36g protein

Hot Dogs (No Bread)

4g net carbs: Black Angus Chili Dog 756 calories, 16g fat, 24g protein
4g net carbs: Black Angus Dog 701 calories, 14g fat, 13g protein
4g net carbs: Fudds Big Dog 710 calories, 17g fat, 25g protein
5g net carbs: Black Angus Chili Cheese Dog 793 calories, 18g fat, 28g protein
5g net carbs: The Big Chili Cheese Dog, easy chile 813 calories, 20g fat, 29g protein
5g net carbs: The Big Chili Dog, easy chili 756 calories, 17g fat, 28g protein

Salads (No Dressing Unless Otherwise Indicated)

3g net carbs: Napa Valley Salad with Grilled Chicken, no apples, no cranberries 517 calories, 6g fat, 24g protein
4g net carbs: Avocado Bacon Salad, no croutons 738 calories, 22g fat, 29g protein
4g net carbs: Grilled Chicken Salad, no croutons 538 calories, 10g fat, 24g protein
5g net carbs: Southern Grilled Chicken Salad, no croutons 665 calories, 11g fat, 19g protein
5g net carbs: Southwest Salad with Nacho Beef, no Tortilla strips 923 calories, 21g fat, 29g protein
6g net carbs: Chicken Caesar Salad with Grilled Chicken & Caesar Dressing, no croutons 799 calories, 10g fat, 17g protein
6g net carbs: Southwest Salad with Grilled Chicken, no Tortilla strips 1048 calories, 20g fat, 26g protein

Salad Dressing (2 oz.)

2g net carbs: Bleu Cheese 360 calories, 38g fat, 2g protein
4g net carbs: Ranch 280 calories, 30g fat, 0g protein

8g net carbs: Balsamic Vinaigrette 120 calories, 10g fat, 0g protein

Sides

2g net carbs: Side Caesar Salad with Caesar Dressing, no croutons 237 calories, 5g fat, 8g protein
2g net carbs: Side Garden Salad, no croutons 101 calories, 3g fat, 9g protein
8g net carbs: Apples[26] 33 calories, 0g fat, 0g protein

DRINKS

0g net carbs: Diet Coke, 16 oz. 0 calories, 0g fat, 0g protein
0g net carbs: Diet Coke Caffeine Free, 16 oz. 0 calories, 0g fat, 0g protein
0g net carbs: Coke Zero Sugar, 16 oz. 0 calories, 0g fat, 0g protein
0g net carbs: Sprite Zero Sugar, 16 oz. 0 calories, 0g fat, 0g protein
0g net carbs: Pibb Zero, 16 oz. 0 calories, 0g fat, 0g protein
0g net carbs: Diet Barq's Root Beer, 16 oz. 0 calories, 0g fat, 0g protein
0g net carbs: Fanta Zero, 16 oz. 0 calories, 0g fat, 0g protein
0g net carbs: Diet Dr. Pepper, 16 oz. 0 calories, 0g fat, 0g protein
0g net carbs: Mello Yellow Zero, 16 oz. 0 calories, 0g fat, 0g protein
0g net carbs: Powerade Zero, 16 oz. 0 calories, 0g fat, 0g protein
3g net carbs: Minute Maid Lemonade Zero Sugar, 16 oz. 10 calories, 0g fat, 0g protein

---

[26] *That's Not Keto!* – You'll find all sorts of surprising foods listed here. I'm not telling you whether you should eat these foods or not. What fits your macros or daily carb spend is up to you. No keto police allowed.

Five Guys

Five Guys earns a *Keto Diet Restaurant Guide* Superstar Award for breaking out the macronutrient information for burger buns and all available toppings. You can analyze each component of the menu item (bun, burger patty, produce, cheese) instead of the actual menu item (Hamburger, Cheeseburger, Bacon Burger). Instead of a customizable nutrition calculator on its website, Five Guys offers a detailed Nutrition & Allergen Information guide. It's super helpful! They forgot to include the hot dog bun, though; *duh!*

Special Order Tips

Order all burgers and sandwiches with "no bread." Be wary of the available "Add-Ons" since they are often an unnecessary source of net carbs. Avoid all fries, potatoes, rice, pasta, bread, etc. Ask the server to substitute a side salad or a side of steamed/grilled vegetables.

Feel free to customize your order. Restaurants are usually happy to accommodate reasonable customer requests.

The exception is when the item has been premade or was prepared off-site. Note that any alterations on your end will change the provided nutrition information. Adjust accordingly.

Author Favorite

Lunch & Dinner: Bunless Bacon Cheeseburger, 16 oz. Diet Coke to drink. 1060 calories, 62g fat, 2g net carbs, 39g protein

LUNCH & DINNER

Meat

0g net carbs: Bacon (2 pieces) 80 calories, 7g fat, 4g protein
0g net carbs: Hamburger Patty 302 calories, 17g fat, 16g protein
1g net carbs: Hot Dog (1) 280 calories, 26g fat, 11g protein

Toppings

0g net carbs: Hot Sauce 0 calories, 0g fat, 0g protein
0g net carbs: Mayonnaise 111 calories, 11g fat, 0g protein
0g net carbs: Mustard 0 calories, 0g fat, 0g protein
1g net carbs: Cheese (1 slice) 70 calories, 6g fat, 4g protein
1g net carbs: Green Peppers 3 calories, 0g fat, 0g protein
1g net carbs: Grilled Mushrooms 19 calories, 0g fat, 0g protein
1g net carbs: Jalapeño Peppers 3 calories, 0g fat, 0g protein
1g net carbs: Lettuce 3 calories, 0g fat, 0g protein
1g net carbs: Pickles 4 calories, 0g fat, 0g protein
2g net carbs: Onions/Grilled Onions 11 calories, 0g fat, 0g protein
2g net carbs: Tomatoes 8 calories, 0g fat, 1g protein
3g net carbs: A.1. Original Steak Sauce 15 calories, 0g fat, 0g protein
4g net carbs: Relish 16 calories, 0g fat, 0g protein
5g net carbs: Ketchup[27] 30 calories, 0g fat, 0g protein
7g net carbs: BBQ Sauce*, .5 oz. 25 calories, 0g fat, 1g protein

DRINKS

0g net carbs: Diet Coke, 16 oz. 0 calories, 0g fat, 0g protein
0g net carbs: Coca-Cola Zero, 16 oz. 0 calories, 0g fat, 0g protein
0g net carbs: Dasani Water Bottle, 16 oz. 0 calories, 0g fat, 0g protein

---

[27] *That's Not Keto!* – You'll find all sorts of surprising foods listed here. I'm not telling you whether you should eat these foods or not. What fits your macros or daily carb spend is up to you. No keto police allowed.

Potbelly Sandwich Shop ◉

Potbelly Sandwich Shop has a fabulous interactive Nutrition Calculator on their website, handily earning them a *Keto Diet Restaurant Guide* Superstar Award! It allows you to experiment with (most) menu components to see an immediate update on the macronutrients in the Nutrition Facts table. That feature alone warms my heart.

Potbelly Sandwich Shop must be a staple in any self-respecting sandwich lover's routine. You won't soon tire of this fun little restaurant with dozens of options (in three different sizes).

Beware that the Bacon and ham appear to have sugar in them (some menu options show higher amounts of carbs when ham or bacon are added to them). Interestingly, not all dishes at Potbelly show an increase in carbs when these ingredients are added (a website glitch?). Hmmm, the jury is still out.

Special Order Tips

Potbelly sandwiches (Skinnys, Originals, and Bigs) come standard with only meat and cheese. After choosing your toppings, add the macronutrients/calories for each to the amount indicated for your standard breadless sandwich.

Order all sandwiches with "no bread." Be wary of the available "Add-Ons" since they are often an unnecessary source of net carbs.

Feel free to customize your order. Restaurants are usually happy to accommodate reasonable customer requests. The exception is when the item has been premade or was prepared off-site. Note that any alterations on your end will change the provided nutrition information. Adjust accordingly.

Avoid all bread, chips, fries, potatoes, rice, pasta, etc. Ask the server to provide a substitute (pickles, side salad, or your pick of low-carb sandwich toppings).

You'll notice some menu items indicate a half-serving size. This was done sparingly. A smaller portion size allowed us to include additional (higher-carb) Potbelly soups and salads.

Author Favorite

Breakfast: Breadless Bigs Ham, Mushroom, Egg & Swiss, easy ham. 22 oz. Iced Tea, unsweetened to drink. 633 calories, 38g fat, 8g net carbs, 31g protein

Lunch & Dinner: Breadless Originals Steakhouse Beef with side (6 oz.) Broccoli Cheddar Soup. 32 oz. Coke Zero Sugar to drink. 650 calories, 47g fat, 12g net carbs, 42g protein

BREAKFAST (No Bread)

2g net carbs: Egg & Cheddar 160 calories, 13g fat, 16g protein
3g net carbs: Bacon, Egg & Cheddar, Skinny 240 calories, 18g fat, 18g protein
3g net carbs: Ham, Mushroom, Egg & Swiss, Skinny 200 calories, 12g fat, 18g protein
3g net carbs: Sausage, Egg & Cheddar, Skinny 400 calories, 34g fat, 20g protein
5g net carbs: Bacon, Egg & Cheddar, BIGS, easy bacon 710 calories, 53g fat, 53g protein
5g net carbs: Sausage, Egg & Cheddar, Original 800 calories, 68g fat, 39g protein
6g net carbs: Bacon, Egg & Cheddar, Originals 470 calories, 35g fat, 35g protein
6g net carbs: Ham, Mushroom, Egg & Swiss, Originals 420 calories, 25g fat, 38g protein
7g net carbs: Breakfast Mediterranean, no hummus 175 calories, 16g fat, 20g protein
8g net carbs: Ham, Mushroom, Egg & Swiss, BIGS, easy ham 630 calories, 38g fat, 31g protein
8g net carbs: Sausage, Egg & Cheddar, BIGS 520 calories, 102g fat, 59g protein

LUNCH & DINNER (No Bread)

5g net carbs: Cheeseburger, bunless 280 calories, 18g fat, 23g protein

Sandwiches, Skinnys[28] (No Bread)

0g net carbs: Grilled Chicken & Cheddar, Skinny 130 calories, 6g fat, 19g protein
1g net carbs: Chicken Salad & Provolone, Skinny 220 calories, 16g fat, 15g protein
1g net carbs: Grilled Chicken Club, Skinny 190 calories, 10g fat, 24g protein
1g net carbs: Skinny Mushroom Melt/Veggie Melt, Skinny 220 calories, 18g fat, 13g protein
1g net carbs: Tuna Salad & Swiss, Skinny 210 calories, 16g fat, 15g protein
2g net carbs: A Wreck®, Skinny 180 calories, 13g fat, 15g protein
2g net carbs: Italian, Skinny 210 calories, 18g fat, 11g protein
2g net carbs: Roast Beef & Provolone, Skinny 150 calories, 9g fat, 15g protein
2g net carbs: Skinny Hammie/Smoked Ham & Swiss, Skinny 140 calories, 9g fat, 15g protein
2g net carbs: Steakhouse Beef, Skinny 240 calories, 17g fat, 18g protein
3g net carbs: Avo Turkey, Skinny 170 calories, 10g fat, 17g protein
3g net carbs: BLTA, Skinny 180 calories, 14g fat, 12g protein
3g net carbs: Skinny T-K-Y/Turkey Breast & Swiss, Skinny 110 calories, 5g fat, 16g protein
4g net carbs: Pizza Melt, Skinny 220 calories, 16g fat, 13g protein
6g net carbs: Mama's Meatball, Skinny 300 calories, 22g fat, 16g protein
6g net carbs: Mediterranean No Chicken, Skinny 110 calories, 6g fat, 6g protein
7g net carbs: Mediterranean, Skinny 180 calories, 7g fat, 21g protein

Toppings for Skinnys (.25 oz. Unless Otherwise Indicated)

0g net carbs: Brown Mustard 10 calories, 0g fat, 0g protein
0g net carbs: Horseradish Mayo 40 calories, 4g fat, 0g protein
0g net carbs: Hot Peppers, .5 oz. 15 calories, 1g fat, 0g protein
0g net carbs: Italian Seasoning, dusting 0 calories, 0g fat, 0g protein
0g net carbs: Lettuce, .75 oz. 0 calories, 0g fat, 0g protein
0g net carbs: Mayo 50 calories, 6g fat, 0g protein
0g net carbs: Oil, 0.08 oz. 20 calories, 2g fat, 0g protein
0g net carbs: Pickles, .5 oz. 0 calories, 0g fat, 0g protein
0g net carbs: Sauerkraut, 1 oz. 5 calories, 0g fat, 0g protein
0g net carbs: Sliced Onions 0 calories, 0g fat, 0g protein
1g net carbs: Potbelly Whole Pickle (1) 25 calories, 0g fat, 1g protein
1g net carbs: Tomato, .75 oz. 0 calories, 0g fat, 0g protein
2g net carbs: Marinara Sauce, 1 oz. 15 calories, 0g fat, 0g protein

Premium Toppings for Skinnys (.5 oz. Unless Otherwise Indicated)

0g net carbs: Artichoke Hearts 5 calories, 0g fat, 0g protein
0g net carbs: Avocado, 1 oz. 45 calories, 4g fat, 1g protein
0g net carbs: Cucumbers 0 calories, 0g fat, 0g protein
0g net carbs: Sliced Mushrooms 0 calories, 0g fat, 0g protein
0g net carbs: Spinach, .25 oz. 0 calories, 0g fat, 0g protein
1g net carbs: Egg Patty 30 calories, 2g fat, 2g protein
1g net carbs: Roasted Red Peppers 5 calories, 0g fat, 0g protein
4g net carbs: Hummus, 1 oz. 60 calories, 4g fat, 2g protein

---

[28] Skinnys sandwiches don't come standard with produce or sauce. Add desired items and calculate carbs accordingly.

Sandwiches, Originals (No Bread)

1g net carbs: Grilled Chicken & Cheddar, Originals 270 calories, 11g fat, 38g protein
2g net carbs: Chicken Salad & Provolone, Originals, no additions 440 calories, 33g fat, 29g protein
2g net carbs: Tuna Salad & Swiss, Originals 420 calories, 32g fat, 30g protein
2g net carbs: Veggie Melt, Originals 440 calories, 35g fat, 26g protein
3g net carbs: Grilled Chicken Club, Originals 390 calories, 20g fat, 48g protein
3g net carbs: Italian, Originals 420 calories, 36g fat, 23g protein
3g net carbs: Roast Beef & Provolone, Originals 310 calories, 18g fat, 30g protein
4g net carbs: A Wreck®, Originals 350 calories, 25g fat, 30g protein
4g net carbs: Smoked Ham & Swiss, Originals 290 calories, 17g fat, 29g protein
4g net carbs: Steakhouse Beef, Originals 480 calories, 35g fat, 36g protein
5g net carbs: Mediterranean, No Chicken, Originals, no hummus 90 calories, 4g fat, 7g protein
6g net carbs: Avo Turkey, Originals 330 calories, 21g fat, 34g protein
6g net carbs: BLTA, Originals 370 calories, 28g fat, 23g protein
6g net carbs: Mediterranean, Originals, no hummus 250 calories, 6g fat, 38g protein
6g net carbs: Turkey Breast & Swiss, Originals 220 calories, 10g fat, 31g protein
7g net carbs: Mama's Meatball, Originals, no marinara 580 calories, 44g fat, 31g protein
8g net carbs: Pizza Melt, Originals 450 calories, 33g fat, 26g protein

Toppings for Originals (.5 oz. Unless Otherwise Indicated)

0g net carbs: Brown Mustard 15 calories, 0g fat, 0g protein
0g net carbs: Italian Seasoning, dusting 0 calories, 0g fat, 0g protein
0g net carbs: Mayo 100 calories, 11g fat, 0g protein
0g net carbs: Oíl, 0.16 oz. 40 calories, 5g fat, 0g protein
0g net carbs: Pickles 0 calories, 0g fat, 0g protein
0g net carbs: Sauerkraut, 1 oz. 5 calories, 0g fat, 0g protein
1g net carbs: Horseradish Mayo 80 calories, 8g fat, 0g protein
1g net carbs: Hot Peppers, 1 oz. 25 calories, 2g fat, 0g protein
1g net carbs: Lettuce, 1.5 oz. 5 calories, 0g fat, 0g protein
1g net carbs: Potbelly Whole Pickle (1) 25 calories, 0g fat, 1g protein
1g net carbs: Sliced Onions 5 calories, 0g fat, 0g protein
1g net carbs: Tomato, 1 oz. 4 calories, 0g fat, 0g protein

Premium Toppings for Originals (1 oz. Unless Otherwise Indicated)

0g net carbs: Avocado, 2.6 oz. 120 calories, 10g fat, 3g protein
1g net carbs: Artichoke Hearts 10 calories, 0g fat, 0g protein
1g net carbs: Cucumbers 0 calories, 0g fat, 0g protein
1g net carbs: Egg Patty (1) 60 calories, 4g fat, 4g protein
1g net carbs: Roasted Red Peppers 10 calories, 0g fat, 1g protein
1g net carbs: Sliced Mushrooms 5 calories, 0g fat, 0g protein
1g net carbs: Spinach, .5 oz. 0 calories, 0g fat, 0g protein
5g net carbs: Coleslaw 15 calories, 1g fat, 2g protein
8g net carbs: Hummus, 2 oz. 120 calories, 7g fat, 4g protein

Sandwiches- Bigs[29] (No Bread)

1g net carbs: Grilled Chicken & Cheddar, BIGS 440 calories, 17g fat, 57g protein
3g net carbs: Chicken Salad & Provolone, BIGS 650 calories, 49g fat, 44g protein
3g net carbs: Tuna Salad & Swiss, BIGS 630 calories, 47g fat, 46g protein
3g net carbs: Veggie Melt, BIGS 650 calories, 53g fat, 39g protein
4g net carbs: Grilled Chicken Club, BIGS 580 calories, 31g fat, 72g protein
5g net carbs: Italian, BIGS 620 calories, 52g fat, 33g protein
5g net carbs: Roast Beef & Provolone, BIGS 460 calories, 28g fat, 45g protein
5g net carbs: Smoked Ham & Swiss, BIGS 430 calories, 26g fat, 44g protein
6g net carbs: A Wreck®, BIGS 530 calories, 38g fat, 45g protein
6g net carbs: BLTA, BIGS, easy bacon 550 calories, 43g fat, 35g protein
6g net carbs: Steakhouse Beef, BIGS 730 calories, 52g fat, 54g protein
7g net carbs: Mediterranean, No Chicken, BIGS, no hummus 140 calories, 6g fat, 11g protein
7g net carbs: Pizza Melt, BIGS, no marinara 630 calories, 48g fat, 39g protein
8g net carbs: Turkey Breast & Swiss, BIGS 320 calories, 15g fat, 47g protein
9g net carbs: Avo Turkey, BIGS 560 calories, 34g fat, 51g protein
9g net carbs: Mediterranean, BIGS, no hummus 370 calories, 10g fat, 57g protein
10g net carbs: Mama's Meatball, BIGS, no marinara 870 calories, 66g fat, 47g protein

Toppings for Bigs (.75 oz. Unless Otherwise Indicated)

0g net carbs: Brown Mustard 25 calories, 0g fat, 0g protein
0g net carbs: Italian Seasoning, dusting 0 calories, 0g fat, 0g protein
0g net carbs: Mayo 150 calories, 17g fat, 0g protein
0g net carbs: Oil, .25 oz. 60 calories, 7g fat, 0g protein
0g net carbs: Pickles 0 calories, 0g fat, 0g protein
0g net carbs: Sauerkraut, 1.5 oz. 10 calories, 0g fat, 0g protein
1g net carbs: Horseradish Mayo 120 calories, 12g fat, 0g protein
1g net carbs: Hot Peppers, 1.5 oz. 40 calories, 3g fat, 0g protein
1g net carbs: Lettuce, 2 oz. 10 calories, 0g fat, 1g protein
1g net carbs: Potbelly Whole Pickle (1) 25 calories, 0g fat, 1g protein
1g net carbs: Sliced Onions, .5 oz. 5 calories, 0g fat, 0g protein
2g net carbs: Diced Red Onion 10 calories, 0g fat, 0g protein
2g net carbs: Tomato, 2 oz. 10 calories, 0g fat, 0g protein

Premium Toppings for Bigs (1.5 oz. Unless Otherwise Indicated)

0g net carbs: Avocado, 4 oz. 180 calories, 16g fat, 4g protein
0g net carbs: Cucumbers, 1 oz. 0 calories, 0g fat, 0g protein
0g net carbs: Sliced Mushrooms 10 calories, 0g fat, 1g protein
1g net carbs: Artichoke Hearts 10 calories, 0g fat, 1g protein
1g net carbs: Egg Patty (1) 60 calories, 4g fat, 4g protein
1g net carbs: Spinach, .5 oz. 0 calories, 0g fat, 0g protein
2g net carbs: Roasted Red Peppers 15 calories, 0g fat, 1g protein
6g net carbs: Hummus, Half-Serving 90 calories, 6g fat, 3g protein

---

[29] Bigs Sandwiches do not come standard with any produce or sauce.

Extra Meat[30] (1 oz. Unless Otherwise Indicated)

0g net carbs: Bacon, Non-Nueske (2 strips) 60 calories, 5g fat, 5g protein
0g net carbs: Chicken Salad 70 calories, 5g fat, 6g protein
0g net carbs: Grilled Chicken 45 calories, 1g fat, 7g protein
0g net carbs: Pepperoni 130 calories, 12g fat, 5g protein
0g net carbs: Tuna Salad 50 calories, 3g fat, 5g protein
1g net carbs: Capicola 60 calories, 4g fat, 5g protein
1g net carbs: Ham 40 calories, 2g fat, 5g protein
1g net carbs: Meatball (1) 80 calories, 6g fat, 5g protein
1g net carbs: Mortadella 110 calories, 10g fat, 4g protein
1g net carbs: Roast Beef 45 calories, 3g fat, 5g protein
1g net carbs: Salami 120 calories, 11g fat, 5g protein
1g net carbs: Sausage 190 calories, 17g fat, 8g protein
1g net carbs: Turkey Breast 25 calories, 1g fat, 5g protein
2g net carbs: Bacon (2 strips) 120 calories, 9g fat, 10g protein
2g net carbs: Roasted Turkey 45 calories, 2g fat, 7g protein

Extra Cheese (.5 oz. Unless Otherwise Indicated)

0g net carbs: Blue Cheese 50 calories, 4g fat, 3g protein
0g net carbs: Cheddar 60 calories, 5g fat, 4g protein
0g net carbs: Mozzarella Cheese 35 calories, 3g fat, 2g protein
0g net carbs: Pepper Jack Cheese 50 calories, 4g fat, 3g protein
1g net carbs: Feta 35 calories, 2g fat, 3g protein
1g net carbs: Provolone Cheese 50 calories, 4g fat, 4g protein
1g net carbs: Swiss Cheese 50 calories, 4g fat, 4g protein
2g net carbs: Cheese Whiz 45 calories, 4g fat, 2g protein

Salads

4g net carbs: Farmhouse with no dressing 430 calories, 24g fat, 34g protein
4g net carbs: Powerhouse without dressing, no hummus 230 calories, 10g fat, 27g protein
5g net carbs: Chicken Salad with no Dressing, no cranberries 330 calories, 23g fat, 22g protein
5g net carbs: Uptown Salad/Apple Walnut Salad without dressing, no Diced Apples, no Dried Cranberry,
    no Glazed Walnuts 250 calories, 11g fat, 32g protein
6g net carbs: Farmhouse with easy Buttermilk Ranch Dressing 610 calories, 41g fat, 36g protein
6g net carbs: Farmhouse, no chicken with easy Buttermilk Ranch Dressing 510 calories, 38g fat, 34g protein
7g net carbs: Powerhouse, easy Buttermilk Ranch dressing, no hummus 490 calories, 37g fat, 23g protein
9g net carbs: Chicken Salad with easy Buttermilk Ranch Dressing, no cranberries 560 calories, 40g fat, 23g
    protein

Salad Add-On Toppings

0g net carbs: Celery Salt dusting 0 calories, 0g fat, 0g protein
0g net carbs: Italian Seasoning dusting 0 calories, 0g fat, 0g protein
1g net carbs: Cucumbers 1 oz. 3 calories, 0g fat, 0g protein

---

[30] Adding extra meat portion to sandwich or salad is optional.

1g net carbs: Diced Red Onion .5 oz. 5 calories, 0g fat, 0g protein
1g net carbs: Grape Tomato 1 oz. 10 calories, 0g fat, 0g protein
7g net carbs: Croutons[31] 14 grams 70 calories, 5g fat, 1g protein

Salad Add-On Premium Toppings (1 oz. Unless Otherwise Indicated)

0g net carbs: Avocado 45 calories 4g fat, 1g protein
0g net carbs: Chopped Bacon 140 calories, 10g fat, 12g protein
0g net carbs: Hard Boiled Egg (1) 45 calories, 3g fat, 4g protein
1g net carbs: Artichoke Hearts 2 oz. 15 calories, 0g fat, 1g protein
2g net carbs: Fresh Strawberries 10 calories, 0g fat, 0g protein
2g net carbs: Garbanzo Beans 25 calories, 0g fat, 1g protein
2g net carbs: Roasted Red Peppers 10 calories, 0g fat, 1g protein
3g net carbs: Candied Walnuts* .5 oz. 90 calories, 8g fat, 2g protein
4g net carbs: Diced Apples* 15 calories, 0g fat, 0g protein
4g net carbs: Hummus 60 calories, 4g fat, 2g protein
5g net carbs: Glazed Walnuts* 200 calories, 19g fat, 4g protein
5g net carbs: Red Grapes* 20 calories, 0g fat, 0g protein
6g net carbs: Dried Cranberry* .25 oz. 25 calories, 0g fat, 0g protein

Salad Dressing (1 oz.)

2g net carbs: Buttermilk Ranch 120 calories, 13g fat, 1g protein
3g net carbs: Potbelly Vinaigrette 110 calories, 10g fat, 0g protein
9g net carbs: Balsamic Vinaigrette 50 calories, 5g fat, 0g protein

Soup (Side, 6 oz)

8g net carbs: Broccoli Cheddar Soup, 6 oz 170 calories, 12g fat, 6g protein
8g net carbs: Chicken Pot Pie Soup*, 6 oz 210 calories, 14g fat, 6g protein
10g net carbs: Garden Vegetable soup, 6 oz 60 calories, 0g fat, 2g protein

Soup (1 Cup)

10g net carbs: Broccoli Cheddar Soup, 1 cup 230 calories, 16g fat, 8g protein

Soup (Extras, .5 oz. Unless Otherwise Indicated)

0g net carbs: Avocado 25 calories, 2g fat, 1g protein
0g net carbs: Cheddar 60 calories, 5g fat, 4g protein
0g net carbs: Chopped Bacon 70 calories, 5g fat, 6g protein
0g net carbs: Sliced Mushrooms 5 calories, 0g fat, 0g protein
0g net carbs: Sliced Onions .25 oz. 0 calories, 0g fat, 0g protein
1g net carbs: Hot Peppers 1 oz. 25 calories, 2g fat, 0g protein
1g net carbs: Roasted Red Peppers 1 oz. 10 calories, 0g fat, 1g protein
3g net carbs: Chili* 1 oz. 30 calories, 2g fat, 2g protein

---

[31] *That's Not Keto!* – You'll find all sorts of surprising foods listed here. I'm not telling you whether you should eat these foods or not. What fits your macros or daily carb spend is up to you. No keto police allowed.

6g net carbs: Oyster Crackers* 35 calories, 1g fat, 0g protein

DRINKS

0g net carbs: Coke Zero Sugar 12 oz. 0 calories, 0g fat, 0g protein
0g net carbs: Coke Zero Sugar 22 oz. 0 calories, 0g fat, 0g protein
0g net carbs: Coke Zero Sugar 32 oz. 0 calories, 0g fat, 0g protein
0g net carbs: Diet Coke 12 oz. 0 calories, 0g fat, 0g protein
0g net carbs: Diet Coca-Cola 22 oz. 0 calories, 0g fat, 0g protein
0g net carbs: Diet Coca-Cola 32 oz. 0 calories, 0g fat, 0g protein
0g net carbs: Diet Coke 12 oz. bottle 0 calories, 0g fat, 0g protein
0g net carbs: Diet Coke 20 oz. bottle 0 calories, 0g fat, 0g protein
0g net carbs: Coke Zero Sugar 12 oz. bottle 0 calories, 0g fat, 0g protein
0g net carbs: Coke Zero Sugar 20 oz. bottle 0 calories, 0g fat, 0g protein
0g net carbs: Diet Dr. Pepper 12 oz. 0 calories, 0g fat, 0g protein
0g net carbs: Diet Dr. Pepper 22 oz. 0 calories, 0g fat, 0g protein
1g net carbs: Diet Dr. Pepper 32 oz. 0 calories, 0g fat, 0g protein
0g net carbs: San Pellegrino Water 16 oz. 0 calories, 0g fat, 0g protein
0g net carbs: Smartwater 16 oz. bottle 0 calories, 0g fat, 0g protein
0g net carbs: Water Bottle 16 oz. bottle 0 calories, 0g fat, 0g protein
0g net carbs: Unsweetened Iced Tea 22 oz. 3 calories, 0g fat, 0g protein
0g net carbs: Unsweetened Iced Tea 32 oz. 5 calories, 0g fat, 0g protein
1g net carbs: Diet Snapple Half & Half 16 oz. bottle 10 calories, 0g fat, 0g protein
5g net carbs: Vitamin Water Zero Sugar Squeezed Lemonade 16 oz. bottle 0 calories, 0g fat, 0g protein

Arby's

Arby's does not have a customizable nutrition calculator. They offer, instead, a Nutrition & Allergen Information PDF on their website, a document with a glaring problem. Arby's only shares macronutrients for one type of bread (4" Sesame Seed Bun). Why is this important? (We aren't eating the bread, after all.) Well, let me explain.

To accurately calculate the nutrition profile of a "breadless" sandwich, you first need to know what information to subtract. How many calories or grams of protein, fat, and carbohydrate are in that bread? Deduct those amounts from the sandwich's advertised nutrition profile (now you know my method). Arby's isn't making this easy for us. One bread? *I don't think so.* Current sandwich offerings include pita, marbled rye, honey wheat, star top bun, onion roll, sub roll, artisan-style roll, slider bun, sourdough, croissant, biscuit, and artisan wraps – not just a sesame seed bun!

Special Order Tips

Order all burgers and sandwiches with "no bread." Be wary of the available "Add-Ons" since they are often an unnecessary source of net carbs. Avoid all fries, potatoes, rice, pasta, bread, etc. Ask the server to substitute a side salad or a side of steamed/grilled vegetables.

Feel free to customize your order. Restaurants are usually happy to accommodate reasonable customer requests. The exception is when the item has been premade or was prepared off-site. Note that any alterations on your end will change the provided nutrition information. Adjust accordingly.

Remember that the chicken nuggets and tenders are breaded and fried.

Author Favorite

Breakfast: Bacon, Egg & Cheese, no bread and no potatoes, with extra bacon and jalapeños toppings. 16 oz. hot coffee, unsweetened, to drink. 545 calories, 27g fat, 6g net carbs, 28g protein

Lunch & Dinner: Breadless Roast Beef Gyro with easy sauce. Roast Chicken Salad with Buttermilk Ranch Dressing and Premium Nuggets (2) on the side. 22 oz. Coca-Cola Zero Sugar to drink. 1105 calories, 69g fat, 18g net carbs, 57g protein

BREAKFAST (No Bread, No Potatoes)

2g net carbs: Bacon, Egg & Cheese 470 calories, 22g fat, 23g protein
3g net carbs: Bacon & Cheese 330 calories, 19g fat, 13g protein
4g net carbs: Ham & Swiss 340 calories, 17g fat, 17g protein
4g net carbs: Ham, Egg & Cheese 460 calories, 18g fat, 26g protein
4g net carbs: Sausage & Cheese 490 calories, 35g fat, 15g protein
5g net carbs: Sausage, Egg & Cheese 630 calories, 38g fat, 24g protein

Breakfast Toppings and Sauces

0g net carbs: Jalapeños, 0.25 oz. 0 calories, 0g fat, 0g protein
0g net carbs: Leaf Lettuce (1 leaf) 0 calories, 0g fat, 0g protein
0g net carbs: Natural Cheddar (1 slice) 80 calories, 6g fat, 5g protein
0g net carbs: Processed Swiss (1 slice) 40 calories, 3g fat, 3g protein
0g net carbs: Red Onion (2 slices) 0 calories, 0g fat, 0g protein
0g net carbs: Smoked Gouda (1 slice) 70 calories, 6g fat, 5g protein
1g net carbs: Bacon (3 half-strips) 70 calories, 5g fat, 5g protein
1g net carbs: Ham 80 calories, 4g fat, 7g protein
1g net carbs: Sausage 130 calories, 13g fat, 9g protein
2g net carbs: Cheddar Cheese Sauce, 0.75 oz. 25 calories, 2g fat, 0g protein
2g net carbs: Tomato (2 slices) 5 calories, 0g fat, 0g protein
3g net carbs: Ketchup[32] (1 packet) 10 calories, 0g fat, 0g protein
5g net carbs: Red Ranch Sauce, 0.5 oz. 70 calories, 6g fat, 0g protein
6g net carbs: Crispy Onions, 0.5 oz. 70 calories, 5g fat, 1g protein

LUNCH & DINNER

Burgers (No Bread)

3g net carbs: Breadless Arby's Melt 330 calories, 12g fat, 18g protein
3g net carbs: Breadless Deluxe Wagyu Steakhouse Burger 410 calories, 43g fat, 39g protein
3g net carbs: Breadless Ham & Swiss Melt 370 calories, 23g fat, 18g protein
3g net carbs: Breadless Super Roast Beef 440 calories, 19g fat, 23g protein
4g net carbs: Breadless Bacon Ranch Wagyu Steakhouse Burger 520 calories, 51g fat, 47g protein
5g net carbs: Breadless Arby-Q® 400 calories, 11g fat, 18g protein

---

[32] *That's Not Keto!* – You'll find all sorts of surprising foods listed here. I'm not telling you whether you should eat these foods or not. What fits your macros or daily carb spend is up to you. No keto police allowed.

Market Fresh® Sandwiches (No Bread)

3g net carbs: Country Style Pork Rib Sandwich, no Onion Strings, easy BBQ sauce 500 calories, 23g fat, 28g protein
4g net carbs: Corned Beef Reuben, easy Sauerkraut 680 calories, 31g fat, 37g protein
5g net carbs: Prime Rib Cheesesteak 630 calories, 27g fat, 52g protein
5g net carbs: Roast Beef Gyro, easy sauce 540 calories, 29g fat, 24g protein
5g net carbs: Roast Turkey & Swiss Sandwich 720 calories, 28g fat, 38g protein
5g net carbs: Roast Turkey, Bacon Ranch Sandwich 810 calories, 35g fat, 45g protein
6g net carbs: Greek Gyro, easy sauce 700 calories, 44g fat, 23g protein
6g net carbs: Roast Turkey Gyro, easy sauce 470 calories, 20g fat, 25g protein
6g net carbs: Spicy Prime Rib Cheesesteak 670 calories, 28g fat, 53g protein

Market Fresh® Wraps (No Tortilla)

4g net carbs: Roast Chicken Club Wrap 650 calories, 35g fat, 41g protein
4g net carbs: Jalapeño Bacon Ranch Roast Chicken Wrap 600 calories, 33g fat, 37g protein
6g net carbs: Creamy Mediterranean Roast Chicken Wrap 540 calories, 29g fat, 32g protein

Slow Roasted Beef Sandwiches (No Bread)

2g net carbs: Classic Roast Beef 360 calories, 14g fat, 23g protein
3g net carbs: Classic Beef 'n Cheddar, no Red Ranch Sauce 450 calories, 20g fat, 23g protein
5g net carbs: Double Beef 'n Cheddar, no Red Ranch Sauce 630 calories, 32g fat, 39g protein
5g net carbs: Double Roast Beef 510 calories, 24g fat, 38g protein
5g net carbs: Half Pound Beef 'n Cheddar, no Red Ranch Sauce 740 calories, 39g fat, 49g protein
5g net carbs: Half Pound Roast Beef 610 calories, 30g fat, 48g protein
5g net carbs: Smokehouse Brisket, no BBQ sauce, no onion strings 350 calories, 22g fat, 28g protein
6g net carbs: Classic French Dip & Swiss 420 calories, 19g fat, 18g protein

Sliders (No Bread, Lettuce Wrapped)

3g net carbs: Grilled Chicken Slider 270 calories, 11g fat, 13g protein
4g net carbs: Jalapeño Roast Beef Slider 220 calories, 9g fat, 12g protein
4g net carbs: Roast Beef Slider 210 calories, 9g fat, 12g protein
4g net carbs: Smokehouse Brisket, no Onion Strings, no BBQ sauce 400 calories, 23g fat, 21g protein
4g net carbs: Turkey Slider 180 calories, 5g fat, 13g protein
5g net carbs: Classic French Dip & Swiss/Au Jus 530 calories, 21g fat, 34g protein
6g net carbs: Grilled Buffalo Chicken Slider 300 calories, 14g fat, 12g protein

Meals (No Bread, with 16 oz. Diet Coke, Substitute Side Salad with Ranch Dressing for Fries)

5g net carbs: Classic Roast Beef Meal 630 calories, 38g fat, 28g protein
5g net carbs: Roast Chicken Entrée Salad Meal 250 calories, 14g fat, 25g protein
6g net carbs: Classic Beef 'N Cheddar Meal, no Red Ranch Sauce 720 calories, 44g fat, 28g protein
6g net carbs: Roast Chicken Bacon Swiss Sandwich Meal, no honey mustard 750 calories, 45g fat, 39g protein
7g net carbs: Corned Beef Reuben Meal, easy Sauerkraut 950 calories, 55g fat, 42g protein

8g net carbs: Double Beef 'N Cheddar Meal, no Red Ranch Sauce 900 calories, 56g fat, 44g protein
8g net carbs: Double Roast Beef Meal 780 calories, 48g fat, 42g protein
8g net carbs: Half Pound Beef 'N Cheddar Meal, no Red Ranch Sauce 1040 calories, 63g fat, 53g protein
8g net carbs: Half Pound Roast Beef Meal 880 calories, 54g fat, 53g protein
8g net carbs: Roast Beef Gyro Meal, easy sauce 810 calories, 53g fat, 29g protein
8g net carbs: Roast Turkey & Swiss Sandwich Meal 990 calories, 52g fat, 43g protein
8g net carbs: Roast Turkey Bacon Ranch Sandwich Meal 1080 calories, 59g fat, 50g protein
8g net carbs: Smokehouse Brisket Meal, no BBQ sauce, no onion strings 620 calories, 46g fat, 33g protein
9g net carbs: Classic French Dip & Swiss Meal 690 calories, 43g fat, 23g protein
9g net carbs: Greek Gyro Meal, easy sauce 970 calories, 68g fat, 57g protein
9g net carbs: Roast Turkey Gyro Meal, easy sauce 740 calories, 44g fat, 30g protein

Sides & Snacks

3g net carbs: Side Salad with Buttermilk Ranch Dressing 270 calories, 24g fat, 5g protein
6g net carbs: Premium Nuggets (2) 105 calories, 5g fat, 8g protein

Dipping Sauces (1 oz. Unless Otherwise Indicated)

1g net carbs: Ranch Dipping Sauce 100 calories, 10g fat, 1g protein
2g net carbs: Buffalo Dipping Sauce 10 calories, 1g fat, 0g protein
3g net carbs: Arby's Sauce®, .5 oz. 14 calories, 0g fat, 0g protein
3g net carbs: Horsey Sauce®, .5 oz. 60 calories, 5g fat, 0g protein
3g net carbs: Spicy Three Pepper® Sauce, .5 oz. 25 calories, 1g fat, 0g protein
5g net carbs: Honey Mustard Dipping Sauce 130 calories, 13g fat, 0g protein
10g net carbs: Tangy Barbeque[33] Dipping Sauce 45 calories, 0g fat, 0g protein

Salads

4g net carbs: Roast Chicken Salad with Buttermilk Ranch Dressing 430 calories, 25g fat, 28g protein

Salad Dressing (1.5 oz.)

2g net carbs: Buttermilk Ranch Dressing 210 calories, 22g fat, 0g protein
2g net carbs: Light Italian Dressing 15 calories, 1g fat, 0g protein
4g net carbs: Balsamic Vinaigrette Dressing 130 calories, 12g fat, 0g protein
7g net carbs: Dijon Honey Mustard Dressing 180 calories, 16g fat, 0g protein

DRINKS

0g net carbs: Diet Coke 16 oz. 0 calories, 0g fat, 0g protein
0g net carbs: Diet Coke 22 oz. 0 calories, 0g fat, 0g protein
0g net carbs: Coca-Cola Zero Sugar 16 oz. 0 calories, 0g fat, 0g protein
0g net carbs: Coca-Cola Zero Sugar 22 oz. 0 calories, 0g fat, 0g protein
0g net carbs: Diet Dr. Pepper 16 oz. 0 calories, 0g fat, 0g protein

---

[33] *That's Not Keto!* – You'll find all sorts of surprising foods listed here. I'm not telling you whether you should eat these foods or not. What fits your macros or daily carb spend is up to you. No keto police allowed.

0g net carbs: Diet Dr. Pepper 22 oz. 0 calories, 0g fat, 0g protein
0g net carbs: Nestle Pure Life 16 oz. Bottled Water 0 calories, 0g fat, 0g protein
1g net carbs: Brewed Iced Tea, unsweetened, 10 oz. 0 calories, 0g fat, 0g protein
2g net carbs: Coffee, unsweetened, 12 oz. 0 calories, 0g fat, 0g protein
3g net carbs: Coffee, unsweetened, 16 oz. 5 calories, 0g fat, 0g protein
3g net carbs: Minute Maid Light Lemonade 16 oz. 10 calories, 0g fat, 0g protein
4g net carbs: Minute Maid Light Lemonade 22 oz. 12 calories, 0g fat, 0g protein

3. Mexican & Asian

Chapter 3

MEXICAN & ASIAN

CHIPOTLE

On The Border

Baja Fresh

Chili's

P.F. Chang's

Benihana

Chipotle ◉

Chipotle has one of the best online menus for dieters in this entire book, so they get a *Keto Diet Restaurant Guide* Superstar Award! Any Mexican restaurant that breaks out the macronutrients for its flour tortillas and taco shells deserves a round of applause, wouldn't you agree? They even have the Keto Salad Bowl listed on its Lifestyle Bowl menu. Click the Nutrition tab on the main page and then Allergen Statement. Next, click the Special Diets tab. Here they list the whole menu and its ingredients and let you know if they're keto safe by a blue "K" placed next to the item.

Special Order Tips

To be safe, I always order my meal as a salad and ask for fajita vegetables and extra lettuce blend. All of the salsas are similar in net carb count but order them on the side (except the tomato pico de gallo) if you are averse to spicy food until you can test their spiciness. Please DO NOT order the healthy-sounding Sofritas (plant-based protein) as your protein since it's high in carbs. Consider ordering double protein (steak, carnitas, chicken, or barbacoa) to make your meal more filling (and expensive) - for us "volume eaters."

All sides of rice, beans, chips, etc. should be substituted with salad, guacamole, or fajita vegetables. Avoid tortillas (both corn and flour), corn salsa, taco shells, chips, beans, and rice (those last few are worth repeating).

You'll notice some menu items indicate a half-serving size. Don't worry; there aren't many! A smaller portion allowed us to include references of (higher-carb) toppings like beans[34] (personally, I don't eat them, but I've come to learn everyone "does keto" a little differently).

Author Favorite

Lunch & Dinner: Steak Salad with double steak with extra lettuce, sour cream, and cheese, 16 oz. Coke Zero to drink. 535 calories, 29g fat, 4g net carbs, 51g protein

LUNCH & DINNER

Bowls (No Rice or Beans Unless Otherwise Indicated)

3g net carbs: Chicken Bowl with extra lettuce, sour cream, and cheese 410 calories, 24g fat, 40g protein

3g net carbs: Steak Bowl with lettuce, sour cream, and cheese 375 calories, 23g fat, 29g protein

6g net carbs: Chicken Keto Bowl, with lettuce, Red Chili Salsa, cheese, and guacamole 555 calories, 37g fat, 40g protein

8g net carbs: Chicken WHOLE30® Bowl, fajita vegetables, Fresh Tomato Salsa, and guacamole 455 calories, 29g fat, 35g protein

8g net carbs: Carnitas Bowl with lettuce, sour cream, Fresh Tomato Salsa, guacamole, cheese 690 calories, 51g fat, 33g protein

8g net carbs: Carnitas Bowl with lettuce, Red-Chili Salsa, cheese, and guacamole 720 calories, 55g fat, 35g protein

8g net carbs: Carnitas Bowl with extra lettuce, Fresh Tomato Salsa, sour cream, and cheese 710 calories, 54g fat, 40g protein

8g net carbs: Barbacoa Bowl with lettuce, fajita vegetables, Fresh Tomato Salsa, guacamole, and cheese 630 calories, 41g fat, 36g protein

8g net carbs: Barbacoa Bowl with lettuce, sour cream, Green-Chili Salsa, guacamole, cheese 590 calories, 36g fat, 36g protein

9g net carbs: Chicken Bowl with lettuce, fajita vegetables, Fresh Tomato Salsa, Guacamole, and cheese 570 calories, 37g fat, 41g protein

9g net carbs: Steak Bowl with extra lettuce, sour cream, Green-Chili Salsa, guacamole, cheese 620 calories, 45g fat, 31g protein

9g net carbs: Barbacoa Bowl with extra lettuce, Fresh Tomato Salsa, sour cream, cheese, and guacamole 655 calories, 46g fat, 34g protein

9g net carbs: Sofritas Bowl with lettuce, sour cream, Green-Chili Salsa, guacamole, cheese 400 calories, 29g fat, 18g protein

9g net carbs: Veggie Bowl with lettuce, sour cream, Green-Chili Salsa, guacamole, cheese 370 calories, 26g fat, 9g protein

9g net carbs: Sofritas Bowl with extra lettuce, sour cream, cheese 380 calories, 27g fat, 16g protein

10g net carbs: Veggie Bowl with extra lettuce, fajita vegetables, Fresh Tomato Salsa, guacamole, and cheese 395 calories, 30g fat, 9g protein

---

[34] *That's Not Keto!* – You'll find all sorts of surprising foods listed here. I'm not telling you whether you should eat these foods or not. What fits your macros or daily carb spend is up to you. No keto police allowed.

Salads (No Rice or Beans Unless Otherwise Indicated)

4g net carbs: Steak Salad with Double Steak with extra lettuce, sour cream, and cheese 535 calories, 29g fat, 51g protein

7g net carbs: Chicken Keto Salad with lettuce, Fresh Tomato Salsa, cheese, and guacamole 560 calories, 37g fat, 41g protein

7g net carbs: Steak Keto Salad with lettuce, Red-Chili Salsa, cheese, and guacamole 535 calories, 36g fat, 30g protein

7g net carbs: Barbacoa Salad with lettuce, easy fajita vegetables, easy Fresh Tomato Salsa, guacamole, cheese, sour cream 670 calories, 47g fat, 33g protein

7g net carbs: Sofritas Salad with lettuce, Fresh Tomato Salsa, cheese, and guacamole 420 calories, 26g fat, 18g protein

7g net carbs: Sofritas Salad with lettuce, Red-Chili Salsa, cheese, and guacamole 400 calories, 24g fat, 16g protein

8g net carbs: Chicken Salad with lettuce, easy queso, sour cream, cheese, and guacamole 705 calories, 50g fat, 45g protein

8g net carbs: Barbacoa Salad with lettuce, Fresh Tomato Salsa, cheese, and guacamole 690 calories, 54g fat, 36g protein

8g net carbs: Veggie Salad with lettuce, Red-Chili Salsa, cheese, and guacamole 470 calories, 35g fat, 10g protein

9g net carbs: Chicken Salad with lettuce, easy black beans, easy cheese, easy sour cream 370 calories, 16g fat, 41g protein

9g net carbs: Steak Salad with lettuce, Fresh Tomato Salsa, guacamole, cheese, sour cream 640 calories, 45g fat, 32g protein

9g net carbs: Carnitas Salad with lettuce, Fresh Tomato Salsa, cheese, and guacamole 490 calories, 32g fat, 14g protein

9g net carbs: Carnitas Salad with lettuce, Red-Chili Salsa, cheese, and guacamole 520 calories, 36g fat, 18g protein

9g net carbs: Veggie Salad with lettuce, easy fajita vegetables, easy Fresh Tomato Salsa, guacamole, cheese, sour cream 487 calories, 39g fat, 12g protein

10g net carbs: Carnitas WHOLE30 Salad with lettuce, fajita vegetables, Fresh Tomato Salsa, and guacamole 500 calories, 34g fat, 27g protein

Protein Fillings

0g net carbs: Carnitas 210 calories, 12g fat, 23g protein
0g net carbs: Chicken 180 calories, 7g fat, 32g protein
0g net carbs: Steak 150 calories, 6g fat, 21g protein
1g net carbs: Barbacoa 170 calories, 7g fat, 24g protein
2g net carbs: Veggie (Includes Guacamole) 235 calories, 22g fat, 2g protein
6g net carbs: Sofritas 150 calories, 10g fat, 8g protein

Beans[35]

7g net carbs: Black Beans*, Half-Serving, 65 calories, 1g fat, 4g protein
7g net carbs: Pinto Beans*, Half-Serving, 65 calories, 1g fat, 4g protein

---

[35] *That's Not Keto!* – You'll find all sorts of surprising foods listed here. I'm not telling you whether you should eat these foods or not. What fits your macros or daily carb spend is up to you. No keto police allowed.

Top It Off

0g net carbs: Romaine Lettuce 5 calories, 0g fat, 0g protein
1g net carbs: Monterey Jack Cheese 110 calories, 8g fat, 6g protein
2g net carbs: Guacamole, reg 230 calories, 22g fat, 2g protein
2g net carbs: Sour Cream 110 calories, 9g fat, 2g protein
3g net carbs: Fresh Tomato Salsa (pico de gallo) 25 calories, 0g fat, 0g protein
3g net carbs: Tomatillo Red-Chili Salsa 30 calories, 0g fat, 0g protein
4g net carbs: Fajita Vegetables 20 calories, 0g fat, 1g protein
4g net carbs: Queso Blanco 120 calories, 9g fat, 5g protein
4g net carbs: Tomatillo Green-Chili Salsa 15 calories, 0g fat, 0g protein

Sides

2g net carbs: Guacamole, side 230 calories, 22g fat, 2g protein
4g net carbs: Guacamole, large 460 calories, 44g fat, 4g protein
7g net carbs: Queso Blanco, side 240 calories, 18g fat, 10g protein

DRINKS

0g net carbs: Coke Zero, 16 oz. 0 calories, 0g fat, 0g protein
0g net carbs: Dasani Bottled Water, 16 oz. 0 calories, 0g fat, 0g protein
0g net carbs: Diet Coke, 16 oz. 0 calories, 0g fat, 0g protein
3g net carbs: Minute Maid Light, 16 oz. 10 calories, 0g fat, 0g protein

On The Border

On The Border is on the right track with its website and its plentiful offerings of keto-friendly menu items. Their "NUTRITION AND ALLERGEN INFORMATION" form (online PDF) does a great job of telling you what the macronutrients are for the base menu item BEFORE tortillas, rice, beans, etc., are added to dishes like Classic Fajitas (lunch and dinner). Classic Tacos and Endless Enchiladas are listed in their base form, but their tortillas need to be removed from the provided online nutrition info. The restaurant's PDF document also itemizes calories, fat, fiber, protein, and carbohydrates for Mexican-dish keto-killers like corn tortillas/crispy taco shells (11 grams of net carbs) or Homemade Flour Tortillas/soft tacos/burritos/enchiladas (15 grams of net carbs). Beware, the Sautéed Vegetables Add-On has 5 grams of net carbs. That is why I recommend easy Sautéed Vegetables with the fajitas.

Special Order Tips

All burritos, tacos, enchiladas, etc., should be ordered without the tortillas, chips, rice, or beans for the provided nutrition information to be accurate. All sides of beans and rice should be swapped for salad greens or a low-carb equivalent (NOT fajita vegetables due to 5 grams of net carbs per Add-On per serving). Be wary of the available "Add-Ons" since they are quite often an unnecessary source of net carbs. The following items are analyzed in their "regular" form as described on the menu. Any alterations will change their calories and macronutrients.

Like with all of the other restaurants in this book, feel free to customize any menu item to your liking. Usually, the restaurants are happy to accommodate their customers (they are used to patrons asking for deletions/substitutions). The exception is when an item is premade with the offending ingredient (think frozen breaded shrimp or pre-seasoned wings).

Author Favorite

Lunch: Border's Best Lunch Steak Fajitas (no tortillas) with guacamole, cheese, and Pico de Gallo. 16 oz. Coke Zero to drink. 525 calories, 40g fat, 5g net carbs, 32g protein

Dinner: Carne Asada without Rice and Beans with House Salad, no croutons on the side. 12 oz. Corona Premier to drink. 789 calories, 50g fat, 16g net carbs, 37g protein

LUNCH (No Tortillas, No Rice, No Beans, No Corn)

Bolder Border Bowls, no rice, no beans, no corn
    7g net carbs: Grilled Portobello 390 calories, 12g fat, 15g protein
    8g net carbs: Grilled Chicken 380 calories, 14g fat, 28g protein
    8g net carbs: Grilled Shrimp 370 calories, 14g fat, 23g protein
    8g net carbs: Grilled Steak 430 calories, 16g fat, 24g protein

Border's Best Lunch Fajitas (Meat Only)

4g net carbs: Steak 360 calories, 26g fat, 24g protein
5g net carbs: Chicken 290 calories, 15g fat, 31g protein

Fajita Condiments

1g net carbs: Guacamole 45 calories, 4g fat, 1g protein
1g net carbs: Mixed Cheese 110 calories, 9g fat, 7g protein
1g net carbs: Pico de Gallo 10 calories, 1g fat, 0g protein
1g net carbs: Shredded Lettuce 5 calories, 0g fat, 0g protein
1g net carbs: Sour Cream 60 calories, 5g fat, 1g protein

DINNER (No Tortillas, No Rice, No Beans)

7g net carbs: Grilled Queso Chicken 520 calories, 25g fat, 42g protein
8g net carbs: Mexican Grilled Chicken 530 calories, 18g fat, 39g protein
9g net carbs: Carne Asada 630 calories, 45g fat, 34g protein

Classic Burrito (No Tortilla, No Rice, No Beans, No Sauce)

6g net carbs: Shredded Beef 320 calories, 17g fat, 23g protein
6g net carbs: Shredded Chicken Tinga 380 calories, 25g fat, 25g protein
7g net carbs: Seasoned Ground Beef 450 calories, 24g fat, 28g protein
8g net carbs: Veggie Burrito without Sauce 370 calories, 14g fat, 17g protein

Classic Fajitas (No Tortilla, No Rice, No Beans, Easy Fajita Vegetables Except When Indicated Otherwise)

3g net carbs: Grilled Shrimp Fajitas 740 calories, 25g fat, 24g protein
4g net carbs: Grilled Steak Fajitas 410 calories, 27g fat, 23g protein

5g net carbs: Grilled Chicken Fajitas 320 calories, 14g fat, 9g protein
5g net carbs: Monterey Ranch Chicken Fajitas, easy sauce 540 calories, 40g fat, 41g protein
6g net carbs: Grande Fajita Trio 700 calories, 49g fat, 36g protein
6g net carbs: Grilled Shrimp Fajitas 420 calories, 38g fat, 20g protein
7g net carbs: El Diablo Veggie Fajitas, 60 calories, 2g fat, 2g protein
8g net carbs: Border Smart Chicken Fajitas 460 calories, 13g fat, 23g protein
8g net carbs: Classic Veggie Fajitas, full-serving, 90 calories, 5g fat, 2g protein

Fajita Condiments

1g net carbs: Guacamole 45 calories, 4g fat, 1g protein
1g net carbs: Mixed Cheese 110 calories, 9g fat, 7g protein
1g net carbs: Shredded Lettuce 5 calories, 0g fat, 0g protein
1g net carbs: Pico de Gallo 10 calories, 1g fat, 0g protein
1g net carbs: Sour Cream 60 calories, 5g fat, 1g protein

Sauce

3g net carbs: Green Chile Sauce 30 calories, 1g fat, 1g protein
4g net carbs: Red Chile Sauce 70 calories, 2g fat, 2g protein
4g net carbs: Sour Cream Sauce 80 calories, 7g fat, 1g protein
6g net carbs: Chile con Carne 110 calories, 5g fat, 6g protein
6g net carbs: Signature Queso 180 calories, 13g fat, 10g protein
7g net carbs: Ranchero Sauce 60 calories, 2g fat, 1g protein

Sides (1 Cup)

8g net carbs: Queso De Espinaca Dip 380 calories, 30g fat, 19g protein
8g net carbs: Signature Queso, Border Style 170 calories, 12g fat, 9g protein
9g net carbs: Queso Blanco Dip 410 calories, 33g fat, 21g protein
10g net carbs: Signature Queso 300 calories, 22g fat, 16g protein
10g net carbs: Smoky Queso Dip 250 calories, 18g fat, 13g protein

Salads (No Dressing)

4g net carbs: House Salad, no croutons 150 calories, 5g fat, 2g protein
7g net carbs: Fajita Salad – Chicken, no corn 410 calories, 20g fat, 36g protein
8g net carbs: Fajita Salad – Steak, no corn 480 calories, 31g fat, 29g protein

Salad Dressing (Quantity Not Specified by Restaurant)

1g net carbs: Avocado Ranch 130 calories, 12g fat, 1g protein
2g net carbs: Ranch 230 calories, 24g fat, 1g protein
3g net carbs: Salsa 20 calories, 0g fat, 1g protein
9g net carbs: Smoked Jalapeño Vinaigrette 120 calories, 10g fat, 0g protein
10g net carbs: Lime Vinaigrette 140 calories, 12g fat, 0g protein

DRINKS

0g net carbs: Diet Coke, 16 oz. 0 calories, 0g fat, 0g protein
0g net carbs: Coke Zero, 16 oz. 0 calories, 0g fat, 0g protein
0g net carbs: Iced Tea, unsweetened, 16 oz. 0 calories, 0g fat, 0g protein
0g net carbs: Coffee, unsweetened, 8 oz. 0 calories, 0g fat, 0g protein
5g net carbs: Juice[36], Tomato, 8 oz. 30 calories, 0g fat, 1g protein

Beer

3g net carbs: Michelob Ultra, 12 oz. 95 calories, 0g fat, 1g protein
3g net carbs: Michelob Ultra, 12 oz. bottle 95 calories, 0g fat, 1g protein
4g net carbs: Michelob Ultra Grande, 16 oz. 130 calories, 0g fat, 1g protein
3g net carbs: Miller Lite, 12 oz. 96 calories, 0g fat, 1g protein
3g net carbs: Miller Lite, 12 oz. bottle 96 calories, 0g fat, 1g protein
4g net carbs: Miller Lite Grande, 16 oz. 130 calories, 0g fat, 1g protein
3g net carbs: Corona Premier, 12 oz. Bottle 90 calories, 0g fat, 1g protein
5g net carbs: Corona Light, 12 oz. Bottle 99 calories, 0g fat, 1g protein
5g net carbs: Coors Light, 12 oz. 102 calories, 0g fat, 1g protein
7g net carbs: Coors Light Grande, 16 oz. 136 calories, 0g fat, 1g protein
7g net carbs: Bud Light, 12 oz. 110 calories, 0g fat, 1g protein
9g net carbs: Bud Light Grande, 16 oz. 147 calories, 0g fat, 2g protein

Wine

4g net carbs: Woodbridge Chardonnay, 6 oz. 150 calories, 0g fat, 0g protein
5g net carbs: House Cabernet, 6 oz. 150 calories, 0g fat, 0g protein
10g net carbs: Sutter Home White Zinfandel, 6 oz. 170 calories, 0g fat, 0g protein

---

[36] *That's Not Keto!* – You'll find all sorts of surprising foods listed here. I'm not telling you whether you should eat these foods or not. What fits your macros or daily carb spend is up to you. No keto police allowed.

Baja Fresh

Baja Fresh does not have a customizable nutrition calculator on its website. Instead, they provide a detailed Nutrition Facts PDF for your reference.

Baja Fresh loses points by offering several items with the new Impossible (meatless) option as the protein. I can't find any macronutrient information for this option online, not even inside their supposedly all-inclusive Nutrition Facts PDF! I would avoid these items until this info is shared because, as we know from other restaurants, these meatless options can have a surprising number of net carbs. I have some Impossible (meatless) menu items quoted below, but I found comparable information (on a reputable source other than the Baja Fresh website) as a helpful cross-reference.

It may not be obvious, but there is a difference between the Veggie menu items and the Roasted Veggies (for items like burritos and bowls, etc.). "Veggie" describes raw fresh lettuce, tomato, and onion with cheese, guacamole, and sour cream (and rice and beans if not eating keto), and the "Roasted Veggies" are roasted bell peppers and onions. Note that the Roasted Veggies contain a minimal amount of net carbs (from the onions and bell peppers).

For some reason, the carnitas is high in net carbs for the fajitas, bowls, and non-tortilla burritos (bowls) that we cover in this section, so I decided not to include any dishes with carnitas. The only way I can see to reduce the net carbs would be to cut back on the sauce, which can get messy. Plus, it's hard to verify the accuracy of a reduced amount, wouldn't you agree? There are several remaining proteins to choose from, so don't fret.

Special Order Tips

Avoid tortillas (corn and flour), hard taco shells, potatoes, chips, corn, corn salsa, beans (black, refried, pinto), and rice. Substitute with salad greens or an equivalent low-carb alternative (ex: guacamole, olives, radishes, steamed/roasted vegetables).

Be wary of the available "Add-Ons" since they are often an unnecessary source of net carbs.

Feel free to customize your order. Restaurants are usually happy to accommodate reasonable customer requests. The exception is when the item has been premade or was prepared off-site. Note that any alterations on your end will change the provided nutrition information. Adjust accordingly.

Don't be alarmed by the mention of a half-serving size. Baja Fresh only has a couple. A smaller portion size allowed us to include (higher-carb) crowd-pleasing soups.

Author Favorite

Breakfast: Breakfast Burrito- Veggie without the tortilla, bread, and potatoes with 16 oz. hot coffee, unsweetened, to drink. 495 calories, 41g fat, 4g net carbs, 37g protein

Lunch & Dinner: Baja Bowl- Grilled Shrimp, substitute roasted vegetables and lettuce for rice and beans with Side Salad, no tortilla strips, and 3 oz. Pronto Guacamole on the side. 32 oz. Diet Dr. Pepper to drink. 860 calories, 34g fat, 11g net carbs, 42g protein

BREAKFAST (No Tortillas, No Bread, No Potatoes)

2g net carbs: Breakfast Burrito- Veggie 420 calories, 29g fat, 30g protein
4g net carbs: Breakfast Burrito- Roasted Veggies 470 calories, 29g fat, 30g protein
4g net carbs: Breakfast Burrito- Bacon 560 calories, 45g fat, 41g protein
5g net carbs: Breakfast Burrito- Sausage 690 calories, 70g fat, 50g protein
5g net carbs: Breakfast Burrito- Steak 510 calories, 47g fat, 55g protein
3g net carbs: Breakfast Americano Grande - Sausage 560 calories, 42g fat, 33g protein
4g net carbs: Breakfast Americano Grande - Bacon 400 calories, 18g fat, 25g protein
5g net carbs: Breakfast Huevos Rancheros 430 calories, 46g fat, 46g protein

Breakfast Sides & Add-Ons

0g net carbs: Bacon (2 slices) 90 calories, 7g fat, 6g protein
0g net carbs: Scrambled Eggs (2) 220 calories, 17g fat, 14g protein
0g net carbs: Steak, 3.5 oz. 60 calories, 3g fat, 5g protein
1g net carbs: Sausage (2 links) 250 calories, 24g fat, 8g protein
2g net carbs: Roasted Veggies 40 calories, 0g fat, 0g protein

LUNCH & DINNER

Favorites (No Tortilla, Substitute Roasted Vegetables and Lettuce for Rice and Beans)

1g net carbs: Baja Bowl- Veggie 490 calories, 13g fat, 16g protein
3g net carbs: Baja Bowl- Grilled Wahoo 670 calories, 20g fat, 39g protein
5g net carbs: Baja Bowl- Grilled Chicken 700 calories, 22g fat, 43g protein
5g net carbs: Baja Bowl- Roasted Veggies 540 calories, 14g fat, 17g protein
5g net carbs: Baja Bowl- Steak 690 calories, 22g fat, 42g protein
6g net carbs: Baja Bowl- Grilled Shrimp 660 calories, 20g fat, 36g protein
3g net carbs: Fajitas- Grilled Chicken 340 calories, 10g fat, 60g protein
3g net carbs: Fajitas- Grilled Wahoo 310 calories, 9g fat, 52g protein
3g net carbs: Fajitas- Steak 340 calories, 11g fat, 59g protein
3g net carbs: Fajitas- Veggie 310 calories, 9g fat, 52g protein
5g net carbs: Fajitas- Shrimp 320 calories, 10g fat, 49g protein
7g net carbs: Fajitas- Roasted Veggies 360 calories, 10g fat, 53g protein

Burritos (No Tortilla, Substitute Roasted Vegetables and Lettuce for Rice and Beans)

2g net carbs: Baja Burrito, Veggie 610 calories, 33g fat, 23g protein
3g net carbs: Baja Burrito, Grilled Wahoo 442 calories, 44g fat, 46g protein
3g net carbs: Baja Burrito, Shrimp 480 calories, 44g fat, 43g protein
4g net carbs: Baja Burrito, Grilled Chicken 520 calories, 46g fat, 50g protein
5g net carbs: Baja Burrito, Steak 410 calories, 45g fat, 48g protein
6g net carbs: Baja Burrito, Roasted Veggies 660 calories, 38g fat, 24g protein
1g net carbs: Burrito Mexicano, Veggie 590 calories, 18g fat, 18g protein
4g net carbs: Burrito Mexicano, Grilled Chicken 800 calories, 27g fat, 45g protein
4g net carbs: Burrito Mexicano, Shrimp 760 calories, 25g fat, 39g protein
5g net carbs: Burrito Mexicano, Grilled Wahoo 770 calories, 25g fat, 42g protein
5g net carbs: Burrito Mexicano, Roasted Veggies 640 calories, 19g fat, 19g protein
5g net carbs: Burrito Mexicano, Steak 790 calories, 26g fat, 44g protein
1g net carbs: Burrito Ultimo, Veggie 360 calories, 41g fat, 24g protein
3g net carbs: Burrito Ultimo, Shrimp 630 calories, 48g fat, 45g protein
4g net carbs: Burrito Ultimo, Grilled Wahoo 630 calories, 48g fat, 48g protein
4g net carbs: Burrito Ultimo, Steak 660 calories, 50g fat, 50g protein
5g net carbs: Burrito Ultimo, Roasted Veggies 410 calories, 42g fat, 25g protein
7g net carbs: Burrito Ultimo, Grilled Chicken 670 calories, 50g fat, 51g protein

1g net carbs: Diablo Burrito, Veggie 500 calories, 34g fat, 24g protein
4g net carbs: Diablo Burrito, Grilled Wahoo 720 calories, 57g fat, 57g protein
5g net carbs: Diablo Burrito, Grilled Chicken 770 calories, 48g fat, 54g protein
5g net carbs: Diablo Burrito, Roasted Veggies 550 calories, 35g fat, 25g protein
5g net carbs: Diablo Burrito, Steak 750 calories, 58g fat, 59g protein
6g net carbs: Diablo Burrito, Shrimp 620 calories, 57g fat, 54g protein
4g net carbs: Fajita Burrito, Steak 980 calories, 52g fat, 51g protein
5g net carbs: Fajita Burrito, Grilled Chicken 690 calories, 52g fat, 52g protein
5g net carbs: Fajita Burrito, Grilled Wahoo 660 calories, 50g fat, 49g protein
5g net carbs: Fajita Burrito, Shrimp 650 calories, 51g fat, 45g protein
1g net carbs: Nacho Burrito, Veggie, no tortilla strips 510 calories, 45g fat, 36g protein
4g net carbs: Nacho Burrito, Grilled Chicken, no tortilla strips 760 calories, 54g fat, 63g protein

4g net carbs: Nacho Burrito, Shrimp, no tortilla strips 720 calories, 52g fat, 57g protein
5g net carbs: Nacho Burrito, Grilled Wahoo, no tortilla strips 630 calories, 52g fat, 60g protein
5g net carbs: Nacho Burrito, Roasted Veggies, no tortilla strips 560 calories, 46g fat, 37g protein
5g net carbs: Nacho Burrito, Steak, no tortilla strips 750 calories, 54g fat, 62g protein
3g net carbs: Veggie Burrito, 580 calories, 36g fat, 32g protein
4g net carbs: Veggie Burrito, Roasted Veggies 650 calories, 41g fat, 54g protein

2g net carbs: Dos Manos, Veggie 520 calories, 38g fat, 32g protein
4g net carbs: Dos Manos, Grilled Chicken 580 calories, 67g fat, 70g protein
4g net carbs: Dos Manos, Grilled Wahoo 530 calories, 69g fat, 78g protein
4g net carbs: Dos Manos, Shrimp 500 calories, 68g fat, 70g protein
5g net carbs: Dos Manos, Steak 570 calories, 67g fat, 68g protein
6g net carbs: Dos Manos, Roasted Veggies 570 calories, 39g fat, 33g protein
4g net carbs: Chicken Caesar Burrito, no tortilla strips 890 calories, 57g fat, 45g protein
8g net carbs: Fuego Impossible Burrito 710 calories, 45g fat, 52g protein

Burrito Add-Ons

3g net carbs: Enchilada® Style Sauce 430 calories, 24g fat, 12g protein

Salads (No Dressing)

2g net carbs: Baja Ensalada- Veggie, no tortilla strips 70 calories, 3g fat, 6g protein
6g net carbs: Baja Ensalada- Grilled Wahoo, no tortilla strips 240 calories, 12g fat, 29g protein
6g net carbs: Baja Ensalada- Roasted Veggies, no tortilla strips 120 calories, 4g fat, 7g protein
6g net carbs: Baja Ensalada- Steak, no tortilla strips 210 calories, 11g fat, 24g protein
7g net carbs: Baja Ensalada- Grilled Chicken, no tortilla strips 60 calories, 11g fat, 25g protein
7g net carbs: Baja Ensalada- Shrimp, no tortilla strips 240 calories, 12g fat, 26g protein
4g net carbs: Baja BBQ Grilled Chicken Salad, no BBQ sauce 400 calories, 17g fat, 27g protein
2g net carbs: Tostada Salad, Veggie, no tortilla shell, no beans 430 calories, 44g fat, 28g protein
5g net carbs: Tostada Salad - Steak, no tortilla shell, no beans 530 calories, 53g fat, 54g protein
6g net carbs: Tostada Salad – Grilled Chicken, no tortilla shell, no beans 520 calories, 53g fat, 55g protein
6g net carbs: Tostada Salad- Roasted Veggies, no tortilla shell, no beans 480 calories, 45g fat, 29g protein
7g net carbs: Tostada Salad - Shrimp, no tortilla shell, no beans 490 calories, 51g fat, 48g protein
6g net carbs: Chile Lime Salad- Grilled Chicken, no tortilla strips, no pico 340 calories, 18g fat, 27g protein
7g net carbs: Chile Lime Salad- Grilled Shrimp, no tortilla strips, no pico 320 calories, 17g fat, 27g protein
7g net carbs: Chile Lime Salad- Steak, no tortilla strips, no pico 325 calories, 14g fat, 24g protein

A La Carte & Sides

2g net carbs: Pronto Guacamole, 3 oz. 130 calories, 10g fat, 2g protein
2g net carbs: Pronto Romaine & Kale Salad, no tortilla strips 90 calories, 4g fat, 4g protein
2g net carbs: Side Salad, no tortilla strips 80 calories, 4g fat, 4g protein
2g net carbs: Smokey Queso Fundido, 1 oz. 60 calories, 4g fat, 3g protein
5g net carbs: Pronto Queso, 3 oz. 190 calories, 14g fat, 9g protein
6g net carbs: Guacamole, 8 oz. 310 calories, 27g fat, 4g protein
6g net carbs: Queso, 4 oz. 235 calories, 19g fat, 13g protein

10g net carbs: Chicken Tortilla Soup[37], Half-Serving 140 calories, 8g fat, 8g protein
10g net carbs: Tortilla Soup*, Half-Serving, 110 calories, 6g fat, 4g protein

Individual Items

0g net carbs: Avocado Slices 45 calories, 4g fat, 1g protein
0g net carbs: Jack Cheese Mix (2 oz.) 220 calories, 18g fat, 14g protein
0g net carbs: Jalapeño Slices 0 calories, 0g fat, 0g protein
0g net carbs: Lettuce Cabbage mix 5 calories, 0g fat, 0g protein
0g net carbs: Lime Wedges 5 calories, 0g fat, 0g protein
1g net carbs: Cheddar & Jack Cheese Blend (2.5 oz.) 270 calories, 22g fat, 17g protein
1g net carbs: Chicken (3.5 oz.) 200 calories, 9g fat, 27g protein
1g net carbs: Cilantro Onion Mix 5 calories, 0g fat, 0g protein
1g net carbs: Diced Tomato 5 calories, 0g fat, 0g protein
1g net carbs: Grilled Wahoo 170 calories, 7g fat, 24g protein
1g net carbs: Shrimp 60 calories, 2g fat, 7g protein
1g net carbs: Steak (3.5 oz.) 200 calories, 9g fat, 26g protein
2g net carbs: Romaine Lettuce 25 calories, 0g fat, 2g protein
4g net carbs: Roasted Veggies (Onions & Bell Peppers- no Tomatoes) 50 calories, 1g fat, 1g protein
5g net carbs: Tortilla Strips* 40 calories, 1g fat, 1g protein

Sauces & Salad Dressing (1 oz.)

0g net carbs: Molcajete Salsa 5 calories, 0g fat, 0g protein
1g net carbs: Avocado Salsa 10 calories, 1g fat, 0g protein
1g net carbs: Cilantro Ranch 90 calories, 9g fat, 1g protein
1g net carbs: Diablo Sauce 70 calories, 7g fat, 0g protein
1g net carbs: Pico de Gallo 5 calories, 0g fat, 0g protein
1g net carbs: Ranch 100 calories, 10g fat, 1g protein
1g net carbs: Salsa Baja 5 calories, 0g fat, 0g protein
1g net carbs: Sour Cream 60 calories, 5g fat, 1g protein
1g net carbs: Vinaigrette 140 calories, 16g fat, 0g protein
2g net carbs: Salsa Roja 10 calories, 0g fat, 0g protein
2g net carbs: Salsa Verde 10 calories, 0g fat, 0g protein
2g net carbs: Six Chile Salsa Crema 25 calories, 1g fat, 1g protein
2g net carbs: Six Chiles Salsa 10 calories, 0g fat, 0g protein
3g net carbs: Corn Avocado Salsa 35 calories, 2g fat, 1g protein
3g net carbs: Mango Salsa 15 calories, 0g fat, 0g protein
4g net carbs: Chili Lime Dressing 120 calories, 11g fat, 0g protein
6g net carbs: BBQ Lime Dressing 110 calories, 10g fat, 0g protein

DRINKS

0g net carbs: Diet Coke 20 oz. 0 calories, 0g fat, 0g protein
0g net carbs: Diet Coke 32 oz. 0 calories, 0g fat, 0g protein
0g net carbs: Diet Coke with Lime 20 oz. 0 calories, 0g fat, 0g protein
0g net carbs: Diet Coke with Lime 32 oz. 0 calories, 0g fat, 0g protein

---

[37] *That's Not Keto!* – You'll find all sorts of surprising foods listed here. I'm not telling you whether you should eat these foods or not. What fits your macros or daily carb spend is up to you. No keto police allowed.

0g net carbs: Caffeine-Free Diet Coke 20 oz. 0 calories, 0g fat, 0g protein
0g net carbs: Caffeine-Free Diet Coke 32 oz. 0 calories, 0g fat, 0g protein
0g net carbs: Coca-Cola Zero 20 oz. 0 calories, 0g fat, 0g protein
0g net carbs: Coca-Cola Zero 32 oz. 0 calories, 0g fat, 0g protein
0g net carbs: Sprite Zero 20 oz. 5 calories, 0g fat, 0g protein
0g net carbs: Sprite Zero 32 oz. 10 calories, 0g fat, 0g protein
0g net carbs: Diet Dr. Pepper 20 oz. 0 calories, 0g fat, 0g protein
1g net carbs: Diet Dr. Pepper 32 oz. 0 calories, 0g fat, 0g protein
2g net carbs: Fresca 20 oz. 0 calories, 0g fat, 0g protein
3g net carbs: Fresca 32 oz. 0 calories, 0g fat, 0g protein
4g net carbs: Minute Maid Light Lemonade 20 oz. 12 calories, 0g fat, 0g protein
5g net carbs: Minute Maid Light Lemonade 32 oz. 15 calories, 0g fat, 0g protein
4g net carbs: Minute Maid Light Pomegranate Lemonade 20 oz. 12 calories, 0g fat, 0g protein
5g net carbs: Minute Maid Light Pomegranate Lemonade 32 oz. 15 calories, 0g fat, 0g protein

1g net carbs: Glaceau Vitaminwater XXX Zero 20 oz. 0 calories, 0g fat, 0g protein
2g net carbs: Glaceau Vitaminwater XXX Zero 32 oz. 5 calories, 0g fat, 0g protein
1g net carbs: Glaceau Fruitwater Black Raspberry 20 oz. 0 calories, 0g fat, 0g protein
2g net carbs: Glaceau Fruitwater Black Raspberry 32 oz. 10 calories, 0g fat, 0g protein
1g net carbs: Glaceau Fruitwater Watermelon Punch 20 oz. 5 calories, 0g fat, 0g protein
2g net carbs: Glaceau Fruitwater Watermelon Punch 32 oz. 10 calories, 0g fat, 0g protein
2g net carbs: Glaceau Vitaminwater Squeezed Zero 20 oz. 5 calories, 0g fat, 0g protein
3g net carbs: Glaceau Vitaminwater Squeezed Zero 32 oz. 10 calories, 0g fat, 0g protein

0g net carbs: Coffee, unsweetened 16 oz. 5 calories, 0g fat, 1g protein
0g net carbs: Gold Peak Diet Black Unsweetened Tea 20 oz. 0 calories, 0g fat, 0g protein
0g net carbs: Gold Peak Diet Black Unsweetened Tea 32 oz. 0 calories, 0g fat, 0g protein
1g net carbs: Gold Peak Diet Green Unsweetened Tea 20 oz. 5 calories, 0g fat, 0g protein
1g net carbs: Gold Peak Diet Green Unsweetened Tea 32 oz. 10 calories, 0g fat, 0g protein
0g net carbs: Gold Peak Premium Unsweetened Tea 20 oz. 0 calories, 0g fat, 0g protein
0g net carbs: Gold Peak Premium Unsweetened Tea 32 oz. 0 calories, 0g fat, 0g protein
0g net carbs: Fuze Unsweetened Tea 20 oz. 0 calories, 0g fat, 0g protein
2g net carbs: Fuze Unsweetened Tea 32 oz. 10 calories, 0g fat, 0g protein
0g net carbs: Honest Freshly Brewed Black Unsweetened Tea 20 oz. 0 calories, 0g fat, 0g protein
0g net carbs: Honest Freshly Brewed Black Unsweetened Tea 32 oz. 0 calories, 0g fat, 0g protein

Chili's

Chili's is a neighborhood Tex-Mex fav. of mine. Fast service and plenty of delicious keto plates or plates that are easily adjusted to make keto, all at reasonable prices. I also get a kick out of the fact that their Big Mouth Burgers come served with a dagger plunged into them from the top. That's wicked.

Any restaurant with two pages of ADULT BEVERAGES on its Nutrition Information listing is tops in my book. Clearly, this place is trying to carve out a niche for itself as the leader in the "Adult Relaxation" category of fast-casual dining eateries. All jokes aside, I find that Chili's is a straight shooter that doesn't overly rely on sugary sauces and hidden ingredients to hoodwink the palate into overconsumption.

Special Order Tips

Order all burgers and sandwiches with "no bread." Be wary of the available "Add-Ons" since they are often an unnecessary source of net carbs.

Avoid all bread, fries, pasta, tortillas (corn and flour), hard taco shells, potatoes, chips, corn, corn salsa, beans (black, refried, pinto), rice, etc. Ask the server to substitute a side salad or a side of steamed/grilled vegetables. Did you know that Chili's offers a side of asparagus and equally delicious, steamed broccoli?

Feel free to customize your order. Restaurants are usually happy to accommodate reasonable customer requests. The exception is when the item has been premade or was prepared off-site. Note that any alterations on your end will change the provided nutrition information. Adjust accordingly.

Author Favorite

Lunch: Bunless Oldtimer® with Cheese Beef Burger with Caesar Salad (Lunch), no croutons on the side. 16 oz. Coca-Cola Zero to drink. 1020 calories, 69g fat, 12g net carbs, 54g protein

Dinner: Bone-In Wings with Buffalo sauce to start. 6 oz. Sirloin with Grilled Avocado with Asparagus on the side. Chilled 12 oz. Truly Hard Seltzer to drink. 1365 calories, 82g fat, 15g net carbs, 168g protein

LUNCH

Big Mouth Burgers (No Bread, No French Fries)

3g net carbs: Double Burger, bunless 790 calories, 48g fat, 44g protein
5g net carbs: Just Bacon Beef Burger, bunless 1030 calories, 71g fat, 55g protein
5g net carbs: Mushroom Swiss Beef Burger, bunless 1010 calories, 70g fat, 52g protein
6g net carbs: Oldtimer® with Cheese Beef Burger, bunless 860 calories, 55g fat, 51g protein
7g net carbs: Alex's Santa Fe Beef Burger, bunless, no spicy Santa Fe sauce 930 calories, 62g fat 51g protein
7g net carbs: Big Mouth® Bites, bunless 1210 calories, 72g fat, 65g protein
7g net carbs: Queso Beef Burger, bunless, no crunchy tortilla strips 940 calories, 62g fat, 51g protein
8g net carbs: Southern Smokehouse Beef Burger, bunless, no Awesome Blossom Petals 1260 calories, 83g fat, 61g protein
8g net carbs: The Boss Beef Burger, bunless, no BBQ Sauce 1130 calories, 107g fat, 92g protein

Burger Substitutes & Add-Ons

0g net carbs: Applewood Smoked Bacon (2 slices) 70 calories, 6g fat, 5g protein
0g net carbs: Classic Beef Patty 510 calories, 39g fat, 38g protein
1g net carbs: Avocado Slices 80 calories, 7g fat, 1g protein
2g net carbs: Sauteed Mushrooms 60 calories, 4g fat, 1g protein
4g net carbs: The Original Chili 150 calories, 9g fat, 9g protein

Entrees (No Bread)

4g net carbs: Tacos Spicy Shrimp, no shells 430 calories, 22g fat, 19g protein
5g net carbs: CA Turkey Club Sandwich, no bread 550 calories, 32g fat, 27g protein
6g net carbs: Lunch Shrimp Fajitas, no rice, no beans, no tortillas, no bell peppers 570 calories, 37g fat, 45g protein
7g net carbs: Bacon Avocado Chicken Sandwich, no bread 620 calories, 33g fat, 44g protein
7g net carbs: Lunch Chicken Fajitas, no rice, no beans, no tortillas, no bell peppers 520 calories, 38g fat, 14g protein

Salads

6g net carbs: Caesar Salad (Lunch Combo), no croutons 160 calories, 14g fat, 3g protein
6g net carbs: House Salad (Lunch Combo), no croutons, no Dressing 70 calories, 3g fat, 3g protein

DINNER

Starters

3g net carbs: Bone-In Wings (6-8), Buffalo 890 calories, 65g fat, 73g protein

Fajitas (Meat Only)

1g net carbs: Grilled Carnitas 240 calories, 18g fat, 17g protein
1g net carbs: Grilled Chicken 160 calories, 4g fat, 30g protein
1g net carbs: Seared Shrimp 60 calories, 2g fat, 11g protein
2g net carbs: Grilled Steak 200 calories, 9g fat, 27g protein

Fajita Add-Ons

1g net carbs: Guacamole, 1 oz. 50 calories, 4g fat, 1g protein
2g net carbs: Pico de Gallo, 1 oz. 45 calories, 2g fat, 4g protein
4g net carbs: White Queso, 1 oz. 150 calories, 12g fat, 6g protein
6g net carbs: Fajita Peppers & Onions 180 calories, 11g fat, 3g protein

Entrees (with Steamed/Grilled Vegetables)

0g net carbs: Classic Ribeye 630 calories, 40g fat, 67g protein
1g net carbs: Classic Sirloin 6 oz. 260 calories, 13g fat, 34g protein
2g net carbs: Classic Sirloin 10 oz. 390 calories, 19g fat, 55g protein
0g net carbs: Add Seared Shrimp, Half-Serving, 30 calories, 1g fat, 6g protein
1g net carbs: Add Seared Shrimp, Full Serving, 60 calories, 2g fat, 11g protein
3g net carbs: Jalapeño-Cheddar Smoked Sausage 380 calories, 31g fat, 21g protein
5g net carbs: Smoked Brisket 290 calories, 22g fat, 16g protein
6g net carbs: Ribs with easy Original BBQ 710 calories, 53g fat, 49g protein
7g net carbs: Ribs with easy House BBQ 720 calories, 53g fat, 49g protein
7g net carbs: Mango-Chile Chicken, no mango glaze, no chopped mango, 510 calories, 20g fat, 36g protein
7g net carbs: Margarita Grilled Chicken, no tortilla strips 650 calories, 17g fat, 55g protein
7g net carbs: Cheesy Bacon BBQ Chicken, no BBQ sauce 370 calories, 18g fat, 40g protein
7g net carbs: Ancho Salmon, no citrus-chili sauce 620 calories, 30g fat, 48g protein
8g net carbs: Sirloin, 6 oz. with Grilled Avocado 340 calories, 16g fat, 38g protein
8g net carbs: Sirloin, 10 oz. with Grilled Avocado 490 calories, 24g fat, 59g protein

Extras

0g net carbs: Cheese, Swiss 80 calories, 7g fat, 6g protein
0g net carbs: Pickles 5 calories, 0g fat, 0g protein
1g net carbs: Avocado Slices 80 calories, 7g fat, 1g protein
1g net carbs: Cheese, American 70 calories, 5g fat, 3g protein
1g net carbs: Cheese, Cheddar 80 calories, 7g fat, 5g protein
1g net carbs: Cheese, Pepper Jack 80 calories, 6g fat, 5g protein
2g net carbs: Fresh Guacamole - Small Side 110 calories, 9g fat, 1g protein
2g net carbs: Salsa 1.5 oz. 10 calories, 0g fat, 0g protein

2g net carbs: Sour Cream 35 calories, 3g fat, 1g protein
2g net carbs: Wing Sauce 1.5 oz. 35 calories, 3g fat, 0g protein
3g net carbs: Fresh Guacamole - Large Side 200 calories, 18g fat, 3g protein
3g net carbs: Gravy, Black Pepper 1.5 oz. 30 calories, 2g fat, 0g protein

Sides

2g net carbs: Asparagus 35 calories, 1g fat, 3g protein
4g net carbs: Steamed Broccoli 40 calories, 0g fat, 3g protein

Soups

9g net carbs: Clam Chowder - Cup 170 calories, 12g fat, 5g protein
10g net carbs: Loaded Baked Potato[38] - Cup 210 calories, 15g fat, 8g protein

Salads

6g net carbs: Caesar Salad, no croutons 310 calories, 27g fat, 5g protein
7g net carbs: Grilled Chicken Salad with Ranch, no corn & black bean salsa, 430 calories, 23g fat, 37g protein
7g net carbs: Santa Fe Chicken Salad with Chicken, no tortilla strips, 570 calories, 44g fat, 36g protein
7g net carbs: Southwestern Chicken Caesar Salad, no tortilla strips 630 calories, 44g fat, 39g protein
7g net carbs: Southwestern Shrimp Caesar Salad, no tortilla strips 530 calories, 42g fat, 21g protein
8g net carbs: House Salad, no croutons without Dressing 140 calories, 60g fat, 6g protein

Salad Dressing (1.5 oz. Unless Otherwise Indicated)

1g net carbs: Bleu Cheese 250 calories, 27g fat, 1g protein
2g net carbs: Avocado Ranch 140 calories, 14g fat, 1g protein
2g net carbs: Bleu Cheese (2 oz.) 330 calories, 35g fat, 1g protein
2g net carbs: Caesar 220 calories, 23g fat, 2g protein
2g net carbs: Ranch 170 calories, 18g fat, 1g protein
2g net carbs: Santa Fe 210 calories, 22g fat, 1g protein
3g net carbs: Ancho Chile Ranch 170 calories, 17g fat, 1g protein
3g net carbs: Avocado Ranch (2 oz.) 190 calories, 19g fat, 1g protein
3g net carbs: Caesar (2 oz.) 290 calories, 31g fat, 2g protein
3g net carbs: Ranch (2 oz.) 230 calories, 23g fat, 2g protein
3g net carbs: Santa Fe (2 oz.) 280 calories, 30g fat, 1g protein
4g net carbs: Ancho Chile Ranch (2 oz.) 220 calories, 22g fat, 2g protein
5g net carbs: Citrus Balsamic Vinaigrette 250 calories, 25g fat, 0g protein
5g net carbs: Honey Lime Vinaigrette 140 calories, 13g fat, 0g protein
6g net carbs: Thousand Island 200 calories, 19g fat, 0g protein
7g net carbs: Citrus Balsamic Vinaigrette (2 oz.) 330 calories, 33g fat, 0g protein
7g net carbs: Honey Lime Vinaigrette (2 oz.) 180 calories, 17g fat, 0g protein
9g net carbs: Thousand Island (2 oz.) 270 calories, 26g fat, 1g protein
10g net carbs: Honey Mustard* 200 calories, 18g fat, 1g protein

---

[38] *That's Not Keto!* – You'll find all sorts of surprising foods listed here. I'm not telling you whether you should eat these foods or not. What fits your macros or daily carb spend is up to you. No keto police allowed.

DRINKS

0g net carbs: Diet Coke 16 oz. 0 calories, 0g fat, 0g protein
0g net carbs: Coca-Cola Zero 16 oz. 0 calories, 0g fat, 0g protein
0g net carbs: Dasani Water 16 oz. bottle 0 calories, 0g fat, 0g protein
0g net carbs: Chili's Premium Blend Coffee, unsweetened 10 oz. 0 calories, 0g fat, 0g protein
0g net carbs: Unsweetened Tea, 8 oz. 0 calories, 0g fat, 0g protein

Beer & Seltzer

2g net carbs: Truly Hard Seltzers 12 oz. 100 calories, 0g fat, 0g protein

3g net carbs: Michelob Ultra 12 oz. 95 calories, 0g fat, 1g protein
3g net carbs: Miller Lite 12 oz. 95 calories, 0g fat, 1g protein
5g net carbs: Coors Light 12 oz. 102 calories, 0g fat, 1g protein
5g net carbs: Corona Light 12 oz. 99 calories, 0g fat, 1g protein
7g net carbs: Bud Light 12 oz. 110 calories, 0g fat, 1g protein

Wine

3g net carbs: Seaglass Pinot Grigio, 5 oz. 123 calories, 0g fat, 0g protein
4g net carbs: Canyon Road Cabernet Sauvignon, 5 oz. 122 calories, 0g fat, 0g protein
4g net carbs: Canyon Road Chardonnay, 5 oz. 122 calories, 0g fat, 0g protein
4g net carbs: Josh Cellars Cabernet Sauvignon, 5 oz. 124 calories, 0g fat, 0g protein
5g net carbs: House White Wine 6 oz. 140 calories, 0g fat, 0g protein
5g net carbs: Red Wine 6 oz. 150 calories, 0g fat, 0g protein
7g net carbs: House White Wine 9 oz. 220 calories, 0g fat, 0g protein
7g net carbs: Red Wine 9 oz. 220 calories, 0g fat, 0g protein

Spirits

10g net carbs: Bloody Mary or Maria 140 calories, 1g fat, 2g protein

P. F. Chang's

P. F. Chang's website is a bit behind the times and only breaks out the calories without mentioning carbs. Somebody tell these guys that they need an update to reflect the new trends that diners are interested in these days. To determine how many net carbs are in each menu item (and its components), we will have to dig into the "Menu Nutritionals" online.

P. F. Chang's is one of those restaurants that is inherently non-keto. Lots of breading and deep frying going on here (think tempura) and lots of sweet sauces. Don't fret; as always, there is almost an infinite number of low-carb personalizations that you can make to get these dishes to "fit" your carb budget.

Special Order Tips

Order all burgers and sandwiches with "no bread." Be wary of the available "Add-Ons" since they are often an unnecessary source of net carbs.

Feel free to customize your order. Restaurants are usually happy to accommodate reasonable customer requests. The exception is when the item has been premade or was prepared off-site. Note that any alterations on your end will change the provided nutrition information. Adjust accordingly.

Avoid all fries, potatoes, rice, pasta, bread, etc. Ask the server to substitute a side salad or a side of steamed/grilled vegetables.

You'll notice some menu items indicate a half-serving size. Don't worry; there will only be a few. A smaller portion size allowed us to include more (higher-carb) crowd-pleasing favorites.

Author Favorite

Lunch: Lunch Bowl of Mongolian Beef, no sweet soy glaze, Substitute Asian Mushrooms, Spinach, and Cabbage for the Rice. 16 oz. Diet Coke to drink. 490 calories, 27g fat, 3g net carbs, 40g protein

Dinner: Start with Northern Style Spare Ribs (6), easy five-spice seasoning/Hot Mustard, and Chile Paste as dips. Kung Pao Shrimp Steamed, remove breading, Asian Caesar Salad, no croutons. Michelob Ultra- 12 oz. bottle. 1860 calories, 93g fat, 22g net carbs, 97g protein

LUNCH

Lunch Bowls (Substitute Asian Mushrooms, Spinach, and Cabbage for Rice)

3g net carbs: Ginger Grilled Chicken with Broccoli 330 calories, 9g fat, 32g protein
3g net carbs: Mongolian Beef, no sweet soy glaze 490 calories, 27g fat, 40g protein
4g net carbs: Sesame Chicken Steamed, easy sauce 540 calories, 20g fat, 35g protein
5g net carbs: Beef & Broccoli, easy sauce 370 19g fat, 22g protein
5g net carbs: Chang's Spicy Chicken steamed, easy sauce, remove breading, 680 calories, 27g fat, 49g protein
5g net carbs: Kung Pao Chicken Steamed, remove breading, 550 calories, 33g fat, 39g protein
5g net carbs: Orange Chicken, remove breading, no sweet citrus chili sauce 670 calories, 34g fat, 34g protein
5g net carbs: Sweet & Sour Chicken, no pineapple, easy sauce 630 calories, 30g fat, 24g protein
6g net carbs: Kung Pao Shrimp Steamed, remove breading, 430 calories, 30g fat, 21g protein

DINNER

Appetizers

2g net carbs: Grilled Dynamite Shrimp, remove breading, 640 calories, 48g fat, 20g protein
4g net carbs: BBQ Pork Spare Ribs (6), super easy Asian barbecue sauce 810 calories, 21g fat, 37g protein
4g net carbs: Chang's Vegetarian Lettuce Wraps, no rice sticks 620 calories, 28g fat, 24g protein
4g net carbs: Chili Garlic Green Beans, no Sichuan preserves, easy red chili sauce 530 calories, 40g fat,
    8g protein
6g net carbs: Chang's Chicken Lettuce Wraps, no rice sticks 710 calories, 27g fat, 38g protein
6g net carbs: Kung Pao Brussel Sprouts, no Kung Pao sauce 720 calories, 42g fat, 16g protein
6g net carbs: Northern Style Spare Ribs (6), easy five-spice seasoning 700 calories, 21g fat, 37g protein
7g net carbs: Edamame, Half-Serving, 200 calories, 8g fat, 37g protein

Dim Sum (Substitute Standard Wrap with Lettuce)

3g net carbs: Lettuce Wrapped Shrimp Dumplings Pan-Fried (6), no chili sauce drizzle 390 calories, 15g fat,
    26g protein
3g net carbs: Lettuce Wrapped Pork Egg Rolls, no sweet and sour mustard sauce (2) 610 calories, 35g fat,
    14g protein
4g net carbs: Lettuce Wrapped Vegetable Spring Rolls, no sweet chili dipping sauce (2) 390 calories, 19g fat,
    4g protein
4g net carbs: Lettuce Wrapped Pork Dumpling Steamed (6), no chili sauce drizzle 460 calories, 21g fat,

19g protein

Main Entrees (Grilled, No Breading)

2g net carbs: Buddha's Feast Steamed, easy sauce 200 calories, 3g fat, 17g protein
3g net carbs: Chang's Spicy Chicken steamed, easy sauce, no breading/remove breading, 560 calories,
      12g fat, 56g protein
3g net carbs: Orange Chicken, no batter, no sweet citrus chili sauce 1160 calories, 59g fat, 65g protein
3g net carbs: Salt & Pepper Prawns, no breading/remove breading, 630 calories, 43g fat, 31g protein
3g net carbs: Sesame Chicken Steamed, easy sauce 600 calories, 14g fat, 62g protein
4g net carbs: Mongolian Beef, no sweet soy glaze 770 calories, 42g fat, 59g protein
4g net carbs: Pepper Steak Steamed, easy Pepper-garlic sauce 440 calories, 21g fat, 33g protein
4g net carbs: Shrimp with Lobster Sauce Steamed, easy sauce, no beans 370 calories, 18g fat, 31g protein
5g net carbs: Beef with Broccoli, easy sauce 670 calories, 33g fat, 50g protein
5g net carbs: Kung Pao Shrimp Steamed, no breading/remove breading, 570 calories, 36g fat, 42g protein
5g net carbs: Ma Po Tofu, no breading/remove breading, easy sauce 910 calories, 59g fat, 58g protein
5g net carbs: Oolong Chilean Sea Bass, easy sauce 560 calories, 35g fat, 34g protein
5g net carbs: Shrimp with Lobster Sauce Steamed, no beans, easy sauce 370 calories, 18g fat, 31g protein
5g net carbs: Stir-Fried Eggplant, no soy glaze 530 calories, 34g fat, 4g protein
6g net carbs: Ginger Grilled Chicken with Broccoli 480 calories, 12g fat, 57g protein
6g net carbs: Kung Pao Chicken Steamed, no breading/remove breading, 720 calories, 39g fat, 67g protein
6g net carbs: Miso Glazed Salmon, easy glaze 660 calories, 37g fat, 49g protein
6g net carbs: Pepper Steak Stir-Fried, easy pepper-garlic sauce 640 calories, 36g fat, 51g protein
7g net carbs: Korean Bulgogi Steak, no potatoes, super easy bulgogi glaze 1330 calories, 57g fat, 87g protein
7g net carbs: Peking Duck, no batter, no flatbread, easy hoisin 2970 calories, 202g fat, 99g protein
7g net carbs: Sweet & Sour Chicken, no pineapple, easy sauce 860 calories, 41g fat, 36g protein

Salads & Soup

4g net carbs: Mandarin Crunch Salad, no oranges, no rice sticks, easy vinaigrette 750 calories, 46g fat,
      14g protein
4g net carbs: Asian Caesar Salad, no croutons 410 calories, 30g fat, 15g protein

Protein Options

0g net carbs: Salmon 240 calories, 16g fat, 22g protein
4g net carbs: Grilled Chicken 160 calories, 5g fat, 22g protein

Soups (1 Cup)

6g net carbs: Wonton Soup, easy wontons 120 calories, 3g fat, 9g protein
6g net carbs: Egg Drop Soup 40 calories, 1g fat, 1g protein
9g net carbs: Hot & Sour Soup 70 calories, 2g fat, 4g protein

Sauces and Dips (1 oz.)

0g net carbs: Hot Mustard 5 calories, 0g fat, 0g protein
1g net carbs: Soy Sauce 8 calories, 0g fat, 1g protein

4g net carbs: Chile Paste 80 calories, 6g fat, 2g protein

DRINKS

0g net carbs: Freshly Brewed Black Iced Tea, unsweetened, 16 oz. 0 calories, 0g fat, 0g protein
0g net carbs: Pot of Full Leaf Tea, 12 oz. (Hot): Organic Green, Dragon Eye Oolong, Ginger Peach, unsweetened 0 calories, 0g fat, 0g protein
0g net carbs: Freshly Brewed Black Coffee, unsweetened, 8 oz. 0 calories, 0g fat, 0g protein
0g net carbs: Diet Coke, 16 oz. 0 calories, 0g fat, 0g protein
0g net carbs: Fiji, 16 oz. bottle 0 calories, 0g fat, 0g protein
0g net carbs: San Pellegrino, 16 oz. bottle 0 calories, 0g fat, 0g protein
1g net carbs: Vitamin Water Zero Sugar XXX, 16 oz. bottle 0 calories, 0g fat, 0g protein

Beer

3g net carbs: Michelob Ultra, 12 oz. bottle 95 calories, 0g fat, 1g protein
5g net carbs: Coors Light, 12 oz. 102 calories, 0g fat, 1g protein
7g net carbs: Bud Light, 12 oz. 110 calories, 0g fat, 1g protein

Wine (6 oz.)

Champagne

3g net carbs: Moet & Chandon Imperial Brut Champagne 115 calories, 0g fat, 0g protein
3g net carbs: Mumm Napa Brut Prestige 125 calories, 0g fat, 0g protein

Riesling

4g net carbs: Chateau Ste. Michelle 144 calories, 0g fat, 0g protein
5g net carbs: Kung Fu Girl 119 calories, 0g fat, 0g protein

Pinot Grigio

4g net carbs: Chloe Wine collection 112 calories, 0g fat, 0g protein
4g net carbs: Santa Margherita 102 calories, 0g fat, 0g protein
5g net carbs: Zenato 110 calories, 0g fat, 0g protein

Sauvignon Blanc

3g net carbs: Cloudy Bay 131 calories, 0g fat, 0g protein
4g net carbs: Kim Crawford 140 calories, 0g fat, 0g protein
4g net carbs: Decoy by Duckhorn 125 calories, 0g fat, 0g protein

Chardonnay

3g net carbs: Kendall-Jackson Vintner's Reserve 123 calories, 0g fat, 0g protein
4g net carbs: 14 Hands 120 calories, 0g fat, 0g protein

4g net carbs: Butter 105 calories, 0g fat, 0g protein
4g net carbs: La Crema 125 calories, 0g fat, 0g protein
4g net carbs: Sonoma-Cutrer 115 calories, 0g fat, 0g protein

Pinot Noir

4g net carbs: Mark West 125 calories, 0g fat, 0g protein
4g net carbs: Meiomi 123 calories, 0g fat, 0g protein

Merlot

4g net carbs: 14 Hands 123 calories, 0g fat, 0g protein
4g net carbs: Francis Coppola Diamond Collection 115 calories, 0g fat, 0g protein

Malbec

4g net carbs: Alamos 122 calories, 0g fat, 0g protein

Red Blend

4g net carbs: Colby Red 110 calories, 0g fat, 0g protein
5g net carbs: Conundrum by Caymus 135 calories, 0g fat, 0g protein

Cabernet Sauvignon

4g net carbs: J Lohr Seven Oaks 126 calories, 0g fat, 0g protein
4g net carbs: Josh Cellars 125 calories, 0g fat, 0g protein
4g net carbs: Oberon by Michael Mondavi Family 128 calories, 0g fat, 0g protein
4g net carbs: Stag's Leap Wine Cellars 118 calories, 0g fat, 0g protein
5g net carbs: 19 Crimes 122 calories, 0g fat, 0g protein

Sake (5 oz. Glass)

4g net carbs: Warm Saké 125 calories, 0g fat, 0g protein
4g net carbs: Gekkeikan 122 calories, 0g fat, 0g protein
5g net carbs: Chilled Saké 124 calories, 0g fat, 0g protein

Benihana

Benihana needs a customizable nutrition calculator on its website. Don't they all? At this time, they have a detailed Nutritional Information PDF that will help you monitor your carb intake.

Most (if not all) of the newer restaurants on this list have customizable nutrition calculators or even a low-carb/keto menu on their website. Needless to say, as an "older restaurant," Benihana does not fit into this category. The food is excellent here, almost everything on the menu is keto-friendly, after all, so I won't complain too much about having to do extra work in the "customization" department.

Special Order Tips

Avoid tempura and order all meals with "no rice." Be wary of the available "Add-Ons" since they are often an unnecessary source of net carbs. Substitute with more salad or grilled vegetables? I never tire of their delicious low-carb medley (fried in butter, no less!).

Feel free to customize your order. Restaurants are usually happy to accommodate reasonable customer requests. The exception is when the item has been premade or was prepared off-site. Note that any alterations on your end will change the provided nutrition information. Adjust accordingly.

You'll notice some menu items indicate a half-serving size. Don't worry; there will only be a few. A smaller portion size allowed us to include more (higher-carb) favorites like a classic Benihana dessert – really!

Author Favorite

Lunch: Lunch Boat Beef, no California Roll, no Tempura, no Steamed Rice, and no Fresh Fruit with 16 oz. Diet Pepsi to drink. 110 calories, 4g fat, 6g net carbs, 13g protein

Dinner: Shrimp Sauté to start. Benihana Special- Lobster Tail. 8 oz. Benihana Hot Sake 450 calories, 3g fat, 10g net carbs, 25g protein

LUNCH

Lunch Entrees (No Sides)

0g net carbs: Hibachi Shrimp (10) 150 calories, 3g fat, 27g protein
1g net carbs: Filet Mignon 200 calories, 9g fat, 30g protein
1g net carbs: Hibachi Chicken 200 calories, 8g fat, 31g protein
1g net carbs: Hibachi Steak 200 calories, 9g fat, 27g protein
3g net carbs: Hibachi Scallops 90 calories, 2g fat, 15g protein
4g net carbs: Beef Julienne, easy teriyaki sauce 160 calories, 6g fat, 19g protein
5g net carbs: Spicy Hibachi Chicken, easy spicy homemade sauce 260 calories, 10g fat, 31g protein

Lunch Entrees Add-Ons

3g net carbs: Benihana Onion Soup 25 calories, 1g fat, 1g protein
4g net carbs: Hibachi Vegetables 40 calories, 1g fat, 1g protein

Lunch Duet (No Sides)

0g net carbs: Chicken 130 calories, 5g fat, 22g protein
0g net carbs: Calamari 120 calories, 6g fat, 16g protein
0g net carbs: Shrimp (5) 70 calories, 2g fat, 14g protein
2g net carbs: Scallops 70 calories, 2g fat, 12g protein
6g net carbs: Beef Julienne 110 calories, 4g fat, 13g protein

Lunch Boat (No California Roll, No Tempura, No Steamed Rice, No Fresh Fruit)

0g net carbs: Lunch Boat Chicken 130 calories, 5g fat, 22g protein
0g net carbs: Lunch Boat Salmon 110 calories, 6g fat, 14g protein
6g net carbs: Lunch Boat Beef 110 calories, 4g fat, 13g protein

Lunch Boat Sides

0g net carbs: Sashimi 70 calories, 1g fat, 17g protein
2g net carbs: Edamame 50 calories, 2g fat, 5g protein
3g net carbs: Benihana Onion Soup 25 calories, 1g fat, 1g protein
3g net carbs: Benihana Salad 90 calories, 8g fat, 2g protein

Sushi Combination (No Rice)

5g net carbs: Tuna Nigiri (1) 40 calories, 0g fat, 5g protein
5g net carbs: Salmon Nigiri (1) 60 calories, 2g fat, 3g protein
5g net carbs: Yellowtail Nigiri (1) 60 calories, 3g fat, 4g protein
5g net carbs: Shrimp Nigiri (1) 30 calories, 0g fat, 3g protein

Sushi Add-Ons

0g net carbs: Ginger 5 calories, 0g fat, 0g protein
0g net carbs: Wasabi 1 calories, 0g fat, 1g protein

Bento Box (No Sides)

0g net carbs: Salmon 232 calories, 14g fat, 25g protein
1g net carbs: Chicken 138 calories, 5g fat, 22g protein
6g net carbs: Steak 122 calories, 4g fat, 14g protein

Bento Box Sides

2g net carbs: Benihana Salad 90 calories, 8g fat, 2g protein
2g net carbs: Edamame 52 calories, 2g fat, 4g protein
3g net carbs: Benihana Onion Soup 25 calories, 1g fat, 1g protein
3g net carbs: Seaweed Salad 28 calories, 1g fat, 1g protein
7g net carbs: Fresh Fruit, 1 oz. 9 calories, 0g fat, 1g protein
8g net carbs: Vegetable Spring Roll 50 calories, 1g fat, 1g protein

Imperial Salad with Ginger Dressing

5g net carbs: Imperial Salad 190 calories, 8g fat, 6g protein
6g net carbs: Imperial Salad with Salmon 300 calories, 17g fat, 37g protein
6g net carbs: Imperial Salad with Chicken 250 calories, 3g fat, 30g protein
6g net carbs: Imperial Salad with Ahi Tuna 210 calories, 4g fat, 40g protein

Sauces (1 oz.)

0g net carbs: Ginger Sauce 10 calories, 0g fat, 2g protein
1g net carbs: Avocado Tartar Sauce 100 calories, 10g fat, 1g protein
1g net carbs: Diablo Sauce 140 calories, 15g fat, 0g protein
2g net carbs: Benihana Original Yum Yum Sauce 170 calories, 19g fat, 0g protein
2g net carbs: Ginger Dressing 60 calories, 6g fat, 0g protein
3g net carbs: Benihana Original Garlic Sauce 90 calories, 10g fat, 1g protein
4g net carbs: Mustard Sauce 110 calories, 10g fat, 2g protein

DESSERT

6g net carbs: Vanilla Ice Cream[39], Half-Serving (1.5 ounces), 50 calories, 3g fat, 1g protein
7g net carbs: Chocolate Ice Cream*, Half-Serving (1.5 ounces), 50 calories, 3g fat, 1g protein
7g net carbs: Green Tea Ice Cream*, Half-Serving (1.5 ounces), 45 calories, 2g fat, 1g protein

DINNER

Warm Appetizers

2g net carbs: Shrimp Sauté 140 calories, 1g fat, 12g protein
4g net carbs: Spicy Sauce Tokyo Wings 690 calories, 70g fat, 82g protein
8g net carbs: Garlic Sauce Tokyo Wings 769 calories, 90g fat, 81g protein
9g net carbs: Edamame 205 calories, 8g fat, 18g protein

Cold Appetizers (No Rice)

2g net carbs: Sashimi Sampler 340 calories, 16g fat, 24g protein
4g net carbs: Chili Ponzu Yellowtail 240 calories, 12g fat, 19g protein
4g net carbs: Seared Tuna, easy Ponzu Sauce 310 calories, 17g fat, 22g protein
4g net carbs: Sushi Sampler 360 calories, 5g fat, 28g protein
4g net carbs: Tuna Poke (Classic or Spicy), no Sweet Soy Sauce 260 calories, 11g fat, 21g protein
5g net carbs: Crispy Spicy Tuna 290 calories, 11g fat, 32g protein

Sashimi Sampler (No Rice)

0g net carbs: Tuna Sashimi 1.8 oz. 50 calories, 1g fat, 12g protein
0g net carbs: Izumidai Sashimi 0.8 oz. 20 calories, 0g fat, 5g protein
0g net carbs: Salmon Sashimi 1.2 oz. 70 calories, 4g fat, 7g protein

Sushi Sampler (No Rice)

1g net carbs: Shrimp Saute (7) 60 calories, 1g fat, 13g protein
5g net carbs: Izumidai Nigiri 0.4 oz. 30 calories, 0g fat, 2g protein
5g net carbs: Salmon Nigiri 0.6 oz. 60 calories, 2g fat, 4g protein
5g net carbs: Shrimp Nigiri 0.4 oz. 30 calories, 0g fat, 3g protein
5g net carbs: Tuna Nigiri 0.6 oz. 40 calories, 0g fat, 5g protein
5g net carbs: Yellowtail Nigiri 0.6 oz. 60 calories, 3g fat, 4g protein
7g net carbs: Chili Ponzu Yellowtail 3.4 oz. 190 calories, 14g fat, 8g protein
7g net carbs: Tuna Tataki 6 oz. 130 calories, 1g fat, 23g protein

Sushi Deluxe (No Rice)

5g net carbs: Albacore Nigiri 0.5 oz. 50 calories, 2g fat, 4g protein

---

[39] *That's Not Keto!* – You'll find all sorts of surprising foods listed here. I'm not telling you whether you should eat these foods or not. What fits your macros or daily carb spend is up to you. No keto police allowed.

5g net carbs: Izumidai Nigiri 0.4 oz. 30 calories, 0g fat, 2g protein
5g net carbs: Octopus Nigiri 0.4 oz. 30 calories, 0g fat, 3g protein
5g net carbs: Salmon Nigiri 0.6 oz. 60 calories, 2g fat, 4g protein
5g net carbs: Tuna Nigiri 0.6 oz. 40 calories, 0g fat, 5g protein
5g net carbs: Yellowtail Nigiri 0.6 oz. 60 calories, 3g fat, 4g protein
6g net carbs: Salmon Roe (Ikura Nigiri) 0.4 oz. 50 calories, 1g fat, 4g protein
8g net carbs: Eel Nigiri 0.6 oz. 50 calories, 1g fat, 2g protein
10g net carbs: Shrimp Nigiri (2) 0.8 oz. 60 calories, 0g fat, 6g protein

Sushi/Sashimi (No Rice)

0g net carbs: Izumidai (Snapper) Sashimi 1.2 oz. 30 calories, 0g fat, 7g protein
0g net carbs: Octopus Sashimi 0.8 oz. 20 calories, 0g fat, 5g protein
0g net carbs: Salmon Sashimi 1.2 oz. 70 calories, 4g fat, 7g protein
0g net carbs: Yellowtail Sashimi 1.2 oz. 80 calories, 5g fat, 8g protein
1g net carbs: Tuna Sashimi 1.8 oz. 50 calories, 0g fat, 13g protein
5g net carbs: Albacore Nigiri 0.5 oz. 60 calories, 2g fat, 4g protein
5g net carbs: Izumidai Nigiri 0.4 oz. 30 calories, 0g fat, 2g protein
5g net carbs: Salmon Nigiri 0.6 oz. 60 calories, 2g fat, 4g protein
5g net carbs: Shrimp Nigiri 0.4 oz. 30 calories, 0g fat, 3g protein
5g net carbs: Tuna Nigiri 0.6 oz. 40 calories, 0g fat, 5g protein
5g net carbs: Yellowtail Nigiri 0.6 oz. 60 calories, 3g fat, 4g protein
8g net carbs: Eel Nigiri 0.6 oz. 50 calories, 1g fat, 2g protein

Small Sashimi (No Rice)

0g net carbs: Albacore Tuna 0.50 oz. 30 calories, 2g fat, 3g protein
0g net carbs: Eel 0.60 oz. 60 calories, 4g fat, 4g protein
0g net carbs: Izumidai - Snapper 0.40 oz. 10 calories, 0g fat, 2g protein
0g net carbs: Kanikama 0.60 oz. 0g fat, 2g protein
0g net carbs: Octopus 0.40 oz. 10 calories, 0g fat, 2g protein
0g net carbs: Salmon 0.60 oz. 35 calories, 2g fat, 3g protein
0g net carbs: Salmon Roe 0.40 oz. 30 calories, 1g fat, 4g protein
0g net carbs: Shrimp 0.40 oz. 10 calories, 0g fat, 2g protein
0g net carbs: Tuna 0.60 oz. 20 calories, 0g fat, 4g protein
0g net carbs: Yellowtail 0.60 oz. 40 calories, 3g fat, 4g protein
2g net carbs: Egg 0.60 oz. 25 calories, 1g fat, 1g protein

5-Course Entrées

Steak & Chicken (No Sides)

1g net carbs: Filet Mignon 250 calories, 11g fat, 36g protein
1g net carbs: Hibachi Chicken 280 calories, 11g fat, 44g protein
1g net carbs: Hibachi Steak 230 calories, 11g fat, 32g protein
3g net carbs: Hibachi Chateaubriand 360 calories, 18g fat, 48g protein
6g net carbs: Spicy Hibachi Chicken, easy spicy homemade sauce 360 calories, 14g fat, 44g protein
7g net carbs: Teriyaki Steak, easy sauce 290 calories, 11g fat, 34g protein
8g net carbs: Teriyaki Chicken, easy sauce 370 calories, 11g fat, 52g protein

Seafood (No Sides)

0g net carbs: Colossal Shrimp (4) 110 calories, 3g fat, 19g protein
0g net carbs: Colossal Shrimp (7) 190 calories, 6g fat, 33g protein
0g net carbs: Hibachi Shrimp (14) 200 calories, 5g fat, 38g protein
1g net carbs: Spicy Hibachi Shrimp 286 calories, 10g fat, 44g protein
7g net carbs: Seafood Diablo, no Japanese udon noodles 275 calories, 10g fat, 49g protein
0g net carbs: Calamari Steak 4 oz. 110 calories, 6g fat, 16g protein
2g net carbs: Scallops 3.5 oz. 70 calories, 2g fat, 12g protein
3g net carbs: Hibachi Scallops 140 calories, 4g fat, 23g protein
4g net carbs: Salmon with Avocado, no sautéed udon noodles 670 calories, 42g fat, 46g protein
6g net carbs: Hibachi Tuna Steak 500 calories, 31g fat, 45g protein
0g net carbs: Lobster Tail (1) 70 calories, 2g fat, 13g protein
0g net carbs: Twin Lobster Tails (2) 130 calories, 3g fat, 25g protein

5-Course Entrée Sides

0g net carbs: Ginger Sauce 10 calories, 0g fat, 2g protein
0g net carbs: Shrimp Appetizer (3) 40 calories, 1g fat, 8g protein
1g net carbs: Hibachi Vegetables- Zucchini 15 calories, 1g fat, 1g protein
2g net carbs: Benihana's Original Yum Yum Sauce 170 calories, 19g fat, 0g protein
3g net carbs: Benihana Onion Soup 6.7 oz. 25 calories, 1g fat, 1g protein
3g net carbs: Benihana Salad 3.8 oz. 90 calories, 8g fat, 2g protein
4g net carbs: Hibachi Vegetables- Onions 25 calories, 1g fat, 1g protein
4g net carbs: Mustard Sauce 110 calories, 2g fat, 2g protein

6-Course Entrées (No Sides)

Specialties (No Sides)

5g net carbs: Spicy Tofu Steak, easy sauce 160 calories, 10g fat, 21g protein

Emperor's Feast (No Sides)

0g net carbs: Filet Mignon 250 calories, 11g fat, 36g protein
0g net carbs: Chicken 130 calories, 5g fat, 22g protein

Rocky's Choice (No Sides)

0g net carbs: Hibachi Steak 240 calories, 11g fat, 32g protein
0g net carbs: Chicken 130 calories, 5g fat, 22g protein

Benihana Trio (No Sides)

0g net carbs: Filet Mignon 200 calories, 9g fat, 30g protein
0g net carbs: Colossal Shrimp (3) 80 calories, 3g fat, 14g protein
0g net carbs: Chicken 130 calories, 5g fat, 22g protein

Benihana Special (No Sides)

0g net carbs: Hibachi Steak 240 calories, 11g fat, 32g protein
0g net carbs: Lobster Tail (1) 70 calories, 2g fat, 13g protein

Benihana Delight (No Sides)

0g net carbs: Chicken 280 calories, 11g fat, 44g protein
0g net carbs: Colossal Shrimp (4) 110 calories, 3g fat, 19g protein

Benihana Excellence (No Sides)

0g net carbs: Colossal Shrimp (4) 110 calories, 3g fat, 19g protein
9g net carbs: Julienne Steak 200 calories, 8g fat, 23g protein

Splash 'N Meadow (No Sides)

0g net carbs: Hibachi Steak 240 calories, 11g fat, 32g protein
0g net carbs: Colossal Shrimp (4) 110 calories, 3g fat, 19g protein

Deluxe Treat (No Sides)

0g net carbs: Filet Mignon 250 calories, 11g fat, 36protein
0g net carbs: Lobster Tail (1) 70 calories, 1g fat, 13protein

Land 'N Sea (No Sides)

0g net carbs: Filet Mignon 250 calories, 11g fat, 36g protein
2g net carbs: Scallops 70 calories, 2g fat, 12g protein

Samurai Treat (No Sides)

0g net carbs: Filet Mignon 250 calories, 11g fat, 36g protein
0g net carbs: Colossal Shrimp (4) 110 calories, 3g fat, 19g protein

Hibachi Supreme (No Sides)

0g net carbs: Lobster Tail (1) 70 calories, 1g fat, 13g protein
2g net carbs: Chateaubriand 370 calories, 18g fat, 48g protein

6-Course Entrée Sides (No Sides)

0g net carbs: Ginger Sauce 1 oz. 10 calories, 0g fat, 2g protein
0g net carbs: Shrimp Appetizer (3) 40 calories, 1g fat, 8g protein
1g net carbs: Hibachi Vegetables- Zucchini 2 oz. 15 calories, 1g fat, 1g protein
1g net carbs: Mushrooms 1.5 oz. 15 calories, 1g fat, 1g protein
2g net carbs: Benihana's Original Yum Yum Sauce 1 oz. 170 calories, 19g fat, 0g protein

3g net carbs: Benihana Onion Soup 6.7 oz. 25 calories, 1g fat, 1g protein
3g net carbs: Benihana Salad 90 calories, 8g fat, 2g protein
4g net carbs: Hibachi Vegetables- Onions 2 oz. 25 calories, 1g fat, 0g protein
4g net carbs: Mustard Sauce 1 oz. 110 calories, 10g fat, 2g protein

Teppan Trio (No Sides)

0g net carbs: Hibachi Shrimp, (14) 200 calories, 5g fat, 38g protein
1g net carbs: Hibachi Chicken 280 calories, 11g fat, 44g protein
7g net carbs: Teriyaki Steak, easy sauce 290 calories, 11g fat, 33g protein

Entrée Complements (Optional Add-On)

0g net carbs: Colossal Shrimp (8) 100 calories, 2g fat, 19g protein
0g net carbs: Lobster Tail (1) 65 calories, 2g fat, 13g protein
1g net carbs: Scallops 70 calories, 2g fat, 12g protein

Sides

0g net carbs: Shrimp Side (3) 40 calories, 1g fat, 8g protein
1g net carbs: Hibachi Vegetables Zucchini 2 oz. 15 calories, 1g fat, 1g protein
1g net carbs: Mushrooms 1.5 oz. 15 calories, 1g fat, 1g protein
3g net carbs: Benihana Onion Soup 6.7 oz. 25 calories, 1g fat, 1g protein
3g net carbs: Benihana Salad 90 calories, 8g fat, 2g protein
3g net carbs: Seaweed Salad 28 calories, 1g fat, 1g protein
4g net carbs: Hibachi Vegetables Onions 2 oz. 25 calories, 1g fat, 0g protein
5g net carbs: Hibachi Vegetables 40 calories, 2g fat, 1g protein

Soup & Salad

0g net carbs: Benihana Onion Soup 25 calories, 1g fat, 1g protein
3g net carbs: Miso Soup 34 calories, 10g fat, 2g protein
3g net carbs: Benihana Salad 90 calories, 8g fat, 2g protein

DESSERT

6g net carbs: Vanilla Ice Cream[40], Half-Serving, 100 calories, 5g fat, 2g protein
7g net carbs: Chocolate Ice Cream*, Half-Serving, 100 calories, 5g fat, 2g protein
7g net carbs: Green Tea Ice Cream*, Half-Serving, 90 calories, 4g fat, 2g protein

DRINKS

0g net carbs: Black Organic Tea unsweetened, 16 oz. 0 calories, 0g fat, 0g protein
0g net carbs: Diet Coke, 16 oz. 0 calories, 0g fat, 0g protein
0g net carbs: Diet Pepsi, 16 oz. 0 calories, 0g fat, 0g protein

---

[40] *That's Not Keto!* – You'll find all sorts of surprising foods listed here. I'm not telling you whether you should eat these foods or not. What fits your macros or daily carb spend is up to you. No keto police allowed.

0g net carbs: Green Tea unsweetened, 16 oz. 0 calories, 0g fat, 0g protein
0g net carbs: Red Flower Tea unsweetened, 16 oz. 0 calories, 0g fat, 0g protein
2g net carbs: Red Bull Sugar-free, 8.4 oz. can 10 calories, 0g fat, 0g protein

Beer & Seltzer

3g net carbs: High Noon Seltzer, 12 oz. can 100 calories, 0g fat, 0g protein

3g net carbs: Michelob Ultra, 12 oz. can 95 calories, 0g fat, 1g protein
5g net carbs: Coors Light, 12 oz. can 102 calories, 0g fat, 1g protein
7g net carbs: Bud Light, 12 oz. can 110 calories, 0g fat, 1g protein
8g net carbs: Kirin Light, 12 oz. bottle 100 calories, 0g fat, 1g protein

Sake

8g net carbs: Benihana Hot Sake, 8 oz. 240 calories, 0g fat, 0g protein

Japanese Artisanal Cold Sake

8g net carbs: Sake Glass, 4 oz. 130 calories, 0g fat, 0g protein

Japanese Premium Spirits

0g net carbs: Yokaichi Mugi Shochu, 2 oz. 80 calories, 0g fat, 0g protein
0g net carbs: Iichiko Silhouette Shochu, 2 oz. 80 calories, 0g fat, 0g protein
0g net carbs: MARS Iwai Tradition, 2 oz. 130 calories, 0g fat, 0g protein
0g net carbs: Yamazaki 18 yrs., 2 oz. 130 calories, 0g fat, 0g protein
0g net carbs: Suntory Whisky TOKITM, 2 oz. 130 calories, 0g fat, 0g protein

Wine

4g net carbs: House White Wine Glass, 6 oz. 150 calories, 0g fat, 0g protein
7g net carbs: House White Wine Carafe, 9 oz. 230 calories, 0g fat, 0g protein

Sparkling & Champagne

1g net carbs: Dom Perignon, 6 oz. glass 75 calories, 0g fat, 0g protein
2g net carbs: Moët & Chandon Brut Imperial, 6 oz. glass 92 carbs 0g fat, 0g protein
3g net carbs: Taittinger Brut 'La Francaise, 6 oz. glass 100 calories, 0g fat, 0g protein

Prosecco

8g net carbs: La Marca, 6 oz. glass 206 calories, 0g fat, 0g protein
8g net carbs: Giuliana, 6 oz. glass 170 calories, 0g fat, 0g protein

Sauvignon Blanc

4g net carbs: Emmolo, 6 oz. glass 180 calories, 0g fat, 0g protein
4g net carbs: Kim Crawford, 6 oz. glass 168 calories, 0g fat, 0g protein
4g net carbs: Joel Gott, 6 oz. glass 165 calories, 0g fat, 0g protein

Chardonnay

4g net carbs: Acacia Winery, 6 oz. glass 182 calories, 0g fat, 0g protein
5g net carbs: Cakebread Cellars, 6 oz. glass 178 calories, 0g fat, 0g protein
5g net carbs: Kendall-Jackson, 6 oz. glass 160 calories, 0g fat, 0g protein
5g net carbs: Columbia Crest, 6 oz. glass 155 calories, 0g fat, 0g protein

Rosé, Pinot Grigio, & Aromatic Whites

4g net carbs: Chloe, 6 oz. glass 112 Calories, 0g fat, 0g protein

Moscato & Riesling

4g net carbs: Chateau Ste. Michelle, 6 oz. glass 130 calories, 0g fat, 0g protein
5g net carbs: Caposaldo, 6 oz. glass 190 calories, 0g fat, 0g protein

Pinot Grigio

3g net carbs: Santa Margherita, 6 oz. glass 165 calories, 0g fat, 0g protein
3g net carbs: Coppola 'Bianco', 6 oz. glass 155 calories, 0g fat, 0g protein

Sauvignon Blanc Blend

3g net carbs: The Whip, 6 oz. glass 160 calories, 0g fat, 0g protein

Cabernet Sauvignon & Blends

4g net carbs: Chimney Rock, 6 oz. glass 190 calories, 0g fat, 0g protein
4g net carbs: Stag's Leap 'Artemis', 6 oz. glass 158 calories, 0g fat, 0g protein

Cabernet Sauvignon

4g net carbs: Louis M. Martini, 6 oz. glass 179 calories, 0g fat, 0g protein
4g net carbs: Hayes Ranch, 6 oz. glass 176 calories, 0g fat, 0g protein

Cabernet

5g net carbs: Franciscan, 6 oz. glass 179 calories, 0g fat, 0g protein

Malbec

4g net carbs: Bodega Norton Reserva, 6 oz. glass 150 calories, 0g fat, 0g protein

Pinot Noir

3g net carbs: Ponzi Vineyards, 6 oz. glass 175 calories, 0g fat, 0g protein
4g net carbs: Meiomi, 6 oz. glass 140 calories, 0g fat, 0g protein
4g net carbs: La Crema, 6 oz. glass 170 calories, 0g fat, 0g protein

Merlot

3g net carbs: Rodney Strong, 6 oz. glass 150 calories, 0g fat, 0g protein
5g net carbs: 14 Hands, 6 oz. glass 150 calories, 0g fat, 0g protein

Spirits

0g net carbs: Shot House Gin, 1.5 oz. 100 calories, 0g fat, 0g protein
0g net carbs: Shot House Rum, 1.5 oz. 100 calories, 0g fat, 0g protein
0g net carbs: Shot House Vodka, 1.5 oz. 100 calories, 0g fat, 0g protein
0g net carbs: Shot House Whiskey, 1.5 oz. 100 calories, 0g fat, 0g protein
2g net carbs: Absolut Cosmo, 9 oz. 180 calories, 0g fat, 0g protein
8g net carbs: Bulleit Rye Old Fashioned, 9 oz. 180 calories, 0g fat, 0g protein

4. Steak & Seafood

CHAPTER 4

STEAK & SEAFOOD

Texas Roadhouse

Logan's Roadhouse

The Capital Grille

Sizzler

Ruth's Chris Steakhouse

Longhorn Steakhouse

Outback Steakhouse

Black Angus

Red Lobster

Bonefish Grill

Texas Roadhouse

Beware that there seem to be some errors on the Texas Roadhouse INTERACTIVE NUTRITION MENU and theNutrition Facts linked from the bottom of the Home page (Nutrition & Allergens). The errors are primarily sides like Green Beans and Steamed Broccoli, which appear to have higher net carb counts (9 grams of net carbs each).

On the bright side, the menu items on the Texas Roadhouse website are customizable, so we can easily adjust them as we wish to get the macronutrients in line. The Nutrition Calculator can be found when the Nutrition & Allergens is clicked at the bottom of the homepage. Too bad the suspected carb errors prevent Texas Roadhouse from securing a spot on the *Keto Diet Restaurant Guide* Superstar List after reviewing this commendable and customizable Nutrition Calculator.

Special Order Tips

Order all burgers and sandwiches with "no bread." Be wary of the available "Add-Ons" since they are often an unnecessary source of net carbs. Avoid all fries, potatoes, rice, pasta, bread, etc. Ask the server to substitute a side salad or a side of steamed/grilled vegetables.

Feel free to customize your order. Restaurants are usually happy to accommodate reasonable customer requests. The exception is when the item has been premade or was prepared off-site. Note that any alterations on your end will change the provided nutrition information. Adjust accordingly.

You'll notice some menu items indicate a half-serving size. Don't worry; there will only be a few! A smaller portion size allowed us to include more (higher-carb) crowd-pleasing favorites and signature dishes from Texas Roadhouse.

Author Favorite

Lunch: Grilled Shrimp, no bread to start with a Pulled Pork Sandwich, breadless, no BBQ sauce. 16 oz. chilled Dasani Bottled Water. 1230 calories, 59g fat, 6g net carbs, 86g protein

Dinner: Grilled Shrimp starter, no bread, with Bleu Cheese Dressing. Road Kill steak entrée with Caesar Side Salad, no croutons on the side. 16 oz. fountain drink; Diet Coke. 1580 calories, 115g fat, 17g net carbs, 81g protein

LUNCH

Starters

2g net carbs: Grilled Shrimp, no bread 360 calories, 19g fat, 18g protein
5g net carbs: Killer Ribs, no BBQ sauce 910 calories, 53g fat, 49g protein
10g net carbs: Texas Red Chili (no beans), Cup 250 calories, 15g fat, 17g protein
10g net carbs: Texas Red Chili (with beans)[41], Cup 210 calories, 10g fat, 16g protein

Dressings, Sauces, and Toppings

4g net carbs: Bleu Cheese Dressing (2 oz.) 280 calories, 30g fat, 2g protein
4g net carbs: Ranch Dressing (2 oz.) 290 calories, 31g fat, 1g protein
5g net carbs: Ranch Dressing (3 oz.) 430 calories, 47g fat, 1g protein
9g net carbs: Cajun Horseradish Sauce (3 oz.) 260 calories, 24g fat, 2g protein
10g net carbs: Texas Red Chili Topping (6 oz.) 220 calories, 12g fat, 15g protein

Burgers & Sandwiches (No Bread, No Side)

3g net carbs: All-American Cheeseburger, bunless 880 calories, 55g fat, 50g protein
4g net carbs: Fried Pork Sandwich, bunless, remove breading from pork chop, no sauce 960 calories, 57g fat, 53g protein
4g net carbs: Pulled Pork Sandwich, breadless, no BBQ sauce 870 calories, 40g fat, 68g protein
5g net carbs: Bacon Cheeseburger, bunless 980 calories, 62g fat, 59g protein
6g net carbs: Mushroom Jack Chicken Sandwich, breadless 710 calories, 30g fat, 63g protein
6g net carbs: Smokehouse Burger, bunless, no BBQ sauce 1,080 calories, 67g fat, 58g protein

Burgers Add-Ons

1g net carbs: Bacon Slices (2) 100 calories, 7g fat, 9g protein

---

[41] *That's Not Keto!* – You'll find all sorts of surprising foods listed here. I'm not telling you whether you should eat these foods or not. What fits your macros or daily carb spend is up to you. No keto police allowed.

DINNER

Starters

2g net carbs: Grilled Shrimp, no bread 360 calories, 19g fat, 18g protein
5g net carbs: Killer Ribs, no BBQ sauce 910 calories, 53g fat, 49g protein
10g net carbs: Texas Red Chili (no beans), Cup 250 calories, 15g fat, 17g protein
10g net carbs: Texas Red Chili (with beans)[42], Cup 210 calories, 10g fat, 16g protein

Dressings, Sauces, and Toppings

4g net carbs: Bleu Cheese Dressing (2 oz.) 280 calories, 30g fat, 2g protein
4g net carbs: Ranch Dressing (2 oz.) 290 calories, 31g fat, 1g protein
5g net carbs: Ranch Dressing (3 oz.) 430 calories, 47g fat, 1g protein
9g net carbs: Cajun Horseradish Sauce (3 oz.) 260 calories, 24g fat, 2g protein
10g net carbs: Texas Red Chili Topping (6 oz.) 220 calories, 12g fat, 15g protein

Hand-Cut Steaks (Filet Medallions & Steak, No Rice, No Sides, Prime Rib Includes Au Jus)

0g net carbs: New York Strip, 12 oz. Traditional Cut 640 calories, 33g fat, 85g protein
1g net carbs: New York Strip, 8 oz. Thick Cut 420 calories, 22g fat, 57g protein
1g net carbs: Prime Rib, 10 oz. 800 calories, 60g fat, 62g protein
1g net carbs: Prime Rib, 12 oz. 950 calories, 72g fat, 74g protein
1g net carbs: Prime Rib, 16 oz. 1,260 calories, 95g fat, 99g protein
0g net carbs: Porterhouse T-Bone 1,040 calories, 54g fat, 139g protein
4g net carbs: Bone-In Ribeye 1,480 calories, 101g fat, 143g protein
4g net carbs: Steak Kabob, no rice 920 calories, 41g fat, 58g protein
2g net carbs: USDA Choice Sirloin, 6 oz. 250 calories, 6g fat, 46g protein
3g net carbs: USDA Choice Sirloin, 8 oz. 340 calories, 8g fat, 61g protein
4g net carbs: USDA Choice Sirloin, 11 oz. 460 calories, 11g fat, 84g protein
6g net carbs: USDA Choice Sirloin, 16 oz. 670 calories, 16g fat, 122g protein
4g net carbs: Dallas Filet, 6 oz. 270 calories, 10g fat, 45g protein
6g net carbs: Dallas Filet, 8 oz. 360 calories, 13g fat, 60g protein
5g net carbs: Filet Medallions, no rice 760 calories, 30g fat, 74g protein
7g net carbs: Road Kill 500 calories, 23g fat, 55g protein
7g net carbs: Ft. Worth Ribeye, 10 oz. 800 calories, 60g fat, 65g protein
8g net carbs: Ft. Worth Ribeye, 12 oz. 960 calories, 72g fat, 78g protein
9g net carbs: Ft. Worth Ribeye, 14 oz. 1,120 calories, 84g fat, 90g protein
10g net carbs: Ft. Worth Ribeye, 16 oz. 1,280 calories, 96g fat, 103g protein

Filet Medallions Sauces (4 oz.)

6g net carbs: Portobello Mushroom Sauce 120 calories, 9g fat, 3g protein
7g net carbs: Peppercorn Sauce 210 calories, 18g fat, 1g protein

---

[42] *That's Not Keto!* – You'll find all sorts of surprising foods listed here. I'm not telling you whether you should eat these foods or not. What fits your macros or daily carb spend is up to you. No keto police allowed.

Prime Rib Sauce Options (2 oz.)

1g net carbs: Au Jus 25 calories, 2g fat, 1g protein
4g net carbs: Creamy Horseradish Sauce 190 calories, 18g fat, 1g protein
8g net carbs: Horseradish 50 calories, 2g fat, 1g protein

Smother Options (for Steaks Less than 11 oz.)

0g net carbs: Monterey Jack Cheese 100 calories, 8g fat, 7g protein
1g net carbs: Bleu Cheese Crumbles 100 calories, 8g fat, 6g protein
1g net carbs: Shrimp 40 calories, 1g fat, 8g protein
2g net carbs: Mushrooms 50 calories, 4g fat, 1g protein
3g net carbs: Brown Smother Gravy 70 calories, 6g fat, 1g protein
3g net carbs: Fire Roasted Green Chile 150 calories, 15g fat, 0g protein
5g net carbs: Cream Smother Gravy 100 calories, 7g fat, 2g protein
5g net carbs: Onions 60 calories, 4g fat, 1g protein

Smother Options (for Steaks 11 oz. and Larger)

0g net carbs: Monterey Jack Cheese 200 calories, 16g fat, 14g protein
1g net carbs: Bleu Cheese Crumbles 100 calories, 8g fat, 6g protein
1g net carbs: Shrimp 40 calories, 1g fat, 8g protein
2g net carbs: Mushrooms 70 calories, 6g fat, 2g protein
4g net carbs: Fire Roasted Green Chile 220 calories, 22g fat, 0g protein
5g net carbs: Brown Smother Gravy 110 calories, 9g fat, 1g protein
7g net carbs: Onions 90 calories, 6g fat, 1g protein
8g net carbs: Cream Smother Gravy 140 calories, 11g fat, 3g protein

Fall-Off-the-Bone Ribs (No Side)

4g net carbs: Fall-Off-the-Bone Ribs – Half-Rack, no BBQ sauce 900 calories, 63g fat, 72g protein
7g net carbs: Fall-Off-the-Bone Ribs – Full-Rack, no BBQ sauce 1,450 calories, 102g fat, 116g protein

Texas Size Combos (No Side)

3g net carbs: Dallas Filet & Grilled Shrimp, no rice 670 calories, 33g fat, 63g protein
3g net carbs: Dallas Filet & Ribs, easy BBQ sauce 820 calories, 49g fat, 90g protein
4g net carbs: Ft. Worth Ribeye 12 oz. & Ribs, easy BBQ sauce 1,510 calories, 111g fat, 122g protein
5g net carbs: Ft. Worth Ribeye 10 oz. & Grilled Shrimp 1,200 calories, 83g fat, 82g protein
5g net carbs: Ft. Worth Ribeye 10 oz. & Ribs, no BBQ sauce 1,350 calories, 99g fat, 109g protein
5g net carbs: Ft. Worth Ribeye 12 oz. & Grilled Shrimp, no rice 1,360 calories, 95g fat, 95g protein
6g net carbs: Sirloin 6 oz. & Grilled Shrimp, no rice 650 calories, 29g fat, 64g protein
6g net carbs: Sirloin 6 oz. & Ribs 800 calories, 45g fat, 90g protein
6g net carbs: Sirloin 8 oz. & Grilled Shrimp, no rice 740 calories, 31g fat, 79g protein
7g net carbs: Sirloin 8 oz. & Ribs 890 calories, 47g fat, 105g protein
6g net carbs: Grilled BBQ Chicken & Sirloin, no BBQ sauce 590 calories, 10g fat, 92g protein
7g net carbs: Grilled BBQ Chicken & Ribs, no BBQ sauce 890 calories, 43g fat, 91g protein

Chicken Specialties (No Side)

4g net carbs: Portobello Mushroom Chicken 430 calories, 20g fat, 58g protein
5g net carbs: Smothered Chicken with Jack Cheese 430 calories, 20g fat, 55g protein
6g net carbs: Green Chile Chicken, easy chili sauce 480 calories, 13g fat, 61g protein
6g net carbs: Sierra Chicken Pasta, substitute steamed vegetables for pasta 1,220 calories, 66g fat, 69g protein
7g net carbs: Grilled BBQ Chicken, easy BBQ sauce 300 calories, 4g fat, 46g protein
7g net carbs: Smothered Chicken with easy Cream Gravy 420 calories, 19g fat, 51g protein
8g net carbs: Herb Crusted Chicken 260 calories, 4g fat, 47g protein

Chicken Critters Dipping Sauce (2 oz. Unless Otherwise Indicated)

2g net carbs: Hot Sauce 140 calories, 14g fat, 0g protein
2g net carbs: Mild Sauce 220 calories, 23g fat, 0g protein
4g net carbs: Ranch 290 calories, 31g fat, 1g protein
6g net carbs: Honey Mustard[43], 1 oz. 160 calories, 32g fat, 0g protein
9g net carbs: Texas Roadhouse Barbecue Sauce*, 1 oz. 50 calories, 0g fat, 0g protein

Country Dinners

3g net carbs: Country Vegetable Plate, choose 4 steamed vegetable side options 250 calories, 15g fat, 20g protein
4g net carbs: Grilled Pork Chops, Single Chop, easy sauce 440 calories, 26g fat, 42g protein
4g net carbs: Pulled Pork Dinner, no bread, no BBQ sauce 890 calories, 41g fat, 80g protein
5g net carbs: Beef Tips with House Side Salad with no dressing, easy gravy, no rice, no potatoes 860 calories, 57g fat, 63g protein
6g net carbs: Beef Tips with Sauteed Mushrooms, easy gravy, no rice, no potatoes 960 calories, 58g fat, 61g protein
6g net carbs: Grilled Pork Chops, Double Chop, easy sauce 730 calories, 38g fat, 82g protein

Country Fried Chicken & Sirloin Gravy Options (6 oz.)

5g net carbs: Brown Gravy, Half-Serving, 3 oz. 110 calories, 8g fat, 1g protein
8g net carbs: Cream Gravy, Half-Serving, 3 oz. 150 calories, 10g fat, 3g protein

Smother Options (Chicken Specialties & Single Pork Chop)

0g net carbs: Monterey Jack Cheese 100 calories, 8g fat, 7g protein
2g net carbs: Mushrooms 50 calories, 4g fat, 1g protein
3g net carbs: Brown Smother Gravy 70 calories, 6g fat, 1g protein
3g net carbs: Fire Roasted Green Chile 150 calories, 15g fat, 0g protein
4g net carbs: Onions 60 calories, 4g fat, 1g protein
5g net carbs: Cream Smother Gravy 100 calories, 7g fat, 2g protein

---

[43] *That's Not Keto!* – You'll find all sorts of surprising foods listed here. I'm not telling you whether you should eat these foods or not. What fits your macros or daily carb spend is up to you. No keto police allowed.

Smother Options (Country Fried Chicken/Sirloin, Double Pork Chop)

0g net carbs: Monterey Jack Cheese 200 calories, 16g fat, 14g protein
2g net carbs: Mushrooms 70 calories, 6g fat, 2g protein
4g net carbs: Fire Roasted Green Chile 220 calories, 22g fat, 0g protein
5g net carbs: Brown Smother Gravy 110 calories, 9g fat, 1g protein
7g net carbs: Onions 90 calories, 6g fat, 1g protein
8g net carbs: Cream Smother Gravy 140 calories, 11g fat, 3g protein

Dockside Favorites (No Side)

2g net carbs: Grilled Salmon, 5 oz. 410 calories, 33g fat, 27g protein
2g net carbs: Grilled Salmon, 8 oz. 560 calories, 42g fat, 45g protein
3g net carbs: Grilled Shrimp Dinner, no rice 670 calories, 37g fat, 32g protein

Dockside Sauce

5g net carbs: Creole Mustard, 3 oz. 450 calories, 49g fat, 0g protein
9g net carbs: Tartar Sauce, 2 oz. 320 calories, 32g fat, 0g protein

Sides & Extras[44]

2g net carbs: Caesar Side Salad, no croutons 440 calories, 43g fat, 6g protein
3g net carbs: Sauteed Mushrooms 120 calories, 11g fat, 3g protein
7g net carbs: House Side Salad 230 calories, 16g fat, 13g protein
8g net carbs: Fresh Vegetables 190 calories, 15g fat, 3g protein
8g net carbs: Steamed Broccoli 210 calories, 16g fat, 5g protein
9g net carbs: Sauteed Onions 150 calories, 10g fat, 2g protein
10g net carbs: Green Beans 100 calories, 4g fat, 6g protein

Sidekicks

2g net carbs: Grilled Shrimp, no bread- Sidekick 270 calories, 9g fat, 18g protein
4g net carbs: Fall-Off-the-Bone Ribs, no BBQ sauce- Sidekick 550 calories, 39g fat, 44g protein

Salads (No Croutons)

2g net carbs: Caesar Salad 440 calories, 43g fat, 6g protein
2g net carbs: House Salad 230 calories, 16g fat, 13g protein
4g net carbs: Grilled Chicken Salad 810 calories, 45g fat, 85g protein
5g net carbs: California Grilled Chicken Salad 970 calories, 46g fat, 74g protein
5g net carbs: Chicken Caesar Salad 1,100 calories, 89g fat, 60g protein
5g net carbs: Grilled Shrimp Salad 660 calories, 43g fat, 52g protein
5g net carbs: Salmon Caesar Salad 1,110 calories, 99g fat, 40g protein
5g net carbs: Shrimp Caesar Salad 940 calories, 86g fat, 26g protein

---

[44] Some of the provided nutrition details for this category appear a bit high to me, but this is the information provided by the restaurant.

5g net carbs: Steakhouse Filet Salad with easy Ranch 1,340 calories, 103g fat, 71g protein
6g net carbs: Grilled Salmon Salad 830 calories, 55g fat, 66g protein

Made-from-Scratch Dressing (3 oz. Unless Otherwise Indicated)

0g net carbs: Oil & Vinegar 410 calories, 42g fat, 0g protein
5g net carbs: Bleu Cheese Dressing 430 calories, 45g fat, 3g protein
5g net carbs: Parmesan Peppercorn Dressing 280 calories, 27g fat, 4g protein
5g net carbs: Ranch Dressing 430 calories, 47g fat, 1g protein
5g net carbs: Thousand Island Dressing, 1 oz. 120 calories, 12g fat, 0g protein
6g net carbs: Caesar Dressing 540 calories, 56g fat, 4g protein
6g net carbs: Low-Fat Ranch Dressing 240 calories, 24g fat, 3g protein

Salad Toppings

0g net carbs: Bacon 70 calories, 4g fat, 6g protein
1g net carbs: Bleu Cheese Crumbles 100 calories, 8g fat, 6g protein

House Salad Made-from-Scratch Dressing (2 oz.)

0g net carbs: Oil & Vinegar 270 calories, 28g fat, 0g protein
3g net carbs: Parmesan Peppercorn Dressing 180 calories, 18g fat, 3g protein
4g net carbs: Bleu Cheese Dressing 280 calories, 30g fat, 2g protein
4g net carbs: Caesar Dressing 360 calories, 37g fat, 3g protein
4g net carbs: Low-Fat Ranch Dressing 160 calories, 16g fat, 2g protein
4g net carbs: Ranch Dressing 290 calories, 31g fat, 1g protein
9g net carbs: Thousand Island Dressing 260 calories, 26g fat, 0g protein

DRINKS

0g net carbs: Diet Coke, 16 oz. 0 calories, 0g fat, 0g protein
0g net carbs: Dasani Bottled Water, 16 oz. 0 calories, 0g fat, 0g protein
0g net carbs: Iced Tea, Original, unsweetened, 16 oz. 0 calories, 0g fat, 0g protein
1g net carbs: Coffee, Decaffeinated, unsweetened, 6 oz. 5 calories, 0g fat, 0g protein
1g net carbs: Coffee, unsweetened, 6 oz. 5 calories, 0g fat, 0g protein
6g net carbs: Iced Tea, Peach, unsweetened, 16 oz. 45 calories, 0g fat, 0g protein
6g net carbs: Iced Tea, Raspberry unsweetened, 16 oz. 40 calories, 0g fat, 0g protein

Wine

5g net carbs: House Red Wine, 6 oz. glass 150 calories, 0g fat, 0g protein
5g net carbs: House White Wine, 6 oz. glass 150 calories, 0g fat, 0g protein
8g net carbs: House Blush Wine, 5 oz. glass 110 calories, 0g fat, 0g protein
8g net carbs: House Red Wine, 9 oz. Texas Pour 230 calories, 0g fat, 0g protein
8g net carbs: House White Wine, 9 oz. Texas Pour 230 calories, 0g fat, 0g protein

Logan's Roadhouse

It appears that Logan's Roadhouse wants to make things difficult for us. They have multiple versions of their menu on their website (under the MENU tab of their Home Page). Can you say *confusing*? There is a "Carolina's Menu," a "California Menu," and a "All Menus," which appears to be a combined menu. I mainly surveyed the "All Menus" when compiling available low-carb options.

Unfortunately, the menu items on Logan's Roadhouse site are not customizable, so we are left to do calculations on our own. They have a detailed Nutritional Menu PDF to help you monitor your carb intake.

Special Order Tips

Order all burgers and sandwiches with "no bread." Be wary of the available "Add-Ons" since they are often an unnecessary source of net carbs. Avoid all fries, potatoes, rice, pasta, bread, etc. Ask the server to substitute a side salad or a side of steamed/grilled vegetables.

Feel free to customize your order. Restaurants are usually happy to accommodate reasonable customer requests. The exception is when the item has been premade or was prepared off-site. Note that any alterations on your end will change the provided nutrition information. Adjust accordingly.

You'll notice some menu items indicate a half-serving size. Don't worry; Logan's Roadhouse has very few. A smaller portion size allowed us to include more (higher-carb) crowd-pleasing favorites.

Author Favorite

Lunch: Logan's Grilled Kickin' Chickin' Salad, no croutons with Blue Cheese Dressing. Bunless Old Fashioned Burger-without cheese. 16 oz. Diet Coke to drink. 1483 calories, 80g fat, 11g net carbs, 123g protein

Dinner: Baby Back Rib Basket, no BBQ sauce with Roadhouse Ranch Dressing, Logan's Wood-Grilled Chicken, no rice with Sautéed Mushrooms and Steamed Broccoli as sides, and a 5 oz. glass of Dark Horse Merlot to top it off. 2037 calories, 123g fat, 21g net carbs, 110g protein

LUNCH

Burgers & Sandwiches (No Bread, No Side)

2g net carbs: Mesquite Grilled Chicken Sandwich, breadless 359 calories, 7g fat, 44g protein
3g net carbs: Choice Rib-Eye Sandwich, breadless 741 calories, 41g fat, 44g protein
3g net carbs: Old Fashioned Burger-without cheese, bunless 581 calories, 30g fat, 46g protein
4g net carbs: Roadhouse Deluxe Burger, bunless 944 calories, 59g fat, 63g protein

Burgers & Sandwich Add-Ons

0g net carbs: Cheddar Cheese 110 calories, 9g fat, 7g protein
0g net carbs: Swiss Cheese 110 calories, 9g fat, 7g protein
0g net carbs: Monterey Jack Cheese 110 calories, 9g fat, 7g protein

Seafood (No Side, No Salad)

0g net carbs: Mesquite Grilled Salmon 663 calories, 62g fat, 29g protein
6g net carbs: Santa Fe Grilled Tilapia 789 calories, 57g fat, 37g protein

Salads (No Dressing)

4g net carbs: Club Combo, Half-Serving, breadless 543 calories, 30g fat, 30g protein
5g net carbs: Logan's Club Salad, no croutons 595 calories, 40g fat, 46g protein
6g net carbs: Grilled Steak Salad, no croutons 672 calories, 37g fat, 71g protein
7g net carbs: Anything and Everything Salad, no cranberries 989 calories, 53g fat, 73g protein
7g net carbs: Logan's Grilled Kickin' Chickin' Salad, no croutons 792 calories, 39g fat, 73g protein
8g net carbs: Mesquite Grilled Chicken Salad, no croutons 649 calories, 35g fat, 69g protein

Salad Dressing

1g net carbs: Blue Cheese Dressing, 1.5 oz. 110 calories, 11g fat, 4g protein
1g net carbs: Ranch Dressing, 1.5 oz. 110 calories, 12g fat, 6g protein
2g net carbs: Caesar Dressing, 1.5 oz. 280 calories, 30g fat, 6g protein
2g net carbs: Parmesan Peppercorn Dressing, 1.5 oz. 260 calories, 28g fat, 6g protein
2g net carbs: Roadhouse Ranch Dressing, 1.5 oz. 100 calories, 10g fat, 4g protein
5g net carbs: Fat-Free Vinaigrette, 1.5 oz. 30 calories, 0g fat, 4g protein
6g net carbs: French Dressing, 1 oz. 160 calories, 13g fat, 11g protein
7g net carbs: Balsamic Vinaigrette, 1 oz. 140 calories, 10g fat, 11g protein

8g net carbs: Thousand Island Dressing, 1 oz. 120 calories, 12g fat, 10g protein

DINNER

Appetizers

1g net carbs: Peel 'N Eat Shrimp-steamed 430 calories, 3g fat, 32g protein
3g net carbs: Baby Back Rib Basket, no BBQ sauce 728 calories, 76g fat, 69g protein
5g net carbs: Wood-Grilled Buffalo Wings 1260 calories, 75g fat, 36g protein
7g net carbs: Deviled Eggs (6) 508 calories, 44g fat, 20g protein
9g net carbs: Yeast Rolls[45] (1), no butter 80 calories, 3g fat, 1g protein

Burgers & Sandwiches (No Bread, No Side Unless Otherwise Indicated)

3g net carbs: All American Cheeseburger no cheese, bunless 680 calories, 40g fat, 46g protein
3g net carbs: All American Cheeseburger with American Cheese, bunless 900 calories, 58g fat, 48g protein
3g net carbs: Chipotle Grilled Chicken Sandwich, breadless 861 calories, 45g fat, 60g protein
3g net carbs: Choice Rib-Eye Sandwich, breadless 741 calories, 41g fat, 44g protein
3g net carbs: Deluxe Grilled Chicken Sandwich, breadless 688 calories, 33g fat, 61g protein
4g net carbs: Buffalo Grilled Chicken Sandwich, breadless 729 calories, 29g fat, 60g protein
4g net carbs: Logan's Club Sandwich, breadless 1085 calories, 59g fat, 61g protein
4g net carbs: Peppercorn Bacon Chicken Sandwich, breadless 860 calories, 48g fat, 48g protein
5g net carbs: Pile High French Dip Au Jus & Creamy Horseradish Sauce, breadless 770 calories, 36g fat, 56g protein
6g net carbs: Bayside Burger with Blackened Shrimp, bunless 850 calories, 35g fat, 50g protein
6g net carbs: Mesquite Grilled Chicken Sandwich, breadless 359 calories, 7g fat, 44g protein
6g net carbs: Original Roadies®, breadless 970 calories, 45g fat, 43g protein
7g net carbs: Roadhouse Deluxe Burger, bunless, no BBQ sauce, easy Brewski Onions® 1120 calories, 73g fat, 64g protein

Ribs & Chops (No Side Unless Otherwise Indicated)

2g net carbs: Fall-off-the-Bone Ribs, Half-Rack, no BBQ sauce 920 calories, 52g fat, 59g protein
3g net carbs: Fall-off-the-Bone Ribs, Full-Rack, no BBQ sauce 1800 calories, 99g fat, 98g protein
4g net carbs: Mesquite Grilled Pork Chops, no Cinnamon Apples 730 calories, 56g fat, 39g protein

Chicken & Seafood (No Side Unless Otherwise Indicated)

4g net carbs: Logan's Wood-Grilled Chicken, no rice 820 calories, 54g fat, 30g protein
5g net carbs: Coastal Carolina Wood-Grilled Shrimp 470 calories, 23g fat, 52g protein
5g net carbs: Mesquite Wood-Grilled Salmon with Dill Sauce, no rice 780 calories, 60g fat, 55g protein
6g net carbs: Santa Fe Grilled Tilapia 641 calories, 60g fat, 68g protein
6g net carbs: Shrimp Stacked Salmon, no potatoes 450 calories, 29g fat, 48g protein

---

[45] *That's Not Keto!* – You'll find all sorts of surprising foods listed here. I'm not telling you whether you should eat these foods or not. What fits your macros or daily carb spend is up to you. No keto police allowed.

Steak & Beef (No Side Unless Otherwise Indicated)

0g net carbs: "The Logan®" 529 calories, 25g fat, 76g protein
0g net carbs: Bone-In Rib Eye 1574 calories, 127g fat, 109g protein
0g net carbs: Filet Mignon 6 oz. 374 calories, 23g fat, 40g protein
0g net carbs: Filet Mignon 9 oz. 510 calories, 29g fat, 59g protein
0g net carbs: New York Strip 16 oz. 685 calories, 32g fat, 91g protein
0g net carbs: Porterhouse 20 oz. 1092 calories, 59g fat, 131g protein
0g net carbs: Rib Eye 16 oz. 1135 calories, 84g fat, 95g protein
0g net carbs: Rib-Eye 12 oz. 876 calories, 66g fat, 71g protein
0g net carbs: Sirloin 6 oz. 335 calories, 19g fat, 42g protein
0g net carbs: Sirloin 8 oz. 380 calories, 17g fat, 56g protein
0g net carbs: T-Bone 16 oz. 894 calories, 50g fat, 105g protein
2g net carbs: Chopped Sirloin Steak 12 oz., no potatoes 607 calories, 32g fat, 79g protein
6g net carbs: Grilled Meatloaf, no Brewski Onions®, no potatoes 800 calories, 54g fat, 49g protein
7g net carbs: Smothered with Brewski Onions, Sauteed Mushrooms, and Gravy 736 calories, 42g fat, 82g protein
8g net carbs: Teriyaki Club Steak 344 calories, 10g fat, 56g protein

Steak Toppers

0g net carbs: Blue Cheese Butter & Bacon 90 calories, 9g fat, 3g protein
0g net carbs: Garlic Butter 140 calories, 12g fat, 5g protein
3g net carbs: Sautéed Mushrooms 60 calories, 5g fat, 8g protein
6g net carbs: Brewski Onions® 40 calories, 6g fat, 12g protein

Sauces (2 oz. Unless Otherwise Indicated)

0g net carbs: Margarine, 1 Tbsp. 400 calories, 44g fat, 0g protein
0g net carbs: Mayonnaise, 1 Tbsp. 100 calories, 11g fat, 0g protein
0g net carbs: Mustard, 1 tsp. 5 calories, 0g fat, 0g protein
0g net carbs: Whipped Butter Blend Margarine, 1 Tbsp. 70 calories, 7g fat, 0g protein
2g net carbs: Texas Petal 320 calories, 34g fat, 0g protein
4g net carbs: Chipotle Ranch 201 calories, 20g fat, 1g protein
5g net carbs: Au Jus 347 calories, 6g fat, 10g protein
5g net carbs: Chipotle Marinade 200 calories, 16g fat, 18g protein
5g net carbs: Horseradish, 1 oz. 200 calories, 18g fat, 0g protein
6g net carbs: Bourbon Glaze*, 1 oz. 90 calories, 7g fat, 0g protein

American Roadhouse Meals (No Side)

1g net carbs: Bayou Popcorn Shrimp with Cocktail Sauce 490 calories, 21g fat, 49g protein
1g net carbs: Southern Fried Fish with Tartar Sauce 1010 calories, 59g fat, 90g protein
2g net carbs: Sirloin, 6 oz. no crispy onions 380 calories, 28g fat, 35g protein
2g net carbs: Steak Tips 230 calories, 13g fat, 31g protein
4g net carbs: Grilled Pork Chop, no BBQ sauce, no crispy onions 380 calories, 15g fat, 19g protein
6g net carbs: Grilled Meatloaf, no potatoes, no Brewski Onions® 600 calories, 39g fat, 37g protein
6g net carbs: Smothered Chopped Steak, no Brewski Onions®, no potatoes 830 calories, 62g fat, 31g protein
6g net carbs: Smothered Steak Tips, no crispy onions 320 calories, 16g fat, 37g protein

Combo Entrees (No Side)

4g net carbs: Filet Mignon & Grilled Shrimp 932 calories, 72g fat, 55g protein

4g net carbs: USDA Choice Sirloin Steak & Grilled Chicken 672 calories, 28g fat, 82g protein

5g net carbs: Fall-Off-the-Bone Ribs & Grilled Chicken, no BBQ sauce 1084 calories, 37g fat, 145g protein

5g net carbs: Grilled Chicken & Mesquite Grilled Shrimp 895 calories, 58g fat, 47g protein

6g net carbs: USDA Choice Sirloin Steak & Fall-Off-the-Bone Ribs, no BBQ sauce 1082 calories, 47g fat, 147g protein

7g net carbs: Fall-Off-the-Bone Ribs & Mesquite Grilled Shrimp, no BBQ sauce 1305 calories, 78g fat, 120g protein

7g net carbs: USDA Choice Sirloin Steak & Mesquite Grilled Shrimp 893 calories, 68g fat, 120g protein

Sides

1g net carbs: Caesar Side Salad, no croutons 230 calories, 19g fat, 12g protein

1g net carbs: House Side Salad without dressing, no croutons 160 calories, 9g fat, 13g protein

2g net carbs: Sautéed Mushrooms 182 calories, 19g fat, 3g protein

3g net carbs: Green Beans 30 calories, 0g fat, 6g protein

5g net carbs: Brewski® Onions 135 calories, 11g fat, 1g protein

5g net carbs: Steamed Broccoli 82 calories, 4g fat, 4g protein

6g net carbs: Fresh Vegetables 45 calories, 1g fat, 3g protein

7g net carbs: Grilled Vegetable Skewer 98 calories, 7g fat, 3g protein

Soup

7g net carbs: Southwest Chicken Tortilla[46], cup, no tortilla strips 72 calories, 3g fat, 4g protein

Salads

3g net carbs: Mesquite-Grilled Chicken without dressing, no croutons 820 calories, 54g fat, 34g protein

4g net carbs: Mesquite-Grilled Chicken Caesar, no croutons 580 calories, 44g fat, 37g protein

4g net carbs: Roadhouse Steak Cobb Salad without dressing, no croutons 750 calories, 53g fat, 26g protein

5g net carbs: Mesquite-Grilled Salmon Caesar, no croutons 760 calories, 60g fat, 45g protein

5g net carbs: Roadhouse Grilled Chicken Cobb without dressing, no croutons 570 calories, 33g fat, 35g protein

6g net carbs: Anything & Everything Salad without dressing, no cranberries 680 calories, 39g fat, 30g protein

Salad Dressing

1g net carbs: Blue Cheese Dressing, 1.5 oz. 110 calories, 11g fat, 4g protein

1g net carbs: Ranch Dressing, 1.5 oz. 110 calories, 12g fat, 6g protein

2g net carbs: Caesar Dressing, 1.5 oz. 280 calories, 30g fat, 6g protein

2g net carbs: Parmesan Peppercorn Dressing, 1.5 oz. 260 calories, 28g fat, 6g protein

2g net carbs: Roadhouse Ranch Dressing, 1.5 oz. 100 calories, 10g fat, 4g protein

5g net carbs: Fat-Free Vinaigrette, 1.5 oz. 30 calories, 0g fat, 4g protein

6g net carbs: French Dressing, 1 oz. 160 calories, 13g fat, 11g protein

---

[46] *That's Not Keto!* – You'll find all sorts of surprising foods listed here. I'm not telling you whether you should eat these foods or not. What fits your macros or daily carb spend is up to you. No keto police allowed.

7g net carbs: Balsamic Vinaigrette, 1 oz. 140 calories, 10g fat, 11g protein
8g net carbs: Thousand Island Dressing, 1 oz. 120 calories, 12g fat, 10g protein

DRINKS

0g net carbs: Diet Coke, 16 oz. 0 calories, 0g fat, 0g protein
0g net carbs: Iced Tea- unsweetened, 16 oz. 10 calories, 0g fat, 0g protein
1g net carbs: Coffee- unsweetened, 5 oz. 5 calories, 0g fat, 0g protein
2g net carbs: Coffee- Decaf- unsweetened, 5 oz. 5 calories, 0g fat, 0g protein
2g net carbs: Sugar-free Red Bull 8.4oz. can 10 calories, 0g fat, 0g protein

Beer & Seltzer (12 oz. Unless Otherwise Indicated)

2g net carbs: Bud Light Seltzer Strawberry 100 calories, 0g fat, 0g protein
3g net carbs: Michelob Ultra 95 calories, 0g fat, 1g protein
3g net carbs: Miller Lite 96 calories, 0g fat, 1g protein
4g net carbs: House Light Draft Beer- 10 oz. 80 calories, 0g fat, 1g protein
5g net carbs: Amstel Light 95 calories, 0g fat, 1g protein
5g net carbs: Coors Light 102 calories, 0g fat, 1g protein
7g net carbs: Bud Light 110 calories, 0g fat, 1g protein
9g net carbs: House Light Draft Beer- 22 oz. 175 calories, 0g fat, 2g protein

Wine (5 oz.)

4g net carbs: 14 Hands Cabernet Sauvignon 120 calories, 0g fat, 0g protein
4g net carbs: House Cabernet 124 calories, 0g fat, 0g protein
4g net carbs: House Chardonnay 132 calories, 0g fat, 0g protein
4g net carbs: House Merlot 130 calories, 0g fat, 0g protein
4g net carbs: Mirassou Chardonnay 120 calories, 0g fat, 0g protein
5g net carbs: Dark Horse Merlot 125 calories, 0g fat, 0g protein
6g net carbs: Berringer White Zinfandel 160 calories, 0g fat, 0g protein
6g net carbs: Ecco Domani Pinot Grigio 140 calories, 0g fat, 0g protein

The Capital Grille

The Capital Grille makes it challenging to decipher the low-carb options. They don't even post entree photos on their website or online menu. Weird, huh? Plus, the description of the offerings is brief. As a result, it's unclear what is included with many of the menu items. Salad dressings are not listed separately in the Menu Nutrition Guide, which is unusual for a restaurant. I recommend that all salads be ordered without (or easy) dressing.

The Capital Grille does not have a customizable nutrition calculator, but they do have a detailed Menu Nutrition Guide PDF on its website. It's somewhat hidden, so rather than poking around, do a Google search for "The Capital Grille nutrition information," and it will be one of the top choices.

Special Order Tips

Order all burgers and sandwiches with "no bread." Be wary of the available "Add-Ons" since they are often an unnecessary source of net carbs. Avoid all fries, potatoes, rice, pasta, bread, etc. Ask the server to substitute a side salad or a side of steamed/grilled vegetables.

Feel free to customize your order. Restaurants are usually happy to accommodate reasonable customer requests. The exception is when the item has been premade or was prepared off-site. Note that any alterations on your end will change the provided nutrition information. Adjust accordingly.

You'll notice some menu items indicate a half-serving size. Don't worry; there will only be a few! Smaller portions allowed us to include more (higher-carb) unique dishes from The Capital Grille.

Author Favorite

Lunch: Shrimp/Prawn (5), easy cocktail sauce to start. Bone-In Dry Aged Strip 14 oz. with Field Greens with Parmesan Vinaigrette. 16 oz. Fresh Brewed Iced Tea, unsweetened, on ice to drink. 841 calories, 49g fat, 14g net carbs, 112g protein

Dinner: Dry Aged Strip au Poivre with Courvoisier Cream with Roasted Wild Mushrooms and Sautéed Spinach with Garlic Confit on the side. Dirty Goose on the rocks to drink. 1280 calories, 62g fat, 13g net carbs, 92g protein

LUNCH

Appetizers

3g net carbs: Caesar Salad, no croutons 420 calories, 27g fat, 14g protein
6g net carbs: Field Greens with Parmesan Vinaigrette 120 calories, 9g fat, 9g protein
7g net carbs: Shrimp/Prawn (5), easy cocktail sauce 170 calories, 1g fat, 26g protein

Burger & Sandwiches (No Bread, No Truffle Fries)

5g net carbs: The Grille's Signature Cheeseburger 640 calories, 58g fat, 49g protein
7g net carbs: Ribeye Steak Sandwich, easy Horseradish Sauce 780 calories, 59g fat, 91g protein

Burger & Sandwich Accompaniments

4g net carbs: Creamy Horseradish Sauce 100 calories, 9g fat, 2g protein

Entrées (No Sides)

0g net carbs: Bone-In Dry Aged Strip 14 oz. 650 calories, 39g fat, 77g protein
2g net carbs: Filet Mignon 8 oz. 390 calories, 23g fat, 43g protein
3g net carbs: Sesame Seared Tuna, no Rice 430 calories, 8g fat, 53g protein
4g net carbs: Boneless Ribeye 14 oz. 890 calories, 65g fat, 72g protein

Entrée Accompaniments

6g net carbs: Creamed Spinach 400 calories, 35g fat, 10g protein

Plates (No Sides)

2g net carbs: Roasted Chicken Breast, no Parmesan Risotto 640 calories, 38g fat, 43g protein
3g net carbs: Mini Tenderloin Sandwiches (2), breadless, no Truffle Fries 530 calories, 30g fat, 31g protein
5g net carbs: Parmesan Crusted Salmon, easy breading 960 calories, 75g fat, 51g protein

Plates Accompaniments

3g net carbs: Caesar Salad, no croutons 420 calories, 27g fat, 14g protein
6g net carbs: Field Greens with Parmesan Vinaigrette 120 calories, 9g fat, 9g protein

Entrée Salads (No Dressing)

4g net carbs: Capital Grille "Cobb" Salad with Sliced Tenderloin, no croutons 680 calories, 49g fat, 18g protein
5g net carbs: Maine Lobster Salad 470 calories, 34g fat, 9g protein
6g net carbs: Salmon with Avocado & Tomato Salad, no Mango 650 calories, 57g fat, 38g protein

Soups

5g net carbs: Lobster Bisque, cup, Half-Serving 160 calories, 13g fat, 10g protein
6g net carbs: New England Clam Chowder, cup, Half-Serving 110 calories, 8g fat, 6g protein

DINNER

Appetizers

3g net carbs: Crab Cocktail 460 calories, 38g fat, 27g protein
4g net carbs: Oysters on the Half (6), no mignonette sauce 130 calories, 1g fat, 4g protein
4g net carbs: Prosciutto-Wrapped Mozzarella with Tomatoes, no crisp crostini 440 calories, 29g fat, 23g protein
6g net carbs: Cold Shellfish Platter, easy shrimp cocktail sauce 430 calories, 3g fat, 24g protein
6g net carbs: Grand Plateau, easy shrimp cocktail sauce 1120 calories, 44g fat, 147g protein
6g net carbs: Smoked Bacon with Tomato Jam 380 calories, 24g fat, 24g protein
7g net carbs: Shrimp/Prawn (5), easy cocktail sauce 170 calories, 1g fat, 26g protein
8g net carbs: Lobster and Crab Cakes- serves 1 410 calories, 36g fat, 16g protein
8g net carbs: Tuna Tartare with Avocado and Sriracha, no mango 130 calories, 3g fat, 16g protein

Bar Plates to Share

1g net carbs: Lollipop Lamb Chops with Herb Oil & Balsamic (serves 2) 180 calories, 12g fat, 26g protein
2g net carbs: Mini Tenderloin Sliders (3), breadless 380 calories, 20g fat, 23g protein
3g net carbs: Sirloin with Sweet Chili Vinaigrette, Wasabi Oil (serves 2) 240 calories, 13g fat, 29g protein

To Share

2g net carbs: Sautéed Spinach with Garlic Confit 30 calories, 3g fat, 2g protein
3g net carbs: Grilled Asparagus with Lemon Mosto 80 calories, 7g fat, 3g protein
4g net carbs: Roasted Wild Mushrooms 140 calories, 14g fat, 3g protein
5g net carbs: Creamed Spinach 200 calories, 17g fat, 3g protein
8g net carbs: Soy Glazed Brussels Sprouts with Bacon 290 calories, 25g fat, 12g protein

Chef's Suggestions

0g net carbs: Tenderloin with Butter Poached Lobster Tails 570 calories, 30g fat, 74g protein
3g net carbs: Parmesan Crusted Tomahawk Veal Chop 930 calories, 57g fat, 100g protein
3g net carbs: Sliced Filet Mignon with Cipollini Onions, no Fig Essence 580 calories, 30g fat, 57g protein
5g net carbs: Porcini-Rubbed Bone-In Ribeye, easy aged balsamic 990 calories, 72g fat, 80g protein
9g net carbs: Bone-In Kona Crusted Strip with Shallot Butter 950 calories, 65g fat, 85g protein

Main Courses

0g net carbs: Dry Aged Strip, 14 oz. 710 calories, 42g fat, 83g protein
3g net carbs: Filet Mignon, 10 oz. 490 calories, 29g fat, 54g protein
4g net carbs: Bone-In Ribeye, 22 oz. 990 calories, 72g fat, 80g protein
5g net carbs: Double Cut Lamb Rib Chops, no glaze/sauce 710 calories, 35g fat, 19g protein
5g net carbs: Dry Aged Strip au Poivre with Courvoisier Cream 730 calories, 41g fat, 85g protein
5g net carbs: Roasted Chicken Breast, no Risotto 840 calories, 44g fat, 29g protein

Seafood

3g net carbs: Sesame Seared Tuna, no gingered rice 500 calories, 8g fat, 68g protein
4g net carbs: Seared Sea Bass with Miso Butter 810 calories, 66g fat, 39g protein
5g net carbs: Citrus Glazed Salmon with Marcona Almonds, easy glaze/sauce 720 calories, 48g fat, 50g protein

Soups & Salads

3g net carbs: Caesar Salad, no croutons 420 calories, 27g fat, 14g protein
5g net carbs: Burrata with Heirloom Tomatoes, easy aged balsamic 850 calories, 62g fat, 23g protein
5g net carbs: Lobster Bisque, cup, Half-Serving 160 calories, 13g fat, 10g protein
6g net carbs: Field Greens with easy Parmesan Vinaigrette 120 calories, 9g fat, 9g protein
6g net carbs: New England Clam Chowder, cup, Half-Serving 110 calories, 8g fat, 6g protein
8g net carbs: Wedge Salad with easy Bleu Cheese and Bacon 590 calories, 54g fat, 18g protein

DRINKS

Non-Alcoholic Beverages

1g net carbs: Fresh Brewed Iced Tea, unsweetened, 16 oz. 0 calories, 0g fat, 1g protein

White Wines

3g net carbs: Cloudy Bay Sauvignon Blanc, 6 oz. 140 calories, 0g fat, 0g protein
3g net carbs: Hartford Court, Russian River Valley, Chardonnay, 6 oz. 145 calories, 0g fat, 0g protein
4g net carbs: Brewer-Clifton, Sta. Rita Hills, 6 oz. 135 calories, 0g fat, 0g protein
4g net carbs: House Wine, White, 6 oz. 150 calories, 0g fat, 0g protein
4g net carbs: Yealands, Sauvignon Blanc, 6 oz. 147 calories, 0g fat, 0g protein
5g net carbs: Santa Margherita Pinot Grigio, Alto Adige, 6 oz. 137 calories, 0g fat, 0g protein

Red Wines

3g net carbs: Siduri, "Sommelier Cuvée," California, Pinot Noir, 6 oz. 125 calories, 0g fat, 0g protein
4g net carbs: Fisher Unity, Cabernet Sauvignon, Napa/Sonoma, CA 2018, 6 oz. 145 calories, 0g fat, 0g protein
4g net carbs: King Estate, Inscription, Willamette Valley, 6 oz. 135 calories, 0g fat, 0g protein
4g net carbs: Penfolds, Bin 28, Kalimna, South Australia, 6 oz. 142 calories, 0g fat, 0g protein
4g net carbs: Robert Hall, Paso Robles, Merlot, 6 oz. 155 calories, 0g fat, 0g protein
4g net carbs: The Prisoner Wine Company, 6 oz. 137 calories, 0g fat, 0g protein
5g net carbs: D'Esclans, Whispering Angel, Côtes de Provence, Rosé, 6 oz. 160 calories, 0g fat, 0g protein

5g net carbs: House Wine, Red, 6 oz. 160 calories, 0g fat, 0g protein
5g net carbs: Penner-Ash, Willamette Valley, 6 oz. 152 calories, 0g fat, 0g protein

Sparkling Wines

4g net carbs: Schramsberg Blanc de Blancs, 6 oz. 155 calories, 0g fat, 0g protein
8g net carbs: House Wine, Sparkling, 5 oz. 120 calories, 0g fat, 0g protein

Cocktails

1g net carbs: Dirty Goose 190 calories, 2g fat, 1g protein
8g net carbs: Stoli Doli 170 calories, 0g fat, 0g protein
8g net carbs: The Bohemian 150 calories, 0g fat, 0g protein

After Dinner Drinks

0g net carbs: Cognac/Brandy, 2 oz. 130 calories, 0g fat, 0g protein
0g net carbs: Grappa, 2 oz. 150 calories, 0g fat, 0g protein
0g net carbs: Scotch, 2 oz. 140 calories, 0g fat, 0g protein
0g net carbs: Tequila, 2 oz. 130 calories, 0g fat, 0g protein
0g net carbs: Whiskey/Bourbon, 2 oz. 160 calories, 0g fat, 0g protein

Sizzler

"Comfort food" pretty much sums up the offerings at Sizzler these days. I usually get a steak here and dive into the endless salad bar for a few bucks more. Don't get any ideas about filling up a doggy bag for later. We found out the hard way that Sizzler frowns upon such behavior. You may have to get creative to get those scrumptious leftovers home for later.

Want to investigate what's being offered? You can search for Sizzler low-carb menu options in the mymenunutrition.com interactive menu. Click ORDER ONLINE at the top of the main page and select your local Sizzler location. Click the third drop-down option, Nutritionals and then click the top choice, Nutrients (Calories, Carbs, Sodium, and more) and reduce the "Carbohydrates" to your desired amount. Then click "Go to Personalized Menu" at the bottom of the page. Easy-peasy.

Special Order Tips

I highly recommend the salad bar. When do you ever have the chance to indulge in a cornucopia of fresh and healthy vegetables? Use your finely honed keto senses (like "Spidey senses") to make careful, low-carb choices.

As for the chicken and steak entrees, here are my two cents. Request meat to be grilled and choose a side of steamed broccoli, House Side Salad with no croutons, Caesar Side Salad with no croutons, or a cup of Vegetable Medley.

As always, when choosing burgers and sandwiches, ask for "no bread." Go bunless or lettuce-wrapped instead. Avoid all fries, potatoes, rice, pasta, bread, etc. Ask the server to substitute a side salad or a side of steamed/grilled vegetables. Be wary of the available "Add-Ons" since they are often an unnecessary source of net carbs.

Feel free to customize your order. Restaurants are usually happy to accommodate reasonable customer requests. The exception is when the item has been premade or was prepared off-site. Note that any alterations on your end will change the provided nutrition information. Adjust accordingly.

You'll notice some menu items indicate a half-serving size. Don't worry; there will only be a few! A smaller portion size allows us to include more (higher-carb) crowd-pleasing favorites (like soup or BBQ ribs) from Sizzler.

Author Favorite

Lunch: Breadless Philly Cheesesteak and breadless Tri-Tip BBQ Sliders, no BBQ sauce with Cucumber Tomato Salad. 16 oz. Diet Coke to drink. 1405 calories, 64g fat, 11g net carbs, 100g protein

Dinner: Classic Steak Trio with grilled shrimp and grilled chicken with Greek Salad. 16 oz. Iced tea to drink. 840 calories, 63g fat, 9g net carbs, 85g protein

LUNCH

Burgers & Sandwiches (No Bread)

2g net carbs: Sizzler Classic 1/3 lb. Burger 660 calories, 36g fat, 30g protein
3g net carbs: Sizzler Classic 1/2 lb. Burger 720 calories, 41g fat, 36g protein
3g net carbs: Grilled Chicken Club Sandwich 580 calories, 14g fat, 50g protein
3g net carbs: Mega Bacon Cheeseburger 790 calories, 48g fat, 41g protein
4g net carbs: Philly Cheesesteak 720 calories, 33g fat, 53g protein
4g net carbs: Tri-Tip BBQ Sliders, no BBQ sauce 660 calories, 27g fat, 40g protein
5g net carbs: Pulled Pork Sandwich, no BBQ sauce 520 calories, 16g fat, 32g protein
6g net carbs: French Dip Sandwich 590 calories, 26g fat, 42g protein
6g net carbs: Smokey Bacon Burger, no BBQ Rub Seasoning, no Onion Straws 745 calories, 53g fat, 45g protein

Salad Bar (2 oz. Unless Otherwise Indicated)

0g net carbs: Blue Cheese Crumbles, 1 oz. 5 calories, 4g fat, 3g protein
0g net carbs: Cheddar Cheese 11 calories, 9g fat, 7g protein
0g net carbs: Eggs, Chopped 5 calories, 4g fat, 4g protein
0g net carbs: Romaine & Iceberg Lettuce Mix 2 calories, 0g fat, 0g protein
0g net carbs: Spinach 2 calories, 0g fat, 0g protein
1g net carbs: Bean Sprouts 6 calories, 0g fat, 0g protein
1g net carbs: Bell Peppers, Green 5 calories, 0g fat, 0g protein
1g net carbs: Black Olives, Sliced, 1 oz. 30 calories, 3g fat, 0g protein
1g net carbs: Broccoli Florets 6 calories, 0g fat, 1g protein
1g net carbs: Cauliflower 8 calories, 0g fat, 0g protein
1g net carbs: Cherry Tomatoes 8 calories, 0g fat, 0g protein
1g net carbs: Cottage Cheese, Low-Fat 1 oz. 25 calories, 0g fat, 4g protein
1g net carbs: Cucumbers, Sliced 5 calories, 0g fat, 0g protein
1g net carbs: Green Beans, 1 oz. 5 calories, 0g fat, 0g protein
1g net carbs: Green Onions, 1 oz. 5 calories, 0g fat, 0g protein
1g net carbs: Jicama 6 calories, 0g fat, 0g protein
1g net carbs: Mushrooms 5 calories, 0g fat, 0g protein
1g net carbs: Parmesan Cheese, 1 oz. 5 calories, 4g fat, 5g protein

1g net carbs: Radishes 5 calories, 0g fat, 0g protein
1g net carbs: Red Cabbage 6 calories, 0g fat, 0g protein
1g net carbs: Spring Lettuce Mix 3 calories, 0g fat, 0g protein
1g net carbs: Strawberries (1 strawberry) 4 calories, 0g fat, 0g protein
1g net carbs: Sunflower Seeds, 1 oz. 20 calories, 1g fat, 4g protein
1g net carbs: Turkey Ham, 1 oz. 38 calories, 3g fat, 4g protein
1g net carbs: Zucchini 6 calories, 0g fat, 0g protein
2g net carbs: Beets, Pickled 8 calories, 0g fat, 0g protein
2g net carbs: Garbanzo Beans, 1 oz. 25 calories, 0g fat, 2g protein
2g net carbs: Kidney Beans[47] 1 oz. 25 calories, 0g fat, 0g protein
3g net carbs: Bacon Bits, 1 oz. 54 calories, 3g fat, 4g protein
3g net carbs: Carrots* 12 calories, 0g fat, 0g protein
3g net carbs: Peas*, 1 oz. 15 calories, 0g fat, 0g protein
3g net carbs: Red Onions 3 calories, 0g fat, 0g protein
4g net carbs: Artichoke Hearts 52 calories, 3g fat, 2g protein
4g net carbs: Grapes*, 4 oz. 15 calories, 0g fat, 0g protein
4g net carbs: Watermelon* (1 wedge) 20 calories, 0g fat, 0g protein
5g net carbs: Croutons*, 1 oz. 30 calories, 5g fat, 2g protein
5g net carbs: Honeydew Melon* (1 wedge) 23 calories, 0g fat, 0g protein
5g net carbs: Roasted Corn* & Peppers 1 oz. 27 calories, 0g fat, 0g protein
6g net carbs: Cantaloupe* (1 wedge) 27 calories, 0g fat, 2g protein
7g net carbs: Pineapple* (1 slice) 30 calories, 0g fat, 0g protein

Salads (4 oz. Unless Otherwise Indicated)

2g net carbs: Greek Salad 50 calories, 4g fat, 12g protein
3g net carbs: Asian Chopped Salad 30 calories, 2g fat, 4g protein
3g net carbs: Caesar Entrée Salad, no croutons, 2 oz. 25 calories, 2g fat, 12g protein
3g net carbs: Creamy Coleslaw, 2 oz. 30 calories, 4g fat, 2g protein
3g net carbs: Cucumber Tomato Salad 25 calories, 4g fat, 7g protein
4g net carbs: Rainbow Slaw Salad, no oranges, no Wonton Garnish 25 calories, 8g fat, 12g protein
4g net carbs: Waldorf Salad* 30 calories, 8g fat, 1g protein
5g net carbs: Carrot Raisin Salad*, 2 oz. 50 calories, 3g fat, 5g protein
5g net carbs: Three Bean Salad*, 2 oz. 25 calories, 5g fat, 4g protein
6g net carbs: Seafood Salad with easy dressing, 2 oz. 30 calories, 6g fat, 8g protein
6g net carbs: Spinach Cranberry* Salad 45 calories, 3g fat, 1g protein

Dressing (2 oz. Unless Otherwise Indicated)

1g net carbs: Ranch Dressing 10 calories, 12g fat, 0g protein
2g net carbs: Bleu Cheese 106 calories, 11g fat, 1g protein
3g net carbs: Italian Dressing 100 calories, 0g fat, 0g protein
4g net carbs: Balsamic Vinaigrette 90 calories, 8g fat, 0g protein
4g net carbs: Caesar 160 calories, 17g fat, 1g protein
5g net carbs: 1000 Island 97 calories, 9g fat, 1g protein
9g net carbs: Honey Mustard* 110 calories, 8g fat, 0g protein

---

[47] *That's Not Keto!* – You'll find all sorts of surprising foods listed here. I'm not telling you whether you should eat these foods or not. What fits your macros or daily carb spend is up to you. No keto police allowed.

Soups (6 oz. Unless Otherwise Indicated)

5g net carbs: Menudo 68 calories, 2g fat, 6g protein
5g net carbs: Vegetable Steak Soup, 3 oz. 55 calories, 8g fat, 2g protein
6g net carbs: Garden Vegetable Soup 35 calories, 0g fat, 2g protein
7g net carbs: Tomato Basil Soup 80 calories, 4g fat, 2g protein
8g net carbs: Chicken Noodle Soup[48] 60 calories, 2g fat, 3g protein
9g net carbs: Broccoli Cheese Soup, Half-Serving, 3 oz. 80 calories, 5g fat, 2g protein

DINNER

Smaller Plates (Vegetable Medley as Side)

1g net carbs: Tri-Tip Sirloin, 6 oz. 310 calories, 14g fat, 44g protein
3g net carbs: Malibu Chicken 440 calories, 18g fat, 36g protein
3g net carbs: Italian Herb Chicken 390 calories, 19g fat, 28g protein

Entrees (No Bread, Vegetable Medley as Side)

0g net carbs: Lemon Herb Chicken- Double 510 calories, 30g fat, 32g protein
0g net carbs: Lemon Herb Chicken- Single 390 calories, 18g fat, 21g protein

1g net carbs: Ribeye 12 oz. 940 calories, 75g fat, 60g protein
3g net carbs: Ribeye 14 oz. 1100 calories, 88g fat, 71g protein

1g net carbs: Tri-Tip Sirloin 8 oz. 340 calories, 16g fat, 48g protein
2g net carbs: Tri-Tip Sirloin 12 oz. 530 calories, 24g fat, 73g protein

5g net carbs: Hibachi Chicken- Single, easy sauce 460 calories, 28g fat, 42g protein
9g net carbs: Hibachi Chicken- Double, easy sauce 570 calories, 39g fat, 55g protein

5g net carbs: Pork Chop- Double, no applesauce 720 calories, 47g fat, 57g protein
5g net carbs: Pork Chop- Single, no applesauce 430 calories, 27g fat, 29g protein
4g net carbs: Malibu Grilled Chicken (Single) 480 calories, 22g fat, 41g protein
7g net carbs: Malibu Grilled Chicken (Double) 590 calories, 28g fat, 58g protein

1g net carbs: Steak & Lobster 720 calories, 51g fat, 62g protein
1g net carbs: The Sizzler Steak, 12 oz. 590 calories, 32g fat, 70g protein
2g net carbs: Cilantro Lime Barramundi, no rice, no sauce 370 calories, 12g fat, 45g protein
2g net carbs: Jumbo Grilled Shrimp Skewers (2) 400 calories, 12g fat, 38g protein
2g net carbs: New York Strip, 12 oz. 980 calories, 81g fat, 75g protein
2g net carbs: Steak & Grilled Shrimp Skewers (2), no rice 620 calories, 42g fat, 44g protein
3g net carbs: Cedar Plank Salmon, no glaze 350 calories, 20g fat, 32g protein
3g net carbs: Double Lobster Tail 460 calories, 14g fat, 40g protein
3g net carbs: Fresh Grilled Salmon 370 calories, 23g fat, 58g protein

---

[48] *That's Not Keto!* – You'll find all sorts of surprising foods listed here. I'm not telling you whether you should eat these foods or not. What fits your macros or daily carb spend is up to you. No keto police allowed.

3g net carbs: Steak & Grilled Malibu Chicken® 820 calories, 63g fat, 51g protein
4g net carbs: Bourbon Peppercorn Sirloin Cut, no crispy onions, easy sauce 540 calories, 26g fat, 37g protein
4g net carbs: Italian Herb Chicken 420 calories, 22g fat, 32g protein
4g net carbs: Steak & Italian Herb Chicken 740 calories, 58g fat, 48g protein
5g net carbs: Bacon Wrapped Sirloin Filets 560 calories, 35g fat, 49g protein
5g net carbs: BBQ Ribs, Half-Rack, super easy BBQ sauce 580 calories, 29g fat, 28g protein
5g net carbs: Chopped Steak, 8 oz. 519 calories, 30g fat, 42g protein
5g net carbs: Classic Steak Trio with grilled shrimp and grilled chicken 790 calories, 59g fat, 73g protein
5g net carbs: Shrimp Scampi Linguine, substitute grilled/steamed vegetables for pasta 580 calories, 21g fat, 28g protein
6g net carbs: BBQ Ribs (3 bones) & BBQ Chicken, 7 oz. super easy BBQ sauce (both) 450 calories, 40g fat, 53g protein
6g net carbs: Big Appetite Trio, grilled 880 calories, 50g fat, 65g protein
6g net carbs: Burgundy Mushroom Sirloin Tips on Vegetable Medley 680 calories, 48g fat, 44g protein
6g net carbs: Tripilicious - Steak, Ribs & Grilled Shrimp, easy BBQ sauce 770 calories, 48g fat, 79g protein
7g net carbs: Steak & Hibachi Chicken 690 calories, 46g fat, 37g protein
8g net carbs: BBQ Ribs, Full-Rack, super easy BBQ sauce 850 calories, 57g fat, 55g protein

Steak Toppings

4g net carbs: Sauteed Button Mushroom 180 calories, 17g fat, 4g protein
6g net carbs: Grilled Onion 80 calories, 6g fat, 1g protein

Butter & Sauces (1.5 oz. Unless Otherwise Indicated)

0g net carbs: Hibachi Sauce 1 oz. 46 calories, 0g fat, 2g protein
0g net carbs: Malibu Sauce 270 calories, 30g fat, 0g protein
0g net carbs: Savory Butter 383 calories, 43g fat, 0g protein
3g net carbs: Burger Sauce 1 oz. 56 calories, 6g fat, 0g protein
3g net carbs: Burgundy Mushroom Sauce 2 oz. 4 calories, 3g fat, 0g protein
4g net carbs: Cocktail Sauce 42 calories, 0g fat, 2g protein
4g net carbs: Garlic Margarine 265 calories, 29g fat, 0g protein
4g net carbs: Lemon Herb Sauce 1 oz. 45 calories, 4g fat, 8g protein
5g net carbs: Dill Tartar Sauce 210 calories, 23g fat, 7g protein
7g net carbs: Honey Butter[49] 276 calories, 27g fat, 0g protein
7g net carbs: Maple Butter* .5 oz. 75 calories, 2g fat, 0g protein
8g net carbs: BBQ Sauce* .5 oz. 30 calories, 0g fat, 0g protein

Additions

0g net carbs: Additional Chicken Breast 170 calories, 8g fat, 16g protein
0g net carbs: Additional Serving Tri-Tip Steak 330 calories, 34g fat, 38g protein
2g net carbs: Additional Serving Sauteed Shrimp 180 calories, 24g fat, 26g protein
3g net carbs: Chicken Wings (12) 540 calories, 25g fat, 18g protein

---

[49] *That's Not Keto!* – You'll find all sorts of surprising foods listed here. I'm not telling you whether you should eat these foods or not. What fits your macros or daily carb spend is up to you. No keto police allowed.

Sides

2g net carbs: Caesar Side Salad, no croutons 145 calories, 6g fat, 7g protein
2g net carbs: House Side Salad, no croutons 160 calories, 6g fat, 8g protein
3g net carbs: Broccoli, 5 oz. 5 calories, 0g fat, 4g protein
6g net carbs: Vegetable Medley 5 oz. 80 calories, 4g fat, 3g protein

DRINKS

0g net carbs: Diet Coke 16 oz. 0 calories, 0g fat, 0g protein
0g net carbs: Aquafina Bottled Water 16 oz. bottle 0 calories, 0g fat, 0g protein
2g net carbs: Iced Tea, unsweetened 16 oz. 0 calories, 0g fat, 0g protein

Ruth's Chris Steak House

Ruth's Chris Steak House claims to have a keto menu, but don't be fooled. They don't even provide the macronutrients for these recommended items. Are we supposed to believe it's keto just because they say so? I prefer more transparency.

Calories are listed for some menu items but not others. You will have to hunt online for this information (or ask your local Ruth's Chris Steak House for help). What a pain! They don't even have a Nutrition Information chart (PDF) accessible on their website.

Special Order Tips

Order all burgers and sandwiches with "no bread." Be wary of the available "Add-Ons" since they are often an unnecessary source of net carbs.

Feel free to customize your order. Restaurants are usually happy to accommodate reasonable customer requests. The exception is when the item has been premade or was prepared off-site. Note that any alterations on your end will change the provided nutrition information. Adjust accordingly.

Avoid all fries, potatoes, rice, pasta, bread, etc. Ask the server to substitute a side salad or a side of steamed/grilled vegetables.

You'll notice some menu items indicate a half-serving size. Don't worry; there will only be a few! A smaller portion size allowed us to include more (higher-carb) signature dishes from Ruth's Chris Steak House.

Author Favorite

Lunch & Dinner: Sizzling Blue Crab Cakes to start. Tournedos and Shrimp with Lettuce Wedge, no croutons. Glass of Chateau Ste. Michelle "Indian Wells" Cabernet Sauvignon. 2230 calories, 222g fat, 12g net carbs, 144g protein

LUNCH & DINNER

Starters

0g net carbs: Chilled Seafood Tower with remoulade sauce, no sriracha-lime, no cocktail sauce 360 calories, 5g fat, 80g protein
0g net carbs: Shrimp Remoulade 350 calories, 27g fat, 25g protein
3g net carbs: Seared Ahi Tuna 100 calories, 2g fat, 19g protein
4g net carbs: Barbecued Shrimp, no toast points 400 calories, 26g fat, 20g protein
4g net carbs: Sizzling Blue Crab Cakes 320 calories, 21g fat, 28g protein
5g net carbs: Spicy Shrimp with Half-Serving of cucumber salad 350 calories, 23g fat, 25g protein
6g net carbs: Traditional Escargot 580 calories, 58g fat, 8g protein
7g net carbs: Lobster Bisque, cup 160 calories, 15g fat, 6g protein
10g net carbs: Crispy Lobster Tail 220 calories, 14g fat, 10g protein

Happy Hour Menu

2g net carbs: Sizzling Jumbo Scallops 340 calories, 35g fat, 37g protein
3g net carbs: Lamb Lollipop Chops, no mango chutney marmalade 410 calories, 45g fat, 32g protein
3g net carbs: Roasted Artisan Grilled Chicken Sandwich, breadless 770 calories, 32g fat, 52g protein
3g net carbs: Seared Ahi Tuna 130 calories, 2g fat, 23g protein
4g net carbs: USDA Prime Burger, bunless 740 calories, 64g fat, 51g protein
5g net carbs: Black and Blue Lettuce Wraps 980 calories, 15g fat, 27g protein
5g net carbs: Steak Sandwich, breadless 1280 calories, 68g fat, 47g protein

Salads

2g net carbs: Chilled Shellfish Salad 240 calories, 4g fat, 8g protein
4g net carbs: Caesar Salad, no croutons 500 calories, 45g fat, 0g protein
4g net carbs: Fresh Mozzarella & Heirloom Tomato Salad, no croutons 230 calories, 13g fat, 11g protein
4g net carbs: Lettuce Wedge, no croutons 210 calories, 5g fat, 0g protein
5g net carbs: Harvest Salad, no croutons, easy dressing 360 calories, 25g fat, 8g protein
5g net carbs: House Salad 180 calories, 5g fat, 0g protein
5g net carbs: Ruth's Chopped Salad, no croutons, no fried onions 370 calories, 18g fat, 13g protein
7g net carbs: Steak House Salad with Thousand Island Dressing, no croutons 150 calories, 34g fat, 28g protein

Entrees (Meat Only)

0g net carbs: Bone-In Filet 470 calories, 24g fat, 62g protein
0g net carbs: Bone-In New York Strip 1010 calories, 75g fat, 80g protein
0g net carbs: Cowboy Ribeye 1690 calories, 73g fat, 75g protein
0g net carbs: Filet 500 calories, 11g fat, 70g protein
0g net carbs: Lamb Chops 860 calories, 70g fat, 56g protein

0g net carbs: New York Strip 1390 calories, 122g fat, 75g protein
0g net carbs: Petite Filet Mignon, 8 oz. 340 calories, 20g fat, 40g protein
0g net carbs: Petite, 6 oz. Filet & Shrimp 210 calories, 20g fat, 0g protein
0g net carbs: Pork Chop 720 calories, 65g fat, 52g protein
0g net carbs: Porterhouse for Two 2260 calories, 169g fat, 186g protein
0g net carbs: Ribeye 1152 calories, 68g fat, 128g protein
0g net carbs: T-Bone 1220 calories, 91g fat, 99g protein
0g net carbs: Tournedos and Shrimp 960 calories, 85g fat, 66g protein
1g net carbs: Stuffed Chicken Breast 720 calories, 45g fat, 82g protein
4g net carbs: Tomahawk for Two 1240 calories, 65g fat, 75g protein
10g net carbs: Beef Tenderloin Brochettes 220 calories, 8g fat, 26g protein

Seafood (Seafood Meat Only)

0g net carbs: Fresh Lobster 110 calories, 1g fat, 21g protein
1g net carbs: King Salmon Fillet 380 calories, 33g fat, 28g protein
2g net carbs: Surf and Turf 420 calories, 40g fat, 32g protein
2g net carbs: Tenderloin & Tails for Two 460 calories, 43g fat, 36g protein
3g net carbs: Seared Ahi Tuna 130 calories, 2g fat, 23g protein
5g net carbs: Chilean Sea Bass, no panko garlic crust 920 calories, 71g fat, 40g protein
6g net carbs: Roasted Vegetable Napoleon, easy sauce 260 calories, 14g fat, 14g protein

Add-Ons

0g net carbs: Cremini Mushrooms 360 calories, 0g fat, 0g protein
0g net carbs: Lobster Tail (1) 190 calories, 0g fat, 12g protein
1g net carbs: Fresh Baby Spinach 90 calories, 0g fat, 4g protein
2g net carbs: Fresh Broccoli 80 calories, 1g fat, 7g protein
2g net carbs: Large Shrimp (6), no spices 229 calories, 0g fat, 10g protein
4g net carbs: Grilled Asparagus, no hollandaise 100 calories, 5g fat, 4g protein
6g net carbs: Roasted Brussels Sprouts, no honey butter 120 calories, 15g fat, 7g protein

Sauces (2 Tbsp)

1g net carbs: Bleu Cheese Crust 40 calories, 4g fat, 6g protein
2g net carbs: Bearnaise Sauce 90 calories, 8g fat, 1g protein
2g net carbs: Hollandaise Sauce 85 calories, 17g fat, 6g protein
3g net carbs: Oscar, easy bearnaise sauce 32 calories, 2g fat, 4g protein
4g net carbs: Ruth's Dipping Trio, no honey soy glaze 170 calories, 2g fat, 17g protein
5g net carbs: Sriracha-Lime Seafood Sauce 270 calories, 27g fat, 1g protein

DRINKS

0g net carbs: Diet Coke, 16 oz. 0 calories, 0g fat, 0g protein
0g net carbs: Coke Zero, 16 oz. 0 calories, 0g fat, 0g protein
0g net carbs: Acqua Panna Natural Spring Water, 16 oz 0 calories, 0g fat, 0g protein
0g net carbs: San Pellegrino Sparkling Natural Mineral Water, 16 oz 0 calories, 0g fat, 0g protein

Beer

3g net carbs: Michelob Ultra 12 oz. 95 calories, 0g fat, 1g protein
3g net carbs: Miller Lite 12 oz. 96 calories, 0g fat, 1g protein
5g net carbs: Coors Light 12 oz. 102 calories, 0g fat, 1g protein
5g net carbs: Corona Light 12 oz. 99 calories, 0g fat, 1g protein
7g net carbs: Bud Light 12 oz. 110 calories, 0g fat, 1g protein

Red Wine

3g net carbs: A To Z Wineworks Pinot Noir 140 calories, 0g fat, 0g protein
3g net carbs: Bishop's Peak "Elevation" Proprietary Red 128 calories, 0g fat, 0g protein
3g net carbs: Meiomi Pinot Noir 133 calories, 0g fat, 0g protein
3g net carbs: Penfolds "Koonunga Hills" Shiraz 132 calories, 0g fat, 0g protein
4g net carbs: Chateau Ste. Michelle "Indian Wells" Cabernet Sauvignon 144 calories, 0g fat, 0g protein
4g net carbs: Hogue Merlot 142 calories, 0g fat, 0g protein
4g net carbs: Left Coast Cellars "Cali's Cuvée" Pinot Noir 136 calories, 0g fat, 0g protein
4g net carbs: Louis Vallon "Res. Ltd Release" Cabernet Sauvignon 120 calories, 0g fat, 0g protein
4g net carbs: Parducci "Ruth's Chris Exclusive Blend" Pinot Noir 136 calories, 0g fat, 0g protein
4g net carbs: Rodney Strong Pinot Noir 127 calories, 0g fat, 0g protein
4g net carbs: Schug Pinot Noir 136 calories, 0g fat, 0g protein
4g net carbs: Seven Falls Merlot 120 calories, 0g fat, 0g protein
4g net carbs: Terrazas De Los Andes "Altos Del Plata" Malbec 140 calories, 0g fat, 0g protein
4g net carbs: Zellerbach Merlot 150 calories, 0g fat, 0g protein
5g net carbs: Matua Valley Pinot Noir 128 calories, 0g fat, 0g protein
5g net carbs: Tapiz Malbec 152 calories, 0g fat, 0g protein
5g net carbs: Terrazas De Los Andes "Altos Del Plata" Cabernet Sauvignon 138 calories, 0g fat, 0g protein

White Wine

3g net carbs: Artesa Chardonnay 130 calories, 0g fat, 0g protein
4g net carbs: Estancia Pinot Grigio 128 calories, 0g fat, 0g protein
4g net carbs: Hahn "Slh" Chardonnay 140 calories, 0g fat, 0g protein
4g net carbs: Lagaria Pinot Grigio 136 calories, 0g fat, 0g protein
4g net carbs: Left Coast Cellars "Truffle Hill" Chardonnay 135 calories, 0g fat, 0g protein
4g net carbs: Parducci "Small Lot Blend" Chardonnay 133 calories, 0g fat, 0g protein
4g net carbs: Sonoma Cutrer "Russian River Ranches" Chardonnay 146 calories, 0g fat, 0g protein
5g net carbs: Alexander Valley Vineyards Chardonnay 139 calories, 0g fat, 0g protein
5g net carbs: Loosen Bros. "Dr. L" Riesling 130 calories, 0g fat, 0g protein
5g net carbs: Rodney Strong "Charlotte's Home" Sauvignon Blanc 140 calories, 0g fat, 0g protein
5g net carbs: Terrazas De Los Andes "Altos Del Plata" Chardonnay 120 calories, 0g fat, 0g protein

Sparkling Wine & Champagne

6g net carbs: Chandon "Classic" Brut 130 calories, 0g fat, 0g protein

Cocktails

0g net carbs: House Rum and Diet Coke 100 calories, 0g fat, 0g protein
0g net carbs: Jack and Diet Coke 100 calories, 0g fat, 0g protein
1g net carbs: Ruth's Manhattan 170 calories, 0g fat, 0g protein
2g net carbs: Dirty Goose Martini 410 calories, 3g fat, 1g protein
7g net carbs: Irish Coffee 190 calories, 5g fat, 1g protein
8g net carbs: Ruth's Coffee 180 calories 7g fat, 1g protein
9g net carbs: Ruth's G&T (Gin & Tonic) 430 calories, 0g fat, 0g protein
10g net carbs: Gambler's Old Fashioned 210 calories, 0g fat, 0g protein

Longhorn Steakhouse

Longhorn Steakhouse has a robust website that includes nutrition information for all menu items and their components (sauces, sides, etc.). Click the desired food or drink and then click "View Nutritional Info" below all the dish options. A window will pop up with the base food item at the top, followed by all the available options and toppings. Surprisingly, only Calories, Total Fat, and Sodium are shown, which doesn't do us much good in keto-land. You will have to visit the Nutritional Guide PDF online for the numbers needed to calculate net carbs.

Special Order Tips

Order all burgers and sandwiches with "no bread." Be wary of the available "Add-Ons" since they are often an unnecessary source of net carbs.

Feel free to customize your order. Restaurants are usually happy to accommodate reasonable customer requests. The exception is when the item has been premade or was prepared off-site. Note that any alterations on your end will change the provided nutrition information. Adjust accordingly.

Avoid all fries, potatoes, rice, pasta, bread, etc. Ask the server to substitute a side salad or a side of steamed/grilled vegetables.

Author Favorite

Lunch: 7-Pepper Sirloin Lunch Salad, no croutons, with easy blue cheese dressing. 16 oz. Diet Coke to drink. 340 calories, 21g fat, 5g net carbs, 24g protein

Dinner: Regular-size order Spicy Grilled Chicken Bites, no chili-ginger sauce, easy ranch on the side. Renegade Sirloin

6 oz. with Redrock Grilled Shrimp(8) and Fresh Steamed Broccoli as a side. LongHorn Old Fashioned with sugar-free sweetener. 1670 calories, 73g fat, 14g net carbs, 156g protein

LUNCH

Handhelds (No Bread)

3g net carbs: The LH Burger, bunless, easy housemade burger sauce 980 calories, 63g fat, 54g protein
3g net carbs: Half-Pound Steakhouse Cheeseburger, bunless 1200 calories, 75g fat, 61g protein
4g net carbs: Maverick Ribeye Sandwich, breadless, easy housemade savory sauce 1050 calories, 62g fat, 63g protein

Steakhouse Lunch Plates (No Bread)

3g net carbs: 7-Pepper Sirloin Lunch Salad, no croutons 250 calories, 13g fat, 23g protein
6g net carbs: Half-Pound Steakhouse Cheeseburger (bunless) and Steamed Broccoli Combo 875 calories, 51g fat, 48g protein
6g net carbs: Half-Pound Steakhouse Cheeseburger (bunless) and Caesar Salad, no croutons Combo 915 calories, 55g fat, 50g protein
6g net carbs: Grilled Chicken & Caesar Salad, no croutons 280 calories, 11g fat, 20g protein
7g net carbs: Half-Pound Steakhouse Cheeseburger (bunless) and Mixed Green Salad with ranch, no Croutons Combo 925 calories, 57g fat, 51g protein
8g net carbs: Half-Pound Steakhouse Cheeseburger (bunless) and Fresh Steamed Asparagus Combo 945 calories, 56g fat, 53g protein

Legendary Steaks (Lunch Portion)

1g net carbs: Fire-Grilled T-Bone 18 oz. 1130 calories, 62g fat, 123g protein
1g net carbs: New York Strip/Kansas City Strip 12 oz. 630 calories, 33g fat, 72g protein
1g net carbs: The LongHorn 22 oz. Porterhouse 1280 calories, 67g fat, 150g protein
2g net carbs: Flo's Filet 6 oz. 330 calories, 15g fat, 37g protein
2g net carbs: Outlaw Ribeye 20 oz. 1250 calories, 87g fat, 94g protein
2g net carbs: Renegade Sirloin 6 oz. 320 calories, 15g fat, 36g protein
2g net carbs: Renegade Sirloin 8 oz. 390 calories, 16g fat, 51g protein
3g net carbs: Flo's Filet 9 oz. 450 calories, 19g fat, 56g protein
3g net carbs: USDA Prime Delmonico 16 oz. 1100 calories, 73g fat, 88g protein
4g net carbs: Ribeye 12 oz. 810 calories, 54g fat, 66g protein
5g net carbs: Chop Steak, easy garlic herb sauce 640 calories, 46g fat, 44g protein
5g net carbs: LongHorn Steak Tips, no sauce 520 calories, 27g fat, 53g protein

Beyond Steak (Lunch Portion)

2g net carbs: Baby Back Ribs, Half-Rack, no BBQ sauce 820 calories, 56g fat, 62g protein
4g net carbs: Baby Back Ribs, Full-Rack, no BBQ sauce 1630 calories, 112g fat, 123g protein

2g net carbs: Redrock Grilled Shrimp, 8 count 160 calories, 3g fat, 30g protein
2g net carbs: LongHorn Salmon 7 oz. 300 calories, 16g fat, 33g protein
3g net carbs: LongHorn Salmon 10 oz. 430 calories, 23g fat, 47g protein
4g net carbs: LongHorn Caesar Salad, no croutons 310 calories, 12g fat, 16g protein

5g net carbs: Steamed Asparagus & Mixed Greens Side Salad with ranch, no croutons 140 calories, 10g fat, 9g protein

5g net carbs: Steamed Broccoli & Caesar Side Salad with Caesar Dressing, no croutons 280 calories, 24g fat, 9g protein

5g net carbs: Parmesan Crusted Chicken, easy Parmesan and garlic cheese crust 9 oz. 650 calories, 36g fat, 68g protein

8g net carbs: Parmesan Crusted Chicken, easy Parmesan and garlic cheese crust 12 oz. 1120 calories, 69g fat, 102g protein

8g net carbs: Steamed Okra, remove breading & Mixed Greens Side Salad with ranch, no croutons 240 calories, 18g fat, 12g protein

DINNER

Appetizers

0g net carbs: Seasoned Steakhouse Wings, no sauce 460 calories, 28g fat, 53g protein
3g net carbs: Spicy Grilled Chicken Bites, no chili-ginger sauce, regular 740 calories, 39g fat, 43g protein
5g net carbs: Spicy Grilled Chicken Bites, no chili-ginger sauce, large 920 calories, 49g fat, 54g protein

Legendary Steaks

1g net carbs: Fire-Grilled T-Bone 18 oz. 1130 calories, 62g fat, 123g protein
1g net carbs: New York Strip/Kansas City Strip 12 oz. 630 calories, 33g fat, 72g protein
1g net carbs: The LongHorn 22 oz. Porterhouse 1280 calories, 67g fat, 150g protein
2g net carbs: Flo's Filet 6 oz. 330 calories, 15g fat, 37g protein
3g net carbs: Flo's Filet 9 oz. 450 calories, 19g fat, 56g protein
2g net carbs: Outlaw Ribeye 20 oz. 1250 calories, 87g fat, 94g protein
2g net carbs: Renegade Sirloin 6 oz. 320 calories, 15g fat, 36g protein
2g net carbs: Renegade Sirloin 8 oz. 390 calories, 16g fat, 51g protein
3g net carbs: USDA Prime Delmonico 16 oz. 1100 calories, 73g fat, 88g protein
4g net carbs: Ribeye 12 oz. 810 calories, 54g fat, 66g protein
5g net carbs: Chop Steak, easy garlic herb sauce 640 calories, 46g fat, 44g protein
6g net carbs: LongHorn Steak Tips, no sauce 620 calories, 34g fat, 64g protein

Grill Master Combos

2g net carbs: Flo's Filet 6 oz. with Lobster Tail 420 calories, 18g fat, 51g protein
4g net carbs: Renegade Sirloin 6 oz. with Redrock Grilled Shrimp 480 calories, 18g fat, 66g protein

Great Steak Additions

0g net carbs: Butter 120 calories, 13g fat, 0g protein
0g net carbs: Lobster Tail 90 calories, 3g fat, 14g protein
1g net carbs: Grilled Shrimp 80 calories, 1g fat, 15g protein
2g net carbs: Butter Sauce 210 calories, 22g fat, 0g protein
2g net carbs: Garlic Butter 230 calories, 26g fat, 1g protein
6g net carbs: Grilled Mushrooms 150 calories, 12g fat, 6g protein
10g net carbs: Parmesan Cheese Crust 390 calories, 30g fat, 17g protein

Beyond Steak

0g net carbs: Cowboy Pork Chops 680 calories, 32g fat, 87g protein
1g net carbs: Baby Back Ribs, Half-Rack, no BBQ sauce 820 calories, 56g fat, 62g protein
2g net carbs: Baby Back Ribs, Full-Rack, no BBQ sauce 1630 calories, 112g fat, 123g protein
2g net carbs: LongHorn Salmon 7 oz. 300 calories, 16g fat, 33g protein
3g net carbs: LongHorn Salmon 10 oz. 430 calories, 23g fat, 47g protein
2g net carbs: Redrock Grilled Shrimp (8) 160 calories, 3g fat, 30g protein
3g net carbs: Redrock Grilled Shrimp (12) 240 calories, 4g fat, 46g protein
3g net carbs: Parmesan Crusted Chicken, easy Parmesan and garlic cheese crust 9 oz. 650 calories, 36g fat, 68g protein
8g net carbs: Parmesan Crusted Chicken, easy Parmesan and garlic cheese crust 12 oz. 1120 calories, 69g fat, 102g protein

Steakhouse Sides & Add-Ons

0g net carbs: Bacon (1 Strip) 130 calories, 12g fat, 7g protein
1g net carbs: Cheese (1 Slice) 80 calories, 6g fat, 5g protein
3g net carbs: Fresh Steamed Broccoli 90 calories, 4g fat, 4g protein
4g net carbs: Fresh Steamed Asparagus 130 calories, 7g fat, 8g protein
5g net carbs: Steamed Okra, remove breading, 310 calories, 19g fat, 5g protein
7g net carbs: Crispy Brussels Sprouts, no seasoning 310 calories, 23g fat, 5g protein

Sauces

3g net carbs: Buffalo Sauce 90 calories, 8g fat, 0g protein
3g net carbs: Avocado-Lime Sauce 220 calories, 23g fat, 1g protein
8g net carbs: Honey Mustard 240 calories, 23g fat, 0g protein

Side Salads

3g net carbs: Mixed Greens Salad, no croutons 140 calories, 8g fat, 6g protein
3g net carbs: Caesar Side Salad with Caesar Dressing, no croutons 250 calories, 19g fat, 6g protein

Steakhouse Salads

5g net carbs: Farm Fresh Field Greens with Grilled Chicken, no croutons 650 calories, 35g fat, 46g protein
5g net carbs: Farm Fresh Field Greens with Grilled Salmon, no croutons 530 calories, 29g fat, 43g protein
5g net carbs: LongHorn Caesar Salad with Grilled Chicken, no croutons 670 calories, 43g fat, 46g protein
5g net carbs: LongHorn Caesar Salad with Salmon, no croutons 800 calories, 55g fat, 45g protein
5g net carbs: 7-Pepper Sirloin Salad, no croutons 490 calories, 26g fat, 45g protein
6g net carbs: Grilled Chicken Cobb Salad 910 calories, 60g fat, 58g protein

Salad Add-Ons

0g net carbs: Sliced Egg 25 calories, 2g fat, 2g protein

Salad Dressing

2g net carbs: Ranch 1.5 oz. 230 calories, 25g fat, 1g protein
3g net carbs: Blue Cheese 1.5 oz. 180 calories, 17g fat, 2g protein
4g net carbs: Ranch 3 oz. 460 calories, 49g fat, 2g protein
6g net carbs: Blue Cheese 3 oz. 350 calories, 34g fat, 4g protein
6g net carbs: White Balsamic Vinaigrette 1.5 oz. 200 calories, 20g fat, 0g protein
8g net carbs: Honey Mustard 1.5 oz. 240 calories, 23g fat, 0g protein

DRINKS

0g net carbs: Diet Coke, 16 oz. 0 calories, 0g fat, 0g protein
0g net carbs: Coke Zero Sugar, 16 oz. 0 calories, 0g fat, 0g protein
0g net carbs: Bottled Water, 16 oz. 0 calories, 0g fat, 0g protein
0g net carbs: Mountain Valley Sparkling Bottled Water, 11.3 oz. 0 calories, 0g fat, 0g protein
0g net carbs: Mountain Valley Bottled Water, 11.3 oz. 0 calories, 0g fat, 0g protein
0g net carbs: Hot Coffee, unsweetened, 8 oz. 0 calories, 0g fat, 0g protein
0g net carbs: Hot Coffee Decaf, unsweetened, 8 oz. 0 calories, 0g fat, 0g protein
0g net carbs: Hot Tea, unsweetened, 8 oz. 0 calories, 0g fat, 0g protein
1g net carbs: Iced Tea, unsweetened, 16 oz. 0 calories, 0g fat, 0g protein

Beer

2g net carbs: Michelob Ultra Gold, 12 oz. bottle 85 calories, 0g fat, 1g protein
3g net carbs: Michelob Ultra, 12 oz. bottle 95 calories, 0g fat, 1g protein
3g net carbs: Miller Lite, 12 oz. bottle 96 calories, 0g fat, 1g protein
5g net carbs: Coors Light, 12 oz. bottle 102 calories, 0g fat, 1g protein
6g net carbs: House Light Draft Beer 12 oz. 100 calories, 0g fat, 1g protein
7g net carbs: Bud Light, 12 oz. bottle 110 calories, 0g fat, 1g protein
8g net carbs: House Light Draft Beer 16 oz. 140 calories, 0g fat, 1g protein

Wine

3g net carbs: Ava Grace Rose, 6 oz. 134 calories, 0g fat, 0g protein
3g net carbs: Ecco Domani Pinot Grigio, 6 oz. 118 calories, 0g fat, 0g protein
4g net carbs: Canyon Road Chardonnay, 6 oz. 142 calories, 0g fat, 0g protein
4g net carbs: Chateau Souverain Merlot, 6 oz. glass 165 calories, 0g fat, 0g protein
4g net carbs: Chateau Ste. Michelle Riesling, 6 oz. 130 calories, 0g fat, 0g protein
4g net carbs: House White, 6 oz. glass 150 calories, 0g fat, 0g protein
4g net carbs: Kim Crawford Sauvignon Blanc, 6 oz. 128 calories, 0g fat, 0g protein
4g net carbs: La Crema Pinot Noir, 6 oz. glass 170 calories, 0g fat, 0g protein
4g net carbs: Sidecar Pinot Noir, 6 oz. glass 150 calories, 0g fat, 0g protein
4g net carbs: Woodbridge by Robert Mondavi Cabernet Sauvignon, 6 oz. glass 130 calories, 0g fat, 0g protein
5g net carbs: Ava Grace Rose, 9 oz. Long Pour 162 calories, 0g fat, 0g protein
5g net carbs: Ecco Domani Pinot Grigio, 9 oz. Long Pour 142 calories, 0g fat, 0g protein
5g net carbs: House Red, 6 oz. glass 160 calories, 0g fat, 0g protein
5g net carbs: Kendall-Jackson Vintner's Reserve Chardonnay, 6 oz. 136 calories, 0g fat, 0g protein
6g net carbs: Canyon Road Chardonnay, 9 oz. Long Pour 182 calories, 0g fat, 0g protein
6g net carbs: Chateau Ste. Michelle Riesling, 9 oz. Long Pour 172 calories, 0g fat, 0g protein

6g net carbs: House White, 9 oz. Long Pour 220 calories, 0g fat, 0g protein
6g net carbs: Kim Crawford Sauvignon Blanc, 9 oz. Long Pour 152 calories, 0g fat, 0g protein
6g net carbs: Sidecar Pinot Noir, 9 oz. Long Pour 185 calories, 0g fat, 0g protein
6g net carbs: Woodbridge by Robert Mondavi Cabernet Sauvignon, 9 oz. Long Pour 180 calories, 0g fat, 0g protein
7g net carbs: Chateau Souverain Merlot, 9 oz. Long Pour 220 calories, 0g fat, 0g protein
7g net carbs: Kendall-Jackson Vintner's Reserve Chardonnay, 9 oz. Long Pour 182 calories, 0g fat, 0g protein
7g net carbs: La Crema Pinot Noir, 9 oz. Long Pour 210 calories, 0g fat, 0g protein
8g net carbs: House Red, Long Pour 230 calories, 0g fat, 0g protein

Spirits

0g net carbs: Jack & Diet Coke 90 calories, 0g fat, 0g protein
3g net carbs: LongHorn Old Fashioned with Sugar-free sweetener 250 calories, 0g fat, 0g protein

Outback Steakhouse

Outback Steakhouse has NOT gotten the memo that *carbs* are what folks are watching these days. They have fancy "Gluten-Free" and "Under 600 Calories" call-outs on their menu, but no mention of carbs? Please update, folks. Keto is here to stay!

Outback Steakhouse does not have a customizable online menu or nutrition calculator. They have a detailed Nutrition Information PDF that will help you monitor your carb intake. Be wary of this resource, however. I found multiple errors on the Outback Steakhouse website regarding the nutritional content of beer. For example, a Rogue Chocolate Stout is listed at 2 grams of net carbs. *I don't think so!*

If you're curious, here is the complete list of errors I found: Heineken, Bottle, 12 oz. 0g net carbs, Kentucky Bourbon Barrel, Bottle, 10 oz., <1g net carb, Rogue Chocolate Stout, Bottle, 22 oz. 2g net carbs, Sam Adams Nitro Coffee Stout, Bottle 1g net carb, Samuel Adams Nitro Coffee Stout, Can, 16 oz. 1g net carb, Summit Saga IPA, Big Bloke 1g net carb, Summit Saga IPA, Middy 1g net carb, Surley Furious IRA, Big Bloke 1g net carb, Surley Furious IRA, Middy 1g net carb, Westmalle Trappist Triple, Bottle, 11.2 oz. 1g net carb.

Special Order Tips

Order all burgers and sandwiches with "no bread." Be wary of the available "Add-Ons" since they are often an unnecessary source of net carbs. Avoid all fries, potatoes, rice, pasta, bread, etc. Ask the server to substitute a side salad or a side of steamed/grilled vegetables. Outback Steakhouse serves amazing grilled asparagus. Give it a try?

Feel free to customize your order. Restaurants are usually happy to accommodate reasonable customer requests. The exception is when the item has been premade or was prepared off-site. Note that any alterations on your end will change the provided nutrition information. Adjust accordingly.

Author Favorite

Lunch & Dinner: Regular size medium spicy Kookaburra Wings with ranch. Bunless Sweet Chook O' Mine Sandwich wrapped in a lettuce leaf, no honey mustard sauce. Baby Back Ribs, Half-Rack, super easy BBQ sauce. 10 oz. chilled Spiked Sugar-free Red Bull with Kettle One to drink. 2360 calories, 217g fat, 13g net carbs, 167g protein

LUNCH & DINNER

Appetizers (Wings Flavored with Spices, Ranch or Blue Cheese Dressing Dip)

2g net carbs: Kookaburra Wings Hot, Small 770 calories, 85g fat, 40g protein
2g net carbs: Kookaburra Wings Medium, Small 770 calories, 85g fat, 40g protein
2g net carbs: Kookaburra Wings Mild, Small 770 calories, 85g fat, 40g protein
3g net carbs: Grilled Shrimp on the Barbie, no bread 550 calories, 44g fat, 33g protein
4g net carbs: Kookaburra Wings Hot, Regular 970 calories, 125g fat, 70g protein
4g net carbs: Kookaburra Wings Medium, Regular 970 calories, 125g fat, 70g protein
4g net carbs: Kookaburra Wings Mild, Regular 970 calories, 125g fat, 70g protein
4g net carbs: Seared Peppered Ahi, Large, super easy sauce 470 calories, 28g fat, 32g protein
5g net carbs: Aussie Twisted Ribs 980 calories, 64g fat, 49g protein
6g net carbs: Three Cheese Steak Dip, no chips 860 calories, 113g fat, 28g protein
7g net carbs: Kookaburra Wings Medium, Family Style (20) 2650 calories, 199g fat, 135g protein
7g net carbs: Kookaburra Wings Mild, Family Style (20) 2650 calories, 199g fat, 135g protein

Sammies & Burgers (No Bread, No Side Dishes Unless Otherwise Indicated)

3g net carbs: The Outbacker Burger without Cheese, bunless 630 calories, 43g fat, 40g protein
4g net carbs: Sweet Chook O' Mine Sandwich, breadless, no honey mustard sauce 820 calories, 56g fat, 50g protein
5g net carbs: Grass-Fed Burger with Aged Cheddar, bunless 820 calories, 65g fat, 46g protein
7g net carbs: Prime Rib Sandwich, breadless 1120 calories, 127g fat, 77g protein

Burger Add-Ons

0g net carbs: Bacon 60 calories, 5g fat, 4g protein
0g net carbs: Cheddar Cheese 160 calories, 14g fat, 10g protein
1g net carbs: American Cheese 100 calories, 9g fat, 5g protein
1g net carbs: Provolone Cheese 200 calories, 15g fat, 15g protein
1g net carbs: Swiss Cheese 170 calories, 14g fat, 13g protein

Signature Steaks (No Side Dishes)

0g net carbs: Victoria's Filet Mignon, 6 oz. 240 calories, 9g fat, 40g protein
1g net carbs: Victoria's Filet Mignon, 8 oz. 320 calories, 12g fat, 53g protein
1g net carbs: Victoria's Filet Mignon, 9 oz. 360 calories, 14g fat, 60g protein
0g net carbs: New York Strip, 12 oz. 810 calories, 62g fat, 63g protein
0g net carbs: New York Strip, 13 oz. 880 calories, 67g fat, 68g protein
2g net carbs: New York Strip, Bone-In 16 oz. 710 calories, 29g fat, 104g protein
0g net carbs: Outback Center-Cut Sirloin, 5 oz. 180 calories, 6g fat, 32g protein

0g net carbs: Outback Center-Cut Sirloin, 6 oz. 210 calories, 7g fat, 38g protein
0g net carbs: Outback Center-Cut Sirloin, 8 oz. 280 calories, 9g fat, 51g protein
1g net carbs: Outback Center-Cut Sirloin, 9 oz. 320 calories, 10g fat, 57g protein
1g net carbs: Outback Center-Cut Sirloin, 10 oz. 350 calories, 11g fat, 63g protein
1g net carbs: Outback Center-Cut Sirloin, 11 oz. 390 calories, 12g fat, 70g protein
1g net carbs: Prime Center-Cut Filet, 11 oz. 440 calories, 17g fat, 73g protein
1g net carbs: Prime New York Strip, 16 oz. 1100 calories, 84g fat, 85g protein
0g net carbs: Ribeye, 12 oz. 630 calories, 40g fat, 66g protein
0g net carbs: Ribeye, 13 oz. 710 calories, 45g fat, 75g protein
0g net carbs: Ribeye, 15 oz. 800 calories, 51g fat, 85g protein
1g net carbs: Ribeye, 16 oz. 1290 calories, 102g fat, 87g protein
0g net carbs: Ribeye, Bone-In, 18 oz. 710 calories, 45g fat, 75g protein
0g net carbs: Slow-Roasted Prime Rib, 12 oz. 1050 calories, 86g fat, 69g protein
0g net carbs: Slow-Roasted Prime Rib, 16 oz. 1400 calories, 114g fat, 92g protein
0g net carbs: Slow-Roasted Prime Rib, 24 oz. 2100 calories, 172g fat, 138g protein
8g net carbs: Outback-Style Prime Rib, 12 oz. 1520 calories, 124g fat, 91g protein
8g net carbs: Outback-Style Prime Rib, 16 oz. 1960 calories, 160g fat, 120g protein
8g net carbs: Melbourne/Porterhouse, 22 oz. 860 calories, 57g fat, 80g protein

Steak N' Mate Combos (No Side Dishes)

2g net carbs: Filet, 6 oz. and Lobster Tail 670 calories, 43g fat, 66g protein
2g net carbs: Filet, 8 oz. and Lobster Tail 750 calories, 46g fat, 80g protein
2g net carbs: Filet, 9 oz. and Lobster Tail 790 calories, 48g fat, 86g protein
4g net carbs: Filet & Shrimp on The Barbie, no rice 660 calories, 24g fat, 55g protein
3g net carbs: Ribeye 12 oz. and Grilled Shrimp on the Barbie, remove breading 940 calories, 75g fat, 86g protein
4g net carbs: Ribeye 13 oz. and 4 Grilled Shrimp on The Barbie, remove breading 1220 calories, 81g fat, 94g protein
5g net carbs: Ribeye 15 oz. and 4 Grilled Shrimp on the Barbie, remove breading 1310 calories, 86g fat, 104g protein
1g net carbs: Sirloin 11 oz. and Grilled Chicken 550 calories, 16g fat, 100g protein
1g net carbs: Sirloin 9 oz. and Grilled Chicken 480 calories, 13g fat, 88g protein
2g net carbs: Sirloin 6 oz. and Grilled Chicken 450 calories, 11g fat, 69g protein
3g net carbs: Sirloin 8 oz. and Grilled Chicken 520 calories, 13g fat, 82g protein
3g net carbs: Sirloin, 10 oz. and Grilled Shrimp on the Barbie, remove breading 870 calories, 46g fat, 82g protein
3g net carbs: Sirloin, 5 oz. and Grilled Shrimp on the Barbie, remove breading 690 calories, 41g fat, 51g protein
3g net carbs: Sirloin, 8 oz. and Grilled Shrimp on the Barbie, remove breading 790 calories, 44g fat, 70g protein
3g net carbs: Sirloin, 9 oz. and Grilled Shrimp on the Barbie, remove breading 830 calories, 45g fat, 76g protein
4g net carbs: Sirloin, 11 oz. and Grilled Shrimp on the Barbie, remove breading 900 calories, 48g fat, 89g protein
4g net carbs: Sirloin, 6 oz. and Grilled Shrimp on the Barbie, remove breading 720 calories, 42g fat, 57g protein
5g net carbs: Sirloin, 11 oz. and Grilled Shrimp on the Barbie, remove breading 900 calories, 48g fat, 89g protein
5g net carbs: Sirloin, 12 oz. and Grilled Shrimp on the Barbie, remove breading 940 calories, 49g fat, 95g protein

Steak Mates

1g net carbs: Lobster Tail, 5 oz. Grilled 430 calories, 34g fat, 27g protein
1g net carbs: Lobster Tail, 5 oz. Steamed 340 calories, 25g fat, 27g protein
2g net carbs: Roasted Garlic Butter Topping 160 calories, 16g fat, 1g protein
3g net carbs: Grilled Shrimp 510 calories, 35g fat, 19g protein
6g net carbs: Baby Back Ribs with easy BBQ sauce 480 calories, 36g fat, 47g protein
6g net carbs: Toowoomba Topping 330 calories, 25g fat, 18g protein
7g net carbs: Grilled Onions 110 calories, 4g fat, 2g protein
7g net carbs: Sautéed 'Shrooms 130 calories, 6g fat, 7g protein

Straight from the Sea (Includes Steamed Vegetables)

1g net carbs: Lobster Tail Entrée (2 tails), 3 oz. Tails 400 calories, 26g fat, 36g protein
1g net carbs: Lobster Tail Entrée (2 tails), 4 oz. Tails 440 calories, 27g fat, 44g protein
1g net carbs: Lobster Tail Entrée (2 tails), 5 oz. Tails 490 calories, 28g fat, 53g protein

1g net carbs: Simply Grilled Mahi 220 calories, 3g fat, 47g protein
2g net carbs: Simply Grilled Salmon, 8oz. 600 calories, 46g fat, 43g protein
3g net carbs: Simply Grilled Halibut 460 calories, 23g fat, 55g protein

3g net carbs: Perfectly Grilled Salmon 10 oz. 720 calories, 54g fat, 55g protein
5g net carbs: Toowoomba Salmon 10 oz. 880 calories, 61g fat, 73g protein
6g net carbs: Botany Bay Halibut 480 calories, 23g fat, 55g protein
6g net carbs: Botany Bay Mahi 400 calories, 21g fat, 42g protein
6g net carbs: Grilled Shrimp on the Barbie Entrée 650 calories, 44g fat, 54g protein
6g net carbs: Toowoomba Salmon 8 oz. 760 calories, 53g fat, 61g protein

The "Not" Steaks (Includes Steamed Vegetables)

2g net carbs: Grilled Chicken on the Barbie, no BBQ sauce 350 calories, 17g fat, 21g protein
2g net carbs: Grilled Pork Chop (1 chop) 230 calories, 33g fat, 27g protein
3g net carbs: Alice Springs Chicken, no honey mustard sauce, 5 oz. 440 calories, 27g fat, 42g protein

5g net carbs: Queensland Chicken & Shrimp Pasta, substitute pasta with steamed vegetables 480
    calories, 32g fat, 28g protein
6g net carbs: Queensland Steak & Shrimp Pasta, substitute pasta with steamed vegetables 520 calories,
    34g fat, 31g protein

3g net carbs: Baby Back Ribs, Half-Rack, super easy BBQ sauce 480 calories, 36g fat, 47g protein
6g net carbs: Baby Back Ribs, Full-Rack, super easy BBQ sauce 720 calories, 47g fat, 64g protein

Sides

3g net carbs: Grilled Asparagus 60 calories, 2g fat, 3g protein
3g net carbs: Fresh Seasonal Veggie (Green Beans) 130 calories, 11g fat, 2g protein
4g net carbs: Fresh Seasonal Veggie (Steamed Broccoli) 150 calories, 10g fat, 6g protein

Soup

10g net carbs: Cream of Broccoli, Cup 200 calories, 14g fat, 5g protein

Big Bowl Salads

4g net carbs: Aussie Cobb Salad without Protein, no croutons (Dressing Not Included) 370 calories, 22g fat, 23g protein

5g net carbs: Asian Salad with Chicken (Dressing Not Included), no fried noodles 360 calories, 7g fat, 53g protein

5g net carbs: Asian Salad with Ahi Tuna (Dressing Not Included), no fried noodles 210 calories, 6g fat, 33g protein

5g net carbs: Brisbane Caesar Salad without Protein, no croutons 410 calories, 34g fat, 10g protein

6g net carbs: Blue Cheese Wedge Salad, no croutons 510 calories, 34g fat, 37g protein

7g net carbs: Steakhouse Salad with Blue Cheese Dressing, no Aussie Crunch, no cinnamon pecans 730 calories, 65g fat, 45g protein

Add-Ons

0g net carbs: Grilled Chicken 160 calories, 4g fat, 31g protein

2g net carbs: Grilled Shrimp 160 calories, 4g fat, 26g protein

Side Salads (No Croutons)

1g net carbs: House Salad with Creamy Blue Cheese Dressing (1.5 oz.) 250 calories, 27g fat, 2g protein

1g net carbs: House Salad with Ranch Dressing (1.5 oz.) 210 calories, 23g fat, 1g protein

2g net carbs: House Salad (Dressing Not Included) 140 calories, 8g fat, 7g protein

2g net carbs: House Salad with Caesar Dressing (1.5 oz.) 200 calories, 21g fat, 3g protein

4g net carbs: Caesar Salad with Caesar Dressing (1.5 oz.) 290 calories, 15g fat, 7g protein

4g net carbs: House Salad with Blue Cheese Vinaigrette (1.5 oz.) 230 calories, 20g fat, 1g protein

4g net carbs: House Salad with easy Balsamic Vinaigrette (1.5 oz.) 80 calories, 5g fat, 0g protein

4g net carbs: House Salad with Mustard Vinaigrette (1.5 oz.) 220 calories, 22g fat, 0g protein

6g net carbs: House Salad with Thousand Island Dressing (1.5 oz.) 250 calories, 25g fat, 0g protein

8g net carbs: House Salad with Honey Mustard Dressing (1 oz.) 230 calories, 20g fat, 1g protein

Salad Dressing

1g net carbs: Blue Cheese Dressing (2 oz.) 340 calories, 35g fat, 3g protein

2g net carbs: Caesar (2 oz.) 270 calories, 28g fat, 4g protein

2g net carbs: Ranch (2 oz.) 280 calories, 30g fat, 1g protein

5g net carbs: Balsamic Vinaigrette (1 oz.) 60 calories, 4g fat, 0g protein

5g net carbs: Blue Cheese Vinaigrette (1 oz.) 240 calories, 19g fat, 2g protein

6g net carbs: Mustard Vinaigrette (2 oz.) 290 calories, 30g fat, 0g protein

6g net carbs: Oil & Vinegar (2 oz.) 280 calories, 28g fat, 0g protein

7g net carbs: Thousand Island (2 oz.) 330 calories, 34g fat, 1g protein

DRINKS

0g net carbs: Diet Coke, 16 oz. 0 calories, 0g fat, 0g protein
0g net carbs: Coke Zero, 16 oz. 0 calories, 0g fat, 0g protein
0g net carbs: Dasani Bottled Water, 16 oz. 0 calories, 0g fat, 0g protein
0g net carbs: Aqua Panna Water, 16 oz. bottle 0 calories, 0g fat, 0g protein
0g net carbs: Perrier Water, 16 oz. bottle 0 calories, 0g fat, 0g protein
0g net carbs: San Pellegrino Water, 16 oz. bottle 0 calories, 0g fat, 0g protein
0g net carbs: Gold Peak Coffee, unsweetened, 8 oz. 0 calories, 0g fat, 0g protein
0g net carbs: Gold Peak Iced Tea, unsweetened, 16 oz. 0 calories, 0g fat, 0g protein
2g net carbs: Red Bull, Sugar-free, 8.4 oz. can 10 calories, 0g fat, 0g protein

Beer & Seltzer

2g net carbs: White Claw- 12 oz. can 100 calories, 0g fat, 0g protein
3g net carbs: Michelob ULTRA Pure Gold, Bottle, 12 oz. 90 calories, 0g fat, 1g protein
3g net carbs: Michelob ULTRA, Bottle, 12 oz. 95 calories, 0g fat, 1g protein
3g net carbs: Miller Light, Bottle, 12 oz. 96 calories, 0g fat, 1g protein
5g net carbs: Amstel Light, Bottle, 12 oz. 95 calories, 0g fat, 1g protein
5g net carbs: Bud Light, Small Bloke 80 calories, 0g fat, 1g protein
5g net carbs: Coors Light, Bottle, 12 oz. 102 calories, 0g fat, 1g protein
5g net carbs: Corona Light, Bottle, 12 oz. 99 calories, 0g fat, 1g protein
7g net carbs: Bud Light, Bottle, 12 oz. 110 calories, 0g fat, 1g protein
7g net carbs: Heineken Light, Bottle, 12 oz. 100 calories, 0g fat, 1g protein
8g net carbs: Bud Light, Middy 130 calories, 0g fat, 1g protein
10g net carbs: Bud Light, Big Bloke 170 calories, 0g fat, 1g protein

Wine

4g net carbs: House Red Wine, 5 oz. 130 calories, 0g fat, 0g protein
4g net carbs: House Rose Wine, 5 oz. 130 calories, 0g fat, 0g protein
4g net carbs: House White Wine, 5 oz. 130 calories, 0g fat, 0g protein
5g net carbs: House Red Wine, 6 oz. 150 calories, 0g fat, 0g protein
5g net carbs: House Sparkling Wine, 6 oz. 150 calories, 0g fat, 0g protein
5g net carbs: House White Wine, 6 oz. 150 calories, 0g fat, 0g protein
7g net carbs: House Red Wine, 9 oz. 230 calories, 0g fat, 0g protein
7g net carbs: House White Wine, 9 oz. 230 calories, 0g fat, 0g protein

Cocktails

0g net carbs: Classic Steakhouse Martini (Absolut) - Rocks/Straight-Up 170 calories, 3g fat, 0g protein
0g net carbs: Classic Steakhouse Martini (Grey Goose) - Rocks/Straight-Up 170 calories, 3g fat, 0g protein
0g net carbs: Classic Steakhouse Martini (Kettle One) - Rocks/Straight-Up 170 calories, 3g fat, 0g protein
0g net carbs: Classic Steakhouse Martini (Stoli) - Rocks/Straight-Up 170 calories, 3g fat, 0g protein
0g net carbs: Classic Steakhouse Martini (Tito's) - Rocks/Straight-Up 170 calories, 3g fat, 0g protein
1g net carbs: Kentucky Bourbon Barrel, Bottle, 10 oz. 160 calories, 0g fat, 3g protein
1g net carbs: Kentucky Bourbon Barrel, Bottle, 11 oz. 180 calories, 0g fat, 3g protein
2g net carbs: Spiked Sugar-free Red Bull with Kettle One, 10 oz. 90 calories, 0g fat, 0g protein
3g net carbs: Spiked Sugar-free Red Bull with Absolut Mandarin, 10 oz. 100 calories, 0g fat, 1g protein

3g net carbs: Spiked Sugar-free Red Bull with Finlandia Raspberry Vodka, 10 oz. 90 calories, 0g fat, 0g protein
4g net carbs: Outback Manhattan 180 calories, 0g fat, 0g protein
6g net carbs: The Strawberry Bull, with Sugar-free Red Bull- 16 oz. 25 calories, 0g fat, 0g protein
6g net carbs: Incredible Hulk 160 calories, 4g fat, 1g protein
7g net carbs: Down Under Mule 110 calories, 0g fat, 0g protein
8g net carbs: Fully Loaded Bloody Mary (Absolut) 150 calories, 3g fat, 1g protein
8g net carbs: Fully Loaded Bloody Mary (Tito's) 150 calories, 3g fat, 1g protein
9g net carbs: Sauza Gold Coast Rita, Rocks 130 calories, 0g fat, 0g protein
9g net carbs: Down Under Sauza Gold Coast 'Rita, Rocks 130 calories, 0g fat, 0g protein
9g net carbs: The Ultimate "Dirty" Martini 190 calories, 6g fat, 0g protein
10g net carbs: Espresso Infused Vodka and White Chocolate Martini 100 calories, 0g fat, 0g protein
10g net carbs: Hawaiian Style 'Rita 220 calories, 0g fat, 0g protein

Black Angus

Black Angus' food tastes terrific. But what's in it? There is a thundering lack of ANY macronutrient information on the restaurant's website. The only resource available is a Nutritional Facts PDF. Adding or subtracting ingredients is a chore. Good thing I did all of the work for you here!

When researching the options at Black Angus, I discovered many discrepancies between what's advertised on the menu online versus the provided Nutrition Facts document. For example, salads appear to have croutons, but there is no mention of those in the PDF. And The Classic Martini? There is no mention of the vermouth/olive brine anywhere. The devil is in the details, Black Angus. Get your act together.

Special Order Tips

Order all burgers and sandwiches with "no bread." Be wary of the available "Add-Ons" since they are often an unnecessary source of net carbs. Avoid all fries, potatoes, rice, pasta, bread, etc. Ask the server to substitute a side salad or a side of steamed/grilled vegetables.

Feel free to customize your order. Restaurants are usually happy to accommodate reasonable customer requests. The exception is when the item has been premade or was prepared off-site. Note that any alterations on your end will change the provided nutrition information. Adjust accordingly.

You'll notice some menu items indicate a half-serving size. Don't worry; there will only be a few! A smaller portion size allowed us to include more (higher-carb) crowd-pleasing favorites from Black Angus.

Author Favorite

Lunch & Dinner: Top Sirloin & Grilled Shrimp with easy Cocktail Sauce with Fresh Green Beans on the side. 16 oz. Diet Pepsi to drink. 983 calories, 76g fat, 12g net carbs, 52g protein

LUNCH & DINNER

Steakhouse Starters

6g net carbs: Jumbo Shrimp Cocktail, easy cocktail sauce 180 calories, 2g fat, 24g protein

Steakhouse Bowls (with Base of House Salad Mix, No Crispy Zucchini)

6g net carbs: Steakhouse Bowl with Grilled Shrimp 590 calories, 34g fat, 20g protein
7g net carbs: Steakhouse Bowl with Grilled Chicken 710 calories, 38g fat, 41g protein
7g net carbs: Steakhouse Bowl with Grilled Salmon 800 calories, 48g fat, 41g protein
7g net carbs: Steakhouse Bowl with Top Sirloin 770 calories, 48g fat, 35g protein

Add-Ons (.5 oz.)

6g net carbs: BBQ Sauce[50] 45 calories, 0g fat, 0g protein
6g net carbs: Teriyaki Sauce* 70 calories, 1g fat, 1g protein
7g net carbs: Honey Sriracha Sauce* 58 calories, 0g fat, 0g protein

Salads & Combos (Lunch Size)

3g net carbs: Fire-Grilled Chicken Caesar Salad, no croutons 620 calories, 37g fat, 45g protein
3g net carbs: Steakhouse Cobb Salad 330 calories, 17g fat, 11g protein
5g net carbs: BBQ Chopped Salad with Steak, no BBQ Sauce, no croutons 840 calories, 44g fat, 53g protein
6g net carbs: BBQ Chopped Salad with Tri-Tip, no BBQ Sauce, no croutons 860 calories, 50g fat, 45g protein
6g net carbs: Steakhouse Cobb Salad with Grilled Chicken 510 calories, 8g fat, 33g protein
6g net carbs: The Vegetable Cobb 280 calories, 18g fat, 22g protein
7g net carbs: BBQ Chopped Salad with BBQ Chicken, no BBQ Sauce, no croutons 770 calories, 39g fat, 51g protein
7g net carbs: Steakhouse Cobb Salad with Filet Mignon 570 calories, 34g fat, 32g protein

Campfire Favorites (Lunch Size, with Garden Salad)

0g net carbs: Tri-Tip Steak 350 calories, 21g fat, 36g protein
1g net carbs: Fire-Grilled Chicken Breast 210 calories, 8g fat, 33g protein
2g net carbs: 6 oz. USDA Prime Wrangler 260 calories, 12g fat, 34g protein
2g net carbs: Flame-Grilled Top Sirloin Steak 318 calories, 21g fat, 31g protein
2g net carbs: Grilled Fresh Salmon 300 calories, 18g fat, 32g protein
7g net carbs: Fire-Grilled Jumbo Shrimp, easy Cocktail Sauce 575 calories, 49g fat, 15g protein

---

[50] *That's Not Keto!* – You'll find all sorts of surprising foods listed here. I'm not telling you whether you should eat these foods or not. What fits your macros or daily carb spend is up to you. No keto police allowed.

7g net carbs: Sesame-Teriyaki Chicken Breast, easy Sesame-Teriyaki 280 calories, 10g fat, 34g protein
8g net carbs: Sesame-Teriyaki Top Sirloin, easy Sesame-Teriyaki 360 calories, 19g fat, 33g protein

Burgers & Sandwiches (No Bread, with Garden Salad Instead of Fries or Onion Rings)

4g net carbs: French Dip Sandwich 880 calories, 33g fat, 63g protein
4g net carbs: Grilled Prime Rib Sandwich 1200 calories, 95g fat, 51g protein
5g net carbs: Bacon & Bleu Cheeseburger 1100 calories, 76g fat, 54g protein
5g net carbs: Chicken, Avocado & Bacon Sandwich 840 calories, 47g fat, 54g protein
5g net carbs: New York Steak Sandwich 1060 calories, 52g fat, 62g protein
5g net carbs: Steakhouse Bacon Cheeseburger, no Onion Rings 1130 calories, 73g fat, 66g protein
6g net carbs: Filet Mignon Sandwich 980 calories, 48g fat, 49g protein
6g net carbs: Mushroom & Swiss Burger 890 calories, 58g fat, 47g protein
6g net carbs: Patty Melt 1060 calories, 67g fat, 52g protein

High Noon Feast (with Garden Salad)

0g net carbs: Filet Mignon Medallions 310 calories, 16g fat, 39g protein
0g net carbs: New York Strip Steak 410 calories, 19g fat, 54g protein
2g net carbs: Baby Back Ribs, Half-Rack, no BBQ sauce 710 calories, 37g fat, 36g protein
3g net carbs: Slow-Roasted Prime Rib 930 calories, 78g fat, 49g protein
6g net carbs: Top Sirloin & Grilled Shrimp 543 calories, 29g fat, 41g protein
7g net carbs: Top Sirloin & Jumbo Shrimp, easy Cocktail Sauce 863 calories, 67g fat, 46g protein

Quick Draw Combo (No Bread, with Garden Salad)

7g net carbs: Chicken Sandwich, Half-Serving, no croutons 520 calories, 35g fat, 32g protein
7g net carbs: French Dip, Half-Serving, no croutons 490 calories, 33g fat, 37g protein
8g net carbs: French Dip, Half-Serving, with Fresh Broccoli 540 calories, 38g fat, 36g protein

Steaks (with Garden Salad)

0g net carbs: Filet Mignon Center-Cut 6 oz. 310 calories, 16g fat, 39g protein
0g net carbs: Filet Mignon Center-Cut 8 oz. 410 calories, 20g fat, 52g protein
0g net carbs: New York Strip Center-Cut 12 oz. 480 calories, 23g fat, 65g protein
0g net carbs: New York Strip Center-Cut 14 oz. 560 calories, 26g fat, 76g protein
0g net carbs: Ribeye Steak 12 oz. 600 calories, 35g fat, 72g protein
0g net carbs: Ribeye Steak 16 oz. 790 calories, 45g fat, 95g protein
0g net carbs: Tri-Tip 8 oz. 450 calories, 27g fat, 48g protein
1g net carbs: 18 oz. Bone-In Ribeye 1030 calories, 83g fat, 72g protein
2g net carbs: Top Sirloin Center-Cut 8 oz. 410 calories, 27g fat, 42g protein
3g net carbs: Top Sirloin Center-Cut 11 oz. 550 calories, 35g fat, 57g protein
3g net carbs: USDA Prime Wrangler 8 oz. 340 calories, 15g fat, 45g protein
4g net carbs: Mushroom & Bleu Filet Mignon 6 oz. 540 calories, 36g fat, 47g protein
4g net carbs: Mushroom & Bleu Filet Mignon 8 oz. 630 calories, 40g fat, 60g protein
4g net carbs: USDA Prime Wrangler 12 oz. 490 calories, 21g fat, 67g protein
6g net carbs: Sesame-Teriyaki Top Sirloin, easy Sesame-Teriyaki Sauce 8 oz. 460 calories, 25g fat, 43g protein
8g net carbs: Sesame-Teriyaki Top Sirloin, easy Sesame-Teriyaki Sauce 12 oz. 510 calories, 29g fat, 52g protein

Prime Rib (with Garden Salad)

3g net carbs: 1/2 Pound Cut 930 calories, 78g fat, 49g protein
3g net carbs: 3/4 Pound Cut 1390 calories, 117g fat, 74g protein
3g net carbs: 1 Pound Cut 1850 calories, 157g fat, 99g protein
4g net carbs: 1 1/2 Pounds Cut - Cowboy Cut 2770 calories, 235g fat, 148g protein

Steakhouse Butters

0g net carbs: Bacon & Bleu 160 calories, 16g fat, 4g protein
1g net carbs: Béarnaise 209 calories, 23g fat, 0g protein
1g net carbs: Bistro Butter 158 calories, 18g fat, 0g protein
1g net carbs: Roasted Jalapeño 130 calories, 14g fat, 0g protein
2g net carbs: Caramelized Shallots & Bleu Cheese 211 calories, 22g fat, 2g protein
10g net carbs: Roasted Garlic & Fresh Herb 240 calories, 23g fat, 2g protein

Toppers

3g net carbs: Sautéed Baby Portabella Mushrooms 120 calories, 12g fat, 2g protein
5g net carbs: Combination of both 130 calories, 12g fat, 2g protein
9g net carbs: Sautéed Sweet Onions 150 calories, 11g fat, 1g protein

Steak & Sea Partners (with Garden Salad)

2g net carbs: Filet Mignon, 6 oz. & Twin Lobster Tails 770 calories, 56g fat, 65g protein
3g net carbs: Prime Rib, 8 oz. & Twin Lobster Tails 1380 calories, 118g fat, 75g protein
3g net carbs: Ribeye, 12 oz. & Twin Lobster Tails 1060 calories, 74g fat, 97g protein
6g net carbs: Filet Mignon, 6 oz. & Grilled Shrimp, easy cocktail sauce 750 calories, 55g fat, 53g protein
6g net carbs: Ribeye, 12 oz. & Grilled Jumbo Shrimp, easy cocktail sauce 1060 calories, 74g fat, 85g protein
7g net carbs: Prime Rib, 8 oz. & Grilled Jumbo Shrimp, easy cocktail sauce 1380 calories, 117g fat, 63g protein

Chicken & Pork (with Garden Salad)

1g net carbs: Fire-Grilled Chicken Breasts 430 calories, 16g fat, 66g protein
4g net carbs: Baby Back Ribs, Half-Rack, no BBQ Sauce 710 calories, 37g fat, 36g protein
4g net carbs: Porterhouse Pork Chop 650 calories, 43g fat, 61g protein
6g net carbs: Baby Back Ribs, Full-Rack, no BBQ Sauce 1310 calories, 74g fat, 73g protein
6g net carbs: BBQ Chicken & Ribs, no BBQ Sauce 980 calories, 46g fat, 69g protein
8g net carbs: Sesame-Teriyaki Chicken Breasts, easy Sesame-Teriyaki sauce 500 calories, 18g fat, 67g protein

Just the Sea (with Garden Salad)

2g net carbs: Grilled Fresh Salmon 390 calories, 23g fat, 41g protein
2g net carbs: Twin Cold-Water Lobster Tails 460 calories, 39g fat, 26g protein
7g net carbs: Grilled Fresh Salmon with Grilled Shrimp, easy cocktail sauce 520 calories, 41g fat, 16g protein
8g net carbs: Fire-Grilled Jumbo Shrimp, easy cocktail sauce 620 calories, 49g fat, 21g protein

Classic Sidekicks

3g net carbs: Fresh Broccoli 120 calories, 10g fat, 3g protein
3g net carbs: Garden Salad, no croutons 90 calories, 2g fat, 3g protein
5g net carbs: Fresh Green Beans 120 calories, 9g fat, 6g protein
6g net carbs: Clam Chowder, Half-Serving, 140 calories, 7g fat, 4g protein
6g net carbs: Loaded Baked Potato Soup[51], Half-Serving, 130 calories, 9g fat, 7g protein
8g net carbs: Steak Soup 90 calories, 3g fat, 6g protein
9g net carbs: Coleslaw 150 calories, 12g fat, 1g protein

Premium Sidekicks

2g net carbs: Grilled Asparagus 60 calories, 4g fat, 3g protein
4g net carbs: Caesar Salad, no croutons 390 calories, 30g fat, 14g protein
4g net carbs: Wedge Salad 340 calories, 30g fat, 13g protein
6g net carbs: Roasted Brussels Sprouts 190 calories, 16g fat, 3g protein

Salads (No Croutons)

4g net carbs: Steakhouse Cobb Salad, easy vinaigrette 230 calories, 27g fat, 11g protein
5g net carbs: Steakhouse Cobb Salad with Grilled Chicken, easy vinaigrette 610 calories, 28g fat, 43g protein
6g net carbs: Steakhouse Cobb Salad with Filet Mignon, easy vinaigrette 670 calories, 24g fat, 42g protein
6g net carbs: Steakhouse Cobb Salad with Fire-Grilled Jumbo Shrimp, easy vinaigrette 660 calories, 31g fat, 39g protein
6g net carbs: Steakhouse Cobb Salad with Grilled Fresh Salmon, easy vinaigrette 700 calories, 28g fat, 42g protein
5g net carbs: BBQ Chopped Salad with Steak, no BBQ Sauce 840 calories, 44g fat, 53g protein
6g net carbs: BBQ Chopped Salad with Tri-Tip, no BBQ Sauce 860 calories, 50g fat, 45g protein
7g net carbs: BBQ Chopped Salad with BBQ Chicken, no BBQ Sauce 770 calories, 39g fat, 51g protein
4g net carbs: Tomato, Mozzarella & Basil Salad 420 calories, 23g fat, 21g protein
6g net carbs: The Vegetable Cobb 280 calories, 28g fat, 22g protein

Salad Dressing

1g net carbs: Bleu Cheese 130 calories, 13g fat, 2g protein
1g net carbs: House Vinaigrette 150 calories, 17g fat, 0g protein
1g net carbs: Ranch 100 calories, 11g fat, 1g protein
5g net carbs: Thousand Island 100 calories, 9g fat, 0g protein
6g net carbs: Honey Mustard* 160 calories, 16g fat, 0g protein

DRINKS

0g net carbs: Diet Pepsi, 16 oz. 0 calories, 0g fat, 0g protein
0g net carbs: San Pellegrino Water, 16 oz. bottle 0 calories, 0g fat, 0g protein

---

[51] *That's Not Keto!* – You'll find all sorts of surprising foods listed here. I'm not telling you whether you should eat these foods or not. What fits your macros or daily carb spend is up to you. No keto police allowed.

0g net carbs: Acqua Panna Water, 16 oz. bottle 0 calories, 0g fat, 0g protein
0g net carbs: Coffee, brewed, unsweetened, 5 oz. 0 calories, 0g fat, 0g protein
0g net carbs: Decaf coffee, unsweetened, 5 oz. 0 calories, 0g fat, 0g protein
0g net carbs: Iced tea, unsweetened, 16 oz. 0 calories, 0g fat, 0g protein

Draft Beer

5g net carbs: Bud Light 14 oz. 120 calories, 0g fat, 1g protein
9g net carbs: Bud Light 23 oz. 200 calories, 0g fat, 2g protein
6g net carbs: Coors Light 14 oz. 120 calories, 0g fat, 1g protein
10g net carbs: Coors Light 23 oz. 200 calories, 0g fat, 1g protein

Bottled Beer

3g net carbs: Miller Light 12 oz. 96 calories, 0g fat, 1g protein
3g net carbs: Michelob Ultra 12 oz. 95 calories, 0g fat, 1g protein
5g net carbs: Coors Light 12 oz. 102 calories, 0g fat, 1g protein
7g net carbs: Heineken Light 12 oz. 100 calories, 0g fat, 1g protein

Red Wine

4g net carbs: Chateau St Jean Pinot Noir 6 oz. 140 calories, 0g fat, 0g protein
4g net carbs: Greg Norman Pinot Noir 6 oz. 140 calories, 0g fat, 0g protein
6g net carbs: Chateau St Jean Pinot Noir 9 oz. 220 calories, 0g fat, 0g protein
6g net carbs: Greg Norman Pinot Noir 9 oz. 220 calories, 0g fat, 0g protein
5g net carbs: Century Cellars Merlot, 6 oz. 140 calories, 0g fat, 0g protein
6g net carbs: Blackstone Merlot, 6 oz. 140 calories, 0g fat, 0g protein
7g net carbs: Century Cellars Merlot, 9 oz. 210 calories, 0g fat, 0g protein
9g net carbs: Blackstone Merlot, 9 oz. 210 calories, 0g fat, 0g protein
5g net carbs: DAOU Cabernet 6 oz. 150 calories, 0g fat, 0g protein
5g net carbs: Mondavi Barrel-Aged Cabernet 6 oz. 150 calories, 0g fat, 0g protein
5g net carbs: Rodney Strong Cabernet 6 oz. 150 calories, 0g fat, 0g protein
6g net carbs: Canyon Road Cabernet 6 oz. 160 calories, 0g fat, 0g protein
6g net carbs: Robert Mondavi Private Cabernet 6 oz. 140 calories, 0g fat, 0g protein
7g net carbs: DAOU Cabernet 9 oz. 220 calories, 0g fat, 0g protein
7g net carbs: Mondavi Barrel-Aged Cabernet 9 oz. 220 calories, 0g fat, 0g protein
7g net carbs: Rodney Strong Cabernet 9 oz. 230 calories, 0g fat, 0g protein
9g net carbs: Canyon Road Cabernet 9 oz. 230 calories, 0g fat, 1g protein
9g net carbs: Robert Mondavi Private Cabernet 9 oz. 210 calories, 0g fat, 0g protein

5g net carbs: Diseño Malbec 6 oz. 140 calories, 0g fat, 0g protein
8g net carbs: Diseño Malbec 9 oz. 220 calories, 0g fat, 0g protein
7g net carbs: Menage a Trois Red Blend 6 oz. 150 calories, 0g fat, 0g protein
10g net carbs: Menage a Trois Red Blend 9 oz. 230 calories, 0g fat, 0g protein

White Wine

3g net carbs: Mionetto Prosecco 187 calories, 0g fat, 0g protein
3g net carbs: Chateau Ste Michelle Chardonnay 6 oz. 180 calories, 0g fat, 0g protein

5g net carbs: Century Cellars Chardonnay 6 oz. 140 calories, 0g fat, 0g protein
5g net carbs: Chateau Ste Michelle Chardonnay 9 oz. 280 calories, 0g fat, 0g protein
5g net carbs: Kendall Jackson Chardonnay 6 oz. 160 calories, 0g fat, 0g protein
7g net carbs: Century Cellars Chardonnay 9 oz. 220 calories, 0g fat, 0g protein

4g net carbs: Ecco Domani Pinot Grigio 6 oz. 140 calories, 0g fat, 0g protein
5g net carbs: Ecco Domani Pinot Grigio 9 oz. 220 calories, 0g fat, 1g protein
4g net carbs: Matua Sauvignon Blanc 6 oz. 130 calories, 0g fat, 0g protein
6g net carbs: Matua Sauvignon Blanc 9 oz. 200 calories, 0g fat, 0g protein
4g net carbs: Kim Crawford 6 oz. 120 calories, 0g fat, 0g protein
6g net carbs: Kim Crawford 9 oz. 170 calories, 0g fat, 0g protein

Favorites

8g net carbs: Mimosa 210 calories, 0g fat, 0g protein

'Ritas

3g net carbs: Cadillac 'Rita 240 calories, 0g fat, 0g protein
4g net carbs: Strawberry 'Rita 215 calories, 0g fat, 0g protein
9g net carbs: Peach 'Rita 235 calories, 0g fat, 0g protein

Marys

8g net carbs: Signature Bloody Mary 170 calories, 2g fat, 2g protein
8g net carbs: Tequila Mary 170 calories, 2g fat, 2g protein

Boilermakers

5g net carbs: All American 220 calories, 0g fat, 1g protein

Classic Cocktails

0g net carbs: Beefeater Martini 250 calories, 2g fat, 0g protein
0g net carbs: Original Texas Tea with Diet Coke 100 calories, 0g fat, 1g protein
0g net carbs: Smirnoff Martini 240 calories, 2g fat, 0g protein
1g net carbs: Top Shelf Martini Ketel One 210 calories, 1g fat, 1g protein
1g net carbs: Top Shelf Martini Tanqueray 220 calories, 1g fat, 1g protein
5g net carbs: Bulls Eye Old Fashioned with sugar-free sweetener 200 calories, 0g fat, 0g protein
7g net carbs: Steakhouse Manhattan 200 calories, 0g fat, 0g protein

Red Lobster

Red Lobster boasts a sleek Interactive Nutrition Calculator that allows you to sort carbs from low to high for each menu category. It's a shame that it doesn't let you customize dishes and add and subtract sides and add-ons. Until they upgrade the tool, use the detailed "Interactive Nutrition Menu" document from the Red Lobster website to learn about each food. This document will help you be in control of your carb intake. Click Nutritional Information at the bottom of the main page, and the Nutrition Calculator and Interactive Nutrition Menu open. Now your search for keto-friendly food may begin!

Special Order Tips

Order all burgers and sandwiches with "no bread." Be wary of the available "Add-Ons" since they are often an unnecessary source of net carbs. Avoid all fries, potatoes, rice, pasta, bread, etc. Ask the server to substitute a side salad or a side of steamed/grilled vegetables.

Feel free to customize your order. Restaurants are usually happy to accommodate reasonable customer requests. The exception is when the item has been premade or was prepared off-site. Note that any alterations on your end will change the provided nutrition information. Adjust accordingly.

You'll notice some menu items indicate a half-serving size. Don't worry; there will only be a couple! Smaller portions allowed us to include popular (higher-carb) signature dishes from Red Lobster.

Author Favorite

Lunch: Bacon-Wrapped Sea Scallops Appetizer to start. Bunless Wagyu Bacon Cheeseburger with Green Beans on the side. 16 oz. unsweetened Iced Tea to drink 1330 calories, 87g fat, 14g net carbs, 76g protein

Dinner: Ultimate Surf & Turf with broccoli and green beans on the side. House Wine- 6 oz. 1130 calories, 64g fat, 17g net carbs, 79g protein

LUNCH

Starters

5g net carbs: Bacon-Wrapped Sea Scallops Appetizer 340 calories, 24g fat, 21g protein
6g net carbs: White Wine and Roasted-Garlic Mussels, no bread 880 calories, 53g fat, 31g protein
7g net carbs: Signature Jumbo Shrimp Cocktail, easy sauce 130 calories, 0g fat, 16g protein

Burgers, Bowls & Sandwiches (No Bread)

3g net carbs: Wagyu Bacon Cheeseburger, bunless 900 calories, 57g fat, 53g protein
6g net carbs: Nashville Hot Grilled Chicken Sandwich, bunless 920 calories, 51g fat, 47g protein
6g net carbs: Grilled Salmon Bowl, no glaze, no quinoa 870 calories, 41g fat, 45g protein
6g net carbs: Baja Shrimp Bowl, no beans, no quinoa rice, no tortilla strips 630 calories, 40g fat, 31g protein

Soups

10g net carbs: New England Clam Chowder-Cup 240 calories, 15g fat, 7g protein

DINNER

Entrees with Steamed/Grilled Vegetables

0g net carbs: Endless Grilled Shrimp (Refill Order) 80 calories, 3g fat, 11g protein
0g net carbs: Wild Caught Dungeness Crab 420 calories, 31g fat, 27g protein
0g net carbs: Wild-Caught Snow Crab Legs 440 calories, 34g fat, 32g protein
1g net carbs: Create Your Own, Atlantic Salmon 310 calories, 19g fat, 32g protein
1g net carbs: Simply Grilled Atlantic Salmon 630 calories, 39g fat, 64g protein
1g net carbs: Simply Grilled Rainbow Trout 490 calories, 22g fat, 67g protein
1g net carbs: Steak-and-Lobster Wednesday 700 calories, 53g fat, 54g protein
1g net carbs: Steaks, 12 oz. NY Strip 600 calories, 36g fat, 66g protein
1g net carbs: Steaks, 7 oz. Sirloin 290 calories, 13g fat, 41g protein
2g net carbs: Steaks, 6 oz. Filet Mignon 270 calories, 14g fat, 34g protein
2g net carbs: Endless Garlic Shrimp Scampi (Refill) 220 calories, 18g fat, 12g protein
3g net carbs: Ultimate Surf & Turf 850 calories, 58g fat, 74g protein
4g net carbs: Lobster, Shrimp & Salmon 710 calories, 50g fat, 57g protein
4g net carbs: Two for Tuesday, Lobster, Shrimp & Salmon 710 calories, 50g fat, 57g protein
4g net carbs: Salmon New Orleans 650 calories, 29g fat, 34g protein
5g net carbs: Create Your Own, Garlic Shrimp Scampi 430 calories, 35g fat, 24g protein
5g net carbs: Endless Garlic Shrimp Scampi (Initial) 430 calories, 35g fat, 24g protein

5g net carbs: Endless Grilled Shrimp (Initial), no rice 220 calories, 10g fat, 25g protein

6g net carbs: Simply Grilled Garlic Shrimp Skewers, no glaze 320 calories, 10g fat, 25g protein

7g net carbs: Baja Shrimp Bowl, no beans, no quinoa, no tortilla strips 630 calories, 70g fat, 41g protein

7g net carbs: Salmon New Orleans 890 calories, 60g fat, 74g protein

7g net carbs: Seaside Shrimp Trio, substitute Walt's Favorite Shrimp with plain grilled shrimp 800 calories, 52g fat, 46g protein

7g net carbs: Ultimate Feast, substitute Walt's Favorite Shrimp with plain grilled shrimp 870 calories, 48g fat, 44g protein

8g net carbs: Lobster Lover's Dream, Substitute linguini with Steamed/Grilled Vegetables 1,130 calories, 57g fat, 63g protein

Pasta (Substitute Steamed/Grilled Vegetables for Pasta)

5g net carbs: Cajun Chicken Linguini Alfredo 670 calories, 34g fat, 43g protein

6g net carbs: Shrimp Linguini Alfredo 790 calories, 32g fat, 33g protein

6g net carbs: Lobster Linguini 720 calories, 29g fat, 38g protein

Sides & Add-Ons

0g net carbs: Snow Crab Legs with lemon and butter 440 calories, 34g fat, 32g protein

1g net carbs: Maine Lobster Tail Add-On 370 calories, 36g fat, 12g protein

2g net carbs: Garlic Shrimp Scampi (No pasta) with garlic sauce and lemon 220 calories, 18g fat, 12g protein

5g net carbs: Broccoli 40 calories, 0g fat, 3g protein

5g net carbs: Crispy Brussels Sprouts, no tortilla strips 280 calories, 17g fat, 11g protein

5g net carbs: Green Beans 90 calories, 6g fat, 2g protein

6g net carbs: Garlic Shrimp Skewers 320 calories, 10g fat, 25g protein

8g net carbs: Coleslaw 110 calories, 8g fat, 2g protein

Salads (No Croutons)

4g net carbs: Classic Caesar Salad 520 calories, 46g fat, 10g protein

5g net carbs: Classic Caesar Salad with Grilled Chicken 720 calories, 50g fat, 48g protein

5g net carbs: Classic Caesar Salad with Seasoned Shrimp 660 calories, 51g fat, 33g protein

5g net carbs: Side Caesar Salad 290 calories, 25g fat, 5g protein

6g net carbs: Classic Caesar Salad with Salmon 830 calories, 65g fat, 41g protein

Salad Dressing & Condiments

0g net carbs: 100% Pure Melted Butter 300 calories, 33g fat, 0g protein

0g net carbs: Butter 80 calories, 8g fat, 0g protein

0g net carbs: Sour Cream 25 calories, 2g fat, 0g protein

0g net carbs: Caesar Dressing 300 calories, 32g fat, 2g protein

2g net carbs: Blue Cheese Dressing 230 calories, 24g fat, 2g protein

2g net carbs: Pico de Gallo 10 calories, 0g fat, 0g protein

2g net carbs: Ranch Dressing 150 calories, 16g fat, 0g protein

4g net carbs: Marinara Sauce 35 calories, 2g fat, 0g protein

4g net carbs: Tartar Sauce 210 calories, 21g fat, 0g protein

8g net carbs: Thousand Island Dressing 210 calories, 19g fat, 0g protein

9g net carbs: Honey Mustard Dressing[52] 200 calories, 18g fat, 0g protein
10g net carbs: Cocktail Sauce* 45 calories, 0g fat, 0g protein
10g net carbs: French Dressing* 180 calories, 16g fat, 0g protein

DRINKS

0g net carbs: Diet Pepsi, 12 oz. can 0 calories, 0g fat, 0g protein
0g net carbs: Coffee, unsweetened 8 oz. 0 calories, 0g fat, 0g protein
1g net carbs: Iced Tea, unsweetened 16 oz. 0 calories, 0g fat, 0g protein

Beer

6g net carbs: 12 oz. House Bottled Beer - Light 100 calories, 0g fat, 1g protein
7g net carbs: 14 oz. House Draft Beer - Light 120 calories, 0g fat, 1g protein
10g net carbs: 20 oz. House Draft Beer - Light 170 calories, 0g fat, 1g protein

Wine

5g net carbs: House Wine-6 oz. 150 calories, 0g fat, 0g protein
7g net carbs: House Wine-9 oz. 220 calories, 0g fat, 0g protein
10g net carbs: Sparkling Wine (Split) 160 calories, 0g fat, 0g protein

Spirits

8g net carbs: Classic Margarita-Rocks 120 calories, 0g fat, 0g protein

---

[52] *That's Not Keto!* – You'll find all sorts of surprising foods listed here. I'm not telling you whether you should eat these foods or not. What fits your macros or daily carb spend is up to you. No keto police allowed.

Bonefish Grill

Bonefish Grill does not have a customizable nutrition calculator on its website, but they have a detailed Nutritional Information PDF to help you monitor your carb intake. Here are a few watch-outs.

I recommend avoiding any of the three Specialty Toppings (entrees): Imperial Topping, Oscar Topping, and Lily's Topping. I cannot find nutrition information about these toppings online, so it's best to stay away.

Special Order Tips

Order all burgers and sandwiches with "no bread." Be wary of the available "Add-Ons" since they are often an unnecessary source of net carbs. Avoid all fries, potatoes, rice, pasta, bread, etc. Ask the server to substitute a side salad or a side of steamed/grilled vegetables. At Bonefish Grill, sauteed asparagus or a side of green beans make an excellent choice.

Feel free to customize your order. Restaurants are usually happy to accommodate reasonable customer requests. The exception is when the item has been premade or was prepared off-site. Note that any alterations on your end will change the provided nutrition information. Adjust accordingly.

You'll notice some menu items indicate a half-serving size. Don't worry; there might be just one or two. A smaller portion size allowed us to include more (higher-carb) crowd-pleasing favorites from the Bonefish Grill.

Author Favorite

Breakfast: Eggs Benedict: Bang Bang Grilled Shrimp with 3 oz. unsweetened Espresso to drink. 825 calories, 42g fat, 13g net carbs, 38g protein

Lunch: Breadless Blackened BFG Fish Sandwich- Grouper with Side Salad- House, no pepitas. 16 oz. Coke Zero to drink. 950 calories, 47g fat, 8g net carbs, 61g protein

Dinner: Ahi Tuna Sashimi, Regular, no sauce to start. Steak & Lobster Tail, 7 oz. Sirloin with Sauteed Asparagus. 1901 Dirty Martini to drink. 1120 calories, 50g fat, 15g net carbs, 99g protein

BREAKFAST

Brunch Specials (No Bread, No Fries)

2g net carbs: BFG Ahi Tuna Steak & Eggs 1060 calories, 76g fat, 65g protein
2g net carbs: BLT: Ahi Tuna 1100 calories, 61g fat, 64g protein
3g net carbs: Omelet: California without Toast 660 calories, 46g fat, 33g protein
4g net carbs: Omelet: Oscar without Toast 640 calories, 42g fat, 32g protein
4g net carbs: Omelet: Oscar, with Egg Whites without Toast 520 calories, 28g fat, 33g protein
5g net carbs: Eggs Benedict: Filet Mignon and Lobster 970 calories, 55g fat, 59g protein
5g net carbs: Eggs Benedict: Traditional 700 calories, 34g fat, 38g protein
5g net carbs: Greens, Eggs & Ham 890 calories, 60g fat, 36g protein
5g net carbs: Omelet: California, with Egg Whites 520 calories, 30g fat, 34g protein
5g net carbs: Traditional Sirloin Steak & Eggs 1050 calories, 77g fat, 60g protein
6g net carbs: BLT: Lobster 980 calories, 51g fat, 45g protein
6g net carbs: Crab Cake Rancheros with Egg, no sauce 970 calories, 81g fat, 28g protein
6g net carbs: Crab Cake Rancheros, no sauce 870 calories, 74g fat, 21g protein
6g net carbs: Eggs Benedict: Bang Bang Grilled Shrimp 780 calories, 40g fat, 37g protein

Brunch Add-Ons

0g net carbs: Fried Egg (1) 100 calories, 8g fat, 7g protein
0g net carbs: Poached Egg (1) 80 calories, 5g fat, 7g protein
0g net carbs: Bacon (3 slices) 90 calories, 7g fat, 7g protein

LUNCH

4g net carbs: Tacos: Blackened Baja Fish (2), no tortillas, no mango salsa 460 calories, 23g fat, 28g protein
4g net carbs: Tacos: Chicken (2), no tortillas 530 calories, 26g fat, 33g protein
4g net carbs: Wagyu Beef Burger, bunless, Half-Serving 490 calories, 28g fat, 13g protein
5g net carbs: Blackened BFG Fish Sandwich – Grouper, no bread 720 calories, 28g fat, 56g protein
5g net carbs: Tacos: Bang Bang Grilled Shrimp (2), no tortillas 660 calories, 48g fat, 23g protein

Lunch Add-On

0g net carbs: Grilled Chicken (1 breast) 120 calories, 1g fat, 26g protein

Salads

3g net carbs: Side Salad, Caesar, no croutons 480 calories, 40g fat, 10g protein
3g net carbs: Side Salad, House, no pepitas 230 calories, 19g fat, 5g protein

DINNER

Starters & Sharing

3g net carbs: Ahi Tuna Poke, no rice 320 calories, 7g fat, 25g protein
3g net carbs: Ahi Tuna Sashimi, Regular, no sauce 340 calories, 17g fat, 35g protein
4g net carbs: Bang Bang Grilled Shrimp 780 calories, 61g fat, 30g protein
4g net carbs: Maryland-Style Crab Cakes, no red remoulade sauce 490 calories, 36g fat, 29g protein
4g net carbs: Mussels Josephine without Bread, easy sauce 710 calories, 37g fat, 31g protein
4g net carbs: Saucy Shrimp (Grilled), easy sauce 1170 calories, 56g fat, 65g protein
5g net carbs: Ahi Tuna Sashimi, Large, no sauce 630 calories, 34g fat, 66g protein
5g net carbs: Imperial Dip, no chips 1160 calories, 96g fat, 43g protein

Seafood Specialties (No Sides)

3g net carbs: Cold Water Lobster Tails (1 Tail, with Butter) 300 calories, 25g fat, 17g protein
3g net carbs: Cold Water Lobster Tails (2 Tails, with Butter) 590 calories, 49g fat, 33g protein
3g net carbs: Scallops & Shrimp Skewer 430 calories, 18g fat, 19g protein
3g net carbs: Pineapple Glazed Shrimp, no pineapple glaze, no risotto 630 calories, 21g fat, 26g protein
3g net carbs: Tacos: Bang Bang Chicken Taco (1) 390 calories, 27g fat, 6g protein
4g net carbs: Crab Crusted Cod, easy breading 440 calories, 17g fat, 53g protein
4g net carbs: Shrimp Rangoon Salmon, no sweet chili sauce, no rice, no panko crumbs 510 calories, 19g fat, 23g protein
4g net carbs: Tacos: Blackened Baja Fish (2) without tortillas, no mango salsa 460 calories, 23g fat, 28g protein
5g net carbs: Tacos: Bang Bang Grilled Shrimp (2) without tortillas 660 calories, 48g fat, 23g protein
6g net carbs: Blackened Salmon Pasta, substitute pasta with Green Beans 1240 calories, 78g fat, 55g protein
6g net carbs: Key West Ahi Tuna, no sweet chili mango vinaigrette 620 calories, 26g fat, 35g protein
6g net carbs: Spicy Tuna Bowl, no rice, no sauce 510 calories, 35g fat, 40g protein
6g net carbs: Tacos: Blackened Baja Fish (3) without tortillas, no mango salsa 690 calories, 34g fat, 42g protein
6g net carbs: Thermidor Gnocchi, substitute Gnocchi with Green Beans 1030 calories, 64g fat, 48g protein
7g net carbs: Pecan Parmesan Crusted Rainbow Trout, easy breading 790 calories, 55g fat, 57g protein
7g net carbs: Tacos: Bang Bang Grilled Shrimp (3) without tortillas 1030 calories, 68g fat, 35g protein
8g net carbs: Cod Imperial 480 calories, 28g fat, 50g protein

From the Land (No Sides)

0g net carbs: Filet Mignon, 7 oz. 280 calories, 15g fat, 39g protein
1g net carbs: Sirloin Steak, 7 oz. 230 calories, 5g fat, 43g protein
4g net carbs: 1/2 Pound BFG Burger, bunless, no special sauce 1420 calories, 88g fat, 63g protein
4g net carbs: Chicken Marsala, easy marsala wine sauce 480 calories, 20g fat, 56g protein
5g net carbs: Fontina Pork Chop, easy wine sauce 920 calories, 52g fat, 89g protein
9g net carbs: Lily's Chicken 490 calories, 23g fat, 62g protein

Grilled Fish (No Sides)

0g net carbs: Ahi Tuna Steak 220 calories, 4g fat, 46g protein
0g net carbs: Atlantic Salmon, Small 330 calories, 19g fat, 39g protein
0g net carbs: Atlantic Salmon, Regular 430 calories, 25g fat, 50g protein
0g net carbs: Chilean Sea Bass, Small 340 calories, 28g fat, 22g protein
0g net carbs: Chilean Sea Bass, Regular 640 calories, 53g fat, 41g protein
0g net carbs: Rainbow Trout 410 calories, 20g fat, 57g protein
1g net carbs: Mahi Mahi, plain 250 calories, 5g fat, 42g protein

Perfect Parings (No Sides)

4g net carbs: Georges Bank Scallops & Shrimp 250 calories, 9g fat, 38g protein
5g net carbs: Steak & Crab Cake, 7 oz. Filet, easy sauce 540 calories, 31g fat, 57g protein
5g net carbs: Steak & Crab Cake, 7 oz. Sirloin, easy sauce 520 calories, 27g fat, 58g protein
5g net carbs: Steak & Lobster Tail, 7 oz. Filet 560 calories, 34g fat, 60g protein
6g net carbs: Steak & Lobster Tail, 7 oz. Sirloin 530 calories, 30g fat, 60g protein
8g net carbs: Lobster Tail & Crab Cake 570 calories, 46g fat, 31g protein
8g net carbs: Mahi Mahi & Shrimp 330 calories, 7g fat, 57g protein

Add-Ons

0g net carbs: Bacon 60 calories, 4g fat, 4g protein
2g net carbs: Sliced Avocado 35 calories, 3g fat, 0g protein

Grilled Fish: Signature Sauces

1g net carbs: Chimichurri Sauce 130 calories, 14g fat, 1g protein
2g net carbs: Lemon Butter 60 calories, 6g fat, 0g protein
4g net carbs: Lime Tomato Garlic 60 calories, 5g fat, 0g protein
7g net carbs: Mango Salsa 30 calories, 0g fat, 0g protein
7g net carbs: Pan Asian Sauce 70 calories, 4g fat, 0g protein

Premium/Signature Sides

2g net carbs: Sautéed Asparagus 45 calories, 3g fat, 2g protein
4g net carbs: Green Beans 50 calories, 3g fat, 2g protein
5g net carbs: Steamed Broccoli 100 calories, 7g fat, 4g protein
6g net carbs: Sauteed Spinach 170 calories, 14g fat, 6g protein
7g net carbs: Coleslaw 160 calories, 14g fat, 1g protein
8g net carbs: Creamed Spinach, no crouton crumb 220 calories, 18g fat, 16g protein

Greens

3g net carbs: Caesar Salad: Side Salad, no croutons 420 calories, 33g fat, 7g protein
5g net carbs: Entrée Large House Salad, no pepitas, easy citrus herb vinaigrette 360 calories, 31g fat, 6g protein
5g net carbs: House Salad: Side Salad, no pepitas, easy citrus herb vinaigrette 230 calories, 19g fat, 5g protein

5g net carbs: Caesar Salad: Entrée Salad, no croutons 480 calories, 40g fat, 10g protein
5g net carbs: Florida Grilled Chicken Cobb Salad, no mango, easy citrus herb vinaigrette 720 calories, 45g fat, 64g protein
7g net carbs: Florida Grilled Shrimp Cobb Salad, no mango, easy citrus herb vinaigrette 640 calories, 52g fat, 27g protein

Greens Add-Ons

0g net carbs: Wood-Grilled Chicken 230 calories, 2g fat, 52g protein
0g net carbs: Wood-Grilled Salmon 330 calories, 19g fat, 39g protein
3g net carbs: Wood-Grilled Shrimp 160 calories, 10g fat, 15g protein

DRINKS

0g net carbs: Bottled Water: Aqua Panna, One Liter 0 calories, 0g fat, 0g protein
0g net carbs: Bottled Water: San Pellegrino, One Liter 0 calories, 0g fat, 0g protein
0g net carbs: Coffee, unsweetened 6 oz. 0 calories, 0g fat, 0g protein
0g net carbs: Coke Zero Sugar, 16 oz. 0 calories, 0g fat, 0g protein
0g net carbs: Diet Coke, with Ice, 16 oz. 0 calories, 0g fat, 0g protein
0g net carbs: Honest Organic Iced Tea: Black Tea, unsweetened 8 oz. with Ice 0 calories, 0g fat, 0g protein
1g net carbs: Hot Tea, unsweetened 6 oz. 0 calories, 0g fat, 0g protein
5g net carbs: Cappuccino, unsweetened 6 oz. 45 calories, 1g fat, 3g protein
7g net carbs: Espresso, unsweetened 3 oz. 45 calories, 2g fat, 1g protein

Beer & Seltzer

2g net carbs: Truly Wild Berry, 12 oz. can 100 calories, 0g fat, 0g protein
3g net carbs: Michelob Ultra, Bottle, 12 oz. 95 calories, 0g fat, 1g protein
3g net carbs: Miller Lite, Bottle, 12 oz. 96 calories, 0g fat, 1g protein
5g net carbs: Coors Light, Bottle, 12 oz. 102 calories, 0g fat, 1g protein
5g net carbs: House Light, Draft, 13 oz. 110 calories, 0g fat, 1g protein
7g net carbs: Bud Light, Bottle, 12 oz. 110 calories, 0g fat, 1g protein

Wine

4g net carbs: House Rose Wine, Glass, 6 oz. 145 calories, 0g fat, 0g protein
5g net carbs: House Red Wine, Glass, 6 oz. 150 calories, 0g fat, 0g protein
5g net carbs: House White Wine, Glass, 6 oz. 130 calories, 0g fat, 0g protein
6g net carbs: House Sparkling Wine, Split, 187 ml 150 calories, 0g fat, 0g protein

Sparkling

2g net carbs: Champagne, France 96 calories, 0g fat, 0g protein
2g net carbs: Chandon Brut Sparkling 187ml Split 120 calories, 0g fat, 0g protein
3g net carbs: Chandon Rosé Sparkling 187ml Split 130 calories, 0g fat, 0g protein
3g net carbs: Veuve Clicquot Yellow Label Brut 110 calories, 0g fat, 0g protein

Interesting Whites

4g net carbs: Jacob's Creek Moscato, Australia 127 calories, 0g fat, 0g protein
4g net carbs: Ecco Domani Pinot Grigio, Italy 137 calories, 0g fat, 0g protein
5g net carbs: Chateau Ste. Michelle Riesling, WA 131 calories, 0g fat, 0g protein
5g net carbs: Santa Margherita Pinot Grigio, Alto Adige, Italy 153 calories, 0g fat, 0g protein

Sauvignon Blanc

3g net carbs: Kim Crawford, Marlborough, New Zealand 149 calories, 0g fat, 0g protein
4g net carbs: Decoy by Duckhorn, Sonoma County 145 calories, 0g fat, 0g protein

Chardonnay

4g net carbs: La Terre, CA 126 calories, 0g fat, 0g protein
4g net carbs: Kendall-Jackson "V.R.," CA 138 calories, 0g fat, 0g protein
4g net carbs: Sonoma-Cutrer, Russian River Ranches 159 calories, 0g fat, 0g protein

Rosé

4g net carbs: Beringer White Zinfandel, CA 125 calories, 0g fat, 0g protein
5g net carbs: Chloe Rosé, Central Coast, CA 131 calories, 0g fat, 0g protein

Pinot Noir

4g net carbs: Acrobat, Willamette Valley, OR 139 calories, 0g fat, 0g protein
4g net carbs: Meiomi, Santa Barbara-Monterey-Sonoma Coast 147 calories, 0g fat, 0g protein
5g net carbs: Silver Gate, CA 129 calories, 0g fat, 0g protein

Interesting Reds

4g net carbs: Villa Antinori "Super Tuscan" Red, Italy 151 calories, 0g fat, 0g protein
4g net carbs: Francis Coppola Black Label Claret, CA 143 calories, 0g fat, 0g protein
5g net carbs: Portillo "Estate Bottled" Malbec, Argentina 133 calories, 0g fat, 0g protein

Merlot/Cabernet

3g net carbs: Columbia Crest "Grand Estates" Merlot, WA 131 calories, 0g fat, 0g protein
4g net carbs: Louis Martini Cabernet Sauvignon, CA 139 calories, 0g fat, 0g protein
4g net carbs: Hess "Allomi" Cabernet Sauvignon, Napa Valley 115 calories, 0g fat, 0g protein

Cocktails

2g net carbs: 1901 Dirty Martini 173 calories, 0g fat, 0g protein
3g net carbs: Infused Manhattan 160 calories, 0g fat, 0g protein
8g net carbs: Smoked Old Fashioned 155 calories, 0g fat, 0g protein

5. Italian & Pizza

CHAPTER 5

ITALIAN & PIZZA

Olive Garden
Romano's Macaroni Grill
Carrabba's Italian Grill
Maggiano's Little Italy
California Pizza Kitchen
Uno Pizzeria & Grill
MOD Pizza
Chuck E. Cheese

Olive Garden

When I think of Olive Garden, my first thoughts always go to their salad. The ripe tomatoes, the crisp lettuce, and the fabulous dressing. Yum. Just navigate around the croutons (or ask the server not to add them to the mix).

Would you believe Olive Garden lists calories on its menu but *not* carbs? *So not helpful, people.* To remedy this, visit the nutrition information PDF for a complete breakdown.

Special Order Tips

All sides of breadsticks and pasta should be substituted with salad or steamed/grilled vegetables. Avoid all noodles, breading, potatoes, croutons, bread, etc. Pro tip: The broccoli at Olive Garden is delicious!

Be wary of the available "Add-Ons" since they are often an unnecessary source of net carbs.

Feel free to customize your order. Restaurants are usually happy to accommodate reasonable customer requests. The exception is when the item has been premade or was prepared off-site. Note that any alterations on your end will change the provided nutrition information. Adjust accordingly.

You'll notice some menu items indicate a half-serving size. Don't worry; there will only be a few. A smaller portion size allowed us to include more (higher-carb) crowd-pleasing favorites like Olive Garden's signature soups.

Author Favorite

Lunch: Salad with Signature Italian Dressing with no croutons to start. Eggplant Parmigiana, remove breading, no bread, steamed vegetables substituted for pasta. Steamed Broccoli on the side. 16 oz. Iced Tea, Fresh Brewed unsweetened over ice to drink. 605 calories, 42g fat, 11g net carbs, 28g protein

Dinner: Salad with Signature Italian Dressing with no croutons to start. Grilled Chicken Margherita, no bread, steamed vegetables substituted for pasta. Steamed Broccoli on the side. Jack & Diet Coke to drink. 695 calories, 37g fat, 10g net carbs, 72g protein

LUNCH (No Bread, Steamed Vegetables Substituted for Pasta)

3g net carbs: Fettuccine Alfredo 410 calories, 27g fat, 15g protein
4g net carbs: Eggplant Parmigiana, remove breading, 460 calories, 32g fat, 21g protein
4g net carbs: Spaghetti with Meat Sauce & Meatballs 680 calories, 17g fat, 30g protein
5g net carbs: Chicken Parmigiana, remove breading, 460 calories, 29g fat, 35g protein
5g net carbs: Shrimp Scampi 480 calories, 19g fat, 20g protein

Salad

3g net carbs: Salad with Signature Italian Dressing, no croutons 110 calories, 10g fat, 3g protein

DINNER (No Bread, Steamed Vegetables Substituted for Pasta)

3g net carbs: 6 oz. Sirloin 530 calories, 32g fat, 57g protein
3g net carbs: Chicken & Shrimp Carbonara 390 calories, 50g fat, 64g protein
3g net carbs: Herb-Grilled Salmon 460 calories, 29g fat, 45g protein
4g net carbs: Herb-Grilled Salmon Coho 360 calories, 15g fat, 50g protein
4g net carbs: Grilled Chicken Margherita 540 calories, 27g fat, 65g protein
4g net carbs: Chicken Scampi 640 calories, 28g fat, 49g protein
5g net carbs: Shrimp Scampi 510 calories, 20g fat, 29g protein
4g net carbs: Fettuccine Alfredo 410 calories, 35g fat, 30g protein
5g net carbs: Chicken Alfredo 570 calories, 56g fat, 81g protein
5g net carbs: Seafood Alfredo 530 calories, 55g fat, 56g protein
6g net carbs: Shrimp Alfredo 450 calories, 55g fat, 63g protein
5g net carbs: Eggplant Parmigiana, remove breading 560 calories, 44g fat, 30g protein
7g net carbs: Chicken Parmigiana, remove breading 660 calories, 52g fat, 63g protein

Dipping Sauces

5g net carbs: Alfredo 440 calories, 43g fat, 8g protein
9g net carbs: Marinara 90 calories, 5g fat, 1g protein
10g net carbs: Five Cheese Marinara 220 calories, 17g fat, 5g protein

Sides

3g net carbs: Steamed Broccoli 35 calories, 0g fat, 4g protein

Add-Ons

1g net carbs: Grilled Chicken 130 calories, 2g fat, 26g protein
1g net carbs: Shrimp 150 calories, 1g fat, 33g protein
2g net carbs: Italian Sausage (2 Links) 470 calories, 39g fat, 27g protein
4g net carbs: Meatballs (3) 480 calories, 40g fat, 23g protein

Soups & Salads

1g net carbs: Salad without Dressing, no croutons 70 calories, 2g fat, 2g protein
3g net carbs: Salad with Signature Italian Dressing, no croutons 110 calories, 10g fat, 3g protein
6g net carbs: Pasta Fagioli Soup[53], Half-Serving, 75 calories, 3g fat, 4g protein
6g net carbs: Zuppa Toscana Soup*, Half-Serving, 110 calories, 8g fat, 4g protein
7g net carbs: Minestrone Soup*, Half-Serving, 55 calories, 1g fat, 3g protein
9g net carbs: Chicken & Gnocchi* Soup, Half-Serving, 120 calories, 6g fat, 5g protein

Dressing

2g net carbs: Italian Dressing 80 calories, 8g fat, 0g protein
2g net carbs: Low-Fat Italian Dressing 30 calories, 2g fat, 0g protein

DRINKS

0g net carbs: Diet Coke, 16 oz. 0 calories, 0g fat, 0g protein
0g net carbs: Coke Zero, 16 oz. 0 calories, 0g fat, 0g protein
0g net carbs: Italian Bottled Water, 16 oz. 0 calories, 0g fat, 0g protein
0g net carbs: Coffee, unsweetened, 8 oz. 0 calories, 0g fat, 0g protein
1g net carbs: Fresh Brewed Tea, unsweetened, 8 oz. 0 calories, 0g fat, 0g protein
1g net carbs: Iced Tea, Fresh Brewed, unsweetened, 16 oz. 0 calories, 0g fat, 0g protein
6g net carbs: Lavazza Espresso, unsweetened, 2 oz. 60 calories, 1g fat, 5g protein
7g net carbs: Raspberry Lemonade, 16 oz. 110 calories, 0g fat, 0g protein

Beer

5g net carbs: House Light Beer,12 oz. bottle 102 calories, 0g fat, 1g protein
6g net carbs: House Light Draft, 16 oz. 140 calories, 0g fat, 1g protein
8g net carbs: House Light Draft, 22 oz. 190 calories, 0g fat, 2g protein

Wine

4g net carbs: Whites and Rosé, 6 oz. Glass 150 calories, 0g fat, 0g protein
5g net carbs: Reds, 6 oz. Glass 160 calories, 0g fat, 0g protein
6g net carbs: Whites and Rosé, 9 oz. Grande Pour 220 calories, 0g fat, 0g protein
8g net carbs: Reds, 9 oz. Grande Pour 230 calories, 0g fat, 0g protein
10g net carbs: Sparkling Prosecco, 6 oz. Glass 160 calories, 0g fat, 1g protein

---

[53] *That's Not Keto!* – You'll find all sorts of surprising foods listed here. I'm not telling you whether you should eat these foods or not. What fits your macros or daily carb spend is up to you. No keto police allowed.

Spirits

0g net carbs: Jack & Diet Coke, 8 oz. 10 calories, 0g fat, 0g protein
6g net carbs: Jack & Coke, 8 oz. 120 calories, 0g fat, 0g protein
9g net carbs: Old Fashioned, 8 oz. 170 calories, 0g fat, 0g protein

Romano's Macaroni Grill

While the food at Romano's Macaroni Grill is outstanding, their website leaves a lot to be desired. You cannot customize nutrition information; worse, only calorie information is provided. Now, if that doesn't frustrate you, this will. Quantities are *unspecified* for most menu options (i.e., "Create Your Own Pasta" and "Adds" – dressing, sauces, and extras). Hello? That makes absolutely no sense.

On the other hand, I must give Romano's Macaroni Grill props for their A La Carte Menu. You can pick your low-carb proteins, sauces, and toppings, and instead of pasta, pair them with a bed of salad greens, spinach, asparagus, or broccolini. Love this!

Special Order Tips

Order all burgers and sandwiches with "no bread." Be wary of the available "Add-Ons" since they are often an unnecessary source of net carbs. Avoid all fries, potatoes, rice, pasta, bread, etc. Ask the server to substitute a side salad or a side of steamed/grilled vegetables.

Feel free to customize your order. Restaurants are usually happy to accommodate reasonable customer requests. The exception is when the item has been premade or was prepared off-site. Note that any alterations on your end will change the provided nutrition information. Adjust accordingly.

Author Favorite

Breakfast: Breakfast Americano with no bread, side of Italian Sausage. 8 oz. Café Mocha with sugar-free sweetener. 1605 calories, 139g fat, 12g net carbs, 72g protein

Lunch & Dinner: Crispy Brussels Sprouts, no balsamic glaze to start. Parmesan-Crusted Chicken Salad, no balsamic glaze, with Grilled Asparagus on the side. 6 oz. glass Drumheller Chardonnay to drink. 1225 calories, 64g fat, 14g net carbs, 74g protein

BREAKFAST (No Bread, No Potatoes)

3g net carbs: Breakfast Americano 915 calories, 79g fat, 36g protein
4g net carbs: Breakfast BLT 580 calories, 66g fat, 44g protein
4g net carbs: Eggs Benedict with Charred Lemon 530 calories, 70g fat, 31g protein
5g net carbs: Eggs Benedict with Basil Pesto Hollandaise 580 calories, 86g fat, 32g protein
6g net carbs: Avocado with Fried Eggs 670 calories, 42g fat, 24g protein

Breakfast Sides

1g net carbs: Eggs (2) 350 calories, 32g fat, 13g protein
1g net carbs: Italian Sausage (1) 580 calories, 52g fat, 26g protein
2g net carbs: Bacon (2 strips) 359 calories, 32g fat, 15g protein

LUNCH & DINNER (No Pasta, Substitute Grilled/Steamed Vegetables)

Antipasti

3g net carbs: Crispy Brussels Sprouts, no balsamic glaze 370 calories, 2g fat, 8g protein
4g net carbs: Caprese Salad, no balsamic glaze 420 calories, 23g fat, 24g protein

Sandwiches (No Bread)

4g net carbs: Italian Pesto Caprese 630 calories, 36g fat, 20g protein
5g net carbs: Grilled Chicken Parmesan, remove breading, 470 calories, 63g fat, 65g protein
6g net carbs: Meatball 680 calories, 73g fat, 56g protein

Carne (Steamed Vegetables on Side, No Pasta, No Bread)

2g net carbs: Grilled Pork Chop 420 calories, 93g fat, 88g protein
3g net carbs: Pork Saltimbocca, easy sauce 500 calories, 67g fat, 108g protein
4g net carbs: Braised Lamb Shank, easy marsala demi-glace 590 calories, 61g fat, 78g protein
4g net carbs: Grilled Steak 550 calories, 94g fat, 72g protein
4g net carbs: Grilled Steak with Oreganata Sauce 620 calories, 85g fat, 73g protein
4g net carbs: Porterhouse Steak 880 calories, 115g fat, 96g protein
7g net carbs: Lamb Braciole, easy sauce 560 calories, 53g fat, 55g protein

Chicken (Steamed Vegetables on Side, No Pasta, No Bread)

4g net carbs: Pollo Caprese, no Balsamic Glaze 500 calories, 22g fat, 50g protein
6g net carbs: San Marino Chicken, no honey pepper glaze, no orzo 680 calories, 34g fat, 30g protein
7g net carbs: Carmela's Chicken 590 calories, 61g fat, 33g protein
7g net carbs: Grilled Chicken Parmesan 610 calories, 62g fat, 79g protein
8g net carbs: Chicken Marsala, no Capellini, easy Marsala Wine Sauce 720 calories, 32g fat, 54g protein
8g net carbs: Chicken Scaloppine, no capellini 660 calories, 76g fat, 61g protein

Seafood (Steamed Vegetables on Side, No Pasta, No Bread)

3g net carbs: Grilled Mahi-Mahi 400 calories, 33g fat, 55g protein
4g net carbs: Shrimp Scampi 480 calories, 88g fat, 35g protein
5g net carbs: Pasta di Mare 330 calories, 43g fat, 55g protein
6g net carbs: Grilled Salmon easy Calabrian Honey Pepper Glaze 630 calories, 45g fat, 61g protein
6g net carbs: Parmesan-Crusted Sole 580 calories, 6g fat, 35g protein
7g net carbs: Shrimp Portofino, no pine nuts, no capellini 330 calories, 38g fat, 36g protein

A La Carte (Substitute Grilled/Steamed Vegetables for Pasta)

Proteins

1g net carbs: Italian Sausage 430 calories, 39g fat, 17g protein
1g net carbs: Shrimp 170 calories, 15g fat, 9g protein
2g net carbs: Scallops 150 calories, 12g fat, 8g protein
3g net carbs: Roasted Chicken 110 calories, 2g fat, 24g protein
8g net carbs: Meatballs 420 calories, 32g fat, 24g protein

Sauces

4g net carbs: Pesto 400 calories, 69g fat, 13g protein
5g net carbs: Garlic Olive Oil 510 calories, 54g fat, 1g protein
10g net carbs: Lemon Butter 430 calories, 37g fat, 6g protein

Toppings (1 oz.)

0g net carbs: Fresh Mushrooms 5 calories, 0g fat, 1g protein
0g net carbs: Fresh Spinach 8 calories, 0g fat, 1g protein
1g net carbs: Broccolini 10 calories, 0g fat, 2g protein
1g net carbs: Roasted Mushrooms 5 calories, 0g fat, 2g protein
1g net carbs: Roasted Tomatoes 15 calories, 1g fat, 0g protein
2g net carbs: Asparagus 8 calories, 0g fat, 2g protein
2g net carbs: Roasted Peppers 10 calories, 0g fat, 0g protein
2g net carbs: Sun-Dried Tomatoes 40 calories, 2g fat, 1g protein
3g net carbs: Mediterranean Olives 15 calories, 4g fat, 18g protein
4g net carbs: Smoked Buffalo Mozzarella 210 calories, 17g fat, 11g protein
8g net carbs: Roasted Garlic 40 calories, 0g fat, 2g protein

Off the Grill

2g net carbs: Grilled Chicken, Small, easy Mediterranean Vinaigrette 300 calories, 16g fat, 25g protein
3g net carbs: Grilled Chicken, Large, easy Mediterranean Vinaigrette 340 calories, 22g fat, 29g protein
4g net carbs: Grilled Chicken, Small, easy Balsamic Glaze 220 calories, 4g fat, 39g protein
6g net carbs: Grilled Chicken, Large, easy Balsamic Glaze 400 calories, 7g fat, 48g protein
2g net carbs: Grilled Salmon, Small 350 calories, 24g fat, 18g protein
3g net carbs: Grilled Salmon, Large 450 calories, 43g fat, 37g protein
3g net carbs: Grilled Sirloin, Small 260 calories, 49g fat, 79g protein
4g net carbs: Grilled Sirloin, Large 340 calories, 56g fat, 92g protein

Sides

1g net carbs: Grilled Asparagus 150 calories, 14g fat, 2g protein
4g net carbs: Crispy Brussels Sprouts, no balsamic glaze 190 calories, 6g fat, 4g protein
4g net carbs: Sautéed Spinach, no croutons 120 calories, 17g fat, 19g protein
6g net carbs: Broccolini 100 calories, 7g fat, 3g protein

Soups

6g net carbs: Italian Herb Soup 70 calories, 2g fat, 4g protein
7g net carbs: Tomato Basil 110 calories, 8g fat, 2g protein
7g net carbs: Tuscan Bean Soup[54], 80 calories, 9g fat, 7g protein

Salads

2g net carbs: Bibb and Bleu with Salmon, no crispy onions 430 calories, 57g fat, 63g protein
2g net carbs: Bibb and Bleu, side, no crispy onions 270 calories, 22g fat, 12g protein
2g net carbs: Fresh Greens, side, no croutons 190 calories, 16g fat, 2g protein
2g net carbs: Italian Chopped, side, easy oreganata dressing 320 calories, 23g fat, 16g protein
2g net carbs: Rosa's Signature Caesar, side, no croutons 240 calories, 20g fat, 7g protein
3g net carbs: Chicken Florentine Salad, side 400 calories, 29g fat, 26g protein
3g net carbs: Rosa's Signature Caesar, no croutons 370 calories, 41g fat, 13g protein
4g net carbs: Bibb and Bleu with Grilled Shrimp, no crispy onions 490 calories, 43g fat, 36g protein
4g net carbs: Bibb and Bleu, no crispy onions 420 calories, 42g fat, 23g protein
4g net carbs: Chicken Florentine Salad 540 calories, 34g fat, 36g protein
4g net carbs: Fresh Greens, no croutons 360 calories, 32g fat, 4g protein
4g net carbs: Italian Chopped, easy oreganata dressing 490 calories, 34g fat, 27g protein
4g net carbs: Rosa's Signature Caesar with Grilled Shrimp, no croutons 440 calories, 42g fat, 26g protein
4g net carbs: Rosa's Signature Caesar with Salmon, no croutons 490 calories, 77g fat, 60g protein
5g net carbs: Bibb and Bleu with Chicken, no crispy onions 480 calories, 43g fat, 61g protein
5g net carbs: Rosa's Signature Caesar with Grilled Chicken, no croutons 430 calories, 41g fat, 51g protein
7g net carbs: Parmesan-Crusted Chicken, no balsamic glaze 480 calories, 48g fat, 64g protein

---

[54] *That's Not Keto!* – You'll find all sorts of surprising foods listed here. I'm not telling you whether you should eat these foods or not. What fits your macros or daily carb spend is up to you. No keto police allowed.

Salad Dressing (2 oz.)

2g net carbs: Creamy Caesar 180 calories, 24g fat, 0g protein
2g net carbs: Buttermilk Ranch 220 calories, 22g fat, 0g protein
6g net carbs: Mediterranean Vinaigrette 160 calories, 18g fat, 0g protein

DRINKS

0g net carbs: Diet Pepsi, 20 oz. 0 calories, 0g fat, 0g protein
0g net carbs: Filtered Coffee, unsweetened 6 oz. 0 calories, 0g fat, 0g protein
0g net carbs: Iced tea, unsweetened 20 oz. 0 calories, 0g fat, 0g protein
3g net carbs: Macchiato, unsweetened 4 oz. 80 calories, 3g fat, 7g protein
4g net carbs: Espresso, unsweetened 4 oz. 90 calories, 3g fat, 6g protein
5g net carbs: Cappuccino, unsweetened 6 oz. 100 calories, 8g fat, 8g protein
6g net carbs: Café Latte, unsweetened 8 oz. 120 calories, 8g fat, 10g protein
7g net carbs: Frizzante, Cucumber, 16 oz. 10 calories, 0g fat, 12g protein
8g net carbs: Café Mocha, unsweetened 8 oz. 110 calories, 8g fat, 10g protein

Beer

3g net carbs: Miller Lite, 12 oz. bottle 96 calories, 0g fat, 1g protein
5g net carbs: Coors Light, 12 oz. bottle 102 calories, 0g fat, 1g protein
7g net carbs: Bud Light, 12 oz. bottle 110 calories, 0g fat, 1g protein

White Wine (6 oz.)

3g net carbs: Sauvignon Blanc, Nobilo 230 calories, 0g fat, 0g protein
3g net carbs: Chardonnay, Drumheller 225 calories, 0g fat, 0g protein
3g net carbs: Chardonnay, Noble Vines 190 calories, 0g fat, 0g protein
4g net carbs: Chardonnay, Rodney Strong 200 calories, 0g fat, 0g protein
3g net carbs: Pinot Grigio, Carletto 219 calories, 0g fat, 0g protein
4g net carbs: Pinot Grigio, Villa Pozzi 210 calories, 0g fat, 0g protein
4g net carbs: Rosé, Chloe, Dry 112 calories, 0g fat, 0g protein
6g net carbs: Moscato, Seven Daughters 120 calories, 0g fat, 0g protein

Red Wine (6 oz.)

3g net carbs: Pinot Noir, Garnet 210 calories, 0g fat, 0g protein
4g net carbs: Pinot Noir, Meiomi 190 calories, 0g fat, 0g protein
4g net carbs: Cabernet Sauvignon, Daou 135 calories, 0g fat, 0g protein
4g net carbs: Cabernet Sauvignon, Francis Ford Coppola Diamond 140 calories, 0g fat, 0g protein
5g net carbs: Cabernet Sauvignon, Josh Cellars, Craftsman Collection 150 calories, 0g fat, 0g protein
5g net carbs: Cabernet Sauvignon, The Federalist 130 calories, 0g fat, 0g protein
4g net carbs: Chianti, Straccali 170 calories, 0g fat, 0g protein
4g net carbs: Skinny Margarita 140 calories, 0g fat, 8g protein
5g net carbs: Merlot, 14 Hands Winery 180 calories, 0g fat, 0g protein
6g net carbs: Red Blend, Z. Alexander Brown Uncaged 170 calories, 0g fat, 0g protein

Carrabba's Italian Grill

Carrabba's Italian Grill does not have a customizable nutrition calculator on its website; however, they have a detailed Master Menu Nutrition Information PDF that will help you monitor your carb intake.

Like all restaurants in this book, feel free to customize any menu item to your liking (but be sure to adjust the carbs). Usually, the restaurants are happy accommodating their customers (they are used to patrons asking for deletions/substitutions by now). The exception is when items are premade with the offending ingredient (think frozen breaded shrimp or pre-seasoned chicken wings).

Special Order Tips

Order all burgers and sandwiches with "no bread." Be wary of the available "Add-Ons" since they are often an unnecessary source of net carbs. Avoid all fries, potatoes, rice, pasta, bread, etc. Ask the server to substitute a side salad or a side of steamed/grilled vegetables.

Author Favorite

Lunch: Lunch Trio Meatballs & Ricotta, Substitute Soup with Grilled Asparagus. Unsweetened Fresh Brewed Iced Tea, 16 oz. 810 calories, 48g fat, 6g net carbs, 44g protein

Dinner: Tomato Caprese with Fresh Burrata, no balsamic glaze to start. Pollo Rosa Maria with Caesar Salad, no croutons, and easy dressing on the side. 8 oz. Mr. C's Dirty Martini to drink. 1530 calories, 98g fat, 14g net carbs, 89g protein

LUNCH

Italian Sandwiches (No Bread)

3g net carbs: Grilled Chicken Caprese Sandwich, no bread, no pine nuts, no walnuts 580 calories, 22g fat, 36g protein

4g net carbs: Caprese Sandwich, no bread, no pine nuts, no walnuts 480 calories, 20g fat, 18g protein

4g net carbs: Steak Sandwich, no bread 920 calories, 47g fat, 57g protein

6g net carbs: Chicken Parmesan Sandwich, no bread, remove breading, easy sauce 620 calories, 18g fat, 44g protein

6g net carbs: Meatball Sandwich, no bread, remove breading, easy sauce 690 calories, 27g fat, 40g protein

Lunch Trio

5g net carbs: Lunch Trio Shrimp Scampi, Substitute Pasta and Soup for Grilled Asparagus and Grilled Broccoli 740 calories, 32g fat, 34g protein

6g net carbs: Lunch Trio Meatballs & Ricotta, Substitute Soup with Grilled Asparagus 810 calories, 48g fat, 44g protein

6g net carbs: Lunch Trio Four-Cheese & Sausage Stuffed Mushrooms, remove breading, easy sauce 750 calories, 38g fat, 32g protein

DINNER

Appetizers

5g net carbs: Meatballs & Ricotta, easy Pomodoro sauce 380 calories, 22g fat, 26g protein

5g net carbs: Shrimp Scampi, no bread, no wine sauce, substitute steamed/grilled vegetables for the Pasta 720 calories, 32g fat, 31g protein

5g net carbs: Tomato Caprese with Fresh Burrata, no balsamic glaze 500 calories, 38g fat, 16g protein

6g net carbs: Cozze in Bianco, No wine sauce 440 calories, 38g fat, 3g protein

7g net carbs: Four-Cheese and Sausage Stuffed Mushrooms, remove breading 290 calories, 22g fat, 15g protein

Pasta (Substitute Steamed/Grilled Vegetables for Pasta)

4g net carbs: Spaghetti with easy Pomodoro Sauce 670 calories, 11g fat, 21g protein

4g net carbs: Spaghetti with Meatballs, easy sauce 1040 calories, 33g fat, 52g protein

6g net carbs: Rigatoni Martino with Chicken, no sun-dried tomatoes, easy sauce 1250 calories, 67g fat, 65g protein

6g net carbs: Rigatoni Martino, no sun-dried tomatoes, easy sauce 1080 calories, 63g fat, 34g protein

7g net carbs: Rigatoni Martino with Sausage, no sun-dried tomatoes, easy sauce 1420 calories, 88g fat, 59g protein

6g net carbs: Linguine Positano with Chicken, easy crushed tomatoes 970 calories, 31g fat, 53g protein

6g net carbs: Linguine Positano with Shrimp, easy crushed tomatoes 870 calories, 29g fat, 36g protein

7g net carbs: Linguine Positano, easy crushed tomatoes 800 calories, 27g fat, 22g protein

6g net carbs: Penne Martino with Chicken, no sun-dried tomatoes, easy sauce 1140 calories, 67g fat, 61g protein

6g net carbs: Penne Martino, no sun-dried tomatoes, easy sauce 970 calories, 63g fat, 30g protein

7g net carbs: Penne Martino with Sausage, no sun-dried tomatoes, easy sauce 1310 calories, 89g fat, 56g protein

5g net carbs: Rigatoni Campagnolo, easy Pomodoro sauce 1050 calories, 50g fat, 53g protein

7g net carbs: Fettuccine Carrabba, no peas 1470 calories, 78g fat, 71g protein

7g net carbs: Linguine Pescatore, easy marinara sauce 820 calories, 11g fat, 56g protein

7g net carbs: Shrimp and Slop Linguine ala Vodka, easy sauce 1100 calories, 36g fat, 53g protein

7g net carbs: Spaghetti with Bolognese Meat Sauce 880 calories, 28g fat, 35g protein

8g net carbs: Fettuccine Weesie, easy sauce 1420 calories, 83g fat, 57g protein

Specialties (Substitute Steamed/Grilled Vegetables for Pasta)

1g net carbs: Tuscan-Grilled Chicken 290 calories, 7g fat, 52g protein

4g net carbs: Chicken Marsala 450 calories, 22g fat, 54g protein

4g net carbs: Chicken Parmesan, remove breading, easy Pomodoro sauce 690 calories, 34g fat, 70g protein

5g net carbs: Chicken Bryan, no sun-dried tomatoes 530 calories, 26g fat, 59g protein

5g net carbs: Chicken Piccata, no flour dusting 300 calories, 17g fat, 28g protein

5g net carbs: Pollo Rosa Maria 540 calories, 28g fat, 65g protein

5g net carbs: Veal Piccata, no flour dusting 380 calories, 16g fat, 46g protein

7g net carbs: Eggplant Parmesan, remove breading, easy Pomodoro sauce 640 calories, 29g fat, 28g protein

8g net carbs: Veal Marsala 430 calories, 21g fat, 47g protein

Seafood (Substitute Steamed/Grilled Vegetables for Pasta)

4g net carbs: Mahi Wulfe, remove breading, no sun-dried tomatoes 360 calories, 16g fat, 38g protein

4g net carbs: Simply Grilled Salmon 620 calories, 43g fat, 52g protein

5g net carbs: Salmon Saporito 740 calories, 54g fat, 57g protein

5g net carbs: Salmon Vazzano 720 calories, 53g fat, 52g protein

5g net carbs: Spiedino Di Mare, remove breading 420 calories, 22g fat, 38g protein

6g net carbs: Grouper DiNisco, remove breading, 950 calories, 49g fat, 79g protein

Combinations (Substitute Steamed/Grilled Vegetables for Pasta)

7g net carbs: Chicken Trio: Chicken Bryan, Pollo Rosa Maria, And Chicken Marsala, no sun-dried tomatoes, easy sauces 780 calories, 39g fat, 89g protein

7g net carbs: The Johnny with 7 oz. Sirloin 700 calories, 42g fat, 68g protein

Steaks and Chops (Substitute Steamed/Grilled Vegetables for Pasta)

0g net carbs: Tuscan-Grilled Ribeye (16 oz.) 820 calories, 63g fat, 60g protein

1g net carbs: Tuscan-Grilled Filet (9 oz.) 640 calories, 47g fat, 50g protein

1g net carbs: Tuscan-Grilled Sirloin (10 oz.) 500 calories, 30g fat, 53g protein

1g net carbs: Tuscan-Grilled Sirloin (7 oz.) 350 calories, 21g fat, 37g protein

1g net carbs: Tuscan-Grilled Pork Chop (1 Chop) 390 calories, 20g fat, 47g protein

3g net carbs: Tuscan-Grilled Pork Chop (2 Chops) 780 calories, 40g fat, 95g protein

5g net carbs: Tuscan Sirloin Marsala, (7 oz.) 510 calories, 36g fat, 39g protein

Steaks & Chops Toppings

1g net carbs: Spicy Sicilian Butter 80 calories, 9g fat, 0g protein
3g net carbs: Marsala Sauce 160 calories, 15g fat, 2g protein
4g net carbs: Ricardo Sauce 70 calories, 4g fat, 0g protein
6g net carbs: Bryan Topping 170 calories, 15g fat, 4g protein
9g net carbs: Ardente 230 calories, 18g fat, 7g protein

Sides

2g net carbs: Steamed Asparagus 25 calories, 0g fat, 2g protein
3g net carbs: Caesar Salad, no croutons, easy dressing 350 calories, 31g fat, 8g protein
3g net carbs: Grilled Asparagus 60 calories, 2g fat, 3g protein
4g net carbs: House Salad, easy dressing 290 calories, 25g fat, 5g protein
4g net carbs: Italian Salad, easy dressing 350 calories, 32g fat, 3g protein
5g net carbs: Sauteed Broccoli 140 calories, 11g fat, 5g protein
7g net carbs: Sauteed Spinach 170 calories, 14g fat, 4g protein

Salads

5g net carbs: Caesar Salad with Chicken, no croutons, easy dressing 810 calories, 62g fat, 43g protein
6g net carbs: Caesar Salad with Shrimp, no croutons, easy dressing 720 calories, 60g fat, 27g protein
6g net carbs: Johnny Rocco Salad 530 calories, 42g fat, 28g protein
8g net carbs: Italian Salad with Chicken, easy dressing 860 calories, 68g fat, 36g protein
8g net carbs: Italian Salad with Shrimp, easy dressing 760 calories, 66g fat, 20g protein

Salad Add-Ons

0g net carbs: Crumbled Gorgonzola 80 calories, 6g fat, 4g protein
8g net carbs: Balsamic Dressing, 1.5 oz. 80 calories, 5g fat, 0g protein

DRINKS

0g net carbs: Diet Coke, 16 oz. 0 calories, 0g fat, 0g protein
0g net carbs: Acqua Panna 500 ml bottled water 0 calories, 0g fat, 0g protein
0g net carbs: Acqua Panna, 1-liter bottled water 0 calories, 0g fat, 0g protein
0g net carbs: San Pellegrino (Small, 500ml) 0 calories, 0g fat, 0g protein
0g net carbs: San Pellegrino (Large, 1 Liter) 0 calories, 0g fat, 0g protein
0g net carbs: Coffee, Regular, unsweetened, 8 oz. 0 calories, 0g fat, 0g protein
0g net carbs: Coffee, Decaf, unsweetened, 8 oz. 0 calories, 0g fat, 0g protein
4g net carbs: Espresso, unsweetened, 3 oz. 25 calories, 1g fat, 1g protein
8g net carbs: Cappuccino, unsweetened, 5 oz. 70 calories, 2g fat, 4g protein
10g net carbs: Caffé Latte, unsweetened, 12 oz. 90 calories, 3g fat, 5g protein

0g net carbs: Fresh Brewed Iced Tea, unsweetened, 16 oz. 0 calories, 0g fat, 0g protein
0g net carbs: Hot Tea, unsweetened, 8 oz. 0 calories, 0g fat, 0g protein
9g net carbs: Flavored Tea, Desert Pear, unsweetened 40 calories, 0g fat, 0g protein
9g net carbs: Flavored Tea, Strawberry, unsweetened 35 calories, 0g fat, 0g protein
9g net carbs: Flavored Tea, White Peach, unsweetened 35 calories, 0g fat, 0g protein

10g net carbs: Flavored Tea, Peach, unsweetened 40 calories, 0g fat, 0g protein
10g net carbs: Flavored Tea, Pomegranate, unsweetened 45 calories, 0g fat, 0g protein

Beer

3g net carbs: Michelob Ultra, 12 oz. Bottle 95 calories, 0g fat, 1g protein
3g net carbs: Miller Lite, 12 oz. Bottle 96 calories, 0g fat, 1g protein
5g net carbs: Coors Light, 12 oz. Bottle 102 calories, 0g fat, 1g protein
7g net carbs: Bud Light, 13 oz. Draft 110 calories, 0g fat, 1g protein
10g net carbs: Bud Light, 19 oz. Draft 170 calories, 0g fat, 1g protein

Wine

5g net carbs: House Red Wine, Glass, 6 oz. 130 calories, 0g fat, 0g protein
7g net carbs: House Red Wine, Glass, 9 oz. 180 calories, 0g fat, 0g protein
5g net carbs: House Rose Wine, Glass, 6 oz. 150 calories, 0g fat, 0g protein
7g net carbs: House Rose Wine, Glass, 9 oz. 230 calories, 0g fat, 0g protein
5g net carbs: House Sparkling Wine, Glass, 6 oz. 140 calories, 0g fat, 0g protein
5g net carbs: House White Wine, Glass, 6 oz. 150 calories, 0g fat, 0g protein
7g net carbs: House White Wine, Glass, 9 oz. 170 calories, 0g fat, 0g protein

Spirits

1g net carbs: Mr. C's Dirty Martini, 8 oz. 130 calories, 1g fat, 0g protein
4g net carbs: Cosmopolitan, 8 oz. 130 calories, 0g fat, 0g protein
7g net carbs: Italian Old-Fashioned with 0g net carb sweetener, 8 oz. 180 calories, 0g fat, 0g protein

Maggiano's Little Italy

Maggiano's Little Italy does not have a customizable nutrition calculator available. Instead, they offer a detailed Nutritional Data PDF (a resource with a few boo-boos).

When researching menu items on Maggiano's Little Italy's website, I discovered several items lacked complete nutrition information. Diavolo Sauce, Red Sauce, White Garlic Herb Sauce, White Wine Butter Sauce, Four-Pepper Relish, and ALL salad dressings, to name a few. To be safe, I recommend you order menu items that do not contain these "mysterious" ingredients.

Special Order Tips

All sandwiches should be ordered "bunless" (without the bread) or "lettuce wrapped" to match the estimated nutrition information provided. Be wary of the available "Add-Ons" since they are often an unnecessary source of net carbs. These items are analyzed in their "regular" form as they are described on the menu. Any alterations will change their calorie and macronutrient amounts.

Avoid all fries, potatoes, rice, pasta, bread, etc. Ask the server to substitute a side salad or a side of steamed/grilled vegetables. Remember that Maggiano's Little Italy serves tasty sides like grilled asparagus and garlic spinach.

Like all other restaurants in this book, feel free to customize any menu item to your liking (be sure to adjust the carbs). Usually, restaurants are happy accommodating their customers (they are used to patrons asking for deletions or substitutions). The exception is when the item is premade with the offending ingredient (think frozen breaded shrimp or pre-seasoned chicken wings).

You'll notice some menu items indicate a half-serving size. Don't worry; there will only be a few! A smaller portion size allowed us to include more (higher-carb) crowd-pleasing favorites like Maggiano's Little Italy signature sandwiches.

Author Favorite

Breakfast: Italian Sausage Frittata, no bread, no potatoes, with bacon on the side. 6 oz. unsweetened Lavazza Cappuccino to drink. 1695 calories, 148g fat, 12g net carbs, 79g protein

Lunch: Breadless Italian Grilled Cheese & Ham Sandwich, Full-Serving, with Roasted Garlic Broccoli, easy seasoning on the side. 16 oz. Diet Coke to drink. 1570 calories, 98g fat, 14g net carbs, 62g protein

Dinner: Beef Tenderloin Medallions, no glaze, substitute Garlic Spinach for the Pasta. 6 oz. House Red Wine to drink. 1420 calories, 52g fat, 13g net carbs, 51g protein

BREAKFAST

Brunch (No Bread, No Potatoes)

4g net carbs: Italian American Breakfast 1300 calories, 79g fat, 67g protein
6g net carbs: Frittata- Italian Sausage 1370 calories, 104g fat, 61g protein
7g net carbs: Frittata- Vegetable 1010 calories, 73g fat, 41g protein
7g net carbs: Benedict- Crab Cake, easy Hollandaise sauce 1470 calories, 110f fat, 47g protein
7g net carbs: Benedict- Smoked Ham, easy Hollandaise sauce 1270 calories, 90g fat, 48g protein
8g net carbs: Benedict- Smoked Salmon & Spinach, easy Hollandaise sauce 1250 calories, 96g fat, 35g protein
8g net carbs: Benedict- The Meatball, easy Hollandaise sauce 1530 calories, 110g fat, 53g protein

Brunch Sides

1g net carbs: Eggs (2) Over-Easy 270 calories, 25g fat, 13g protein
1g net carbs: Eggs (2) Over-Hard 270 calories, 25g fat, 13g protein
1g net carbs: Eggs (2) Poached 140 calories, 9g fat, 13g protein
1g net carbs: Eggs (2) Scrambled 270 calories, 25g fat, 13g protein
1g net carbs: Egg Sunny Side-Up (2) 270 calories, 25g fat, 13g protein
2g net carbs: Bacon (2 strips) 280 calories, 24g fat, 16g protein
4g net carbs: Italian Sausage (1) 300 calories, 25g fat, 15g protein
8g net carbs: Smoked Ham (1 slice) 270 calories, 12g fat, 31g protein

LUNCH

Sandwiches (No Bread, No Potatoes)

4g net carbs: Chicken Parmesan, Half-Serving, remove breading, 830 calories, 43g fat, 32g protein
6g net carbs: Chicken Parmesan, Full-Serving, remove breading, 1290 calories, 68g fat, 55g protein
4g net carbs: Lemon & Herb Salmon Club, Half-Serving 990 calories, 60g fat, 37g protein
6g net carbs: Lemon & Herb Salmon Club, Full-Serving 1620 calories, 102g fat, 65g protein
4g net carbs: Italian Grilled Cheese & Ham, Half-Serving 870 calories, 50g fat, 33g protein

6g net carbs: Italian Grilled Cheese & Ham, Full-Serving 1370 calories, 83g fat, 57g protein

5g net carbs: Meatball, Half-Serving, easy marinara 1180 calories, 70g fat, 53g protein
7g net carbs: Meatball, Full-Serving, easy marinara 1990 calories, 122g fat, 97g protein

3 for $15 (Choose 1 Side Salad, 1 Entrée, 1 Drink)

Side Salad (Choose One)

2g net carbs: Side Caesar Salad, no Garlic Croutons 280 calories, 26g fat, 7g protein
7g net carbs: Side Maggiano's Salad 300 calories, 26g fat, 9g protein

Entrée (Substitute Fresh Grilled Asparagus or Garlic Spinach for Pasta)

3g net carbs: Spaghetti with easy Marinara 840 calories, 26g fat, 23g protein
5g net carbs: Spaghetti with Meat Sauce 930 calories, 28g fat, 37g protein
5g net carbs: Fettuccine Alfredo with Chicken 620 calories, 45g fat, 21g protein
6g net carbs: Eggplant Parmesan, remove breading 980 calories, 45g fat, 29g protein

Lunch-Sized Entrees

4g net carbs: Chicken Frances, no breading/remove breading 790 calories, 37g fat, 71g protein
4g net carbs: Chicken Marsala, no breading/remove breading 690 calories, 26g fat, 60g protein
4g net carbs: Shrimp Fra Diavolo 410 calories, 13g fat, 36g protein
4g net carbs: Veal Piccata, no breading/remove breading 670 calories, 20g fat, 66g protein
5g net carbs: Shrimp Scampi 920 calories, 55g fat, 43g protein
5g net carbs: Veal Marsala, no breading/remove breading 720 calories, 26g fat, 65g protein
6g net carbs: Chicken Parmesan, no breading/remove breading, easy marinara 690 calories, 25g fat, 70g protein
6g net carbs: Chicken Piccata, no breading/remove breading 650 calories, 25g fat, 63g protein
8g net carbs: Jumbo Lump Crab Cakes 790 calories, 69g fat, 22g protein

DINNER

Appetizers

6g net carbs: Bruschetta Classic Tomato Relish, no bread 80 calories, 5g fat, 2g protein

Classic Pasta (Substitute Fresh Grilled Asparagus or Garlic Spinach for Pasta)

3g net carbs: Spaghetti with easy Marinara 840 calories, 26g fat, 23g protein
4g net carbs: Spaghetti & Meatball with easy Marinara Sauce 1160 calories, 45g fat, 47g protein
5g net carbs: Spaghetti with Meat Sauce 930 calories, 28g fat, 37g protein
5g net carbs: Spaghetti & Meatball with Meat Sauce 1250 calories, 47g fat, 61g protein
5g net carbs: Fettuccine Alfredo 730 calories, 39g fat, 17g protein
5g net carbs: Fettuccine Alfredo with Chicken 620 calories, 45g fat, 21g protein
7g net carbs: Taylor Street Baked Ziti 1400 calories, 76g fat, 55g protein

Specialty Pasta (Substitute Fresh Grilled Asparagus or Garlic Spinach for Pasta)

3g net carbs: Chicken & Spinach Manicotti 1020 calories, 64g fat, 77g protein
5g net carbs: Orecchiette Chicken Pesto 1560 calories, 84g fat, 78g protein
6g net carbs: Eggplant Parmesan, remove breading, 980 calories, 45g fat, 29g protein
6g net carbs: Mediterranean Spaghetti 860 calories, 27g fat, 24g protein
7g net carbs: Our Famous Rigatoni "D" 1610 calories, 92g fat, 71g protein
7g net carbs: Rigatoni Arrabbiata with Sausage 1460 calories, 89g fat, 47g protein
8g net carbs: Rigatoni Arrabbiata with Chicken 1250 calories, 65g fat, 54g protein

Chicken (Substitute Fresh Grilled Asparagus or Garlic Spinach for Pasta)

5g net carbs: Chicken Marsala, no breading/remove breading 1170 calories, 67g fat, 67g protein
6g net carbs: Chicken Frances, no breading/remove breading 1030 calories, 59g fat, 74g protein
6g net carbs: Chicken Parmesan, no breading/remove breading, easy marinara 1290 calories, 59g fat, 80g protein
7g net carbs: Chicken Piccata, no breading/remove breading 1180 calories, 71g fat, 70g protein

Seafood (Substitute Fresh Grilled Asparagus or Garlic Spinach for Pasta)

3g net carbs: Twin Cold Water Lobster Tails 970 calories, 88g fat, 44g protein
4g net carbs: Alaskan Cod, remove breading, 830 calories, 66g fat, 41g protein
4g net carbs: Chef KB's Lobster Carbonara 1590 calories, 91g fat, 64g protein
5g net carbs: Linguine & Clams with easy White Sauce 1600 calories, 88g fat, 73g protein
6g net carbs: Linguine & Clams with easy Red Sauce 1480 calories, 68g fat, 74g protein
6g net carbs: Salmon Lemon & Herb 800 calories, 66g fat, 47g protein
6g net carbs: Salmon Oscar 1160 calories, 86g fat, 77g protein
6g net carbs: Shrimp Scampi 1270 calories, 76g fat, 72g protein
7g net carbs: Linguine di Mare 1350 calories, 43g fat, 102g protein
7g net carbs: Shrimp Fra Diavolo 820 calories, 26g fat, 72g protein
8g net carbs: Tuscan Shrimp & Chicken 1860 calories, 100g fat, 121g protein
9g net carbs: Jumbo Lump Crab Cakes 1150 calories, 102g fat, 32g protein

Steak & Veal (Substitute Fresh Grilled Asparagus or Garlic Spinach for Pasta)

2g net carbs: Center-Cut Filet Mignon 850 calories, 47g fat, 61g protein
4g net carbs: Beef Tenderloin Medallions, no glaze 920 calories, 58g fat, 60g protein
4g net carbs: Make it Oscar Style 530 calories, 40g fat, 28g protein
4g net carbs: Surf & Turf, no breading/remove breading 1120 calories, 92g fat, 71g protein
4g net carbs: Veal Parmesan, no breading/remove breading 1690 calories, 79g fat, 98g protein
5g net carbs: Filet Mignon & Asparagus Risotto 1040 calories, 73g fat, 44g protein
5g net carbs: New York Strip 1120 calories, 67g fat, 84g protein
5g net carbs: Prime Ribeye 1870 calories, 149g fat, 70g protein
5g net carbs: Veal Piccata, no breading/remove breading 1200 calories, 66g fat, 73g protein
6g net carbs: Make it Contadina Style 630 calories, 45g fat, 30g protein
7g net carbs: Make it Al Forno Style 520 calories, 44g fat, 17g protein
7g net carbs: Veal Marsala, no breading/remove breading 1200 calories, 66g fat, 73g protein
7g net carbs: Veal Porterhouse 1570 calories, 111g fat, 97g protein

Sides

3g net carbs: Fresh Grilled Asparagus 70 calories, 4g fat, 5g protein
4g net carbs: Garlic Spinach 90 calories, 7g fat, 4g protein
8g net carbs: Roasted Garlic Broccoli, easy seasoning 200 calories, 15g fat, 5g protein

Salads

2g net carbs: Caesar Salad - Side, no croutons 280 calories, 26g fat, 7g protein
5g net carbs: Caesar Salad - Combo, no croutons 590 calories, 53g fat, 14g protein
6g net carbs: Caesar Salad - Entrée, no croutons 810 calories, 72g fat, 20g protein

4g net carbs: Chopped Salad - Side, easy dressing 480 calories, 24g fat, 9g protein
6g net carbs: Chopped Salad – Combo, easy dressing 880 calories, 27g fat, 16g protein
7g net carbs: Chopped Salad - Entrée, easy dressing 1250 calories, 34g fat, 24g protein
4g net carbs: Maggiano's Salad - Combo 660 calories, 59g fat, 15g protein
6g net carbs: Maggiano's Salad - Entrée 940 calories, 83g fat, 24g protein
7g net carbs: Maggiano's Salad - Side 300 calories, 26g fat, 9g protein

4g net carbs: Spinach Salad - Side, easy dressing 400 calories, 36g fat, 8g protein
6g net carbs: Spinach Salad - Combo, easy dressing 600 calories, 54g fat, 13g protein
8g net carbs: Spinach Salad - Entrée, easy dressing 820 calories, 73g fat, 18g protein
5g net carbs: Italian Tossed Salad - Combo, no croutons, easy dressing 480 calories, 42g fat, 8g protein
5g net carbs: Italian Tossed Salad - Side, no croutons, easy dressing 140 calories, 12g fat, 3g protein
7g net carbs: Italian Tossed Salad - Entrée, no croutons, easy dressing 700 calories, 62g fat, 11g protein
6g net carbs: Grilled Chicken Caprese Salad, no glaze, easy dressing 810 calories, 60g fat, 41g protein
8g net carbs: Grilled Salmon Salad, no croutons, no Snap Peas, no glaze, easy dressing 740 calories, 45g fat, 40g protein

Salad Add-Ons

0g net carbs: Salmon 250 calories, 15g fat, 28g protein
0g net carbs: Shrimp 90 calories, 3g fat, 16g protein
1g net carbs: Chicken 160 calories, 6g fat, 26g protein
7g net carbs: Crispy Calabrian Shrimp 190 calories, 11g fat, 15g protein

Soups

6g net carbs: Clam Chowder Manhattan Cup 70 calories, 8g fat, 5g protein
7g net carbs: Minestrone[55] Cup 90 calories, 5g fat, 4g protein
8g net carbs: Clam Chowder New England Cup 110 calories, 9g fat, 2g protein
8g net carbs: Tuscan Chicken Sausage Soup* Cup 100 calories, 4g fat, 6g protein

DRINKS

0g net carbs: Coke Zero, 16 oz. 0 calories, 0g fat, 0g protein

---

[55] *That's Not Keto!* – You'll find all sorts of surprising foods listed here. I'm not telling you whether you should eat these foods or not. What fits your macros or daily carb spend is up to you. No keto police allowed.

0g net carbs: Diet Coke, 16 oz. 0 calories, 0g fat, 0g protein
0g net carbs: Fresh Roasted Lavazza Coffee, unsweetened, 8 oz. 5 calories, 0g fat, 0g protein
0g net carbs: Harvey & Son's Hot Tea, unsweetened, 8 oz. 0 calories, 0g fat, 0g protein
1g net carbs: Lavazza Espresso, unsweetened, 3 oz. 5 calories, 0g fat, 0g protein
2g net carbs: Iced Tea, unsweetened, 16 oz. 5 calories, 0g fat, 0g protein
4g net carbs: Lavazza Cappuccino, unsweetened, 6 oz. 45 calories, 20g fat, 2g protein

Beer

3g net carbs: Bottle Miller Lite 12 oz. 96 calories, 0g fat, 1g protein
4g net carbs: Draft Miller Light 16 oz. 130 calories, 0g fat, 1g protein
5g net carbs: Bottle Coors Light 12 oz. 102 calories, 0g fat, 1g protein
7g net carbs: Bottle Bud Light 12 oz. 110 calories, 0g fat, 1g protein
9g net carbs: Draft Bud Light 16 oz. 140 calories, 0g fat, 1g protein

Wine

4g net carbs: House White Wine, 6 oz. 140 calories, 0g fat, 0g protein
5g net carbs: House Red Wine, 6 oz. 150 calories, 0g fat, 0g protein
7g net carbs: House Red Wine, 9 oz. 220 calories, 0g fat, 0g protein
7g net carbs: House White Wine, 9 oz. 210 calories, 0g fat, 0g protein

Spirits

7g net carbs: Mimosa 130 calories, 0g fat, 0g protein
7g net carbs: Old Fashioned 190 calories, 0g fat, 0g protein
8g net carbs: Bloody Mary Bourbon 210 calories, 40g fat, 3g protein
8g net carbs: Signature Barrel Aged Cocktail 150 calories, 0g fat, 0g protein
9g net carbs: Bloody Mary Vodka 160 calories, 15g fat, 3g protein
10g net carbs: Negroni 240 calories, 0g fat, 0g protein

California Pizza Kitchen

California Pizza Kitchen earns a *Keto Diet Restaurant Guide* Superstar Award by having a super-easy online tool that lists menu options based on nutrition (calories/carbs), allergies, or lifestyle (vegetarian).

Who would have thought that some PIZZA would have made it on the list of keto-approved options available at CPK? Look for yourself; they're in the Dinner section under Pizza (One Slice). *But before you get too excited.* Note the serving size. ONE slice, people (not the whole pie – I've made that mistake!). Slow your roll and savor every bite. Our best friend, the cauliflower, has again saved the day with this fabulous CPK "Cauliflower Crust."

Special Order Tips

Order all burgers and sandwiches with "no bread." Be wary of the available "Add-Ons" since they are often an unnecessary source of net carbs.

Feel free to customize your order. Restaurants are usually happy to accommodate reasonable customer requests. The exception is when the item has been premade or was prepared off-site. Note that any alterations on your end will change the provided nutrition information. Adjust accordingly.

Avoid all fries, potatoes, rice, pasta, bread, etc. Ask the server to substitute a side salad or a side of steamed/grilled vegetables.

You'll notice some menu items indicate a half-serving size. Don't worry; there aren't very many. In this instance, we did not initiate the modification. These half-serving offerings come directly from the California Pizza Kitchen's menu.

Author Favorite

Lunch: Full-size Breadless California Club- Turkey with lunch size The Mediterranean Salad, no Garbanzo Beans. 16 oz. Diet Coke to drink. 720 calories, 52g fat, 10g net carbs, 41g protein

Dinner: Petite Wedge salad to start. Fire-Grilled Ribeye, no potatoes. 16 oz. Freshly Brewed Iced Tea with sugar-free sweetener. 730 calories, 50g fat, 11g net carbs, 29g protein

LUNCH

Sandwiches (No Bread)

Oven Roasted Turkey and Brie, no honey-mustard, no apple
    2g net carbs: Half-Serving 410 calories, 17g fat, 23g protein
    4g net carbs: Full-Serving 810 calories, 35g fat, 46g protein
California Club- Chicken
    4g net carbs: Half-Serving 390 calories, 21g fat, 18g protein
    8g net carbs: Full-Serving 760 calories, 40g fat, 36g protein
California Club- Turkey
    3g net carbs: Half-Serving 250 calories, 17g fat, 18g protein
    7g net carbs: Full-Serving 490 calories, 33g fat, 36g protein
Grilled Veggie with easy sun-dried tomato aioli
    3g net carbs: Half-Serving 310 calories, 15g fat, 9g protein
    5g net carbs: Full-Serving 610 calories, 31g fat, 19g protein

Sandwich & Salad (No Bread)

3g net carbs: Grilled Veggie Sandwich & Classic Caesar, no croutons 490 calories, 29g fat, 14g protein
6g net carbs: Grilled Veggie Sandwich & The Mediterranean, no Garbanzo Beans 540 calories, 34g fat, 14g protein
4g net carbs: Oven-Roasted Turkey and Brie, no honey-mustard, no apple & Classic Caesar, no croutons 590 calories, 32g fat, 28g protein
5g net carbs: Oven-Roasted Turkey and Brie, no honey-mustard, no apple & The Mediterranean, no Garbanzo Beans 640 calories, 36g fat, 28g protein
5g net carbs: California Club Sandwich, Turkey & Classic Caesar, no croutons 430 calories, 31g fat, 23g protein
6g net carbs: California Club Sandwich, Turkey & The Mediterranean, no Garbanzo Beans 480 calories, 36g fat, 23g protein
6g net carbs: California Club Sandwich, Chicken & Classic Caesar, no croutons 570 calories, 35g fat, 23g protein

7g net carbs: California Club Sandwich, Chicken & The Mediterranean, no Garbanzo Beans 630 calories, 40g fat, 23g protein

Pasta & Salad (Substitute Steamed/Grilled Vegetables for Pasta)

4g net carbs: Spaghetti Bolognese & Classic Caesar Salad, no croutons 520 calories, 38g fat, 19g protein
4g net carbs: Tomato Basil Spaghetti with Goat Cheese and Classic Caesar Salad, no croutons 600 calories, 43g fat, 1g protein
4g net carbs: Tomato Basil Spaghetti with shrimp & Classic Caesar Salad, no croutons 560 calories, 40g fat, 15g protein
4g net carbs: Tomato Basil Spaghetti & Classic Caesar Salad, no croutons 560 calories, 40g fat, 15g protein
6g net carbs: Tomato Basil Spaghetti & The Mediterranean Salad, no Garbanzo Beans 580 calories, 46g fat, 15g protein
7g net carbs: Tomato Basil Spaghetti with Goat Cheese & The Mediterranean Salad, no Garbanzo Beans 610 calories, 45g fat, 18g protein
7g net carbs: Tomato Basil Spaghetti with shrimp & The Mediterranean Salad, no Garbanzo Beans 580 calories, 36g fat, 21g protein
7g net carbs: Spaghetti Bolognese & The Mediterranean Salad, no Garbanzo Beans 560 calories, 34g fat, 21g protein

Lunch Size Pastas (Substitute Steamed/Grilled Vegetables for Pasta)

2g net carbs: Tomato Basil Spaghetti 380 calories, 26g fat, 10g protein
2g net carbs: Tomato Basil Spaghetti with shrimp 390 calories, 28g fat, 12g protein
3g net carbs: Tomato Basil Spaghetti with Goat Cheese 410 calories, 31g fat, 15g protein
4g net carbs: Spaghetti Bolognese 360 calories, 24g fat, 13g protein

Lunch Size Salads

2g net carbs: Classic Caesar, no croutons 180 calories, 14g fat, 5g protein
3g net carbs: The Mediterranean Salad, no Garbanzo Beans 230 calories, 19g fat, 5g protein

Power Bowls

Banh Mi Bowl, no Quinoa
   2g net carbs: with Oil & Vinegar 580 calories, 40g fat, 34g protein
   4g net carbs: with No Dressing 450 calories, 26g fat, 34g protein
   5g net carbs: with Bleu Cheese 680 calories, 50g fat, 37g protein
   5g net carbs: with Caesar 590 calories, 47g fat, 35g protein
   5g net carbs: with Herb Ranch 630 calories, 44g fat, 35g protein
   5g net carbs: with Mustard Herb Vinaigrette 710 calories, 55g fat, 35g protein
   5g net carbs: with Poblano Ranch 560 calories, 38g fat, 35g protein
   7g net carbs: with easy Champagne Vinaigrette 680 calories, 50g fat, 34g protein
   7g net carbs: with easy Chili Lime Vinaigrette 620 calories, 43g fat, 35g protein
   8g net carbs: with easy Dijon Balsamic Vinaigrette 630 calories, 43g fat, 35g protein
Santa Fe Bowl, no Beans, no corn, no pepitas
   3g net carbs: with easy Dijon Balsamic Vinaigrette 530 calories, 43g fat, 25g protein
   4g net carbs: with No Dressing 350 calories, 26g fat, 34g protein
   5g net carbs: with Bleu Cheese 580 calories, 50g fat, 37g protein

5g net carbs: with Caesar 490 calories, 47g fat, 35g protein
5g net carbs: with Champagne Vinaigrette 580 calories, 50g fat, 37g protein
5g net carbs: with Chili Lime Vinaigrette 520 calories, 43g fat, 37g protein
5g net carbs: with Herb Ranch 530 calories, 44g fat, 35g protein
5g net carbs: with Mustard Herb Vinaigrette 610 calories, 55g fat, 35g protein
5g net carbs: with Oil & Vinegar 480 calories, 40g fat, 34g protein
5g net carbs: with Poblano Ranch 460 calories, 38g fat, 35g protein

Salads

Roasted Veggie Salad with Bleu Cheese, no corn, no sun-dried tomatoes
    4g net carbs: Half-Serving 360 calories, 27g fat, 7g protein
    6g net carbs: Full-Serving 730 calories, 55g fat, 13g protein
Classic Caesar Salad, no croutons
    4g net carbs: Half-Serving 340 calories, 27g fat, 9g protein
    6g net carbs: Full-Serving 530 calories, 40g fat, 17g protein
Waldorf Chicken Salad with Mustard Herb Vinaigrette, no grapes, no apples, no candied walnuts
    3g net carbs: Half-Serving 560 calories, 47g fat, 27g protein
    6g net carbs: Full-Serving 720 calories, 64g fat, 54g protein
Thai Crunch Salad with easy Mustard Herb Vinaigrette, no wontons, no rice sticks, no Thai peanut dressing
    4g net carbs: Half-Serving 490 calories, 36g fat, 28g protein
    7g net carbs: Full-Serving 680 calories, 73g fat, 55g protein
California Cobb Salad with easy bleu cheese dressing
    6g net carbs: Half-Serving 510 calories, 40g fat, 27g protein
    9g net carbs: Full-Serving 1020 calories, 79g fat, 53g protein
Italian Chopped Salad, no garbanzo Beans
    4g net carbs: Half-Serving 450 calories, 41g fat, 24g protein
    7g net carbs: Full-Serving 810 calories, 82g fat, 48g protein

Salad Dressing (1.5 oz.)

1g net carbs: Bleu Cheese 230 calories, 24g fat, 3g protein
1g net carbs: Caesar 140 calories, 14g fat, 1g protein
1g net carbs: Herb Ranch 170 calories, 17g fat, 1g protein
1g net carbs: Mustard Herb Vinaigrette 260 calories, 29g fat, 1g protein
1g net carbs: Poblano Ranch 110 calories, 12g fat, 1g protein
3g net carbs: Oil & Vinegar 130 calories, 14g fat, 0g protein
6g net carbs: Champagne Vinaigrette 230 calories, 24g fat, 0g protein
6g net carbs: Chili Lime Vinaigrette 170 calories, 17g fat, 1g protein
7g net carbs: Dijon Balsamic Vinaigrette 180 calories, 16g fat, 1g protein

DINNER

Small Plates Salad

4g net carbs: Petite Wedge 270 calories, 26g fat, 6g protein
6g net carbs: Crispy Artichoke Salad 350 calories, 31g fat, 9g protein

Small Plates Salad Add-On

0g net carbs: California Olive Oil with Mediterranean Herbs (1/2 oz.) 110 calories, 13g fat, 0g protein

Main Plates

3g net carbs: West Coast Burger "The WCB," bunless, no potatoes 280 calories, 21g fat, 17g protein
4g net carbs: Cedar Plank Salmon, no succotash, no corn 350 calories, 17g fat, 22g protein
6g net carbs: Fire-Grilled Ribeye, no potatoes 460 calories, 24g fat, 23g protein
7g net carbs: Chicken Piccata, no pasta 330 calories, 26g fat, 25g protein

Pasta (Substitute Steamed/Grilled Vegetables for Pasta)

3g net carbs: Chicken & Shrimp Kung Pao Spaghetti with easy sauce 590 calories, 37g fat, 28g protein
3g net carbs: Chicken Kung Pao Spaghetti with easy sauce 590 calories, 37g fat, 28g protein
4g net carbs: Shrimp Kung Pao Spaghetti with easy sauce 580 calories, 37g fat, 26g protein
4g net carbs: Shrimp Scampi Zucchini 480 calories, 26g fat, 27g protein
4g net carbs: Tomato Basil Spaghetti 450 calories, 52g fat, 20g protein
4g net carbs: Tomato Basil Spaghetti with shrimp 460 calories, 52g fat, 22g protein
5g net carbs: Bolognese Spaghetti 670 calories, 45g fat, 23g protein
5g net carbs: Garlic Cream Shrimp Fettuccine 750 calories, 80g fat, 32g protein
5g net carbs: Jambalaya Linguini Fini 730 calories, 51g fat, 57g protein
6g net carbs: Chicken Tequila Fettuccine, no lime sauce 710 calories, 67g fat, 39g protein
6g net carbs: Garlic Cream Chicken & Shrimp Fettuccine 740 calories, 86g fat, 30g protein
6g net carbs: Garlic Cream Chicken Fettuccine 760 calories, 84g fat, 30g protein

Pizza (One Slice)

8g net carbs: Avocado Super Green, Cauliflower Crust 140 calories, 10g fat, 2g protein
8g net carbs: Five Cheese and Fresh Tomato, Cauliflower Crust 140 calories, 8g fat, 7g protein
8g net carbs: Pepperoni, Cauliflower Crust 140 calories, 8g fat, 6g protein
8g net carbs: Wild Mushroom, Cauliflower Crust 120 calories, 7g fat, 5g protein
9g net carbs: California Club, Cauliflower Crust 190 calories, 11g fat, 10g protein
9g net carbs: Carne Asada, Cauliflower Crust 160 calories, 10g fat, 9g protein
9g net carbs: Mushroom Pepperoni Sausage, Cauliflower Crust 150 calories, 9g fat, 7g protein
9g net carbs: Shrimp Scampi, Cauliflower Crust 140 calories, 8g fat, 7g protein
10g net carbs: Spicy Milano Pizza, Cauliflower Crust 200 calories, 12g fat, 10g protein
10g net carbs: Sicilian, Cauliflower Crust 180 calories, 11g fat, 10g protein
10g net carbs: Spicy Chipotle Chicken, Cauliflower Crust 170 calories, 11g fat, 9g protein
10g net carbs: The Works, Cauliflower Crust 160 calories, 10g fat, 7g protein
10g net carbs: Hawaiian, Cauliflower Crust 130 calories, 6g fat, 9g protein

Soups

5g net carbs: Tomato Basil Bisque, no croutons 230 calories, 27g fat, 3g protein

DRINKS

0g net carbs: Diet Coke, 16 oz. 0 calories, 0g fat, 0g protein
0g net carbs: Coke Zero, 16 oz. 0 calories, 0g fat, 0g protein
1g net carbs: Fresca, 16 oz. 0 calories, 0g fat, 0g protein
10g net carbs: Sparkling Berry, Lemon, 16 oz. 40 calories, 0g fat, 0g protein
0g net carbs: Acqua Panna, 16 oz. bottle 0 calories, 0g fat, 0g protein
0g net carbs: San Pellegrino Sparkling, 16 oz. bottle 0 calories, 0g fat, 0protein
0g net carbs: Coffee, unsweetened, 8 oz. 0 calories, 0g fat, 0g protein
0g net carbs: Tazo Hot Teas, unsweetened, 8 oz. 0 calories, 0g fat, 0g protein
0g net carbs: Freshly Brewed Iced Tea, unsweetened, 16 oz. 0 calories, 0g fat, 0g protein

Beer & Seltzer

2g net carbs: Truly Lime Hard Seltzer, 12 oz. 100 calories, 0g fat, 0g protein
2g net carbs: Truly Wild Berry Hard Seltzer, 12 oz. 100 calories, 0g fat, 0g protein
3g net carbs: Miller Lite, 12 oz. 96 calories, 0g fat, 1g protein
5g net carbs: Coors Light, 12 oz. 102 calories, 0g fat, 1g protein
7g net carbs: Bud Light, 12 oz. 110 calories, 0g fat, 1g protein

Wine

3g net carbs: M. Chapoutier Belleruche Rose, 6 oz. 153 calories, 0g fat, 0g protein
3g net carbs: Mark West Pinot Noir, 6 oz. 152 calories, 0g fat, 0g protein
4g net carbs: Meiomi Pinot Noir, 6 oz. 140 calories, 0g fat, 0g protein
4g net carbs: La Crema Pinot Noir, 6 oz. 148 calories, 0g fat, 0g protein
4g net carbs: Francis Ford Coppola "Diamond Collection" Merlot, 6 oz. 162 calories, 0g fat, 1g protein
5g net carbs: Tamari Reserva Malbec, 6 oz. 147 calories, 0g fat, 0g protein
5g net carbs: Colby Red Blend, 6 oz. 152 calories, 0g fat, 0g protein
3g net carbs: Nobilo Sauvignon Blanc, 6 oz. 157 calories, 0g fat, 0g protein
4g net carbs: Kim Crawford Sauvignon Blanc, 6 oz. 168 calories, 0g fat, 0g protein
5g net carbs: Clos Du Bois Chardonnay, 6 oz. 162 calories, 0g fat, 0g protein
5g net carbs: Kendall-Jackson Vintner's Reserve Chardonnay, 6 oz. 160 calories, 0g fat, 0g protein
7g net carbs: Wine Flight (3), 3 oz. glasses 220 calories, 0g fat, 1g protein
8g net carbs: La Marca Prosecco (1 split) 160 calories, 0g fat, 1g protein

Spirits

0g net carbs: Woodford Old Fashioned 200 calories, 0g fat, 10g protein

Uno Pizzeria & Grill

Pizza on keto? Right here, folks! For this reason alone, Uno Pizzeria & Grill has earned a *Keto Diet Restaurant Guide* Superstar Award. They have a cauliflower crust available (Thin Crust only), enabling them to offer several pizza options at 5 to 7 grams of net carbs per slice, "Individual Size." That's just magical, Uno Pizzeria. We appreciate your initiative!

Uno Pizzeria & Grill offers a detailed "Nutritional Information" document on its website, which makes informed decision-making much more accessible. Though not a nutrition calculator, it's still valuable and worthy of mention.

Special Order Tips

Order all burgers and sandwiches "bunless" (without the bread) or "lettuce wrapped" to match the estimated nutrition information provided. Be wary of the available "Add-Ons" since they are often an unnecessary source of net carbs. These items are analyzed in their "regular" form as described on the menu. Any alterations will change their calorie and macronutrient amounts.

Avoid all fries, potatoes, rice, pasta, bread, etc. Ask the server to substitute a side salad or a side of steamed/grilled vegetables. Maybe try the steamed broccoli? This is a great alternative provided by Uno Pizzeria & Grill. Yummy.

Feel free to customize your order. Restaurants are usually happy to accommodate reasonable customer requests. The exception is when the item has been premade or was prepared off-site. Note that any alterations on your end will change the provided nutrition information. Adjust accordingly.

You'll notice some menu items indicate a half-serving size. Don't worry; there will only be a few. A smaller portion size allowed us to include more (higher-carb) crowd-pleasing favorites like soups or chilis.

Author Favorite

Lunch & Dinner: Grilled Shrimp with super easy Orange Cilantro Dipping Sauce to start. Rattlesnake Pasta, substitute steamed/roasted vegetables for pasta with Caesar side salad, no croutons on the side. Towering (Long Island) Iced Tea with Diet Pepsi cocktail on ice to drink. 970 calories, 91g fat, 16g net carbs, 105g protein

LUNCH & DINNER

Appetizers

4g net carbs: Buffalo Wings 1130 calories, 89g fat, 71g protein
7g net carbs: Grilled Shrimp with super easy Orange Cilantro Dipping Sauce 200 calories, 1g fat, 32g protein

Burgers & Sandwiches (No Bread)

3g net carbs: 1/2 lb. Uno Burger 1000 calories, 72g fat, 46g protein
6g net carbs: 1/2 lb. Uno Burger Gluten-Sensitive 1030 calories, 74g fat, 45g protein
3g net carbs: 1/2 lb. Cheddar Burger 1110 calories, 81g fat, 53g protein
6g net carbs: 1/2 lb. Cheddar Burger Gluten-Sensitive 1140 calories, 83g fat, 52g protein
3g net carbs: Bacon Cheddar Burger 1350 calories, 99g fat, 71g protein
6g net carbs: Bacon Cheddar Burger Gluten-Sensitive 1380 calories, 101g fat, 70g protein
4g net carbs: Aged Cheddar & Mushroom Burger 1120 calories, 81g fat, 53g protein
7g net carbs: Classic Beyond Burger, no Ketchup 560 calories, 32g fat, 26g protein
8g net carbs: Nashville Hot Burger 1210 calories, 84g fat, 58g protein

5g net carbs: BBQ Bacon Chicken Sandwich, super easy BBQ sauce 910 calories, 43g fat, 74g protein
6g net carbs: Caprese Sandwich, easy balsamic 450 calories, 18g fat, 21g protein
8g net carbs: Grilled Chicken Parm. Sandwich, remove breading, easy marinara 940 calories, 48g fat, 65g protein

Thin Crust Pizza Slice (Individual Size)

5g net carbs: Cheese Please! Cauliflower Crust 80 calories, 4g fat, 5g protein
5g net carbs: Super Roni Cauliflower Crust 120 calories, 8g fat, 7g protein
6g net carbs: Veggie Extravaganza Cauliflower Crust 100 calories, 6g fat, 6g protein

6g net carbs: Windy City Works Cauliflower Crust 120 calories, 8g fat, 7g protein
6g net carbs: Spicy Hawaiian Cauliflower Crust, no pineapple, easy red chili sauce 120 calories, 6g fat, 6g protein
7g net carbs: BBQ Chicken Cauliflower Crust, easy BBQ sauce 100 calories, 4g fat, 7g protein
7g net carbs: Margherita, easy housemade pizza sauce 103 calories, 2g fat, 5g protein

Create Your Own Cauliflower Thin Crust Slice (Individual Size Slice, 10 Inch)

Cauliflower Thin Crust Slice (Crust Only, Individual Size Slice, 10 Inch)

2g net carbs: Cauliflower Thin Crust (Only) 80 calories, 2g fat, 4g protein

Sauce

1g net carbs: Alfredo Sauce 10 calories, 4g fat, 0g protein
1g net carbs: Pesto Sauce 45 calories, 4g fat, 1g protein
2g net carbs: Tomato Sauce 5 calories, 0g fat, 0g protein

Free Toppings[56]

0g net carbs: Anchovies 30 calories, 1g fat, 4g protein
0g net carbs: Chicken 80 calories, 2g fat, 12g protein
0g net carbs: Eggplant 15 calories, 0g fat, 0g protein
0g net carbs: Meatballs 80 calories, 5g fat, 5g protein
0g net carbs: Pepperoni 50 calories, 4g fat, 2g protein
0g net carbs: Roasted Veggies 10 calories, 0g fat, 0g protein
0g net carbs: Sausage 240 calories, 20g fat, 13g protein
0g net carbs: Spinach 0 calories, 0g fat, 0g protein
1g net carbs: Bacon 140 calories, 11g fat, 7g protein
1g net carbs: Extra Cheese 20 calories, 7g fat, 7g protein
1g net carbs: Fresh Mozzarella 20 calories, 4g fat, 3g protein
1g net carbs: Goat Cheese 80 calories, 5g fat, 6g protein
1g net carbs: Ham 100 calories, 4g fat, 6g protein
1g net carbs: Jalapeños 5 calories, 0g fat, 0g protein
1g net carbs: Kalamata Olives 40 calories, 5g fat, 0g protein
1g net carbs: Mushrooms 0 calories, 0g fat, 1g protein
1g net carbs: Pesto 45 calories, 4g fat, 1g protein
2g net carbs: Black Olives 50 calories, 5g fat, 0g protein
2g net carbs: Broccoli 15 calories, 1g fat, 1g protein
2g net carbs: Extra Tomato Sauce 5 calories, 0g fat, 0g protein
2g net carbs: Feta Cheese 70 calories, 6g fat, 5g protein
2g net carbs: Onions 10 calories, 0g fat, 0g protein
2g net carbs: Peppers (Bell) 15 calories, 0g fat, 1g protein
2g net carbs: Ricotta 100 calories, 7g fat, 7g protein
3g net carbs: Hamburger 210 calories, 15g fat, 18g protein

---

[56] Quantity not specified by restaurant. If I had to guess, I would say per 1 Tbsp./per slice of pizza.

3g net carbs: Pineapple[57] 40 calories, 0g fat, 0g protein
3g net carbs: Seasoned Garlic 60 calories, 1g fat, 2g protein

Extra-Charge Toppings[58]

0g net carbs: Anchovies 30 calories, 1g fat, 4g protein
0g net carbs: Chicken 80 calories, 2g fat, 12g protein
0g net carbs: Eggplant 15 calories, 0g fat, 0g protein
0g net carbs: Meatballs 80 calories, 5g fat, 5g protein
0g net carbs: Pepperoni 50 calories, 4g fat, 2g protein
0g net carbs: Roasted Veggies 10 calories, 0g fat, 0g protein
0g net carbs: Sausage 240 calories, 20g fat, 13g protein
0g net carbs: Spinach 0 calories, 0g fat, 0g protein
1g net carbs: Bacon 140 calories, 11g fat, 7g protein
1g net carbs: Extra Cheese 90 calories, 7g fat, 7g protein
1g net carbs: Fresh Mozzarella 90 calories, 7g fat, 7g protein
1g net carbs: Goat Cheese 80 calories, 5g fat, 6g protein
1g net carbs: Ham 100 calories, 4g fat, 6g protein
1g net carbs: Jalapeños 5 calories, 0g fat, 0g protein
1g net carbs: Kalamata Olives 40 calories, 5g fat, 0g protein
1g net carbs: Mushrooms 0 calories, 0g fat, 1g protein
1g net carbs: Pesto 45 calories, 4g fat, 1g protein
2g net carbs: Broccoli 15 calories, 1g fat, 1g protein
2g net carbs: Feta Cheese 70 calories, 6g fat, 5g protein
2g net carbs: Green (Bell) Peppers 15 calories, 0g fat, 1g protein
2g net carbs: Onions 10 calories, 0g fat, 0g protein
2g net carbs: Tomato Sauce 5 calories, 0g fat, 0g protein
3g net carbs: Hamburger 210 calories, 15g fat, 18g protein
3g net carbs: Pineapple* 40 calories, 0g fat, 0g protein
3g net carbs: Seasoned Garlic 60 calories, 1g fat, 2g protein

Pasta (Substitute Steamed/Roasted Vegetables for Pasta)

5g net carbs: Regular Mac & Cheese 640 calories, 43g fat, 70g protein
5g net carbs: Romano-Grilled Chicken Parm, remove breading, easy marinara 660 calories, 39g fat, 82g
    protein
6g net carbs: Buffalo Chicken Mac & Cheese 700 calories, 63g fat, 96g protein
6g net carbs: Rattlesnake Pasta 710 calories, 70g fat, 67g protein
6g net carbs: Shrimp Scampi, easy sauce 690 calories, 54g fat, 44g protein
7g net carbs: Chicken Spinoccoli, easy tomato sauce 760 calories, 62g fat, 77g protein
7g net carbs: Classic Spaghetti & Meatball, easy marinara 800 calories, 79g fat, 51g protein
7g net carbs: Grilled Chicken & Broccoli Alfredo 650 calories, 73g fat, 68g protein

---

[57] *That's Not Keto!* – You'll find all sorts of surprising foods listed here. I'm not telling you whether you should eat these foods or not. What fits your macros or daily carb spend is up to you. No keto police allowed.

[58] Quantity not specified by restaurant. If I had to guess, I would say per 1 Tbsp./per slice of pizza.

Steak, Seafood & Chicken

0g net carbs: Lemon Basil Salmon 490 calories, 38g fat, 40g protein
0g net carbs: Top Sirloin Steak 560 calories, 37g fat, 52g protein
1g net carbs: Grilled Shrimp & Sirloin 690 calories, 45g fat, 66g protein
2g net carbs: Lemon Herb Chicken Skewers 440 calories, 28g fat, 40g protein
2g net carbs: Tuscan Chimichurri Cap Steak 590 calories, 31g fat, 52g protein
3g net carbs: Baked Haddock, remove breading, 530 calories, 33g fat, 48g protein
3g net carbs: Sirloin Tips 470 calories, 27g fat, 62g protein
4g net carbs: Mediterranean Chicken, no mashed potatoes 460 calories, 21g fat, 49g protein
6g net carbs: Baked Fish & Chips, remove breading, 550 calories, 53g fat, 32g protein
6g net carbs: Grilled Chicken Tender Platter, remove breading, 700 calories, 46g fat, 72g protein

Sides

2g net carbs: Steamed Broccoli 70 calories, 6g fat, 3g protein
6g net carbs: Roasted Seasonal Vegetables 70 calories, 4g fat, 2g protein

Soup

7g net carbs: Broccoli & Cheddar Soup, Half-Serving, no soup crackers 155 calories, 10g fat, 6g protein

Side Salads (Includes Salad Dressing Unless Otherwise Indicated)

2g net carbs: House Side Salad (Excludes Dressing), no croutons 90 calories, 5g fat, 2g protein
4g net carbs: House Side Salad Gluten Sensitive, no croutons 25 calories, 0g fat, 1g protein
2g net carbs: Caesar Side Salad, no croutons 220 calories, 19g fat, 5g protein
3g net carbs: Caesar Side Salad Gluten Sensitive, no croutons 160 calories, 15g fat, 4g protein
6g net carbs: Berry & Goat Cheese Side Salad, no berries, no grapes, no honey, easy dressing 170 calories, 10g fat, 4g protein
7g net carbs: Wedge Side Salad 230 calories, 19g fat, 7g protein

Signature Salads (Includes Salad Dressing Unless Otherwise Indicated)

2g net carbs: House Salad, no croutons 270 calories, 13g fat, 14g protein
3g net carbs: Berry & Goat Cheese Salad, no berries, easy dressing 240 calories, 21g fat, 7g protein
3g net carbs: Grilled Chicken Caesar Salad with anchovies, no croutons 590 calories, 44g fat, 37g protein
3g net carbs: Grilled Chicken Caesar Salad, no croutons 560 calories, 41g fat, 33g protein
3g net carbs: Grilled Chicken House Salad, no croutons 390 calories, 18g fat, 27g protein
4g net carbs: Berry & Goat Cheese Grilled Chicken Salad, no berries, easy dressing 340 calories, 28g fat, 17g protein
4g net carbs: Grilled Chicken Caesar Salad, Gluten Sensitive, no croutons 440 calories, 32g fat, 32g protein
4g net carbs: Italian Chopped Salad, no croutons, easy dressing 540 calories, 28g fat, 32g protein
6g net carbs: Grilled Chicken Italian Chopped Salad, no croutons, easy dressing 680 calories, 48g fat, 42g protein
7g net carbs: Chopped Honey Grilled Chicken Salad with Avocado Ranch Dressing, no spaghetti 720 calories, 40g fat, 33g protein

Salad Dressing

1g net carbs: Bleu Cheese 210 calories, 23g fat, 1g protein
1g net carbs: Caesar 200 calories, 20g fat, 3g protein
1g net carbs: Greek 130 calories, 2g fat, 0g protein
2g net carbs: Avocado Ranch 140 calories, 15g fat, 0g protein
3g net carbs: Balsamic Vinaigrette 160 calories, 16g fat, 0g protein
3g net carbs: Ranch 170 calories, 18g fat, 0g protein
5g net carbs: Low-Fat Vinaigrette 60 calories, 4g fat, 0g protein
7g net carbs: Low-Fat Honey Vinaigrette, Half-Serving, 40 calories, 2g fat, 0g protein
9g net carbs: Honey Mustard[59] 200 calories, 18f 3g fat, 0g protein

DRINKS

0g net carbs: Diet Pepsi, 16 oz. 0 calories, 0g fat, 0g protein
0g net carbs: Spring Water, 16 oz. bottle 0 calories, 0g fat, 0g protein
0g net carbs: Sparkling Water, 16 oz. bottle 0 calories, 0g fat, 0g protein
0g net carbs: Iced Tea, unsweetened, 16 oz. 0 calories, 0g fat, 0g protein
0g net carbs: Coffee, unsweetened, 8 oz. 0 calories, 0g fat, 0g protein
2g net carbs: Red Bull, Sugar-free 8.4 oz. 10 calories, 0g fat, 0g protein

Beer & Seltzer

2g net carbs: Bud Light Seltzer Lemonade Strawberry, 12 oz. can 100 calories, 0g fat, 0g protein
2g net carbs: Bud Light Seltzer Black Cherry, 12 oz. can 100 calories, 0g fat, 0g protein
2g net carbs: White Claw Hard Seltzer, 12 oz. can 100 calories, 0g fat, 0g protein

0g net carbs: Budweiser Next- Zero Carb, 12 oz. bottle 0 calories, 0g fat, 1g protein
3g net carbs: Michelob ULTRA, 12 oz. bottle 95 calories, 0g fat, 1g protein
3g net carbs: Miller Lite, 12 oz. bottle 96 calories, 0g fat, 1g protein
4g net carbs: Miller Lite 16oz. Draft 130 calories, 0g fat, 1g protein
6g net carbs: Miller Lite 22oz. Draft 176 calories, 0g fat, 2g protein

5g net carbs: Amstel Light, 12 oz. bottle 95 calories, 0g fat, 1g protein
5g net carbs: Coors Light, 12 oz. bottle 102 calories, 0g fat, 1g protein
5g net carbs: Corona Light, 12 oz. bottle 99 calories, 0g fat, 1g protein
7g net carbs: Coors Light 16oz. Draft 140 calories, 0g fat, 1g protein
9g net carbs: Coors Light 22oz. Draft 193 calories, 0g fat, 2g protein

7g net carbs: Heineken Light, 12 oz. bottle 100 calories, 0g fat, 1g protein
7g net carbs: Bud Light, 12 oz. bottle 110 calories, 0g fat, 1g protein
9g net carbs: Bud Light 16oz. Draft 147 calories, 0g fat, 1g protein
10g net carbs: Bud Light 22oz. Draft 188 calories, 0g fat, 2g protein

---

[59] *That's Not Keto!* – You'll find all sorts of surprising foods listed here. I'm not telling you whether you should eat these foods or not. What fits your macros or daily carb spend is up to you. No keto police allowed.

White Wine

3g net carbs: Canyon Road Chardonnay (House), 5 oz. 150 calories, 0g fat, 0g protein
5g net carbs: Kendall-Jackson Chardonnay, 5 oz. 140 calories, 0g fat, 0g protein
3g net carbs: Mezzacorona Pinot Grigio, 5 oz. 130 calories, 0g fat, 0g protein
3g net carbs: Stemmari Dry Rosé, 5 oz. 120 calories, 0g fat, 0g protein
4g net carbs: Nobilo Sauvignon Blanc, 5 oz. 120 calories, 0g fat, 0g protein
7g net carbs: Beringer White Zinfandel, 5 oz. 130 calories, 0g fat, 0g protein

Red Wine

3g net carbs: Mark West Pinot Noir, 5 oz. 140 calories, 0g fat, 0g protein
4g net carbs: Blackstone Merlot, 5 oz. 140 calories, 0g fat, 0g protein
4g net carbs: Canyon Road Cabernet (House), 5 oz. 160 calories, 0g fat, 0g protein
4g net carbs: J. Lohr Cabernet Sauvignon, 5 oz. 150 calories, 0g fat, 0g protein
5g net carbs: Ruffino Chianti, 5 oz. 170 calories, 0g fat, 0g protein
5g net carbs: Tilia Malbec, 5 oz. 150 calories, 0g fat, 0g protein

Spirits

0g net carbs: Basil Hayden Manhattan 230 calories, 0g fat, 0g protein
0g net carbs: Knob Creek Old Fashioned 240 calories, 0g fat, 1g protein
0g net carbs: Now That's a Martini Grey Goose Vodka 270 calories, 0g fat, 0g protein
0g net carbs: Now That's a Martini Hendrick's Gin 270 calories, 0g fat, 0g protein
1g net carbs: Towering (Long Island) Iced Tea, with Diet Pepsi 40 calories, 1g fat, 1g protein
3g net carbs: Cucumber Mint Seltzer Spritzer 90 calories, 2g fat, 2g protein
5g net carbs: Absolut Bloody Mary 370 calories, 11g fat, 10g protein

MOD Pizza

If you want to go the pizza route at MOD Pizza, the only way to make this happen is by going "crustless." Choose the size, low-carb sauce, cheese, meat, and veggies you like, and eat this creation with a fork. When ordering, make it VERY CLEAR that you want *no crust* AT ALL. Otherwise, the salad route is a more traditional order, and you won't get those stares from both staff and customers.

The figures quoted for this restaurant are for crustless pizzas and for the whole pizza (Mini/MOD). Mini and MOD are the only 2 pizza choices since the Mega is only a thicker crust, and we are going crustless here. Don't even think of finding refuge with the Gluten-Friendly Crust. It has almost twice the net carbs as the standard crust. Unfortunately, the cauliflower crust isn't much help, either. It has virtually the same amount of net carbs as the regular flour crust (MOD- 11-inch). Good try, though, MOD Pizza.

Special Order Tips

MOD Pizza does not have a customizable nutrition calculator on its website. Instead, they provide a detailed "Nutritional Information" page that will help you be in control of your carb intake. I very much appreciate what they've done here. They have broken out the macronutrients for ALL crust options and ALL possible toppings.

Feel free to customize your order. Restaurants are usually happy to accommodate reasonable customer requests. The exception is when the item has been premade or was prepared off-site. Note that any alterations on your end will change the provided nutrition information. Adjust accordingly.

Avoid all fries, potatoes, rice, pasta, bread, etc. Ask the server to substitute a side salad or a side of steamed/grilled vegetables.

Author Favorite

Lunch & Dinner: Greek Mega Salad, no chickpeas. 16 oz. Diet Coke to drink. 760 calories, 54g fat, 7g net carbs, 22g protein

LUNCH & DINNER

Crustless Pizza (Whole Pizza, Mini/MOD)

Calexico (No Crust)
    2g net carbs: Mini 160 calories, 11g fat, 8g protein
    3g net carbs: MOD 330 calories, 24g fat, 28g protein
Dillon James (No Crust)
    4g net carbs: Mini 160 calories, 11g fat, 12g protein
    6g net carbs: MOD 320 calories, 20g fat, 17g protein
Jasper (No Crust)
    1g net carbs: Mini 130 calories, 9g fat, 11g protein
    4g net carbs: MOD 270 calories, 17g fat, 23g protein
Lucy Sunshine (No Crust)
    5g net carbs: Mini 130 calories, 8g fat, 9g protein
    7g net carbs: MOD 270 calories, 16g fat, 19g protein
Dominic (No Crust)
    3g net carbs: Mini 100 calories, 7g fat, 6g protein
    6g net carbs: MOD 190 calories, 13g fat, 11g protein
Tristan (No Crust)
    1g net carbs: Mini 160 calories, 12g fat, 10g protein
    3g net carbs: MOD 310 calories, 24g fat, 20g protein
Mad Dog (No Crust)
    2g net carbs: Mini 40 calories, 18g fat, 9g protein
    2g net carbs: MOD 470 calories, 35g fat, 32g protein
Wilbur/Red Eye (No Crust)
    6g net carbs: Mini 220 calories, 15g fat, 13g protein
Amelia/Layover (No Crust)
    3g net carbs: Mini 250 calories, 17g fat, 17g protein
    6g net carbs: MOD 460 calories, 34g fat, 31g protein
Maddy (No Crust)
    1g net carbs: Mini 100 calories, 6g fat, 7g protein
    3g net carbs: MOD 200 calories, 14g fat, 15g protein
Willow - Flash Mod (No Crust)
    3g net carbs: Mini 140 calories, 11g fat, 9g protein
    5g net carbs: MOD 280 calories, 20g fat, 18g protein
Willow (Vegan) - Flash Mod (No Crust)
    9g net carbs: Mini 180 calories, 14g fat, 5g protein

Build Your Own Crustless Pizza (Mini, 6-inch Pizza & MOD, 11-inch pizza)

Sauce (1 Tbsp, Mini, 6-inch Pizza)

0g net carbs: Extra Virgin Olive Oil 120 calories, 14g fat, 0g protein

1g net carbs: Pesto 50 calories, 4g fat, 1g protein
1g net carbs: Spicy Calabrian Chili Red Sauce 20 calories, 1g fat, 0g protein
1g net carbs: White Sauce 10 calories, 0g fat, 0g protein
2g net carbs: Red Sauce 5 calories, 0g fat, 0g protein
3g net carbs: Garlic Rub 10 calories, 0g fat, 1g protein
8g net carbs: BBQ Sauce[60] 30 calories, 0g fat, 0g protein

Sauce (2 Tbsp, MOD, 11-inch Pizza)

0g net carbs: Extra Virgin Olive Oil 240 calories, 28g fat, 0g protein
2g net carbs: Pesto 90 calories, 8g fat, 2g protein
2g net carbs: Spicy Calabrian Chili Red Sauce 40 calories, 2g fat, 0g protein
2g net carbs: White Sauce 15 calories, 0g fat, 0g protein
5g net carbs: Red Sauce 15 calories, 0g fat, 0g protein
5g net carbs: Garlic Rub 15 calories, 0g fat, 1g protein

Cheese (2 Tbsp, Mini, 6-inch Pizza)

1g net carbs: Asiago 50 calories, 4g fat, 4g protein
1g net carbs: Cheddar 55 calories, 5g fat, 3g protein
1g net carbs: Gorgonzola 50 calories, 4g fat, 3g protein
1g net carbs: Mozzarella 45 calories, 4g fat, 4g protein
1g net carbs: Feta 35 calories, 3g fat, 2g protein
1g net carbs: Parmesan 70 calories, 4g fat, 5g protein
1g net carbs: Ricotta 50 calories, 4g fat, 4g protein
4g net carbs: Dairy-Free Cheese 40 calories, 3g fat, 1g protein

Cheese (4 Tbsp, MOD, 11-inch Pizza)

1g net carbs: Asiago 110 calories, 8g fat, 8g protein
1g net carbs: Cheddar 110 calories, 9g fat, 6g protein
1g net carbs: Gorgonzola 100 calories, 8g fat, 6g protein
1g net carbs: Mozzarella 90 calories, 7g fat, 7g protein
2g net carbs: Feta 70 calories, 6g fat, 5g protein
2g net carbs: Parmesan 130 calories, 9g fat, 10g protein
2g net carbs: Ricotta 100 calories, 7g fat, 7g protein
8g net carbs: Dairy-Free Cheese 80 calories, 5g fat, 1g protein

Meat (2 Tbsp, Mini, 6-inch Pizza)

0g net carbs: Anchovies (3) 20 calories, 1g fat, 2g protein
0g net carbs: Mild Sausage 120 calories, 10g fat, 6g protein
0g net carbs: Pepperoni (3 slices) 30 calories, 2g fat, 1g protein
1g net carbs: Bacon 70 calories, 6g fat, 3g protein
1g net carbs: Grilled Chicken 35 calories, 1g fat, 6g protein
1g net carbs: Red Thai Curry Chicken 40 calories, 1g fat, 6g protein

---

[60] *That's Not Keto!* – You'll find all sorts of surprising foods listed here. I'm not telling you whether you should eat these foods or not. What fits your macros or daily carb spend is up to you. No keto police allowed.

1g net carbs: Salami (3 slices) 45 calories, 4g fat, 3g protein
1g net carbs: Spicy Chicken Sausage 45 calories, 3g fat, 6g protein
1g net carbs: Canadian Bacon (3 slices) 25 calories, 1g fat, 4g protein
1g net carbs: Egg – scrambled 40 calories, 2g fat, 4g protein
1g net carbs: Plant-Based Italian Sausage 45 calories, 3g fat, 3g protein
2g net carbs: Ground Beef 110 calories, 7g fat, 9g protein

Meat (4 Tbsp, MOD, 11-inch Pizza)

0g net carbs: Anchovies (6) 30 calories, 1g fat, 4g protein
0g net carbs: Mild Sausage 240 calories, 20g fat, 13g protein
0g net carbs: Pepperoni (5 slices) 50 calories, 4g fat, 2g protein
1g net carbs: Bacon 140 calories, 11g fat, 7g protein
1g net carbs: Grilled Chicken 70 calories, 2g fat, 12g protein
1g net carbs: Red Thai Curry Chicken 80 calories, 2g fat, 12g protein
1g net carbs: Salami (5 slices) 90 calories, 8g fat, 5g protein
1g net carbs: Spicy Chicken Sausage 90 calories, 5g fat, 11g protein
2g net carbs: Canadian Bacon (5 slices) 50 calories, 1g fat, 9g protein
2g net carbs: Egg – scrambled 80 calories, 4g fat, 7g protein
2g net carbs: Plant-Based Italian Sausage 90 calories, 6g fat, 6g protein
3g net carbs: Ground Beef 210 calories, 15g fat, 18g protein

Veggies & Good Stuff (2 Tbsp Unless Otherwise Indicated, Mini, 6-inch Pizza)

0g net carbs: Arugula 0 calories, 0g fat, 0g protein
0g net carbs: Basil – fresh chopped 0 calories, 0g fat, 0g protein
0g net carbs: Sea Salt (per tsp) 0 calories, 0g fat, 0g protein
0g net carbs: Spinach 0 calories, 0g fat, 0g protein
1g net carbs: Black Olives 25 calories, 3g fat, 0g protein
1g net carbs: Broccoli – roasted 10 calories, 1g fat, 1g protein
1g net carbs: Green Bell Peppers 5 calories, 0g fat, 0g protein
1g net carbs: Jalapeños 3 calories, 0g fat, 0g protein
1g net carbs: Mushrooms 0 calories, 0g fat, 1g protein
1g net carbs: Oregano (per tsp) 0 calories, 0g fat, 0g protein
1g net carbs: Rosemary – fresh chopped 5 calories, 0g fat, 0g protein
1g net carbs: Sea Salt & Pepper (per tsp) 0 calories, 0g fat, 0g protein
1g net carbs: Tomatoes – diced 5 calories, 0g fat, 0g protein
2g net carbs: Garlic – chopped (per Tbsp) 5 calories, 0g fat, 1g protein
2g net carbs: Red Onion 5 calories, 0g fat, 0g protein
2g net carbs: Red Peppers – roasted 10 calories, 0g fat, 1g protein
2g net carbs: Serrano Peppers 10 calories, 0g fat, 0g protein
2g net carbs: Tomatoes – sliced (5) 10 calories, 0g fat, 1g protein
4g net carbs: Artichokes 15 calories, 0g fat, 1g protein
4g net carbs: Corn[61] – roasted 20 calories, 1g fat, 1g protein
4g net carbs: Garlic – roasted 30 calories, 1g fat, 1g protein
4g net carbs: Mama Lil's Sweet Hot Peppas 25 calories, 0g fat, 0g protein
5g net carbs: Pineapple* 20 calories, 0g fat, 0g protein

---

[61] *That's Not Keto!* – You'll find all sorts of surprising foods listed here. I'm not telling you whether you should eat these foods or not. What fits your macros or daily carb spend is up to you. No keto police allowed.

Veggies & Good Stuff (4 Tbsp Unless Otherwise Indicated, MOD, 11-inch Pizza)

0g net carbs: Arugula 0 calories, 0g fat, 0g protein
0g net carbs: Basil – fresh chopped 0 calories, 0g fat, 0g protein
0g net carbs: Sea Salt (per tsp) 0 calories, 0g fat, 0g protein
0g net carbs: Spinach 0 calories, 0g fat, 0g protein
1g net carbs: Jalapeños 5 calories, 0g fat, 0g protein
1g net carbs: Mushrooms 0 calories, 0g fat, 1g protein
1g net carbs: Oregano (per tsp) 0 calories, 0g fat, 0g protein
1g net carbs: Rosemary – fresh chopped 10 calories, 0g fat, 0g protein
1g net carbs: Sea Salt & Pepper (per tsp) 0 calories, 0g fat, 0g protein
2g net carbs: Black Olives 50 calories, 5g fat, 0g protein
2g net carbs: Broccoli – roasted 15 calories, 1g fat, 1g protein
2g net carbs: Green Bell Peppers 5 calories, 0g fat, 0g protein
2g net carbs: Serrano Peppers 10 calories, 0g fat, 0g protein
2g net carbs: Tomatoes – diced 10 calories, 0g fat, 0g protein
3g net carbs: Garlic – chopped (per Tbsp) 15 calories, 0g fat, 1g protein
3g net carbs: Red Onion 10 calories, 0g fat, 0g protein
3g net carbs: Red Peppers – roasted 15 calories, 0g fat, 1g protein
3g net carbs: Tomatoes – sliced (5) 20 calories, 0g fat, 1g protein
8g net carbs: Artichokes 30 calories, 0g fat, 2g protein
8g net carbs: Corn* – roasted 45 calories, 1g fat, 1g protein
8g net carbs: Mama Lil's Sweet Hot Peppas 50 calories, 0g fat, 0g protein
9g net carbs: Garlic – roasted 60 calories, 1g fat, 2g protein
10g net carbs: Pineapple* 40 calories, 0g fat, 0g protein

Finishing Sauces (1/2 Tbsp, Mini, 6-inch Pizza)

0g net carbs: hot buffalo sauce 0 calories, 0g fat, 0g protein
1g net carbs: pesto drizzle 25 calories, 3g fat, 1g protein
1g net carbs: ranch finish 25 calories, 3g fat, 0g protein
1g net carbs: red sauce dollops 5 calories, 0g fat, 0g protein
1g net carbs: sri-rancha sauce 20 calories, 2g fat, 0g protein
4g net carbs: balsamic fig glaze* 15 calories, 0g fat, 0g protein
4g net carbs: bbq* swirl 15 calories, 0g fat, 0g protein

Finishing Sauces (1 Tbsp, MOD, 11-inch Pizza)

0g net carbs: hot buffalo sauce 0 calories, 0g fat, 0g protein
1g net carbs: pesto drizzle 45 calories, 5g fat, 1g protein
1g net carbs: ranch finish 50 calories, 6g fat, 0g protein
1g net carbs: red sauce dollops 5 calories, 0g fat, 0g protein
2g net carbs: sri-rancha sauce 35 calories, 3g fat, 0g protein
8g net carbs: balsamic fig glaze[62] 30 calories, 0g fat, 0g protein
8g net carbs: bbq swirl* 30 calories, 0g fat, 0g protein

---

[62] *That's Not Keto!* – You'll find all sorts of surprising foods listed here. I'm not telling you whether you should eat these foods or not. What fits your macros or daily carb spend is up to you. No keto police allowed.

Dipping Sauces (3 Tbsp)

0g net carbs: Hot Buffalo Sauce 0 calories, 0g fat, 0g protein
2g net carbs: Pesto 140 calories, 14g fat, 3g protein
3g net carbs: Ranch 160 calories, 18g fat, 1g protein
4g net carbs: Red Sauce 20 calories, 0g fat, 1g protein
6g net carbs: Sri-Rancha 100 calories, 9g fat, 1g protein

Salads (No Dressing)

3g net carbs: Italian Chop Mini, no chickpeas 310 calories, 25g fat, 10g protein
5g net carbs: Italian Chop Mod, no chickpeas 470 calories, 36g fat, 20g protein
7g net carbs: Italian Chop Mega, no chickpeas 950 calories, 71g fat, 39g protein
5g net carbs: Greek Mini, no chickpeas 270 calories, 21g fat, 6g protein
6g net carbs: Greek Mod, no chickpeas 380 calories, 27g fat, 11g protein
7g net carbs: Greek Mega, no chickpeas 760 calories, 54g fat, 22g protein
4g net carbs: Garden Mini, no croutons 150 calories, 11g fat, 1g protein
6g net carbs: Garden Mod, no croutons 170 calories, 12g fat, 2g protein
8g net carbs: Garden Mega, no croutons 320 calories, 23g fat, 4g protein
4g net carbs: Caesar Mini, no croutons 480 calories, 41g fat, 12g protein
5g net carbs: Caesar Mod, no croutons 680 calories, 52g fat, 23g protein
7g net carbs: Caesar Mega, no croutons 1360 calories, 104g fat, 46g protein
3g net carbs: Fall Harvest Salad Mini, no croutons 180 calories, 11g fat, 5g protein
5g net carbs: Fall Harvest Salad MOD, no croutons 360 calories, 22g fat, 9g protein
7g net carbs: Fall Harvest Salad Mega, no croutons 720 calories, 43g fat, 18g protein

Salad Dressing (1 Tbsp Unless Indicated Otherwise)

0g net carbs: Blue Cheese 90 calories, 9g fat, 0g protein
0g net carbs: Extra Virgin Olive Oil 120 calories, 14g fat, 0g protein
0g net carbs: Italian 70 calories, 8g fat, 0g protein
0g net carbs: Oil and Vinegar 60 calories, 7g fat, 0g protein
0g net carbs: Red Wine Vinegar 65 calories, 0g fat, 0g protein
1g net carbs: Balsamic 60 calories, 6g fat, 0g protein
1g net carbs: Caesar 100 calories, 10g fat, 1g protein
1g net carbs: Ranch 50 calories, 6g fat, 0g protein
2g net carbs: Greek Herb & Tahini 50 calories, 5g fat, 0g protein
3g net carbs: Honey Lime 60 calories, 6g fat, 0g protein
3g net carbs: Lemon Vinaigrette (3 Tbsp) 140 calories, 1g fat, 1g protein
3g net carbs: Zesty Roma 45 calories, 4g fat, 0g protein

DRINKS

0g net carbs: Diet Coke, 16 oz. 0 calories, 0g fat, 0g protein
0g net carbs: Diet Coke, 24 oz. 0 calories, 0g fat, 0g protein
0g net carbs: Coke Zero, 16 oz. 0 calories, 0g fat, 0g protein
0g net carbs: Coke Zero, 24 oz. 0 calories, 0g fat, 0g protein
1g net carbs: Hot Tea, Unsweetened, 8 oz. 0 calories, 0g fat, 0g protein
1g net carbs: Iced Gold Peak, Unsweetened Black Tea, 16 oz. 0 calories, 0g fat, 0g protein

Chuck E. Cheese

Chuck E. Cheese[63] has been known to prepare a crustless pizza so peruse all available "Build Your Own Pizza" cheeses, sauces, and toppings and build your own Keto Cravin' Pizza or check out one of their Specialty Pizzas and order it up "crustless." Can I get an Amen for this effort?

Feel free to customize any menu item to your liking, but be sure to adjust the carbs. Restaurants are happy to make reasonable substitutions for their customers. The exception is when an item is premade with the offending ingredient (think frozen breaded shrimp or pre-seasoned chicken wings).

Chuck E. Cheese does not have a customizable nutrition calculator on its website. Instead, they offer a detailed "Nutritionals" PDF to help you be in control of your carb intake. How do you find this helpful document? Start at the restaurant's main page. Locate "Pizza & More" at the top of the main page and then scroll almost to the very bottom. Click "Download Nutrition Information PDF" for a hyperlink to page one of the PDF, where macronutrients are itemized.

Special Order Tips

If you're deadset on ordering a "real" pizza slice with a crust, consider an Individual Size slice of pizza made with the Smart Flour Gluten-Free Crust. It has 9 grams of net carbs (for the crust only). Toppings are additional.

---

[63] Noodle this one over. The website uses the "Chuck E. Cheese" branding, while the restaurant signage uses "Chuck E. Cheese's." *Which one is it?*

Watch out for the Wings at Chuck E. Cheese. Both the boneless and traditional wings are higher in net carbs. If you must, choose traditional wings (no deep-fried coating) and be careful of sauces. Most contain sugar. Your best bet for dipping is either ranch or blue cheese dressing.

Author Favorite

Lunch & Dinner: 1 Individual Size slice of "Crustless" Supreme pizza with a side of Small Wings- Plain, no glaze or sauce. 16 oz. Lipton Unsweetened Iced Tea to drink. 620 calories, 38g fat, 4g net carbs, 52g protein

LUNCH & DINNER

Sandwiches (No Bread)

2g net carbs: Breadless Chicken Bacon Ranch Sub 1/2 Sandwich 290 calories, 13g fat, 21g protein
2g net carbs: Breadless Italian Sub 1/2 Sandwich 290 calories, 14g fat, 17g protein
3g net carbs: Breadless Ham & Cheese Sub 1/2 Sandwich 280 calories, 13g fat, 18g protein

Specialty Pizzas (Smart Flour Gluten-Free Crust, Individual Size, 1 Slice)

9g net carbs: "5 Meat", 1 Slice 130 calories, 7g fat, 7g protein
9g net carbs: Supreme, 1 Slice 130 calories, 6g fat, 5g protein
9g net carbs: Veggie 1 Slice 100 calories, 4g fat, 4g protein

Crustless Specialty Pizza (1 Slice, Individual Size)

0g net carbs: "5 Meat", 1 Slice, Individual Size 70 calories, 6g fat, 3g protein
0g net carbs: Supreme, 1 Slice, Individual Size 70 calories, 5g fat, 1g protein
0g net carbs: Veggie, 1 Slice, Individual Size 40 calories, 3g fat, 0g protein

Build Your Own Pizza (Individual Size)

Crust (1 Slice)

9g net carbs: Smart Flour Gluten-Free Crust, 1 Slice, Individual Size 45 calories, 1g fat, 0g protein

Cheese

0g net carbs: Mozzarella, Individual Size, 1 Slice 30 calories, 2g fat, 2g protein
0g net carbs: Extra Mozzarella, Individual Size, 1 Slice 20 calories, 1g fat, 2g protein

Sauces

0g net carbs: Red, Individual Size, 1 Slice 0 calories, 0g fat, 0g protein

Toppings (on 1 Slice, Individual Size)

0g net carbs: Bacon 20 calories, 1g fat, 2g protein
0g net carbs: Beef 15 calories, 1g fat, 1g protein
0g net carbs: Black Olives 10 calories, 1g fat, 0g protein
0g net carbs: Canadian Bacon 5 calories, 0g fat, 1g protein
0g net carbs: Chicken 5 calories, 0g fat, 1g protein
0g net carbs: Fresh Spinach 0 calories, 0g fat, 0g protein
0g net carbs: Green Peppers 0 calories, 0g fat, 0g protein
0g net carbs: Jalapeños 0 calories, 0g fat, 0g protein
0g net carbs: Mushrooms 0 calories, 0g fat, 0g protein
0g net carbs: Pepperoni 15 calories, 1g fat, 1g protein
0g net carbs: Red Onion 0 calories, 0g fat, 0g protein
0g net carbs: Sausage 15 calories, 1g fat, 1g protein
0g net carbs: Tomato 0 calories, 0g fat, 0g protein

Traditional Wings (Bone-In)

4g net carbs: Small Wings, Plain, no breading/remove breading 12 oz. 2 servings 550 calories, 33g fat, 51g protein
7g net carbs: Medium Wings, Plain, no breading/remove breading 24 oz. 4 servings 1110 calories, 66g fat, 103g protein

Wing Sauces & Celery

0g net carbs: Celery (4 Pieces) 5 calories, 0g fat, 0g protein
1g net carbs: Celery (8 Pieces) 15 calories, 0g fat, 1g protein
2g net carbs: Celery (12 Pieces) 20 calories, 0g fat, 1g protein
2g net carbs: Celery (16 Pieces) 25 calories, 0g fat, 1g protein
1g net carbs: Blue Cheese Dressing 1.5 oz. 260 calories, 28g fat, 1g protein
3g net carbs: Blue Cheese Dressing 4 oz. 690 calories, 75g fat, 3g protein
2g net carbs: Medium Lite Ranch Dressing 1.5 oz. 110 calories, 11g fat, 1g protein
2g net carbs: Small Lite Ranch Dressing 1.5 oz. 110 calories, 11g fat, 1g protein
6g net carbs: Large Lite Ranch Dressing 4 oz. 290 calories, 29g fat, 2g protein

Sides

2g net carbs: Chicken, grilled 3 oz. 110 calories, 3g fat, 23g protein
3g net carbs: Garden Side Salad 23 calories, 2g fat, 9g protein
7g net carbs: Rotini Pasta Salad[64] 2 oz. 70 calories, 4g fat, 2g protein
8g net carbs: Carrots* 4 oz. 45 calories, 0g fat, 1g protein
9g net carbs: Mandarin Oranges* 2 oz. 30 calories, 0g fat, 1g protein
10g net carbs: Macaroni Salad* 2 oz. 120 calories, 7g fat, 2g protein

---

[64] *That's Not Keto!* – You'll find all sorts of surprising foods listed here. I'm not telling you whether you should eat these foods or not. What fits your macros or daily carb spend is up to you. No keto police allowed.

Dipping Sauces (1.5 oz.)

1g net carbs: Blue Cheese Dressing 260 calories, 28g fat, 1g protein
1g net carbs: Buffalo Sauce 35 calories, 3g fat, 0g protein
2g net carbs: Lite Ranch Dressing 110 calories, 11g fat, 1g protein
2g net carbs: Red Pizza Sauce 15 calories, 0g fat, 1g protein

Salad Bar

0g net carbs: Bacon Bits 1 Tbsp 60 calories, 4g fat, 5g protein
0g net carbs: Black Olives 1 Tbsp 15 calories, 1g fat, 0g protein
0g net carbs: Cheddar Cheese 1 Tbsp 25 calories, 2g fat, 2g protein
0g net carbs: Eggs (1) 70 calories, 4g fat, 6g protein
0g net carbs: Jalapeños 1 Tbsp 0 calories, 0g fat, 0g protein
0g net carbs: Mushrooms, 1 tong load, 5 calories, 0g fat, 0g protein
0g net carbs: Parmesan Cheese 1 Tbsp 35 calories, 2g fat, 2g protein
0g net carbs: Spinach 1 Cup 5 calories, 0g fat, 1g protein
0g net carbs: Turkey 1 Tbsp 30 calories, 2g fat, 2g protein
0g net carbs: Yellow Squash (3 Slices) 0 calories, 0g fat, 0g protein
0g net carbs: Zucchini (3 Slices) 0 calories, 0g fat, 0g protein
1g net carbs: Broccoli, 1 tong load, 5 calories, 0g fat, 0g protein
1g net carbs: Carrots[65] (3) 5 calories, 0g fat, 0g protein
1g net carbs: Cauliflower, 1 tong load, 5 calories, 0g fat, 0g protein
1g net carbs: Cucumbers (2 Slices) 0 calories, 0g fat, 0g protein
1g net carbs: Grape Tomatoes (3) 5 calories, 0g fat, 0g protein
1g net carbs: Green Peppers (3 Slices) 5 calories, 0g fat, 0g protein
1g net carbs: Lettuce Mix 1 Cup 10 calories, 0g fat, 1g protein
1g net carbs: Orange* (1 Slice) 5 calories, 0g fat, 0g protein
1g net carbs: Red Onion (3 Slices) 5 calories, 0g fat, 0g protein
1g net carbs: Romaine Lettuce 1 Cup 10 calories, 0g fat, 1g protein
1g net carbs: Strawberry Jell-O Parfait* 1/2 Cup 5 calories, 0g fat, 0g protein
1g net carbs: Sunflower Seeds 1 Tbsp 50 calories, 4g fat, 2g protein
2g net carbs: Cantaloupe 1 oz. 10 calories, 0g fat, 0g protein
2g net carbs: Croutons* 1 Tbsp 15 calories, 1g fat, 0g protein
2g net carbs: Strawberries (2) 10 calories, 0g fat, 0g protein
2g net carbs: Watermelon* 1 oz. 10 calories, 0g fat, 0g protein
3g net carbs: Grapes* 0.5 oz. 10 calories, 0g fat, 0g protein
3g net carbs: Honeydew 1 oz. 10 calories, 0g fat, 0g protein
4g net carbs: Crackers* (2 Crackers) 30 calories, 1g fat, 0g protein
5g net carbs: Beets 1/2 Cup 35 calories, 0g fat, 1g protein
5g net carbs: Cottage Cheese 1/2 Cup 110 calories, 5g fat, 12g protein
6g net carbs: Garlic Sesame Sticks* 1 Tbsp 80 calories, 5g fat, 1g protein
6g net carbs: Potato Salad*, Red Skin 1/2 Cup 80 calories, 5g fat, 1g protein
7g net carbs: Potato Salad*, Diced with Egg 1/2 Cup 70 calories, 3g fat, 1g protein
9g net carbs: Cranberries* 1 Tbsp 35 calories, 0g fat, 0g protein

---

[65] *That's Not Keto!* – You'll find all sorts of surprising foods listed here. I'm not telling you whether you should eat these foods or not. What fits your macros or daily carb spend is up to you. No keto police allowed.

Salad Dressing

0g net carbs: Blue Cheese 1 Tbsp 90 calories, 9g fat, 0g protein
0g net carbs: Olive Oil 1 Tsp 40 calories, 4g fat, 0g protein
0g net carbs: Red Wine Vinegar 1 Tsp 0 calories, 0g fat, 0g protein
1g net carbs: Balsamic Vinaigrette 1 Tbsp 60 calories, 6g fat, 0g protein
1g net carbs: Buttermilk Ranch 1 Tbsp 60 calories, 6g fat, 0g protein
1g net carbs: Caesar 1 Tbsp 60 calories, 6g fat, 0g protein
1g net carbs: Lite Northern Italian 1 Tbsp 25 calories, 2g fat, 0g protein
1g net carbs: Lite Ranch 1 Tbsp 35 calories, 3g fat, 0g protein
2g net carbs: Thousand Island 1 Tbsp 60 calories, 6g fat, 0g protein

DRINKS

0g net carbs: Diet Pepsi, 16 oz. 0 calories, 0g fat, 0g protein
0g net carbs: Lipton Unsweetened Iced Tea, 16 oz. 0 calories, 0g fat, 0g protein

6. Americana

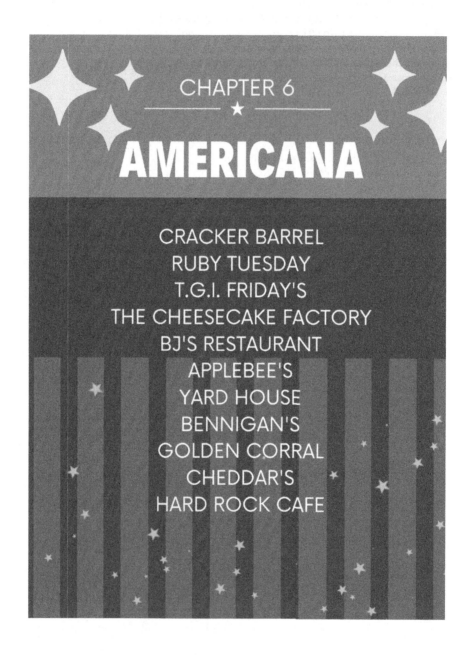

CHAPTER 6

★

AMERICANA

CRACKER BARREL
RUBY TUESDAY
T.G.I. FRIDAY'S
THE CHEESECAKE FACTORY
BJ'S RESTAURANT
APPLEBEE'S
YARD HOUSE
BENNIGAN'S
GOLDEN CORRAL
CHEDDAR'S
HARD ROCK CAFE

Cracker Barrel

Cracker Barrel is the first restaurant I've come across that provides a table of contents for their NUTRITIONAL FACTS N' FIGURES PDF. How amazing is that? (It's the little things that get me excited.) None of the other restaurants covered in this book have seen fit to provide such a helpful tool. You can see the macronutrients for individual ingredients and even side dishes. Gravy, Grits, and Green Beans? Yep. They're all in there. Thank you, Cracker Barrel. For this, I award you a *Keto Diet Restaurant Guide* Superstar badge of honor.

Special Order Tips

Order all burgers and sandwiches with "no bread." Be wary of the available "Add-Ons" since they are often an unnecessary source of net carbs. Avoid all fries, potatoes, rice, pasta, bread, etc. Ask the server to substitute a side salad or a side of steamed/grilled vegetables. Maybe give the Cracker Barrel turnip greens, steamed broccoli, or country green beans a try?

Feel free to customize your order. Restaurants are usually happy to accommodate reasonable customer requests. Note that any alterations on your end will change the provided nutrition information. Adjust accordingly. You'll notice some menu items indicate a half-serving size. Don't worry; there aren't very many. A smaller portion size allowed us to include more (higher-carb) crowd-pleasing favorites from Cracker Barrel. Some are surprising!

Author Favorite

Breakfast: Double Meat Breakfast, no grits, no biscuits. 10 oz. Traditional Espresso Latte, unsweetened. 890 calories, 64g fat, 8g net carbs, 55g protein

Lunch & Dinner: Country House Salad with grilled chicken, no croutons with 2 oz. Dill Pickle Ranch Dressing. Spicy Grilled Catfish: 1 fillet, Fresh Steamed Broccoli and Turnip Greens on the side. Freshly Brewed Iced Tea, 32 oz. with sugar-free sweetener (optional) to drink. 875 calories, 53g fat, 13g net carbs, 63g protein

BREAKFAST (No Fried Apples, No Hashbrown Casserole, No Biscuits, No Sawmill Gravy, No Grits)

2g net carbs: Eggs-in-the-Basket 430 calories, 21g fat, 20g protein
3g net carbs: Double Meat Breakfast 740 calories, 61g fat, 49g protein
4g net carbs: Grandpa's Country Fried Breakfast®, no breaded chicken 230 calories, 12g fat, 15g protein
4g net carbs: Old Timer's Breakfast 230 calories, 12g fat, 15g protein
4g net carbs: Smokehouse Breakfast® 230 calories, 12g fat, 15g protein
4g net carbs: Uncle Herschel's Favorite® 230 calories, 12g fat, 15g protein
5g net carbs: Country Morning Breakfast 230 calories, 12g fat, 15g protein
5g net carbs: Sunrise Sampler ® 920 calories, 55g fat, 49g protein
6g net carbs: The Cracker Barrel's Country Boy Breakfast® 660 calories, 35g fat, 37g protein

All The Fixin's

0g net carbs: Butter (1 pat) 35 calories, 4g fat, 0g protein
4g net carbs: Sugar-free Syrup 10 calories, 0g fat, 0g protein
6g net carbs: Sawmill Gravy, 1 oz. 80 calories, 5g fat, 3g protein

Sunrise Specials (No Bread)

3g net carbs: Egg Sandwich, no bread 470 calories, 26g fat, 20g protein
3g net carbs: One Egg n' Bacon or Sausage, no bread 390 calories, 20g fat, 13g protein
6g net carbs: Southwestern Scramble, no bread 1000 calories, 63g fat, 47g protein

Breakfast Side Plates

3g net carbs: Grilled Southwest Sausage: one link 250 calories, 22g fat, 10g protein
0g net carbs: Sirloin Steak, no gravy 600 calories, 28g fat, 37g protein
0g net carbs: Thick-Sliced Bacon: three slices 210 calories, 17g fat, 14g protein
1g net carbs: Grilled Catfish 130 calories, 5g fat, 19g protein
1g net carbs: Hamburger Steak seasoned with garlic butter 440 calories, 31g fat, 36g protein

1g net carbs: Sugar Cured Ham 220 calories, 15g fat, 18g protein
2g net carbs: Smoked Sausage Patties: two patties 240 calories, 19g fat, 13g protein
3g net carbs: Country Ham Sampler 140 calories, 6g fat, 16g protein
5g net carbs: Hickory-Smoked Country Ham 270 calories, 13g fat, 33g protein
6g net carbs: Grilled Southwest Sausage: two links 510 calories, 43g fat, 20g protein
1g net carbs: Turkey Sausage: two patties 110 calories, 6g fat, 13g protein
8g net carbs: Fried Catfish 400 calories, 32g fat, 18g protein

Breakfast Side Plates - Tasty Alternatives

2g net carbs: Eggs (2) any way you like 'em 150 calories, 10g fat, 14g protein
2g net carbs: Scrambled Egg Whites (2) 60 calories, 0g fat, 11g protein
8g net carbs: Fresh Seasonal Fruit[66], Half-Serving, 35 calories, 0g fat, 1g protein
10g net carbs: Coarse Ground Grits*, Half-Serving, 45 calories, 3g fat, 2g protein

LUNCH & DINNER

Sandwich n' Burger Platters (No Bread)

2g net carbs: The Barrel Cheeseburger 650 calories, 38g fat, 28g protein
2g net carbs: The Barrel Cheeseburger with bacon 680 calories, 40g fat, 30g protein
5g net carbs: Smoky Homestyle Grilled Chicken BLT 800 calories, 33g fat, 48g protein

Downhome Daily Dinner Specials (No Bread)

7g net carbs: Tuesday- Meatloaf, Half-Serving, 260 calories, 17g fat, 35g protein
5g net carbs: Wednesday- Broccoli Cheddar Chicken, easy sauce 690 calories, 44g fat, 40g protein
7g net carbs: Thursday- Turkey n' Dressing, no dressing, no Sweet Potato Casserole 820 calories, 31g fat,
    45g protein
6g net carbs: Friday- Fish Fry Cod Fillets: 4 pieces, remove breading, with tartar sauce 730 calories, 29g fat,
    45g protein
5g net carbs: Saturday- Southern Fried Pork Chops, remove breading, 1040 calories, 72g fat, 53g protein
6g net carbs: Sunday- Pot Roast Supper 550 calories, 20g fat, 52g protein

Cracker Barrel Favorites (No Bread)

1g net carbs: Spicy Grilled Catfish (2 Fillets) 260 calories, 11g fat, 38g protein
2g net carbs: Roast Beef, no glaze, no sauce 480 calories, 29g fat, 45g protein
5g net carbs: Fried Catfish (2 Fillets) remove breading 810 calories, 57g fat, 38g protein
5g net carbs: Grilled Chicken Tenders (6 pieces) 270 calories, 7g fat, 48g protein
5g net carbs: Homestyle Grilled Chicken Breasts with easy turkey gravy 740 calories, 60g fat, 74g protein
6g net carbs: Country Fried Steak, remove breading, with Brown Gravy 600 calories, 28g fat, 37g protein
7g net carbs: Meatloaf, Half-Serving, 260 calories, 17g fat, 17g protein

---

[66] *That's Not Keto!* – You'll find all sorts of surprising foods listed here. I'm not telling you whether you should eat these foods or not. What fits your macros or daily carb spend is up to you. No keto police allowed.

Southern Suppers

5g net carbs: Chile Jack Grilled Chicken, easy sauce 440 calories, 18g fat, 56g protein

Ham

2g net carbs: Sugar Cured Ham 440 calories, 29g fat, 36g protein
7g net carbs: Hickory-Smoked Country Ham, easy glaze 540 calories, 26g fat, 66g protein
7g net carbs: Barrel-Cut Sugar Ham[67] 1020 calories, 55g fat, 109g protein

Home Cooked Classics (No Bread)

1g net carbs: Hamburger Steak: seasoned with garlic butter 440 calories, 31g fat, 36g protein
1g net carbs: Spicy Grilled Catfish: 1 fillet 130 calories, 5g fat, 19g protein
7g net carbs: Hamburger Steak Smothered with Sautéed Onions and Gravy 450 calories, 33g fat, 38g protein
8g net carbs: Country Vegetable Plate (Four Vegetable Country Sides) 260 calories, 14g fat, 12g protein
8g net carbs: Fried Catfish: 1 fillet 400 calories, 32g fat, 18g protein

Southern Suppers (No Bread)

1g net carbs: Grilled Sirloin Steak 350 calories, 17g fat, 49g protein
6g net carbs: Lemon Pepper Grilled Rainbow Trout: 2 fillets 330 calories, 14g fat, 43g protein

Country Sides

0g net carbs: Hatch Valley Green Chiles 25 calories, 0g fat, 0g protein
2g net carbs: Brown Gravy 20 calories, 1g fat, 1g protein
2g net carbs: Fresh Steamed Broccoli 40 calories, 0g fat, 4g protein
2g net carbs: Turkey Gravy 10 calories, 1g fat, 1g protein
2g net carbs: Turnip Greens 100 calories, 4g fat, 10g protein
3g net carbs: Sawmill Gravy 40 calories, 2g fat, 1g protein
4g net carbs: Country Green Beans 60 calories, 3g fat, 1g protein
7g net carbs: Coleslaw, Half-Serving, 125 calories, 10g fat, 0g protein
7g net carbs: Pinto Beans*, Half-Serving, 70 calories, 1g fat, 5g protein
8g net carbs: Fresh Seasonal Fruit*, Half-Serving, 50 calories, 0g fat, 1g protein

Country Salads (No Dressing, No Crackers, No Croutons)

3g net carbs: House Salad 260 calories, 15g fat, 12g protein
4g net carbs: Country Chef Salad 480 calories, 26g fat, 39g protein
4g net carbs: Country House Salad with grilled chicken 350 calories, 17g fat, 28g protein
4g net carbs: Homestyle Grilled Chicken Salad 470 calories, 21g fat, 46g protein

---

[67] *That's Not Keto!* – You'll find all sorts of surprising foods listed here. I'm not telling you whether you should eat these foods or not. What fits your macros or daily carb spend is up to you. No keto police allowed.

Salad Dressing (2.5 oz. with Entrée Salads)

2g net carbs: Dill Pickle Ranch 320 calories, 34g fat, 2g protein
3g net carbs: Blue Cheese Dressing 310 calories, 32g fat, 3g protein
3g net carbs: Buttermilk Ranch 240 calories, 25g fat, 1g protein
10g net carbs: Dijon Honey Mustard[68] 280 calories, 26g fat, 1g protein

Salad Dressing (2 oz. Unless Otherwise Indicated with House Salad)

2g net carbs: Blue Cheese Dressing 250 calories, 26g fat, 2g protein
2g net carbs: Buttermilk Ranch 190 calories, 20g fat, 1g protein
2g net carbs: Dill Pickle Ranch 250 calories, 27g fat, 2g protein
5g net carbs: Balsamic Herb Vinaigrette, 1 oz. 70 calories, 6g fat, 0g protein
8g net carbs: Dijon Honey Mustard* 220 calories, 21g fat, 1g protein

Soups

7g net carbs: Pot Roast Soup cup 100 calories, 5g fat, 7g protein
9g net carbs: Chicken Noodle* Soup cup 100 calories, 4g fat, 7g protein
10g net carbs: Beef n' Noodle* Soup cup 120 calories, 4g fat, 10g protein
10g net carbs: Turkey Noodle* Soup cup 120 calories, 1g fat, 16g protein

Toppings

0g net carbs: Butter (1 pat) 35 calories, 4g fat, 0g protein
0g net carbs: Bacon Pieces: 0.5 oz. 70 calories, 6g fat, 5g protein
1g net carbs: Colby Cheese Shreds: 1 oz. 110 calories, 9g fat, 7g protein
1g net carbs: Sour Cream: 1 oz. 60 calories, 5g fat, 1g protein

Sauces

2g net carbs: Tartar Sauce, 1 oz. 140 calories, 14g fat, 0g protein
8g net carbs: Cocktail Sauce*, 1 oz. 35 calories, 0g fat, 0g protein

DRINKS

0g net carbs: Diet Coke, 16 oz. 0 calories, 0g fat, 0g protein
0g net carbs: Coca-Cola Zero Sugar, 16 oz. 0 calories, 0g fat, 0g protein
1g net carbs: Hot Tea, unsweetened, 10 oz. 0 calories, 0g fat, 0g protein
2g net carbs: Freshly Brewed Unsweetened Iced Tea, 32 oz. 5 calories, 0g fat, 0g protein
1g net carbs: Freshly Brewed Premium Coffee, unsweetened, 10 oz. 0 calories, 0g fat, 0g protein
1g net carbs: Freshly Brewed Premium Decaf Coffee, unsweetened, 10 oz. 0 calories, 0g fat, 0g protein
5g net carbs: Traditional Espresso Latte, unsweetened, 10 oz. 140 calories, 3g fat, 6g protein
5g net carbs: Traditional Espresso Iced Latte, unsweetened, 16 oz. 90 calories, 3g fat, 6g protein

---

[68] *That's Not Keto!* – You'll find all sorts of surprising foods listed here. I'm not telling you whether you should eat these foods or not. What fits your macros or daily carb spend is up to you. No keto police allowed.

Ruby Tuesday

Ruby Tuesday has a very robust interactive nutrition calculator that allows you to sort by "Food Allergies or Restrictions," "Lifestyle Options," and/or "Nutritional Goals" (carbs). That's just cool in my book. This nifty calculator earns Ruby Tuesday a *Keto Diet Restaurant Guide* Superstar Award. Congratulations!

Special Order Tips

Order all burgers and sandwiches with "no bread." Be wary of the available "Add-Ons" since they are often an unnecessary source of net carbs. Avoid all fries, potatoes, rice, pasta, bread, etc. Ask the server to substitute a side salad or a side of steamed/grilled vegetables. Ruby Tuesday offers yummy low-carb alternatives. Maybe try their steamed broccoli, grilled zucchini, or one of my personal favorites, roasted baby Bellas?

Feel free to customize your order. Restaurants are usually happy to accommodate reasonable customer requests.

The exception is when the item has been premade or was prepared off-site (for example, frozen breaded shrimp or chicken wings). Note that any alterations on your end will change the provided nutrition information. That makes sense, right? Adjust accordingly (add or subtract the changes you made). You don't want to be caught slippin', folks!

Author Favorite

Lunch & Dinner: Chicken Wings with Ranch Dressing to start. Top Sirloin & Grilled Shrimp with Steamed Broccoli and Grilled Zucchini on the side and a 12 oz. Michelob Ultra to drink. 1015 calories, 91g fat, 9g net carbs, 89g protein

LUNCH & DINNER

Appetizers

2g net carbs: Chicken Wings with Ranch Dressing 570 calories, 72g fat, 46g protein
5g net carbs: Cheddar Cheese Queso 650 calories, 55g fat, 25g protein
7g net carbs: Shrimp Fondue 520 calories, 36g fat, 27g protein
7g net carbs: Spinach Artichoke Dip 420 calories, 34g fat, 15g protein

Burgers & Sandwiches (No Bread, No Fries, No Tots)

2g net carbs: Ruby's Cheeseburger 620 calories, 35g fat, 39g protein
4g net carbs: Bacon Cheeseburger 770 calories, 45g fat, 42g protein
5g net carbs: Cheeseburger Sliders (2), no sauce, no croutons, no corn, 470 calories, 34g fat, 18g protein
5g net carbs: Philly Cheesesteak Hoagie 660 calories, 36g fat, 29g protein
5g net carbs: Turkey Burger 610 calories, 35g fat, 31g protein
6g net carbs: Grilled Chicken Sandwich 510 calories, 20g fat, 38g protein
6g net carbs: Smokehouse Burger, no BBQ Sauce, no Onion Rings 910 calories, 48g fat, 48g protein

Entrees (Grilled or Steamed Vegetables as Side, No Bread, No Pasta)

0g net carbs: Grilled Salmon, no sauce or glaze 330 calories, 22g fat, 39g protein
4g net carbs: Hickory Bourbon Salmon, super easy Hickory Bourbon Glaze 240 calories, 4g fat, 29g protein
4g net carbs: Shrimp Scampi Pasta, easy sauce 720 calories, 35g fat, 31g protein
2g net carbs: Blackened Tilapia 200 calories, 7g fat, 42g protein
5g net carbs: Blackened Shrimp and Sausage 580 calories, 36g fat, 36g protein
6g net carbs: New Orleans Seafood 340 calories, 15g fat, 40g protein
7g net carbs: Parmesan Shrimp Pasta, easy sauce 650 calories, 41g fat, 33g protein

0g net carbs: Rib Eye 730 calories, 56g fat, 56g protein
1g net carbs: Rib Eye & Grilled Shrimp 810 calories, 62g fat, 64g protein
3g net carbs: Rib Eye & Ribs, Half-Rack, no Spicy Glaze 800 calories, 70g fat, 71g protein
8g net carbs: Rib Eye & Hickory Bourbon Chicken, easy Hickory Bourbon Glaze 910 calories, 62g fat, 81g protein
2g net carbs: Top Sirloin & Grilled Shrimp 330 calories, 18g fat, 41g protein
2g net carbs: Top Sirloin 290 calories, 17g fat, 32g protein
4g net carbs: Smothered BBQ Sirloin, easy BBQ Jus, no crispy onions 340 calories, 8g fat, 32g protein
7g net carbs: Asiago Sirloin & Grilled Shrimp 470 calories, 30g fat, 43g protein
7g net carbs: Hickory Bourbon Bacon Sirloin, easy Hickory Bourbon Bacon Sauce 290 calories, 10g fat, 30g

protein

3g net carbs: Grilled Chicken Fresco 320 calories, 19g fat, 33g protein
5g net carbs: Grilled Chicken Carbonara, easy sauce 540 calories, 37g fat, 32g protein
5g net carbs: Hickory Bourbon Chicken, super easy Hickory Bourbon Glaze 250 calories, 5g fat, 31g protein
6g net carbs: Asiago Bacon Chicken 450 calories, 26g fat, 44g protein
6g net carbs: Chicken & Broccoli Pasta, easy sauce 640 calories, 34g fat, 33g protein
7g net carbs: Smoky Mountain Chicken, no BBQ sauce 420 calories, 24g fat, 45g protein
4g net carbs: Baby Back Ribs, Half-Rack, no Spicy Glaze- Nashville Hot 580 calories, 42g fat, 44g protein
4g net carbs: Baby Back Ribs, Half-Rack, no Hickory Bourbon Glaze- Texas Dusted 580 calories, 42g fat, 44g protein
8g net carbs: Baby-Back Rib, Full-Rack, no Spicy Glaze- Nashville Hot 870 calories, 74g fat, 79g protein

Sides

1g net carbs: Steamed Broccoli 60 calories, 4g fat, 4g protein
2g net carbs: Grilled Zucchini 20 calories, 1g fat, 1g protein
2g net carbs: Roasted Baby Bellas 100 calories, 6g fat, 4g protein
7g net carbs: Coleslaw (1/4 cup) 120 calories, 9g fat, 1g protein
9g net carbs: Cauliflower Au Gratin[69], no Crispy Onions 400 calories, 32g fat, 9g protein

Soups (4 oz.)

9g net carbs: Chicken Corn Chowder* Soup 150 calories, 9g fat, 7g protein
9g net carbs: Broccoli & Cheese Soup 150 calories, 10g fat, 4g protein

Salads

2g net carbs: Potato Salad* (1/2 cup) 150 calories, 1g fat, 1g protein
3g net carbs: Backyard BBQ Grilled Chicken Salad, no corn, no black beans 560 calories, 28g fat, 28g protein
3g net carbs: Cucumber Salad (1/2 cup) 45 calories, 4g fat, 1g protein
5g net carbs: Ruby's Grilled Chicken Caesar Salad, no croutons 500 calories, 32g fat, 42g protein
6g net carbs: Hickory Bourbon BBQ Chicken Cobb Salad, no corn 660 calories, 42g fat, 47g protein
6g net carbs: Phillipsburg Broccoli Salad (1/2 cup) 110 calories, 8g fat, 2g protein
10g net carbs: Quinoa Salad* (1/2 cup) 100 calories, 6g fat, 3g protein

Garden Bar Toppings (1 Tbsp Unless Indicated Otherwise)

0g net carbs: Bacon Pieces 30 calories, 2g fat, 3g protein
0g net carbs: Diced Eggs 20 calories, 2g fat, 2g protein
0g net carbs: Diced Ham 10 calories, 0g fat, 2g protein
0g net carbs: Pepperoncini 0 calories, 0g fat, 0g protein
0g net carbs: Pico de Gallo 0 calories, 0g fat, 0g protein
1g net carbs: Banana Peppers 5 calories, 0g fat, 0g protein
1g net carbs: Black Olives 15 calories, 2g fat, 0g protein
1g net carbs: Edamame 10 calories, 0g fat, 1g protein

---

[69] *That's Not Keto!* – You'll find all sorts of surprising foods listed here. I'm not telling you whether you should eat these foods or not. What fits your macros or daily carb spend is up to you. No keto police allowed.

1g net carbs: Green Peas[70] 5 calories, 0g fat, 0g protein
1g net carbs: Jalapeño Peppers 0 calories, 0g fat, 0g protein
2g net carbs: Crispy Onions 25 calories, 2g fat, 0g protein
2g net carbs: Garbanzo Beans 15 calories, 0g fat, 1g protein
3g net carbs: Beets, Pickled 20 calories, 0g fat, 1g protein
3g net carbs: Corn* 25 calories, 1g fat, 0g protein
3g net carbs: Sunflower Seeds 100 calories, 8g fat, 3g protein
7g net carbs: Dried Cranberries* 25 calories, 0g fat, 0g protein
8g net carbs: Grapes* (1/2 cup) 30 calories, 0g fat, 0g protein

Cheese Toppings (1 Tbsp)

0g net carbs: Shredded Cheddar Cheese 30 calories, 3g fat, 2g protein
0g net carbs: Shredded Mozzarella Blend 25 calories, 2g fat, 2g protein
1g net carbs: Shredded Parmesan Cheese 20 calories, 2g fat, 2g protein

Salad Dressings (2 Tbsp)

1g net carbs: Buttermilk Blue Cheese 180 calories, 19g fat, 2g protein
1g net carbs: Ranch Dressing 120 calories, 13g fat, 1g protein
2g net carbs: Lite Ranch Dressing 100 calories, 9g fat, 1g protein
3g net carbs: Balsamic Vinaigrette 90 calories, 9g fat, 0g protein
3g net carbs: Cilantro Lime Vinaigrette 130 calories, 13g fat, 0g protein
3g net carbs: Golden Italian Dressing 100 calories, 0g fat, 0g protein
4g net carbs: Balsamic Vinegar 20 calories, 0g fat, 0g protein
4g net carbs: Thousand Island 90 calories, 0g fat, 0g protein
5g net carbs: Honey Mustard Dressing* 100 calories, 8g fat, 0g protein
6g net carbs: French* 120 calories, 11g fat, 0g protein

DRINKS

0g net carbs: Diet Coke, 16 oz. 0 calories, 0g fat, 0g protein
0g net carbs: Coke Zero, 16 oz. 0 calories, 0g fat, 0g protein
3g net carbs: Minute Maid Light, 16 oz. 10 calories, 0g fat, 0g protein
0g net carbs: Dasani Bottled Water, 16 oz. 0 calories, 0g fat, 0g protein
0g net carbs: Twining's Hot Tea, 8 oz. unsweetened 0 calories, 0g fat, 0g protein
0g net carbs: Black Coffee, 8 oz. unsweetened 0 calories, 0g fat, 0g protein

Beer & Seltzer

2g net carbs: Truly Hard Seltzer, 12 oz. 100 calories, 0g fat, 0g protein

3g net carbs: Michelob Ultra, 12 oz. 95 calories, 0g fat, 1g protein
3g net carbs: Miller Light, 12 oz. 96 calories, 0g fat, 1g protein
5g net carbs: Coors Light, 12 oz. 102 calories, 0g fat, 1g protein
7g net carbs: Bud Light, 12 oz. 110 calories, 0g fat, 1g protein

---

[70] *That's Not Keto!* – You'll find all sorts of surprising foods listed here. I'm not telling you whether you should eat these foods or not. What fits your macros or daily carb spend is up to you. No keto police allowed.

Wine

4g net carbs: Canyon Road Chardonnay, 5 oz. 126 calories, 0g fat, 0g protein
4g net carbs: Canyon Road Cabernet Sauvignon, 5 oz. 122 calories, 0g fat, 0g protein

Spirits

0g net carbs: Jack and Diet Coke, 10 oz. 100 calories, 0g fat, 4g protein
0g net carbs: Rum and Diet Coke, 10 oz. 100 calories, 0g fat, 4g protein
3g net carbs: Dirty Martini, 4 oz. with lower net carb dry vermouth 140 calories, 0g fat, 5g protein

T.G.I. Friday's

It's a challenge to celebrate the weekend at T.G.I. Friday's. What low-carb foods should you order? The tempting menu isn't much help. Many of the offerings are breaded, fried, or sauce-laden dishes. With no customizable nutrition calculator available, you're left to scrutinize the Nutritional Values PDF and hope for the best. (Good thing you have this book!)

Special Order Tips

Order all burgers and sandwiches with "no bread." Be wary of the available "Add-Ons" since they are often an unnecessary source of net carbs.

Feel free to customize your order. Restaurants are usually happy to accommodate reasonable customer requests. The exception is when the item has been premade or was prepared off-site. Note that any alterations on your end will change the provided nutrition information. Adjust accordingly.

Avoid all fries, potatoes, rice, pasta, bread, etc. Ask the server to substitute a side salad or a side of steamed/grilled vegetables. At T.G.I. Friday's, you can even order a side of celery (with ranch dressing for dipping). How cool is that?

Author Favorite

Breakfast: Omelet Spinach Florentine. 16 oz. Freshly Brewed Gold Peak Iced Tea, Unsweetened 660 calories, 58g fat, 14g net carbs, 37g protein

Lunch & Dinner: World Wing Quad Bone-In Baked Wings with Buffalo Sauce to start. Simply Grilled Salmon with Lemon-Butter Broccoli & Cheese on the side. FRIDAYS Ultimate Long Island Tea with Diet Coke, easy Grand Marnier to drink. 1760 calories, 131g fat, 15g net carbs, 95g protein

BREAKFAST (No Bread)

9g net carbs: Egg BLT Sandwich, no bread 670 calories, 80g fat, 43g protein

Omelets

7g net carbs: Steak 6 oz. & Eggs Fried (2) 720 calories, 57g fat, 46g protein
8g net carbs: Omelet Bacon Cheddar 790 calories, 73g fat, 47g protein
8g net carbs: Omelet Spinach Florentine 640 calories, 58g fat, 37g protein
8g net carbs: Steak 6 oz. & Eggs Scrambled (2) 760 calories, 59g fat, 49g protein

Sides

0g net carbs: Sausage (3 links) 200 calories, 20g fat, 5g protein
1g net carbs: Bacon (3 slices) 120 calories, 8g fat, 11g protein
9g net carbs: Fruit[71] 50 calories, 0g fat, 1g protein

LUNCH & DINNER

Burgers (No Bread, No French Fries)

7g net carbs: Beyond Meat Cheeseburger 860 calories, 52g fat, 44g protein
7g net carbs: Cheeseburger 770 calories, 52g fat, 34g protein
8g net carbs: Loaded Cheese Fry Burger, no bacon-cheese fries, no potato skin 840 calories, 93g fat, 55g protein
8g net carbs: Philly Cheesesteak Burger, no bell peppers, no egg roll 850 calories, 67g fat, 48g protein
9g net carbs: Bacon Cheeseburger, no sauce 790 calories, 61g fat, 41g protein

Burger Substitutions

1g net carbs: Beef Patty 370 calories, 30g fat, 21g protein
6g net carbs: Beyond Meatless Patty 400 calories, 27g fat, 30g protein

Burger Add-Ons

0g net carbs: Avocado 60 calories, 5g fat, 1g protein
1g net carbs: Bacon (1.5 slices) 60 calories, 4g fat, 5g protein

Gluten-Friendly Burgers (No Bread)

7g net carbs: Lettuce Wrap Cheeseburger without Side 500 calories, 40g fat, 28g protein
8g net carbs: Lettuce Wrap Spicy Reaper Burger without Side 590 calories, 48g fat, 28g protein

---

[71] *That's Not Keto!* – You'll find all sorts of surprising foods listed here. I'm not telling you whether you should eat these foods or not. What fits your macros or daily carb spend is up to you. No keto police allowed.

9g net carbs: Lettuce Wrap Bacon Cheeseburger without Side 560 calories, 44g fat, 31g protein

Gluten-Friendly Burger Add-Ons

0g net carbs: Avocado 60 calories, 5g fat, 1g protein
1g net carbs: Bacon 60 calories, 4g fat, 5g protein

Sandwiches (No Bread)

7g net carbs: Bacon Ranch Grilled Chicken Sandwich, breadless 760 calories, 35g fat, 28g protein

Entrees (No Pasta)

5g net carbs: Sizzling Chicken & Shrimp 730 calories, 61g fat, 59g protein
6g net carbs: Simply Grilled Salmon 560 calories, 36g fat, 36g protein
7g net carbs: Sizzling Chicken & Cheese 730 calories, 50g fat, 63g protein
8g net carbs: Chicken & Broccoli Alfredo Tortelloni, Swap Pasta with Steamed/Grilled Vegetables 790 calories, 53g fat, 68g protein
8g net carbs: Cajun Shrimp & Chicken Pasta, Swap Pasta with Steamed/Grilled Vegetables 540 calories, 28g fat, 53g protein

Sides

0g net carbs: World Wing Quad Bone-In Baked Wings with Buffalo Sauce 990 calories, 88g fat, 53g protein
0g net carbs: Wings Traditional Frank's Buffalo without Dressing 620 calories, 55g fat, 34g protein
1g net carbs: Celery (24 sticks) 15 calories, 0g fat, 1g protein
6g net carbs: Lemon-Butter Broccoli & Cheese 120 calories, 7g fat, 5g protein
6g net carbs: Lemon-Butter Broccoli 90 calories, 5g fat, 4g protein
7g net carbs: Wings Traditional Chile-Lime without Dressing 700 calories, 61g fat, 35g protein
9g net carbs: Wings Traditional Garlic Parm without Dressing 940 calories, 87g fat, 35g protein

Sides Add-Ons

1g net carbs: Bleu Cheese Dressing, 1.25 oz. 200 calories, 21g fat, 2g protein
1g net carbs: Ranch Dressing, 1.25 oz. 130 calories, 14g fat, 1g protein
3g net carbs: World Wing Quad Dipping Sauce (Marinara Only) 35 calories, 2g fat, 1g protein

Salads (No Dressing Unless Otherwise Indicated)

4g net carbs: Side House Salad, no breadstick, no croutons 90 calories, 4g fat, 4g protein
4g net carbs: Caesar Salad Without Protein, no croutons 600 calories, 54g fat, 11g protein
5g net carbs: Caesar Salad with Grilled Chicken, no croutons 790 calories, 59g fat, 45g protein
5g net carbs: Million Dollar Cobb Salad with Grilled Chicken with Ranch, no carrots 1000 calories, 75g fat, 66g protein
7g net carbs: Million Dollar Cobb Salad Without Protein with Ranch 820 calories, 70g fat, 31g protein

Salad Protein Options

1g net carbs: Grilled Chicken 190 calories, 5g fat, 35g protein
2g net carbs: Sirloin, 6 oz. 170 calories, 7g fat, 25g protein
6g net carbs: Beyond Meat Patty 400 calories, 27g fat, 30g protein
6g net carbs: Grilled Salmon 280 calories, 15g fat, 29g protein

Salad Add-Ons

0g net carbs: Sautéed Shrimp 200 calories, 16g fat, 13g protein
3g net carbs: Crispy Fried Shrimp (6) 150 calories, 8g fat, 13g protein

Salad Dressing (1.25 oz.)

1g net carbs: Blue Cheese 200 calories, 21g fat, 2g protein
1g net carbs: Caesar 190 calories, 20g fat, 1g protein
1g net carbs: Ranch 130 calories, 14g fat, 1g protein
4g net carbs: Balsamic Vinaigrette 190 calories, 19g fat, 0g protein
5g net carbs: BBQ Ranch 110 calories, 9g fat, 1g protein
7g net carbs: Sesame Citrus 160 calories, 15g fat, 0g protein
8g net carbs: Honey Mustard[72] 190 calories, 17g fat, 0g protein
9g net carbs: Low-Fat Balsamic Vinaigrette 50 calories, 2g fat, 0g protein

DRINKS

0g net carbs: Diet Coke, 16 oz. 0 calories, 0g fat, 0g protein
0g net carbs: Coke Zero,16 oz. 0 calories, 0g fat, 0g protein
0g net carbs: Dasani Bottled Water, 16 oz. 0 calories, 0g fat, 0g protein
0g net carbs: Perrier Bottled Water, 16 oz. 0 calories, 0g fat, 0g protein
6g net carbs: Freshly Brewed Gold Peak Iced Tea, unsweetened, 16 oz. 20 calories, 0g fat, 0g protein

Beer

3g net carbs: Michelob Ultra 12 oz. 95 calories, 0g fat, 1g protein
3g net carbs: Miller Lite 12 oz. 96 calories, 0g fat, 1g protein
5g net carbs: Coors Light 12 oz. 102 calories, 0g fat, 1g protein
7g net carbs: Bud Light 12 oz. 110 calories, 0g fat, 1g protein

Wine

3g net carbs: Ecco Domani Pinot Grigio, 5 oz. 123 calories, 0g fat, 0g protein
4g net carbs: 14 Hands Merlot, 5 oz. 123 calories, 0g fat, 0g protein
4g net carbs: Canyon Road Cabernet, 5 oz. 122 calories, 0g fat, 0g protein
4g net carbs: Josh Cellars Cabernet Sauvignon, 5 oz. 124 calories, 0g fat, 0g protein
4g net carbs: Kendall-Jackson Chardonnay, 5 oz. 130 calories, 0g fat, 0g protein

---

[72] *That's Not Keto!* – You'll find all sorts of surprising foods listed here. I'm not telling you whether you should eat these foods or not. What fits your macros or daily carb spend is up to you. No keto police allowed.

5g net carbs: Dark Horse Chardonnay, 5 oz. 125 calories, 0g fat, 0g protein

Spirits

3g net carbs: FRIDAY'S Ultimate Long Island Tea with Diet Coke, easy Grand Marnier 90 calories, 0g fat, 1g protein
3g net carbs: FRIDAY'S Ultimate Around the World LIT with Diet Coke, easy Cointreau 105 calories, 0g fat, 1g protein
6g net carbs: House Bloody Mary 120 calories, 1g fat, 1g protein
10g net carbs: Michelada 100 calories, 0g fat, 3g protein

The Cheesecake Factory 👍

Who doesn't have fond memories of past sugary escapades at The Cheesecake Factory? (I know I put a hurtin' on many a slice of cheesecake back in the day.) But don't let the desserts confuse you. Besides its namesake specialty (cheesecake), this place has TONS of low-carb options. They even have a sugar-free cheesecake offering, served with or without strawberries and whipped cream. Let me tell you; it's delicious! This slice of heaven ranks high on my once-in-a-while treat list. At 20 grams net carbs per slice, Low-Licious Cheesecake is nothing short of a miracle. Share it with a friend, and *bam!* You're right at 10 grams of net carbs.

The Cheesecake Factory doesn't have nutrition information (calories/carbohydrates) next to the menu items, which is disappointing. But, lucky for them, I'm going to look the other way. Their Low-Licious Cheesecake saved the day! They earned the prestigious *Keto Diet Restaurant Guide* Superstar Award.

Special Order Tips

Order all burgers and sandwiches with "no bread." Be wary of the available "Add-Ons" since they are often an unnecessary source of net carbs. Avoid all fries, potatoes, rice, pasta, bread, etc. Ask the server to substitute a side salad or a side of steamed/grilled vegetables. How does a side of tomato slices, broccoli, green beans, asparagus, or spinach sound to you? All are available to order at The Cheesecake Factory.

You'll notice some menu items indicate a half-serving size. Don't worry; there will only be a few! A smaller portion size allowed us to include more (higher-carb) classic favorites.

Don't be fooled by the deceiving Impossible Burger (Breadless). The 4 oz. patty alone has 6 grams of net carbs.

Feel free to customize your order. Restaurants are usually happy to accommodate reasonable customer requests. The exception is when the item has been premade or was prepared off-site. Note that any alterations on your end will change the provided nutrition information. Adjust accordingly.

Author Favorite

Breakfast: California Omelet with 16 oz. Cold Brew Iced Coffee over ice with sugar-free sweetener. 1145 calories, 96g fat, 8g net carbs, 57g protein

Lunch: Small Green Salad, no croutons to start. Breadless California Cheesesteak with a 16 oz. Diet Dr. Pepper to drink. 970 calories, 55g fat, 8g net carbs, 63g protein

Dinner: Hibachi Steak, no Bread, Steamed Vegetables substituted for Pasta, Potatoes, and Rice. Green Beans and Sauteed Spinach on the side with a tiny bite of Low-Licious Cheesecake (not counted in macronutrients – *scandalous!*). SkinnyLicious® The Well-Mannered Dirty Martini to drink. 1220 calories, 72g fat, 14g net carbs, 70g protein

BREAKFAST (No Potatoes, No Bread)

Eggs & More (No Bread)

3g net carbs: Farm Fresh Eggs (2) 260 calories, 20g fat, 17g protein
3g net carbs: Farm Fresh Eggs (2) with Avocado Slices 300 calories, 23g fat, 17g protein
4g net carbs: Farm Fresh Eggs (2) with Grilled Ham 430 calories, 25g fat, 49g protein
7g net carbs: Farm Fresh Eggs (2) with Old Smokehouse® Bacon 470 calories, 36g fat, 29g protein
5g net carbs: Breadless Brioche Breakfast Sandwich 400 calories, 36g fat, 42g protein
6g net carbs: Factory Huevos Rancheros 520 calories, 43g fat, 54g protein
2g net carbs: Plain Omelet 610 calories, 57g fat, 22g protein
5g net carbs: Loco Moco, no rice 650 calories, 34g fat, 81g protein
6g net carbs: Breakfast Burrito, no tortilla 750 calories, 28g fat, 88g protein
8g net carbs: California Omelet 1140 calories, 96g fat, 57g protein

Factory Create an Omelet

0g net carbs: Avocado 40 calories, 3g fat, 0g protein
0g net carbs: Bacon 140 calories, 13g fat, 5g protein
0g net carbs: Ham 60 calories, 1g fat, 12g protein

0g net carbs: Spinach 5 calories, 0g fat, 1g protein
0g net carbs: Swiss Cheese 220 calories, 17g fat, 17g protein
1g net carbs: Cheddar Cheese 230 calories, 19g fat, 13g protein
1g net carbs: Fontina Cheese 180 calories, 14g fat, 13g protein
1g net carbs: Fresh Mushrooms 15 calories, 0g fat, 2g protein
1g net carbs: Fresh Tomato 10 calories, 0g fat, 0g protein
1g net carbs: Green Onions 5 calories, 0g fat, 0g protein
1g net carbs: Jack Cheese 210 calories, 18g fat, 12g protein
2g net carbs: Asparagus 25 calories, 1g fat, 2g protein
3g net carbs: Bell Peppers 15 calories, 0g fat, 1g protein
3g net carbs: Red Onions 10 calories, 0g fat, 0g protein
3g net carbs: Roasted Peppers 20 calories, 0g fat, 1g protein
6g net carbs: Spinach, Mushroom, Bacon, and Cheese Omelet 700 calories, 57g fat, 41g protein

Breakfast Accompaniments

0g net carbs: Sliced Avocado 40 calories, 3g fat, 0g protein
3g net carbs: Sliced Tomatoes 25 calories, 0g fat, 1g protein

Saturday & Sunday Brunch (No Potatoes, No Bread)

5g net carbs: Brunch Combo 510 calories, 23g fat, 30g protein
5g net carbs: Eggs Benedict with Canadian Bacon and Hollandaise 530 calories, 46g fat, 38g protein
6g net carbs: Breadless Monte Cristo Sandwich 580 calories, 14g fat, 69g protein
7g net carbs: Jambalaya & Eggs 480 calories, 41g fat, 43g protein

LUNCH (No Bread)

Hamburgers (No Bread)

2g net carbs: Classic Burger 480 calories, 87g fat, 66g protein
3g net carbs: Old Fashioned Burger 540 calories, 22g fat, 46g protein
4g net carbs: Americana Cheeseburger, no Crunchy Potato Crisps 530 calories, 93g fat, 60g protein
4g net carbs: Mushroom Burger 610 calories, 102g fat, 65g protein
4g net carbs: Stuffed Cheddar Burger 660 calories, 31g fat, 59g protein
5g net carbs: Bacon-Bacon Cheeseburger 850 calories, 116g fat, 78g protein
5g net carbs: French Dip Cheeseburger 690 calories, 50g fat, 62g protein
6g net carbs: Green Chile Cheeseburger 720 calories, 80g fat, 61g protein
6g net carbs: Smokehouse BBQ Burger, no Crispy Onion Strings, easy BBQ sauce 680 calories, 97g fat,
    68g protein
7g net carbs: Factory Turkey Burger 680 calories, 76g fat, 52g protein
9g net carbs: Impossible Burger 670 calories, 53g fat, 35g protein
9g net carbs: Veggie Burger 650 calories, 27g fat, 26g protein
3g net carbs: SkinnyLicious® Hamburger 570 calories, 30g fat, 35g protein
4g net carbs: SkinnyLicious® Grilled Turkey Burger 560 calories, 30g fat, 29g protein

Sandwiches (No Bread)

3g net carbs: The Club 540 calories, 30g fat, 56g protein

4g net carbs: Cuban Sandwich 640 calories, 25g fat, 71g protein
4g net carbs: Fresh Turkey Sandwich, Half-Serving 590 calories, 43g fat, 32g protein
5g net carbs: BBQ Kalua Pork, easy BBQ sauce 930 calories, 45g fat, 59g protein
5g net carbs: California Cheesesteak 710 calories, 30g fat, 61g protein
5g net carbs: Chicken-Almond Salad Sandwich, Half-Serving 530 calories, 48g fat, 28g protein
5g net carbs: Grilled Chicken and Avocado Club 690 calories, 32g fat, 82g protein
6g net carbs: Chicken Salad Sandwich 630 calories, 28g fat, 50g protein
6g net carbs: Spicy Grilled Chicken Sandwich, Spicy Buffalo Sauce 710 calories, 56g fat, 62g protein
7g net carbs: Spicy Grilled Chicken Sandwich, Chipotle Mayo 680 calories, 65g fat, 60g protein
3g net carbs: SkinnyLicious® Spicy Grilled Chicken Sandwich 560 calories, 27g fat, 25g protein
4g net carbs: SkinnyLicious® Turkey & Avocado Sandwich 550 calories, 26g fat, 38g protein

Lunch Specials (No Bread, No Croutons)

Renee's Special (Half-Serving of a Sandwich, a Cup of Soup, and a Small Salad)
    4g net carbs: Fresh Turkey Sandwich, Half-Serving, 590 calories, 43g fat, 32g protein
    5g net carbs: Chicken-Almond Salad Sandwich, Half-Serving, 530 calories, 48g fat, 28g protein
    6g net carbs: Cream of Broccoli Soup, cup, Half-Serving, 180 calories, 16g fat, 5g protein
    3g net carbs: Small Green Salad, no croutons 260 calories, 25g fat, 2g protein
    4g net carbs: Small Caesar Salad, no croutons 440 calories, 38g fat, 8g protein

Lunch Specials (No Bread, Steamed Vegetables Substituted for Pasta or Potatoes)

3g net carbs: Fettuccini Alfredo with Shrimp 540 calories, 27g fat, 41g protein
5g net carbs: Fettuccini Alfredo with Chicken 580 calories, 37g fat, 36g protein
2g net carbs: Miso Salmon with easy Miso Sauce, no peas, no rice 500 calories, 24g fat, 46g protein
3g net carbs: Factory Burrito Grande, no tortilla, no rice, no black beans 480 calories, 23g fat, 22g protein
3g net carbs: Four Cheese Pasta, easy marinara sauce 290 calories, 19g fat, 22g protein
3g net carbs: Pasta Da Vinci with Madeira Wine Sauce 383 calories, 33g fat, 39g protein
3g net carbs: Shrimp with Angel Hair 360 calories, 32g fat, 25g protein
4g net carbs: Bistro Grilled Shrimp Pasta 620 calories, 27g fat, 38g protein
4g net carbs: Chicken Madeira with easy sauce 375 calories, 26g fat, 32g protein
4g net carbs: Chicken Riesling 490 calories, 27g fat, 32g protein
4g net carbs: Evelyn's Favorite Pasta 591 calories, 31g fat, 41g protein
4g net carbs: Famous Factory Meatloaf, no mashed potatoes, no corn 410 calories, 18g fat, 27g protein
4g net carbs: Fresh Grilled Salmon 550 calories, 19g fat, 50g protein
4g net carbs: Herb Crusted Filet of Salmon 770 calories, 34g fat, 48g protein
4g net carbs: Louisiana Chicken Pasta 335 calories, 30g fat, 30g protein
4g net carbs: Pasta Pomodoro with easy marinara sauce 340 calories, 28g fat, 27g protein
4g net carbs: Thai Glazed Salmon, no glaze 380 calories, 31g fat, 52g protein
5g net carbs: Chicken & Broccoli Pasta 520 calories, 26g fat, 43g protein
5g net carbs: Chicken Marsala and Mushrooms with easy Marsala Wine Sauce 520 calories, 28g fat, 38g protein
5g net carbs: Spicy Chicken Chipotle Pasta, no honey glaze, no peas 410 calories, 19g fat, 37g protein
5g net carbs: Thai Coconut-Lime Chicken, no snow peas, no pineapple 545 calories, 21g fat, 41g protein
6g net carbs: Chicken Piccata 600 calories, 48g fat, 52g protein
6g net carbs: Crusted Chicken Romano 540 calories, 32g fat, 38g protein
6g net carbs: Pasta Carbonara, no peas 360 calories, 25g fat, 38g protein
6g net carbs: Spaghetti and Meatballs 310 calories, 34g fat, 34g protein

Lunch Salads (No Dressing Unless Otherwise Stated)

3g net carbs: Small Green Salad, no croutons 260 calories, 25g fat, 2g protein
3g net carbs: Cobb Salad 540 calories, 24g fat, 74g protein
4g net carbs: Small Caesar Salad, no croutons 440 calories, 38g fat, 8g protein
6g net carbs: Sheila's Chicken and Avocado Salad with Balsamic Vinaigrette, no tortilla strips 670 calories,
    30g fat, 43g protein

Salad Dressing (1 Tbsp)

1g net carbs: Balsamic Vinaigrette 80 calories, 7g fat, 0g protein
1g net carbs: Blue Cheese Dressing 60 calories, 5g fat, 1g protein
1g net carbs: Caesar Dressing 80 calories, 7g fat, 1g protein
1g net carbs: Cilantro Dressing 60 calories, 6g fat, 1g protein
1g net carbs: Ranch Dressing 70 calories, 7g fat, 0g protein
1g net carbs: Shallot Vinaigrette 90 calories, 9g fat, 0g protein
1g net carbs: SkinnyLicious® Mustard Vinaigrette 15 calories, 1g fat, 0g protein
2g net carbs: Thousand Island Dressing 70 calories, 7g fat, 0g protein
3g net carbs: Barbeque Ranch Dressing 80 calories, 7g fat, 0g protein
3g net carbs: SkinnyLicious® Sesame Soy Dressing 20 calories, 0g fat, 0g protein
4g net carbs: Citrus Honey Dressing[73] 60 calories, 4g fat, 0g protein
4g net carbs: Spicy Peanut Vinaigrette 60 calories, 4g fat, 1g protein
5g net carbs: Ketchup* 20 calories, 0g fat, 0g protein
6g net carbs: Chinese Plum* Dressing 60 calories, 4g fat, 0g protein

DINNER

Small Plates/Appetizers

2g net carbs: Ahi Carpaccio, Serves 2-4, 250 calories, 9g fat, 63g protein
4g net carbs: Bunless Roadside Sliders, (4) 400 calories, 35g fat, 48g protein
4g net carbs: Grilled Dynamite Shrimp (no tempura) 350 calories, 17g fat, 19g protein
4g net carbs: Stuffed Mushrooms, no Wine Sauce 410 calories, 42g fat, 15g protein
4g net carbs: Buffalo Wings, no breading/remove breading 420 calories, 69g fat, 29g protein
5g net carbs: Fire-Roasted Fresh Artichoke, easy garlic dip- serves 2-4 480 calories, 31g fat, 10g protein
6g net carbs: Thai Lettuce Wraps, easy carrots, no Coconut Curry Noodles, no Sweet Red Chili sauce
    370 calories, 8g fat, 15g protein
7g net carbs: Little House Salad 260 calories, 25g fat, 2g protein
8g net carbs: Crispy Brussels Sprouts, no Vermont Maple Butter Glaze 450 calories, 15g fat, 7g protein
8g net carbs: Edamame 100 calories, 3g fat, 8g protein

Appetizer Salads

2g net carbs: Tossed Green Appetizer Salad, no croutons, no dressing 110 calories, 1g fat, 4g protein
3g net carbs: Tossed Green Appetizer Salad with easy Ranch Dressing, no croutons 410 calories, 26g fat,
    5g protein

---

[73] *That's Not Keto!* – You'll find all sorts of surprising foods listed here. I'm not telling you whether you should eat these foods or not. What fits your macros or daily carb spend is up to you. No keto police allowed.

4g net carbs: Tossed Green Appetizer Salad with easy Balsamic Vinaigrette, no croutons 480 calories, 25g fat, 5g protein

4g net carbs: Tossed Green Appetizer Salad with easy Blue Cheese Dressing, no croutons 350 calories, 26g fat, 11g protein

4g net carbs: Tossed Green Appetizer Salad with easy SK Mustard Vinaigrette, no croutons 200 calories, 11g fat, 5g protein

4g net carbs: Tossed Green Appetizer Salad with easy Thousand Island Dressing, no croutons 450 calories, 37g fat, 4g protein

4g net carbs: Caesar Appetizer Salad, no croutons 470 calories, 16g fat, 15g protein

5g net carbs: Caesar Appetizer Salad with Grilled Chicken, no croutons 540 calories, 17g fat, 54g protein

6g net carbs: Greek Appetizer Salad, easy Vinaigrette 440 calories, 20g fat, 16g protein

7g net carbs: Factory Chopped Appetizer Salad, no corn, no apples 530 calories, 29g fat, 35g protein

Specialties (No Bread, Steamed Vegetables Substituted for Pasta, Potatoes, or Rice)

4g net carbs: Chicken Madeira 620 calories, 35g fat, 78g protein

4g net carbs: Island Style Ahi Poke Bowl with Kale-Cashew Salad 420 calories, 20g fat, 42g protein

4g net carbs: White Chicken Chili[74], easy beans 540 calories, 16g fat, 49g protein

5g net carbs: Chicken Piccata 550 calories, 44g fat, 78g protein

5g net carbs: Grilled Chicken Bellagio 700 calories, 29g fat, 88g protein

6g net carbs: Chicken Marsala and Mushrooms 510 calories, 33g fat, 8g protein

6g net carbs: Chicken Riesling 550 calories, 41g fat, 77g protein

6g net carbs: Factory Burrito Grande, no tortilla, no black beans 560 calories, 56g fat, 52g protein

6g net carbs: Famous Factory Meatloaf, no corn 660 calories, 56g fat, 72g protein

7g net carbs: Thai Coconut-Lime Chicken with easy Thai Coconut-Curry Sauce, no peas, no pineapple 410 calories, 44g fat, 72g protein

Pasta (No Bread, Steamed Vegetables Substituted for Pasta)

3g net carbs: Tomato Basil Pasta 410 calories, 18g fat, 63g protein

4g net carbs: Baked Rigatoni 550 calories, 42g fat, 72g protein

4g net carbs: Evelyn's Favorite Pasta 590 calories, 30g fat, 34g protein

4g net carbs: Fettuccini Alfredo 350 calories, 24g fat, 53g protein

4g net carbs: Pasta with Shrimp and Sausage 580 calories, 30g fat, 70g protein

4g net carbs: Shrimp with Angel Hair 570 calories, 24g fat, 53g protein

5g net carbs: Cajun Jambalaya Pasta 560 calories, 32g fat, 12g protein

5g net carbs: Farfalle with Chicken and Roasted Garlic, no peas 420 calories, 48g fat, 81g protein

5g net carbs: Pasta Carbonara with Chicken, no peas 450 calories, 30g fat, 78g protein

5g net carbs: Pasta Napoletana with easy sauce 480 calories, 32g fat, 65g protein

6g net carbs: Chicken and Broccoli Pasta 510 calories, 31g fat, 68g protein

6g net carbs: Fettuccini Alfredo with Chicken 380 calories, 35g fat, 59g protein

6g net carbs: Four Cheese Pasta with Chicken with easy sauce 450 calories, 27g fat, 76g protein

6g net carbs: Pasta da Vinci 560 calories, 36g fat, 72g protein

7g net carbs: Spaghetti and Meatballs 440 calories, 44g fat, 66g protein

---

[74] *That's Not Keto!* – You'll find all sorts of surprising foods listed here. I'm not telling you whether you should eat these foods or not. What fits your macros or daily carb spend is up to you. No keto police allowed.

Seafood (No Bread, Steamed Vegetables Substituted for Pasta, Potatoes, or Rice)

3g net carbs: Fresh Grilled Salmon 420 calories, 16g fat, 63g protein
3g net carbs: Grilled Shrimp Platter 640 calories, 21g fat, 40g protein
3g net carbs: Shrimp Scampi 690 calories, 37g fat, 45g protein
4g net carbs: Carolina Grilled Salmon 660 calories, 19g fat, 63g protein
4g net carbs: Herb Crusted Filet of Salmon 530 calories, 33g fat, 64g protein
5g net carbs: Miso Salmon, no peas, easy miso 610 calories, 31g fat, 64g protein
5g net carbs: Seared Ahi Tuna, easy miso 490 calories, 20g fat, 44g protein
5g net carbs: Shrimp and Chicken Gumbo 740 calories, 38g fat, 45g protein
5g net carbs: Thai Glazed Salmon with easy glaze 480 calories, 21g fat, 70g protein
4g net carbs: Jamaican Black Pepper Shrimp, no black beans, no plantains, no pineapple 450 calories, 27g fat, 67g protein
5g net carbs: Jamaican Black Pepper Chicken, no black beans, no plantains, no pineapple 480 calories, 29g fat, 90g protein
8g net carbs: Jamaican Black Pepper Chicken and Shrimp, no black beans, no plantains, no pineapple 520 calories, 33g fat, 72g protein
4g net carbs: Macadamia Crusted Fresh Hawaiian Fish - Mahi 470 calories, 25g fat, 64g protein
5g net carbs: Macadamia Crusted Fresh Hawaiian Fish - Salmon 660 calories, 32g fat, 65g protein
6g net carbs: Macadamia Crusted Fresh Hawaiian Fish - Ahi 420 calories, 26g fat, 79g protein
6g net carbs: Macadamia Crusted Fresh Hawaiian Fish - Ono 410 calories, 26g fat, 75g protein
4g net carbs: Sesame Crusted Fresh Hawaiian Fish - Mahi 470 calories, 32g fat, 88g protein
5g net carbs: Sesame Crusted Fresh Hawaiian Fish - Ahi 490 calories, 27g fat, 96g protein
5g net carbs: Sesame Crusted Fresh Hawaiian Fish - Salmon 420 calories, 26g fat, 83g protein

Factory Combinations (No Bread, Steamed Vegetables Substituted for Pasta, Potatoes, or Rice)

6g net carbs: Shrimp Scampi and Grilled Salmon 490 calories, 27g fat, 56g protein
6g net carbs: Chicken Madeira and Shrimp Scampi 530 calories, 35g fat, 62g protein
7g net carbs: Chicken Madeira and Steak Diane 570 calories, 36g fat, 89g protein
7g net carbs: Shrimp Scampi and Steak Diane 440 calories, 54g fat, 72g protein

Steaks & Chops (No Bread, Steamed Vegetables Substituted for Pasta, Potatoes, or Rice)

2g net carbs: Carne Asada Steak with easy Creamy Ranchero Sauce, no corn 520 calories, 22g fat, 58g protein
3g net carbs: Chargrilled New York Steak 480 calories, 26g fat, 63g protein
3g net carbs: Filet Mignon 450 calories, 29g fat, 73g protein
3g net carbs: Hibachi Steak 570 calories, 34g fat, 57g protein
4g net carbs: Grilled Rib-Eye Steak 520 calories, 37g fat, 74g protein
4g net carbs: Steak Diane 580 calories, 27g fat, 76g protein

Sides

4g net carbs: Small Caesar Salad, no croutons 340 calories, 28g fat, 8g protein
5g net carbs: Broccoli 280 calories, 4g fat, 8g protein
5g net carbs: Green Beans 150 calories, 12g fat, 3g protein
5g net carbs: Grilled Asparagus 120 calories, 8g fat, 5g protein

6g net carbs: Sauteed Spinach 250 calories, 20g fat, 9g protein
6g net carbs: Small Green Salad, includes croutons*, 260 calories, 25g fat, 2g protein

Salads

3g net carbs: Caesar Salad, no croutons 400 calories, 14g fat, 21g protein
4g net carbs: Caesar Salad with Grilled Chicken, no croutons 500 calories, 19g fat, 30g protein
3g net carbs: Cobb Salad 540 calories, 24g fat, 74g protein
4g net carbs: SkinnyLicious® Factory Chopped Salad, no croutons 430 calories, 30g fat, 35g protein
5g net carbs: Seared Tuna Tataki Salad, no glaze 480 calories, 29g fat, 42g protein
6g net carbs: Almond-Crusted Salmon Salad, no Quinoa, no Cranberries 560 calories, 26g fat, 56g protein
5g net carbs: Sheila's Chicken and Avocado Salad, no tortilla strips with Shallot Vinaigrette 690 calories,
    16g fat, 64g protein

Salad Toppings

0g net carbs: Chargrilled Steak 200 calories, 7g fat, 34g protein
0g net carbs: Grilled Chicken 220 calories, 7g fat, 39g protein
2g net carbs: Avocado 160 calories, 14g fat, 2g protein
2g net carbs: Grilled Salmon 220 calories, 12g fat, 26g protein
2g net carbs: Grilled Shrimp 90 calories, 1g fat, 18g protein

Salad Dressing & Condiments (1 Tbsp)

1g net carbs: Balsamic Vinaigrette 80 calories, 7g fat, 0g protein
1g net carbs: Blue Cheese Dressing 60 calories, 5g fat, 1g protein
1g net carbs: Caesar Dressing 80 calories, 7g fat, 1g protein
1g net carbs: Cilantro Dressing 60 calories, 6g fat, 1g protein
1g net carbs: Ranch Dressing 70 calories, 7g fat, 0g protein
1g net carbs: Shallot Vinaigrette 90 calories, 9g fat, 0g protein
1g net carbs: SkinnyLicious® Mustard Vinaigrette 15 calories, 1g fat, 0g protein
2g net carbs: Thousand Island Dressing 70 calories, 7g fat, 0g protein
3g net carbs: Barbeque Ranch Dressing 80 calories, 7g fat, 0g protein
3g net carbs: SkinnyLicious® Sesame Soy Dressing 20 calories, 0g fat, 0g protein
4g net carbs: Citrus Honey Dressing[75] 60 calories, 4g fat, 0g protein
4g net carbs: Spicy Peanut Vinaigrette 60 calories, 4g fat, 1g protein
5g net carbs: Ketchup* 20 calories, 0g fat, 0g protein
6g net carbs: Chinese Plum Dressing* 60 calories, 4g fat, 0g protein

Soup

6g net carbs: Cream of Broccoli Soup, cup, Half-Serving, 180 calories, 16g fat, 5g protein

---

[75] *That's Not Keto!* – You'll find all sorts of surprising foods listed here. I'm not telling you whether you should eat these foods or not. What fits your macros or daily carb spend is up to you. No keto police allowed.

DRINKS

0g net carbs: Diet Coke, 16 oz. 0 calories, 0g fat, 0g protein
0g net carbs: Coca-Cola Zero Sugar, 16 oz. 0 calories, 0g fat, 0g protein
0g net carbs: Sprite Zero, 16 oz. 0 calories, 0g fat, 0g protein
0g net carbs: Diet Dr. Pepper, 16 oz. 0 calories, 0g fat, 0g protein
0g net carbs: Fiji Natural Artesian Water, 16 oz. 0 calories, 0g fat, 0g protein
0g net carbs: San Pellegrino Water, 16 oz. 0 calories, 0g fat, 0g protein

Hot Drinks & Espressos (Unsweetened)

0g net carbs: Certified Organic Black and Herb Teas, 8 oz. 0 calories, 0g fat, 0g protein
1g net carbs: Freshly Brewed Coffee, 8 oz. 5 calories, 0g fat, 0g protein
1g net carbs: Café, 8 oz. 10 calories, 0g fat, 0g protein
4g net carbs: Café Cortadito, 1 oz. 15 calories, 1g fat, 1g protein
9g net carbs: Café con Leche, 8 oz. 100 calories, 5g fat, 5g protein
5g net carbs: Cappuccino with Unsweetened Almond Milk, 6 oz. 70 calories, 3g fat, 7g protein
1g net carbs: Double Espresso, 6 oz. 5 calories, 0g fat, 0g protein
6g net carbs: Cafe Latte with Unsweetened Almond Milk, 12 oz. 15 calories, 2g fat, 3g protein
8g net carbs: Small Cafe Mocha with Unsweetened Almond Milk and unsweetened chocolate, 8 oz.
    25 calories, 3g fat, 6g protein

Cold Teas & Coffees

0g net carbs: Freshly Brewed Black, Green, or Tropical Iced Teas, 12 oz. 0 calories, 0g fat, 0g protein
0g net carbs: Cold Brew Iced Coffee, 16 oz. 5 calories, 0g fat, 0g protein

Beer

5g net carbs: House Draft Light Beer (glass), 12 oz. 100 calories, 0g fat, 1g protein
5g net carbs: House Bottled Light Beer, 12 oz. 100 calories, 0g fat, 1g protein

White Wine

5g net carbs: White Wine (6 .5 oz.) 160 calories, 0g fat, 0g protein
7g net carbs: White Wine (9 oz.) 220 calories, 0g fat, 0g protein

Red Wine

5g net carbs: Red Wine (6 .5 oz.) 160 calories, 0g fat, 0g protein
7g net carbs: Red Wine (9 oz.) 220 calories, 0g fat, 0g protein

Sparkling Wine

4g net carbs: Sparkling Wine (5 .5 oz.) 130 calories, 0g fat, 0g protein
9g net carbs: Sparkling Wine Bottle 375ml 300 calories, 0g fat, 0g protein

Skinnylicious® Cocktails

0g net carbs: The Well-Mannered Dirty Martini, 10 oz. 250 calories, 6g fat, 1g protein
6g net carbs: SkinnyLicious® Long Island Iced Tea, 12 oz. 110 calories, 0g fat, 0g protein
9g net carbs: SkinnyLicious® Cosmopolitan, 10 oz. 110 calories, 0g fat, 0g protein

Well Drinks (1.5 oz.)

0g net carbs: Well Bourbon 80 calories, 0g fat, 0g protein
0g net carbs: Well Gin 80 calories, 0g fat, 0g protein
0g net carbs: Well Rum 80 calories, 0g fat, 0g protein
0g net carbs: Well Scotch 80 calories, 0g fat, 0g protein
0g net carbs: Well Tequila 80 calories, 0g fat, 0g protein
0g net carbs: Well Vodka 80 calories, 0g fat, 0g protein

BJ's Restaurant

Do you want to know how much of a vegetable lover I have become while on my keto journey? Check this out. I began to crave Brussels sprouts. Seriously! My go-to order at BJ's Restaurant is the Honey Sriracha Brussels Sprouts with no honey glaze. I have no idea about their secret cooking method, but boy, have I tried to emulate it. These balls of deliciousness melt in your mouth.

Special Order Tips

Order all burgers and sandwiches with "no bread." Be wary of the available "Add-Ons" since they are often an unnecessary source of net carbs. Avoid all fries, potatoes, rice, pasta, buns, bread, etc. Ask the server to substitute a side salad or a side of steamed/grilled vegetables. Are you feeling brave? Order Turmeric-Roasted Cauliflower from the small bites menu. BJ's Restaurant knows how to serve it up!

Low-carb side dishes at BJ's Restaurant are garlic-roasted vegetables, asparagus, broccoli, avocado slices, and sauteed green beans. Despite the rumors, zoodles are no longer offered at this restaurant. Dang.

Feel free to customize your order. Restaurants are usually happy to accommodate reasonable customer requests. The exception is when the item has been premade or was prepared off-site. Note that any alterations on your end will change the provided nutrition information. Adjust accordingly.

You'll notice some menu items indicate a half-serving size. Don't worry; there will only be a few. A smaller portion size allowed us to include more (higher-carb) crowd-pleasing favorites from BJ's Restaurant.

Author Favorite

Breakfast: Enlightened Veggie Omelet with extra Avocado. 6 oz. Coffee, unsweetened, to drink. 350 calories, 16g fat, 4g net carbs, 23g protein

Lunch: Ahi Poke, no rice, no sauce to start. Meat Lover's Piadina, no piadina with Turmeric-Roasted Cauliflower as a side. 16 oz. Unsweetened Sunset Peach Tea over ice to drink. 1830 calories, 102g fat, 16g net carbs, 73g protein

Dinner: BJ'S Original Wings, 10 Piece with Lemon Pepper Sesame Dry Rub and ranch dip. Bunless Hickory Brisket and Bacon Burger, no sauce, with Sauteed Green Beans on the side. 16 oz. Diet Coke to drink. 2460 calories, 163g fat, 19g net carbs, 102g protein

BREAKFAST[76] (No Bread)

3g net carbs: Enlightened Veggie Omelet 250 calories, 8g fat, 22g protein
6g net carbs: BJ's California Scramble, no bread 810 calories, 69g fat, 53g protein
10g net carbs: BJ's Breakfast Flatbread Pizza (with Crust) (1 slice) 190 calories, 12g fat, 9g protein

0g net carbs: Eggs (2) Any Style 310 calories, 21g fat, 19g protein
5g net carbs: Eggs (2) Any Style with Sausage 630 calories, 43g fat, 33g protein
6g net carbs: Eggs (2) Any Style with Bacon 640 calories, 31g fat, 27g protein
6g net carbs: Eggs (2) Any Style with Ham 610 calories, 25g fat, 33g protein

6g net carbs: Classic Breakfast Sandwich with Sausage, no bread 740 calories, 87g fat, 49g protein
7g net carbs: Classic Breakfast Sandwich with Bacon, no bread 950 calories, 46g fat, 42g protein
7g net carbs: Classic Breakfast Sandwich with Ham, no bread 920 calories, 40g fat, 48g protein

Breakfast Add-Ons

1g net carbs: Avocado 100 calories, 8g fat, 1g protein
2g net carbs: Bacon (3 slices) 140 calories, 11g fat, 8g protein
2g net carbs: Ham (1 slice) 110 calories, 5g fat, 14g protein
2g net carbs: Sausage Link (1) 520 calories, 52g fat, 14g protein
8g net carbs: Strawberry Topping[77] 50 calories, 0g fat, 1g protein

LUNCH

Apps

4g net carbs: Honey Sriracha Brussels Sprouts, no honey glaze 220 calories, 6g fat, 11g protein
5g net carbs: Chicken Lettuce Wraps, no wontons 490 calories, 19g fat, 31g protein
7g net carbs: Ahi Poke, no rice, no sauce 320 calories, 10g fat, 32g protein
7g net carbs: Spinach Stuffed Mushrooms, Half-Serving, 150 calories, 10g fat, 6g protein

---

[76] Note that some BJ's Restaurant locations may not serve breakfast.

[77] *That's Not Keto!* – You'll find all sorts of surprising foods listed here. I'm not telling you whether you should eat these foods or not. What fits your macros or daily carb spend is up to you. No keto police allowed.

Starter Salads

3g net carbs: Small Caesar Salad, no croutons 340 calories, 25g fat, 10g protein
5g net carbs: Wedge Salad 320 calories, 31g fat, 6g protein
7g net carbs: House Salad (No Dressing) 80 calories, 4g fat, 5g protein
8g net carbs: Fresh Mozzarella and Tomato Salad 260 calories, 18g fat, 14g protein

Wings (No Sauce with Lemon Pepper Sesame Dry Rub)

4g net carbs: Boneless Chicken Wings, 1 lb., remove breading, 870 calories, 41g fat, 34g protein
5g net carbs: Bone-In Wings (10) 750 calories, 57g fat, 50g protein
6g net carbs: BJ'S Original Wings (10) 560 calories, 45g fat, 23g protein

Sauces & Rubs

0g net carbs: Lemon Pepper Sesame Dry Rub 0 calories, 0g fat, 0g protein
1g net carbs: Ranch Dressing 120 calories, 13g fat, 1g protein
3g net carbs: Hot and Spicy Buffalo 20 calories, 0g fat, 1g protein
4g net carbs: EXXXXtra Hot Buffalo 30 calories, 0g fat, 1g protein
5g net carbs: Sriracha Dry Rub 30 calories, 0g fat, 1g protein
8g net carbs: Garlic Parmesan 420 calories, 42g fat, 0g protein

BJ'S Flatbread Appetizer Pizza (With Crust, One Slice)

9g net carbs: Slice California Club Flatbread Pizza[78] 110 calories, 6g fat, 5g protein
9g net carbs: Slice Margherita Fresca Flatbread Pizza* 100 calories, 5g fat, 5g protein
10g net carbs: Slice Pepperoni Extreme Flatbread Pizza* 110 calories, 6g fat, 4g protein

BJ'S Snacks and Small Bites

2g net carbs: Brewhouse Meatballs, no marinara sauce 480 calories, 43g fat, 25g protein
2g net carbs: Turmeric-Roasted Cauliflower 280 calories, 18g fat, 7g protein
8g net carbs: Pirahna Pale Ale Chili*, Cup, no tortilla strips 800 calories, 36g fat, 34g protein

Entrees (with Grilled/Steamed Vegetables as Side)

5g net carbs: Lunch Enlightened Lemon Thyme Chicken, no rice 490 calories, 16g fat, 45g protein
6g net carbs: Italian Chicken Piadina, no piadina 1100 calories, 64g fat, 37g protein
7g net carbs: Caprese Piadina, no piadina 960 calories, 51g fat, 33g protein
7g net carbs: Chicken Bacon Ranch Piadina, no piadina 1240 calories, 74g fat, 46g protein
7g net carbs: Steak & Cheese Piadina, no piadina 1020 calories, 55g fat, 37g protein
8g net carbs: Meat Lover's Piadina, no piadina 1190 calories, 74g fat, 34g protein

---

[78] *That's Not Keto!* – You'll find all sorts of surprising foods listed here. I'm not telling you whether you should eat these foods or not. What fits your macros or daily carb spend is up to you. No keto police allowed.

Pastas (Substitute Grilled/Steamed Vegetables for Pasta)

6g net carbs: Lunch Grilled Chicken Alfredo, no pasta, easy sauce 680 calories, 34g fat, 36g protein
7g net carbs: Lunch Jumbo Spaghetti and Meatballs, no pasta, super easy marinara sauce 850 calories, 43g fat, 29g protein

DINNER (Served with a Grilled/Steamed Vegetable Side)

Burgers (No Bread, No Fries)

3g net carbs: Classic Burger, bunless 1180 calories, 66g fat, 49g protein
4g net carbs: BJ's Bacon Cheeseburger, bunless 1350 calories, 80g fat, 59g protein
4g net carbs: Enlightened Barbeque Bison Burger, bunless, no BBQ sauce 670 calories, 33g fat, 31g protein
5g net carbs: Bacon-Guacamole Deluxe Burger, bunless 1420 calories, 85g fat, 60g protein
5g net carbs: Enlightened Turkey Burger, bunless, no cranberries 750 calories, 45g fat, 38g protein
6g net carbs: Bistro Burger, bunless, no sauce 1350 calories, 76g fat, 59g protein
6g net carbs: Mushroom Swiss Burger, bunless 1600 calories, 10g fat, 59g protein
7g net carbs: Hickory Brisket and Bacon Burger, bunless, no BBQ sauce 1700 calories, 99g fat, 76g protein

Brewhouse Burgers (No Bread, No Fries)

3g net carbs: Brewhouse Burger, bunless 1090 calories, 60g fat, 43g protein
6g net carbs: Brewhouse Bacon Cheeseburger, bunless 1260 calories, 74g fat, 54g protein
7g net carbs: Black and Bleuhouse Burger, bunless 1240 calories, 73g fat, 50g protein

Burger Add-Ons

0g net carbs: American Cheese 170 calories, 13g fat, 7g protein
0g net carbs: Cheddar Cheese 170 calories, 14g fat, 11g protein
0g net carbs: Loaded Burger Patty 380 calories, 26g fat, 35g protein
1g net carbs: Avocado 100 calories, 8g fat, 1g protein
1g net carbs: Brewhouse Burger Patty 290 calories, 19g fat, 26g protein
1g net carbs: Housemade Guacamole 90 calories, 8g fat, 1g protein
8g net carbs: Cup BJ's Pirahna® Pale Ale Chili[79], no tortilla strips 800 calories, 36g fat, 34g protein

Sandwiches (No Bread, No Fries)

3g net carbs: California Chicken Club Sandwich, Half-Serving, no bread 830 calories, 44g fat, 39g protein
5g net carbs: California Chicken Club Sandwich, no bread 1310 calories, 69g fat, 73g protein
5g net carbs: Classic Prime Rib Dip, no bread 1640 calories, 118g fat, 45g protein
6g net carbs: Brewhouse Philly, no bread, no coleslaw 890 calories, 90g fat, 63g protein
6g net carbs: Slow Roasted Turkey Club, no bread 1560 calories, 99g fat, 55g protein

---

[79] *That's Not Keto!* – You'll find all sorts of surprising foods listed here. I'm not telling you whether you should eat these foods or not. What fits your macros or daily carb spend is up to you. No keto police allowed.

Steaks & Slow Roasted Menu

3g net carbs: Baby Back Pork Ribs, Half-Rack, no BBQ sauce 710 calories, 34g fat, 25g protein
4g net carbs: BJ's Classic Rib-Eye 1080 calories, 67g fat, 106g protein
4g net carbs: Chimichurri Grilled Chicken, easy sauce 840 calories, 45g fat, 44g protein
4g net carbs: Slow-Roasted Tri-Tip, no BBQ sauce 590 calories, 22g fat, 49g protein
4g net carbs: Tri-Tip Combo with Grilled Chicken 710 calories, 22g fat, 76g protein
4g net carbs: Tri-Tip Combo with Grilled Shrimp 910 calories, 47g fat, 62g protein
4g net carbs: Tri-Tip Combo with Ribs, no BBQ sauce 1070 calories, 50g fat, 61g protein
5g net carbs: Baby Back Pork Ribs, Full-Rack, no BBQ sauce 900 calories, 68g fat, 50g protein
5g net carbs: Prime Rib Dinner 1310 calories, 106g fat, 79g protein
6g net carbs: Double Bone-In Pork Chop 610 calories, 38g fat, 55g protein
6g net carbs: New Orleans Jambalaya, no rice 1330 calories, 70g fat, 69g protein
7g net carbs: Bacon Jam Rib-Eye, no jam 810 calories, 55g fat, 45g protein
7g net carbs: Parmesan-Crusted Chicken 1330 calories, 76g fat, 89g protein

Seafood

2g net carbs: Broiled Salmon 820 calories, 45g fat, 51g protein
3g net carbs: Pacific Poke, no Soba Noodles 610 calories, 17g fat, 41g protein
4g net carbs: Fried Mahi-Mahi Tacos, no taco shells 800 calories, 35g fat, 25g protein
5g net carbs: Cajun Shrimp Tacos, no taco shells 710 calories, 36g fat, 36g protein
5g net carbs: Shrimp and Arugula Pita Tacos, no pitas 830 calories, 38g fat, 42g protein
6g net carbs: Flame-Broiled Mahi-Mahi Tacos, no taco shells 680 calories, 35g fat, 31g protein
7g net carbs: Fresh Atlantic Salmon (Blackened), no rice 880 calories, 50g fat, 48g protein
7g net carbs: Fresh Atlantic Salmon (Flame-Broiled), no rice 860 calories, 52g fat, 48g protein

Housemade Sides

0g net carbs: Garlic-Roasted Vegetables 200 calories, 3g fat, 0g protein
1g net carbs: Avocado 100 calories, 8g fat, 1g protein
2g net carbs: Asparagus 30 calories, 0g fat, 2g protein
4g net carbs: Broccoli 40 calories, 0g fat, 3g protein
4g net carbs: Brussels Sprouts, no honey sauce 160 calories, 4g fat, 9g protein
5g net carbs: Sauteed Green Beans 80 calories, 4g fat, 2g protein

Add-Ons

0g net carbs: Flame-Broiled Salmon 390 calories, 25g fat, 40g protein
0g net carbs: Grilled Chicken Breast 220 calories, 6g fat, 39g protein
1g net carbs: Turkey Burger Patty 170 calories, 4g fat, 20g protein
3g net carbs: Meatball 270 calories, 18g fat, 23g protein
4g net carbs: Blackened Chicken 240 calories, 6g fat, 40g protein
4g net carbs: Blackened Shrimp 250 calories, 10g fat, 35g protein
6g net carbs: Blackened Salmon 410 calories, 25g fat, 40g protein

$6 Take Home Entrees (Substitute Steamed/Grilled Vegetables for Pasta)

2g net carbs: $6 Vegetarian Turmeric Cauliflower, no quinoa 420 calories, 8g fat, 12g protein

3g net carbs: $6 Grilled Chicken Alfredo (Take Home Entrée) 680 calories, 34g fat, 36g protein
4g net carbs: $6 Fire-Roasted Barbacoa Chicken, no rice, no beans (Take Home Entrée) 530 calories, 15g fat, 53g protein
5g net carbs: $6 Jumbo Spaghetti and Meatballs, super easy marinara (Take Home Entrée) 720 calories, 38g fat, 25g protein
6g net carbs: $6 Spicy Peanut Chicken, no Soba Noodles, no peanut sauce (Take Home Entrée) 860 calories, 49g fat, 29g protein

Pasta Favorites (Substitute Steamed/Grilled Vegetables for Pasta)

2g net carbs: Italiano Vegetable Penne 300 calories, 18g fat, 18g protein
6g net carbs: Italiano Vegetable Penne with Blackened Chicken 640 calories, 34g fat, 37g protein
6g net carbs: Italiano Vegetable Penne with Cajun Shrimp 650 calories, 38g fat, 33g protein
6g net carbs: Italiano Vegetable Penne with Grilled Chicken 620 calories, 34g fat, 37g protein
5g net carbs: Grilled Chicken Alfredo, easy sauce 1460 calories, 71g fat, 59g protein
6g net carbs: Shrimp Scampi Pasta, easy sauce 860 calories, 100g fat, 57g protein
5g net carbs: Lemon Thyme Chicken 630 calories, 19g fat, 60g protein
5g net carbs: Mediterranean-Spiced Chicken Entree 750 calories, 50g fat, 49g protein
6g net carbs: Enlightened Fire-Roasted Barbacoa Chicken, no rice, no beans 520 calories, 15g fat, 51g protein
6g net carbs: Enlightened Mediterranean Chicken Pita Tacos, no pita bread 830 calories, 34g fat, 45g protein
8g net carbs: Jumbo Spaghetti and Meatballs, super easy marinara sauce 960 calories, 62g fat, 55g protein
8g net carbs: Spicy Peanut Chicken, no Soba Noodles, no peanut sauce 1040 calories, 61g fat, 45g protein

Salads

4g net carbs: Santa Fe Salad, no corn, no tortilla strips 840 calories, 61g fat, 55g protein
5g net carbs: Santa Fe Salad with Blackened Salmon, no corn, no tortilla strips 910 calories, 81g fat, 55g protein
5g net carbs: Santa Fe Salad with Cajun Shrimp, no corn, no tortilla strips 950 calories, 66g fat, 50g protein
5g net carbs: Santa Fe Salad with Grilled Chicken, no corn, no tortilla strips 920 calories, 61g fat, 55g protein
6g net carbs: Santa Fe Salad with Flame-Broiled Salmon, no corn, no tortilla strips 990 calories, 81g fat, 55g protein
4g net carbs: Grilled Chicken Antipasto Salad, easy dressing 790 calories, 51g fat, 61g protein
5g net carbs: House Salad, no croutons 590 calories, 5g fat, 23g protein
6g net carbs: Derby-Style Cobb Salad, easy dressing 940 calories, 69g fat, 52g protein
6g net carbs: Tri-Tip Wedge Salad, no croutons 1300 calories, 91g fat, 53g protein
7g net carbs: House Wedge Salad 610 calories, 7g fat, 25g protein
6g net carbs: House Caesar Salad with Cajun Shrimp, no croutons 1060 calories, 74g fat, 57g protein
6g net carbs: House Caesar Salad, no croutons 510 calories, 64g fat, 23g protein
7g net carbs: House Caesar Salad with Blackened Salmon, no croutons 1220 calories, 89g fat, 62g protein
7g net carbs: House Caesar Salad with Flame Broiled Salmon, no croutons 1200 calories, 89g fat, 62g protein
8g net carbs: House Caesar Salad with Grilled Chicken, no croutons 1030 calories, 70g fat, 62g protein
8g net carbs: Fresh Mozzarella and Tomato Salad 670 calories, 8g fat, 38g protein
8g net carbs: Seared Ahi Salad, no croutons 570 calories, 31g fat, 30g protein

Salad Dressings

1g net carbs: Avocado Ranch Dressing 130 calories, 12g fat, 0g protein
2g net carbs: Bleu Cheese Dressing 180 calories, 20g fat, 2g protein

2g net carbs: Italian Dressing 170 calories, 18g fat, 0g protein
2g net carbs: Ranch Dressing 170 calories, 17g fat, 0g protein
2g net carbs: Santa Fe Dressing 170 calories, 17g fat, 0g protein
3g net carbs: Caesar Dressing 200 calories, 20g fat, 3g protein
5g net carbs: Oil & Vinegar 210 calories, 21g fat, 0g protein
6g net carbs: Balsamic Vinaigrette 160 calories, 15g fat, 0g protein
6g net carbs: BBQ Ranch Dressing 140 calories, 12g fat, 0g protein
6g net carbs: Thousand Island Dressing 200 calories, 20g fat, 0g protein
8g net carbs: Honey Mustard Dressing[80] 240 calories, 24g fat, 0g protein
9g net carbs: Rice Wine Vinaigrette 170 calories, 15g fat, 1g protein
10g net carbs: Strawberry Vinaigrette 70 calories, 4g fat, 0g protein

DRINKS

0g net carbs: Diet Pepsi, 16 oz. 0 calories, 0g fat, 0g protein
0g net carbs: Diet Dr. Pepper, 16 oz. 0 calories, 0g fat, 0g protein
0g net carbs: Coffee, unsweetened, 6 oz. 0 calories, 0g fat, 0g protein
0g net carbs: Decaf Coffee, unsweetened, 6 oz. 0 calories, 0g fat, 0g protein
0g net carbs: Green Iced Tea, unsweetened, 16 oz. 0 calories, 0g fat, 0g protein
0g net carbs: Hot Tea, unsweetened, 6 oz. 0 calories, 0g fat, 0g protein
0g net carbs: Iced Tea, unsweetened, 16 oz. 0 calories, 0g fat, 0g protein
0g net carbs: Sunset Peach Tea, 16 oz. 0 calories, 0g fat, 0g protein
2g net carbs: Tropical, Iced Tea, unsweetened, 16 oz. 10 calories, 0g fat, 0g protein
6g net carbs: Raspberry Sparkling Water, 16 oz. 30 calories, 0g fat, 0g protein
8g net carbs: Cucumber Mint Sparkling Water, 16 oz. 40 calories, 0g fat, 0g protein

Beer & Seltzer

2g net carbs: Truly Hard Seltzer Strawberry Lemonade, 12 oz. can 100 calories, 0g fat, 0g protein
2g net carbs: Truly Hard Seltzer Wild Berry, 12 oz. can 100 calories, 0g fat, 0g protein
5g net carbs: BJ's Oasis® Amber, 12 oz. 160 calories, 0g fat, 3g protein
9g net carbs: BJ's LightSwitch® Lager, 12 oz. 240 calories, 0g fat, 3g protein

Wine

4g net carbs: Apothic Red Winemaker's Blend, 5 oz. 220 calories, 0g fat, 0g protein
4g net carbs: Cupcake Light-Hearted Rose, 5 oz. 180 calories, 0g fat, 0protein
4g net carbs: Dark Horse Cabernet Sauvignon, 5 oz. 140 calories, 0g fat, 0g protein
5g net carbs: Dark Horse Chardonnay, 5 oz. 210 calories, 0g fat, 0g protein
6g net carbs: Ecco Domani Pinot Grigio, 5 oz. 225 calories, 0g fat, 0g protein

---

[80] *That's Not Keto!* – You'll find all sorts of surprising foods listed here. I'm not telling you whether you should eat these foods or not. What fits your macros or daily carb spend is up to you. No keto police allowed.

Applebee's

Applebee's is cruisin' for a bruisin' right out of the gate with only *breaded* chicken wings and *breaded* chicken strips on the menu. I'm unimpressed, fellas. Where are the unbreaded, grilled, or baked chicken options? Us keto folks demand more.

The customizable Nutrition Calculator on Applebee's website is almost fantastic enough to provide them with redemption. It can make burgers and sandwiches breadless, which is pretty darn cool.

Special Order Tips

Order all burgers and sandwiches with "no bread." Be wary of the available "Add-Ons" since they are often an unnecessary source of net carbs.

Don't be fooled by the Impossible Burger Patty. It has 5 grams of net carbs, whereas the Impossible Patty (Quesadilla Burger) has 6 grams of net carbs. Interesting.

Feel free to customize your order. Restaurants are usually happy to accommodate reasonable customer requests. The exception is when the item has been premade or was prepared off-site. Note that any alterations on your end will change the provided nutrition information. Adjust accordingly.

Avoid all fries, potatoes, rice, pasta, bread, etc. Ask the server to substitute a side salad or a side of steamed/grilled vegetables. Need a suggestion? How about an Applebee's side dish of steamed broccoli or garlicky green beans?

Author Favorite

Lunch: Breadless The Prime Rib Dipper with House Salad with easy Blue Cheese, no croutons. 16 oz. Diet Mountain Dew. 1470 calories, 24g fat, 11g net carbs, 64g protein

Dinner: Double Crunch Bone-In Wings, baked, with no batter, with Blue Cheese Dressing to start. Shrimp 'N Parmesan Sirloin with Garlicky Green Beans and Homestyle Cheesy Broccoli on the side. House Salad with Ranch, no croutons. 2220 calories, 55g fat, 25g net carbs, 145g protein

LUNCH

Appetizers

3g net carbs: Double Crunch Bone-In Wings (10), baked with no batter 580 calories, 9g fat, 60g protein

Wing Dressing

1g net carbs: Blue Cheese 200 calories, 4g fat, 1g protein
3g net carbs: Ranch 150 calories, 3g fat, 1g protein
3g net carbs: Classic Hot Buffalo 210 calories, 8g fat, 1g protein
3g net carbs: Extra Hot Buffalo 220 calories, 8g fat, 1g protein
4g net carbs: Garlic Parmesan 400 calories, 10g fat, 3g protein

$12.99 Bunless Burger Bundle (No Bread, Steamed Broccoli Instead of Fries)

5g net carbs: Classic Burger 510 calories, 39g fat, 34g protein
5g net carbs: Classic Cheeseburger 610 calories, 47g fat, 39g protein
6g net carbs: Classic Bacon Cheeseburger 700 calories, 54g fat, 46g protein
9g net carbs: Quesadilla Burger, no tortilla, no pico de gallo 1,030 calories, 82g fat, 61g protein
9g net carbs: Whisky Bacon Burger, no crispy onions, no Whisky Infused Sauce 760 calories, 59g fat,
    51g protein

Handcrafted Burgers (No Bread)

2g net carbs: Classic Burger 410 calories, 31g fat, 31g protein
2g net carbs: Classic Cheeseburger 510 calories, 39g fat, 36g protein
3g net carbs: Classic Bacon Cheeseburger 600 calories, 46g fat, 43g protein
6g net carbs: Quesadilla Burger, no tortilla, no pico de gallo 930 calories, 74g fat, 58g protein
6g net carbs: Whisky Bacon Burger, no crispy onions, no Whisky Infused Sauce 660 calories, 51g fat,
    48g protein
7g net carbs: Impossible Cheeseburger 340 calories, 21g fat, 25g protein

Burger Substitutions & Add-Ons

0g net carbs: Chicken Breast Patty 190 calories, 1g fat, 40g protein
1g net carbs: Lettuce Cup 5 calories, 0g fat, 0g protein
1g net carbs: Bacon (3 strips) 100 calories, 2g fat, 7g protein
1g net carbs: Burger Patty 410 calories, 13g fat, 32g protein
5g net carbs: Impossible Burger Patty 230 calories, 13g fat, 19g protein
6g net carbs: Impossible Patty (Quesadilla Burger) 240 calories, 14g fat, 19g protein

Sandwiches & More (No Bread, Steamed Broccoli Substituted for Fries)

6g net carbs: Chicken Fajita Lettuce Rollup 790 calories, 27g fat, 62g protein

7g net carbs: Bacon Cheddar Grilled Chicken Sandwich, no bread, no BBQ ranch 920 calories, 19g fat, 69g protein

7g net carbs: Clubhouse Grille, no bread, no honey BBQ sauce 1,430 calories, 20g fat, 56g protein

7g net carbs: Oriental Grilled Chicken Lettuce Wrap, no crunchy rice noodles 1,190 calories, 17g fat, 59g protein

8g net carbs: The Prime Rib Dipper, no bread 1,340 calories, 22g fat, 58g protein

Side Salads

3g net carbs: House Salad with easy Blue Cheese, no croutons 130 calories, 2g fat, 6g protein

5g net carbs: Caesar Salad, no croutons 230 calories, 4g fat, 5g protein

Salad Dressing

1g net carbs: Bleu Cheese 200 calories, 4g fat, 1g protein

1g net carbs: Lemon Olive Oil Vinaigrette 150 calories, 3g fat, 0g protein

2g net carbs: Caesar 200 calories, 3g fat, 1g protein

3g net carbs: Mexi-Ranch 140 calories, 3g fat, 1g protein

3g net carbs: Ranch 150 calories, 2g fat, 1g protein

5g net carbs: Fat-Free Italian 20 calories, 0g fat, 0g protein

7g net carbs: Thousand Island 230 calories, 4g fat, 1g protein

DINNER

Steaks & Ribs (Substitute Grilled/Steamed Vegetables as Side)

4g net carbs: Top Sirloin, 6 oz. 580 calories, 9g fat, 42g protein

5g net carbs: Top Sirloin, 8 oz. 660 calories, 11g fat, 53g protein

6g net carbs: Ribeye, 12 oz. 980 calories, 25g fat, 68g protein

6g net carbs: Bourbon Street Steak 820 calories, 12g fat, 52g protein

5g net carbs: Applebee's Riblets Plate, super easy Honey BBQ sauce 880 calories, 14g fat, 53g protein

7g net carbs: Applebee's Riblets Platter, super easy Honey BBQ sauce 1,290 calories, 22g fat, 83g protein

6g net carbs: Shrimp 'N Parmesan Sirloin 940 calories, 26g fat, 67g protein

Chicken (Substitute Grilled/Steamed Vegetables as Side)

4g net carbs: Grilled Chicken Breast 570 calories, 7g fat, 48g protein

6g net carbs: Grilled Oriental Chicken Salad, no rice noodles, easy Oriental vinaigrette 670 calories, 12g fat, 51g protein

6g net carbs: Bourbon Street Chicken & Shrimp 780 calories, 8g fat, 55g protein

6g net carbs: Fiesta Lime Chicken, no rice, no tortilla strips 1,170 calories, 14g fat, 60g protein

Seafood (Substitute Grilled/Steamed Vegetables as Side)

4g net carbs: Blackened Cajun Salmon 630 calories, 8g fat, 44g protein

Salads (No Breadstick)

4g net carbs: Blackened Shrimp Caesar Salad, no croutons 880 calories, 12g fat, 33g protein
5g net carbs: Grilled Chicken Caesar Salad, no croutons 990 calories, 12g fat, 56g protein
5g net carbs: Tuscan Garden Chicken Salad, no bruschetta tomatoes 580 calories, 6g fat, 45g protein
6g net carbs: Grilled Chicken Tender Salad, no honey Dijon mustard dressing 1,010 calories, 17g fat, 61g protein

Salad Dressing

1g net carbs: Bleu Cheese 200 calories, 4g fat, 1g protein
1g net carbs: Lemon Olive Oil Vinaigrette 150 calories, 3g fat, 0g protein
2g net carbs: Caesar 200 calories, 3g fat, 1g protein
3g net carbs: Mexi-Ranch 140 calories, 3g fat, 1g protein
3g net carbs: Ranch 150 calories, 2g fat, 1g protein
5g net carbs: Fat-Free Italian 20 calories, 0g fat, 0g protein
7g net carbs: Thousand Island 230 calories, 4g fat, 1g protein

Pasta (Substitute Grilled/Steamed Vegetables for Pasta)

6g net carbs: Classic Blackened Shrimp Alfredo 710 calories, 44g fat, 57g protein
6g net carbs: Three-Cheese Chicken Penne, no bruschetta tomatoes 920 calories, 40g fat, 77g protein
8g net carbs: Classic Broccoli Chicken Alfredo 820 calories, 45g fat, 80g protein

Bowls (No Rice, No Corn Salsa, No Tortilla Strips)

6g net carbs: Southwest Chicken Bowl with extra greens 820 calories, 6g fat, 54g protein
6g net carbs: Tex-Mex Shrimp Bowl with extra greens 710 calories, 4g fat, 30g protein

Sides

3g net carbs: Steamed Broccoli 100 calories, 4g fat, 3g protein
5g net carbs: Homestyle Cheesy Broccoli 210 calories, 10g fat, 9g protein
7g net carbs: Garlicky Green Beans 160 calories, 4g fat, 2g protein

DRINKS

0g net carbs: Diet Coke, 16 oz. 0 calories, 0g fat, 0g protein
0g net carbs: Caffeine-Free Diet Coke, 16 oz. 0 calories, 0g fat, 0g protein
0g net carbs: Coke Zero, 16 oz. 0 calories, 0g fat, 0g protein
0g net carbs: Diet Pepsi, 16 oz. 0 calories, 0g fat, 0g protein
0g net carbs: Caffeine-Free Diet Pepsi, 16 oz. 0 calories, 0g fat, 0g protein
0g net carbs: Diet Sierra Mist, 16 oz. 0 calories, 0g fat, 0g protein
1g net carbs: Diet Mountain Dew, 16 oz. 5 calories, 0g fat, 0g protein

0g net carbs: IBC Diet Root Beer, 16 oz. 0 calories, 0g fat, 0g protein
3g net carbs: Minute Maid Lemonade Light, 16 oz. 10 calories, 0g fat, 0g protein
0g net carbs: Sugar-free Lemonade, 16 oz. 5 calories, 0g fat, 0g protein
0g net carbs: Tropicana Light Lemonade, 16 oz. 5 calories, 0g fat, 0g protein
2g net carbs: Red Bull, Sugar-free, 8.4 oz. can 10 calories, 0g fat, 0g protein
0g net carbs: Bubly Sparkling Water, Lime, 12 oz. can 0 calories, 0g fat, 0g protein
0g net carbs: Bubly Sparkling Water, Orange, 12 oz. can 0 calories, 0g fat, 0g protein
0g net carbs: Sobe Life Water, Yumberry Pomegranate, 16 oz. 0 calories, 0g fat, 0g protein
0g net carbs: Dasani Water Bottled Water, 16 oz. 0 calories, 0g fat, 0g protein
0g net carbs: Perrier Sparkling Water, 16 oz. 0 calories, 0g fat, 0g protein
0g net carbs: Lipton Unsweetened Iced Tea, 16 oz. 0 calories, 0g fat, 0g protein
0g net carbs: Brewed Hot Tea, Unsweetened, 8 oz. 0 calories, 0g fat, 0g protein
2g net carbs: Brewed Iced Tea Unsweetened, 16 oz. 0 calories, 0g fat, 0g protein
0g net carbs: Fresh Brewed Coffee Unsweetened, 8 oz. 0 calories, 0g fat, 0g protein
0g net carbs: Fresh Brewed Decaf Coffee Unsweetened, 8 oz. 0 calories, 0g fat, 0g protein

Beer & Seltzer

2g net carbs: Bud Light Seltzer, Strawberry, 12 oz. can 100 calories, 0g fat, 0g protein
2g net carbs: Bud Light Seltzer, Black Cherry, 12 oz. can 100 calories, 0g fat, 0g protein
2g net carbs: Bud Light Seltzer, Lemon Lime, 12 oz. can 100 calories, 0g fat, 0g protein
2g net carbs: Bud Light Seltzer, Mango, 12 oz. can 100 calories, 0g fat, 0g protein

3g net carbs: Michelob Ultra, 12 oz. bottle 95 calories, 0g fat, 1g protein
3g net carbs: Miller Lite, 12 oz. bottle 96 calories, 0g fat, 1g protein
5g net carbs: Coors Light, 12 oz. bottle 102 calories, 0g fat, 1g protein
7g net carbs: Bud Light, 12 oz. bottle 110 calories, 0g fat, 1g protein

Wine

4g net carbs: Kendall Jackson Vintner's Reserve Chardonnay, 5 oz. glass 122 calories, 0g fat, 0g protein
4g net carbs: Robert Mondavi Woodbridge Cabernet, 5 oz. glass 135 calories, 0g fat, 1g protein
5g net carbs: Josh Cellars Cabernet, 5 oz. glass 125 calories, 0g fat, 0g protein
5g net carbs: Robert Mondavi Woodbridge Chardonnay, 5 oz. glass 128 calories, 0g fat, 0g protein

Spirits

0g net carbs: Jack and Diet Coke 95 calories, 0g fat, 0g protein
0g net carbs: House Rum and Diet Coke 90 calories, 0g fat, 0g protein

Yard House

I'm guessing keto hasn't caught on here yet. Yard House only lists gluten sensitive, vegan-friendly, and vegetarian as dietary restrictions. Maybe they'll catch on soon and update their website. Let's hope so.

The menu items online for Yard House are not customizable, so we are left to do all the math on our own. "View Nutritional Info" becomes visible when an individual menu item is clicked. But only calories are listed. *Hmpf.* Until that changes, thank your lucky stars for this book. Otherwise, only the Food & Beverage Nutrition Guide PDF can clarify what you're eating.

Special Order Tips

Order all burgers and sandwiches with "no bread." Be wary of the available "Add-Ons" since they are often an unnecessary source of net carbs.

Feel free to customize your order. Restaurants are usually happy to accommodate reasonable customer requests. The exception is when the item has been premade or was prepared off-site. Note that any alterations on your end will change the provided nutrition information. Adjust accordingly.

Avoid all fries, potatoes, rice, pasta, bread, etc. Ask the server to substitute a side salad or a side of steamed/grilled vegetables. Be sure to check out the baby broccoli and zoodle dishes at Yard House. Yes, you read that correctly. Yard House offers zucchini noodles!

Don't be misled into thinking that the meatless (Gardein™) options are a "10 grams of net carbs or less" possibility. They are higher in carbs (30+ grams of net carbs for an appetizer serving of unflavored wings for some reason). Thus, STAY AWAY.

Author Favorite

Lunch & Dinner: Ahi Sashimi, easy soy vinaigrette, 3 Lettuce Wrapped Carne Asada Tacos, easy salsa. 2 Dirty Ketel Martinis 1470 calories, 68g fat, _12g net carbs_, 19g protein

LUNCH & DINNER

Appetizers

2g net carbs: Four Cheese Spinach Dip, no bread, no chips 220 calories, 14g fat, 14g protein
4g net carbs: Chicken Lettuce Wraps, no wonton cup, no sweet chili 770 calories, 37g fat, 42g protein
5g net carbs: Lemon Pepper Wings (Crispy Traditional) 1100 calories, 75g fat, 3g protein
6g net carbs: Ahi Sashimi, easy soy vinaigrette 470 calories, 30g fat, 16g protein
6g net carbs: Buffalo Wings (Crispy Traditional) 1280 calories, 92g fat, 5g protein
6g net carbs: Poke Nachos, no wontons, no sweet soy-ginger sauce, no truffle sauce 870 calories, 59g fat, 9g protein
7g net carbs: Spicy Tuna Stack, easy sauce 550 calories, 33g fat, 6g protein
8g net carbs: Hot & Spicy Edamame, easy sauce 490 calories, 36g fat, 10g protein
8g net carbs: Steamed Edamame 180 calories, 8g fat, 0g protein

Soups & Starter Salads

4g net carbs: House Salad, no croutons 430 calories, 29g fat, 12g protein
4g net carbs: Traditional Caesar, no croutons 410 calories, 34g fat, 3g protein
7g net carbs: Kale & Romaine Caesar, no raisins, no pistachios, no croutons 540 calories, 39g fat, 12g protein

Prime Burgers (with Pickle, No Bread, No Side)

2g net carbs: Hamburger, bunless 1030 calories, 69g fat, 11g protein
3g net carbs: Classic Cheeseburger, bunless 1080 calories, 71g fat, 11g protein
4g net carbs: Pepper Jack Burger, bunless 1150 calories, 75g fat, 11g protein
6g net carbs: BBQ Bacon Cheddar Burger, bunless, super easy BBQ sauce 1370 calories, 91g fat, 26g protein

Burger Add-Ons

1g net carbs: Avocado 70 calories, 6g fat, 0g protein
1g net carbs: Applewood Bacon (3 strips) 210 calories, 18g fat, 0g protein
1g net carbs: Pickles 0 calories, 0g fat, 0g protein

Sandwiches (with Pickle, No Bread, No Side)

5g net carbs: Double Decker BLT, breadless 1140 calories, 78g fat, 16g protein
5g net carbs: Grilled Chicken & Avocado Sandwich, breadless 1120 calories, 74g fat, 12g protein
6g net carbs: "Everything-Crusted" Ahi, breadless, easy sauce 1020 calories, 62g fat, 14g protein
6g net carbs: House Cheesesteak, breadless, no onion strings, easy sauce 1260 calories, 66g fat, 9g protein
6g net carbs: Stacked Turkey Club, breadless 1360 calories, 85g fat, 19g protein
7g net carbs: Korean BBQ Cheesesteak, breadless, no gochujang 1390 calories, 75g fat, 23g protein

Sandwich Add-Ons

1g net carbs: Avocado 70 calories, 6g fat, 0g protein
1g net carbs: Applewood Bacon (3 strips) 210 calories, 18g fat, 0g protein

Lettuce Wrapped Street Tacos

2g net carbs: Lettuce Wrapped Blackened Shrimp Taco (1), easy salsa 210 calories, 11g fat, 1g protein
2g net carbs: Lettuce Wrapped Carne Asada Taco (1), easy salsa 240 calories, 12g fat, 1g protein
3g net carbs: Lettuce Wrapped Vampire Taco (1), easy salsa 470 calories, 31g fat, 3g protein
4g net carbs: Lettuce Wrapped Grilled Fish Taco (1), easy salsa 240 calories, 14g fat, 1g protein
7g net carbs: Lettuce Wrapped Grilled Korean Beef Taco (1), no gochujang 340 calories, 20g fat, 7g protein

Steaks (with Steamed Vegetables on the Side)

1g net carbs: Bone-In Rib Eye, 20 oz. 1390 calories, 81g fat, 14g protein
1g net carbs: Bone-In Rib Eye, 20 oz. with Shrimp 1530 calories, 83g fat, 14g protein
4g net carbs: Pepper Crusted Filet, 8 oz., no carrots 1080 calories, 67g fat, 22g protein

Bowls (No Brown Rice, No Red Quinoa)

4g net carbs: Steak Bowl 520 calories, 19g fat, 13g protein
4g net carbs: Chicken Bowl 500 calories, 16g fat, 13g protein
5g net carbs: Shrimp Bowl 440 calories, 13g fat, 14g protein

House Favorites & Seafood

1g net carbs: Grilled Salmon, no sweet glaze 420 calories, 37g fat, 45g protein
5g net carbs: Grilled Shrimp Zoodle Bowl, no wine 470 calories, 31g fat, 10g protein
5g net carbs: Sesame-Crusted Ahi, no rice, easy sauce 670 calories, 38g fat, 5g protein
6g net carbs: Lobster Garlic Zoodles, no honey 1090 calories, 55g fat, 18g protein
5g net carbs: Spicy Jambalaya, small, easy sauce, no pasta, no rice 740 calories, 58g fat, 6g protein
7g net carbs: Spicy Jambalaya, large, no sauce, no pasta, no rice 1310 calories, 109g fat, 9g protein

Entree Salads

2g net carbs: Kale & Romaine Caesar, small, no raisins, no pistachios, no croutons 540 calories, 39g fat, 12g protein
4g net carbs: Kale & Romaine Caesar, regular, no raisins, no pistachios, no croutons 700 calories, 50g fat, 15g protein
5g net carbs: Kale & Romaine Caesar with Shrimp, small, no raisins, no pistachios, no croutons 680 calories, 42g fat, 12g protein
6g net carbs: Kale & Romaine Caesar with Shrimp, regular, no raisins, no pistachios, no croutons 840 calories, 53g fat, 15g protein
5g net carbs: Kale & Romaine Caesar with Salmon, small, no raisins, no pistachios, no croutons 940 calories, 64g fat, 12g protein
6g net carbs: Kale & Romaine Caesar with Salmon, regular, no raisins, no pistachios, no croutons 1100 calories, 75g fat, 15g protein

7g net carbs: Kale & Romaine Caesar with Chicken, small, no raisins, no pistachios, no croutons 740 calories, 45g fat, 12g protein
8g net carbs: Kale & Romaine Caesar with Chicken, regular, no raisins, no pistachios, no croutons 900 calories, 56g fat, 15g protein

4g net carbs: Cobb Salad with Grilled Shrimp, small, no corn 550 calories, 36g fat, 6g protein
6g net carbs: Cobb Salad with Grilled Shrimp, regular, no corn 880 calories, 62g fat, 11g protein
4g net carbs: Cobb Salad, small, no corn 410 calories, 34g fat, 6g protein
5g net carbs: Cobb Salad, regular, no corn 740 calories, 60g fat, 11g protein
5g net carbs: Cobb Salad with Grilled Chicken, small, no corn 610 calories, 40g fat, 6g protein
7g net carbs: Cobb Salad with Grilled Chicken, regular, no corn 940 calories, 66g fat, 11g protein
5g net carbs: Cobb Salad with Salmon, small, no corn 820 calories, 59g fat, 6g protein
6g net carbs: Cobb Salad with Salmon, regular, no corn 1140 calories, 85g fat, 11g protein

6g net carbs: Ahi Crunchy Salad, small, no wontons 410 calories, 27g fat, 8g protein
8g net carbs: Ahi Crunchy Salad, regular, no wontons 780 calories, 52g fat, 17g protein
6g net carbs: Poke Salad, no wantons 730 calories, 52g fat, 14g protein

Sides

2g net carbs: Baby Broccoli 35 calories, 0g fat, 4g protein
2g net carbs: Steamed Edamame 40 calories, 2g fat, 0g protein
4g net carbs: House Salad 60 calories, 3g fat, 5g protein
6g net carbs: Steamed Mixed Vegetables 50 calories, 0g fat, 5g protein

DRINKS

0g net carbs: Diet Coke, 16 oz. 0 calories, 0g fat, 0g protein
0g net carbs: Coke Zero Sugar, 16 oz. 0 calories, 0g fat, 0g protein
0g net carbs: Topo Chico Sparkling, 16 oz. 0 calories, 0g fat, 0g protein
1g net carbs: House-Brewed Iced Tea, unsweetened (all flavors), 16 oz. 0 calories, 0g fat, 0g protein
1g net carbs: Hot Tea, unsweetened (all flavors), 6 oz. 0 calories, 0g fat, 0g protein
2g net carbs: Sugar-free Red Bull, 8.4 oz. can 10 calories, 0g fat, 0g protein
0g net carbs: Coffee, unsweetened, 6 oz. 0 calories, 0g fat, 0g protein
6g net carbs: Espresso, unsweetened, 3 oz. 30 calories, 0g fat, 0g protein

Beer & Seltzer

3g net carbs: Hard Seltzer, Pint (16 oz.) 130 calories, 0g fat, 0g protein
4g net carbs: Hard Seltzer, 23 oz. 190 calories, 0g fat, 0g protein

6g net carbs: House Light Lager, Pint (16 oz.) 130 calories, 0g fat, 1g protein
8g net carbs: House Light Lager, 23 oz. 180 calories, 0g fat, 1g protein

Wine

4g net carbs: House White, 6 oz. 150 calories, 0g fat, 2g protein
6g net carbs: House White, 9 oz. 220 calories, 0g fat, 3g protein
5g net carbs: House Red, 6 oz. 160 calories, 0g fat, 1g protein

8g net carbs: House Red, 9 oz. 230 calories, 0g fat, 2g protein
8g net carbs: House Sparkling, 5.25 oz. 130 calories, 0g fat, 8g protein

Spirits

0g net carbs: Dirty Ketel Martini 140 calories, 1g fat, 0g protein
8g net carbs: Hendrick's Elderflower Tonic 140 calories, 0g fat, 8g protein
8g net carbs: Tito's Bloody Mary 190 calories, 2g fat, 4g protein

Bennigan's

I'll be honest; Bennigan's leaves much to be desired regarding low-carb options. Lots of breaded and deep-fried food here. Even the broccoli is breaded –for cryin' out loud! Temptation is everywhere. Not even the restaurant's website can steer you in the right direction. All customizations must be figured out by cross-comparing entrée descriptions with the online menu. Sheez. Needless to say, picking out low options is *complicated* while dining at Bennigan's. They simply do not provide clear Nutrition Information.

Special Order Tips

Order all burgers and sandwiches with "no bread." Be wary of the available "Add-Ons" since they are often an unnecessary source of net carbs. Avoid all fries, potatoes, rice, pasta, bread, etc. Ask the server to substitute a side salad or a side of steamed/grilled vegetables.

Feel free to customize your order. Restaurants are usually happy to accommodate reasonable customer requests. The exception is when the item has been premade or was prepared off-site. Note that any alterations on your end will change the provided nutrition information. Adjust accordingly.

Author Favorite

Lunch & Dinner: Broccoli Bites (remove breading) as an appetizer. Entrée choice is Smothered Chicken with Broccoli Sauté and Roasted Brussels Sprouts, with no maple on the side. 6 oz. glass of Pinot Grigio, Ecco Domani to drink. 1818 calories, 87g fat, 29g net carbs, 101g protein

LUNCH & DINNER

Crowd Pleasers

2g net carbs: Bennigan's Premium Buffalo Wings 175 calories, 18g fat, 21g protein
4g net carbs: Cheeseburger Pub Bites, bunless, no onion rings 290 calories, 27g fat, 31g protein
5g net carbs: Mangia Mozzarella 115 calories, 15g fat, 14g protein
6g net carbs: Mix and Match; Mangia Mozzarella and Cheeseburger Pub Bites, bunless, no onion rings
  405 calories, 64g fat, 65g protein
7g net carbs: Broccoli Bites, remove breading, 286 calories, 19g fat, 13g protein
9g net carbs: Mix and Match; Broccoli Bites and Bennigan's Premium Buffalo Wings 461 calories, 37g fat,
  34g protein

Celebrated Sandwiches (No Bread)

3g net carbs: The Original Irish Dip 570 calories, 36g fat, 21g protein
3g net carbs: Turkey O'Toole, easy honey Dijon dressing 670 calories, 32g fat, 31g protein
4g net carbs: The Classic Reuben, easy sauerkraut 590 calories, 42g fat, 38g protein
5g net carbs: Bennigan's Club 570 calories, 33g fat, 46g protein
5g net carbs: Cajun Chicken O'Toole, easy honey Dijon dressing 615 calories, 50g fat, 36g protein
6g net carbs: Bennigan's Club™ with Garden Salad, no croutons 630 calories, 55g fat, 37g protein
6g net carbs: Kilkenny's Country Grilled Chicken Wrap, easy honey Dijon dressing, no tortilla 480 calories,
  27g fat, 41g protein

The Prime Burgers (No Bread)

3g net carbs: The Classic Burger 620 calories, 56g fat, 31g protein
4g net carbs: Spicy Chipotle Burger 634 calories, 59g fat, 41g protein
6g net carbs: The B.O.M.B. no marmalade, 764 calories, 66g fat, 45g protein
7g net carbs: GUINNESS Glazed Bacon Burger, easy glaze 794 calories, 62g fat, 51g protein
7g net carbs: St. Brigid Burger 664 calories, 64g fat, 49g protein
7g net carbs: The Big Irish 824 calories, 72g fat, 52g protein
7g net carbs: BBQ Bacon Cheddar Burger, easy BBQ sauce 844 calories, 72g fat, 58g protein
8g net carbs: The Irishman, easy glaze, easy whiskey cream sauce 894 calories, 76g fat, 63g protein

Legendary Favorites (Salad or Steamed Vegetable as Side)

2g net carbs: Char-Grilled Flat Iron Steak 490 calories, 29g fat, 55g protein
3g net carbs: Oh, Baby™ Back Ribs, Half-Rack, no BBQ Sauce 510 calories, 34g fat, 25g protein
4g net carbs: Cajun Seasoned Grilled Salmon Fillet 350 calories, 17g fat, 22g protein
4g net carbs: Danny Boy Chicken 620 calories, 12g fat, 43g protein
4g net carbs: Pork Chop, no glaze or sauce, 445 calories, 26g fat, 42g protein
4g net carbs: Simple Grilled Salmon Fillet 340 calories, 17g fat, 22g protein
5g net carbs: Oh, Baby™ Back Ribs, Full-Rack, no BBQ Sauce 900 calories, 64g fat, 50g protein
6g net carbs: Cajun Chicken & Shrimp, no pasta, no bread 780 calories, 8g fat, 55g protein
6g net carbs: The Irishman Chicken, no Whiskey Glaze 740 calories, 14g fat, 49g protein

Steak & Ale Classics

2g net carbs: Kensington Club® Grilled, 8oz. Top Sirloin 430 calories, 29g fat, 49g protein
6g net carbs: Smothered Chicken 810 calories, 18g fat, 59g protein

Sides

2g net carbs: Caesar Salad, no croutons 265 calories, 32g fat, 7g protein
3g net carbs: Garden Salad, no croutons 270 calories, 24g fat, 4g protein
3g net carbs: Seasonal Vegetables 150 calories, 4g fat, 2g protein
6g net carbs: Roasted Brussels Sprouts, no maple 340 calories, 31g fat, 10g protein
7g net carbs: Broccoli Sauté 260 calories, 19g fat, 19g protein

Salads

3g net carbs: Loaded Grilled Chicken Cobb Salad 410 calories, 14g fat, 29g protein
4g net carbs: Steakhouse Salad, no croutons 615 calories, 28g fat, 33g protein
5g net carbs: Steakhouse Salad with Extra steak, no croutons 710 calories, 32g fat, 43g protein
5g net carbs: Baby Spinach & Bacon Salad, no raisins, easy sweet pepper vinaigrette 390 calories, 16g fat, 29g protein
5g net carbs: Ultimate Buffalo Grilled Chicken Salad 550 calories, 20g fat, 33g protein
6g net carbs: Grilled Shrimp Baby Spinach & Bacon Salad, no raisins, easy sweet pepper vinaigrette 480 calories, 24g fat, 36g protein
7g net carbs: Grilled Chicken Baby Spinach & Bacon Salad, no raisins, easy sweet pepper vinaigrette 510 calories, 28g fat, 43g protein
7g net carbs: Kilkenny's Country Grilled Chicken Salad, easy honey Dijon Dressing 640 calories, 33g fat, 53g protein

Salad Dressing

0g net carbs: Caesar 240 calories, 32g fat, 2g protein
0g net carbs: Oil and Vinegar 65 calories, 4g fat, 0g protein
1g net carbs: Housemade Ranch 90 calories, 10g fat, 1g protein
1g net carbs: Chunky Bleu Cheese 130 calories, 13g fat, 2g protein
2g net carbs: Lite Italian 70 calories, 7g fat, 0g protein
5g net carbs: Sweet Pepper Vinaigrette 170 calories, 7g fat, 0g protein
6g net carbs: Bennigan's Smoky Honey Dijon 150 calories, 16g fat, 0g protein
6g net carbs: Thousand Island 110 calories, 10g fat, 0g protein

DRINKS

0g net carbs: Dasani Bottled Water, 16 oz. 0 calories, 0g fat, 0g protein
0g net carbs: Gold Peak Iced Tea, unsweetened, 16 oz. 0 calories, 0g fat, 0g protein
0g net carbs: Hot Tea, unsweetened, 5 oz. 0 calories, 0g fat, 0g protein
0g net carbs: Coffee, unsweetened, 5 oz. 0 calories, 0g fat, 0g protein
0g net carbs: Diet Coke, 16 oz. 0 calories, 0g fat, 0g protein
0g net carbs: Coke Zero, 16 oz. 0 calories, 0g fat, 0g protein
2g net carbs: Red Bull Sugar-free, 8.4 oz. can 10 calories, 0g fat, 0g protein

Beer

3g net carbs: Michelob Ultra, 12 oz. bottle 95 calories, 0g fat, 1g protein
3g net carbs: Miller Lite, 12 oz. can 96 calories, 0g fat, 1g protein
5g net carbs: Coors Light, 12 oz. can 102 calories, 0g fat, 1g protein
5g net carbs: Corona Light, 12 oz. Bottle 99 calories, 0g fat, 1g protein
7g net carbs: Bud Light, 12 oz. can 110 calories, 0g fat, 1g protein

White Wine

3g net carbs: Pinot Grigio, Ecco Domani, 6 oz. 122 calories, 0g fat, 0g protein
4g net carbs: White Zinfandel, Pacific Bay, 6 oz. 133 calories, 0g fat, 0g protein
4g net carbs: Chardonnay, Cupcake, 6 oz. 150 calories, 0g fat, 0g protein
4g net carbs: Chardonnay, Kendall-Jackson, 6 oz. 120 calories, 0g fat, 0g protein
4g net carbs: Chardonnay, Fetzer, 6 oz. 135 calories, 0g fat, 0g protein
6g net carbs: Moscato, Woodbridge, 6 oz. 120 calories, 0g fat, 0g protein

Red Wine

3g net carbs: Pinot Noir, Cellar 8, 6 oz. 122 calories, 0g fat, 0g protein
4g net carbs: Cabernet Sauvignon, Little Black Dress, 6 oz. 130 calories, 0g fat, 0g protein
4g net carbs: Cabernet Sauvignon, Rodney Strong Sonoma County, 6 oz. 125 calories, 0g fat, 0g protein
5g net carbs: Cabernet Sauvignon, Fetzer, 6 oz. 119 calories, 0g fat, 0g protein
5g net carbs: Red Blend, Black Forest Cupcake, 6 oz. 160 calories, 0g fat, 0g protein
6g net carbs: Malbec, Alamos, 6 oz. 172 calories, 0g fat, 0g protein
6g net carbs: Merlot, Blackstone, 6 oz. 140 calories, 0g fat, 0g protein

Spirits

0g net carbs: The Skinny Leprechaun 220 calories, 0g fat, 0g protein

Golden Corral

Golden Corral offers a unique Nutrition Facts search engine on its website. It even has filters for "sugar-free," "breakfast," "salad," and "bread." A snappy little feature that is fun to play around with, but overall, not very helpful. Let me explain. The Nutrition Facts engine lists only the entrée's name with its macronutrients. Ingredients are broken down for *some* menu items but not others. What gives? Golden Corral is lacking in ingredient transparency. Less than half are found on the Nutrition Facts. I call that sneaky.

Special Order Tips

Remove rolls or bread from burgers and sandwiches - "no bread." To keep carb intake as low as possible, avoid all fries, potatoes, rice, pasta, crackers, beans, tortillas, sweet sauces, etc.

Beware of the sugar-free desserts. Sugar is just one part of the equation, remember? They may still contain regular white flour, a source of high carbs. Personally, I take a bite of each (they're free, right?) and call it a day.

It's easy to overindulge at buffets. One trick I've learned is to spend as much time as possible at the salad bar (before heading to higher-carb entrees, sides, and sugar-free desserts). Also, drinking water, as opposed to diet soda, can help fill you up.

Enjoy the wealth of low-carb vegetables available at Golden Corral. From collard greens to cauliflower, sauerkraut to spinach, even the pickiest eaters will find a satisfying dish.

Author Favorite

Breakfast: Classic Breakfast Combo - Bacon and Sausage, no bread, no potatoes. 12 oz. Gold Peak Tea, Unsweetened on ice to drink. 610 calories, 44g fat, 2g net carbs, 24g protein

Lunch & Dinner: Baked Fish with Piccata Sauce with 1/2 cup Okra and Tomato Stew on the side. 16 oz. Coca-Cola Zero Sugar to drink. 210 calories, 12g fat, 6g net carbs, 15g protein

BREAKFAST (No Bread, No Potatoes)

1g net carbs: Made-to-Order Eggs, (1) 130 calories, 11g fat, 6g protein
2g net carbs: Chorizo and Eggs- 1/2 cup 200 calories, 16g fat, 13g protein
2g net carbs: Classic Breakfast Combo - Bacon and Sausage 610 calories, 44g fat, 24g protein
2g net carbs: Scrambled Eggs- 1/2 cup 180 calories, 14g fat, 11g protein
3g net carbs: Avocado Egg and Cheese Sandwich 390 calories, 17g fat, 21g protein
3g net carbs: Omelet 260 calories, 23g fat, 12g protein
4g net carbs: Sausage Breakfast Bowl 530 calories, 34g fat, 26g protein
4g net carbs: Two Egg Breakfast - Bacon and Turkey Sausage 450 calories, 30g fat, 22g protein
4g net carbs: Southwest Breakfast Burrito, no tortilla 510 calories, 30g fat, 20g protein
5g net carbs: Southwest Breakfast Bowl 500 calories, 37g fat, 19g protein
5g net carbs: Chorizo and Egg Burrito, no tortilla 310 calories, 18g fat, 16g protein
6g net carbs: Sausage and Egg Burrito, no tortilla 320 calories, 19g fat, 16g protein
6g net carbs: Sausage Skillet- 1/2 cup 270 calories, 21g fat, 7g protein
6g net carbs: Steak and Eggs 530 calories, 38g fat, 42g protein
7g net carbs: Egg and Sausage Breakfast Skillet 130 calories, 8g fat, 8g protein
8g net carbs: Egg and Sausage Casserole- 1/2 cup 240 calories, 16g fat, 14g protein
8g net carbs: Eggs Benedict, easy Hollandaise 320 calories, 23g fat, 9g protein

Breakfast Add-Ons

0g net carbs: Bacon (3 strips) 60 calories, 4g fat, 4g protein
0g net carbs: Sausage Patties (1) 80 calories, 7g fat, 5g protein
0g net carbs: Sausage Patty (4) 300 calories, 27g fat, 18g protein
1g net carbs: Sausage Crumbles, 1 oz. 120 calories, 11g fat, 4g protein
1g net carbs: Sausage Links (1) 120 calories, 11g fat, 5g protein
1g net carbs: Sausage Links (2) 230 calories, 21g fat, 9g protein
2g net carbs: Crabmeat, Surimi, 1 Tbsp 251 calories, 0g fat, 1g protein
3g net carbs: Down Home Fried Bacon (2 strips) 130 calories, 10g fat, 4g protein
4g net carbs: Sausage Gravy, 2 oz. 80 calories, 7g fat, 2g protein
4g net carbs: Turkey Sausage (4) 320 calories, 20g fat, 32g protein
6g net carbs: Sugar-free Syrup, 2 Tbsp 15 calories, 0g fat, 0g protein
9g net carbs: Blueberry Pancakes[81] (1) 80 calories, 4g fat, 2g protein
9g net carbs: Pancakes* (1) 80 calories, 4g fat, 2g protein

---

[81] *That's Not Keto!* – You'll find all sorts of surprising foods listed here. I'm not telling you whether you should eat these foods or not. What fits your macros or daily carb spend is up to you. No keto police allowed.

LUNCH & DINNER

Burgers (No Bread)

2g net carbs: Cheeseburger, 4 oz. 530 calories, 27g fat, 28g protein
3g net carbs: Cheeseburger, 6 oz. 580 calories, 33g fat, 36g protein
4g net carbs: Cheeseburger, 8 oz. 720 calories, 39g fat, 47g protein
4g net carbs: Mini Steakburger, no BBQ sauce 260 calories, 14g fat, 17g protein
4g net carbs: Mini Bacon Steakburger, no BBQ sauce 260 calories, 14g fat, 17g protein

Chicken/Turkey Sandwiches (No Bread)

2g net carbs: Buffalo Chicken Sandwich 200 calories, 9g fat, 9g protein
2g net carbs: Chicken Bistro Melt 320 calories, 17g fat, 18g protein
2g net carbs: Mini Grilled Chicken Sandwich 200 calories, 9g fat, 9g protein
4g net carbs: Grilled Chicken and Avocado Sandwich 290 calories, 16g fat, 14g protein
4g net carbs: Nashville Grilled Chicken Sandwich 870 calories, 63g fat, 23g protein
4g net carbs: Turkey Bistro Sandwich with Bacon 350 calories, 19g fat, 23g protein
5g net carbs: Farm House Grilled Chicken Sandwich, no sauce 630 calories, 40g fat, 26g protein

Chicken/Turkey Dishes (No Bread, No Potatoes, Choose Steamed Vegetables as Side)

0g net carbs: Buffalo Wings with Frank's RedHot Sauce (3) 180 calories, 12g fat, 16g protein
0g net carbs: Carved Turkey, Dark Meat, 3 oz. 180 calories, 9g fat, 23g protein
0g net carbs: Carved Turkey, White Meat, 3 oz. 170 calories, 7g fat, 24g protein
0g net carbs: Chicken Strips, 3 oz. 80 calories, 1g fat, 17g protein
0g net carbs: Chicken Wings (10) 400 calories, 27g fat, 36g protein
0g net carbs: Chicken Wings (5) 160 calories, 11g fat, 14g protein
0g net carbs: Chicken Wings, Hot (10) 330 calories, 22g fat, 29g protein
0g net carbs: Chicken Wings, Hot (5) 170 calories, 11g fat, 15g protein
0g net carbs: Golden Roasted Chicken (Dark Meat), 3 oz. 160 calories, 9g fat, 19g protein
0g net carbs: Golden Roasted Chicken (White Meat), 3 oz. 140 calories, 6g fat, 22g protein
0g net carbs: Grilled Chicken Breast, 10 oz. 430 calories, 11g fat, 83g protein
0g net carbs: Hot Buffalo Chicken Wings (3) 180 calories, 12g fat, 16g protein
0g net carbs: Mild Buffalo Chicken Wings (3) 180 calories, 12g fat, 16g protein
0g net carbs: Rotisserie Chicken, 1 piece 310 calories, 15g fat, 43g protein
0g net carbs: Smoked Chicken (Dark Meat), 3 oz. 170 calories, 11g fat, 18g protein
0g net carbs: Smoked Chicken (White Meat), 3 oz. 150 calories, 6g fat, 23g protein
0g net carbs: Spicy Garlic Chicken Legs (1) 140 calories, 7g fat, 18g protein

1g net carbs: Chicken Machaca, 3 oz. 120 calories, 6g fat, 15g protein
1g net carbs: Hot Buffalo Chicken Legs (1) 150 calories, 7g fat, 18g protein
1g net carbs: Mild Buffalo Chicken Legs (1) 150 calories, 7g fat, 18g protein
1g net carbs: Roasted Grilled Bone-in Chicken, 3 oz. 160 calories, 9g fat, 20g protein
1g net carbs: Spicy Garlic Wings (3) 180 calories, 12g fat, 16g protein
1g net carbs: Spicy Garlic Wings (3) 180 calories, 12g fat, 16g protein
1g net carbs: Turkey Sausage (1) 80 calories, 5g fat, 8g protein
2g net carbs: Carved Turkey Breast, 3 oz. 110 calories, 6g fat, 15g protein
2g net carbs: Smoked BBQ Wings (3) 180 calories, 11g fat, 17g protein

2g net carbs: Smothered Grilled Chicken (1) 200 calories, 10g fat, 27g protein
2g net carbs: Spicy Ranch Chicken Breast (1) 280 calories, 15g fat, 33g protein
2g net carbs: Turkey Sausage (side) (2) 160 calories, 10g fat, 16g protein
3g net carbs: BBQ Chicken Wings (3) 180 calories, 12g fat, 15g protein
3g net carbs: Boneless Nashville Chicken Wings, no glaze/sauce (2) 190 calories, 6g fat, 19g protein
3g net carbs: Bourbon Street Chicken Burrito Bowl (no tortilla), easy sauce 570 calories, 30g fat, 32g protein
3g net carbs: Bourbon Street Chicken Wings, no glaze/sauce (3) 190 calories, 12g fat, 16g protein
3g net carbs: Bourbon Street Chicken, easy sauce, 3 oz. 170 calories, 9g fat, 19g protein
3g net carbs: Buffalo Grilled Chicken, 18 oz. 740 calories, 62g fat, 56g protein
3g net carbs: Chicken Enchiladas, no tortillas (1) 190 calories, 11g fat, 11g protein
3g net carbs: Chicken Lemonata (1) 140 calories, 6g fat, 15g protein
3g net carbs: Orange Chicken, super easy sauce, 1 cup 390 calories, 15g fat, 25g protein
3g net carbs: Pulled Chicken in Poultry Gravy, 3 oz. 80 calories, 2g fat, 14g protein
3g net carbs: Smoked BBQ Turkey Breast, 3 oz. 120 calories, 4g fat, 19g protein
3g net carbs: Turkey Slices with Poultry Gravy, 3 oz. 90 calories, 4g fat, 11g protein

4g net carbs: BBQ Chicken Breasts (Baked Bone-In) (1) 350 calories, 12g fat, 55g protein
4g net carbs: BBQ Chicken Legs (1) 150 calories, 7g fat, 18g protein
4g net carbs: Boneless Chicken Wings (2) 180 calories, 6g fat, 20g protein
4g net carbs: Bourbon Street Chicken Bowl, no glaze/sauce 400 calories, 18g fat, 29g protein
4g net carbs: Chicken Cacciatore (1) 280 calories, 18g fat, 23g protein
4g net carbs: Chicken Fajitas, 3 oz. 60 calories, 1g fat, 6g protein
4g net carbs: Honey Sesame Glazed Wings, easy sauce (3) 200 calories, 13g fat, 16g protein
4g net carbs: Nashville Hot Grilled Chicken Thighs (1) 520 calories, 29g fat, 20g protein
4g net carbs: Spicy Pagoda Chicken, super easy sauce, 1 cup 240 calories, 10g fat, 17g protein
4g net carbs: Turkey Stacker, breadless 400 calories, 21g fat, 20g protein

5g net carbs: Baked BBQ Chicken Legs (1) 140 calories, 7g fat, 16g protein
5g net carbs: BBQ Chicken Thighs (Baked Bone-In) (1) 350 calories, 24g fat, 28g protein
5g net carbs: Boneless Franks Red Hot Chicken Wings (2) 180 calories, 7g fat, 22g protein
5g net carbs: Chicken Parmesan, remove breading (1 piece) 240 calories, 11g fat, 17g protein
5g net carbs: Chicken Piccata (1) 220 calories, 13g fat, 19g protein
5g net carbs: Chicken Wings, BBQ, easy BBQ sauce (5) 200 calories, 11g fat, 15g protein
5g net carbs: Grilled BBQ Chicken (1) 140 calories, 2g fat, 17g protein
5g net carbs: Ranch Grilled Chicken- Homeward, 18 oz. 610 calories, 48g fat, 34g protein
5g net carbs: Sweet and Sour Chicken, super easy sauce, 1 cup 240 calories, 10g fat, 17g protein
5g net carbs: Sweet Buffalo Chicken Thigh, easy sauce (1) 400 calories, 26g fat, 36g protein
5g net carbs: Teriyaki Honey Pineapple Chicken Wings, easy BBQ sauce (3) 190 calories, 12g fat, 16g protein

6g net carbs: Boneless Buffalo Chicken Wings (2) 180 calories, 8g fat, 18g protein
6g net carbs: Honey Teriyaki Chicken Breasts (Baked Bone-in), easy sauce (1) 360 calories, 12g fat, 55g protein
6g net carbs: Lemon Herb Chicken, easy glaze/sauce, 1 cup 190 calories, 9g fat, 14g protein
6g net carbs: Pulled BBQ Chicken, easy BBQ sauce, 3 oz. 110 calories, 1g fat, 14g protein
6g net carbs: Teriyaki Chicken Breasts (Baked Bone-in), easy BBQ sauce (1) 350 calories, 12g fat, 55g protein
6g net carbs: Turkey with easy Stuffing (1) 110 calories, 5g fat, 6g protein

7g net carbs: Baked Honey Teriyaki Chicken Legs, easy sauce (1) 150 calories, 7g fat, 16g protein
7g net carbs: Baked Teriyaki Chicken Legs, easy sauce (1) 150 calories, 7g fat, 16g protein
7g net carbs: Breaded Chicken Wings (3) 280 calories, 19g fat, 18g protein
7g net carbs: Chicken Stuffed Burrito Bowl (no tortilla) 300 calories, 18g fat, 17g protein
7g net carbs: Honey Teriyaki Chicken Thighs, easy sauce (1) 360 calories, 24g fat, 28g protein

7g net carbs: Honey Teriyaki Pineapple Chicken Legs, easy sauce (1) 160 calories, 7g fat, 18g protein

7g net carbs: Teriyaki Chicken Thighs (Baked Bone-in), easy BBQ sauce (1) 360 calories, 24g fat, 28g protein

8g net carbs: Chicken Pot Pie (1) 150 calories, 8g fat, 5g protein

8g net carbs: Chicken Quesadillas (1) 130 calories, 8g fat, 5g protein

8g net carbs: Lightly-Breaded Chicken Tenders (1) 150 calories, 7g fat, 13g protein

8g net carbs: Mandarin Orange Chicken Breasts (Baked Bone-in), easy sauce (1) 360 calories, 12g fat, 55g protein

9g net carbs: Baked Mandarin Orange Chicken Legs, easy sauce (1) 160 calories, 7g fat, 16g protein

9g net carbs: Chicken Gizzards (3) 160 calories, 10g fat, 9g protein

9g net carbs: Hickory Bourbon Chicken Legs, easy sauce (1) 170 calories, 7g fat, 18g protein

9g net carbs: Mandarin Orange Chicken Thighs (Baked Bone-in), easy sauce (1) 370 calories, 24g fat, 28g protein

10g net carbs: Chicken Wings, BBQ, easy BBQ sauce (10) 360 calories, 22g fat, 29g protein

Beef Sandwiches/Hot Dogs (No Bread)

2g net carbs: Braised Beef Sandwich 430 calories, 32g fat, 32g protein

2g net carbs: Mini Hot Dog 160 calories, 8g fat, 5g protein

3g net carbs: Patty Melt 460 calories, 23g fat, 20g protein

3g net carbs: Roast Beef Stacker 480 calories, 27g fat, 27g protein

4g net carbs: Hot Dogs with Onions & Peppers (1) 310 calories, 22g fat, 9g protein

4g net carbs: Meatloaf Sandwich All Beef, easy ketchup 460 calories, 23g fat, 18g protein

4g net carbs: Mini BBQ Brisket Sandwich, easy BBQ sauce 150 calories, 7g fat, 4g protein

4g net carbs: Philly Cheese Braised Beef Sandwich 560 calories, 24g fat, 39g protein

4g net carbs: Philly Steak Sandwich 360 calories, 20g fat, 21g protein

5g net carbs: Meatloaf Sandwich, easy ketchup 440 calories, 21g fat, 18g protein

5g net carbs: Philly Cheesesteak Meatballs (2) with easy sauce 180 calories, 15g fat, 12g protein

5g net carbs: Smokehouse Beef Flatbread, no BBQ sauce 170 calories, 10g fat, 10g protein

5g net carbs: Smokehouse Sandwich, no BBQ sauce 630 calories, 40g fat, 26g protein

Beef Dishes (No Bread, No Potatoes, Choose Steamed Vegetables as Side)

0g net carbs: Barbacoa, no BBQ sauce- 3 oz. 270 calories, 23g fat, 18g protein

0g net carbs: BBQ Beef, no BBQ sauce- 3 oz. 120 calories, 5g fat, 18g protein

0g net carbs: Chuck Tips- 3 oz. 140 calories, 5g fat, 21g protein

0g net carbs: Portobello Mushroom Carved Sirloin- 3 oz. 150 calories, 10g fat, 16g protein

0g net carbs: Ribeye- 3 oz. 170 calories, 9g fat, 23g protein

0g net carbs: Roast Beef (inside round)- 3 oz. 110 calories, 3g fat, 19g protein

0g net carbs: Sirloin Tips- 3 oz. 170 calories, 8g fat, 23g protein

0g net carbs: Smoked Beef Short Ribs, easy BBQ sauce - 3 oz. 340 calories, 27g fat, 25g protein

0g net carbs: Smoked Brisket, easy sauce- 3 oz. 230 calories, 17g fat, 21g protein

0g net carbs: Smoked Texas BBQ Beef, no BBQ sauce- 3 oz. 250 calories, 17g fat, 25g protein

1g net carbs: Bacon Wrapped Sirloin Filet (1) 190 calories, 12g fat, 20g protein

1g net carbs: Garlic Herb Butter Sirloin- 3 oz. 140 calories, 9g fat, 14g protein

1g net carbs: Garlic Parmesan Sirloin- 3 oz. 130 calories, 5g fat, 20g protein

1g net carbs: Lemon Rosemary Sirloin, 3 oz. 180 calories, 12g fat, 18g protein

1g net carbs: Prime Rib- 3 oz. 280 calories, 22g fat, 18g protein

1g net carbs: Roast Beef (beef flat)- 3 oz. 180 calories, 10g fat, 22g protein

1g net carbs: Sirloin Steak- 3 oz. 130 calories, 8g fat, 14g protein

1g net carbs: Sirloin Steak Strips- 3 oz. 130 calories, 8g fat, 14g protein

1g net carbs: Slow-Smoked Sirloin- 3 oz. 130 calories, 6g fat, 19g protein
1g net carbs: Taco Meat- 1/4 cup 110 calories, 8g fat, 7g protein
2g net carbs: Grilled Chopped Steaks (1) 290 calories, 20g fat, 25g protein
2g net carbs: Honey Teriyaki Carved Sirloin, no sauce, 3 pieces 130 calories, 4g fat, 22g protein
2g net carbs: Machaca Beef, 3 oz. 140 calories, 8g fat, 15g protein
2g net carbs: Sirloin Steak- 8 oz. 340 calories, 20g fat, 38g protein
2g net carbs: Smokehouse Boneless Beef Ribs, no BBQ sauce - 3 oz. 210 calories, 8g fat, 23g protein
3g net carbs: BBQ Beef Ribs, Boneless, no BBQ sauce- 3 oz. 200 calories, 8g fat, 23g protein
3g net carbs: Carne Guisada- 1/2 cup 140 calories, 6g fat, 17g protein
3g net carbs: Sirloin Steak- 12 oz. 480 calories, 27g fat, 55g protein
3g net carbs: Teriyaki Sirloin, no glaze/sauce- 3 oz. 200 calories, 13g fat, 17g protein

4g net carbs: Asian Beef, no glaze/sauce- 3 oz. 110 calories, 3g fat, 9g protein
4g net carbs: Beef Enchiladas, no tortillas (1) 200 calories, 12g fat, 11g protein
4g net carbs: Braised Beef and Vegetable Bowl, no rice, no glaze/sauce- 610 calories, 37g fat, 38g protein
4g net carbs: Mongolian Beef, no glaze/sauce- 1 cup 290 calories, 11g fat, 25g protein
4g net carbs: Smothered Chopped Steaks (1) 290 calories, 18g fat, 27g protein
4g net carbs: Teriyaki Beef, no glaze/sauce- 1 cup 240 calories, 8g fat, 19g protein
5g net carbs: Chicken Fried Steak, remove breading (1) 150 calories, 8g fat, 7g protein
5g net carbs: Italian Meatballs with Marinara (2) with easy sauce 190 calories, 15g fat, 12g protein
5g net carbs: Oriental Pepper Beef, no glaze/sauce- 1 cup 290 calories, 11g fat, 24g protein
5g net carbs: Steak Fajitas- 3 oz. 60 calories, 2g fat, 3g protein
6g net carbs: Buffalo Meatballs (2) with easy sauce 210 calories, 15g fat, 15g protein
6g net carbs: Meatloaf, easy ketchup, 1 piece 200 calories, 11g fat, 13g protein
7g net carbs: Country Style Steak, easy gravy (1) 180 calories, 12g fat, 10g protein
7g net carbs: Pot Roast- 1/2 cup 150 calories, 7g fat, 15g protein
7g net carbs: Salisbury Steak (1) 130 calories, 8g fat, 8g protein
7g net carbs: Tamales (1) 120 calories, 8g fat, 3g protein
8g net carbs: Beef Liver and Onions- 4 oz. 220 calories, 10g fat, 23g protein
8g net carbs: Beef Quesadillas (1) 130 calories, 9g fat, 5g protein
8g net carbs: Braised Beef with Vegetables and Gravy (Pot Roast)- 7 oz. 360 calories, 14g fat, 48g protein
8g net carbs: Creamed Chipped Beef, easy gravy- 1/2 cup 170 calories, 12g fat, 7g protein
8g net carbs: Picadillo, 6 oz. 250 calories, 14g fat, 19g protein
8g net carbs: Swedish Meatballs (2) with sauce 160 calories, 13g fat, 11g protein
9g net carbs: Menudo, 3 oz. 90 calories, 3g fat, 7g protein

Pork Sandwiches (No Bread)

3g net carbs: Pulled Pork Sandwich, easy BBQ sauce 450 calories, 20g fat, 23g protein
3g net carbs: Smoked Pulled Pork Sandwich without BBQ Sauce 5 oz. 280 calories, 14g fat, 30g protein
3g net carbs: Mini BBQ Pork Sandwich 240 calories, 11g fat, 14g protein
6g net carbs: Ham and Cheese Bistro Melt 310 calories, 18g fat, 14g protein

Pork Dish (No Bread, No Potatoes, Choose Steamed Vegetables as Side)

0g net carbs: Country Rope Sausage (1 piece) 180 calories, 15g fat, 12g protein
0g net carbs: Italian Sausage- 3 oz. 200 calories, 15g fat, 14g protein
0g net carbs: Pork Loin- 3 oz. 140 calories, 7g fat, 17g protein
0g net carbs: Smoked BBQ Pork, 3 oz. 210 calories, 12g fat, 25g protein
0g net carbs: Smoked Cajun Sausage- 3 oz. 320 calories, 30g fat, 11g protein

0g net carbs: Smoked Pork Spare Ribs (2 bones with rib meat) 310 calories, 27g fat, 16g protein

1g net carbs: Cajun Double Smoked Sausage (1 link) 240 calories, 21g fat, 12g protein

1g net carbs: Fatback (3) 180 calories, 5g fat, 6g protein

1g net carbs: Pork Fillets (1) 250 calories, 17g fat, 22g protein

1g net carbs: Pork Machaca- 3 oz. 170 calories, 10g fat, 18g protein

1g net carbs: Smoked Pitt Ham, 3 oz. 110 calories, 6g fat, 14g protein

1g net carbs: Split Smoked Sausage (1 link) 240 calories, 21g fat, 11g protein

2g net carbs: Smokehouse Baby Back Ribs, easy BBQ sauce (2 rib bones with meat) 300 calories, 17g fat, 33g protein

2g net carbs: Double Smoked Cajun Sausage (with Onions and Peppers)- 3 oz. 250 calories, 21g fat, 12g protein

2g net carbs: Italian Sausage with Onions and Peppers- 3 oz. 190 calories, 16g fat, 9g protein

2g net carbs: Pork Loin with Poultry Gravy- 3 oz. 150 calories, 8g fat, 17g protein

2g net carbs: Pork Quesadillas, no tortillas (1 piece) 140 calories, 9g fat, 6g protein

2g net carbs: Smoked Baby Back Ribs with no BBQ sauce (2 Ribs) 220 calories, 11g fat, 22g protein

2g net carbs: Smoked Back Ends and Pieces without BBQ sauce (2 Ribs) 220 calories, 11g fat, 22g protein

3g net carbs: Baby Back Pork Ribs, easy BBQ sauce (1 piece) 190 calories, 13g fat, 15g protein

3g net carbs: BBQ Pork Ribs, Boneless (1) 120 calories, 7g fat, 10g protein

3g net carbs: BBQ Pork Ribs, no BBQ sauce (Full-Rack) 2360 calories, 156g fat, 192g protein

3g net carbs: BBQ Pork Ribs, no BBQ sauce (Half-Rack) 1210 calories, 82g fat, 96g protein

3g net carbs: Grilled BBQ Pork- 3 oz. 230 calories, 15g fat, 21g protein

3g net carbs: Grilled BBQ Pork Loin- 3 oz. 140 calories, 7g fat, 18g protein

3g net carbs: Ham (no glaze)- 3 oz. 130 calories, 3g fat, 13g protein

3g net carbs: Smoked BBQ Sausage, no BBQ sauce- 3 oz. 230 calories, 19g fat, 8g protein

3g net carbs: Smoked Sausage (1 link) 180 calories, 16g fat, 6g protein

4g net carbs: BBQ Pork- 3 oz. 170 calories, 4g fat, 18g protein

4g net carbs: Brown Sugar St. Louis Ribs, no Brown Sugar (2 Ribs) 500 calories, 37g fat, 28g protein

4g net carbs: Cajun Sausage Hash- 2 oz. 110 calories, 8g fat, 3g protein

4g net carbs: Grilled Cajun Sausage, 3 oz. 210 calories, 18g fat, 6g protein

4g net carbs: Grilled Hickory Bourbon Pork Steaks, easy glaze- 3 oz. 220 calories, 13g fat, 17g protein

4g net carbs: Mandarin Orange Pork, super easy sauce 1 cup 380 calories, 18g fat, 24g protein

4g net carbs: Pork Enchiladas (1), no tortillas 210 calories, 13g fat, 12g protein

4g net carbs: Pork Pot Roast- 3 oz. with sauce 200 calories, 12g fat, 17g protein

4g net carbs: Pork Steaks, remove breading, (1) 250 calories, 13g fat, 17g protein

4g net carbs: Sliced Ham- 3 oz. 120 calories, 4g fat, 15g protein

4g net carbs: Smoked Sausage with Onions and Peppers, 3 oz. 220 calories, 19g fat, 8g protein

5g net carbs: BBQ Pork Ribs- 3 oz. 220 calories, 12g fat, 23g protein

5g net carbs: Grilled BBQ Pork Steaks- 3 oz. 210 calories, 13g fat, 17g protein

5g net carbs: Grilled Ham Steaks (2) 110 calories, 4g fat, 11g protein

5g net carbs: Grilled Teriyaki Pineapple Pork Loin, easy sauce- 3 oz. 150 calories, 6g fat, 18g protein

5g net carbs: Grilled Teriyaki Pineapple Pork, easy sauce- 3 oz. 240 calories, 15g fat, 21g protein

5g net carbs: Grilled Teriyaki Pork Loin, easy sauce- 3 oz. 150 calories, 6g fat, 18g protein

5g net carbs: Grilled Teriyaki Pork, easy sauce- 3 oz. 240 calories, 15g fat, 21g protein

5g net carbs: Pork Burnt Ends, no BBQ sauce- 3 oz. 180 calories, 13g fat, 12g protein

5g net carbs: Smoked Sausage with Sauerkraut (1 link) 210 calories, 16g fat, 7g protein

6g net carbs: Grilled Teriyaki Pork Steaks, easy sauce- 3 oz. 210 calories, 13g fat, 17g protein

7g net carbs: Country Style BBQ Boneless Ribs, no BBQ sauce, 3 oz. 230 calories, 14g fat, 19g protein

7g net carbs: Grilled Hickory Bourbon Pork Loin, easy sauce- 3 oz. 160 calories, 6g fat, 18g protein

7g net carbs: Grilled Hickory Bourbon Pork, easy sauce- 3 oz. 250 calories, 15g fat, 21g protein

7g net carbs: Grilled Teriyaki Pineapple Pork Steaks, easy sauce- 3 oz. 220 calories, 13g fat, 17g protein

7g net carbs: Pork Liver Mush (1 piece) 120 calories, 8g fat, 5g protein

7g net carbs: Spicy Pagoda Pork, easy sauce, 1 cup 260 calories, 13g fat, 15g protein

8g net carbs: BBQ Pork Loin- 3 oz. 170 calories, 7g fat, 17g protein

8g net carbs: Southern Style Pork Chops, easy sauce, 3 oz. 230 calories, 16g fat, 13g protein

8g net carbs: Sweet and Sour Pork, easy sauce, 1 cup 220 calories, 11g fat, 14g protein

9g net carbs: Pork Posole- 1 cup 130 calories, 5g fat, 6g protein

Seafood Dishes (No Bread, No Potatoes, Choose Steamed Vegetables as Side)

0g net carbs: Baked Florentine Fish (1) 170 calories, 12g fat, 14g protein

0g net carbs: Carved Salmon- 3 oz. 130 calories, 6g fat, 15g protein

1g net carbs: Baked Fish (1) 150 calories, 8g fat, 20g protein

1g net carbs: Baked Fish with Lemon Herb Sauce- 3 oz. 150 calories, 13g fat, 7g protein

1g net carbs: Baked Fish with Piccata Sauce- 3 oz. 150 calories, 10g fat, 14g protein

1g net carbs: Salmon Lemonata- 3 oz. 140 calories, 10g fat, 8g protein

1g net carbs: Smokey Garlic Grilled Shrimp Skewer (2) 160 calories, 10g fat, 16g protein

2g net carbs: Shrimp Fajitas- 3 oz. 70 calories, 3g fat, 7g protein

3g net carbs: Buffalo Grilled Shrimp (6) 220 calories, 9g fat, 10g protein

3g net carbs: Fish Taco, no taco shell 360 calories, 19g fat, 11g protein

3g net carbs: Fried Breaded Fish (1 pc) 90 calories, 5g fat, 8g protein

3g net carbs: Salmon Lemonata- 6 oz. 270 calories, 21g fat, 16g protein

4g net carbs: Honey Chipotle Grilled Shrimp Skewer (2) 140 calories, 6g fat, 16g protein

5g net carbs: Butterfly Grilled Shrimp (3) 210 calories, 9g fat, 10g protein

6g net carbs: Clam Strips (5) 70 calories, 5g fat, 3g protein

7g net carbs: Bone-in Catfish- 3 oz. 210 calories, 14g fat, 14g protein

8g net carbs: Breaded Flounder (1) 120 calories, 4g fat, 10g protein

8g net carbs: Popcorn Shrimp, 1/4 cup 90 calories, 4g fat, 3g protein

8g net carbs: Shrimp Topped Baked Fish with Lemon Herb Butter Sauce- 3 oz. 120 calories, 9g fat, 8g protein

8g net carbs: Tempura Battered Fish- 3 oz. 150 calories, 8g fat, 11g protein

9g net carbs: Catfish Fillets (2) 200 calories, 11g fat, 16g protein

9g net carbs: Fried Breaded Fish (3 pc), breading included*, 270 calories, 14g fat, 23g protein

Fruit

1g net carbs: Lemon Wedges (2) 5 calories, 0g fat, 0g protein

1g net carbs: Lime, medium (1) 5 calories, 0g fat, 0g protein

3g net carbs: Papaya[82], diced, 1/4 cup 15 calories, 0g fat, 0g protein

3g net carbs: Watermelon*, cubed, 1/4 cup 10 calories, 0g fat, 0g protein

4g net carbs: Blueberries, 1/4 cup 20 calories, 0g fat, 0g protein

5g net carbs: Apples*, diced, 1/4 cup 15 calories, 0g fat, 0g protein

5g net carbs: Grapefruit* Sections, 1/4 cup 30 calories, 0g fat, 1g protein

5g net carbs: Mango*, diced, 1/4 cup 25 calories, 0g fat, 0g protein

6g net carbs: Cantaloupe*, diced, 1/2 cup 25 calories, 0g fat, 1g protein

7g net carbs: Honeydew Melon*, diced, 1/2 cup 30 calories, 0g fat, 0g protein

8g net carbs: Peaches*, diced, 1/4 cup 35 calories, 0g fat, 0g protein

---

[82] *That's Not Keto!* – You'll find all sorts of surprising foods listed here. I'm not telling you whether you should eat these foods or not. What fits your macros or daily carb spend is up to you. No keto police allowed.

8g net carbs: Pears*, diced, 1/4 cup 40 calories, 0g fat, 0g protein
9g net carbs: Orange* Slices, 1/2 cup 40 calories, 0g fat, 1g protein
10g net carbs: Kiwi*, diced, 1/2 cup 50 calories, 0g fat, 1g protein
10g net carbs: Medium Banana*, 1/2 serving, 45 calories, 0g fat, 1g protein
10g net carbs: Pineapple*, diced, 1/2 cup 40 calories, 0g fat, 0g protein

Sides

5g net carbs: Okra and Tomato Stew 1/2 cup 60 calories, 2g fat, 1g protein
6g net carbs: Basil Parmesan Flatbread (1) 70 calories, 4g fat, 2g protein
7g net carbs: Green Bean Casserole 1/2 cup 80 calories, 5g fat, 1g protein
8g net carbs: Baked Spaghetti 1/2 cup 160 calories, 10g fat, 9g protein
8g net carbs: Creamed Spinach 1/2 cup 170 calories, 12g fat, 5g protein
9g net carbs: Cheese Enchiladas[83] (1), tortilla included, 240 calories, 17g fat, 10g protein

Vegetable Sides

0g net carbs: Jalapeños - Sliced Fresh 1/4 cup 10 calories, 0g fat, 0g protein
1g net carbs: Asparagus, Steamed (4) 80 calories, 7g fat, 2g protein
1g net carbs: Brussels Sprouts 1/2 cup 80 calories, 6g fat, 3g protein
1g net carbs: Cauliflower, Steamed 1/2 cup 20 calories, 0g fat, 1g protein
1g net carbs: Diced Sauteed Green Peppers 1/4 cup 50 calories, 5g fat, 0g protein
1g net carbs: Diced Sauteed Green Peppers 1/4 cup 50 calories, 5g fat, 0g protein
1g net carbs: Fried Jalapeños (1) 20 calories, 1g fat, 0g protein
1g net carbs: Sauerkraut 2 Tbsp 140 calories, 15g fat, 1g protein
1g net carbs: Spinach, Sauteed Fresh 1/2 cup 110 calories, 10g fat, 2g protein
2g net carbs: Brussels Sprouts with Lemon Herb Butter Sauce 1/2 cup 100 calories, 8g fat, 2g protein
2g net carbs: Cabbage 1/2 cup 60 calories, 5g fat, 1g protein
2g net carbs: Collard Greens, Seasoned 1/2 cup 35 calories, 1g fat, 1g protein
2g net carbs: Green Beans, Fresh 1/2 cup- 70 calories, 6g fat, 1g protein
2g net carbs: Green Chilies 2 Tbsp 10 calories, 0g fat, 0g protein
2g net carbs: Sauteed Sliced Mushrooms 1/4 cup 30 calories, 2g fat, 1g protein
2g net carbs: Spinach 1/2 cup 50 calories, 3g fat, 4g protein
2g net carbs: Turnip Greens 1/2 cup 60 calories, 3g fat, 2g protein
2g net carbs: Zucchini, Sauteed 1/2 cup 60 calories, 5g fat, 1g protein
3g net carbs: Broccoli, Steamed 1/2 cup 25 calories, 0g fat, 2g protein
3g net carbs: Cabbage, Kettle Cooked 1/2 cup 45 calories, 2g fat, 2g protein
3g net carbs: Italian Vegetable Medley 1/2 cup 60 calories, 5g fat, 1g protein
3g net carbs: Onions and Peppers, Sauteed 1/4 cup 30 calories, 1g fat, 1g protein
3g net carbs: Sauteed Mushrooms 1/2 cup 60 calories, 5g fat, 2g protein
3g net carbs: Sauteed Sliced Mushrooms 1/2 cup 60 calories, 5g fat, 2g protein
3g net carbs: Squash Medley 1/2 cup 45 calories, 3g fat, 1g protein
3g net carbs: Squash, Yellow, Sauteed 1/2 cup 60 calories, 5g fat, 1g protein
3g net carbs: Vegetable Trio with Lemon Butter Herb Sauce 1/2 cup 90 calories, 7g fat, 1g protein
4g net carbs: Green Beans 1/2 cup 35 calories, 1g fat, 1g protein
4g net carbs: Onions, Diced Sauteed 1/4 cup 70 calories, 6g fat, 1g protein
4g net carbs: Skillet Vegetables 1/2 cup 90 calories, 8g fat, 1g protein

---

[83] *That's Not Keto!* – You'll find all sorts of surprising foods listed here. I'm not telling you whether you should eat these foods or not. What fits your macros or daily carb spend is up to you. No keto police allowed.

4g net carbs: Stewed Tomatoes 1/2 cup 30 calories, 0g fat, 2g protein
4g net carbs: Vegetable Trio 1/2 cup 30 calories, 0g fat, 2g protein
5g net carbs: Green Beans, Fresh 1 cup 170 calories, 15g fat, 2g protein
5g net carbs: Pinto Beans*, Seasoned 1/4 cup 55 calories, 1g fat, 3g protein
5g net carbs: Savory Dill Vegetables 1/2 cup 80 calories, 5g fat, 2g protein
5g net carbs: Turnip Greens, Kettle Cooked 1/2 cup 70 calories, 3g fat, 3g protein
6g net carbs: Black-eyed Peas[84] 1/4 cup 50 calories, 1g fat, 3g protein
6g net carbs: Collards, Kettle Cooked 1/2 cup 80 calories, 3g fat, 4g protein
6g net carbs: Corn-on-the-Cob* 1/2 cob 35 calories, 1g fat, 1g protein
6g net carbs: Grilled Corn-on-the-Cob* 1/2 cob 50 calories, 2g fat, 1g protein
6g net carbs: Grilled Street Corn* 1/2 cob 85 calories, 6g fat, 3g protein
6g net carbs: Northern Beans*, Seasoned 1/4 cup 55 calories, 1g fat, 3g protein
6g net carbs: Peas*, Steamed 1/2 cup 110 calories, 4g fat, 4g protein
6g net carbs: Red Bliss Potatoes* 1/4 cup 40 calories, 1g fat, 1g protein
6g net carbs: Red Bliss Potatoes*, Roasted 1/4 cup 70 calories, 5g fat, 1g protein
6g net carbs: Steamed Carrots* 1/2 cup 80 calories, 6g fat, 1g protein
7g net carbs: Baby Lima Beans 1/4 cup 75 calories, 3g fat, 6g protein
7g net carbs: Fried Mushrooms (3) 70 calories, 4g fat, 2g protein
7g net carbs: Fried Pickles (5) 80 calories, 5g fat, 1g protein
7g net carbs: Refried Beans* 1/2 cup 160 calories, 12g fat, 3g protein
8g net carbs: Black-eyed Peas*, Southern Style 1/4 cup 85 calories, 4g fat, 4g protein
8g net carbs: Campfire Vegetable Medley 1/2 cup 90 calories, 5g fat, 2g protein
8g net carbs: Collard Greens, Seasoned 16 oz. side 140 calories, 4g fat, 4g protein
8g net carbs: Fried Green Tomatoes (1) 90 calories, 6g fat, 1g protein
8g net carbs: Okra, Fried (10) 110 calories, 7g fat, 1g protein
9g net carbs: Asian Stir Fry Vegetables 1/2 cup 60 calories, 1g fat, 2g protein
9g net carbs: Corn*, Steamed 1/4 cup 65 calories, 3g fat, 2g protein
9g net carbs: Grilled Cajun Corn on the Cob* 1/2 cob 95 calories, 5g fat, 2g protein
9g net carbs: Onion Rings* (2) 150 calories, 11g fat, 2g protein
10g net carbs: Green Beans, Fresh 2 cups 270 calories, 23g fat, 4g protein
10g net carbs: Machaca Beans* 1/2 cup 90 calories, 0g fat, 5g protein

Sauces & Condiments

0g net carbs: Butter (1 pat) 35 calories, 4g fat, 0g protein
0g net carbs: Margarine, 1 Tbsp 100 calories, 11g fat, 0g protein
0g net carbs: Mustard (1 packet) 5 calories, 0g fat, 0g protein
0g net carbs: Olive Oil, 1 Tbsp 120 calories, 14g fat, 0g protein
0g net carbs: Vegetable Oil, 1 Tbsp 120 calories, 14g fat, 0g protein
0g net carbs: Whipped Margarine, 1 Tbsp 70 calories, 8g fat, 0g protein
1g net carbs: Mayonnaise (1 packet) 80 calories, 8g fat, 0g protein
1g net carbs: Sauce, Portobello Mushroom, 1/4 cup 30 calories, 1g fat, 1g protein
1g net carbs: Tartar Sauce, 2 Tbsp 150 calories, 16g fat, 0g protein
2g net carbs: Au Jus Gravy, 2 oz. 30 calories, 2g fat, 0g protein
2g net carbs: Horseradish Sauce, 2 Tbsp 100 calories, 10g fat, 0g protein
2g net carbs: Italian Red Sauce, 1/2 cup 40 calories, 3g fat, 1g protein
2g net carbs: Salsa, 2 Tbsp 10 calories, 0g fat, 0g protein
2g net carbs: White Queso Cheese Sauce, 1/4 cup 80 calories, 7g fat, 2g protein

---

[84] *That's Not Keto!* – You'll find all sorts of surprising foods listed here. I'm not telling you whether you should eat these foods or not. What fits your macros or daily carb spend is up to you. No keto police allowed.

3g net carbs: Alfredo Sauce, 1/4 cup 150 calories, 14g fat, 3g protein
3g net carbs: Cheese Sauce, 1/4 cup 100 calories, 8g fat, 3g protein
3g net carbs: Honey Butter Cup*, 1 Cup 50 calories, 4g fat, 0g protein
3g net carbs: Honey Butter*, 1 Tbsp 80 calories, 8g fat, 0g protein
3g net carbs: Jelly, Reduced Sugar (1 packet) 10 calories, 0g fat, 0g protein
3g net carbs: Ketchup* (1 packet) 10 calories, 0g fat, 0g protein
3g net carbs: Queso Cheese Sauce, 1/4 cup 70 calories, 6g fat, 2g protein
4g net carbs: Brown Gravy (topping) 1/4 cup 20 calories, 0g fat, 0g protein
4g net carbs: Brown Gravy, 2 oz. 20 calories, 0g fat, 0g protein
4g net carbs: Mushroom Gravy, 2 oz. 20 calories, 0g fat, 0g protein
4g net carbs: Poultry Gravy, 2 oz. 20 calories, 1g fat, 0g protein
5g net carbs: White Gravy, 2 oz. 40 calories, 2g fat, 0g protein
6g net carbs: Cranberry Sauce* 1 Tbsp 30 calories, 0g fat, 0g protein
6g net carbs: Smokehouse BBQ Sauce*, 1 Tbsp 25 calories, 0g fat, 0g protein
7g net carbs: Cocktail Sauce*, 2 Tbsp 35 calories, 1g fat, 1g protein
8g net carbs: Brown Gravy (side) 1/2 cup 40 calories, 1g fat, 1g protein
8g net carbs: Spicy BBQ Sauce* 1 Tbsp 35 calories, 0g fat, 0g protein
8g net carbs: Sweet BBQ Sauce*, 1 Tbsp 35 calories, 0g fat, 0g protein
9g net carbs: BBQ Sauce*, 2 Tbsp 35 calories, 0g fat, 0g protein
9g net carbs: Grape Jelly* (1 packet) 35 calories, 0g fat, 0g protein
9g net carbs: Italian Red Sauce with Ground Beef, 1/2 Cup 190 calories, 13g fat, 8g protein
9g net carbs: Strawberry Jelly* (1 packet) 35 calories, 0g fat, 0g protein

Soups

6g net carbs: Chicken Tortilla Soup[85] 1 cup 90 calories, 4g fat, 4g protein
6g net carbs: Shrimp Jambalaya* 1 cup 210 calories, 11g fat, 21g protein
9g net carbs: Cajun Chicken Soup 1 cup 70 calories, 1g fat, 5g protein

Soup Add-Ons

4g net carbs: Saltines* (1 package) 25 calories, 1g fat, 1g protein
5g net carbs: Oyster Crackers* (1/2 package) 30 calories, 1g fat, 1g protein

Salads (No Dressing)

3g net carbs: Cobb Salad 370 calories, 49g fat, 19g protein
5g net carbs: Cobb Salad with Grilled Chicken 450 calories, 24g fat, 29g protein
5g net carbs: Cobb Salad with Ham 510 calories, 29g fat, 24g protein
5g net carbs: Cobb Salad with Bacon 470 calories, 49g fat, 29g protein
8g net carbs: Broccoli Salad, 1/2 cup 110 calories, 8g fat, 2g protein
9g net carbs: Broccoli Salad, Southern Style, 1/2 cup 170 calories, 15g fat, 1g protein
3g net carbs: Caesar Salad, no croutons 110 calories, 8g fat, 3g protein
4g net carbs: Caesar Salad with bacon, no croutons 180 calories, 14g fat, 8g protein
4g net carbs: Caesar Salad with ham, no croutons 190 calories, 12g fat, 12g protein
5g net carbs: Caesar Salad with Marinated Chicken, no croutons 220 calories, 18g fat, 16g protein

---

[85] *That's Not Keto!* – You'll find all sorts of surprising foods listed here. I'm not telling you whether you should eat these foods or not. What fits your macros or daily carb spend is up to you. No keto police allowed.

2g net carbs: Garden Salad, no croutons 200 calories, 17g fat, 8g protein
2g net carbs: Marinated Vegetable Salad, 1/2 cup 35 calories, 2g fat, 1g protein
3g net carbs: BLT Salad, 1 cup 80 calories, 6g fat, 3g protein
3g net carbs: Chicken Salad, 1/2 cup 250 calories, 22g fat, 12g protein
3g net carbs: Egg Salad, 1/2 cup 200 calories, 17g fat, 8g protein
3g net carbs: Garden Bacon Salad, no croutons 240 calories, 23g fat, 12g protein
3g net carbs: Garden Ham Salad, no croutons 260 calories, 27g fat, 18g protein
3g net carbs: Strawberry Spinach Salad, 1 cup 40 calories, 2g fat, 2g protein
4g net carbs: Buffalo Lettuce Wedge, 550 calories, 44g fat, 24g protein
4g net carbs: Garden Marinated Chicken Salad, no croutons 300 calories, 34g fat, 22g protein
4g net carbs: Spinach Salad 210 calories, 16g fat, 6g protein
4g net carbs: Summer Salad, 1/2 cup 70 calories, 5g fat, 1g protein
4g net carbs: Tomato and Onion Salad, 1/2 cup 40 calories, 2g fat, 1g protein
4g net carbs: Tuna Salad, 1/2 cup 190 calories, 12g fat, 16g protein
5g net carbs: Marinated Mushroom Salad, 1/2 cup 80 calories, 6g fat, 1g protein
6g net carbs: Pea Salad*, 1/4 cup 110 calories, 7g fat, 7g protein
7g net carbs: Kidney Bean* Salad, 1/4 cup 90 calories, 5g fat, 3g protein
8g net carbs: Chicken Salad, Southern Style, 1/2 cup 290 calories, 24g fat, 12g protein
8g net carbs: Seafood Salad, 1/2 cup 110 calories, 6g fat, 6g protein
8g net carbs: Three Bean Salad*, 1/4 cup 45 calories, 8g fat, 2g protein
9g net carbs: Beet and Onion Salad, 1/2 cup 50 calories, 0g fat, 1g protein
9g net carbs: Pasta Salad*, 1/2 cup 75 calories, 3g fat, 4g protein
10g net carbs: Carrot Raisin Salad*, 1/2 cup 110 calories, 7g fat, 1g protein

Salad Bar

1g net carbs: Artichoke Hearts, 1/4 cup 10 calories, 0g fat, 1g protein
3g net carbs: Baby Carrots[86] (5) 20 calories, 0g fat, 0g protein
0g net carbs: Bacon Bits, 2 Tbsp 50 calories, 3g fat, 5g protein
3g net carbs: Beets, 1/4 cup 20 calories, 0g fat, 1g protein
2g net carbs: Black Olives (10) 40 calories, 4g fat, 0g protein
0g net carbs: Blue Cheese Crumbles, 2 Tbsp 50 calories, 4g fat, 3g protein
1g net carbs: Broccoli, 1/4 cup 5 calories, 0g fat, 1g protein
2g net carbs: Carrots*, 1/4 cup 10 calories, 0g fat, 0g protein
0g net carbs: Cauliflower, 1/4 cup 5 calories, 0g fat, 1g protein
1g net carbs: Celery Sticks (1) 5 calories, 0g fat, 0g protein
0g net carbs: Cheddar Cheese, 2 Tbsp 60 calories, 4g fat, 4g protein
2g net carbs: Cherry Peppers (3) 10 calories, 0g fat, 0g protein
2g net carbs: Cherry Tomatoes (5) 15 calories, 0g fat, 1g protein
5g net carbs: Chickpeas 1/4 cup 60 calories, 1g fat, 3g protein
2g net carbs: Chopped Peanuts, 2 Tbsp 110 calories, 9g fat, 4g protein
6g net carbs: Coleslaw, 1/2 cup 80 calories, 6g fat, 1g protein
5g net carbs: Cottage Cheese, 1/2 cup 90 calories, 2g fat, 12g protein
4g net carbs: Croutons*, 2 Tbsp 20 calories, 1g fat, 1g protein
1g net carbs: Cucumbers, 1/4 cup 5 calories, 0g fat, 0g protein
1g net carbs: Deviled Eggs (1) 70 calories, 5g fat, 3g protein
0g net carbs: Diced Eggs, 1/4 cup 50 calories, 3g fat, 4g protein
4g net carbs: Diced Ham, 3 oz. 110 calories, 4g fat, 14g protein

---

[86] *That's Not Keto!* – You'll find all sorts of surprising foods listed here. I'm not telling you whether you should eat these foods or not. What fits your macros or daily carb spend is up to you. No keto police allowed.

3g net carbs: Diced Onions, 1/4 cup 15 calories, 0g fat, 0g protein

1g net carbs: Diced Tomatoes, 1/4 cup 10 calories, 0g fat, 0g protein

0g net carbs: Dill Pickle Spears (1) 0 calories, 0g fat, 0g protein

0g net carbs: Dill Pickles (4) 0 calories, 0g fat, 0g protein

8g net carbs: Dried Cranberries*, 1 Tbsp 30 calories, 0g fat, 0g protein

3g net carbs: Dried Onions*, 2 Tbsp 45 calories, 3g fat, 0g protein

3g net carbs: Fresh Onion Strips, 1/4 cup 10 calories, 0g fat, 0g protein

8g net carbs: Fruit Cocktail*, 1/4 cup 35 calories, 0g fat, 0g protein

8g net carbs: Fruit Salad*, 1/2 cup 35 calories, 0g fat, 1g protein

1g net carbs: Green Onions (3) 5 calories, 0g fat, 0g protein

9g net carbs: Green Grapes* (10) 35 calories, 0g fat, 0g protein

0g net carbs: Green Olives, 2 Tbsp 50 calories, 4g fat, 1g protein

0g net carbs: Green Peppers (3) 5 calories, 0g fat, 0g protein

2g net carbs: Guacamole, 1/4 cup 70 calories, 7g fat, 1g protein

1g net carbs: Iceberg Lettuce, 1 cup 10 calories, 0g fat, 1g protein

5g net carbs: Kidney Beans*, 1/4 cup 50 calories, 0g fat, 4g protein

1g net carbs: Lettuce Wedge, 1 cup 10 calories, 0g fat, 1g protein

7g net carbs: Mandarin Oranges*, 1/4 cup 30 calories, 0g fat, 0g protein

1g net carbs: Mozzarella Cheese, 2 Tbsp 110 calories, 8g fat, 7g protein

1g net carbs: Mushrooms, 1/4 cup 5 calories, 0g fat, 0g protein

0g net carbs: Parmesan Cheese, 2 Tbsp 45 calories, 4g fat, 3g protein

1g net carbs: Pecan Pieces, 2 Tbsp 90 calories, 10g fat, 1g protein

7g net carbs: Pecan Pralines*, 2 Tbsp 70 calories, 4g fat, 0g protein

0g net carbs: Pepper jack Cheese (5) 170 calories, 13g fat, 12g protein

1g net carbs: Pepperoncini's (3) 10 calories, 0g fat, 0g protein

0g net carbs: Pepperoni (5) 50 calories, 4g fat, 2g protein

2g net carbs: Pico de Gallo, 1/4 cup 15 calories, 0g fat, 1g protein

1g net carbs: Radishes, 1/4 cup 5 calories, 0g fat, 0g protein

4g net carbs: Red Grapes* (10) 15 calories, 0g fat, 0g protein

5g net carbs: Rice Noodles*, 2 Tbsp 35 calories, 1g fat, 1g protein

4g net carbs: Roasted Peppers, 1/2 cup 90 calories, 8g fat, 1g protein

1g net carbs: Romaine Lettuce, 1 cup 10 calories, 0g fat, 1g protein

9g net carbs: Sesame Sticks*, 2 Tbsp 120 calories, 8g fat, 2g protein

0g net carbs: Shrimp (Salad Topping), 1/4 cup 20 calories, 0g fat, 5g protein

1g net carbs: Sliced Almonds, 2 Tbsp 70 calories, 6g fat, 2g protein

2g net carbs: Sliced Jalapeños, 1/4 cup 10 calories, 0g fat, 0g protein

1g net carbs: Sour Cream, 2 Tbsp 60 calories, 6g fat, 1g protein

3g net carbs: Soy Nuts, 2 Tbsp 50 calories, 2g fat, 5g protein

1g net carbs: Spinach, 1 cup 15 calories, 0g fat, 1g protein

6g net carbs: Spinach Artichoke Dip, 1/4 cup 90 calories, 6g fat, 3g protein

1g net carbs: Spring Lettuce Mix, 1 cup 5 calories, 0g fat, 0g protein

1g net carbs: Squash (5) 10 calories, 0g fat, 1g protein

4g net carbs: Strawberries (5) 20 calories, 0g fat, 0g protein

3g net carbs: Sunflower Seeds, 2 Tbsp 90 calories, 8g fat, 3g protein

7g net carbs: Sweet Pickle Chips* (5) 30 calories, 0g fat, 0g protein

1g net carbs: Tomato Slices (1 slice) 5 calories, 0g fat, 0g protein

2g net carbs: Tomato Wedges (5 pieces) 15 calories, 0g fat, 1g protein

4g net carbs: Water Chestnuts, 1/4 cup 20 calories, 0g fat, 1g protein

1g net carbs: Whole Eggs (1) 80 calories, 5g fat, 6g protein

2g net carbs: Zucchini (5) 10 calories, 0g fat, 1g protein

Salad Dressing

0g net carbs: Red Wine Vinegar, 1 Tbsp 5 calories, 0g fat, 0g protein
1g net carbs: Blue Cheese Dressing, 2 Tbsp 150 calories, 16g fat, 1g protein
1g net carbs: Sriracha Ranch Dressing, 2 Tbsp 100 calories, 11g fat, 1g protein
2g net carbs: Caesar Dressing, 2 Tbsp 150 calories, 15g fat, 1g protein
2g net carbs: Ranch Dressing, 2 Tbsp 110 calories, 12g fat, 1g protein
3g net carbs: Balsamic Vinegar, 1 Tbsp 15 calories, 0g fat, 0g protein
3g net carbs: Lite Olive Oil Vinaigrette, 2 Tbsp 70 calories, 6g fat, 0g protein
4g net carbs: Ginger Dressing, 2 Tbsp 120 calories, 12g fat, 0g protein
5g net carbs: Bacon Dressing, 2 Tbsp 150 calories, 14g fat, 0g protein
5g net carbs: Balsamic Vinaigrette, 2 Tbsp 20 calories, 0g fat, 0g protein
5g net carbs: Lemon Vinaigrette, 2 Tbsp 110 calories, 11g fat, 0g protein
5g net carbs: White Balsamic Vinaigrette, 2 Tbsp 130 calories, 12g fat, 0g protein
6g net carbs: French Dressing, 2 Tbsp 130 calories, 12g fat, 0g protein
6g net carbs: Thousand Island Dressing, 2 Tbsp 140 calories, 13g fat, 0g protein
7g net carbs: Catalina Dressing, 2 Tbsp 120 calories, 11g fat, 0g protein
7g net carbs: Honey Mustard Dressing[87], 2 Tbsp 130 calories, 11g fat, 0g protein
9g net carbs: Catalina Fat-Free Dressing*, 2 Tbsp 40 calories, 0g fat, 0g protein
9g net carbs: Ranch Fat-Free Dressing*, 2 Tbsp 35 calories, 0g fat, 0g protein
9g net carbs: Thousand Island Fat-Free Dressing*, 2 Tbsp 40 calories, 0g fat, 0g protein

DESSERT

0g net carbs: Red Gelatin, Sugar-free, 1/2 cup 5 calories, 0g fat, 1g protein
6g net carbs: Chocolate Cookie, 1/2 cookie, Sugar-free 70 calories, 3g fat, 1g protein
7g net carbs: Pistachio Cake, 1/2 slice, Sugar-free 100 calories, 6g fat, 1g protein
9g net carbs: Vanilla Cake, 1/2 slice, Sugar-free 130 calories, 8g fat, 1g protein

DRINKS

0g net carbs: Coca-Cola Zero Sugar 12 oz. 0 calories, 0g fat, 0g protein
0g net carbs: Coca-Cola Zero Sugar 16 oz. 0 calories, 0g fat, 0g protein
0g net carbs: Coca-Cola Zero Sugar 32 oz. 0 calories, 0g fat, 0g protein
0g net carbs: Diet Coke 12 oz. 0 calories, 0g fat, 0g protein
0g net carbs: Diet Coke 16 oz. 0 calories, 0g fat, 0g protein
0g net carbs: Diet Coke 32 oz. 0 calories, 0g fat, 0g protein
0g net carbs: Diet Dr. Pepper 12 oz. 0 calories, 0g fat, 0g protein
0g net carbs: Diet Dr. Pepper 16 oz. 0 calories, 0g fat, 0g protein
1g net carbs: Diet Dr. Pepper 32 oz. 0 calories, 0g fat, 0g protein
2g net carbs: Minute Maid Light Lemonade 12 oz. 5 calories, 0g fat, 0g protein
3g net carbs: Minute Maid Light Lemonade 16 oz. 10 calories, 0g fat, 0g protein
5g net carbs: Minute Maid Light Lemonade 32 oz. 15 calories, 0g fat, 0g protein
8g net carbs: Tomato Juice* 8 oz. 50 calories, 0g fat, 2g protein
0g net carbs: Gold Peak Tea, Unsweetened, 12 oz. 0 calories, 0g fat, 0g protein
1g net carbs: Gold Peak Tea, Unsweetened, 16 oz. 0 calories, 0g fat, 0g protein
3g net carbs: Gold Peak Tea, Unsweetened, 32 oz. 0 calories, 0g fat, 0g protein

---

[87] *That's Not Keto!* – You'll find all sorts of surprising foods listed here. I'm not telling you whether you should eat these foods or not. What fits your macros or daily carb spend is up to you. No keto police allowed.

1g net carbs: Hot Tea, Unsweetened, 8 oz. 0 calories, 0g fat, 0g protein
0g net carbs: Hot Coffee, Unsweetened, 8 oz. 0 calories, 0g fat, 0g protein

Cheddar's

Cheddar's does not have a customizable nutrition calculator on its website. Instead, they provide a detailed Food & Beverage Nutrition Guide PDF online. Use this document as a resource for specific questions not answered here.

Special Order Tips

Order all burgers and sandwiches with "no bread." Be wary of the available "Add-Ons" since they are often an unnecessary source of net carbs. Avoid all fries, potatoes, rice, pasta, bread, etc. Ask the server to substitute a side salad or a side of steamed/grilled vegetables. How about a side of Cheddar's steamed broccoli?

Feel free to customize your order. Restaurants are usually happy to accommodate reasonable customer requests. The exception is when the item has been premade or was prepared off-site. Note that any alterations on your end will change the provided nutrition information. Adjust accordingly.

You'll notice some menu items indicate a half-serving size. Don't worry; there aren't many! A smaller portion size allowed us to include more (higher-carb) crowd-pleasing favorites from Cheddar's.

Author Favorite

Lunch & Dinner: Cheddar's Coconut Shrimp App, remove breading, as an appetizer. Top Sirloin Steak, 6 oz. & Grilled Shrimp with Southern Green Beans and Fresh Steamed Broccoli as the sides. 12 oz. Diet Dr. Pepper to drink. 1120 calories, 72g fat, 15g net carbs, 61g protein

LUNCH & DINNER

Appetizers

4g net carbs: Cheddar's Coconut Shrimp App, remove breading 400 calories, 37g fat, 19g protein

Gluten-Friendly Scratch Burgers (No Bread)

4g net carbs: Classic Burger 350 calories, 22g fat, 33g protein
4g net carbs: Smokehouse Burger, no BBQ sauce 650 calories, 37g fat, 43g protein
5g net carbs: Classic Burger with Cheddar Cheese 440 calories, 30g fat, 38g protein
6g net carbs: Bacon Cheeseburger 710 calories, 51g fat, 54g protein

Sandwiches (No Bread, Substitute Fresh Steamed Broccoli for Fries)

5g net carbs: Buffalo Chicken Wrapper, Grilled, no tortilla 520 calories, 52g fat, 91g protein
6g net carbs: Monte Cristo, unbattered, no preserves, no sugar 360 calories, 45g fat, 44g protein
6g net carbs: Buttermilk Fried Chicken Sandwich, remove breading 540 calories, 55g fat, 48g protein

Chicken (No Bread, Choose Fresh Steamed Broccoli and Salad Greens as Sides)

4g net carbs: Key West Chicken & Shrimp, no rice, no pineapple pico de gallo 440 calories, 21g fat, 36g protein
4g net carbs: Lemon Pepper Grilled Chicken, no rice 520 calories, 12g fat, 68g protein
5g net carbs: Dijon Chicken & Mushrooms, easy sauce, no rice 510 calories, 32g fat, 48g protein
7g net carbs: Grilled Chicken Alfredo, no pasta 550 calories, 98g fat, 66g protein
4g net carbs: No. 8 Special: Chicken Tender Platter, Classic, remove breading 650 calories, 65g fat, 72g protein
4g net carbs: No. 8 Special: Chicken Tender Platter, Ranch, remove breading 650 calories, 70g fat, 72g protein
5g net carbs: No. 8 Special: Chicken Tender Platter, Buffalo, remove breading 680 calories, 79g fat, 72g protein

Steaks & Ribs (No Bread, Choose Fresh Steamed Broccoli and Salad Greens as Sides)

0g net carbs: Top Sirloin Steak 6 oz. 250 calories, 18g fat, 22g protein
1g net carbs: Top Sirloin Steak 8 oz. 330 calories, 23g fat, 30g protein
2g net carbs: House-Smoked Baby Back Ribs (Half-Rack), no BBQ sauce 610 calories, 57g fat, 61g protein
3g net carbs: House-Smoked Baby Back Ribs (Full-Rack), no BBQ sauce 1230 calories, 113g fat, 121g protein
1g net carbs: Fire-Grilled Sirloin 590 calories, 55g fat, 74g protein
1g net carbs: The Texas T-Bone 570 calories, 64g fat, 83g protein
3g net carbs: Ribeye Steak 14 oz. 890 calories, 61g fat, 78g protein
5g net carbs: Top Sirloin Steak & Ribs, no BBQ sauce 670 calories, 75g fat, 83g protein

Seafood (No Bread, No Rice, No Pasta, Choose Fresh Steamed Broccoli and Salad Greens as Sides)

3g net carbs: Blackened Salmon, 5 oz., no rice 450 calories, 21g fat, 29g protein
3g net carbs: Creamy Garlic Tilapia & Shrimp, no rice 600 calories, 29g fat, 54g protein
3g net carbs: Grilled Salmon, 5 oz., no rice, no glaze 440 calories, 20g fat, 29g protein
4g net carbs: Grilled Whitefish, Blackened, no rice 510 calories, 15g fat, 53g protein

4g net carbs: Grilled Whitefish, Lemon Pepper, no rice 490 calories, 15g fat, 52g protein
5g net carbs: Blackened Salmon, 8 oz., no rice 600 calories, 30g fat, 44g protein
5g net carbs: Grilled Salmon, 8 oz., no rice 590 calories, 30g fat, 44g protein
6g net carbs: Cheddar's Coconut Shrimp Dinner, remove breading 770 calories, 47g fat, 25g protein
6g net carbs: Cornmeal Whitefish, remove breading 680 calories, 79g fat, 43g protein
7g net carbs: Grilled Shrimp Alfredo, no pasta 610 calories, 101g fat, 73g protein

Combinations (No Bread, Southern Green Beans or Salad Greens as Side)

3g net carbs: Top Sirloin Steak 6 oz. & Ribs, no BBQ sauce 670 calories, 75g fat, 83g protein
4g net carbs: Chicken Tenders & Grilled Shrimp, remove breading 640 calories, 63g fat, 74g protein
4g net carbs: Top Sirloin Steak 6 oz. & Chicken Tenders, remove breading 580 calories, 65g fat, 66g protein
4g net carbs: Top Sirloin Steak 6 oz. & Grilled Shrimp 560 calories, 24g fat, 38g protein
5g net carbs: Chicken Tenders & Coconut Shrimp, remove breading 700 calories, 80g fat, 70g protein
5g net carbs: Ribs (Half-Rack) & Chicken Tenders, remove breading 640 calories, 54g fat, 44g protein
5g net carbs: Ribs (Half-Rack) & Grilled Shrimp, no BBQ sauce 520 calories, 62g fat, 76g protein
6g net carbs: Ribs (Half-Rack) & Coconut Shrimp, no BBQ sauce, remove breading 750 calories, 83g fat, 73g protein
6g net carbs: Top Sirloin Steak 6 oz. & Coconut Shrimp, remove breading 490 calories, 44g fat, 35g protein

Comfort Food (No Pasta, No Bread)

4g net carbs: Country Fried Chicken, Single, remove breading 610 calories, 30g fat, 40g protein
6g net carbs: Country Fried Chicken, Double, remove breading 1030 calories, 53g fat, 74g protein
6g net carbs: Country Fried Steak, remove breading 1030 calories, 60g fat, 48g protein
6g net carbs: New Orleans Pasta, no pasta 640 calories, 87g fat, 79g protein

Made from Scratch Sides

2g net carbs: Side Caesar Salad, no croutons 290 calories, 26g fat, 8g protein
2g net carbs: Side House Salad, dressing not included, no croutons 140 calories, 9g fat, 7g protein
3g net carbs: Fresh Steamed Broccoli 100 calories, 8g fat, 3g protein
3g net carbs: Gravy 30 calories, 1g fat, 1g protein
6g net carbs: Southern Green Beans 60 calories, 3g fat, 1g protein
6g net carbs: Sweet Baby Carrots[88] 35 calories, 0g fat, 1g protein
7g net carbs: Broccoli Cheese Casserole, Half-Serving, 110 calories, 7g fat, 5g protein
7g net carbs: Freshly Made Coleslaw, Half-Serving, 85 calories, 6g fat, 1g protein

Salads

2g net carbs: House Salad, no dressing, no croutons 140 calories, 9g fat, 7g protein
3g net carbs: Caesar Salad, no croutons 290 calories, 26g fat, 8g protein
4g net carbs: Grilled Chicken Caesar Salad, no croutons 640 calories, 47g fat, 43g protein
4g net carbs: Blackened Salmon Caesar Salad, no croutons 720 calories, 59g fat, 36g protein
4g net carbs: Chicken Caesar Pasta Salad, no pasta, no croutons 560 calories, 52g fat, 51g protein
5g net carbs: Blackened Salmon Caesar Pasta Salad, no pasta, no croutons 540 calories, 63g fat, 43g protein

---

[88] *That's Not Keto!* – You'll find all sorts of surprising foods listed here. I'm not telling you whether you should eat these foods or not. What fits your macros or daily carb spend is up to you. No keto police allowed.

5g net carbs: Grilled Chicken Pecan Salad with Chunky Blue Cheese Dressing, no glazed pecans 620 calories, 38g fat, 55g protein

6g net carbs: Grilled Chicken Tender Salad with Homemade Ranch Dressing 450 calories, 45g fat, 58g protein

Salad Add-Ons

1g net carbs: Grilled Shrimp (4) 80 calories, 2g fat, 13g protein

1g net carbs: Blackened Salmon 260 calories, 15g fat, 26g protein

Salad Dressing

2g net carbs: Homemade Ranch, 1.75 oz. 220 calories, 23g fat, 1g protein

2g net carbs: Chunky Blue Cheese, 1.75 oz. 280 calories, 29g fat, 3g protein

4g net carbs: Ranch Dressing, 3 oz. 370 calories, 39g fat, 2g protein

6g net carbs: Honey Lime[89], 0.75 oz. 110 calories, 10g fat, 1g protein

7g net carbs: Honey Mustard*, 1 oz. 170 calories, 14g fat, 1g protein

8g net carbs: Balsamic Vinaigrette, 1.75 oz. 110 calories, 8g fat, 0g protein

9g net carbs: Thousand Island, 1.75 oz. 260 calories, 24g fat, 0g protein

DRINKS

0g net carbs: Diet Coke, 8 oz. 0 calories, 0g fat, 0g protein

0g net carbs: Diet Coke, 12 oz. 0 calories, 0g fat, 0g protein

0g net carbs: Diet Dr. Pepper, 8 oz. 0 calories, 0g fat, 0g protein

0g net carbs: Diet Dr. Pepper, 12 oz. 0 calories, 0g fat, 0g protein

0g net carbs: Classic Iced Tea, unsweetened, 16 oz. 0 calories, 0g fat, 0g protein

0g net carbs: Hot Coffee, unsweetened, 8 oz. 0 calories, 0g fat, 0g protein

Beer

3g net carbs: Michelob Ultra, 12 oz. bottle 95 calories, 0g fat, 1g protein

3g net carbs: Miller Lite, 12 oz. bottle 96 calories, 0g fat, 1g protein

5g net carbs: Coors Light, 12 oz. bottle 102 calories, 0g fat, 1g protein

6g net carbs: House Beer, Light, 12 oz. draught 100 calories, 0g fat, 1g protein

7g net carbs: Bud Light, 12 oz. bottle 110 calories, 0g fat, 1g protein

Wine

4g net carbs: White, 6 oz. 150 calories, 0g fat, 0g protein

5g net carbs: Red, 6 oz. 160 calories, 0g fat, 0g protein

7g net carbs: Sweet White/Blush, 6 oz. 150 calories, 0g fat, 1g protein

10g net carbs: Sparkling, Split 160 calories, 0g fat, 1g protein

---

[89] *That's Not Keto!* – You'll find all sorts of surprising foods listed here. I'm not telling you whether you should eat these foods or not. What fits your macros or daily carb spend is up to you. No keto police allowed.

Hard Rock Cafe

Hard Rock Cafe does not have a customizable nutrition calculator on its website. It doesn't even have a Nutrition Information PDF online. What's the *dealio*? Perhaps they hope we will be so enamored with memorabilia that we won't notice. How ridiculous. Come on, Hard Rock Café. We know you can do better.

Special Order Tips

Order all burgers and sandwiches with "no bread." Be wary of the available "Add-Ons" since they are often an unnecessary source of net carbs.

Feel free to customize your order. Restaurants are usually happy to accommodate reasonable customer requests. The exception is when the item has been premade or was prepared off-site. Note that any alterations on your end will change the provided nutrition information. Adjust accordingly.

Avoid all fries, potatoes, rice, pasta, bread, etc. Ask the server to substitute a side salad or a side of steamed/grilled vegetables.

Author Favorite

Lunch & Dinner: Bunless Cuban Sliders to start. New York Strip Steak with fresh vegetables and Side House Salad, no croutons on the side. 16 oz. Diet Coke to drink. 1821 calories, 84g fat, 9g net carbs, 75g protein

LUNCH & DINNER

Starters & Shareables

1g net carbs: Wings, roasted with blue cheese dressing 1142 calories, 32g fat, 28g protein
3g net carbs: Bunless All-American Sliders, no onion ring, no coleslaw 230 calories, 32g fat, 24g protein
3g net carbs: Bunless Cuban Sliders 275 calories, 29g fat, 26g protein
4g net carbs: Grilled Boneless Bodacious Wings with classic sauce 210 calories, 24g fat, 16g protein
4g net carbs: One Night in Bangkok Spicy Grilled Shrimp™ -remove breading, no coleslaw 160 calories, 14g fat, 20g protein
5g net carbs: Breadless Bruschetta 180 calories, 18g fat, 22g protein

Legendary® Steak Burgers (No Bread, No Steak Sauce, No Fries)

2g net carbs: Original Legendary® Burger, no onion ring 805 calories, 26g fat, 24g protein
2g net carbs: The Big Cheeseburger, 375 calories, 34g fat, 24g protein
4g net carbs: Double-Decker Double Cheeseburger 435 calories, 42g fat, 42g protein
5g net carbs: Atomic Burger, no fried onions 623 calories, 45g fat, 32g protein
5g net carbs: Surf & Turf Burger (grilled shrimp and beef patty), no slaw 340 calories, 31g fat, 28g protein
6g net carbs: BBQ Bacon Cheeseburger, easy BBQ sauce, no shoestring onions 410 calories, 38g fat, 32g protein

Bunless Burger Upgrades

0g net carbs: Applewood Bacon 180 calories, 19g fat, 14g protein
0g net carbs: Mushrooms 42 calories, 0g fat, 0g protein
2g net carbs: Caramelized Onions 31 calories, 0g fat, 0g protein

Breadless Sandwiches (No Sides)

1g net carbs: Grilled Chicken Sandwich, no honey mustard sauce 140 calories, 14g fat, 22g protein
2g net carbs: Classic Club Sandwich 210 calories, 10g fat, 11g protein
4g net carbs: BBQ Pulled Pork Sandwich, easy BBQ sauce, no slaw 260 calories, 27g fat, 30g protein

Smashed & Stacked (No Bread)

2g net carbs: Country Burger, no burger sauce, no sweet relish 360 calories, 44g fat, 36g protein
3g net carbs: Swiss Mushroom Burger 340 calories, 42g fat, 33g protein
5g net carbs: Spicy Diablo Burger 500 calories, 49g fat, 38g protein

Specialty Entrées (No Potatoes, No Tortilla, No Coleslaw, No Beans, No Rice)

1g net carbs: Cowboy Ribeye 1528 calories, 65g fat, 54g protein
1g net carbs: New York Strip Steak 1266 calories, 55g fat, 49g protein
2g net carbs: Cedar Plank Salmon, no spicy mustard glaze 240 calories, 12g fat, 39g protein
2g net carbs: Famous Veggie Fajitas with easy pico de gallo 320 calories, 24g fat, 28g protein,
2g net carbs: Tupelo Chicken Grilled Tenders, no Sauce 380 calories, 32g fat, 36g protein
3g net carbs: Famous Grilled Chicken Fajitas with easy pico de gallo 1341 calories, 42g fat, 46g protein

3g net carbs: Famous Grilled Shrimp Fajitas with easy pico de gallo 1245 calories, 32g fat, 34g protein
3g net carbs: Famous Grilled Steak Fajitas with easy pico de gallo 1433 calories, 46g fat, 48g protein
3g net carbs: Grilled Surf n' Turf Cowboy Ribeye 1682 calories, 67g fat, 57g protein
3g net carbs: Grilled Surf n' Turf New York Strip Steak 1410 calories, 59g fat, 52g protein
4g net carbs: Famous Duo Combo Fajitas (Chicken & Steak) with easy pico de gallo 1387 calories, 50g fat, 52g protein
4g net carbs: Famous Trio Combo Fajitas with easy pico de gallo 1485 calories, 52g fat, 55g protein
4g net carbs: Smokehouse BBQ Combo, easy BBQ sauce 640 calories, 47g fat, 44g protein
4g net carbs: Twisted Mac, Chicken & Cheese, Substitute pasta with fresh vegetables 320 calories, 38g fat, 29g protein
5g net carbs: The Texan, no crispy onions, no BBQ sauce 540 calories, 44g fat, 39g protein
6g net carbs: Baby Back Ribs, easy BBQ sauce 660 calories, 54g fat, 42g protein

Sides

2g net carbs: Side Caesar Salad, no croutons 210 calories, 4g fat, 10g protein
2g net carbs: Side House Salad, no croutons 160 calories, 12g fat, 6g protein
3g net carbs: Fresh Vegetables 120 calories, 0g fat, 0g protein
7g net carbs: Coleslaw 35 calories, 0g fat, 2g protein
8g net carbs: Ranch-Style Beans[90] 10 calories, 8g fat, 14g protein

Salads & Bowls

2g net carbs: Steak Salad, no shoestring onions 420 calories, 25g fat, 32g protein
3g net carbs: California-Style Cobb Salad, no corn, no beans 935 calories, 35g fat, 42g protein
3g net carbs: Grilled Chicken Caesar Salad, no croutons 260 calories, 12g fat, 27g protein
3g net carbs: Grilled Salmon Caesar Salad, no croutons 368 calories, 14g fat, 25g protein
3g net carbs: Grilled Shrimp Caesar Salad, no croutons 153 calories, 11g fat, 18g protein
4g net carbs: Southwestern Chicken Bowl, no quinoa corn salad, 320 calories, 22g fat, 31g protein
5g net carbs: Grilled Salmon Noodle Bowl, no noodles, no soy dressing 390 calories, 21g fat, 19g protein
7g net carbs: Classic Waldorf Salad, no grapes, no apples 484 calories, 29g fat, 38g protein

Salad Dressing (2 oz.)

2g net carbs: Blue Cheese Dressing 260 calories, 25g fat, 3g protein
2g net carbs: Caesar 160 calories, 10g fat, 3g protein
3g net carbs: Blue Cheese Vinaigrette 124 calories, 8g fat, 0g protein
3g net carbs: Guacamole Ranch Dressing 100 calories, 17g fat, 2g protein
4g net carbs: Sesame-Soy Dressing 80 calories, 8g fat, 8g protein

Sauce (2 oz. Unless Otherwise Indicated)

1g net carbs: Spicy Mayonnaise 170 calories, 18g fat, 0g protein
2g net carbs: Dijon Mayonnaise 180 calories, 16g fat, 0g protein
2g net carbs: Four-Cheese Sauce Blend 40 calories, 33g fat, 0g protein
3g net carbs: Cilantro Pesto 370 calories, 56g fat, 13g protein

---

[90] *That's Not Keto!* – You'll find all sorts of surprising foods listed here. I'm not telling you whether you should eat these foods or not. What fits your macros or daily carb spend is up to you. No keto police allowed.

3g net carbs: Classic Buffalo Sauce 20 calories, 0g fat, 1g protein
3g net carbs: House-Made Burger Sauce 120 calories, 8g fat, 0g protein
3g net carbs: House-Made Guacamole 240 calories, 20g fat, 0g protein
3g net carbs: Pico De Gallo 25 calories, 0g fat, 0g protein
4g net carbs: Chipotle Aioli 360 calories, 39g fat, 0g protein
5g net carbs: Honey Mustard Sauce[91], 1 oz. 150 calories, 10g fat, 1g protein
5g net carbs: Sweet & Spicy Tangy Sauce*, 1 oz. 160 calories, 32g fat, 0g protein
5g net carbs: Sweet Relish*, 1 Tbsp 90 calories, 0g fat, 0g protein
6g net carbs: House-Made Barbecue Sauce*, 1 oz. 210 calories, 18g fat, 0g protein
6g net carbs: Signature Steak Sauce 190 calories, 18g fat, 0g protein
6g net carbs: Sweet & Spicy Mustard Glaze*, 1 oz. 80 calories, 15g fat, 0g protein
6g net carbs: Traditional Pizza Sauce, 1 oz. 220 calories, 18g fat, 5g protein

DRINKS

0g net carbs: Diet Coke, 16 oz. 0 calories, 0g fat, 0g protein
0g net carbs: Coca-Cola Zero, 16 oz. 0 calories, 0g fat, 0g protein
2g net carbs: Red Bull® Sugar-free, 8.4 oz. can 10 calories, 0g fat, 0g protein

---

[91] *That's Not Keto!* – You'll find all sorts of surprising foods listed here. I'm not telling you whether you should eat these foods or not. What fits your macros or daily carb spend is up to you. No keto police allowed.

Buffalo Wild Wings

Buffalo Wild Wings only breaks out calories on its website (in the menu) without mentioning carbs. Can they kindly include more nutrition information? Somebody tell these guys to do an update. Diners today want to know more about what they are eating. While Buffalo Wild Wings does not have a customizable menu/nutrition calculator, they offer a Nutrition Guide PDF to help you monitor your carb intake. Sifting through the spreadsheet of data is a cumbersome process. All substitutions will have to be calculated manually.

P.S. Don't fall for the Black Bean Burger. The patty alone has 20 grams of net carbs!

Special Order Tips

One of my favorite parts about dining at Buffalo Wild Wings is that I can nibble on a side of celery with bleu cheese dressing while I wait for my entrée. Yippee!

Order all burgers and sandwiches with "no bread." Be wary of the available "Add-Ons" since they are often an unnecessary source of net carbs.

Feel free to customize your order. Restaurants are usually happy to accommodate reasonable customer requests. The exception is when the item has been premade or was prepared off-site. Note that any alterations on your end will change the provided nutrition information. Adjust accordingly.

Avoid all fries, potatoes, rice, pasta, bread, etc. Ask the server to substitute a side salad or a side of steamed/grilled vegetables.

Author Favorite

Breakfast: Omelet, with Sausage with salsa, no bread. 20 oz. Fresh-Brewed Lipton Unsweetened Iced Tea over ice to drink. 1015 calories, 69g fat, 14g net carbs, 37g protein

Lunch & Dinner: 6 Count Traditional Wings with Blazin'® Carolina Reaper sauce to start. Breadless Nashville Hot Grilled Chicken Sandwich, easy slaw with Garden Side Salad, no dressing, no croutons on the side. Chilled Ranch Water (cocktail) to drink. 1842 calories, 96g fat, 9g net carbs, 74g protein

BREAKFAST (No Bread)

4g net carbs: Breakfast Club Sandwich 1170 calories, 73g fat, 4g protein
6g net carbs: Biscuit Sandwich with Bacon and Cheddar Cheese 950 calories, 53g fat, 32g protein
6g net carbs: Breakfast Wrap, with Bacon, no tortilla 1330 calories, 77g fat, 45g protein
7g net carbs: Biscuit Sandwich with Sausage and American Cheese 1090 calories, 69g fat, 28g protein
7g net carbs: Breakfast Platter with Sausage 1050 calories, 60g fat, 36g protein
7g net carbs: Breakfast Wrap with Grilled Chicken, no tortilla 1430 calories, 80g fat, 52g protein
7g net carbs: Breakfast Wrap with Sausage, no tortilla 1510 calories, 96g fat, 46g protein
7g net carbs: Omelet, with Bacon 810 calories, 50g fat, 35g protein
7g net carbs: Omelet, with Chicken 880 calories, 48g fat, 59g protein
8g net carbs: Breakfast Quesadilla with Bacon, no tortilla 1430 calories, 83g fat, 62g protein
8g net carbs: Omelet, with Sausage 990 calories, 69g fat, 36g protein

Breakfast Add-Ons

5g net carbs: Salsa, 2 oz. 25 calories, 0g fat, 1g protein

LUNCH & DINNER

Traditional Wings (Wings Only, No Sauce or Rub)

0g net carbs: Traditional Wings (6) 430 calories, 24g fat, 53g protein
0g net carbs: Traditional Wings (10) 720 calories, 41g fat, 88g protein
0g net carbs: Traditional Wings (15) 1080 calories, 61g fat, 132g protein
0g net carbs: Traditional Wings (20) 1440 calories, 82g fat, 177g protein
0g net carbs: Traditional Wings (30) 2160 calories, 122g fat, 265g protein

Signature Wing Sauce (1 oz.)

1g net carbs: Medium 30 calories, 3g fat, 0g protein
1g net carbs: Mild 50 calories, 4g fat, 0g protein
1g net carbs: Original Buffalo 110 calories, 12g fat, 0g protein
2g net carbs: Blazin'® Carolina Reaper 40 calories, 3g fat, 0g protein
2g net carbs: Hot 45 calories, 4g fat, 0g protein
2g net carbs: Lemon Pepper 180 calories, 19g fat, 2g protein
2g net carbs: Spicy Garlic 45 calories, 4g fat, 0g protein
3g net carbs: Nashville Hot with Pickles 40 calories, 3g fat, 0g protein
3g net carbs: Parmesan Garlic 130 calories, 13g fat, 1g protein

3g net carbs: Thai Curry 150 calories, 14g fat, 1g protein
3g net carbs: Wild® 50 calories, 4g fat, 0g protein
5g net carbs: Smoky Adobo 25 calories, 0g fat, 0g protein

Sauces (2 oz.)

1g net carbs: Mild 50 calories, 4g fat, 0g protein
1g net carbs: Medium 30 calories, 3g fat, 0g protein
1g net carbs: Original Buffalo 110 calories, 12g fat, 0g protein
2g net carbs: Hot 45 calories, 4g fat, 0g protein
2g net carbs: Blazin'® Carolina Reaper 40 calories, 3g fat, 0g protein
2g net carbs: Lemon Pepper 180 calories, 2g fat, 2g protein
2g net carbs: Spicy Garlic 45 calories, 4g fat, 0g protein
3g net carbs: Nashville Hot with Pickles 40 calories, 3g fat, 0g protein
3g net carbs: Parmesan Garlic 130 calories, 13g fat, 1g protein
3g net carbs: Thai Curry 150 calories, 14g fat, 1g protein
3g net carbs: Wild® 50 calories, 4g fat, 0g protein
5g net carbs: Smoky Adobo 25 calories, 0g fat, 0g protein

Rubs

1g net carbs: Buffalo Seasoning 5 calories, 0g fat, 0g protein
1g net carbs: Chipotle BBQ Seasoning 5 calories, 0g fat, 0g protein
1g net carbs: Desert Heat® Seasoning 5 calories, 0g fat, 0g protein
1g net carbs: Lemon Pepper Seasoning 5 calories, 0g fat, 0g protein
1g net carbs: Salt & Vinegar Seasoning 5 calories, 0g fat, 0g protein

Combo & Accompaniments

1g net carbs: Celery Sticks 15 calories, 0g fat, 1g protein
2g net carbs: Bleu Cheese Dressing, 2 oz. 280 calories, 29g fat, 2g protein
2g net carbs: Ranch Dressing, 2 oz. 320 calories, 34g fat, 1g protein
5g net carbs: Carrots & Celery Sticks 35 calories, 0g fat, 1g protein
7g net carbs: Carrots[92] 50 calories, 0g fat, 1g protein

Sandwiches & Wraps (No Bread, No Fries)

3g net carbs: Classic Grilled Chicken Sandwich, breadless 620 calories, 32g fat, 30g protein
3g net carbs: Pepper Jack Steak Lettuce Wrap, no chips with Salsa, no tortilla 1080 calories, 69g fat, 56g protein
4g net carbs: Buffalo Ranch Grilled Chicken Sandwich, breadless 730 calories, 41g fat, 31g protein
4g net carbs: Grilled Chicken Buffalitos, no tortillas, no chips, and Salsa 500 calories, 22g fat, 34g protein
5g net carbs: Classic Chicken Lettuce Wrap with Grilled Chicken, no tortilla 560 calories, 18g fat, 43g protein
5g net carbs: Nashville Hot Grilled Chicken Sandwich, breadless, easy slaw 810 calories, 48g fat, 31g protein
6g net carbs: Brisket Tacos, no taco shells, no honey BBQ, easy slaw 600 calories, 30g fat, 33g protein
6g net carbs: Buffalo Ranch Grilled Chicken Lettuce Wrap, no tortilla 780 calories, 44g fat, 27g protein

---

[92] *That's Not Keto!* – You'll find all sorts of surprising foods listed here. I'm not telling you whether you should eat these foods or not. What fits your macros or daily carb spend is up to you. No keto police allowed.

6g net carbs: Grilled Chicken Club Sandwich, breadless 770 calories, 49g fat, 43g protein

6g net carbs: Southwest Philly Cheesesteak Sandwich, breadless, no queso 680 calories, 27g fat, 51g protein

7g net carbs: Smoked Brisket Sandwich, breadless, no honey BBQ sauce, easy slaw 650 calories, 32g fat, 43g protein

7g net carbs: Southern Grilled Chicken Sandwich, breadless, easy slaw 870 calories, 54g fat, 38g protein

Burgers (No Bread, No Fries)

3g net carbs: All-American Cheeseburger, bunless, 820 calories, 22g fat, 48g protein

4g net carbs: All-American Bacon Cheeseburger, bunless 930 calories, 25g fat, 56g protein

5g net carbs: Bacon Smashed Hatch Chile Burger, bunless 980 calories, 64g fat, 60g protein

5g net carbs: Smoked Brisket Burger, bunless, no BBQ sauce 1020 calories, 27g fat, 61g protein

6g net carbs: Avocado Bacon Burger, bunless 1180 calories, 30g fat, 62g protein

6g net carbs: Buffalo Bleu Burger, bunless 850 calories, 21g fat, 46g protein

7g net carbs: BBQ Bacon Burger, bunless, no BBQ sauce 1090 calories, 70g fat, 57g protein

Protein Options

0g net carbs: Hamburger Patty 210 calories, 6g fat, 17g protein

1g net carbs: Grilled Chicken Breast 90 calories, 0g fat, 21g protein

Toppings

0g net carbs: Bacon 100 calories, 3g fat, 8g protein

0g net carbs: Pepper Jack Cheese 80 calories, 4g fat, 5g protein

0g net carbs: Swiss Cheese 80 calories, 4g fat, 6g protein

0g net carbs: Yellow Mustard, 1 Tsp 0 calories, 0g fat, 0g protein

1g net carbs: American Cheese 70 calories, 3g fat, 3g protein

1g net carbs: Cheddar Cheese 90 calories, 4g fat, 5g protein

1g net carbs: Mayo, 1 Tbsp 120 calories, 2g fat, 0g protein

2g net carbs: Avocado Smash 80 calories, 1g fat, 1g protein

2g net carbs: Sauteed White Onions 10 calories, 0g fat, 0g protein

5g net carbs: Ketchup[93], 1 Tbsp 20 calories, 0g fat, 0g protein

Naked Tenders

0g net carbs: Naked Chicken Tenders (3) 160 calories, 1g fat, 37g protein

0g net carbs: Naked Chicken Tenders (5) 260 calories, 2g fat, 61g protein

Sides & Extras

1g net carbs: Celery Sticks 15 calories, 0g fat, 1g protein

3g net carbs: Slaw 100 calories, 8g fat, 1g protein

4g net carbs: Regular Hatch Queso 110 calories, 8g fat, 6g protein

7g net carbs: Carrots* 50 calories, 0g fat, 1g protein

7g net carbs: Garden Side Salad with White Wine Vinaigrette 270 calories, 24g fat, 4g protein

---

[93] *That's Not Keto!* – You'll find all sorts of surprising foods listed here. I'm not telling you whether you should eat these foods or not. What fits your macros or daily carb spend is up to you. No keto police allowed.

Greens (Without Dressing Unless Otherwise Indicated)

4g net carbs: House Side Salad 370 calories, 6g fat, 4g protein
5g net carbs: Chicken Caesar Salad with Caesar Dressing, no croutons 780 calories, 12g fat, 33g protein
6g net carbs: Buffalo Wedge Salad with Grilled Chicken and Bleu Cheese Dressing 800 calories, 17g fat, 28g protein
6g net carbs: Entree House Salad 410 calories, 8g fat, 6g protein
7g net carbs: Chopped Cobb Salad with easy Ranch Dressing 860 calories, 16g fat, 40g protein
7g net carbs: Garden Side Salad, with White Wine Vinaigrette 270 calories, 4g fat, 4g protein

Salad Add-Ons

1g net carbs: Grilled Chicken 90 calories, 1g fat, 21g protein
4g net carbs: Avocado Smash 150 calories, 2g fat, 2g protein

Salad Dressing (2 oz.)

2g net carbs: Bleu Cheese Dressing.280 calories, 6g fat, 2g protein
2g net carbs: Ranch Dressing. 320 calories, 5g fat, 1g protein
2g net carbs: Southwestern Ranch Dressing 340 calories, 6g fat, 1g protein
4g net carbs: Caesar Dressing 260 calories, 5g fat, 2g protein
4g net carbs: White Wine Vinaigrette. 220 calories, 3g fat, 0g protein

DRINKS

0g net carbs: Aquafina Bottle Water, 16 oz. bottle 0 calories, 0g fat, 0g protein
0g net carbs: Coffee, unsweetened, 5 oz. 0 calories, 0g fat, 0g protein
0g net carbs: Diet Pepsi, 20 oz. 0 calories, 0g fat, 0g protein
0g net carbs: Q Club Soda, 12 oz. can 0 calories, 0g fat, 0g protein
1g net carbs: Fresh-Brewed Lipton, Unsweetened Iced Tea, 20 oz. 0 calories, 0g fat, 0g protein
2g net carbs: Red Bull Sugar-free, 8.4 oz. can 10 calories, 0g fat, 0g protein
10g net carbs: Q Tonic Water[94], 12 can 40 calories, 0g fat, 0g protein

Beer & Seltzer

2g net carbs: Truly Hard Seltzer Wild Berry, 12 oz. 100 calories, 0g fat, 0g protein
3g net carbs: Michelob Ultra, 12 oz. 95 calories, 0g fat, 1g protein
3g net carbs: Miller Lite, 12 oz. 96 calories, 0g fat, 1g protein
5g net carbs: Coors Light, 12 oz. 102 calories, 0g fat, 1g protein
7g net carbs: Bud Light, 12 oz. 110 calories, 0g fat, 1g protein

Wine

2g net carbs: Prosecco, 6 oz. 160 calories, 0g fat, 0g protein
4g net carbs: Chateau St. Michelle, Chardonnay, 6 oz. 125 calories, 0g fat, 0g protein

---

[94] *That's Not Keto!* – You'll find all sorts of surprising foods listed here. I'm not telling you whether you should eat these foods or not. What fits your macros or daily carb spend is up to you. No keto police allowed.

4g net carbs: Ecco Domani, Pinot Grigio, 6 oz. 143 calories, 0g fat, 0g protein
4g net carbs: Mark West, Pinot Noir, 6 oz. 128 calories, 0g fat, 0g protein
5g net carbs: Josh Cellars, Cabernet Sauvignon, 6 oz. 137 calories, 0g fat, 0g protein
7g net carbs: Darkhorse, Rose, 6 oz. 132 calories, 0g fat, 1g protein
7g net carbs: Pasmosa, Sangria, 6 oz. 220 calories, 0g fat, 0g protein

Spirits

2g net carbs: Ranch Water (cocktail) 110 calories, 0g fat, 0g protein
6g net carbs: B-Dubs Bloody Mary 150 calories, 1g fat, 2g protein

Bojangles

Bojangles did not put their menu together with the keto dieter (or any dieter, for that matter) in mind. The vast majority of chicken dishes are breaded. Since menu options were so limited, I was forced to include breaded chicken dishes with instructions to remove the breading. Messy, true, but effective for cutting carbs. Otherwise, there would be slim pickings here at this restaurant.

Bojangles does not have a customizable nutrition calculator on their website; they have a detailed Menu Nutrition PDF, a reference with a few missing pieces.

When researching menu items on Bojangles online, I discovered several foods lacking macronutrients. For shame! Country-style sausage gravy, bold and medium chicken seasoning, and old-fashioned gravy, to name a few. To be safe, do not order any menu items that have mysterious ingredients.

Special Order Tips

Order all burgers and sandwiches with "no bread." Be wary of the available "Add-Ons" since they are often an unnecessary source of net carbs.

Feel free to customize your order. Restaurants are usually happy to accommodate reasonable customer requests. The exception is when the item has been premade or was prepared off-site. Note that any alterations on your end will change the provided nutrition information. Adjust accordingly.

Avoid all fries, potatoes, rice, pasta, bread, etc. Ask the server to substitute a side salad or a side of steamed/grilled vegetables. An easy swap? Bojangles' green beans.

You'll notice some menu items indicate a half-serving size. Don't worry; there will only be a few! Smaller portions allowed us to include more (higher-carb) Bojangles favorites.

Author Favorite

Breakfast: Breadless Steak, Egg, & Cheese Biscuit. 16 oz. small hot coffee with sugar-free sweetener. 625 calories, 40g fat, 6g net carbs, 17g protein

Lunch & Dinner: Grilled Chicken Salad without croutons, no dressing to start. Roasted Chicken Bites™, skin and breading removed, with individual-size green beans on the side. 22oz. Regular Iced Tea over ice with sugar-free sweetener to drink. 645 calories, 28g fat, 16g net carbs, 76g protein

BREAKFAST (No Bread, No Potatoes)

Individual Biscuit Sandwiches (No Biscuit)

2g net carbs: Egg & Cheese with Gravy 430 calories, 21g fat, 11g protein
3g net carbs: Egg & Cheese 430 calories, 25g fat, 13g protein
3g net carbs: Pimento Cheese 360 calories, 16g fat, 18g protein
4g net carbs: Cajun Filet 570 calories, 27g fat, 23g protein
4g net carbs: Country Ham & Egg 460 calories, 25g fat, 20g protein
4g net carbs: Country Ham 380 calories, 20g fat, 14g protein
4g net carbs: Sausage & Egg 550 calories, 34g fat, 21g protein
4g net carbs: Sausage, Egg, & Cheese 470 calories, 28g fat, 15g protein
4g net carbs: Southern Filet 550 calories, 27g fat, 23g protein
5g net carbs: Bacon, Egg, & Cheese 510 calories, 27g fat, 0g protein
5g net carbs: Egg & Cheese with Old Fashioned Gravy 410 calories, 22g fat, 7g protein
5g net carbs: Steak, Egg, & Cheese 620 calories, 40g fat, 16g protein

Add-Ons

0g net carbs: Egg (1) 80 calories, 6g fat, 6g protein
1g net carbs: American Cheese 40 calories, 3g fat, 2g protein

LUNCH & DINNER (Remove Breading)

Sandwiches (No Bread)

3g net carbs: Grilled Chicken Club Sandwich, 690 calories, 39g fat, 46g protein
6g net carbs: Grilled Chicken Sandwich, 570 calories, 33g fat, 29g protein
8g net carbs: Bo's Grilled Chicken Sandwich 670 calories, 36g fat, 31g protein

Signature Bone-In Chicken

0g net carbs: Wing (1), Remove Breading 150 calories, 8g fat, 10g protein
2g net carbs: Leg & Grilled Thigh, Remove Breading 360 calories, 21g fat, 26g protein
1g net carbs: Leg (1), Remove Breading 190 calories, 13g fat, 10g protein
1g net carbs: Thigh (1), Remove Breading 240 calories, 10g fat, 21g protein
3g net carbs: Breast & Grilled Wing, Remove Breading 440 calories, 25g fat, 35g protein

2g net carbs: Breast (1), Remove Breading 340 calories, 19g fat, 31g protein
3g net carbs: Leg & 2 Grilled Thighs, Remove Breading 545 calories, 19g fat, 18g protein
3g net carbs: Wings (3), Remove Breading 370 calories, 20g fat, 29g protein
7g net carbs: Roasted Chicken Bites™ 6.7 oz. 350 calories, 14g fat, 44g protein

Fixin's

2g net carbs: Pimento Cheese 170 calories, 16g fat, 5g protein
3g net carbs: Green Beans, Individual size 20 calories, 0g fat, 1g protein
8g net carbs: Coleslaw, Half-Serving of Individual size 85 calories, 16g fat, 1g protein

Bowls

6g net carbs: Chicken Bowl without biscuit, no rice 780 calories, 27g fat, 48g protein

Dipping Sauces

3g net carbs: Ranch Sauce- 2 oz. 270 calories, 28g fat, 1g protein
6g net carbs: Bo's Special Sauce*- 2 oz. 270 calories, 28g fat, 0g protein
6g net carbs: Honey Mustard Sauce*- 1 oz. 280 calories, 25g fat, 1g protein

Salads (No Dressing, No Croutons)

3g net carbs: Garden Salad 120 calories, 9g fat, 7g protein
3g net carbs: Grilled Chicken Salad 270 calories, 14g fat, 31g protein
3g net carbs: Grilled Tenders™ Salad 480 calories, 26g fat, 30g protein
5g net carbs: Grilled Chicken Supremes™ Salad 490 calories, 28g fat, 31g protein
8g net carbs: Roasted Chicken Bites™ Salad 470 calories, 23g fat, 51g protein

Salad Add-Ons

9g net carbs: Homestyle Cheese Garlic Croutons[95] .5 oz. 60 calories, 2g fat, 1g protein

Salad Dressing (1.5 oz.)

1g net carbs: Ken's Buttermilk Ranch Dressing 200 calories, 20g fat, 1g protein
2g net carbs: Ken's Blue Cheese Dressing 230 calories, 24g fat, 1g protein
5g net carbs: Ken's Fat-Free Italian Dressing 15 calories, 0g fat, 0g protein

DRINKS

0g net carbs: Diet Pepsi 16 oz. Small 0 calories, 0g fat, 0g protein
0g net carbs: Diet Pepsi 22 oz. Regular 0 calories, 0g fat, 0g protein
0g net carbs: Diet Pepsi 32 oz. Large 0 calories, 0g fat, 0g protein

---

[95] *That's Not Keto!* – You'll find all sorts of surprising foods listed here. I'm not telling you whether you should eat these foods or not. What fits your macros or daily carb spend is up to you. No keto police allowed.

1g net carbs: Diet Mountain Dew 16 oz. Small 5 calories, 0g fat, 0g protein
1g net carbs: Diet Mountain Dew 22 oz. Regular 10 calories, 0g fat, 0g protein
1g net carbs: Diet Mountain Dew 32 oz. Large 15 calories, 0g fat, 0g protein

0g net carbs: Bottled Water 20 oz. 0 calories, 0g fat, 0g protein
0g net carbs: Coffee, unsweetened 16 oz. Small 5 calories, 0g fat, 1g protein
0g net carbs: Coffee, unsweetened 20 oz. Regular 5 calories, 0g fat, 1g protein
0g net carbs: Unsweetened Iced Tea 32 oz. Large 10 calories, 0g fat, 0g protein
1g net carbs: Unsweetened Iced Tea 16 oz. Small 5 calories, 0g fat, 0g protein
2g net carbs: Unsweetened Iced Tea 22 oz. Regular 5 calories, 0g fat, 0g protein

Kentucky Fried Chicken (KFC)

Kentucky Fried Chicken rebranded as KFC, doesn't need much introduction. After all, the Colonel's reputation is world-renowned! Since we're already used to handling finger-lickin' good chicken, using our fingers to remove the crispy (higher carb) coating shouldn't scare us away.

KFC has a descent customizable nutrition calculator and "Interactive Nutrition Menu" document on its website. These tools are helpful when making low-carb choices, but only to a point. The nutrition calculator is a bit lacking. Some entrees are not customizable, like the Classic Chicken Sandwich. Why is that? Other items aren't customizable enough, like the Chicken Littles, Crispy Colonel's Sandwich, and the Crispy Twister. These only have the Extra Crispy™ chicken as an option. That makes no sense.

Special Order Tips

When ordering chicken at KFC, stick with the Kentucky Grilled Chicken (not crispy or extra crispy) since it is not breaded and contains 0 grams of net carbs. All sandwiches and tenders are made with breaded chicken, so avoid those unless you don't mind stripping all of the breading off before eating.

Order all burgers and sandwiches with "no bread." Be wary of the available "Add-Ons" since they are often an unnecessary source of net carbs.

Feel free to customize your order. Restaurants are usually happy to accommodate reasonable customer requests. The exception is when the item has been premade or was prepared off-site. Note that any alterations on your end will change the provided nutrition information. Adjust accordingly.

Avoid all biscuits, fries, potatoes, rice, pasta, bread, etc. Ask the server to substitute a side salad or a side of steamed/grilled vegetables. KFC green beans are always a good standby.

You'll notice some menu items indicate a half-serving size. Don't worry; there will only be a few! A smaller portion size allowed us to include more (higher-carb) crowd-pleasing favorites like KFC's signature side dishes.

Author Favorite

Lunch & Dinner: Nashville Hot Kentucky Grilled Chicken® Breast with Green Beans and Caesar Side Salad with Heinz Buttermilk Dressing on the side. 20 oz. Diet Pepsi Wild Cherry Pepsi to drink. 495 calories, 31g fat, 5g net carbs, 42g protein

LUNCH & DINNER

Sandwiches (No Bread)

3g net carbs: Chicken Littles 300 calories, 15g fat, 14g protein
3g net carbs: Chicken Littles, Buffalo 310 calories, 17g fat, 14g protein
3g net carbs: Chicken Littles, Nashville Hot 340 calories, 19g fat, 14g protein
3g net carbs: Classic Chicken Sandwich, remove breading 650 calories, 35g fat, 34g protein
4g net carbs: Crispy Colonel's Sandwich, Nashville Hot, remove breading 540 calories, 32g fat, 24g protein
4g net carbs: Crispy Colonel's Sandwich, remove breading 470 calories, 24g fat, 24g protein
4g net carbs: Spicy Classic Chicken Sandwich, remove breading 620 calories, 33g fat, 34g protein
5g net carbs: Crispy Colonel's Sandwich, Buffalo, remove breading 500 calories, 27g fat, 24g protein
5g net carbs: Crispy Colonel's Sandwich, Honey BBQ, remove breading 510 calories, 25g fat, 24g protein
5g net carbs: Crispy Twister®, remove breading 630 calories, 34g fat, 28g protein
5g net carbs: Honey BBQ Sandwich, no honey BBQ sauce 350 calories, 3g fat, 24g protein
7g net carbs: Chicken Littles, Honey BBQ 320 calories, 15g fat, 14g protein

Original Recipe Chicken

3g net carbs: Original Recipe® Chicken Breast, remove breading 390 calories, 21g fat, 39g protein
3g net carbs: Original Recipe® Chicken Drumstick 130 calories, 8g fat, 12g protein
3g net carbs: Original Recipe® Chicken Thigh, remove breading 280 calories, 19g fat, 19g protein
3g net carbs: Original Recipe® Chicken Whole Wing 130 calories, 8g fat, 10g protein

Extra Crispy Chicken

3g net carbs: Extra Crispy™ Chicken Breast, remove breading 530 calories, 35g fat, 35g protein
3g net carbs: Extra Crispy™ Chicken Thigh, remove breading 330 calories, 23g fat, 22protein
5g net carbs: Extra Crispy™ Chicken Drumstick 170 calories, 12g fat, 10g protein
5g net carbs: Extra Crispy™ Chicken Whole Wing 170 calories, 13g fat, 10g protein

Kentucky Grilled Chicken

0g net carbs: Kentucky Grilled Chicken® Breast 210 calories, 7g fat, 38g protein
0g net carbs: Kentucky Grilled Chicken® Drumstick 80 calories, 4g fat, 11g protein
0g net carbs: Kentucky Grilled Chicken® Thigh 150 calories, 9g fat, 17g protein
0g net carbs: Kentucky Grilled Chicken® Whole Wing 70 calories, 3g fat, 9g protein

Spicy Crispy Chicken

3g net carbs: Spicy Crispy Chicken Breast, remove breading 350 calories, 20g fat, 30g protein
3g net carbs: Spicy Crispy Chicken Thigh, remove breading 270 calories, 20g fat, 13g protein
4g net carbs: Spicy Crispy Chicken Drumstick 130 calories, 8g fat, 9g protein
5g net carbs: Spicy Crispy Chicken Whole Wing 120 calories, 8g fat, 7g protein

Extra Crispy Tenders

5g net carbs: Beyond Fried Chicken Nugget (1) 80 calories, 4g fat, 6g protein
8g net carbs: Extra Crispy™ Tender (1 order) 140 calories, 7g fat, 10g protein
8g net carbs: Nashville Hot Extra Crispy™ Tender (1 order) 220 calories, 16g fat, 10g protein

Kentucky Fried Wings (1 Wing)

3g net carbs: Kentucky Fried Wings- Buffalo 100 calories, 7g fat, 5g protein
3g net carbs: Kentucky Fried Wings- No sauce, 80 calories, 6g fat, 5g protein
4g net carbs: Kentucky Fried Wings- Nashville Hot 130 calories, 11g fat, 5g protein
8g net carbs: Kentucky Fried Wings- Honey BBQ[96] 100 calories, 6g fat, 5g protein

Nashville Hot Chicken

0g net carbs: Nashville Hot Kentucky Grilled Chicken® Drumstick 100 calories, 6g fat, 11g protein
0g net carbs: Nashville Hot Kentucky Grilled Chicken® Thigh 180 calories, 12g fat, 17g protein
1g net carbs: Nashville Hot Kentucky Grilled Chicken® Breast 260 calories, 12g fat, 38g protein
1g net carbs: Nashville Hot Kentucky Grilled Chicken® Whole Wing 90 calories, 6g fat, 9g protein
3g net carbs: Nashville Hot Extra Crispy™ Chicken Thigh, remove breading 500 calories, 40g fat, 22g protein
3g net carbs: Nashville Hot Spicy Crispy Chicken Thigh, remove breading 390 calories, 32g fat, 13g protein
4g net carbs: Nashville Hot Extra Crispy™ Chicken Breast, remove breading 470 calories, 40g fat, 35g protein
4g net carbs: Nashville Hot Spicy Crispy Chicken Breast, remove breading 440 calories, 40g fat, 31g protein
4g net carbs: Nashville Hot Spicy Crispy Chicken Whole Wing 180 calories, 15g fat, 8g protein
5g net carbs: Nashville Hot Extra Crispy™ Chicken Drumstick 250 calories, 21g fat, 11g protein
5g net carbs: Nashville Hot Extra Crispy™ Chicken Whole Wing 290 calories, 25g fat, 10g protein
5g net carbs: Nashville Hot Spicy Crispy Chicken Drumstick 190 calories, 14g fat, 9g protein

Homestyle Sides (Individual)

2g net carbs: Green Beans 25 calories, 0g fat, 1g protein
10g net carbs: Coleslaw 170 calories, 12g fat, 10g protein

Salads (No Dressing, No Croutons)

1g net carbs: Caesar Side Salad 40 calories, 2g fat, 3g protein
1g net carbs: House Side Salad 15 calories, 0g fat, 1g protein

---

[96] *That's Not Keto!* – You'll find all sorts of surprising foods listed here. I'm not telling you whether you should eat these foods or not. What fits your macros or daily carb spend is up to you. No keto police allowed.

Salad Dressing

1g net carbs: Heinz Buttermilk Dressing 160 calories, 17g fat, 0g protein
2g net carbs: Marzetti Light Italian Dressing 15 calories, 1g fat, 0g protein
4g net carbs: KFC Creamy Parmesan Caesar Dressing 260 calories, 26g fat, 2g protein
8g net carbs: Hidden Valley The Original Ranch Fat-Free Dressing 35 calories, 0g fat, 1g protein

Dipping Sauces & Condiments

0g net carbs: Colonel's Buttery Spread 35 calories, 4g fat, 0g protein
1g net carbs: Lemon Juice Packet, 5 calories, 0g fat, 0g protein
2g net carbs: Ranch Dipping Sauce Cup 130 calories, 14g fat, 0g protein
5g net carbs: KFC Sauce Dipping Sauce Cup 90 calories, 8g fat, 0g protein
6g net carbs: Honey Mustard Dipping Sauce Cup[97] 110 calories, 9g fat, 0g protein
8g net carbs: Honey Sauce* Packet 30 calories, 0g fat, 0g protein
8g net carbs: Ketchup* 30 calories, 0g fat, 0g protein
9g net carbs: Grape Jelly* Packet 35 calories, 0g fat, 0g protein
9g net carbs: Strawberry Jam* Packet 35 calories, 0g fat, 0g protein
10g net carbs: BBQ Dipping Sauce* Cup 45 calories, 0g fat, 0g protein

DRINKS

0g net carbs: Diet Pepsi, 12 oz. 0 calories, 0g fat, 0g protein
0g net carbs: Diet Pepsi, 16 oz. 0 calories, 0g fat, 0g protein
0g net carbs: Diet Pepsi, 20 oz. 0 calories, 0g fat, 0g protein
1g net carbs: Diet Pepsi, 30 oz. 0 calories, 0g fat, 0g protein
0g net carbs: Diet Pepsi Wild Cherry Pepsi, 12 oz. 0 calories, 0g fat, 0g protein
0g net carbs: Diet Pepsi Wild Cherry Pepsi, 16 oz. 0 calories, 0g fat, 0g protein
0g net carbs: Diet Pepsi Wild Cherry Pepsi, 20 oz. 0 calories, 0g fat, 0g protein
1g net carbs: Diet Pepsi Wild Cherry Pepsi, 30 oz. 0 calories, 0g fat, 0g protein
0g net carbs: Pepsi Zero Sugar, 12 oz. 0 calories, 0g fat, 0g protein
0g net carbs: Pepsi Zero Sugar, 16 oz. 0 calories, 0g fat, 0g protein
0g net carbs: Pepsi Zero Sugar, 20 oz. 0 calories, 0g fat, 0g protein
1g net carbs: Pepsi Zero Sugar, 30 oz. 0 calories, 0g fat, 0g protein
0g net carbs: Diet Dr. Pepper, 12 oz. 0 calories, 0g fat, 0g protein
0g net carbs: Diet Dr. Pepper, 16 oz. 0 calories, 0g fat, 0g protein
0g net carbs: Diet Dr. Pepper, 20 oz. 0 calories, 0g fat, 0g protein
1g net carbs: Diet Dr. Pepper, 30 oz. 0 calories, 0g fat, 0g protein
0g net carbs: Diet Sierra Mist, 12 oz. 0 calories, 0g fat, 0g protein
0g net carbs: Diet Sierra Mist, 16 oz. 0 calories, 0g fat, 0g protein
0g net carbs: Diet Sierra Mist, 20 oz. 0 calories, 0g fat, 0g protein
0g net carbs: Diet Sierra Mist, 30 oz. 5 calories, 0g fat, 0g protein
0g net carbs: Diet Mountain Dew, 12 oz. 0 calories, 0g fat, 0g protein
1g net carbs: Diet Mountain Dew, 16 oz. 5 calories, 0g fat, 0g protein
1g net carbs: Diet Mountain Dew, 20 oz. 10 calories, 0g fat, 0g protein
1g net carbs: Diet Mountain Dew, 30 oz. 15 calories, 0g fat, 0g protein

---

[97] *That's Not Keto!* – You'll find all sorts of surprising foods listed here. I'm not telling you whether you should eat these foods or not. What fits your macros or daily carb spend is up to you. No keto police allowed.

0g net carbs: Lipton Brisk No Calorie Peach Iced Green Tea, 12 oz. 0 calories, 0g fat, 0g protein
0g net carbs: Lipton Brisk No Calorie Peach Iced Green Tea, 16 oz. 0 calories, 0g fat, 0g protein
0g net carbs: Lipton Brisk No Calorie Peach Iced Green Tea, 20 oz. 5 calories, 0g fat, 0g protein
0g net carbs: Lipton Brisk No Calorie Peach Iced Green Tea, 30 oz. 10 calories, 0g fat, 0g protein
0g net carbs: Lipton Brisk Unsweetened No Lemon Iced Tea, 12 oz. 0 calories, 0g fat, 0g protein
0g net carbs: Lipton Brisk Unsweetened No Lemon Iced Tea, 16 oz. 0 calories, 0g fat, 0g protein
0g net carbs: Lipton Brisk Unsweetened No Lemon Iced Tea, 20 oz. 0 calories, 0g fat, 0g protein
0g net carbs: Lipton Brisk Unsweetened No Lemon Iced Tea, 30 oz. 0 calories, 0g fat, 0g protein
0g net carbs: Tropicana Light Lemonade, 12 oz. 0 calories, 0g fat, 0g protein
0g net carbs: Tropicana Light Lemonade, 16 oz. 5 calories, 0g fat, 0g protein
0g net carbs: Tropicana Light Lemonade, 20 oz. 5 calories, 0g fat, 0g protein
0g net carbs: Tropicana Light Lemonade, 30 oz. 10 calories, 0g fat, 0g protein
0g net carbs: Sobe Lifewater Yumberry Pomegranate, 12 oz. 0 calories, 0g fat, 0g protein
0g net carbs: Sobe Lifewater Yumberry Pomegranate, 16 oz. 0 calories, 0g fat, 0g protein
0g net carbs: Sobe Lifewater Yumberry Pomegranate, 20 oz. 0 calories, 0g fat, 0g protein
1g net carbs: Sobe Lifewater Yumberry Pomegranate, 30 oz. 5 calories, 0g fat, 0g protein

Popeyes

Popeyes will surely disappoint any keto'er due to its disgraceful lack of low-carb options. Shrimp, chicken, and fish sandwiches are breaded, and nuggets are "hand-battered and breaded in buttermilk coating." Prepare to get your hands dirty. If not removing breading, keto-friendly meat options at Popeyes are limited to the Blackened Tenders.

Popeyes does not have a customizable nutrition calculator on its website. They offer a Nutritional Information document, but it is too general. Sandwich breads are not itemized separately (only biscuits). This lack of specificity makes determining calories and macronutrients for breadless sandwiches a guessing game. Good thing I have experience in this area!

On the positive side, Popeyes provides nutrition information for meal and combo components. Click on almost any item from the online menu and select "Nutritional Information" near the bottom of the page. A pop-up window will appear with the available options. Pretty cool!

Special Order Tips

Order all burgers and sandwiches with "no bread." Be wary of the available "Add-Ons" since they are often an unnecessary source of net carbs.

Feel free to customize your order. Restaurants are usually happy to accommodate reasonable customer requests. The exception is when the item has been premade or was prepared off-site. Note that any alterations on your end will change the provided nutrition information. Adjust accordingly.

Avoid all fries, potatoes, rice, pasta, bread, etc. Ask the server to substitute a side salad or a side of steamed/grilled vegetables. Note that Popeyes's lowest net carb side dishes are green beans and coleslaw.

Author Favorite

Breakfast: Breadless Egg (1) & Sausage (1) Biscuit with 10 oz. Hot Coffee, unsweetened to drink. 390 calories, 22g fat, 4g net carbs, 20g protein

Lunch & Dinner: 3 Handcrafted Spicy Blackened Tenders- to start. Breadless Spicy Chicken Sandwich, breading removed, with Green Beans and Jalapeños on the side. 22 oz. Iced Tea with sugar-free sweetener to drink. 610 calories, 46g fat, 15g net carbs, 57g protein

BREAKFAST (No Bread)

3g net carbs: Breadless Bacon (3 strips) Biscuit 200 calories, 12g fat, 8g protein
3g net carbs: Breadless Egg (2) Biscuit 310 calories, 15g fat, 13g protein
3g net carbs: Breadless Sausage (2 links) Biscuit 340 calories, 18g fat, 13g protein
4g net carbs: Breadless Chicken Biscuit 290 calories, 14g fat, 17g protein
4g net carbs: Breadless Egg (1) & Sausage (1 link) Biscuit 390 calories, 22g fat, 20g protein
4g net carbs: Breadless Sausage (2 links) & Gravy Biscuit 310 calories, 14g fat, 10g protein

LUNCH & DINNER

Tenders & Nuggets

2g net carbs: Handcrafted Tenders (3), Blackened 170 calories, 2g fat, 26g protein
3g net carbs: Handcrafted Tenders (5), Blackened 283 calories, 3g fat, 43g protein
5g net carbs: Handcrafted Tenders (8), Blackened 453 calories, 8g fat, 69g protein
9g net carbs: Nuggets[98] (4), breading included 111 calories, 6g fat, 11g protein
10g net carbs: Handcrafted Tenders (10), Blackened 570 calories, 10g fat, 90g protein

Signature Chicken (Classic or Spicy)

2g net carbs: Wing* (Drumette) with breading 110 calories, 4g fat, 5g protein
4g net carbs: Leg* (1) with breading 160 calories, 9g fat, 14g protein
5g net carbs: Breast (1), remove breading 480 calories, 31g fat, 34g protein
6g net carbs: Thigh* (1) with breading 280 calories, 21g fat, 24g protein

Sandwiches & Wraps (No Bread, No Wrap)

3g net carbs: Loaded Chicken Wrap, remove breading 310 calories, 12g fat, 14g protein
6g net carbs: Chicken Sandwich-Classic, remove breading 380 calories, 42g fat, 28g protein
6g net carbs: Chicken Sandwich-Spicy, remove breading 380 calories, 42g fat, 28g protein

Signature Sides

0g net carbs: Jalapeños 5 calories, 0g fat, 0g protein

---

[98] *That's Not Keto!* – You'll find all sorts of surprising foods listed here. I'm not telling you whether you should eat these foods or not. What fits your macros or daily carb spend is up to you. No keto police allowed.

5g net carbs: Green Beans 55 calories, 2g fat, 3g protein
6g net carbs: Coleslaw, Regular Size, Half-Serving, 70 calories, 5g fat, 1g protein

Signature Dipping Sauces (1 oz. Unless Otherwise Indicated)

1g net carbs: Tartar 140 calories, 15g fat, 0g protein
2g net carbs: Bayou Buffalo™ 60 calories, 6g fat, 2g protein
2g net carbs: Blackened Ranch 118 calories, 13g fat, 1g protein
3g net carbs: Buttermilk Ranch 150 calories, 15g fat, 0g protein
4g net carbs: Mardi Gras Mustard™ 100 calories, 8g fat, 1g protein
5g net carbs: Wild Honey Mustard[99] 130 calories, 12g fat, 1g protein
6g net carbs: Boldbq™*, .75 oz. 40 calories, 0g fat, 0g protein
7g net carbs: Creole Cocktail* 30 calories, 0g fat, 0g protein
9g net carbs: Sweet Heat®* .5 oz. 36 calories, 0g fat, 0g protein

DRINKS

0g net carbs: Seltzer Water, 22 oz. 0 calories, 0g fat, 0g protein
0g net carbs: Seltzer Water, 30 oz. 0 calories, 0g fat, 0g protein
0g net carbs: Seltzer Water, 40 oz. 0 calories, 0g fat, 0g protein
0g net carbs: Sugar-free Ginger Ale, 22 oz. 0 calories, 0g fat, 0g protein
0g net carbs: Sugar-free Ginger Ale, 30 oz. 0 calories, 0g fat, 0g protein
0g net carbs: Sugar-free Ginger Ale, 40 oz. 0 calories, 0g fat, 0g protein
0g net carbs: Unsweetened Iced Tea, 22 oz. 0 calories, 0g fat, 0g protein
0g net carbs: Unsweetened Iced Tea, 30 oz. 0 calories, 0g fat, 0g protein
0g net carbs: Unsweetened Iced Tea, 40 oz. 0 calories, 0g fat, 0g protein
0g net carbs: Unsweetened Hot Coffee, 10 oz. 0 calories, 0g fat, 0g protein
0g net carbs: Diet Coke, 22 oz. 0 calories, 0g fat, 0g protein
0g net carbs: Diet Coke, 30 oz. 0 calories, 0g fat, 0g protein
0g net carbs: Diet Coke, 40 oz. 0 calories, 0g fat, 0g protein
0g net carbs: Coca-Cola Zero Sugar, 22 oz. 0 calories, 0g fat, 0g protein
0g net carbs: Coca-Cola Zero Sugar, 30 oz. 0 calories, 0g fat, 0g protein
0g net carbs: Coca-Cola Zero Sugar, 40 oz. 0 calories, 0g fat, 0g protein
0g net carbs: Diet Pepsi, 22 oz. 0 calories, 0g fat, 0g protein
1g net carbs: Diet Pepsi, 30 oz. 0 calories, 0g fat, 0g protein
1g net carbs: Diet Pepsi, 40 oz. 0 calories, 0g fat, 0g protein

---

[99] *That's Not Keto!* – You'll find all sorts of surprising foods listed here. I'm not telling you whether you should eat these foods or not. What fits your macros or daily carb spend is up to you. No keto police allowed.

Chick-fil-A

Chick-fil-A effortlessly claims a *Keto Diet Restaurant Guide* Superstar Award for its comprehensive, customizable nutrition calculator. Tailoring an order to suit your needs is a snap. And have you tried their grilled Chick-fil-A Nuggets? *Delish.* I must say that Chick-fil-A wins "Best in Show" for this book. They make enjoying a keto-friendly lunch easy.

Special Order Tips

Order all burgers and sandwiches with "no bread." Be wary of the available "Add-Ons" since they are often an unnecessary source of net carbs.

Feel free to customize your order. Restaurants are usually happy to accommodate reasonable customer requests. The exception is when the item has been premade or was prepared off-site. Note that any alterations on your end will change the provided nutrition information. Adjust accordingly.

All sides of fries, hash browns, bread, etc. should be substituted with the Kale Crunch Side or a Side Salad with Garden Herb Ranch Dressing, no bell peppers, no charred tomato to match the provided nutrition information.

You'll notice some menu items indicate a half-serving size. Don't worry; there will only be a few! Smaller portions allowed us to include more (higher-carb) Chick-fil-A favorite sides.

Author Favorite

Breakfast: Scramble Bowl with grilled fillet, no hash browns, and 16 oz. Vanilla Iced Coffee, unsweetened, to drink. 170 calories, 16g fat, 5g net carbs, 19g protein

Lunch & Dinner: Cobb Salad- Spicy Grilled Chicken, no corn with Lemon Caesar Vinaigrette Dressing. 20 oz. Diet Dr. Pepper to drink. 450 calories, 31g fat, 5g net carbs, 27g protein

BREAKFAST (No Bread, No Potatoes)

1g net carbs: Bacon, Egg & Cheese Breakfast Bowl 130 calories, 10g fat, 11g protein
1g net carbs: Egg White Grill 150 calories, 6g fat, 21g protein
1g net carbs: Grilled Chicken Breakfast Bowl 160 calories, 10g fat, 13g protein
1g net carbs: Sausage, Egg & Cheese Breakfast Bowl 280 calories, 29g fat, 18g protein
2g net carbs: Chicken, Egg & Cheese Breakfast Bowl 150 calories, 11g fat, 11g protein
2g net carbs: Grilled Nuggets Chick-n-Minis™ with cheese 160 calories, 13g fat, 19g protein
4g net carbs: Scramble Bowl 170 calories, 16g fat, 19g protein
4g net carbs: Scramble Bowl with grilled fillet 170 calories, 16g fat, 19g protein
5g net carbs: Scramble Bowl with sausage 180 calories, 22g fat, 16g protein
6g net carbs: Fruit Cup[100], Half-Serving, 30 calories, 0g fat, 1g protein

LUNCH & DINNER

Sandwiches and Wraps (No Bread, No Wrap, No Tortilla)

1g net carbs: Grilled Nuggets 60 calories, 3g fat, 25g protein
2g net carbs: Chick-fil-A Cool Wrap 250 calories, 13g fat, 42g protein
2g net carbs: Chick-fil-A Grilled Chicken Sandwich 240 calories, 17g fat, 29g protein
2g net carbs: Spicy Grilled Chicken Sandwich 260 calories, 19g fat, 28g protein
3g net carbs: Chick-fil-A Grilled Chicken Club Sandwich 320 calories, 22g fat, 37g protein
3g net carbs: Spicy Grilled Deluxe Sandwich 350 calories, 25g fat, 33g protein
4g net carbs: Chick-fil-A Grilled Deluxe Sandwich 300 calories, 22g fat, 32g protein

Sandwich Toppings

0g net carbs: Bacon (1 strip) 50 calories, 3g fat, 4g protein
0g net carbs: Colby Jack Cheese 80 calories, 7g fat, 5g protein
0g net carbs: Pepper Jack Cheese 80 calories, 6g fat, 4g protein
0g net carbs: Pickles 0 calories, 0g fat, 0g protein
1g net carbs: American Cheese 50 calories, 4g fat, 3g protein

---

[100] *That's Not Keto!* – You'll find all sorts of surprising foods listed here. I'm not telling you whether you should eat these foods or not. What fits your macros or daily carb spend is up to you. No keto police allowed.

1g net carbs: Lettuce 5 calories, 0g fat, 0g protein
1g net carbs: Tomato 5 calories, 0g fat, 0g protein

Dipping Sauces (1 oz. Unless Otherwise Indicated)

0g net carbs: Cilantro Lime Sauce 140 calories, 14g fat, 0g protein
1g net carbs: Garden Herb Ranch Sauce 140 calories, 15g fat, 1g protein
1g net carbs: Zesty Buffalo Sauce 18 calories, 2g fat, 0g protein
3g net carbs: Honey Roasted BBQ Sauce[101] 60 calories, 5g fat, 0g protein
6g net carbs: Barbeque Sauce*, .5 oz. 22 calories, 0g fat, 0g protein
6g net carbs: Honey Mustard Sauce* 25 calories, 0g fat, 0g protein
6g net carbs: Sweet and Spicy Sriracha Sauce* 22 calories, 0g fat, 0g protein
7g net carbs: Chick-fil-A Sauce* 140 calories, 13g fat, 0g protein
7g net carbs: Polynesian Sauce* 55 calories, 3g fat, 0g protein

Proteins

0g net carbs: Grilled Chicken Breakfast Filet (1) 60 calories, 1g fat, 13g protein
0g net carbs: Bacon (1 strip) 50 calories, 3g fat, 4g protein
1g net carbs: Sausage (1 link) 240 calories, 22g fat, 11g protein
4g net carbs: Spicy Grilled Chicken Filet (1) 130 calories, 13g fat, 23g protein
6g net carbs: Chick-fil-A Grilled Chicken Filet (1) 125 calories, 6g fat, 12g protein
8g net carbs: Sausage Breakfast Filet (1) 160 calories, 8g fat, 15g protein

Salads (No Roasted Corn, No Bell Peppers, No Charred Tomato)

4g net carbs: Cobb Salad, no chicken 350 calories, 9g fat, 22g protein
4g net carbs: Spicy Southwest Salad, no chicken, no beans, no tortilla strips 290 calories, 9g fat, 23g protein
5g net carbs: Cobb Salad, Grilled Chicken Filet 440 calories, 21g fat, 46g protein
5g net carbs: Cobb Salad, Grilled Nuggets 430 calories, 20g fat, 47g protein
5g net carbs: Cobb Salad, Spicy Grilled Chicken 450 calories, 31g fat, 27g protein
6g net carbs: Spicy Southwest Salad, Grilled Chicken Filet, no beans, no tortilla strips 390 calories, 19g fat, 33g protein
6g net carbs: Spicy Southwest Salad, Grilled Nuggets, no beans, no tortilla strips 400 calories, 20g fat, 34g protein
6g net carbs: Spicy Southwest Salad, Grilled Spicy Chicken Filet, no beans, no tortilla strips 405 calories, 21g fat, 33g protein

Salad Dressing (2 oz. Unless Otherwise Indicated)

0g net carbs: Lemon Caesar Vinaigrette Dressing 0 calories, 0g fat, 0g protein
2g net carbs: Avocado Lime Ranch Dressing 310 calories, 32g fat, 1g protein
2g net carbs: Creamy Salsa Dressing 290 calories, 31g fat, 1g protein
2g net carbs: Garden Herb Ranch Dressing 280 calories, 29g fat, 1g protein
3g net carbs: Light Italian Dressing 25 calories, 1g fat, 0g protein
5g net carbs: Light Balsamic Vinaigrette Dressing, .5 oz. 40 calories, 2g fat, 0g protein

---

[101] *That's Not Keto!* – You'll find all sorts of surprising foods listed here. I'm not telling you whether you should eat these foods or not. What fits your macros or daily carb spend is up to you. No keto police allowed.

8g net carbs: Zesty Apple Cider Vinaigrette Dressing .5 oz. 115 calories, 10g fat, 0g protein
9g net carbs: Fat-Free Honey Mustard Dressing, .5 oz. 45 calories, 0g fat, 0g protein

Salad Toppings

1g net carbs: Chili Lime Pepitas 80 calories, 7g fat, 4g protein
6g net carbs: Crispy Bell Peppers 80 calories, 6g fat, 1g protein
7g net carbs: Lemon Parmesan Panko* 70 calories, 2g fat, 3g protein
7g net carbs: Seasoned Tortilla Strips* 70 calories, 4g fat, 1g protein
10g net carbs: Harvest Nut Granola[102], .5 oz 70 calories, 0g fat, 1g protein

Sides

4g net carbs: Side Salad with Garden Herb Ranch Dressing, no bell peppers, no charred tomato 140 calories,
   10g fat, 6g protein
6g net carbs: Buddy Fruits® Apple Sauce*, Half-Serving, 22 calories, 0g fat, 0g protein
6g net carbs: Kale Crunch Side 120 calories, 9g fat, 3g protein
7g net carbs: Fruit Cup*, Half-Serving, 30 calories, 0g fat, 1g protein
9g net carbs: Chicken Noodle Soup*, Half-Serving, 70 calories, 2g fat, 5g protein

Soup Toppings

5g net carbs: Saltines* 25 calories, 1g fat, 0g protein

DRINKS

0g net carbs: Diet Coke, 8 oz. 0 calories, 0g fat, 0g protein
0g net carbs: Diet Coke, 12 oz. 0 calories, 0g fat, 0g protein
0g net carbs: Diet Coke, 20 oz. 0 calories, 0g fat, 0g protein
0g net carbs: Coke Zero Sugar, 8 oz. 0 calories, 0g fat, 0g protein
0g net carbs: Coke Zero Sugar, 12 oz. 0 calories, 0g fat, 0g protein
0g net carbs: Coke Zero Sugar, 20 oz. 0 calories, 0g fat, 0g protein
0g net carbs: Diet Dr. Pepper, 8 oz. 0 calories, 0g fat, 0g protein
0g net carbs: Diet Dr. Pepper, 12 oz. 0 calories, 0g fat, 0g protein
0g net carbs: Diet Dr. Pepper, 20 oz. 0 calories, 0g fat, 0g protein
0g net carbs: DASANI Bottled Water, 16 oz. bottle 0 calories, 0g fat, 0g protein
9g net carbs: Honest Kids Apple Juice*, 6 oz. 35 calories, 0g fat, 0g protein
0g net carbs: Freshly-Brewed Iced Tea Unsweetened, 7 oz. 0 calories, 0g fat, 0g protein
0g net carbs: Freshly-Brewed Iced Tea Unsweetened, 12 oz. 0 calories, 0g fat, 0g protein
0g net carbs: Freshly-Brewed Iced Tea Unsweetened, 15 oz. 0 calories, 0g fat, 0g protein
0g net carbs: Hot Coffee, unsweetened, 12 oz. 0 calories, 0g fat, 0g protein
0g net carbs: Iced Coffee, unsweetened, 16 oz. 0 calories, 0g fat, 0g protein
0g net carbs: Vanilla Iced Coffee, unsweetened, 16 oz. 0 calories, 0g fat, 0g protein

---

[102] *That's Not Keto!* – You'll find all sorts of surprising foods listed here. I'm not telling you whether you should eat these foods or not. What fits your macros or daily carb spend is up to you. No keto police allowed.

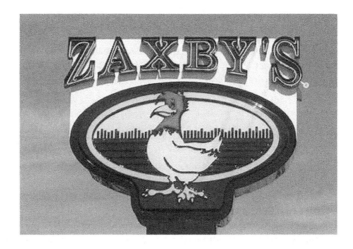

Zaxby's

Being a classic "chicken joint," expect lots of breaded and fried food on the menu at Zaxby's. To cut back on carbs, you'll have to remove the coating. Otherwise, choose an entrée like the Grilled Chicken Sandwich or traditional bone-in wings (neither are breaded). The Chicken Fingerz™ and boneless wings are only lightly breaded, but you'll still want to avoid that outside layer. You can always ask for a grilled chicken breast substitution when ordering a breaded chicken meal.

Zaxby falls short in the transparency department. Their Nutritional and Allergen Information PDF does not itemize sandwich bread separately (except for the Texas Toast), making it difficult for us to calculate calories and macronutrients for a breadless sandwich. Zaxby's does not have a customizable nutrition calculator on its website.

Special Order Tips

Order all burgers and sandwiches with "no bread." Be wary of the available "Add-Ons" since they are often an unnecessary source of net carbs.

Feel free to customize your order. Restaurants are usually happy to accommodate reasonable customer requests. The exception is when the item has been premade or was prepared off-site. Note that any alterations on your end will change the provided nutrition information. Adjust accordingly.

Avoid all fries, potatoes, rice, pasta, bread, etc. Ask the server to substitute a side salad or a side of steamed/grilled vegetables.

Author Favorite

Lunch & Dinner: Buffalo Traditional Wings & Things Plate, no bread, breading removed, easy sauce, and 1 oz. Insane™ dip. 22 oz. Iced Tea, unsweetened on ice to drink. 567 calories, 49g fat, 8g net carbs, 49g protein

LUNCH & DINNER

Sandwich Meals & Sandwiches (No Bread, Substitute Salad for Fries)

3g net carbs: Cajun Club Blackened Chicken Sandwich Only 300 calories, 31g fat, 46g protein
3g net carbs: Grilled Chicken Sandwich Only 540 calories, 26g fat, 43g protein
3g net carbs: Zaxby's Club Sandwich Only, remove breading 320 calories, 28g fat, 43g protein
4g net carbs: 3 Nibblerz™ Sandwich Only, remove breading 340 calories, 29g fat, 40g protein
4g net carbs: Cajun Club Blackened Chicken Sandwich Meal 340 calories, 35g fat, 51g protein
4g net carbs: Zaxby's Signature Sandwich Only with easy Spicy Zax Sauce, remove breading 570 calories, 42g fat, 45g protein
4g net carbs: Zaxby's Club Sandwich Meal, remove breading 350 calories, 32g fat, 48g protein
4g net carbs: Zaxby's Signature Sandwich Only with easy Zax Sauce, remove breading 580 calories, 43g fat, 45g protein
5g net carbs: Grilled Chicken Sandwich Meal 580 calories, 30g fat, 47g protein
5g net carbs: Kickin' Chicken Sandwich Only, remove breading 330 calories, 41g fat, 37g protein
6g net carbs: 3 Nibblerz Sandwich Meal®, remove breading 380 calories, 31g fat, 45g protein
6g net carbs: Kickin' Chicken Sandwich Meal, remove breading 370 calories, 45g fat, 41g protein
8g net carbs: Zaxby's Signature Sandwich Meal with easy Zax Sauce, remove breading 710 calories, 57g fat, 49g protein
8g net carbs: Zaxby's Signature Sandwich Meal with easy Spicy Zax Sauce, remove breading 700 calories, 56g fat, 49g protein

Most Popular (No Bread, Substitute Salad for Fries)

4g net carbs: Traditional Wings Meal, remove breading 410 calories, 18g fat, 24g protein
5g net carbs: Boneless Wings Meal, remove breading 400 calories, 21g fat, 26g protein
5g net carbs: Buffalo Chicken Fingerz™ Plate (4), remove breading 620 calories, 68g fat, 49g protein
5g net carbs: Great 8 Boneless Wings Meal, remove breading 520 calories, 57g fat, 32g protein
5g net carbs: Traditional Wings & Things, remove breading 430 calories, 36g fat, 37g protein
6g net carbs: Boneless Wings & Things, remove breading 480 calories, 38g fat, 62g protein
7g net carbs: Big Zax Snak Meal, remove breading 460 calories, 52g fat, 38g protein
7g net carbs: Buffalo Big Zax Snak Meal, remove breading 480 calories, 54g fat, 39g protein
7g net carbs: Buffalo Boneless Wings & Things, remove breading 520 calories, 41g fat, 63g protein
7g net carbs: Buffalo Chicken Fingerz™ Plate (5), remove breading 650 calories, 73g fat, 59g protein
7g net carbs: Buffalo Traditional Wings & Things, remove breading, easy sauce 550 calories, 48g fat, 48g protein
7g net carbs: Traditional Wings Meal (5) remove breading 670 calories, 65g fat, 47g protein
8g net carbs: Chicken Fingerz™ Plate (4) with easy Zax Sauce®, remove breading 660 calories, 66g fat, 49g protein
8g net carbs: Chicken Fingerz™ Plate (5) with easy Zax Sauce®, remove breading 680 calories, 71g fat, 59g protein
9g net carbs: Chicken Fingerz™ Plate (6) with easy Zax Sauce®, remove breading 700 calories, 93g fat, 69g protein

10g net carbs: Buffalo Chicken Fingerz™ Plate (6), remove breading 690 calories, 97g fat, 70g protein

1 Boneless Wing (with Sauce When Indicated)

4g net carbs: Boneless Wing, No Sauce 70 calories, 3g fat, 5g protein
5g net carbs: Boneless Wing, HHM 80 calories, 5g fat, 5g protein
5g net carbs: Boneless Wing, Insane 70 calories, 4g fat, 5g protein
5g net carbs: Boneless Wing, Nuclear 70 calories, 4g fat, 5g protein
5g net carbs: Boneless Wing, Original 70 calories, 3g fat, 5g protein
5g net carbs: Boneless Wing, Tongue Torch 70 calories, 3g fat, 5g protein
5g net carbs: Boneless Wing, Wimpy 70 calories, 3g fat, 5g protein
6g net carbs: Boneless Wing, Teriyaki[103], 70 calories, 2g fat, 5g protein
7g net carbs: Boneless Wing, BBQ* 80 calories, 3g fat, 5g protein
7g net carbs: Boneless Wing, Sweet & Spicy* 80 calories, 4g fat, 5g protein

1 Traditional Wing (with Sauce When Indicated)

1g net carbs: Traditional Wing, Insane 80 calories, 5g fat, 8g protein
1g net carbs: Traditional Wing, No Sauce 80 calories, 5g fat, 8g protein
1g net carbs: Traditional Wing, Nuclear 80 calories, 5g fat, 8g protein
1g net carbs: Traditional Wing, Original 80 calories, 5g fat, 8g protein
1g net carbs: Traditional Wing, Tongue Torch 80 calories, 5g fat, 8g protein
2g net carbs: Traditional Wing, HHM 100 calories, 7g fat, 8g protein
2g net carbs: Traditional Wing, Wimpy 80 calories, 5g fat, 8g protein
3g net carbs: Traditional Wing, BBQ* 90 calories, 5g fat, 8g protein
3g net carbs: Traditional Wing, Sweet & Spicy* 90 calories, 5g fat, 8g protein
3g net carbs: Traditional Wing, Teriyaki* 90 calories, 5g fat, 8g protein

5 Traditional Wings (with Sauce When Indicated)

3g net carbs: Traditional Wings, No Sauce 380 calories, 24g fat, 38g protein
4g net carbs: Traditional Wings, Original 410 calories, 27g fat, 38g protein
5g net carbs: Traditional Wings, Insane 400 calories, 25g fat, 39g protein
5g net carbs: Traditional Wings, Nuclear 400 calories, 25g fat, 39g protein
5g net carbs: Traditional Wings, Tongue Torch 400 calories, 24g fat, 38g protein
8g net carbs: Traditional Wings, HHM 480 calories, 33g fat, 39g protein
8g net carbs: Traditional Wings, Wimpy 410 calories, 24g fat, 39g protein

10 Traditional Wings (with Sauce When Indicated)

6g net carbs: Traditional Wings, No Sauce 760 calories, 48g fat, 76g protein
6g net carbs: Traditional Wings, Original 820 calories, 54g fat, 77g protein
10g net carbs: Traditional Wings, Tongue Torch 790 calories, 49g fat, 77g protein
10g net carbs: Traditional Wings, Nuclear 800 calories, 49g fat, 77g protein
10g net carbs: Traditional Wings, Insane 800 calories, 49g fat, 78g protein

---

[103] *That's Not Keto!* – You'll find all sorts of surprising foods listed here. I'm not telling you whether you should eat these foods or not. What fits your macros or daily carb spend is up to you. No keto police allowed.

18 Traditional Wings

10g net carbs: Traditional Wings, No Sauce 1530 calories, 97g fat, 153g protein

1 Chicken Fingerz (with Sauce Unless Otherwise Indicated)

4g net carbs: Chicken Fingerz, No Sauce 100 calories, 4g fat, 10g protein
5g net carbs: Chicken Fingerz, Insane 100 calories, 4g fat, 10g protein
5g net carbs: Chicken Fingerz, Nuclear 100 calories, 5g fat, 10g protein
5g net carbs: Chicken Fingerz, Original 110 calories, 5g fat, 10g protein
5g net carbs: Chicken Fingerz, Tongue Torch 100 calories, 4g fat, 10g protein
6g net carbs: Chicken Fingerz, HHM 130 calories, 7g fat, 10g protein
6g net carbs: Chicken Fingerz, Wimpy 100 calories, 5g fat, 10g protein
8g net carbs: Chicken Fingerz, Teriyaki[104], 110 calories, 4g fat, 10g protein
9g net carbs: Chicken Fingerz, BBQ* 120 calories, 4g fat, 10g protein
9g net carbs: Chicken Fingerz, Sweet & Spicy* 120 calories, 5g fat, 10g protein

Sauces (1.5 oz. Unless Otherwise Indicated)

2g net carbs: Ranch Sauce 190 calories, 20g fat, 1g protein
3g net carbs: Tongue Torch® 20 calories, 0g fat, 0g protein
4g net carbs: BBQ* .75 oz. 30 calories, 0g fat, 0g protein
5g net carbs: Spicy Zax Sauce® 170 calories, 16g fat, 1g protein
5g net carbs: Zax Sauce® 180 calories, 18g fat, 1g protein
7g net carbs: Honey Mustard* 180 calories, 16g fat, 1g protein
9g net carbs: Marinara Sauce 80 calories, 4g fat, 1g protein

Sauces (8 oz.)

2g net carbs: Original 250 calories, 25g fat, 1g protein
8g net carbs: Ranch 1010 calories, 105g fat, 5g protein

Wing Dip (1 oz.)

0g net carbs: Original 30 calories, 3g fat, 0g protein
1g net carbs: Insane™ 17 calories, 1g fat, 1g protein
1g net carbs: Nuclear™ 15 calories, 1g fat, 1g protein
3g net carbs: Hot Honey Mustard* 45 calories, 8g fat, 1g protein
4g net carbs: Wimpy™ 22 calories, 0g fat, 1g protein

Wing Dip (2 oz.)

0g net carbs: Original 60 calories, 6g fat, 0g protein
3g net carbs: Insane™ 35 calories, 1g fat, 1g protein
3g net carbs: Nuclear™ 30 calories, 1g fat, 1g protein

---

[104] *That's Not Keto!* – You'll find all sorts of surprising foods listed here. I'm not telling you whether you should eat these foods or not. What fits your macros or daily carb spend is up to you. No keto police allowed.

7g net carbs: Hot Honey Mustard* 180 calories, 16g fat, 1g protein
8g net carbs: Wimpy™ 45 calories, 0g fat, 1g protein

Sides

3g net carbs: Extra Chicken Fingerz, remove breading 80 calories, 12g fat, 12g protein
4g net carbs: The Nibbler, breadless, remove breading 220 calories, 14g fat, 18g protein
10g net carbs: Coleslaw, side 140 calories, 10g fat, 1g protein

Zalads® (No Dressing, No Bread, No Fried Onions)

2g net carbs: The Garden Blue Zalad 270 calories, 22g fat, 16g protein
2g net carbs: The Garden Cobb Zalad 330 calories, 34g fat, 26g protein
3g net carbs: The Garden House Zalad 280 calories, 25g fat, 17g protein
3g net carbs: The Grilled Cobb Zalad 340 calories, 36g fat, 31g protein
4g net carbs: The Blackened Blue Zalad 330 calories, 24g fat, 27g protein
4g net carbs: The Grilled House Zalad 310 calories, 27g fat, 32g protein
6g net carbs: The Buffalo Blue Zalad, easy sauce 380 calories, 35g fat, 41g protein

Salad Dressing (1.25 oz. Per Packet)

1g net carbs: Caesar 90 calories, 9g fat, 2g protein
1g net carbs: Lite Ranch 90 calories, 8g fat, 1g protein
1g net carbs: Ranch 160 calories, 16g fat, 1g protein
2g net carbs: Blue Cheese 180 calories, 19g fat, 1g protein
3g net carbs: Mediterranean 140 calories, 13g fat, 0g protein
3g net carbs: Thousand Island 230 calories, 23g fat, 1g protein
5g net carbs: Honey Mustard[105] 150 calories, 14g fat, 1g protein
6g net carbs: Lite Vinaigrette 35 calories, 1g fat, 0g protein

DRINKS

0g net carbs: Diet Coke, 12 oz. 0 calories, 0g fat, 0g protein
0g net carbs: Diet Coke, 16 oz. 0 calories, 0g fat, 0g protein
0g net carbs: Diet Coke, 22 oz. 0 calories, 0g fat, 0g protein
0g net carbs: Coke Zero, 12 oz. 0 calories, 0g fat, 0g protein
0g net carbs: Coke Zero, 16 oz. 0 calories, 0g fat, 0g protein
0g net carbs: Coke Zero, 22 oz. 0 calories, 0g fat, 0g protein
0g net carbs: Iced Tea, unsweetened, 12 oz. 0 calories, 0g fat, 0g protein
0g net carbs: Iced Tea, unsweetened, 16 oz. 0 calories, 0g fat, 0g protein
0g net carbs: Iced Tea, unsweetened, 22 oz. 0 calories, 0g fat, 0g protein

---

[105] *That's Not Keto!* – You'll find all sorts of surprising foods listed here. I'm not telling you whether you should eat these foods or not. What fits your macros or daily carb spend is up to you. No keto police allowed.

Raising Cane's Chicken Fingers

Raising Cane's is pretty much a keto dieter's purgatory. All the available chicken is breaded and fried. There's no way around it. You've got to roll up your sleeves and remove the breading. Not ideal, but "what cha gonna do"?

Raising Cane's Chicken Fingers does not have a customizable nutrition calculator on its website. Instead, they offer a detailed Nutrition Content PDF.

Special Order Tips

Order chicken sandwiches "bunless" (without the bread) or "lettuce wrapped" to match the estimated nutrition information provided. Be wary of the available "Add-Ons" since they are often an unnecessary source of net carbs. Unless I state otherwise, these items are analyzed in their "regular" form as described on the menu. Any alterations will change their total calorie and macronutrient amounts.

Feel free to customize your order. Usually, restaurants are happy to accommodate reasonable customer requests. The exception is when items have been premade or prepared off-site (think frozen breaded shrimp or chicken wings).

You'll notice some menu items indicate a half-serving size. Otherwise, there wouldn't be many options at Raising Cane's Chicken Fingers. (I even threw in a kid's meal as evidence of my desperation.)

Avoid all fries, buns, sugary sauces, etc.

Author Favorite

Lunch & Dinner: Breadless Chicken Sandwich, breading removed, with coleslaw, Half-Serving, on the side. 22 oz. Coke Zero to drink. 430 calories, 21g fat, 10g net carbs, 39g protein

LUNCH & DINNER

Individual Items

4g net carbs: Chicken Finger (1) 130 calories, 6g fat, 13g protein
5g net carbs: Breadless Chicken Sandwich, remove breading 380 calories, 18g fat, 38g protein
6g net carbs: Cane's Sauce 190 calories, 19g fat, 0g protein
5g net carbs: Coleslaw, Half-Serving 50 calories, 3g fat, 1g protein

Combos (with Coleslaw- Half-Serving, No Fries, No Bread, No Cane's Sauce, No Drink)

8g net carbs: Kids Combo, remove breading 330 calories, 15g fat, 29g protein
9g net carbs: 3 Finger Combo, remove breading 320 calories, 18g fat, 47g protein
9g net carbs: Box Combo, remove breading 250 calories, 21g fat, 61g protein
9g net carbs: Caniac Combo, remove breading 640 calories, 36g fat, 89g protein
10g net carbs: Breadless Chicken Sandwich, remove breading 380 calories, 18g fat, 52g protein

DRINKS

0g net carbs: Diet Coke, Kids 12 oz. 0 calories, 0g fat, 0g protein
0g net carbs: Diet Coke, Regular 22 oz. 0 calories, 0g fat, 0g protein
0g net carbs: Diet Coke, Large 32 oz. 0 calories, 0g fat, 0g protein
0g net carbs: Coke Zero, Kids 12 oz. 0 calories, 0g fat, 0g protein
0g net carbs: Coke Zero, Regular 22 oz. 0 calories, 0g fat, 0g protein
0g net carbs: Coke Zero, Large 32 oz. 0 calories, 0g fat, 0g protein
0g net carbs: Unsweetened Tea, Kids 12 oz. 0 calories, 0g fat, 0g protein
0g net carbs: Unsweetened Tea, Regular 22 oz. 0 calories, 0g fat, 0g protein
0g net carbs: Unsweetened Tea, Large 32 oz. 0 calories, 0g fat, 0g protein

Boston Market

Boston Market earns a *Keto Diet Restaurant Guide* Superstar Award for several reasons. First up, their slow-roasted rotisserie chicken is *dee-licious*. And there are so many low-carb sides available! Affordable and healthy, the menu at Boston Market is comfort food at its finest.

Bonus point to Boston Market for NOT having breaded or fried chicken on its menu. They make it easy to choose keto-friendly foods. Be sure to check out the customizable Nutrition Calculator on the Boston Market website. Located in the Nutrition Portal, this nifty tool lets you remove bread from sandwiches, sauce from entrée, or whatever your keto-heart desires. Ingredients can be added, removed, or in most cases, swapped out for a lower-carb option.

Boston Market was known as Boston Chicken until 1995. This gives you an idea of where their loyalties lie: chicken, chicken, and more chicken.

Special Order Tips

Order all burgers and sandwiches with "no bread." Be wary of the available "Add-Ons" since they are often an unnecessary source of net carbs.

Feel free to customize your order. Restaurants are usually happy to accommodate reasonable customer requests. The exception is when the item has been premade or was prepared off-site. Note that any alterations on your end will change the provided nutrition information. Adjust accordingly.

Avoid all fries, potatoes, rice, pasta, bread, etc. Ask the server to substitute a side salad or a side of steamed/grilled vegetables. May I suggest the steamed broccoli? Boston Market makes it just right.

You'll notice some menu items indicate a half-serving size. Don't worry; there aren't very many. A smaller portion allowed us to include a few more (higher-carb) Boston Market signature sandwiches and soups.

Author Favorite

Lunch: Breadless Full Rotisserie Chicken Carver with Chicken Caesar Salad (entree size), ranch dressing, and no croutons. 20 oz. bottle of chilled Dasani water to drink. 1320 calories, 100g fat, 11g net carbs, 46g protein

Dinner: Nashville Hot Rotisserie Chicken, Half Chicken with Regular Steamed Broccoli and Chicken Caesar Salad as Sides. 20 oz. bottle chilled Diet Coke to drink. 745 calories, 50g fat, 9g net carbs, 63g protein

LUNCH

Market Bowls (No Rice, No Corn Relish, No Potatoes, Includes Side of Steamed Vegetables)

1g net carbs: Roasted Turkey Breast Bowl 330 calories, 13g fat, 25g protein
3g net carbs: Roasted Turkey Bowl 390 calories, 18g fat, 26g protein
3g net carbs: Southwest Chicken Bowl 520 calories, 15g fat, 26g protein
4g net carbs: Cheeseburger Bowl, no mac and cheese, no BBQ sauce 410 calories, 23g fat, 22g protein
4g net carbs: Rotisserie Chicken Bowl 410 calories, 18g fat, 34g protein
4g net carbs: Vegetarian Bowl 470 calories, 14g fat, 9g protein
5g net carbs: Pulled Rotisserie Chicken Cheddar Mashed Bowl 430 calories, 23g fat, 31g protein
9g net carbs: Home Style Meatloaf Bowl 580 calories, 36g fat, 29g protein
9g net carbs: Meatloaf Bowl 460 calories, 39g fat, 38g protein

Boston Carver Sandwiches (No Bread)

1g net carbs: Chicken Salad Carver 540 calories, 46g fat, 26g protein
1g net carbs: Chicken Salad Carver, Half-Serving 270 calories, 23g fat, 13g protein
2g net carbs: Chicken Avocado Club, Half-Serving 390 calories, 31g fat, 22g protein
2g net carbs: Nashville Hot Rotisserie Chicken Sandwich 430 calories, 12g fat, 42g protein
2g net carbs: Rotisserie Chicken Carver, Half-Serving 320 calories, 25g fat, 20g protein
3g net carbs: Roasted Turkey Carver, Half-Serving 315 calories, 26g fat, 17g protein
3g net carbs: Southwest Chicken Carver, Half-Serving, no corn 390 calories, 31g fat, 22g protein
4g net carbs: Chicken Avocado Club 770 calories, 63g fat, 44g protein

4g net carbs: Rotisserie Chicken Carver 640 calories, 50g fat, 40g protein
4g net carbs: Vegetarian Sandwich 950 calories, 63g fat, 28g protein
5g net carbs: Roasted Turkey Carver 630 calories, 52g fat, 34g protein
5g net carbs: Southwest Chicken Carver, no corn 770 calories, 62g fat, 45g protein

Sliders (No Bread)

1g net carbs: Chicken & Cheddar Slider, no BBQ sauce 200 calories, 17g fat, 10g protein
1g net carbs: Chicken Chipotle Ranch Slider 130 calories, 10g fat, 10g protein
1g net carbs: Turkey & Cheddar Slider 210 calories, 18g fat, 11g protein
5g net carbs: BBQ Meatloaf Cheddar Slider, no BBQ sauce 130 calories, 10g fat, 4g protein

Salads (No Dressing) & Soups

2g net carbs: Caesar Side Salad, no croutons 70 calories, 4g fat, 5g protein
2g net carbs: House Side Salad, no croutons 45 calories, 2g fat, 3g protein
3g net carbs: Chicken Caesar Salad, no croutons 280 calories, 10g fat, 40g protein
4g net carbs: Southwest Cobb Side Salad, no corn relish 110 calories, 8g fat, 4g protein
9g net carbs: Chicken Noodle Soup[106], Half-Serving, 120 calories, 5g fat, 8g protein
9g net carbs: Southwest Cobb Salad, no corn relish 410 calories, 24g fat, 39g protein

Salad Dressing

2g net carbs: Ranch Dressing 200 calories, 20g fat, 1g protein
3g net carbs: Caesar Dressing 180 calories, 18g fat, 3g protein
4g net carbs: Chipotle Ranch Dressing 290 calories, 29g fat, 2g protein

DINNER

Starters

2g net carbs: Holiday Spinach Artichoke Dip 45 calories, 3g fat, 2g protein

Individual Meals (Includes Side of Steamed Vegetables)

2g net carbs: Holiday Turkey Breast 140 calories, 4g fat, 24g protein
4g net carbs: Roasted Turkey Breast, Large 230 calories, 6g fat, 42g protein
4g net carbs: Roasted Turkey Breast, Regular 160 calories, 4g fat, 30g protein
3g net carbs: Holiday Spiral Ham 100 calories, 6g fat, 8g protein

3g net carbs: Rotisserie Chicken, Quarter White Chicken (1 Breast) 270 calories, 11g fat, 43g protein
4g net carbs: Rotisserie Chicken, Half Chicken 500 calories, 24g fat, 70g protein
4g net carbs: Rotisserie Chicken, Quarter White Chicken (1 Breast), Skinless 210 calories, 5g fat, 40g protein
4g net carbs: Rotisserie Chicken, Three Piece Dark Chicken (2 Thigh, 1 Drum) 390 calories, 23g fat, 43g protein
4g net carbs: Rotisserie Chicken, Whole Chicken 950 calories, 48g fat, 130g protein

---

[106] *That's Not Keto!* – You'll find all sorts of surprising foods listed here. I'm not telling you whether you should eat these foods or not. What fits your macros or daily carb spend is up to you. No keto police allowed.

4g net carbs: Rotisserie Chicken, Three Piece Dark Chicken (2 Drum, 1 Thigh), Skinless 300 calories, 16g fat, 37g protein

5g net carbs: Nashville Hot Rotisserie Chicken, Half Chicken 460 calories, 27g fat, 51g protein

5g net carbs: Nashville Hot Rotisserie Chicken, Three Piece Dark Chicken (2 Drumsticks, 1 Thigh) 460 calories, 30g fat, 38g protein

5g net carbs: Nashville Hot Rotisserie Chicken, Quarter White Chicken 470 calories, 24g fat, 44g protein

6g net carbs: Nashville Hot Rotisserie Chicken, Three Piece Dark Chicken (2 Thighs, 1 Drumstick) 550 calories, 36g fat, 44g protein

6g net carbs: Rotisserie Chicken, Half All-Dark Chicken 270 calories, 25g fat, 49g protein

6g net carbs: Rotisserie Chicken, Half All-White Chicken 510 calories, 22g fat, 72g protein

6g net carbs: Rotisserie Chicken, Quarter Dark Chicken (1 Thigh & 1 Drumstick) 230 calories, 13g fat, 27g protein

6g net carbs: Rotisserie Chicken and BBQ Ribs (Quarter-White Chicken and Quarter-Rack Ribs) 670 calories, 39g fat, 77g protein

6g net carbs: Parmesan Rotisserie, Quarter White Chicken, easy breading 370 calories, 15g fat, 46g protein

6g net carbs: Parmesan Rotisserie, Quarter Dark Chicken (1 Thigh, 2 Drumsticks), easy breading 400 calories, 21g fat, 41g protein

6g net carbs: Parmesan Rotisserie, Quarter Dark Chicken (2 Thighs, 1 Drumstick), easy breading 490 calories, 28g fat, 47g protein

9g net carbs: Parmesan Rotisserie, Half Chicken, easy breading 590 calories, 28g fat, 73g protein

5g net carbs: Roasted Garlic & Herb Chicken, Half Chicken, no glaze, no toasted herb crunch 650 calories, 35g protein

5g net carbs: Roasted Garlic & Herb White, Quarter Chicken, no glaze, no toasted herb crunch 420 calories, 22g fat, 45g protein

6g net carbs: Roasted Garlic & Herb Dark, Quarter Dark Chicken (1 Thigh, 2 Drumsticks), no glaze, no toasted herb crunch 450 calories, 27g fat, 40g protein

6g net carbs: Roasted Garlic & Herb Dark, Quarter Dark Chicken (2 Thighs, 1 Drumstick), no glaze, no toasted herb crunch 540 calories, 34g fat, 46g protein

5g net carbs: Sesame Chicken, Quarter Dark Chicken, easy sauce/glaze 400 calories, 17g fat, 43g protein

5g net carbs: Sesame Three Piece Dark Chicken (2 Drum, 1 Thigh), easy sauce/glaze 430 calories, 23g fat, 38g protein

5g net carbs: Sesame Three Piece Dark Chicken (2 Thigh, 1 Drum), easy sauce/glaze 520 calories, 30g fat, 44g protein

6g net carbs: Sesame Chicken, Half Chicken, easy sauce/glaze 630 calories, 30g fat, 70g protein

6g net carbs: Grilled Country Chicken with White Gravy, Half Chicken 480 calories, 27g fat, 41g protein

6g net carbs: Grilled Country Chicken with White Gravy, Quarter White Chicken 430 calories, 24g fat, 44g protein

7g net carbs: Creamy Garlic, Half Chicken 550 calories, 27g fat, 72g protein

7g net carbs: Creamy Garlic, Quarter White Chicken 320 calories, 14g fat, 45g protein

7g net carbs: Creamy Garlic, Three Piece Dark Chicken (2 Drumsticks, 1 Thigh) 350 calories, 20g fat, 39g protein

7g net carbs: Creamy Garlic, Three Piece Dark Chicken (2 Thigh, 1 Drumstick) 440 calories, 26g fat, 45g protein

7g net carbs: Grilled Country Chicken with White Gravy, Three Piece Dark Chicken (2 Drumsticks, 1 Thigh) 460 calories, 30g fat, 38g protein

7g net carbs: Grilled Country Chicken with White Gravy, Three Piece Dark Chicken (2 Thighs, 1 Drumstick) 550 calories, 36g fat, 44g protein

7g net carbs: Lemon Piccata, 3pc Dark Chicken, no capers, easy white wine sauce 510 calories, 24g fat, 51g protein

7g net carbs: Lemon Piccata, Half All-Dark Chicken, no capers, easy white wine sauce 490 calories, 28g fat, 52g protein

7g net carbs: Lemon Piccata, Half All-White Chicken, no capers, easy white wine sauce 500 calories, 28g fat, 50g protein

7g net carbs: Lemon Piccata, Half Chicken, no capers, easy white wine sauce 480 calories, 24g fat, 48g protein

8g net carbs: Lemon Piccata, Quarter White Chicken, no capers, easy white wine sauce 465 calories, 21g fat, 46g protein

4g net carbs: Rotisserie Prime Rib 630 calories, 47g fat, 55g protein

8g net carbs: Rotisserie Prime Rib with Beef Au Jus and Horseradish 690 calories, 50g fat, 56g protein

7g net carbs: Complete Comfort Combo, Half-Serving of chicken and roasted turkey 630 calories, 24g fat, 41g protein

8g net carbs: Meatloaf, Regular, no ketchup 470 calories, 33g fat, 26g protein

Ribs (No BBQ Sauce, No Cornbread)

5g net carbs: Baby Back Ribs, Half-Order, 800 calories, 57g fat, 68g protein

6g net carbs: Baby Back Ribs, Half-Order & Rotisserie Chicken, 1/4 Chicken 1,070 calories, 68g fat, 111g protein

10g net carbs: Baby Back Ribs, Full-Order, 1600 calories, 114g fat, 135g protein

Sides

2g net carbs: Steamed Broccoli, Regular 35 calories, 0g fat, 4g protein

3g net carbs: All-White Rotisserie Chicken Salad 420 calories, 24g fat, 23g protein

4g net carbs: Fresh Steamed Vegetables, Regular 60 calories, 3g fat, 2g protein

5g net carbs: Steamed Broccoli, Large 60 calories, 0g fat, 7g protein

6g net carbs: Bacon Brussel Sprouts, no seasoning 240 calories, 15g fat, 7g protein

9g net carbs: Creamed Spinach 240 calories, 17g fat, 11g protein

9g net carbs: Fresh Steamed Vegetables, Large 140 calories, 8g fat, 5g protein

Side Salads (No Dressing)

2g net carbs: Caesar Side Salad, no croutons 70 calories, 4g fat, 5g protein

2g net carbs: House Side Salad, no croutons 45 calories, 2g fat, 3g protein

4g net carbs: Southwest Cobb Side Salad, no corn relish 110 calories, 8g fat, 4g protein

Salads (No Dressing) & Soups

2g net carbs: Caesar Side Salad, no croutons 70 calories, 4g fat, 5g protein

2g net carbs: House Side Salad, no croutons 45 calories, 2g fat, 3g protein

3g net carbs: Chicken Caesar Salad, no croutons 280 calories, 10g fat, 40g protein

4g net carbs: Southwest Cobb Side Salad, no corn relish 110 calories, 8g fat, 4g protein

9g net carbs: Chicken Noodle Soup, Half-Serving, 120 calories, 5g fat, 8g protein

9g net carbs: Southwest Cobb Salad, no corn relish 410 calories, 24g fat, 39g protein

Salad Dressing

2g net carbs: Ranch Dressing 200 calories, 20g fat, 1g protein
3g net carbs: Caesar Dressing 180 calories, 18g fat, 3g protein
4g net carbs: Chipotle Ranch Dressing 290 calories, 29g fat, 2g protein

Sauces

2g net carbs: Beef Au Jus 10 calories, 0g fat, 0g protein
2g net carbs: Beef Gravy 10 calories, 0g fat, 0g protein
2g net carbs: Poultry Gravy 10 calories, 0g fat, 0g protein
2g net carbs: Southwest Chipotle Pesto Sauce 90 calories, 9g fat, 1g protein
6g net carbs: Horseradish 60 calories, 3g fat, 0g protein
10g net carbs: Zesty Barbecue[107] (mild) 40 calories, 0g fat, 0g protein

DRINKS

0g net carbs: Diet Coke, 20 oz. bottle 0 calories, 0g fat, 0g protein
0g net carbs: Dasani, 20 oz. bottle 0 calories, 0g fat, 0g protein

---

[107] *That's Not Keto!* – You'll find all sorts of surprising foods listed here. I'm not telling you whether you should eat these foods or not. What fits your macros or daily carb spend is up to you. No keto police allowed.

Dickey's Barbecue Pit

Due to its thorough, user-friendly, customizable Nutritional Calculator, Dickey's Barbecue Pit earns itself a *Keto Diet Restaurant Guide* Superstar Award. Give it a try. Click "Nutritional & Allergen Info" at the bottom of the restaurant website. See how it lets you remove the bread from your sandwich or offending (high-carb) sauce from your meat plate? I love this calculator. There is virtually no limit to its usefulness.

Special Order Tips

Be careful what meats you order here. Read the meat section carefully because some innocent-sounding entrees at Dickey's Barbecue Pit are NOT low-carb. A serving of ham has 8 grams of net carbs, and Smoked Chicken contains 9 grams of net carbs. What gives? I suspect the BBQ sauce is causing foul play. Error on the side of caution. Order meats with easy (light) sauce or no sauce.

Is the meat too dry for your liking? Consider the Buffalo BBQ sauce (1 gram of net carb per 2 oz. serving) or

Buffalo Hot BBQ sauce (2 grams of net carbs per 2 oz. serving). Compare these stats to Dickey's Original BBQ sauce (12 grams of net carbs per 2 oz. serving). What a difference!

Another item to be wary of is a typically low-carb ingredient: Ranch dressing at Dickey's Barbecue Pit contains a whopping 8 grams of net carbs per serving. Wow. That's triple the usual amount.

Order all sandwiches with "no bread." Be wary of the available "Add-Ons" since they are often an unnecessary source of net carbs. Avoid all buns, rolls, potatoes, fries, onion rings, rice, pasta (that includes mac and cheese, folks!), bread, etc. Ask the server to substitute a side salad or a side of steamed/grilled vegetables. How about a side of pickles?

Feel free to customize your order. Restaurants are usually happy to accommodate reasonable customer requests. The exception is when the item has been premade or was prepared off-site. Note that any alterations on your end will change the provided nutrition information. Adjust accordingly.

You'll notice some menu items indicate a half-serving size. Don't worry; there aren't very many. A smaller portion size allowed us to include more (higher-carb) crowd-pleasing favorites like soups or chilis.

Author Favorite

Lunch & Dinner: Chopped Beef Brisket Plate with Individual size Green Beans and Individual size Brisket Chili on the side. 16 oz. Diet Coke to drink. 596 calories, 40g fat, 11g net carbs, 41g protein

LUNCH & DINNER

Sandwiches (No Bread)

1g net carbs: Brisket Double Cheese Sandwich, no Mac and Cheese 367 calories, 29g fat, 26g protein
1g net carbs: Burnt Ends Sandwich, no BBQ sauce 369 calories, 29g fat, 26g protein
2g net carbs: The Westerner with cheese with Chopped Beef Brisket and Red Hot Pork and Beef Sausage 580 calories, 47g fat, 33g protein
2g net carbs: Red Hot Pork and Beef Sausage Link Classic Sandwich with Cheese 460 calories, 39g fat, 21g protein
2g net carbs: Smoked Turkey Classic Sandwich 120 calories, 4g fat, 18g protein
3g net carbs: Jalapeño Cheddar Kielbasa Sliders (2) 286 calories, 24g fat, 12g protein
4g net carbs: Cuban Sandwich 463 calories, 36g fat, 28g protein
4g net carbs: The Lil' Hoagie, no BBQ sauce 618 calories, 18g fat, 29g protein
4g net carbs: Wild Westerner Sandwich, no BBQ sauce, no Onion Rings 532 calories, 42g fat, 32g protein
6g net carbs: Big Barbecue Sandwich, no BBQ sauce 775 calories, 28g fat, 39g protein
7g net carbs: Barbecue Ranch Bird Sandwich, no BBQ sauce, no onion rings 214 calories, 10g fat, 25g protein
7g net carbs: Carolina Style Brisket Sandwich, no BBQ sauce 359 calories, 26g fat, 22g protein
7g net carbs: Hawaiian Pulled Pork Sandwich, easy BBQ sauce 320 calories, 25g fat, 30g protein
7g net carbs: Pit Dip (Smoked Beef Brisket) Sandwich, easy Smoky Beef Dip 397 calories, 29g fat, 27g protein
7g net carbs: Texas Hot Style Smoked Pork Butt Sandwich 250 calories, 15g fat, 20g protein
8g net carbs: Kickin' Buffalo Chicken Sandwich, no Cabbage Slaw 223 calories, 10g fat, 25g protein

Meat Plates (Meat Only)

1g net carbs: Chopped Beef Brisket Plate 431 calories, 32g fat, 32g protein

1g net carbs: Smoked Beef Brisket Plate 431 calories, 32g fat, 32g protein
2g net carbs: Smoked Pork Butt Plate 329 calories, 23g fat, 30g protein
2g net carbs: Texas Style Chopped Beef Brisket Plate, 4 oz. 334 calories, 42g fat, 32g protein
3g net carbs: Polish Style Kielbasa Plate 480 calories, 42g fat, 24g protein
3g net carbs: Red Hot Pork and Beef Sausage Link Plate 570 calories, 48g fat, 24g protein
3g net carbs: Sliced Beef Brisket Plate, 6 oz. 501 calories, 33g fat, 47g protein
3g net carbs: Smoked Turkey Plate 180 calories, 6g fat, 27g protein
3g net carbs: Southern Pulled Pork Plate, 4 oz. 297 calories, 34g fat, 28g protein
3g net carbs: Texas Style Chopped Beef Brisket Plate, 6 oz. 501 calories, 46g fat, 47g protein
4g net carbs: Sliced Beef Brisket Plate, 4 oz. 334 calories, 26g fat, 32g protein
5g net carbs: Southern Pulled Pork Plate, 6 oz. 445 calories, 36g fat, 42g protein
5g net carbs: The Pork Ribs Plate, no BBQ sauce 562 calories, 40g fat, 29g protein
6g net carbs: Jalapeño Cheddar Kielbasa Plate 570 calories, 48g fat, 24g protein
7g net carbs: The Quarter Plate 1531 calories, 29g fat, 61g protein
8g net carbs: Ham Plate 240 calories, 10g fat, 26g protein
9g net carbs: Smoked Chicken Plate 198 calories, 4g fat, 30g protein

Meats by the Pound (1 Pound, Unless Otherwise Indicated)

1g net carbs: Smoked Beef Brisket 1149 calories, 86g fat, 84g protein
1g net carbs: Chopped Beef Brisket 1149 calories, 86g fat, 84g protein
4g net carbs: Smoked Pork Butt 878 calories, 60g fat, 80g protein
5g net carbs: Ham, Quarter-Serving 160 calories, 7g fat, 17g protein
6g net carbs: Pork Ribs, no BBQ sauce 1498 calories, 107g fat, 78g protein
6g net carbs: Sliced Beef Brisket 1335 calories, 65g fat, 126g protein
6g net carbs: Smoked Chicken, no glaze 529 calories, 10g fat, 80g protein
8g net carbs: Jalapeño Cheddar Kielbasa, Half-Serving 760 calories, 64g fat, 32g protein
8g net carbs: Polish Style Kielbasa 1280 calories, 112g fat, 64g protein
8g net carbs: Red Hot Pork and Beef Sausage 1520 calories, 128g fat, 64g protein
8g net carbs: Smoked Turkey 480 calories, 16g fat, 72g protein

Fall Off the Bone Ribs (No BBQ Sauce)

4g net carbs: St Louis Style Pork Ribs Platter (6 Piece), no BBQ sauce 935 calories, 67g fat, 48g protein
6g net carbs: St Louis Style Pork Ribs Platter (9 Piece), no BBQ sauce 1402 calories, 100g fat, 72g protein
8g net carbs: St Louis Style Pork Ribs Platter (12 Piece), no BBQ sauce 1869 calories, 133g fat, 97g protein

Pit Smoked Wings

3g net carbs: Smoked Wings (9) with Hot Buffalo sauce and Dill Pickle Slices 329 calories, 23g fat, 26g protein
4g net carbs: Smoked Wings (12) with Buffalo and Dill Pickle Slices 443 calories, 31g fat, 34g protein
4g net carbs: Smoked Wings (18) with Lemon Pepper Rub and Dill Pickle Slices 628 calories, 44g fat, 51g protein
5g net carbs: Smoked Wings (24) with Rib Rub and Dill Pickle Slices 836 calories, 59g fat, 67g protein
5g net carbs: Smoked Wings (6) with ranch and Dill Pickle Slices 426 calories, 37g fat, 17g protein

Sides

2g net carbs: Caesar Side Salad, no croutons 96 calories, 8g fat, 2g protein

3g net carbs: Green Beans, Individual 43 calories, 2g fat, 1g protein
4g net carbs: Green Beans, Large 48 calories, 3g fat, 1g protein
4g net carbs: Green Beans, Medium 46 calories, 3g fat, 1g protein
5g net carbs: Creamed Spinach, Individual 155 calories, 11g fat, 6g protein
5g net carbs: Creamed Spinach, Medium 161 calories, 12g fat, 6g protein
7g net carbs: Brisket Chili[108], Individual size 122 calories, 6g fat, 8g protein
7g net carbs: Creamed Spinach, Large 175 calories, 15g fat, 8g protein
7g net carbs: Green Beans with Bacon- 5 oz. 105 calories, 9g fat, 4g protein

Salads

5g net carbs: Garden Salad, no croutons 501 calories, 26g fat, 27g protein
6g net carbs: Chicken Caesar Salad, no croutons, no dinner roll, no glaze on chicken 375 calories, 24g fat, 21g protein
8g net carbs: Smokehouse Salad, no BBQ sauce 969 calories, 34g fat, 58g protein

Add-Ons

0g net carbs: Cheddar Cheese (1 slice) 80 calories, 7g fat, 5g protein
0g net carbs: Pickles (1) 17 calories, 0g fat, 0g protein
2g net carbs: Pickled Jalapeños 10 calories, 0g fat, 0g protein
3g net carbs: Fresh Onions 16 calories, 0g fat, 1g protein
5g net carbs: Add a Rib (1) 155 calories, 11g fat, 8g protein

Sauces (2 oz. Unless Otherwise Indicated)

1g net carbs: Buffalo Barbecue Sauce* 15 calories, 1g fat, 1g protein
2g net carbs: Buffalo Hot Barbecue Sauce* 19 calories, 1g fat, 1g protein
6g net carbs: Original Barbecue Sauce*, 1 oz. 25 calories, 0g fat, 0g protein
6g net carbs: Spicy Barbecue Sauce*, 1 oz. 27 calories, 0g fat, 5protein
7g net carbs: Texas Hot Barbecue Sauce* 37 calories, 1g fat, 0g protein
9g net carbs: Carolina Barbecue Sauce* 41 calories, 1g fat, 0g protein

DRINKS

0g net carbs: Diet Coke, 16 oz. 0 calories, 0g fat, 0g protein
0g net carbs: Diet Coke, 32 oz. 0 calories, 0g fat, 0g protein
0g net carbs: Coke Zero, 16 oz. 0 calories, 0g fat, 0g protein
0g net carbs: Coke Zero, 32 oz. 0 calories, 0g fat, 0g protein
0g net carbs: Iced Tea, unsweetened, 16 oz. 0 calories, 0g fat, 0g protein
0g net carbs: Iced Tea, unsweetened, 32 oz. 0 calories, 0g fat, 0g protein

---

[108] *That's Not Keto!* – You'll find all sorts of surprising foods listed here. I'm not telling you whether you should eat these foods or not. What fits your macros or daily carb spend is up to you. No keto police allowed.

Famous Dave's

Famous Dave's does not have a customizable nutrition calculator on its website. They do have a detailed Nutrition Guide PDF online. This document will help you stay in control of your carb intake.

Special Order Tips

Order all burgers and sandwiches with "no bread." Be wary of the available "Add-Ons" since they are often an unnecessary source of net carbs.

Feel free to customize your order. Restaurants are usually happy to accommodate reasonable customer requests. The exception is when the item has been premade or was prepared off-site. Note that any alterations on your end will change the provided nutrition information. Adjust accordingly.

Avoid all fries, potatoes, rice, pasta, bread, etc. Ask the server to substitute a side salad or a side of steamed/grilled vegetables.

You'll notice a handful of menu items indicate a half-serving size. Don't worry; there will only be a few! A smaller portion size allowed us to include more (higher-carb) crowd-pleasing favorites like soups or signature sides.

Author Favorite

Lunch: Bunless Dave's Favorite Burger, no Sassy sauce with Jalapeño Cheddar Sausage (1) and Garden Side Salad on the side. 16 oz. Diet Pepsi to drink. 1620 calories, 114g fat, 7g net carbs, 90g protein

Dinner: Traditional Wing Basket (wings only) to start. Texas Beef Brisket with Farmhouse Side Salad, no croutons, and

Brussels Sprouts on the side. 16 oz. Unsweetened Iced Tea to drink. 1590 calories, 103g fat, 11g net carbs, 90g protein

LUNCH (No Bread)

Bunless Burgers (No Bread, No Sides)

2g net carbs: Double Stack Cheese Burger with Cheddar 1020 calories, 68g fat, 62g protein
3g net carbs: Dave's Favorite Burger, no Sassy sauce 1100 calories, 72g fat, 67g protein
3g net carbs: Devil's Spit® Burger, no Spit sauce 970 calories, 75g fat, 72g protein
4g net carbs: Ultimate Burger, no BBQ sauce 1240 calories, 78g fat, 78g protein

Breadless Sandwiches (No Bread, No Sides)

4g net carbs: BBQ Sandwich with BBQ Pulled Chicken, no BBQ sauce 630 calories, 29g fat, 33g protein
4g net carbs: BBQ Sandwich with Texas Beef Brisket, no BBQ sauce 600 calories, 28g fat, 43g protein
5g net carbs: BBQ Sandwich with Georgia Chopped Pork, no BBQ sauce 640 calories, 32g fat, 40g protein

Lunch Sandwich/Salad Add-Ons

1g net carbs: Skirt Steak 180 calories, 12g fat, 19g protein
2g net carbs: Grilled Chicken Breast 110 calories, 2g fat, 25g protein

Meat Platters (No Sides, No Corn Bread)

1g net carbs: Country-Roasted Chicken (1/4 chicken) 450 calories, 27g fat, 50g protein
2g net carbs: Cedar Plank Salmon (1) 420 calories, 25g fat, 35g protein
2g net carbs: Georgia Chopped Pork, 4 oz. 530 calories, 30g fat, 37g protein
2g net carbs: Jalapeño Cheddar Sausage (1) 420 calories, 36g fat, 21g protein
2g net carbs: Texas Beef Brisket, 4 oz. 490 calories, 26g fat, 40g protein
3g net carbs: BBQ Roasted Chicken (1/4 chicken), no BBQ sauce 580 calories, 28g fat, 51g protein
3g net carbs: Southside Rib Tips with Pickled Onions and Hellfire Pickles, 6 oz., no BBQ sauce 640 calories, 38g fat, 52g protein
4g net carbs: Burnt Ends, 6 oz., no BBQ sauce 480 calories, 25g fat, 45g protein
4g net carbs: Shrimp Skewer 150 calories, 2g fat, 23g protein
5g net carbs: BBQ Pulled Chicken, 4 oz., no BBQ sauce 390 calories, 18g fat, 23g protein
5g net carbs: St. Louis-Style Spareribs (3) 480 calories, 34g fat, 35g protein

Sauce (2 oz. Unless Otherwise Indicated)

1g net carbs: Remoulade Sauce 340 calories, 40g fat, 0g protein
4g net carbs: Spicy Pickle Tartar Sauce 290 calories, 30g fat, 0g protein
5g net carbs: Southside BBQ Sauce*, .5 oz. 130 calories, 6g fat, 1g protein
5g net carbs: Texas Pit, .5 oz. 80 calories, 1g fat, 1g protein
6g net carbs: Buffalo Sauce, 1 oz. 110 calories, 7g fat, 0g protein
6g net carbs: Comeback Sauce 250 calories, 28g fat, 0g protein
6g net carbs: Devil's Spit®, .5 oz. 110 calories, 1g fat, 1g protein
6g net carbs: White BBQ Sauce* 360 calories, 36g fat, 0g protein
6g net carbs: Wilbur's Revenge®, .5 oz. 100 calories, 1g fat, 1g protein

7g net carbs: Blackberry BBQ Sauce*, .5 oz. 130 calories, 0g fat, 1g protein
7g net carbs: Rich & Sassy®, .5 oz. 130 calories, 1g fat, 1g protein
7g net carbs: Sweet & Zesty®, .5 oz. 140 calories, 0g fat, 1g protein
8g net carbs: Georgia Mustard 40 calories, 0g fat, 1g protein

Salads (No Croutons, No Dressing & Easy BBQ Sauce Unless Otherwise Indicated)

1g net carbs: Dave's Sassy BBQ Salad with Grilled Chicken, no potatoes, 110 calories, 2g fat, 25g protein
1g net carbs: Dave's Sassy BBQ Salad with Grilled Shrimp Skewers, no potatoes 150 calories, 2g fat, 23g protein
1g net carbs: Dave's Sassy BBQ Salad with Grilled Skirt Steak, no potatoes 370 calories, 23g fat, 37g protein
1g net carbs: Dave's Sassy BBQ Salad with Texas Beef Brisket, no potatoes 330 calories, 18g fat, 37g protein
1g net carbs: Dave's Sassy BBQ Salad, meatless, no shoestring potatoes 310 calories, 21g fat, 15g protein
6g net carbs: Dave's Sassy BBQ Salad with BBQ Pulled Chicken, no potatoes 240 calories, 11g fat, 20g protein
6g net carbs: Dave's Sassy BBQ Salad with Georgia Chopped Pork, no potatoes 360 calories, 23g fat, 34g protein
2g net carbs: Caesar Salad with Grilled Chicken with Caesar Dressing 110 calories, 2g fat, 25g protein
3g net carbs: Caesar Salad with Grilled Shrimp Skewers with Caesar Dressing 150 calories, 2g fat, 23g protein
3g net carbs: Caesar Salad, Meatless, with Caesar Dressing 470 calories, 39g fat, 9g protein
4g net carbs: Caesar Salad with Grilled Skirt Steak with Caesar Dressing 370 calories, 23g fat, 37g protein
4g net carbs: Caesar Salad with Texas Beef Brisket with Caesar Dressing 330 calories, 18g fat, 37g protein
5g net carbs: Caesar Salad with Georgia Chopped Pork with Caesar Dressing 360 calories, 23g fat, 34g protein
6g net carbs: Caesar Salad with BBQ Pulled Chicken with Caesar Dressing 240 calories, 11g fat, 20g protein

Salad Dressing

1g net carbs: Bleu Cheese Dressing 240 calories, 25g fat, 2g protein
2g net carbs: Ranch Dressing 220 calories, 23g fat, 1g protein
3g net carbs: Bacon Bleu Cheese Dressing 150 calories, 14g fat, 1g protein
4g net carbs: Fat-Free Italian Dressing 20 calories, 0g fat, 0g protein
9g net carbs: Honey BBQ Dressing[109] 100 calories, 7g fat, 0g protein
10g net carbs: Honey Mustard Dressing* 220 calories, 21g fat, 0g protein

DINNER

Smokin' Starters (No Sauce Unless Otherwise Indicated)

0g net carbs: Farmhouse Traditional Wings, 1/2 lb. (wings only) 360 calories, 24g fat, 35g protein
0g net carbs: Farmhouse Traditional Wings, 1 lb. (wings only) 720 calories, 48g fat, 70g protein
0g net carbs: Traditional Wing Basket (wings only) 630 calories, 42g fat, 62g protein
3g net carbs: Stack of Breadless Beef Sliders 1120 calories, 57g fat, 49g protein
4g net carbs: Stack of Breadless Chicken Sliders 1170 calories, 52g fat, 44g protein
7g net carbs: Southside Rib Tips, easy sauce 1540 calories, 98g fat, 139g protein

---

[109] *That's Not Keto!* – You'll find all sorts of surprising foods listed here. I'm not telling you whether you should eat these foods or not. What fits your macros or daily carb spend is up to you. No keto police allowed.

Wing Sauce (2 oz. Unless Otherwise Indicated)

1g net carbs: Remoulade Sauce 340 calories, 40g fat, 0g protein
4g net carbs: Spicy Pickle Tartar Sauce 290 calories, 30g fat, 0g protein
5g net carbs: Southside BBQ Sauce[110], .5 oz. 130 calories, 6g fat, 1g protein
5g net carbs: Texas Pit, .5 oz. 80 calories, 1g fat, 1g protein
6g net carbs: Buffalo Sauce, 1 oz. 110 calories, 7g fat, 0g protein
6g net carbs: Comeback Sauce 250 calories, 28g fat, 0g protein
6g net carbs: Devil's Spit®, .5 oz. 110 calories, 1g fat, 1g protein
6g net carbs: White BBQ Sauce* 360 calories, 36g fat, 0g protein
6g net carbs: Wilbur's Revenge®*, .5 oz. 100 calories, 1g fat, 1g protein
7g net carbs: Blackberry BBQ Sauce*, .5 oz. 130 calories, 0g fat, 1g protein
7g net carbs: Rich & Sassy®, .5 oz. 130 calories, 1g fat, 1g protein
7g net carbs: Sweet & Zesty®*, .5 oz. 140 calories, 0g fat, 1g protein
8g net carbs: Georgia Mustard 40 calories, 0g fat, 1g protein

Build Your Own Breadless Burger or Sandwich

Choose Your Meat

0g net carbs: Beef Burger Patty 670 calories, 39g fat, 40g protein
0g net carbs: Grilled Chicken Breast 380 calories, 11g fat, 31g protein
4g net carbs: BBQ Pulled Chicken, easy sauce 580 calories, 23g fat, 31g protein
4g net carbs: Georgia Chopped Pork, easy sauce 730 calories, 38g fat, 49g protein
4g net carbs: Texas Beef Brisket 690 calories, 33g fat, 52g protein
5g net carbs: Beyond Meat Burger Patty 540 calories, 30g fat, 26g protein

Choose Your Toppings

0g net carbs: Jalapeños 0 calories, 0g fat, 0g protein
0g net carbs: Lettuce 0 calories, 0g fat, 0g protein
0g net carbs: Monterey Jack Cheese 210 calories, 17g fat, 14g protein
0g net carbs: Pepper-Jack Cheese 180 calories, 14g fat, 10g protein
0g net carbs: Smoked Bacon (4 strips) 160 calories, 16g fat, 13g protein
1g net carbs: American Cheese 130 calories, 12g fat, 7g protein
1g net carbs: Red Onion 5 calories, 0g fat, 0g protein
1g net carbs: Tomato 5 calories, 0g fat, 0g protein
2g net carbs: Cheddar Cheese 230 calories, 19g fat, 13g protein
3g net carbs: Comeback Sauce 150 calories, 15g fat, 0g protein
3g net carbs: Memphis-Style (Creamy Coleslaw) 40 calories, 2g fat, 0g protein
4g net carbs: Hot Link Sausage (1) 590 calories, 52g fat, 26g protein
7g net carbs: Spicy Hell-Fire Pickles 25 calories, 0g fat, 0g protein
8g net carbs: Dave's Cheesy Mac & Cheese[111] 60 calories, 3g fat, 3g protein

---

[110] *That's Not Keto!* – You'll find all sorts of surprising foods listed here. I'm not telling you whether you should eat these foods or not. What fits your macros or daily carb spend is up to you. No keto police allowed.

[111] *That's Not Keto!* – You'll find all sorts of surprising foods listed here. I'm not telling you whether you should eat these foods or not. What fits your macros or daily carb spend is up to you. No keto police allowed.

Breadless Burgers (No Bread, No Sides)

2g net carbs: Double Stack Cheese Burger with Cheddar 1020 calories, 68g fat, 62g protein
3g net carbs: Dave's Favorite Burger, no Sassy sauce 1100 calories, 72g fat, 67g protein
3g net carbs: Devil's Spit® Burger, no Spit sauce 970 calories, 75g fat, 72g protein
4g net carbs: Ultimate Burger, no BBQ sauce 1240 calories, 78g fat, 78g protein

Breadless Sandwiches (No Bread, No Sides)

3g net carbs: Cajun Grilled Chicken Sandwich 1190 calories, 78g fat, 46g protein
3g net carbs: Iris' Comeback Grilled Chicken Sandwich 620 calories, 33g fat, 32g protein
4g net carbs: BBQ Sandwich with BBQ Pulled Chicken, no BBQ sauce 630 calories, 29g fat, 33g protein
4g net carbs: BBQ Sandwich with Texas Beef Brisket, no BBQ sauce 600 calories, 28g fat, 43g protein
5g net carbs: BBQ Sandwich with Georgia Chopped Pork, no BBQ sauce 640 calories, 32g fat, 40g protein

Pasta Dishes (Pasta Substituted with Steamed Broccoli)

1g net carbs: Alfredo Pasta Grilled Skirt Steak 370 calories, 23g fat, 37g protein
2g net carbs: Alfredo Pasta Grilled Chicken 110 calories, 2g fat, 25g protein
3g net carbs: Alfredo Pasta BBQ Pulled Chicken, easy BBQ sauce 240 calories, 11g fat, 20g protein
4g net carbs: Alfredo Pasta Texas Beef Brisket 330 calories, 18g fat, 37g protein
5g net carbs: Alfredo Pasta Georgia Chopped Pork 360 calories, 23g fat, 34g protein
9g net carbs: Alfredo Pasta Grilled Shrimp Skewers 150 calories, 2g fat, 23g protein

Award-Winning Ribs (No Sides, No Corn Bread Muffin)

Naked Ribs:
    0g net carbs: 4 bones 580 calories, 40g fat, 54g protein
    0g net carbs: 6 bones 880 calories, 60g fat, 81g protein
    0g net carbs: 9 bones 1310 calories, 90g fat, 122g protein
    0g net carbs: 12 bones 1750 calories, 120g fat, 163g protein
St. Louis-Style Spareribs, Sauced with Rich & Sassy®:
    1g net carbs: 1 bone 160 calories, 11g fat, 12g protein
    6g net carbs: 4 bones 640 calories, 46g fat, 47g protein
    7g net carbs: 9 bones, easy sauce 1430 calories, 103g fat, 106g protein
    9g net carbs: 6 bones 960 calories, 69g fat, 71g protein
Baby Back Ribs Original-style with Dave's Rib Rub and Sweet & Zesty®:
    5g net carbs: Half Baby 560 calories, 37g fat, 50g protein
    10g net carbs: Big Baby 1120 calories, 74g fat, 100g protein
Memphis-style with herbs and spices, and vinegar:
    0g net carbs: Half Baby 620 calories, 45g fat, 53g protein
    0g net carbs: Big Baby 1230 calories, 90g fat, 107g protein

The Meats (No Sides, No Corn Bread Muffin)

0g net carbs: Country-Roasted Chicken (1/4 chicken) 450 calories, 27g fat, 50g protein
2g net carbs: Cedar Plank Salmon (1) 420 calories, 25g fat, 35g protein
2g net carbs: Jalapeño Cheddar Sausage (1) 420 calories, 36g fat, 21g protein
3g net carbs: Burnt Ends, 6 oz., easy sauce 480 calories, 25g fat, 45g protein

3g net carbs: Texas Beef Brisket, 4 oz., easy sauce 490 calories, 26g fat, 40g protein
4g net carbs: Southside Rib Tips with Pickled Onions and Hellfire Pickles, 6 oz., easy sauce 640 calories, 38g fat, 52g protein
5g net carbs: BBQ Pulled Chicken, 4 oz., easy sauce 390 calories, 18g fat, 23g protein
5g net carbs: St. Louis-Style Spareribs (3) 480 calories, 34g fat, 35g protein
6g net carbs: BBQ Roasted Chicken (1/4 chicken), easy sauce 580 calories, 28g fat, 51g protein
6g net carbs: Sweetwater Catfish Fingers with Remoulade (4), easy sauce 570 calories, 44g fat, 21g protein
7g net carbs: Georgia Chopped Pork, 4 oz., easy sauce 530 calories, 30g fat, 37g protein
9g net carbs: Shrimp Skewer 150 calories, 2g fat, 23g protein

The Farmhouse (with Steamed Broccoli, No Potatoes, No Corn Bread Muffin)

2g net carbs: Cedar Plank Salmon 830 calories, 41g fat, 42g protein
2g net carbs: Grilled Chicken Breast 640 calories, 19g fat, 57g protein
3g net carbs: Skirt Steak & Ribs 1350 calories, 84g fat, 64g protein
3g net carbs: Skirt Steak & Shrimp 1020 calories, 51g fat, 52g protein
4g net carbs: Skirt Steak & Chicken 990 calories, 51g fat, 53g protein
4g net carbs: Skirt Steak with Onion Strings 1060 calories, 61g fat, 47g protein
5g net carbs: Chicken & Shrimp 670 calories, 19g fat, 55g protein

Sides

2g net carbs: Caesar Side Salad with Caesar Dressing, no croutons 220 calories, 18g fat, 4g protein
3g net carbs: Farmhouse Side Salad, no croutons 310 calories, 24g fat, 16g protein
3g net carbs: Garden Side Salad, no croutons 100 calories, 6g fat, 2g protein
4g net carbs: Fresh-Steamed Broccoli 60 calories, 4g fat, 2g protein
5g net carbs: Brussels Sprouts 160 calories, 11g fat, 8g protein
6g net carbs: Creamy Coleslaw, Half-Serving, 60 calories, 7g fat, 1g protein

Salads (No Croutons, No Dressing & Easy BBQ Sauce Unless Otherwise Indicated)

1g net carbs: Dave's Sassy BBQ Salad with Grilled Chicken, no potatoes, 110 calories, 2g fat, 25g protein
1g net carbs: Dave's Sassy BBQ Salad with Grilled Shrimp Skewers, no potatoes 150 calories, 2g fat, 23g protein
1g net carbs: Dave's Sassy BBQ Salad with Grilled Skirt Steak, no potatoes 370 calories, 23g fat, 37g protein
1g net carbs: Dave's Sassy BBQ Salad with Texas Beef Brisket, no potatoes 330 calories, 18g fat, 37g protein
1g net carbs: Dave's Sassy BBQ Salad, meatless, no shoestring potatoes 310 calories, 21g fat, 15g protein
6g net carbs: Dave's Sassy BBQ Salad with BBQ Pulled Chicken, no potatoes 240 calories, 11g fat, 20g protein
6g net carbs: Dave's Sassy BBQ Salad with Georgia Chopped Pork, no potatoes 360 calories, 23g fat, 34g protein
2g net carbs: Caesar Salad with Grilled Chicken with Caesar Dressing 110 calories, 2g fat, 25g protein
3g net carbs: Caesar Salad with Grilled Shrimp Skewers with Caesar Dressing 150 calories, 2g fat, 23g protein
3g net carbs: Caesar Salad, Meatless, with Caesar Dressing 470 calories, 39g fat, 9g protein
4g net carbs: Caesar Salad with Grilled Skirt Steak with Caesar Dressing 370 calories, 23g fat, 37g protein
4g net carbs: Caesar Salad with Texas Beef Brisket with Caesar Dressing 330 calories, 18g fat, 37g protein
5g net carbs: Caesar Salad with Georgia Chopped Pork with Caesar Dressing 360 calories, 23g fat, 34g protein
6g net carbs: Caesar Salad with BBQ Pulled Chicken with Caesar Dressing 240 calories, 11g fat, 20g protein

Salad Dressing (1.5 oz. Unless Otherwise Indicated)

1g net carbs: Bleu Cheese Dressing 240 calories, 25g fat, 2g protein
2g net carbs: Ranch Dressing 220 calories, 23g fat, 1g protein
3g net carbs: Caesar Dressing 170 calories, 16g fat, 2g protein
4g net carbs: Fat-Free Italian Dressing 20 calories, 0g fat, 0g protein
5g net carbs: Honey BBQ Dressing[112], .5 oz. 50 calories, 4g fat, 0g protein
6g net carbs: Ranch & Sassy 200 calories, 19g fat, 1g protein
7g net carbs: Honey Mustard Dressing*, 1 oz. 100 calories, 10g fat, 0g protein

Sauce (2 oz. Unless Otherwise Indicated)

1g net carbs: Remoulade Sauce 340 calories, 40g fat, 0g protein
4g net carbs: Spicy Pickle Tartar Sauce 290 calories, 30g fat, 0g protein
5g net carbs: Southside BBQ Sauce*, .5 oz. 130 calories, 2g fat, 1g protein
5g net carbs: Texas Pit, .5 oz. 20 calories, 0g fat, 1g protein
6g net carbs: Buffalo Sauce, 1 oz. 55 calories, 4g fat, 0g protein
6g net carbs: Comeback Sauce 250 calories, 28g fat, 0g protein
6g net carbs: Devil's Spit®, .5 oz. 30 calories, 1g fat, 1g protein
6g net carbs: White BBQ Sauce* 360 calories, 36g fat, 0g protein
6g net carbs: Wilbur's Revenge®, .5 oz. 25 calories, 0g fat, 1g protein
7g net carbs: Blackberry BBQ Sauce*, .5 oz. 30 calories, 0g fat, 1g protein
7g net carbs: Rich & Sassy®, .5 oz. 30 calories, 1g fat, 1g protein
7g net carbs: Sweet & Zesty®, .5 oz. 40 calories, 0g fat, 1g protein

DESSERT

10g net carbs: Vanilla Ice Cream[113]* (1 scoop) 90 calories, 5g fat, 2g protein

DRINKS

0g net carbs: Diet Pepsi, 16 oz. 0 calories, 0g fat, 0g protein
0g net carbs: Fresh-Brewed Unsweetened Iced Tea, 16 oz. 0 calories, 0g fat, 0g protein

---

[112] *That's Not Keto!* – You'll find all sorts of surprising foods listed here. I'm not telling you whether you should eat these foods or not. What fits your macros or daily carb spend is up to you. No keto police allowed.

[113] I seriously triple-checked this information on the Famous Dave's website. I was like, "NO FREAKIN' WAY!"

Index

A Letter from the Laskas

Dear Readers,

We want to thank you for reading the *Keto Diet Restaurant Guide* and being part of the DIRTY, LAZY, KETO community. Would you like more support on your low-carb journey? Sign up for our free e-newsletter. It's full of helpful ketosis tips and tricks, keto-friendly recipes, links to instructional videos, and loads of weight loss inspiration. BONUS: Look for the free starter keto grocery list *inside* your welcome email. (There is no charge to receive the newsletter – unsubscribe anytime.)

https://dirtylazyketo.com/

Are you finding the DIRTY, LAZY, KETO books to be helpful? We would be so grateful if you could write a review. Your thoughts mean the world to us and inspire new readers to try this amazing lifestyle!

#KetoOn

Stephanie and Bill

About the Authors

USA TODAY–bestselling author and creator of DIRTY, LAZY, KETO Stephanie Laska doesn't just talk the talk; she walks the walk. She is one of the few keto authors who has successfully lost half of her body weight (140 pounds!) and maintained that weight loss for almost a decade. Her mission is to help as many people as possible fight obesity one carb at a time.

Stephanie's honest sass and fresh approach to the keto diet breaks all the traditional dieting rules. You might have caught her cooking debut with Al Roker on NBC's *Today* show or seen her on the covers of *Woman's World*. Her story has been celebrated in articles and images shared by Parade, Fox News, US News & World Report, New York Post, Reader's Digest, Yahoo! News, First for Women, Woman's World, Muscle & Fitness: Hers, Men's Journal, Keto for You, runDisney, and Costco Connection. Stephanie participated in the USA TODAY Storyteller's project and has appeared multiple times on CBS Good Day Sacramento. She has run a dozen marathons—most notably the New York City Marathon as a sponsored athlete for PowerBar. Not bad for a girl who ran her first mile (as in ever!) at close to age forty.

Want the "full story" on how you, too, can lose weight for good? Check out the blockbuster *DIRTY, LAZY, KETO (revised and expanded): Get Started Losing Weight While Breaking the Rules* (St. Martin's Essentials, 2020). This guidebook started an international trend to help hundreds of thousands of fans lose weight in a revolutionary new way.

Alongside her co-author and husband, William Laska (and official taste-testers, children Charlotte and Alex), Stephanie has created a series of support tools: *The DIRTY, LAZY, KETO® 5-Ingredient Cookbook* (Simon & Schuster, 2021), *The DIRTY, LAZY, KETO® No Time to Cook Cookbook* (Simon & Schuster, 2021), *The DIRTY, LAZY, KETO® Dirt Cheap Cookbook* (Simon & Schuster, 2020), *The DIRTY, LAZY, KETO® Cookbook* (Simon & Schuster, 2020) and *DIRTY, LAZY, KETO® Fast Food Guide* (2018) – more to come!

Stephanie also hosts a free podcast, *DIRTY, LAZY, KETO Podcast by Stephanie Laska,* available for watching on the DIRTY, LAZY, KETO YouTube channel or for audio only on Apple Podcasts, Spotify, or wherever you listen to podcasts.

Stephanie and Bill reside in sunny California. When they aren't talking about their third child (DIRTY, LAZY, KETO), the Laskas enjoy bobbing in the ocean, traveling "on the cheap," and shopping at thrift stores.

Keep in Touch with DLK

For additional free resources, visit https://dirtylazyketo.com/

Listen to the author directly on the free podcast *DIRTY, LAZY, KETO by Stephanie Laska*, available on YouTube or wherever you listen to podcasts.

youtube.com/DIRTYLAZYKETOStephanieLaska
facebook.com/dirtylazyketo
instagram.com/dirtylazyketo
pinterest.com/dirtylazyketo
twitter.com/140lost
amazon.com/Stephanie-Laska/e/B075C2FMGV

DLK

THE FULL COLLECTION

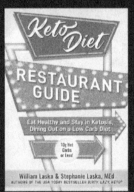

dirtylazyketo.com